15:26 Greenwood 12 - 68

COLOMBIA AND THE UNITED STATES
1765-1934

DR. ENRIQUE OLAYA HERRERA

COLOMBIA
AND THE UNITED STATES
1765-1934

By

E. Taylor Parks

GREENWOOD PRESS, PUBLISHERS
NEW YORK   1968

To

Lois Annie Ferry
Lois Ferry Parks
and
Richard Ferry Parks

PREFACE

DURING the era following the World War, Colombia achieved marked stability and assumed a leading rôle in Inter-American affairs. After having had in the last century at least ten general revolutions, seventy local uprisings, seven national constitutions, and some fifty presidents and acting-presidents, the nation seems now to have arrived politically. The orderly presidential elections of 1930 and 1934 indicate the end of political apprenticeship and the vindication of the belief of the founders of the republic that Colombians are capable of self-government.

Strategically, Colombia is of great importance to the United States. It faces both the Atlantic and Pacific oceans, it long possessed the Isthmus of Panama, and it still possesses territory very near both termini of the canal. The distance from its northern coast to New Orleans is only 1,400 miles, and to New York only 1,900 miles.

With a population of 8,573,126 and a domain of approximately 476,916 square miles, Colombia is now ranked by some as third in population and area among the South American states. It is nearly twice the size of the state of Texas, over nine times that of North Carolina, and more than seven times that of all New England. It is larger than the combined areas of Great Britain, France, Belgium, and Italy.

In recent years Colombia's foreign trade has enjoyed a phenomenal growth. Exports to the United States alone in 1923 were greater than the entire national trade of 1913. The total volume of some $50,000,000 of the latter year reached $273,688,701 in 1928. Of this amount, some eighty per cent of the exports went to and some forty-five per cent of the imports came from the United States.

In the production of coffee Colombia ranks second to Brazil. This commodity represents sixty per cent of the exports, and of this amount some eighty-five per cent come to the United States. Colombia is the chief producer of emeralds. Its output of platinum is exceeded only by Russia. It is also rich in gold, silver, coal, and salt deposits. Petroleum production increased from 323,000 barrels in 1923 to 20,384,000 in 1929. An American authority on minerals classifies Colombia as "the richest section of the globe now above water." The North American investment of approximately $300,000,-000 in the exploitation and development of the area certainly indicates faith in Colombia's future.

Naturally, Colombia has not escaped the effects of the world depression. Its imports from the United States decreased from $64,249,146 in 1928 to $10,581,000 in 1931-32, while its exports to the United States decreased from $100,721,464 to $69,182,000 during the same period. Even in the midst of the depression, however, Brazil was the only South American nation having a greater volume of trade with the United States. As for the future, Colombia possesses great recuperative powers in its unexploited mineral wealth.

Since the international relations of a state are comprehensible only in the light of internal history, I have devoted considerable space to Colombia's colonial heritage, its heroic struggle for independence, its early political evolution as a republic, its dissolution into present-day Colombia, Venezuela, and Ecuador, and its difficulties in maintaining peace on both the Mainland and the Isthmus of Panama.

Colombia's extensive domain, its wealth of natural resources, its possession of the strategically important Isthmus, and the intellectual stature of its early statesmen naturally made the new republic a leader among the liberated colonies of Spain. Colombia was the first of these colonies to be recognized as independent.

The United States led in recognizing this status. North American political influence over and commercial interest in Colombia extend far back into the colonial era of New Granada. With independence established, it was quite natural that the non-competitive nature of the exports of each to the other—along with early Yankee interest in a trans-isthmian communication—should place the two nations on friendly terms. However, certain unsettled claims, Colombian discrimination against American importation of products of non-American manufacture, and a few unfortunate clashes in national temperaments delayed any satisfactory permanent treaty arrangement between the two.

The Treaty of 1846 seemingly solved the difficulty by providing for Colombia's removal of discriminating tariffs and the United States guarantee of the neutrality of the Isthmus of Panama. However, the conflicting interpretations of this convention—still in force, except Article XXXV—proved a source of misunderstanding for more than fifty years. Yet neither party saw fit or dared to discontinue the arrangement. Meanwhile, the United States canal policy had evolved from a mere approval of any interoceanic canal constructed for international use to a demand for American official ownership, construction, and control of a canal by way of the Panama route.

American activities during and immediately following the Panama Revolution of 1903 caused a pronounced Colombian coolness towards the United States. Intelligent leaders in both nations, realizing the importance of mutual friendship and commerce, were untiring in their efforts to reëstablish friendly relations. However, it was not until 1921 that a satisfactory formula was agreed upon. The subsequent business boom in both countries was temporarily retarded by the unprecedented depression. World economic recovery will undoubtedly impart new life to Colombo-American trade.

The lack of an acceptable name to particularize citizens of the United States of America has necessitated my using the incorrect (and much resented in Hispanic America) term, "American." Some monotony and criticism have been avoided, I hope, by the use of "Yankee." This, however, is variously interpreted in North America. When writing in general terms, I have employed "Colombia"; when discussing its history and diplomacy, I have used the official title of the nation during the period concerned.

Two other difficulties were encountered: (1) choosing the surnames of Hispanic Americans in cases where practice permitted two or more possibilities, (2) deciding what Spanish words had become sufficiently Anglicized to warrant the omission of the usual accent marks or a change in spelling. In many cases, my judgment may have been faulty.

In the preparation of this study, Professor J. Fred Rippy has contributed much by his wise counsel and stimulating criticism. To Professor P. M. Hamer, I wish to express my thanks for valuable suggestions furnished during the earlier stages of the work. I am grateful also to Professor Tennessee Jenkins who was the first to interest me in the study of inter-American relations. In the collection of materials, I am indebted to the staffs of the State Department Archives, the Pan American Union, the Filson Club, and the following libraries: Duke University, Library of Congress, University of Tennessee, Carson and Newman College, Lawson-McGhee (Knoxville, Tenn.), Shreve Memorial (Shreveport, La.), and the University of South Carolina.

The maps were prepared by Dr. Ben F. Lemert of the Department of Economics, Duke University. Valuable aid has been rendered also by the following: Charles Lyon Chandler, Raimundo Rivas, José M. Coronado, Nicolás García Samudio, R. O. Rivera, William Watts Ball, Thomas Maney, R. P. Lemly, Mrs. Laura Bidlack, and Mrs. James T. Du Bois.

Of course, I alone am responsible for statements and conclusions contained in this study.

E. T. PARKS

Berea, Kentucky
August 1, 1934

TABLE OF CONTENTS

PART I

INTRODUCTION

CHAPTER   PAGE

I Colonial Heritage.................................. 3

Discovery and Settlement—A Heterogeneous Pedigree—An "Alien" Absolutism—An Irrational Economic System—A Powerful, Exacting, and Reactionary Church—Parallels and Contrasts between Colonial Colombia and the Thirteen English Colonies—The Aftermath

PART II

FROM COLONY TO REPUBLIC

II Accumulating Discontent and Incipient Revolts, 1765-1800 19

The Quito Uprising—*Los Comuneros*—*Los Precursores:* Espejo, Nariño, España and Gual

III The Case of Colonial Independence Before Foreign Councils, 1790-1806.......................... 33

Early European Interest and Activities—Early North American Attitude and Influence—Miranda: Patriot and "Promoter of Revolutions"—Miranda and the Nootka Sound Controversy —A Pawn on the International Chessboard—The Venezuelan Expedition of 1806

IV The Emergence of La Gran Colombia, 1806-1822.... 55

The British Chameleon Policy—Napoleon Underrates Spanish Nationalism—England Casts Its Lot with Spain—The Spanish Revolt Spreads to New Granada—Quito Launches the Revolution—Caracas Follows—Revolutionary Contagion Pervades the Viceroyalty—"*La Patria Boba*"—The Reconquest of New Granada—The Triumph of Patriot Arms

V Sundry Revolutionary Relations, 1810-1824......... 73

Yankees in the Patriot Service—The First American Mission; Commercial and Charitable—Privateers, Seizures, and Unsettled Claims

VI The Evolution of the Recognition Policy of the United States, 1810-1822..................... 86

Solicitous Rebels and Interested Spectators—Recognition Considered—Adams Advises Caution—Clay Embarrasses the Administration—The Patriot Agents Blunder——Torres and Recognition—Europe Follows in Granting Recognition

[xiii]

PART III

COLOMBIA AMONG THE NATIONS

CHAPTER   PAGE

VII An Era of Transient Greatness, 1822-1830 109

Laying the Constitutional Foundation—Signs of Progress and
Leadership—The Yankee Suspects the Briton—Development of
Commercial Contacts—Ill Omens—The Páez Rebellion—Re-
publicanism vs. Monarchism—The Dissolution of La Gran
Colombia

VIII On the Margin of World Politics, 1822-1826 124

The Monroe Doctrine—The First Treaty with the United
States—The Contemplated Invasion of Cuba—The Panama
Congress.

PART IV

ANTECEDENTS OF THE TREATY OF 1846

IX Clashes of Temperaments, 1826-1846 151

The Watts Letter—The Unfortunate Harrison Mission—Temporary Rapprochement—The Formation of New Granada—The
Return of Santander—National Renaissance—The Abrupt Departure of Chargé Semple

X Claims and Commerce, 1822-1848 165

Unsuccessful Claims Negotiations—The Removal of Early
Commercial Discrimination—Adverse Legislation; Commerce
on the Wane—Prolonged Negotiations for an Equal Trade
Footing—The Yankee Defective Consular System—The Volume of Trade

XI The Growth of the Canal Idea, 1500-1842 178

"The Secret of the Strait"—Initial Spanish Interest—The
Idea Becomes International—La Gran Colombia Considers a
Canal—The Yankees Manifest an Interest—The Biddle Mission—The Proverbial Yankee Persistence—The Second Secession of the Isthmus

XII The Isthmus Guaranteed; Discrimination
Abolished, 1842-1848 194

New Granada Seeks a Foreign Guarantee—European Nego-
tiations Fail—Washington Assumes a Defensive Attitude—
The Treaty of 1846—American Hesitancy: Granadian Anxiety
—Suspicion and Reaction

PART V

RELATIONS UNDER THE TREATY OF 1846

XIII Isthmian Disturbances and American
Interventions, 1846-1903 219

Explosive Possibilities—The Panama Riot—North American
Forces Intervene—The Isthmians Talk Secession—The Idea of
a Yankee Protectorate—The Isthmus as a Federal Department

CHAPTER PAGE

XIV The Guarantee of an Open and Free Transit,
1848-1903 235
Passenger, Tonnage, and Mail Taxes—The Passage of American Troops across the Isthmus—The Transporting of Prisoners across the Isthmus—The Use of American Troops to Maintain an Open Transit

XV The Guarantee of Isthmian Neutrality, 1848-1903 . . 250
The Threatened Flores Expedition—The Period of Mutual
Storm and Stress—Article XXXV Interpreted—American In-
tervention; Not a Duty But a Right

XVI The Growth of Commerce, 1845-1903 262
Trade Prospers—Dangers Encountered—President Arthur Ad-
vocates Reciprocity—Retaliatory Reciprocity—Improved Trade
Relations

XVII Yankee Economic Adventures in Colombia,
1846-1903 272
The Panama Railroad Company—The Chiriquí Improvement
Company—Other Isthmian Transportation Adventures—Sundry
Investments on the Isthmus—Adventures on the Mainland

XVIII The Protection of United States Citizens and
Interests, 1845-1861 285
Continued Efforts to Adjust Claims—A Firmer Policy—The
Treaties of 1857 and 1864

XIX The Protection of United States Citizens and
Interests *(continued)*, 1861-1903 303
Circumstances Compel Consistency—Colombia's Growing Inde-
pendence—The Cartagena Riot—The Montijo Arbitration—
The Colón Fire Claims—Colombia's Successful Denial of Li-
ability for Colón Claims—Continued Diplomatic and Military
Intervention

PART VI

THE EVOLUTION OF THE AMERICAN CANAL POLICY

XX National Self-Interest Conditioned by Interna-
tional Expediency, 1848-1866 323
The Yankees Scan the Entire Isthmus—The Clayton-Bulwer
Treaty—American Self-Interest Dependent on Temporary Self-
Denial—Granada Internally Weak: America Aggressive—
American Policy Temporarily Embarrassed—Panama in the
Limelight

CHAPTER   PAGE

XXI WASHINGTON ENTHUSIASTIC: BOGOTÁ RETICENT,
    1866-1872 338
    General Revival of Canal Interest—Mosquera and the British
    —London Refuses a Guarantee; Washington Approached—
    Seward Enthusiastic, But to No Avail—Grant's Futile Efforts

XXII WASHINGTON RETICENT: BOGOTÁ ANXIOUS, 1872-1880. . 351
    Unsuccessful Nicaraguan Negotiations—An American Delivers
    Panama to the French—Ferdinand de Lesseps—American Op-
    position Aroused

XXIII POLICY OF AMERICAN CONTROL ADOPTED AND
    ABANDONED, 1880-1888 362
    De Lesseps Fails to Convert the Americans—The Protocol of
    1881—Washington's Fear of a European Guarantee—Efforts
    to Modify the Clayton-Bulwer Treaty—Cleveland Turns
    Provincial—The Bankruptcy of the French Canal Company

XXIV THE POLICY OF GOVERNMENTAL CONSTRUCTION AND
    CONTROL, 1889-1903 378
    Nicaragua to the Fore—Opposition to Extension of Panama
    Concession—"Canal Insanity (Furor Canaliensis)"—Nicara-
    gua vs. Panama—Great Britain Agrees to American Control—
    The Panama Route Chosen—Negotiations with Colombia

PART VII

THE PANAMA REVOLUTION AND ITS AFTERMATH

XXV A CASE IN INTERNATIONAL MORALITY 395
    The Essential Facts: (A) Colombia rejects the Hay-Herrán
    Treaty (B) Panama plans secession (C) The Revolution is
    staged (D) The independence of Panama is recognized (E)
    Colombia is prevented from suppressing the revolt (F) Wash-
    ington refuses arbitration; *International Law and Equity:*
    (A) The equality of sovereign states under international law
    (B) Treaty-making powers and duties of sovereign states
    (C) Mutual rights and obligations under the Treaty of 1846
    (D) American actions during the Panama Revolution (E)
    Recognition of the new republic (F) American refusal to arbi-
    trate; *American "Interests and Safety"; The Interests of
    "Collective Civilization"*

XXVI CIRCUITOUS INDEMNITY VS. ARBITRATION, 1903-1913. . 427
    Early Reconciliation Efforts of Reyes—Temporary Renuncia-
    tion of Arbitration and Indemnity—American Agreement to
    Partial Arbitration

CHAPTER   PAGE

XXVII Oil and Ideals, 1913-1921..................... 440
Democratic Penance for Rooseveltian Sins—American Reception of the New Treaty—Forces Behind the Treaty—The
Treaty Before the Senate—Oil Enters Diplomacy—"A Smell
of Oil in the August Chamber"

PART VIII

RAPPROCHEMENT

XXVIII Recent Relations, 1922-1934................. 461
Colombian Economic Renaissance—Colombo-American Rapprochement—Yankee Petroleros Enter Colombia—Unexpected
Complications—The State Department to the Rescue—Extensive Loans—The New Régime—America's Interest in Colombia's Future

Appendices 481

Bibliography 492

Index 531

MAPS AND ILLUSTRATIONS

PAGE

DR. ENRIQUE OLAYA HERRERA....................*frontispiece*

COLOMBIA: COLONIAL AND NATIONAL...............facing 18

UNVEILING TABLET TO MEMORY OF DON
    MANUEL TORRES...........................facing 103

PROPOSED ISTHMIAN CANAL ROUTES...............facing 322

"A GREAT CONSCIENCE AWAKENER"..............facing 451

PRESIDENT-ELECT LÓPEZ AND SECRETARY OF
    STATE HULL................................facing 480

ABBREVIATIONS

A. H. A. A. R.—American Historical Association, *Annual Report*
A. H. R.—*The American Historical Review*
Annals—*The Annals* (American Academy of Political and Social Science)
A. S. P. F. R.—*American State Papers: Foreign Relations*
B. F. S. P.—*British and Foreign State Papers*
B. P. A. U.—*Bulletin* (Pan American Union)
Col.—Colombia (volumes containing early notes from Colombian agents to State Department)
Con. Let.—Consular Letters
Con. Rep.—*Consular Reports*
Cong. Rec.—*Congressional Record*
Desp. Col. ⎫
Desp. G. B. ⎬ Despatches from Ministers ⎰ Colombia / Great Britain / Prussia
Desp. Prussia ⎭

Desp. Col.		Colombia
Desp. G. B.	Despatches from Ministers	Great Britain
Desp. Prussia		Prussia

Dom. Let.—Domestic Letters
For. Rel.—*Foreign Relations* (earlier volumes, *Diplomatic Correspondence*)
H. A. H. R.—*The Hispanic American Historical Review*
H. Doc.—*House Documents*
H. Ex. Doc.—*House Executive Documents*
H. Jour.—*House Journal*
H. Rep.—*House Reports*

Inst. Col.		Colombia
Inst. G. B.		Great Britain
Inst. Mex.	Instructions to Ministers	Mexico
Inst. Russia		Russia
Inst. Sp.		Spain

Inst. to Con.—Instructions to Consuls
Misc. Let.—Miscellaneous Letters
Monthly Con. Rep.—*Monthly Consular Reports*
Monthly Con. and Trade Rep.—*Monthly Consular and Trade Reports*
Niles' Reg.—*Niles' Register*
Notes from Col. Leg.—Notes from Colombian Legation

Notes to Col. Leg.—Notes to Colombian Legation
Notes to For. Leg.—Notes to Foreign Legations (except Colombia)
Sen. Doc.—Senate Documents
Sen. Ex. Doc.—Senate Executive Documents
Sen. Ex. Jour.—Senate Executive Journal
Sen. Jour.—Senate Journal
Sen. Misc. Doc.—Senate Miscellaneous Documents
Specl. Agts. Ser.—Special Agents Series

COLOMBIA AND THE UNITED STATES
1765-1934

Part I

INTRODUCTION

CHAPTER I

COLONIAL HERITAGE

At the very gates of the Panama Canal—lost to her by her own short-sightedness and the prompt but high-handed energy of the President of the United States, Colonel Roosevelt—lies a country of lofty mountains and snow-capped summits, of fertile, temperate valleys and plateaux, of riotously tropical coasts and lowlands, of extensive natural pastures and of thousands of miles of virgin forests; a country rich with promise of vast mineral wealth, whose varied climate is capable of nurturing the vegetation of every zone, yet which lies fallow for lack of highways and railroads; a country teeming with interest to the historian and the archaeologist, possessing a literature and culture second to none in the New World, and whose capital proudly bears the title of the "Athens of South America," yet where the mass of the people are illiterate and in whose remote forests roam savage tribes who have never looked upon the face of white man—in short, a country of boundless possibilities and of the strangest contrasts. This is the Republic of Colombia.[1]

COLOMBIA, situated as it is in the northwest portion of South America, with extensive coastlines and excellent harbors on both the Atlantic and Pacific oceans, enjoys a privileged geographic position on that continent. Its proximity to the Isthmus of Panama and the fact that it exercised more or less control over this commercially and strategically valuable and much coveted region for upwards of a century and a half (1740-1903) have tended to keep Colombia almost continually in the international limelight and have made it an important factor in world affairs.

DISCOVERY AND SETTLEMENT

Columbus discovered the islands of Trinidad, Tobago, and Margarita and then touched the South American mainland in 1498. He skirted the coast of Panama four years later, but Alonso de Ojeda, Juan de la Cosa, and

[1] Phanor James Eder, *Colombia*, p. 2. The terms, Colombia and New Granada, are used interchangeably in this chapter.

[3]

Amerigo Vespucci were the first to explore the coast of present-day Colombia. In 1499 they sailed westward from what is now Guiana to Lake Maracaibo and thence to Cabo de la Vela. The following year Juan de la Cosa and Rodrigo de Bastidas completed the running of the northern coast line.[2]

The territory extending from Cabo de la Vela to the Gulf of Urabá (now Darién) was granted under the name of "Nueva Andalucía" to Ojeda in 1508. The following year he attempted to establish a colony near the Cartagena harbor, but hostile Indians caused him to move westward to the shores of the Gulf of Urabá, where he founded San Sebastián de Urabá in 1510. However, failure to receive necessary reinforcements and supplies caused the abandonment of the town. Shortly thereafter Martín Fernández de Enciso, an associate of Ojeda, attempted another settlement, Santa María la Antigua de Darién.[3]

In the meanwhile, Diego de Nicuesa had received a grant of land west of the Gulf of Urabá, including present-day Panama and Central America, under the name of "Castilla de Oro." After a mutiny in the colony of Antigua and the overthrow of Enciso by Vasco Núñez de Balboa, Nicuesa was asked to take over the governorship, since the colony was actually in the territory of Castilla de Oro. However, on Nicuesa's arrival (1511) the colonists refused to receive him. This left Balboa master of the situation. After his discovery of the Pacific (1513) he applied to the Crown for the governorship of Castilla de Oro. But his request arrived too late (1514), since Pedro Arias Dávila had already been appointed governor of Darién and was on his way to the colony. In 1519 Pedrarias (the name by which the gov-

[2] Eder, *op. cit.*, p. 13; Mary Wilhelmine Williams, *The People and Politics of Latin America*, pp. 108-109.

[3] Eder, *op. cit.*, pp. 13-14; Jesús María Henao y Gerardo Arrubla, *Historia de Colombia*, p. 53.

ernor is best known) founded the city of Panama and made it the seat of government.[4]

The establishment of permanent towns on the Spanish Main and in the interior followed. Nuevo Toledo (Cumaná) was founded in 1520; Santa Marta, 1525; Santa Ana de Coro, 1527; Cartagena, 1533; Santiago de Guayaquil, 1535; Popayán, 1536; Santiago de Cali, 1536; Santa Fé de Bogotá, 1538; Pasto, 1539; Tunja, 1539; Neiva, 1539; Vélez, 1539 (destroyed later but reëstablished in 1612); Quito, 1541; San Bonifacio de Ibagué, 1550; Barquisimeto, 1552; Valencia, 1556; Truxillo, 1556; Honda, 1565; Santiago de León de Caracas, 1567; Maracaibo, 1571; Ocaña, 1573; San Sebastián de los Reyes, 1585; Bucaramanga, 1622; Barranquilla, 1629; Nuestra Señora de la Candelaria de Medellín, 1675; Socorro, 1681 —all in the Viceroyalty of New Granada, which included approximately present-day Colombia, Venezuela, Ecuador, and Panama.[5]

The population of this area is reported to have been 2,900,000 in 1810[6] and 2,644,600 in 1822[7]—at the beginning and the end of the revolutionary period, respectively.[8]

A HETEROGENEOUS PEDIGREE

New Granadian society was composed originally of three distinct groups: the Spaniards, the Indians, and the Negroes. Out of the sensuality of the first two grew

[4] Henao y Arrubla, *op. cit.*, chap. i; Williams, *op. cit.*, pp. 112-113; Eder, *op. cit.*, pp. 15-16.

[5] Henao y Arrubla, *op. cit.*, pp. 88, 89, 107, 108, 115, 173, 190, 191, 222; F. Depons, *Travels in South America during the Years of 1801, 1802, 1803 and 1804*, I, 36, 38, 49; Williams, *op. cit.*, pp. 129-131; *Encyclopaedia Britannica* (14th ed.), X, 945; XVIII, 857.

[6] William Pilling, *The Emancipation of South America*, p. 296.

[7] G. Mollien, *Travels in the Republic of Colombia in the Years 1822 and 1823*, p. 352. It is difficult to determine whether this estimate includes Ecuador.

[8] Henao y Arrubla, *op. cit.*, p. 518, accept the approximate figure of 3,000,000 for 1825. A Colombian official source gives the population of Colombia proper in 1825 as 1,223,598 (*Censo de población de la República de Colombia* [1918], Bogotá, 1924, p. 441).

a fourth, the mestizos. The early introduction of Negro slaves made for still greater racial heterogeneity. The union of these with the Spaniards and the Indians resulted in two more groups: the mulattoes and the zambos, respectively. The further union of these hybrids with the original groups and with other hybrids naturally produced innumerable racial shadings.

The royal prohibition of the emigration of unmarried women, except the daughters and servants of prospective settlers, to the colony naturally encouraged the growth of the mestizo class. In fact, the Crown favored this miscegenation as the best method of creating a uniform race in America,[9] but disapproved of the union of the Negro and the Indian. In spite of royal discouragement of this hybridization, the zambo was not uncommon in the colony. Mulattoes likewise constituted a large group of the population.[10]

Neither harmony nor a large degree of social equality existed between the groups. In granting permission to emigrate to the colony, the Crown considered Catholic orthodoxy of more importance than personal character.[11] Usually the settlers were of the warlike and adventure-loving type, similar to the *conquistadores*. And until 1701 there were rigorous laws against foreigners entering the colony.[12] The few Peninsular Spaniards residing there monopolized the high political and ecclesiastical offices and looked with no slight degree of contempt on the other groups. Even the creoles—those born of Spanish parents in the colony—were considered inferior by this social, political, and ecclesiastical ruling class.[13]

[9] Bernard Moses, *Spanish America on the Eve of Emancipation*, p. 100.

[10] *Ibid.*, pp. 100-101; Williams, *op. cit.*, p. 230.

[11] Only those who were able to prove that none of their forebears for the past two generations had been punished by the Inquisition were permitted to migrate (Williams, *op. cit.*, p. 228).

[12] Herman G. James and Percy A. Martin, *The Republics of Latin America*, p. 58.

[13] Parents actually made a distinction between their own children born in Spain and those born after migrating to the colony.

As many of the creoles became wealthy and well educated, this ostracism was deeply resented. Spanish arrogance and utter lack of sympathy created among them "excessive vanity and overbearing manners," which in turn led to a broadening of the breach between them and the Crown and the making of common cause with the mestizos. A large number of these influential and dangerous creoles were won over to the Crown by the sale of "patents of nobility," and many of the Indians and mestizos by the bestowal or sale of "patents of whiteness."[14]

However, these measures only temporarily retarded the growth and progress of the discontented groups, who later were to wage the War of Independence against both Spain and the Peninsular Spaniards in the colony. One of the greatest problems of republican Colombia has been the welding together of the diverse races and hybrids—possessing varied antecedents, history, traditions, and culture—into a harmonious social and political unity.

AN "ALIEN" ABSOLUTISM

The early period of the colonial régime—under the Viceroyalty of Peru—was one of "bewildering confusion of authority, civil and ecclesiastical," and the early officials, as a rule, were not only inefficient but corrupt and cruel. The Crown attempted reform (1564) by appointing a governor and captain general of New Granada, who was to be "absolutely independent of the viceroys of Peru and endowed with correspondingly large powers." For almost two centuries—1564 to 1740, with the exception of a few years after 1718—the colony retained this status. The Viceroyalty of New Granada was established in 1740, including the Captaincies General of New Granada and Venezuela and the *Audiencias* of Quito and Panama. This territorial arrangement and viceregal ad-

[14] Moses, *Spanish America on the Eve of Emancipation*, pp. 113-114; James and Martin, *op. cit.*, p. 60.

ministration continued, with slight modification, until the independence movement of the nineteenth century.[15]

Since the colony was considered by the Sovereign as his personal *hacienda* and in no wise the property of the Spanish nation, all administrative and judicial authority rested in his person. In Spain he delegated the larger portion of this to the *Consejo de Indias* and in New Granada, during the late colonial period, to royally appointed viceroys. But all officials held their positions at his pleasure.[16]

The Peninsular Spaniards practically dominated colonial officialdom. Of the seven hundred and fifty-four viceroys, captains general, governors, and presidents in all the Spanish colonies, only eighteen were creoles. The Spaniards "were the lords of the soil, owners of the mines and factories, the great political, ecclesiastical, and military functionaries; they monopolized the riches and honours."[17] Thus New Granadians became politically impotent outcasts in the land of their birth, where the foreigner (Peninsular Spaniard) held sway.

AN IRRATIONAL ECONOMIC SYSTEM

The administration of colonial economic affairs centered in the *Casa de Contratación* which supervised all emigration and trade. By very early decrees foreigners were forbidden to enter the colony, and the movements of Spaniards and American colonials were restricted.[18]

Large portions of the royal *hacienda* were granted to court favorites, and other large tracts to Spanish monop-

[15] William Spence Robertson, *The Rise of the Spanish-American Republics*, p. 4; Bernard Moses, *Spain's Declining Power in South America*, pp. 50-55; Eder, *op. cit.*, p. 24; Thomas C. Dawson, *The South American Republics*, II, 419; Henao y Arrubla, *op. cit.*, vol. I, *passim.*

[16] Henao y Arrubla, *op. cit.*, pp. 164-165.

[17] Bernard Moses, *The Spanish Dependencies in South America*, II, 398-399; John Holladay Latané, *The United States and Latin America*, p. 12, places the figure as eight natives out of seven hundred and sixty-two high officials.

[18] Williams, *op. cit.*, pp. 165-166; Bernard Moses, "The Casa de Contratación de Seville," *A. H. A. A. R.* (1894), pp. 93-123.

olists on the profit-sharing basis. The small independent farmer was almost unknown. The cultivation of products competing with those of Spain was strictly forbidden. Likewise manufacturing was restricted to articles not produced in the mother country. The pearl fisheries were required to pay a tax of one-fifth of their profits and the mining interests forced to contribute a royalty of one-fifth to two-thirds on their output. In fact, there was scarcely an industry which was not either burdened with oppressive taxes or controlled by a ruthless monopoly.[19]

Legal trade could be conducted only with Spain and even then was restricted to the colonial ports of Vera Cruz, Porto Bello, and Cartagena, and to the Spanish port of Seville—later to Cádiz. This was true until late in the colonial régime. Commercial contact was made with Spain, during most of the period, only once each year. A fleet of Spanish merchantmen protected by an armed convoy usually sailed in the late summer, spent the winter in American waters, arrived at Cartagena in time for the annual March fair, and returned to Spain in the spring.[20]

Prior to 1550 trade was reasonably free from excessive duties. However, after this, until nearly the end of the eighteenth century, the exorbitant export and import duties, in both the colony and Spain, sapped the colonial wealth, alienated colonial patriotic affection, strangled legal commercial activity, and led to the growth of an enormous volume of smuggling.

Piracy began very soon after discovery. French freebooters captured merchant and treasure ships, plundered seacoast towns, and desecrated churches and cemeteries. Nor were the "Elizabethan Sea-Dogs" inactive

[19] Latané, *op. cit.*, p. 11; Williams, *op. cit.*, pp. 171-173.
[20] *Ibid.*, pp. 168-170; Latané, *op. cit.*, pp. 11-12. New Granada, Peru, Guatemala, and Mexico were granted the right to trade with each other in 1774 (Moses, *The Spanish Dependencies*, II, 359).

in gathering wealth at the expense of Spain.   The
French, English, and Dutch, with bases on Jamaica,
Curaçao, and other islands of the West Indies, played
havoc with colonial trade and spread terror among the
inhabitants of the Mainland.[21] The small and inefficient
Spanish navy was almost helpless, especially after the
defeat of the Armada in 1588.

Since Spain, then, was unable to protect its colonial
interests and trade monopoly and its home industries
were insufficient to supply the colonial demand, secret and
illegal trade was most welcome to both the colonists ánd
the English, French, and Dutch merchants.   There resulted "a curious species of trader—half merchant, half
pirate, and necessarily always a smuggler—who sailed
the Spainish Main,"[22] prepared to seize merchant ships
and smuggle the captured wares into the nearby colony
or even carry on direct trade between England and the
Spanish Indies. Since Spain did not supply the growing
needs of the colonists and the smuggler's price was far
less than that of the legal merchant, illicit trade flourished.

The English Asiento Contract of 1713[23] simplified
the process of smuggling and actually gave it dignity.
Charles III, after the Peace of Paris in 1763, attempted
to reform the economic system by encouraging agriculture, industry, and commerce in Spain and opening additional ports in both Spain and the colony.   But it was
too late.

A POWERFUL, EXACTING, AND REACTIONARY CHURCH

With the *conquistadores* came the Roman Catholic
priests. Fray Bartolomé de Las Casas accompanied the
expedition of Alonso de Ojeda; and his cousin, Father
Domingo de Las Casas, ascended the Magdalena with
Jiménez de Quesada (1536) and later said the first mass

---

[21] Eder, *op. cit.*, pp. 28-29.

[22] James Harvey Robinson and Charles A. Beard, *The Development of Modern Europe*, I, 136.

[23] Incorporated in the Treaty of Utrecht (1713).

in the newly founded city of Santa Fé de Bogotá. The first bishop to arrive in the colony was Fray Juan de Quevedo, who (1514) accompanied Pedrarias Dávila, the new governor of Darién. Pedrarias was advised by the Council of the Indies to "hear the bishops and priests who, with less passion and less hopes of getting anything from the Indians, would be more impartial."

The first Colombian See was established at Santa María la Antigua de Darién and later transferred to Panama. Fray Tomás Ortiz and twenty Dominican missionaries arrived at Santa Marta in 1529. Sees were founded at Santa Marta in 1531; Cartagena, 1533; and Popayán, 1547. The Jesuits came before the end of the century.[24] And by 1610 the Holy Tribunal of the Inquisition was established in Cartagena. The introduction of the Index and the suppression of free speech naturally followed.[25]

The piety of Ferdinand and Isabella and their immediate successors and the preoccupation of the Pope with the Protestant Secession in Europe made it possible for the Spanish Crown to secure control of ecclesiastical patronage and supervision. The *Cámara de Indias* was set up in 1600 to regulate the clergy and their activities. Thus the ecclesiastical rôle was "played under royal direction," and the Church soon "became the strong right arm of the crown—and its most important instrument of control."[26]

However, nominal subordination to the crown did not necessarily mean subordination to the colonial political officials. The maintenance of separate courts; the ac-

[24] Depons, *op. cit.*, I, 13, 15; H. C. Lea, *The Inquisition in the Spanish Dependencies*, p. 453; Henao y Arrubla, *op. cit.*, pp. 157-160; Rodolfo Osvaldo Rivera, "Education in Colombia: Its Historical Development and Present Satus" (thesis, Duke University), pp. 35-62.

[25] See J. Toribio Medina, *Historia del Tribunal de la Inquisición de Cartagena*, and Lea, *op. cit.* The works of 5,420 authors were put on the prohibited list (Depons, *op. cit.*, I, 325).

[26] Williams, *op. cit.*, pp. 179-180.

cumulation of enormous wealth from tithes, royal gifts, and private donations; the enjoyment of a peculiar relationship with the colonists (many of them disgruntled) gave the clergy power far beyond their numbers. During the seventeenth century it became customary for the bishop rather than the *audiencia* to choose the temporary viceroys, and in the following century an archbishop actually held the viceregal office (1782-1788).[27]

The Church was not only powerful in political affairs, but it dominated the educational, social, and religious life and outlook of the people. All schools were under its supervision.[28] Only the one religion was permitted to be taught or practiced—the Inquisition saw to that. Marriages came under church jurisdiction. The Index was supposed to keep out liberal religious and political books and pamphlets. Individual thought was not only discouraged but stifled, and the offender punished. Unquestioned obedience to church dogma and practice was thus enforced.

This does not mean, however, that the clergy did not perform valiant service on the missionary frontier, supply a real need in the establishment of schools, and contribute somewhat to colonial welfare, but it does mean that the colonial "strong right arm of the Crown" proved to be a reactionary and not a progressive force in the new republic. Its relinquishment of power has always been forced, reluctant, and resentful.[29]

PARALLELS AND CONTRASTS BETWEEN COLONIAL COLOMBIA

AND THE THIRTEEN ENGLISH COLONIES

The dates of discovery of what are now called the Republic of Colombia and the United States almost co-

[27] *Ibid.*, p. 180; Henao y Arrubla, *op. cit.*, p. 282.

[28] In 1767 the Jesuits conducted thirteen colleges, while the Dominicans and Franciscans operated ten (J. M. Vergara y Vergara, *Historia de la literatura en la Nueva Granada*, pp. 62-65).

[29] See José Manuel Groot, *Historia Eclesiástica y civil de Nueva Granada*, I; Juan Pablo Restrepo, *La iglesia y el estado en Colombia*.

incide. However, permanent settlements in Colombia precede those in the United States by nearly a century.

The aborigines of Colombia (especially around Bogotá), when the Spaniards came, were a semi-civilized people with a fairly well-ordered government and with permanent cities and towns. The North American territory, when the early settlers arrived, was inhabited by half-savage, nomadic tribes, with no well-organized government and no cities or towns of any consequence. Many of the first emigrants to Colombia were Spaniards of high birth. For the most part they were mere soldiers of fortune, defiant, proud, and cruel to the extreme with utter contempt for manual labor. They had no intention of making homes and rearing families in the newly found country, but desired only to loot, rob, and destroy.

In the main, the early settlers in the English colonies were of the so-called middle class and came more to attain religious and economic freedom and to make homes than simply to acquire wealth at the expense of more backward people. The permanent rewards of labor were prized more highly than the temporary rewards of conquest, especially since the latter were meager in this region.

The Indians were incorporated into Colombian colonial society, although deprived of the title to most of their lands and generally reduced to economic vassalage. However, the Church made a conscious effort to attract them by building splendid structures, by giving to their religious processions a certain mysticism and splendor, and by permitting the continuance of certain superstitious practices after conversion. Owing to the shortage of marriageable *señoritas* and the natural sexual excesses of tropical adventurers, an ethnic hodgepodge resulted from the contact of the white man with the red and black.

The North American colonists made no place in their

society for the Indians. The lands of the natives were
either purchased or seized. The Indians themselves were
destroyed or ruthlessly pushed back by the westward
movement of the pioneers. Some slight efforts were
made towards their Christianization, but usually they
were considered as beyond the pale. Instead of attempting to attract the Indians into the churches, the North
Americans attended worship armed against them. Inter-
marriage with the Indians was rare. Thus the North
Americans, although possibly appearing more cruel,
were early able to produce a fairly harmonious social and
political unity.

The monarchal principles of Spain were transferred
to Colombia (New Granada) in their entirety. The
Peninsular functionaries placed personal ambition and
royal will above popular welfare. The native Colombians, being excluded from responsible offices, never
acquired experience in law-making and constitution-
drafting. Laws were made, and taxes and customs
levied and collected without their consent.

On the other hand, the colonists of North America
early began to assert the right of self-government. The
Virginia House of Burgesses met in 1619—just twelve
years after the planting of the colony at Jamestown but
nearly two centuries before any such meeting in Colombia. The colonial assemblies voted the internal taxes and
customs with only slight interference from the English
Crown. The policies of the Crown officials were often
modified at the desire or demand of these bodies. The
royal charters held by several of the colonies served as
constitutional examples when independence was established. Independence, therefore, was followed by orderly
national and state government founded on constituencies
already educated in the art of self-government.

During the colonial period New Granada was unable
to build up any appreciable amount of trade on account

of the Spanish commercial restrictions and trade monop-
olies. On the other hand, the British trade laws were
lenient enough to permit the North American colonies to
enjoy a considerable and very profitable trade.

New Granada, like the Thirteen Colonies, was the
first on its continent to strike for independence from the
mother country. However, its various cities and provinces declared themselves free before they united in the
fight against Spain. In North America, union preceded
the formal Declaration of Independence. "The English colonies . . . renounced allegiance to their sovereign
more through fear of future oppression than on account
of burdens actually imposed."[30] The United States was
never colonial in the Spanish sense of the term, since it
was never subjected to the ecclesiastical tyranny, the
oppressive economic system, the political vassalage, and
the studied insults, which New Granada was forced to
endure. It emerged from the colonial state as one strong
union, while Colombia, after shaking off the Spanish rule,
became one of the many separate and independent republics of South America.

THE AFTERMATH

These inherited factors early brought about internal
conflicts. The great Liberator Bolívar on his deathbed,
exclaimed: "Treaties are paper; constitutions, books;
elections, combats; liberty, anarchy, and life itself a tor-
ment."[31] This seems almost a forecast of subsequent
Colombian history, which has been until recently a record
of revolutions and counter revolutions, of the swinging of
the pendulum of government from ultra-republicanism to
dictatorship and back again, of the struggle between nationalism and localism, and of the strife between the
Church and the State for supremacy. The people knew

[30] Latané, *op. cit.*, p. 3.
[31] William R. Shepherd, *The Hispanic Nations of the New World: A Chronicle of Our Southern Neighbors* (New Haven, Yale University Press, 1921), p. 66.

how to submit but not how to govern, how to endure the rule of a tyrant but not how to control themselves properly after being freed. They had been chained by ignorance and superstition and knew not how to think for themselves.

With such ill-preparation for self-government, there is little wonder that greed and passion have often run riot and that liberty has many times given way to license. It would probably have been better for the Colombians if they could have gained their freedom by degrees. Freedom without preparation for self-government forced them to run before they had learned to walk, to write before they had learned their A B C's, and to assume a "developed stage without first having had the preliminaries."[32] The achievement of separation from Spain did not simultaneously establish real independence and self-government. These have been the products of long years of development and experience.

Any treatment, analysis, evaluation, or judgment of Colombian international relations which omits the consideration of this colonial heritage obviously would be not only unfair but false.

[32] Federico Alfonso Pezet, *Contrast in the Development of Nationality in Anglo-America and Latin America*, p. 13.

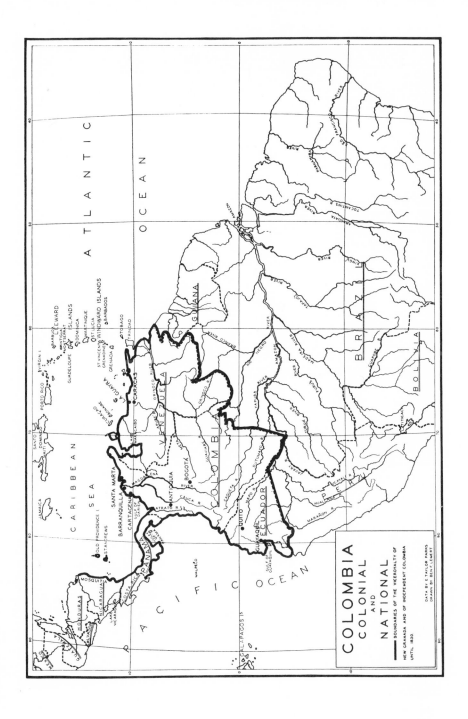

COLOMBIA
COLONIAL
AND
NATIONAL

—— BOUNDARIES OF THE VICEROYALTY OF
NEW GRANADA AND OF INDEPENDENT COLOMBIA
UNTIL 1830.

DATA BY E TAYLOR PARKS
DRAWN BY BEN CLEMERT

Chapter II

ACCUMULATING DISCONTENT AND INCIPIENT REVOLTS
(1765-1800)

RUMBLINGS of discontent were heard in the Viceroyalty of New Granada long before the North American and the French revolutions. A Negro attempted to establish a monarchy at Santa Marta in 1555; the revolt of Gonzalo Oyón occurred in Popayán in 1560; another disturbance followed in 1580; a mulatto was declared king in Venezuela in 1711; the creoles rebelled against the operations of the monopoly of the *"Compañía Guipuzcoana de Caracas"* in 1733; Bogotá experienced a disturbance in 1740; the people of Panaquire (Venezuela) rose against monopoly in 1749; and Quito suffered a revolutionary convulsion in 1765.[1]

THE QUITO UPRISING (1765)

The creole-mestizo masses of Quito revolted against the government alcohol monopoly in 1765. The disorder was so violent that Juan Días Herrera, the viceregal representative, was forced to request the mediation of the Jesuits, and the royal *audiencia* was compelled to promise not only relief from economic oppression but also pardon to all the rebels. The viceregal ratification of the general amnesty brought the four months' dis-

---

[1] Bartolomé Mitre, *Historia de San Martín y de la emancipación Sud-Americana*, pp. 35-37; J. A. Vargas Jurado, *Tiempos coloniales*, p. 21; José Felix Blanco, *Documentos para la historia de la vida pública de Libertador de Colombia, Perú y Bolivia*, I, 228; Moses, *Spanish Dependencies in South America*, II, 350 ff., 400. The captaincy general of Venezuela became practically independent of the viceroyalty in 1777. However, since the two were reunited under the Republic of Colombia, this chapter treats the entire area as a unit.

turbance to an end, but not before the creole-mestizo
faction had come to a realization of the possibilities of
its strength. The expulsion of the Jesuits two years later
and the acquisition of a large portion of their confiscated
property by the creoles and mestizos "loosened the hitherto firm hold of Europeans on both the material and
spiritual interests" of the colonists.[2]

Los Comuneros (1781-1784)

As a consequence of the Franco-American Alliance of
1778, Spain dutifully followed her ally, the next year, in
war against Great Britain. This move naturally placed
new and heavier burdens on the depleted Spanish treasury and, in turn, increased the already excessive financial
exactions on the Spanish colonials. The subsequent royal
edicts aroused vigorous opposition, especially in the province of Socorro, where a group refused (1781) to bear
the burden.

The disorder was temporarily quelled by the decision
of the *cabildo* to suspend the collection of the taxes.
However, the discontent spread into other localities,
where tax administrators were attacked and government
property destroyed indiscriminately.

The following month the malcontents, some 6,000
strong, assembled in Socorro and began an organized
resistance by electing José Francisco Berbeo as their
chief and three others of their number to serve with him
on a commission or *comun*. The *Comuneros* proceeded
to make military preparations. At Puente Real they
went so far as to declare themselves independent, choosing a council of war and a secretary of state, and casting
about for a monarch.[3]

The Indians of the Pamplona district were aroused,

---

[2] Moses, *Spain's Declining Power*, pp. 98-103.

[3] Joaquín de Finestrad, *El vassallo instruído*, p. 149.

"solemnly published the proclamation of Tupac Amarú,"[4] and swore obedience to him as "Emperor of America."[5] Since the government at Bogotá was ill-prepared to resist the advance of the *Comuneros* and their Indian allies, they agreed to a capitulation proposed by the insurgents.[6]

Following this fancied victory the *Comuneros* disbanded. The government, its arm having been strengthened by the arrival of troops from Cartagena, proceeded to crush the Indian disaffection with unusual brutality. Such action led to a new revolt under the leadership of José Antonio Galán. However, during the early months of 1782 this was also stamped out, and the leaders were executed or imprisoned. The government then proceeded to repudiate the capitulations,[7] without fear of any dangerous opposition.

Juan Bautista Morales—chosen by Berbeo in 1781 to secure English assistance for the *Comuneros*—and Antonio Pitá arrived in London in February, 1784, to purchase supplies for a new revolution. Since England was at peace with Spain (Treaty of Versailles, 1783), the Spanish ambassador was officially advised of their revolutionary activities.[8] In the meanwhile, Luis Vidalle of Curaçao had proceeded to London to secure English support. On May 12, 1784, he presented his credentials, signed by Vicente de Aguiar and Dionisio Contreras— *"hombres de talento, ricos y respetables."* He was authorized to declare to the British Ministry that a new revolution was ripe in Bogotá, Maracaibo, Santa Marta, and Cartagena, and that his entire territory would be

---

[4] An Inca, Tupac Amarú, had initiated a rather formidable revolt in Peru in November, 1780. See Moses, *Spain's Declining Power*, pp. 174-203.

[5] Manuel Briceño, *Los comuneros*, p. 64.

[6] Moses, *Spain's Declining Power*, p. 218; Briceño, *op. cit.*, pp. 119-137. 119-137.

[7] *Ibid.*, pp. 183-187. See also Blanco, *Documentos*, I, 146, 157, 158, 162 ff., 171-177; Gonzalo Bulnes, *Nacimiento de las repúblicas Americanas*, I, 52-67.

[8] *Los comuneros* (Biblioteca de historia nacional, IV, apéndice, p. 448; Briceño, *op. cit.*, p. 227; Moses, *Spain's Declining Power*, pp. 215, 225.

"delivered to His Britannic Majesty without reserving to
. . . [themselves] anything except . . . [their] religion,
and the same privileges that an English subject . . .
[was] entitled to."[9] Vidalle asserted that the *Comunero* movement had been closely associated with the
Tupac Amarú revolt of Peru and that it had the hearty
support of the masses, who were "looking forward with
anxiety to their separation from Spain."[10] The only
condition to the proposed and anticipated transfer of
allegiance was certain material assistance for which New
Granada would pay cash.[11]

Since Spain, as an ally of France, had rendered
assistance to the revolutionary colonies of North America, it seemed plausible that England would hasten to get
revenge by aiding the Spanish colonies. But the ministry was slow to act, and Vidalle was arrested and imprisoned by the Spanish authorities. Morales attempted
to proceed with the negotiations but to no avail.[12]

Opinions differ as to whether or not the New Granadians were aiming at independence so early. Restrepo
sees in the movement no spirit or conception of independence;[13] and Bulnes contends that there was no
connection between the *revuelta indígena* of Tupac
Amarú and the *sublevación proletaria* of New Granada,
and that the movement apparently had nothing to do
with the origin of independence.[14] On the other hand,
Briceño points out that the *proposiciones* submitted
to the British Ministry were actually drawn up by Jorge
Lozano de Peralta and that false names were put to the
document in order to conceal the identity of Lozano and
Berbeo. It would seem, then, that the leaders of the
Comuneros had become advocates of independence; in

[9] Briceño, *op. cit.*, pp. 227-231; *Los comuneros*, apéndice, p. 448.

[10] Briceño, *op. cit.*, pp. 231-237.

[11] *Ibid.*   [12] *Ibid.*, p. 94.

[13] José Manuel Restrepo, *Historia de la revolución de la república de
Colombia*, I, 19.

[14] Bulnes, *op. cit.*, I, 56, 67.

which case, New Granada would deserve the honor of having launched the movement and Lozano the title of *"El Padre de la Independencia."*[15]

In its inception the revolt undoubtedly did not aim beyond relief from economic oppression. However, the declaration of the Indians of Pamplona, the radical actions of the *Comuneros* of Puente Real, and the *proposiciones* of Vidalle to the British ministry seem to indicate that in New Granada many were gradually beginning to look forward "with anxiety to their separation from Spain." The Tupac Amarú uprising in Peru and considerable disturbance in Chile[16] clearly show that discontent was widespread in the Spanish colonies by the end of the North American War of Independence. It was little wonder, then, that the Spanish premier saw in it all "food for thought and fear" and suggested to his monarch a sort of American "Imperial Federation System."[17]

Los Precursores (1790-1800)

The year 1790, however, may be considered as marking the actual initiation of the movement for New Granadian independence. The early revolts certainly did not have independence as their motive. Nor were the masses ready to follow the *Comuneros* in their project to separate from Spain and come under British rule. But the viceroy of New Granada, the president of Quito, and the captain general of Venezuela were, in 1790, warning Madrid "that principles of liberty and independence, most dangerous to Spanish sovereignty, were beginning to ferment in the American minds."[18] It was also in this year that Francisco de Miranda of Caracas first presented his plan of emancipation to the British ministry.[19]

[15] Briceño, *op. cit.*, p. 93.

[16] In 1781 Chile sent delegates to Great Britain to secure 6,000 soldiers for a revolution and offered as compensation certain commercial concessions.

[17] Charles Lyon Chandler, *Inter-American Acquaintances*, pp. 4-5.

[18] Blanco, *Documentos*, I, 228.

[19] W. Spence Robertson, *The Life of Miranda* (1929), I, 99.

The *Precursores* were launching an under-cover movement, which was to result eventually in colonial independence.

Strange as it may seem, one of the earliest of the precursors was a Quito Indian, Francisco Javier Eugenio Santa Cruz y Espejo. His radical pronouncements brought him to Bogotá for trial on a charge of slander. While there he came in contact with the revolutionist, Antonio Nariño, who, it is thought, explained to him a project of organizing literary and patriotic societies which later were to serve as centers of revolutionary propaganda. Here he also met Francisco Antonio Zea, who was to serve later as New Granadian representative at the British Court, and Juan Pío Montúfar, who led the Quito revolution in 1809.[20]

Upon their return to Quito, Espejo and Montúfar founded *"La sociedad patriótica o escuela de la concordia,"* ostensibly to encourage intellectual development. In 1792 Espejo established a fortnightly periodical, *Primicias de la cultura de Quito.* The publication was not ultra-radical in character, but it called forth the bitter opposition of a powerful minority. And after the appearance of seven issues its publication ceased.[21]

This defeat of his program of intellectual development, which he felt was a necessary antecedent of independence, did not prevent Espejo from evolving a rather complete scheme of colonial emancipation and future national political organization. This scheme—according to Archbishop González Suárez—advocated a well-timed general uprising throughout the colonies and a unified coöperative struggle against Spain. After emancipation each colony was to become an autonomous republic governed only by those born in the colony. Foreigners were not to be expelled, but in government and public admin-

[20] Bulnes, *op. cit.,* I, 69-70, 76.
[21] *Ibid.,* I, 71.

istration they, especially the Spaniards, were to be totally excluded from participation.[22]

The discovery of this plan, owing to an indiscretion of Espejo himself, led to his arrest and imprisonment. However, before he came to trial, he was taken ill, and died near the close of 1795. Although his scheme seems to have been lost sight of temporarily, the similarity of its principles to those of the subsequent Monroe Doctrine and Bolívar's "Pan-Latin-Americanism" is very striking.[23]

An intellectual and liberal awakening was also quite evident in Bogotá. The Spanish choice of certain liberal and learned viceroys actually aided the movement. Printing presses were introduced (the only one in Bogotá had disappeared with the expulsion of the Jesuits); the Royal Library was opened to the public; and a newspaper, *Papel periódico de la cuidad de Santa Fé de Bogotá*, was established in 1791. This was followed by other periodicals: *Correo curioso, El redactor americano, Alternativo del redactor,* and *Semanario del nuevo reino del Granada.* A public theater was opened in 1793, and the literary clubs, *"Eutropélico"* and *"Buen Gusto,"* flourished.

Education was now actively encouraged by the viceregal government, by the colleges of El Rosario and San Bartolomé, and by the Seminary of Popayán. The famous scientist, José Celestino Mutis, carried on his investigations and trained young scholars.[24] The colonial mind was becoming so inquisitive and so eager for contact with the great thinkers and movements of the day that Spanish restrictions and barriers were no longer able to keep out the political and philosophical ideas which had actuated the revolutionary movements of North America and France.

[22] *Ibid.,* I, 76-77. [23] *Ibid.,* I, 77.
[24] Henao y Arrubla, *op. cit.,* pp. 264, 285 ff., 296-297, 301-302, 311, 313; Blanco, *Documentos,* I, 232.

It was in the midst of these liberalizing and invigorating forces that Antonio Nariño established his *"Club literario"* in 1789 and presided over it until 1794. This club, supposedly for the discussion of literary and cultural topics, appeared quite harmless at first, but "that which is innocent under a régime of liberty is not under one of despotism."[25] Among Nariño's effects, when later confiscated, were found, intended for the walls of the society hall, the following mottoes: *"Quitó al cielo el rayo y de las manos el cetro a los tiranos"* and *"Es verdaderamente libre aquel que no necesita poner los brazos de otro al fin de los suyos para hacer su voluntad."*[26] Cervallos claims that the *"Club literario"* of Bogotá and the *"Escuela de la concordia"* of Quito kept in close contact with each other "for the purpose of instigating and diffusing certain ideas of independence."[27]

It seems quite apparent that Nariño, while remaining intimate with the viceroy and holding the position of treasurer of tithes, was consciously striving towards the ultimate independence of the colony. Through his friend, Captain Rodríquez (Ramírez) de Arellano of the Vice-regal Guards, Nariño secured a copy of Galart de Montjoie's *Histoire de l'assemblée constituante* (3 vols.). From the third volume he translated "The Declaration of the Rights of Man," and with his private press published (1794) a spurious second edition bearing a Spanish imprint.[28] The work was distributed only among a limited group of his friends. However, one Francisco Carrasco saw a copy and reported the matter to the viceroy, who almost immediately proceeded against Nariño.

[25] *El precursor: documentos sobre la vida pública y privada del General Antonio Nariño*, p. 16.
[26] Bulnes, *op. cit.*, I, 104. The former refers to Benjamin Franklin; the latter is copied from Rousseau's works.
[27] Quoted in *ibid.*, I, 104.
[28] *Ibid.*, I, 103-105; *El precursor: documentos*, pp. 3-15. This would give the publication additional prestige and at the same time might conceal the identity of the real publisher.

When Nariño learned that action would be taken, he destroyed all available copies.[29]

An official examination of his library of 6,000 volumes, which was ordered confiscated, disclosed a portrait of Benjamin Franklin and works of such philosophers as Voltaire, Rousseau, Raynal, Montesquieu—*"todos malos,"* agreed the *audiencia*.[30] Along with Nariño were tried ten others on charges varying from criticizing the government to inciting revolution, and from speaking favorably of the French philosophers and the United States Constitution to endeavoring to secure foreign aid for a revolution.[31] Nariño was convicted despite his able defense conducted by José Antonio Ricaurte.[32] He was sentenced to ten years' imprisonment in Africa, was exiled for life, and was deprived of all his property by confiscation. The cases of the other ten were referred to the *Consejo Supremo de Indias* in Spain. This body later set them free and permitted them to return to their country and professions.[33]

By the judicious use of money Nariño was able to effect his escape during the confusion which attended his arrival at the port of Cádiz, and to make his way to the home of a friend, Esteban de Amador. Thence he proceeded to Madrid, Paris, and London.[34] The next six months were spent in attempted negotiations for foreign

[29] Moses, *Spain's Declining Power*, p. 283. C. E. Chapman, *Colonial Hispanic America*, p. 221, says that thousands of copies were printed and "reached the most distant points of South America."

[30] Jules Mancini, *Bolívar y la emancipación de las colonias Españolas desde los orígines hasta 1815*, p. 81; Bulnes, *op. cit.*, I, 107. For a list of his books, see *El precursor: documentos*, pp. 164-179, 184-191.

[31] *Ibid.*, pp. 111-143.

[32] *Ibid.*, pp. 51-110. Ricaurte was arrested in August, 1795, and sent to prison, where he died May 9, 1804. His beliefs and actions seemed to coincide with his defense arguments too well. L. Marroquín, *Precursores (Centenario de Cundinamarca)*, pp. 67, 77, 152.

[33] Moses, *Spain's Declining Power*, p. 285; *El precursor: documentos*, p. 142.

[34] Nariño to Viceroy, Aug. 13, 1797, *ibid.*, pp. 213 ff.; Bulnes, *op. cit.*, pp. 113-116; Mancini, *op. cit.*, pp. 89-94; Henao y Arrubla, *op. cit.*, pp. 305-306; Moses, *Spain's Declining Power*, pp. 285-287.

assistance in his emancipation scheme. In Paris (June-July, 1796) he was assured by Tallien[35] of French secret sympathy, but was denied aid because France and Spain were at peace.[36]

His two letters to William Pitt, on arrival in London, were not answered. However, through two commercial friends, Campbell and Chort, Nariño secured conferences with Lord Liverpool. The latter was willing to furnish sufficient assistance for a successful revolt on condition that the new kingdom be delivered over to Great Britain —Vidalle had made such an offer in 1784. However, Nariño was not ready to go that far. He countered by offering certain commercial advantages in return for assistance. This offer Lord Liverpool accepted.[37]

Returning by way of Paris, Nariño arrived secretly at Bogotá early in 1797. After a few days in the capital he visited the neighboring towns, trying to stir up revolutionary fervor, but to no avail.[38] The masses were not ready. His presence in Bogotá, when discovered, caused a near panic. Under the protection of the archbishop he surrendered himself to the viceroy, and was incarcerated. Penitently he told of his wanderings abroad, his negotiations with Tallien and Pitt, and his attempted purchase of arms from a merchant of Philadelphia; and he sought to convince the viceroy of his conversion to the royal cause:

If resentment led me to the edge of the precipice, I assure your Excellency that from today forward my obligation and the recognition of his great goodness will lead me even to shedding the last drop of my blood in the service of the king. . . . I implore his sovereign piety . . . that . . . restoring me to his royal confidence . . . I may remain in such a state that by my works

[35] Former president of the National Assembly and member of Committee of Public Safety, but at this time merely a member of the Council of Five Hundred.

[36] *El precursor: documentos*, p. 217.

[37] Bulnes, *op. cit.*, I, 113-114; Henao y Arrubla, *op. cit.*, p. 305.

[38] *Ibid.*, p. 305.

I may be able to give evidence of my repentance and of being able to come to the support of my disgraced country.[39]

After receiving further assurance, the viceroy, on September 11, 1797, granted Nariño amnesty. But the king refused to approve it and ordered his imprisonment until the close of the war.[40] Thus Nariño was removed from the field of activity until the actual outbreak of the revolution.

The current revolutionary philosophy was striking deep root also among the creoles of Venezuela. On hearing that it had been proposed in the French National Assembly to introduce into the Spanish colonies a manifesto designed to arouse the inhabitants to follow the French example, the *Consejo de Indias* issued an order (1793) forbidding the circulation of political books and papers, "whose prime object ... [was] the spirit of independence and irreligion." Four years later the Audiencia of Caracas specifically forbade the circulation of *Derechos del hombre y del cuidadano*.[41]

Meanwhile, a rebellion in the city of Coro was vigorously crushed (1795),[42] and the viceroy (May 13, 1796) wrote to the "Prince of Peace," expressing uneasiness and venturing to offer certain suggestions as to the methods of preventing "new commotions."[43] The administration of the new viceroy, Pedro Mendinueta (1797-1803), was one of such commotion and unrest that he warned his official successor:

One of the greatest concerns of the government is the maintenance of internal order, submission to the Magistrates, and public peace. Communication with foreigners through contraband trade; the introduction of books and papers prohibited as pernicious to religion and the state; ill-directed reading; certain

[39] *El precursor: documentos,* p. 233.
[40] *Ibid.,* pp. 223-233, 238-263, 270-271; Moses, *Spain's Declining Power,* pp. 289-290; Blanco, *Documentos,* I, 257, 285-286, 288-294, 296-308, 310, 323.
[41] Blanco, *Documentos,* I, 247-248, 327-328.   [42] *Ibid.,* I, 256-261.
[43] *Ibid.,* I, 282-283.

flattering maxims imperfectly understood; a philosophical fanaticism; and more than all a spirit of fondness for novelty, has turned some heads and made them adopt various notions, which they indiscreetly announce as their own concepts. Herein, is found the origin of the changes occurring in the capital.[44]

Less than six months after Mendinueta assumed power and while Nariño was pleading for re-instatement in the good graces of the Crown, a general revolution aiming at the erection of an independent republic was being fomented in La Guayra and Caracas.[45]

In 1796 the San Blas Conspiracy, an attempt to set up a Spanish republic, was discovered in Madrid and four of its leaders condemned to prison *"en lugares mal sanos"* in Spanish America.[46] These prisoners—Juan Bautista Picornell, Sebastián Andrés, Manuel Cortés, and José Laz—were considered "martyrs of liberty and victims of Spanish despotism" by the creoles of La Guayra, where they were incarcerated temporarily. With the connivance of the prison officials and local malcontents, the condemned conspirators escaped in June, 1797. Picornell and Cortés hid in La Guayra, and Andrés fled to Caracas, where he was recaptured. The conspirators in La Guayra were joined by José María España and Manuel Gual, both men of local importance and wealth, the latter a retired army officer. Picornell and Cortés, after assisting in the maturing of the plans, fled to the Dutch, French, and English West Indies for the purpose of securing foreign support.[47]

However, before this could be obtained, the indiscretion of one Montesinos y Rico caused the discovery of the revolutionary plans in Caracas.[48] These plans had

---

[44] *Relaciones de mando,* pp. 584-585.

[45] Blanco, *Documentos,* I, 287, 294-295, 309; II, 323, 331-383. For good secondary accounts, see Bulnes, *op. cit.,* I, 120-126; Moses, *Spain's Declining Power,* pp. 315-317.

[46] Blanco, *Documentos,* I, 285.

[47] *Ibid.,* I, 285; Bulnes, *op. cit.,* I, 121.

[48] *Ibid.,* I, 122; Blanco, *Documentos,* I, 363.

provided for the formation of both local and general governmental juntas and the calling of a congress in the name of the *"pueblo americano"* for the purpose of declaring Venezuela independent. Even the colors of the national flag had been chosen and a sort of New Granadian *Marseillaise* or *Soneto Americano* composed: *"Viva nuestro pueblo; viva la igualdad, la ley, la justicia y la liberdad."*[49]

The aged captain general, thoroughly frightened, concentrated all available troops in the disaffected areas and requested reinforcements from Spain. The customary tedious investigation followed. Although the leaders had fled beyond Spanish jurisdiction, approximately one hundred conspirators were arrested and convicted.[50] España himself returned to La Guayra during the early part of 1799. Betrayed there by one of his servants, he was captured and executed.[51]

Picornell had escaped to Curaçao (Dutch), Guadalupe (French), then Trinidad (English, since the early months of 1797). The authorities of none of these, however, would return the fugitive to Spanish jurisdiction. While in Trinidad, he published *Derechos del hombre*—including an *"infame prólogo"* and a national anthem, *"Caramañola Americana"*—and circulated it profusely along the Venezuelan coast.[52] From Trinidad also Gual wrote Miranda (July 12, 1799) that since the "miscarriage of ... [their] attempt, the desire of independence ... [had] but increased."[53]

The British governor of Trinidad, Sir Thomas Picton —true to the spirit of Lord Liverpool's conversations

[49] Viceroy Carbonell to Prince of Peace, Aug. 28, 1797, *ibid.*, I, 311-319; Bulnes, *op. cit.*, I, 122-123.

[50] *Ibid.*, I, 123-126.

[51] R. M. Baralt y R. Díaz, *Resumen de la historia de Venezuela*, I, 14-15.

[52] Bulnes, *op. cit.*, I, 123-124, 126. Some 12,000 copies of the pamphlet were published. William Spence Robertson, ''Francisco de Miranda and the Revolutionizing of Spanish America,'' *A. H. A. A. R.* (1907), p. 224. Hereinafter referred to as Robertson, *Miranda* (1907).

[53] Quoted by Moses, *Spain's Declining Power*, p. 316.

with Nariño in 1796 and in accordance with British instructions of April 8, 1797—issued a manifesto to all the
"cabildos y habitantes de la costa firma," assuring them
of British assistance in "the securing of their independence, without pretention to any rights of sovereignty over
their country, or intermeddling in their political, civil,
or religious rights."[54] Since this was issued twenty days
before the date set for the revolt in Caracas, the accusation that Picton was the counsellor[55] of the revolution
may have some justification. At any rate, the captain
general (November 21, 1798) warned a Caracan council
of war:

Our situation, gentlemen, is truly deplorable! An expedition
threatens the whole coast, and all the coast is without defense;
and the king's fleet, blockaded in his ports, cannot come to our
support. And *the people* already wearied with our government,
look up to the English as their protectors and friends.[56]

In London, Francisco de Miranda was employing all
of his arts of diplomacy to make this threatened expedition a reality.

[54] Blanco, *Documentos,* I, 284; Mancini, *op. cit.,* p. 95.
[55] Bulnes, *op. cit.,* I, 124.
[56] Address of Nov. 21, 1798, quoted by Moses, *Spain's Declining Power,*
p. 323.

CHAPTER III

THE CASE OF COLONIAL INDEPENDENCE
BEFORE FOREIGN COUNCILS
(1790-1806)

OUT of the bitter rivalries and the greed of the era of discovery and exploration grew the European desire for commercial and political advantages in the Caribbean Sea and on the Spanish Main.

EARLY EUROPEAN INTEREST AND ACTIVITIES

The "Elizabethan Sea-Dogs" played havoc with early Spanish commerce, and the seventeenth-century buccaneers attacked and plundered the towns of Porto Bello, Maracaibo, Cartagena, Panama, and Guayaquil.[1] In 1648 Thomas Gage pointed out the advantages of the Spanish Main and attempted to arouse English interest in its seizure.[2] He urged Cromwell, six years later, to attack the area. The governor of Barbados, Thomas Modyford (or Muddiford), advocated a similar move. These men undoubtedly influenced Cromwell's decision to send out his West Indian expedition of 1655.[3]   ✳

During the first half of the next century the English attacked Porto Bello (1739), Cartagena (1741), and La Guayra (1743),[4] but retained none of them in the Treaty of Aix-la-Chapelle (1748). In the same year of the attack on Cartagena, Stephen Deveros proposed a British alliance with the Spanish American colonists. Trade and commerce, not conquest, were his aims. To make the

[1] Robertson, *Miranda* (1907), pp. 195-197; Moses, *Spanish Dependencies*, II, 105, 106, 109.

[2] Thomas Gage, *A New Survey of the West Indies; or the English-American, His Travels by Sea and Land* (London, 1677).

[3] Frank Strong, "The Causes of Cromwell's West Indian Expedition," *A. H. R.*, IV, 228 ff.

[4] Moses, *The Spanish Dependencies*, II, 339, 341, 348.

proposal seem more altruistic, he added that "it well . . .
[became] a free people to place others in the same condition with themselves."[5]

France soon began to suspect the British of efforts to
revolutionize Spanish America and in 1756 considered a
plan proposed by M. Bertrand to prevent it. Other
projects were presented in 1768 and 1770.[6] But the signing of the Family Compact with Spain (1761) and the
loss of its North American colonies (Treaty of Paris,
1763) had lessened French interest in the Spanish Main.
Plans designed for the reacquisition of the Louisiana
Territory had much greater appeal.

In December of the year of the North American Declaration of Independence, Captain Kaye proposed that
the British furnish aid to the Spanish colonists in return
for "free and exclusive trade and commerce" and the
possession of the seacoast. Since one colonial revolution
at a time was quite sufficient, Britain did not seriously
consider the plan until three years later, when Spain
joined France in assisting the English colonies in their
struggle for independence. Actual attacks on Louisiana
and Darién seem to have been contemplated but never
executed. Governor Pownall (1780) thought that the
colonies were already "growing too much for Spain to
manage."[7]

British influence and interest encouraged the colonists
themselves to present numerous projects during the next
four years.[8] However, the peace treaties of 1783 brought
a change in British attitude. The Spanish ambassador,
as already noted, was advised of the revolutionary activities of the New Granadians, Morales and Pitá, and
Vidalle's offer of allegiance to the British crown in re-

        [5] Stephen Deveros, "Some Thoughts Relating to Our Conquest in
America" (June 6, 1741), endorsed in Admiral Vernon's hand, *A. H. R.*,
IV, 323-328.
        [6] Robertson, *Miranda* (1907), pp. 210-211.
        [7] *Ibid.*, pp. 198-200.   [8] *Ibid.*, pp. 202-211.

turn for certain material assistance was rejected.[9] When Miranda arrived in London in the early part of 1785, he talked with certain influential men, but did not approach the British government.[10] However, Spain, not entirely convinced of this change of heart, warned the viceroy against English agents in Caracas.[11]

EARLY NORTH AMERICAN ATTITUDE AND INFLUENCE

In North America certain New England churchmen— John Cotton, Roger Williams, William Hooke, and John Higginson—were early convinced of the "religious necessity of driving the Spaniards from America." It is entirely probable that Roger Williams, who lived in England for three years (1651-1654) in close touch with Cromwell, helped to influence the latter's decision to send the West Indian expedition of 1655.[12] The participation of some 3,000 colonials in the British attack on Cartagena (1741)[13] might indicate an increased North American interest in that area during the early eighteenth century.

At any rate, scarcely had United States independence been recognized (1783) when the Spanish premier, Aranda, wrote his king:

This Federal Republic has been born a pigmy, so to speak, and has needed the aid of states as powerful as Spain and France to attain her independence. The time will come when she will be a giant, and even a colossus, much to be feared in those vast regions. Then she will forget the benefits that she received from both powers and will only think of aggrandizing herself.[14]

That Aranda was correct in his prophecy is somewhat evidenced by Jefferson's letter from Paris, less than three years later:

[9] See *supra,* chap. ii. [10] See *infra,* p. 38.

[11] Robertson, *Miranda* (1907), p. 209.

[12] Frank Strong, ''The Causes of Cromwell's West Indian Expedition,'' *loc. cit.,* pp. 239 ff. Gage represented the economic and Williams the religious motive of the expedition.

[13] Richard Bache, *Notes on Colombia Taken in the Years of 1822-23,* p. 276.

[14] Memorial of 1783, quoted by Chandler, *op. cit.,* pp. 4-5.

Those countries [Spanish America] cannot be in better hands. My fear is that they [Spanish] are too feeble to hold them till our population can be sufficiently advanced to gain it from them piece by piece.[15]

Even Jefferson's later political opponents at home, although cautious, were willing to entertain independence proposals.[16] Sir Home Popham claimed to believe that Miranda (1783-1784) laid his plans before Generals Washington, Knox, and Hamilton, "who promised him every assistance and gave him assurance of raising troops in the province of New England, provided he could persuade Great Britain to assist with her navy."[17] Although official assistance was certainly not promised, John Adams wrote from London (1786) that it was the "fixed opinion" there that a revolution in South America would be "agreeable to the United States" and that it was expected that the North Americans would not only fail to do anything "to prevent it" but would exert themselves "to promote it."[18]

The London *Political Herald and Review* (1785) contained the observation that "the flame which was kindled in North America" had spread into the Spanish dominions and the example of the former had become "the great subject of discourse and the grand object of emulation."[19] By the Spanish royal order of May 18, 1791, the circulation of all medals alluding in any way to North American independence was prohibited in the colonies. Three years later the Colombian patriot Nariño admitted "working in accordance with the constitution of Philadelphia" and in 1797 told the viceroy that he had negotiated with P. Conlon of the same city for revolu-

---

[15] Jefferson to Archibald Stuart, Jan. 25, 1786, Paul L. Ford (ed.), *The Works of Thomas Jefferson*, IV, 188; V, 23.

[16] See *infra*, pp. 46-50.

[17] Memorandum of Sir Home Popham, Oct. 14, 1804, Carlos A. Villanueva, *Napoleón y la independencia de América*, pp. 334 ff.

[18] Adams to Jay, May 28, 1786, quoted by Chandler, *op. cit.*, p. 9.

[19] Quoted by *ibid.*, p. 8.

tionary supplies.[20] The following year an exiled Jesuit priest, Juan Pablo Vizcardo y Guzmán, died in London and left with the American minister a manuscript on Spanish American independence. This was published in 1799 at Philadelphia.[21] Manuel Truxillo y Torres— destined to be the first Colombian representative recognized by the United States—had already taken up his residence in the same city.[22]

MIRANDA: PATRIOT AND "PROMOTER OF REVOLUTIONS"

Miranda—said to be the only individual who participated in "the struggle for the independence of the United States, the French Revolution, and the emancipation of South America"—was a creole, born (1750) and educated in Caracas, Viceroyalty of New Granada. At the age of twenty-one he went to Spain, where his father purchased for him a commission in the army. A decade later, as a captain in the Spanish service, he took part in the Pensacola campaign of the North American revolution.[23]

While in Cuba (1781-1782) he corresponded with certain disgruntled Caracans in regard to relief from the "insupportable and infamous oppression" of Spain. In order to escape trial for this and for alleged participation in contraband trade, he escaped to the shores of the Carolinas in June, 1783. The next eighteen months were spent in touring the States, where he visited, among other places, Charleston, Philadelphia, New York, and Boston.[24]

During his journey to the eastern cities of the Union

[20] *Ibid.*, pp. 16-18.

[21] Juan Pablo Vizcardo y Guzmán, *Lettres aux Espagnols-Americains*, Philadelphia, 1799, reprinted in Carlos A. Villanueva, *Napoleón y la independencia de América*, pp. 295-321.

[22] Raimundo Rivas, *Relaciones internacionales entre Colombia y los Estados Unidos, 1810-1850*, p. 12.

[23] Much of the following general account is based on Professor Robertson's two biographies of Miranda, whose manuscripts are in the process of publication by the Venezuelan government.

[24] Robertson, *Miranda* (1929), I, 28 ff.

he met George Washington, Alexander Hamilton, Thomas Paine, Colonel William Smith, and Henry Knox. It was with Knox (1784) that Miranda seems to have formulated his first Spanish American independence plan, which included the use of 5,000 New England troops and was dependent on English coöperation.[25] He impressed the leading Americans as a "great general and master of military science." Hamilton soon became "one of his most intimate friends and confidential advisers." The emancipation of South America was his "constant topic" of conversation.[26]

Leaving a copy of a cipher with Knox,[27] he set out for England in the latter part of 1784. A few months later he was found in conference with Lords Howe, Shelbourne, and Sidney; Henry Melton (M.P.); and a former lord of the admiralty.[28] The *Political Herald and Review* reported the presence in London of a Spanish American who coveted "the glory of being the deliverer of his country."[29] However, instead of submitting his project to the British government at this time, he set out on an extensive continental tour.

MIRANDA AND THE NOOTKA SOUND CONTROVERSY

On returning to London (June, 1789) Miranda set about his work in earnest. The Nootka Sound Controversy[30] between England and Spain offered an opportunity for the presentation of his emancipation scheme to the British cabinet. His first conference with William Pitt was secured on February 14, 1790.[31] Certain trade

[25] *Ibid.*, I, 39, 42, 43, 54; William Spence Robertson (ed.), *The Diary of Francisco de Miranda (1783-4).*
[26] Adams to James Lloyd, March 6, 1815, C. F. Adams (ed.), *The Works of John Adams*, X, 134 ff.
[27] Robertson, *Miranda* (1929), I, 54.
[28] Robertson, *Miranda* (1907), p. 253.
[29] Quoted by Robertson, *Miranda* (1907), p. 257.
[30] See W. R. Manning, "The Nootka Sound Controversy," *A. H. A. A. R.* (1904).
[31] Robertson, *Miranda* (1907), pp. 264, 272.

concessions were offered in return for British military and naval aid in the independence struggle. The conversation went even to the point of discussing a suitable form of government for the freed colonies.[32] Pitt approved the scheme in case war should result with Spain.[33]

However, France—the Revolution was already in progress—notified Spain that it was not bound by the Family Compact to render aid in a war against Great Britain.[34] This warning produced in Spain a more conciliatory mood which not only made the settlement of the controversy relatively easy, but brought Spain gradually into an *entente* with England against France.[35]

Shortly after Miranda's return to London and before his conference with Pitt, he had written to Knox (then the American secretary of war) in regard to American coöperation. Evidently he received no reply, for he wrote again on March 15, 1790. Two weeks later he frantically appealed: "Pray, is your Roman plan of military legions approved or not?" Knox finally answered these letters but failed to commit either himself or his government.[36] Probably the responsibility of office had cooled his revolutionary ardor.

Miranda was not the only one interested in Anglo-American coöperation. Acting under official instructions, the Canadian governor sent Major Beckwick to ascertain the American attitude towards the sending of troops across their territory for an attack on New Orleans and the Spanish Floridas. Washington's cabinet was divided in its attitude towards the possible contenders—Hamilton being pro-British; Jefferson, pro-Span-

[32] Robertson, *Miranda* (1929), I, 99.

[33] Robertson, *Miranda* (1907), pp. 268, 272.

[34] Louis Martin Sears, *History of American Foreign Relations*, pp. 56-59.

[35] In 1796 Spain exchanged the English alliance for a French *entente*, under which it remained until its revolt against Napoleon in 1808.

[36] Miranda to Knox, Aug. 30, 1789, March 29, 1790, Knox to Miranda, Sept. 5, 1790, quoted by Robertson, *Miranda* (1907), pp. 277, 279; (1929), I, 95, 110.

ish; and Knox, rather non-committal, yet ready to consider inducements from either party—but all agreed that neutrality was best for American interests.[37]

Any other policy would have been difficult, since the United States had causes of complaint against both England and Spain.[38] Even neutrality might prove difficult, if England should choose to violate it by sending troops across to attack Spanish possessions or if there should appear the possibility of English control of the Mississippi. Decadent Spain was a more desirable western neighbor. However, the settlement of the Nootka Sound Controversy saved Washington from the dilemma.

A PAWN ON THE INTERNATIONAL CHESSBOARD

Although the danger of an Anglo-Spanish war had passed, neither Pitt nor Miranda was ready to give up the independence project. The latter was placed on the British payroll and continued in close touch with the British cabinet and certain leading Americans.[39]

In 1792 Miranda's field of activity was shifted to Paris. While presumably there on a short visit, the tender of the rank of major general and the promise of the consideration of his emancipation scheme caused him to enter the French service. So enthusiastic was he after conference with Dumouriez, Kersaint, and Brissot that he wrote Knox:

You will see . . . how things are coming to maturity; and the Period advancing when our dear Country America shall become that glorious part of the globe, that nature intended her to be—and those schemes our patriotism suggested to our minds in our Semposiums [*sic*] at Boston, are not far from being realized.[40]

---

[37] See Manning, *op. cit.*, pp. 412-423.
[38] See A. C. McLaughlin, ''The Western Posts and the British Debts,'' *A. H. A. A. R.* (1894), pp. 413-414.
[39] Robertson, *Miranda* (1907), pp. 285, 288.
[40] Miranda to Knox, Nov. 4, 1792, quoted, *ibid.*, p. 291.

About the same time he assured Hamilton that the time was ripe

. . . for the execution of those grand and beneficial projects we had in contemplation when in our conversations at New York the love of our country exalted our minds with those Ideas, for the sake of unfortunate Colombia.[41]

However, his enthusiasm was to be short-lived, since the defeat of the French forces in the battle of Neerwinden (March 18, 1793) brought him before the revolutionary tribunal on the charge of treason. Although acquitted of the charge, he was soon re-arrested, kept in prison until after the death of Robespierre, and closely watched thereafter until his departure for London on January 3, 1798.

During his residence in Paris, Miranda held numerous conferences with James Monroe (United States minister to France and an ardent Republican), Thomas Paine, Colonel William Smith, and another American named Stephen Sayre. Smith then conferred with Secretary Jefferson in regard to American coöperation in Miranda's scheme and delivered a letter from Lebrun to be given to President Washington.[42] However, Washington's proclamation of neutrality[43] in the renewed Anglo-French struggle and the subsequent unfortunate mission of Citizen Genêt made Franco-American coöperation improbable. The weakness of the new republic, the divergent attitudes of the political factions, and the fact that the United States held grievances against all three of the major powers involved in the struggle made neutrality perhaps the wisest course.

Spain's separate peace (August, 1796), its alliance with France, and its subsequent declaration of war on England (October, 1796) revived British interest in the

---

[41] Miranda to Hamilton, Nov. 4, 1792, quoted by Robertson, *Miranda* (1929), I, 126.

[42] Robertson, Miranda (1907), pp. 292, 299, 303, 305; (1929), I, 149, 158.

[43] April 22, 1793.

revolutionizing of Spanish America. A new plan of attack was drawn up by Nicholas Vansittart; the Island of Trinidad was actually taken in February, 1797;[44] and the governor of Trinidad (four months later) assured the *cabildos* and inhabitants on the Mainland of British assistance in "the securing of their independence." This assurance, given on the eve of the discovery of the España-Gual conspiracy, might even indicate British connivance.[45]

During the very month of the British seizure of Trinidad the Cuban patriot, Pedro José Caro, arrived in London from Paris—probably sent by Miranda—and soon presented a project to Pitt. Since it was felt that the Province of Santa Fé (New Granada) was the ripest for revolution, Caro suggested that a British squadron and 30,000 men be sent to Cartagena and at least 5,000 men to the Isthmus along with additional supplies.[46]

The delay in securing immediate British coöperation brought Miranda to London the following January (1798). He was well received by Pitt, and his suggestion of an alliance between Great Britain, the United States, and Spanish America seemed to have been enthusiastically approved.[47] Miranda lost little time in calling on the American minister, Rufus King, who had already received "several hints and suggestions from high authority" that had led him to believe that Great Britain was "desirous of attempting to separate So[uth] America from Spain" with the "probable coöperation" of the United States. King listened attentively to the unfolding of Miranda's plan, but thought it "wholly improper in any degree" to commit himself or his country.[48]

[44] Robertson, *Miranda* (1907), pp. 309, 311, 313-315.
[45] Spain, suspecting English plots, had warned the Caracan authorities.
[46] Robertson, *Miranda* (1929), I, 167; M. Romero, "The United States and the Liberation of the Spanish American Colonies," *N. Amer. Rev.*, CLXV, 70 ff.
[47] Robertson, *Miranda* (1929), I, 168.
[48] Memorandum, Jan. 30, 1798, Charles R. King (ed.), *The Life and Correspondence of Rufus King*, III, 555-557.

Numerous conferences followed. But King, not knowing the sentiments of his government, remained a bit hesitant, especially after Lord Grenville remarked that he "did not much like the scheme" and that, "if Spain sh[oul]d be able to preserve her independence and prevent a Revolution in her Gov[ernmen]t, they sh[oul]d not enter into the project." England held as its aim the preventing of the French use of Spanish American resources in case Spain fell under its power. In the latter event, the British would "immediately open their views and commence a negotiation upon the subject with the U[nited] S[tates]."[49]

Miranda seems not to have been advised of the British decision.[50] He proceeded to draw up a preamble to the "Triple Alliance" and to dispatch Caro to Trinidad and New Granada to advise the colonists of his progress.[51] Even King interpreted certain British preparations on Trinidad as a sign that "South America . . . [would] soon pass through a revolution."[52] However, the British cabinet not only did not give aid at this time but apparently made no effort to negotiate with the United States. Although Miranda was detained and again paid a subsidy, the idea of a triple treaty faded away.[53]

During the spring of 1799 Governor Thomas Picton of Trinidad aroused the British cabinet again by proposing an attack on the Mainland. This, he thought, "would probably become the center of a General Movement." He was keeping Manuel Gual there in readiness, and suggested that Miranda might also be employed.[54]

On September 30 Miranda forwarded certain doc-

---

[49] Memoranda, Feb. 1, 8, 12, 15, 1798, *ibid.*, III, 558-561.

[50] Robertson, *Miranda* (1907), p. 324.

[51] Robertson, *Miranda* (1929), I, 171, 174.

[52] King to Secretary Pickering, April 6, 1798, J. Adams, *Works*, VIII, 586.

[53] Robertson, *Miranda* (1929), I, 185-186; (1907), p. 339.

[54] Picton to Dundas, April 21, 1799, quoted by Robertson, *Miranda* (1907), p. 342 n.

uments to the British secretary of state for war, Dundas,
and requested a conference. One of these documents—
a letter from Gual to Miranda—declared that the time to
strike was at hand and that "the smallest assistance at
the outset would be sufficient, and it might be obtained
in these islands by a simple order from the English Ministers."[55] In an accompanying memorial Gual pleaded
that only "four or six thousand stands of arms, as many
uniforms . . . a few pieces of field artillery, a small quan-
tity of ammunition, about two hundred regular troops . . .
and two frigates for a few days" were necessary "to
overturn the colossal dominion of the Spanish Government, which . . . [was] ready to fall from its own weakness."[56]

Four days later, in submitting the material to the
cabinet, Dundas expressed himself as ordinarily opposed
to revolution, but warned his colleagues that the United
States search for markets might lead it to promote one.
Since revolution was almost inevitable, the question was:
Should England "interpose" and be a "party in the business" or should it permit this vast empire "to revolutionize itself without guidance or control, or any direction
given to their endeavors"?[57] Lord Grenville opposed
coöperation with either Miranda or the United States,
since he feared the consequences of a revolution.[58] Wind-
ham distrusted Miranda and had little confidence in the
United States, but felt that the danger of colonial revolution might be used as the means of detaching Spain
from France and securing constitutions for the colonies.[59]

These frank expressions of lack of confidence in the
United States were quite in contrast to Pitt's early de-

---

[55] Miranda to Dundas, Sept. 30, 1799; Gual to Miranda, July 12, 1799,
Charles W. Vane (ed.), *Correspondence, Despatches, and Other Papers of
Viscount Castlereagh*, VII, 273-275.

[56] Memorial of Manuel Gual, May 2, 1799, *Castlereagh Correspondence*,
VII, 276-279.

[57] *Ibid.*, VII, 284-285.   [58] *Ibid.*, VII, 285.

[59] *Ibid.*, VII, 285-286.

sire for coöperation. When Miranda's independence project was considered again in 1801 by the new Addington Ministry, the United States was left entirely out of the plans. England seemed able and willing to proceed alone.[60] However, the Treaty of Amiens (1802) brought peace with Spain and, naturally, the discontinuance of negotiations with Miranda.

This willingness on the part of Miranda to proceed without North American aid was not evident in early 1798. Scarcely had he re-opened negotiations with Pitt before he forwarded a letter to Hamilton[61] and began his long series of frequent conversations with King. During March and April he wrote twice to President Adams, attempting to convince him that the project had the entire approval of the British cabinet and was only awaiting the expected American break with France.[62] Two other letters to Hamilton soon followed. Miranda expressed the hope that his friend would not fail him when the proper time came. He feared that Knox had lost interest but asked Hamilton to sound General Harry Lee as to his attitude.[63]

In the meanwhile, the French refusal to receive the new American Federalist minister, Charles Coatesworth Pinckney, had led to Adams's decision to send John Marshall and Elbridge Gerry to join him in a new mission to secure compensation for the French destruction of American commerce. The insults shown these commissioners, Talleyrand's attempt to secure a bribe for the negotiation of a treaty, and the resultant publication of the ''X. Y. Z.'' correspondence by the United States aroused pub-

[60] Robertson, *Miranda* (1929), I, 223, 232; *King Correspondence*, IV, 262.
[61] Miranda to Hamilton, Feb. 7, 1798, Robertson, *Miranda* (1907), p. 321.
[62] Miranda to Adams, March 24, 1798; April 28, 1798, Adams, *Works*, VIII, 569-572; Robertson, *Miranda* (1907), p. 327.
[63] Miranda to Hamilton, April 6, 1798, June 7, 1798, *ibid*.

lic opinion against France.[64]   An open break seemed so near that some military preparations were actually made.[65]   A sort of "war fever" seized the nation.

From London, King expressed his fear that, if England did not revolutionize the Spanish American colonies, France would soon control them.[66]   However, on the same day, Secretary Pickering warned him that "threatening as . . . [was] the aspect of our affairs with France, the President . . . [did] not deem it expedient at this time to make any advances to Great Britain"; in case of hostilities, American public opinion might be aroused sufficiently to suggest such a treaty with England, but not until then.[67]

King, in a series of letters to Hamilton, then pointed out the danger of the United States being drawn into the struggle for self-preservation.   He felt the American measures should be "bold and active," since such would be not only the "most certain means of safety, but would promise the acquisition of great and lasting advantages." In American hands rested "the destiny of the New World," and the United States had "a right and it . . . [was its] duty to deliberate and act, not as secondaries but Principals."   Hamilton replied that this had been his view since the time that a "decisive rupture" had become evident.[68]   King then proceeded to impress Miranda that America was "rising with scorn and arms" against France.[69]

Possessing this encouraging news, Miranda wrote his third letter to President Adams and sent another to

[64] See Albert J. Beveridge, *The Life of John Marshall*, II, 215-373.

[65] War was never actually declared, but nearly two years of dilatory sea fighting did take place.

[66] King to Pinckney, Marshall, and Gerry, April 2, 1798, *King Correspondence*, II, 300.

[67] Pickering to King, April 2, 1798, *ibid.*, II, 296.

[68] *King Correspondence*, II, 656-657.

[69] King to Miranda, Aug. 1, 1798, quoted by Robertson, *Miranda* (1929), I, 179.

Hamilton, expressing his impatience at the latter's long delay.[70] Hamilton had made a note on the back of Miranda's letter of February 7 to the effect that he would not answer it because he considered the latter an "intriguing adventurer." However, he admitted that when Miranda formerly visited the United States he might have "expressed ideas favorable" to his project and have given "an opinion that it was one to which the United States would look with favor."[71]

Before the receipt of Miranda's letter, however, Hamilton had written King:

I wish it much to be undertaken, but I should be glad that the principal agency was in the United States—they to furnish the whole land force necessary. The command in this case would very naturally fall upon me. . . . Are we as yet mature for this undertaking? Not quite. But we ripen fast, and it may (I think) be rapidly brought to maturity, if an efficient negotiation for the purpose is at once set on foot. . . . Great Britain alone cannot ensure the accomplishment of the object. I have some time since advised certain preliminary steps to prepare the way consistently with national character and justice.[72]

Accompanying this, went a note to Miranda expressing approval of Anglo-American coöperation, advising of the mobilization of 12,000 troops, and prophesying effective American support by the following winter. However, he warned that personally he could give no assistance unless the entire plan received American official approval.[73] Both King and Miranda in their over-enthusiasm assured him of the British unqualified sanction, and Miranda added that "only the *fiat* of your

[70] Miranda to Adams, Aug. 17, 1798, Adams, *Works*, VIII, 581; Miranda to Hamilton, Aug. 16, 1798, Robertson, *Miranda* (1907), p. 328.

[71] *Ibid.*, pp. 251, 327.

[72] Hamilton to King, Aug. 22, 1798, John C. Hamilton (ed.), *The Works of Alexander Hamilton*, VI, 347.

[73] Hamilton to Miranda, Aug. 22, 1798, *ibid.*, VI, 348.

illustrous President" was awaited for them "to depart like lightning."[74]

In a final letter to Knox, Miranda made an effort to arouse his long-cooled revolutionary ardor:

In fine, everything seems to favor the execution of our projects of the year 1784. I expect that you will carry out your promises and that I shall soon have the honor of taking you to our country.[75]

Probably Knox could not be aroused, but Hamilton's enthusiasm grew apace. Before the end of the year, after outlining American military preparations, he wrote:

This, you perceive, looks to offensive operations. If we are to engage in war, our game will be to attack where we can. France is not to be considered as separated from her ally. Tempting objects will be within our grasp.[76]

In June of the following year he suggested to Secretary McHenry:

It is desirable to complete and prepare the land force which has been provided for by law. Besides eventual security against invasion, we ought certainly to look to the possession of the Floridas and Louisiana, and we ought to squint at South America.[77]

Thus it seems that in 1798-1799 it was Hamilton, instead of Jefferson, who favored depriving Spain of her colonies "piece by piece." The Jeffersonians, usually pro-French, were now trying to avert war with France. Between the two extremes stood President Adams. Owing to the activities of Picton and Gual at Trinidad, Miranda's negotiations in London, and the desire of Pitt for

[74] King to Hamilton, Oct. 20, 1798, *King Correspondence*, II, 662; Miranda to King, Oct. 19, 1798, quoted by Robertson, *Miranda* (1907), p. 330.

[75] Miranda to Knox, Oct. 19, 1798, quoted by Robertson, *Miranda* (1929), I, 183.

[76] Hamilton to Gunn, Dec. 22, 1798, Hamilton, *Works*, V, 184.

[77] Hamilton to McHenry, June 27, 1799, *ibid.*, V, 283.

Anglo-American coöperation, President Adams's approval might have set the revolutionary forces in motion. However, lacking confidence in the British ministry—especially in Pitt—Adams feared that the whole affair was merely a plot to draw the United States into a war with France and an alliance with England.[78] The letters from Miranda were locked in his desk unanswered.[79] Pickering ceased replying to King's fevered despatches, and Adams, hearing that Talleyrand would receive a new American mission, sent (1799) William Van Murray, William R. Davie, and Oliver Ellsworth to negotiate a treaty. At the price of Federalist unity, and probably his presidential re-election, Adams secured peace with France and possibly postponed the Spanish American revolution.

THE VENEZUELAN EXPEDITION OF 1806

The English declaration of war (May, 1803) against France and the possibility of a rupture with Spain revived again Miranda's hope of securing British assistance. Pitt came back into power in May of the following year. And five months later (October, 1804) Spain declared war on England. However, the British policy towards Spanish America did not change with the ministry. It continued to be one of keeping Miranda in England in readiness to arouse a revolution, if desired, and to prevent a revolution, if Spain could be separated from France.

Growing impatient at British promises and getting an inkling that the North American relations with Spain were not satisfactory, Miranda set out for New York. On arrival there (November 9, 1805) he soon made contact with Rufus King, Colonel William Smith, Commodore Lewis, and two influential merchants (Samuel Ogden and Christopher Gore) and forwarded a letter to

---

[78] Adams to James Lloyd, March 6, 26, 27, 29, 30, 1815, Adams, *Works*, X, 134-152.

[79] Adams to Lloyd, March 29, 1815, *ibid.*, X, 146-149.

his old friend Henry Knox.[80]   On the advice of King, he decided to proceed to Washington for interviews with President Jefferson and Secretary Madison.

The strained relations with Spain[81] made Miranda "a rather welcome guest" in Washington.[82]   He met and dined with Jefferson, visited Vice-President Clinton, held numerous conferences with Madison, and announced on his return to New York (December 29) that his plan had the "tacit approbation and good wishes" of the American government, on condition that the law was not "openly violated."[83]   Commodore Truxton, Doctor Thompson (of the State Department), and Jonathan Dayton (ex-senator of New Jersey) were informed of the details of the project.[84]

Preparations were rushed. The services of the ship *Leander* were secured, guns and ammunition procured and placed on board, and some two hundred volunteers enlisted. As shown by accounts written by several surviving members of the expedition,[85] various artifices were used to lure men into the service. The air of mystery surrounding the entire movement and the intimation that it was being secretly supported by the government drew many otherwise hesitant ones into it. The *Leander* put to sea on February 2, 1806.

After a few days out, Miranda appeared on deck for the first time; many did not even know that he was

[80] Robertson, *Miranda* (1929), I, 289-294.

[81] Due to unlawful seizures, suppression of the *entrepôt* of New Orleans in 1802, unsettled boundary of the Louisiana Territory, and American desire for Texas and the Floridas.

[82] Charles E. Hill, *James Madison*, p. 66.

[83] *King Correspondence*, IV, 577-581; Robertson, *Miranda* (1929), I, 295-298.

[84] Robertson, *Miranda* (1907), p. 366.

[85] John Edsall, *Incidents in the Life of John Edsall;* John A. Sherman, *A General Account of Miranda's Expedition;* James Biggs, *The History of Don Francisco de Miranda's Attempt to Effect a Revolution in South America;* Moses Smith, *History of the Adventures and Sufferings of Moses Smith;* E. E. Sparks (ed.), "The Diary and Letters of Henry Ingersoll, Prisoner at Cartagena, 1806-1809," *A. H. R.*, III, 674-702.

aboard. The *Leander* was halted (February 12) by the
British ship *Cleopatra,* but was allowed to proceed after
a conference with the captain. The next few days were
spent in organizing the few men into the nucleus of a
"Colombian army." A month later the "Colombian
flag" was raised. At Jacmel, Santo Domingo, the two
schooners, *Bacchus* and *Bee,* were chartered, and the
Venezuelan coast was reached by the latter part of
April.[86]

A warning from the Spanish minister in Washington
had given the colonial authorities ample time to prepare
for the defense. The expedition encountered (April 28)
two armed Spanish vessels. After a few shots the
Leander fled and the other two vessels and some sixty
men were captured. Receiving British reinforcements
from Admiral Cochrane at Barbados, Miranda returned,
landed (August 3), and captured the forts and the town
of Coro. However, the failure of the colonials to rally
to his standard and the gradual weakening of British
support forced him to abandon the entire project.[87]

The prisoners from the *Bacchus* and the *Bee* were
first carried to Puerto Cabello.[88] After a trial in true
Spanish fashion, ten were condemned to be hanged, be-
headed, and quartered. Three others were ordered held
at Cartagena until the king's pleasure was known, and
the remainder were sentenced to imprisonment for terms
of eight and ten years.[89]

From Cartagena these victims sent two memorials to
the American government.[90] One was presented to Congress in 1808 and a relief appropriation asked, but the
bill was defeated by the vote of 50 to 30. It was recon-

[86] Moses, *Spain's Declining Power,* pp. 331-334; Latané, *The United States and Latin America,* pp. 20-21.

[87] Moses, *Spain's Declining Power,* pp. 334-336.

[88] "The Diary and Letters of Henry Ingersoll," *A. H. R.,* III, 681.

[89] *Ibid.,* III, 682; Sherman, *A General Account of Miranda's Expedition,* pp. 67-69.

[90] Moses Smith, *op. cit.,* p. 66.

sidered in June, 1809, but the debate drifted into the discussion of whether or not the Jefferson administration had connived with Miranda. An appropriation would have been interpreted by many as an admission of previous official approval of the expedition. The measure was finally defeated in the House of Representatives only by the vote of the speaker.[91]

Both the Spanish and French ministers protested against the American attitude towards the expedition. Madison, denying any official connivance, assured them that investigations had already been ordered and the guilty parties would be punished to the full extent of the law.[92] Some prosecutions followed, the most famous being those of William Smith and Samuel G. Ogden in the federal district court of New York.[93] After a twelve-day trial, two independent juries rendered a verdict of "Not Guilty" in both cases.[94] Since so much "political capital" was made of the incident, it was little wonder that the Jeffersonian forces opposed the voting of relief to the unfortunate prisoners.

The exact relation of the government to the affair has been a subject of much debate. Many felt, at the time, that the acquittal of Smith and Ogden amounted to the government's conviction. Henry Ingersoll—one of the Cartagena prisoners—believed that Jefferson "not only knew but aided the cursed expedition."[95] King claimed that Madison impressed Miranda with the idea that "although the government would not sanction, it

[91] *A. S. P. F. R.*, III, 256 ff.; *Annals of Cong.* (10.2), pp. 488-491, 511, 896-898; (11.1), pp. 161, 257, 269-315. British pressure later brought about the release of those who survived the imprisonment ordeal.

[92] Robertson, *Miranda* (1907), pp. 370-373.

[93] Smith's own son, a grandson of former President Adams, went on the expedition (Adams, *Works*, X, 157).

[94] Ogden to Miranda, July 28, 1806, *Castlereagh Correspondence*, VII, 416.

[95] "The Diary and Letters of Henry Ingersoll," *A. H. R.*, III, 692; Katharine Roof, *Colonel William Smith and Lady*, pp. 265-273.

would wink" at his movements; therefore he thought it undoubtedly guilty of "unworthy conduct."[96]

A few days before sailing, Miranda, in a note to Jefferson, expressed the hope that the latter's "happy predictions" of the "future destiny of . . . [their] dear Colombia" might soon be accomplished under his "auspices and by the generous efforts" of the Colombians; and advised Madison that he had attempted to conform "in everything to the intention of the Government," which he hoped had been "apprehended and observed with exactness and discretion."[97]

Madison—while admitting that Miranda had told him, in general terms, of his intention to revolutionize Spanish America—claimed that Miranda "was merely listened to, with an avowal at first on his part that nothing more was expected." However, when it became evident that the possibility of an open rupture between the United States and Spain had led Miranda to believe that "some positive encouragement" might be secured, he was "expressly told" that the official willingness to listen must not be interpreted as a decision to conduct hostilities against Spain (if such became necessary) in any "underhand and illicit way but in a way consistent with the laws of war, and becoming our [American] national character."[98]

Jefferson denounced as "an absolute falsehood" any statement to the effect that he "countenanced" the expedition. He was equally satisfied that the same was true of the charge against Madison. "To know as much of it as we could," he added, "was our duty, but not to encourage it."[99] Later he wrote the new Spanish minister:

[96] Undated memorandum and King to Gore, March 9, 1806, *King Correspondence*, IV, 529-530, 581.

[97] Miranda to Jefferson, to Madison, Jan. 22, 1806, *ibid.*, IV, 583-584.

[98] Madison to Armstrong, March 15, 1806, G. Hunt (ed.), *The Writings of James Madison*, VII, 202.

[99] Jefferson to William Duane, March 22, 1806, *The Writings of Thomas Jefferson*, Memorial ed., XI, 96.

We had no suspicion that he [Miranda] expected to engage men here, but merely to purchase military stores. Against this there was no law, nor consequently any authority for us to interpose obstacles. On the other hand, we deemed it improper to betray his voluntary communication to the agents of Spain.[100]

The Spanish agents did not furnish the needed information until too late for the American officials to prevent the sailing of the *Leander*. However, Smith, the surveyor of the New York port, was removed and would have been punished for his complicity in the expedition but for the protection of New York citizens, "who by their impudent falsehoods and calumnies were able to overbear the minds of the jurors"[101]—the greater part of whom were "bitterest Federalists."[102]

It would be difficult, if not impossible, either to prove or disprove official coöperation or connivance.[103] In either case, however, the expedition was not wholly "an American enterprise." Although American "neglect" permitted the *Leander* to sail and a federal official (Smith) rendered direct assistance, more than one half of Miranda's force (August 3) was British. And even the attack on Coro would have been impossible except for British supplies and naval support.[104] Hence, the first organized effort to free the Viceroyalty of New Granada was made by Anglo-American forces under creole leadership.

[100] Jefferson to Don Valentine de Foronda, Oct. 4, 1809, *ibid.*, XII, 319.
[101] *Ibid.*, XII, 319.
[102] F. B. Sawvel (ed.), *The Complete Anas of Thomas Jefferson*, p. 244.
[103] Spain (July, 1806) advanced a claim for damages due to the expedition. The fact that the *Leander* sailed from New York was thought sufficient to place responsibilty. This claim was not entirely renounced until the Treaty of 1819 (Robertson, *Miranda*, 1907, pp. 394-396).
[104] *Ibid.*, p. 396.

Chapter IV

THE EMERGENCE OF LA GRAN COLOMBIA
(1806-1822)

AFTER the failure of his expedition Miranda fled to Trinidad and reëstablished contacts with British officials in the West Indies, as well as with influential friends in London. The news of the formation of the Portland cabinet, including Lord Castlereagh, and the expressed desire of Castlereagh to discuss the emancipation project with him brought Miranda back to London in December, 1807.[1]

THE BRITISH CHAMELEON POLICY

In the meanwhile, British official circles had been astir with Spanish American discussions. Sir Arthur Wellesley (February, 1807) drew up a plan of attack on the Spanish Main.[2] Castlereagh presented his views to the Cabinet for discussion. England was faced, he thought, with the alternative of either conquest or emancipation.[3] He rather opposed the former as prejudicial to future British commerce but favored the latter on condition that a stable government could be created to replace Spanish dominion. A preference for a monarchy under a French Bourbon, probably Louis Philippe, was expressed. In any scheme Castlereagh felt that the British should not present themselves "in any other light than as auxiliaries and protectors." Furthermore, British policy should be determined greatly by the turn of things on the continent.[4]

Miranda lost little time, on his arrival in London, in

[1] Robertson, *Miranda* (1929), II, 1-5.
[2] Robertson, *Miranda* (1907), p. 401.
[3] British forces had attacked Buenos Aires in 1806, as well as assisted Miranda.
[4] Memo., *Castlereagh Correspondence*, VII, 314-324.

seeing Castlereagh.[5] He reported that the people of Caracas and Santa Fé (Bogotá) still favored independence and were much disturbed over rumors from both France and Spain "that the Island of Puerto Rico and the province of Caracas, by secret stipulations with Spain . . . [were] already ceded to France." The presence of "180 French troops already established" at Caracas had greatly increased these apprehensions. He now claimed "from his Majesty's Ministers that assistance so long ago and so repeatedly promised."[6]

This proffered assistance now seemed about to become a reality. The governor of Jamaica was instructed "to make every exertion for preventing the American colonies of Spain from falling into the hands of France." If they desired to declare themselves independent—either under a Bourbon king or a government of their own choice—he was to assure them of the British guarantee of their independence.[7] Furthermore, the British were preparing, under the command of Sir Arthur Wellesley, a large military expedition to proceed against the Spanish colonies in case conditions in Spain did not indicate greater success for their arms there.[8]

NAPOLEON UNDERRATES SPANISH NATIONALISM

Spain—an ally of France since 1796—had been gradually becoming subservient to the dominant will of the "Little Corsican." The Treaty of Fontainbleau (1807) had permitted the passage of the Napoleonic troops over its territory for the invasion of Portugal.[9] The spirited opposition of the Spanish heir apparent, Don Fernando, to the policies of his father led to the abdication of the latter in favor of his son.

[5] Miranda to Castlereagh, Jan. 3, 1808, *ibid.*, VII, 403.
[6] Miranda to Castlereagh, Jan. 10, 1808, *ibid.*, VII, 405-422.
[7] Castlereagh to Duke of Manchester, June 4, 1808, *ibid.*, VI, 364-368.
[8] Robertson, *Miranda* (1929), II, 18-19; Melville to Castlereagh, June 8, 1808, *Castlereagh Correspondence*, VII, 442-448.
[9] To escape humiliation at the hands of Napoleon, the Portuguese Royal Family (Braganza), with a British escort, sailed for Brazil.

These unsettled conditions furnished Napoleon the desired pretext for intervention. His troops had already occupied Pamplona, and Joachim Murat had been appointed his military representative in Spain. Murat now refused to recognize Ferdinand VII and marched his troops into Madrid on March 23, 1808. Napoleon then came forward as arbiter between father and son and persuaded both—under duress—to renounce all rights to the Spanish throne. Soon thereafter Joseph Bonaparte was declared "King of Spain and the Indies."[10]

In the meanwhile, the revolt of the *Dos de Mayo* had occurred in Madrid and governmental juntas had sprung up in Asturias and Galicia.[11] These juntas—without a king, government, or army—formally declared war on France and dispatched agents to London for the purpose of securing monetary, material, and military assistance.[12]

ENGLAND CASTS ITS LOT WITH SPAIN

The British cabinet recognized in Spanish affairs the long-desired "turn" of things, which was to decide its policy. The agents were promised assistance; the governor of Jamaica was instructed "to suspend any measure tending to divide and therefore to weaken" the Spanish monarchy and to circulate no material in the Spanish colonies tending to reflect "on the conduct of the Spanish Court"; peace with Spain was declared (July 4); and eight days later the last of Wellesley's command of 9,000 sailed from the Irish coast for Spain.[13] The Spanish revolt "put a new face on European politics," and England decided that Napoleon could be crushed more effectively on the Peninsula than in Spanish America.

[10] Henao y Arrubla, *op. cit.*, pp. 314-315; Latané, *The United States and Latin America*, pp. 26-27.

[11] Other Spanish districts soon followed (William Spence Robertson, "The Juntas of 1808 and the Spanish Colonies," *Eng. Hist. Rev.*, XXXI, 576).

[12] *Ibid.*, pp. 576-579; *Castlereagh Correspondence*, VI, 363-364.

[13] *Ibid.*, VI, 375; *Eng. Hist. Rev.*, XXXI, 579-580.

THE SPANISH REVOLT SPREADS TO NEW GRANADA

The Spaniards lost little time, after the arrival of the British troops, in setting up the *Junta Central* and dispatching Captain Juan José Pando y Sanllorente to inform New Granada of the situation in Spain. On arrival at Bogotá (September 3) he found unmistakable evidences of colonial loyalty. Ferdinand VII was acknowledged as lawful king, war was declared against Napoleon, and 500,000 pesos were contributed for Spanish defense.[14]

The appearance of two French officials at Caracas (July, 1808) caused a near riot. They were forced to flee for their lives. The Caracans vigorously declared their loyalty to the new sovereign. Later the cities of Caracas, La Guayra, Maracaibo, Coro, Puerta Cabello, Barcelona, Cumaná, and Guayana made contributions for the defense of Spain.[15]

A British agent who arrived about the same time to advise of the complete reversal of British policy caused no such commotion.[16] Even the colonial fast-disappearing sense of loyalty to the Spanish sovereign was outraged by Napoleon's usurpation. Since the colony had always been the personal *hacienda* of the king, the colonials were not willing to recognize any ties whatever to the existing Spanish government. The spread of the propaganda (1809) that Joseph Bonaparte desired colonial separation from Spain and promised a constitution similar to that of the United States[17] did not change this attitude. Hatred and fear of Napoleon were too deep-rooted.

The *Junta Central* decreed (January 22, 1809) that the colonies were an integral part of the Spanish empire and would be permitted representation. The viceregal government at Bogotá then recognized the *Junta* and

[14] *Ibid.*, XXXI, 582; J. M. Caballero, ''Días de la independencia,'' *La patria boba*, pp. 109-111; Henao y Arrubla, *op. cit.*, p. 316.

[15] Blanco, *Documentos*, II, 161-163, 166-167, 182.

[16] *Ibid.*, II, 166-167.   [17] Chandler, *op. cit.*, p. 55.

chose Don José Narváez of Cartagena as its member. But Narváez was cautious and did not hasten to Spain.[18] Many felt that one representative was not proportional to the importance of the colony in the empire.[19]

In January, 1810, the *Junta* provided for a regency of five members to arrange for the meeting of a *Cortes* of representatives from both Spain and the colonies. This conservative regency was soon replaced by a more radical one, "responsible and subservient" to the *Cortes*. Numerous innovations followed, the greatest being the famous Constitution of 1812, which encroached greatly on the royal prerogatives.[20]

However, the liberal reforms of the Peninsula were not extended to the colonies. The *Cortes* of 1810 met before the colonial representatives arrived. The Regency, upon the establishment of provisional juntas by the colonies themselves, attempted to restrict colonial trade and even went so far as to stigmatize the colonials as rebels and traitors against Spanish legitimate authority.[21]

QUITO LAUNCHES THE REVOLUTION

Early on the morning of August 10, 1809, Count Ruiz de Castilla, President of Quito, was awakened to receive a letter from the *junta suprema de gobierno* advising him of the establishment of a provisional government. The new junta declared its loyalty to Ferdinand VII and invited Bogotá to follow its example.[22] But disagreement within the body led three months later to the reinstatement of Count Luis on the promise of a general amnesty. On the arrival of royal troops from Lima,

---

[18] Henao y Arrubla, *op. cit.*, p. 317; Charles E. Chapman, *A History of Spain*, p. 492.

[19] Blanco, *Documentos*, II, 373. Under this plan all the colonies would have had only twelve to Spain's thirty-six representatives (Henao y Arrubla, *op. cit.*, p. 320).

[20] *Ibid.*, p. 321; Chapman, *A History of Spain*, p. 493.

[21] Latané, *The United States and Latin America*, p. 29.

[22] Blanco, *Documentos*, II, 241.

Guayaquil, and Bogotá, however, the amnesty was ignored and some eighty-four rebels were sentenced to death or outlawed.[23]

The continued persecution led to another uprising on August 2, 1810, and the massacre of nearly three hundred citizens by Spanish soldiers. The news of the Caracas (April) and the Bogotá (July) revolts caused much official uneasiness. But order was soon restored, and Quito remained under Spanish authority until 1822.[24] Although the first to launch the revolution, the Presidency of Quito (now Ecuador) was one of the last to drive out the Spanish forces.

CARACAS FOLLOWS

For almost a score of years Caracas and its seaport, La Guayra, had been exposed to French ·and North American revolutionary philosophy and to English (West Indian) "unofficial" separation propaganda. After the ill-fated expedition of 1806, Miranda had returned to London, still hoping to secure English official assistance. In Caracas the people were being prepared for revolution, not only by leading liberals but also by four newly established periodicals. The very press used by Miranda in 1806 was employed by Mateo Gallagher and Jaime Lamb, two years later, to publish the first Venezuelan newspaper, *Gaceta de Caracas*.[25]

The colonial temper had so changed since the establishment of the Regency that, when its agents suggested (April 18, 1810) recognition, almost irresistible revolutionary forces were set in motion. The *cabildo* of Caracas accepted the resignation of the captain general, assumed control, and declared its loyalty to Ferdinand.

[23] *Ibid.*, II, 237-243; Henao y Arrubla, *op. cit.*, pp. 17-18; W. B. Stevenson, *A Historical and Descriptive Narrative of Twenty Years' Residence in South America*, III, 11-25.

[24] *Ibid.*, III, 26-45; Blanco, *Documentos*, II, 573-579.

[25] *Ibid.*, II, 176-177; Robertson, *Miranda* (1929), II, 104-105.

A supreme governmental junta was created, and agents were dispatched to both the United States and Great Britain to secure assistance.[26]

The *Cortes,* evidently fearing the outcome of the colonial unrest,[27] declared (February 9, 1811) that the colonists were on an equality with the Peninsular Spaniards in rights and *Cortes* representation, all colonial trade restrictions were to be removed, and all colonial offices were thereafter to be open to creoles.[28] These concessions a year earlier might have been effectual, but now the movement was too well under way. Miranda had already returned (December, 1810) to Caracas, and before the conciliatory news reached there, the first Venezuelan congress was in session.[29]

This congress of representatives from the provinces of Barcelona, Barinas, Caracas, Cumaná, Margarita, Mérida, and Trujillo soon began a spirited discussion of self-government and on July 5 sanctioned the "Solemn Act of Independence" for the United Provinces of Venezuela. However, before the document was signed by all the representatives, the cry of "Death to Traitors! Long live the King and the Inquisition!" was heard.[30] The promulgation of a constitution in December failed to check the reactionary forces. Soon the royalists under Domingo de Monteverde were practically in control of Coro and Maracaibo, and were preparing to advance against Caracas.[31]

In the midst of the patriot confusion came the earthquake of Holy Thursday (March 26, 1812) with its ap-

[26] *Ibid.,* II, 72-75; Blanco, *Documentos,* II, 377-401, 403-414; W. R. Manning (ed.), *Diplomatic Correspondence of the United States concerning the Independence of the Latin American Republics,* II, 1143.

[27] The United States commercial agent at La Guayra was convinced that a "large portion of the people" desired independence (Lowry to Smith, Nov. 30, 1810, Con. Let., La Guayra, I).

[28] Robertson, *Miranda* (1929), II, 104.

[29] *Ibid.,* II, 94, 106.   [30] *Ibid.,* II, 106, 117, 120, 130.

[31] *Ibid.,* II, 138-145.

palling destruction of life and property.[32] Since the catastrophe came on a religious feast day and many at worship were buried under church ruins, there was a tendency among the more devout to interpret it as God's vengeance visited upon them for their rebellion. The fact that the patriot centers suffered very severely, while the royalist stronghold of Coro was scarcely harmed, increased the popular superstition and prepared fertile soil for royalist propaganda.[33]

The patriot cause was so discredited that even the imposing of the death penalty for deserters failed to check the reactionary tendencies. Miranda was placed in supreme command of the patriot army and given dictatorial powers. Martial law was declared and frantic preparation for defense made. However, the royalist advance to Valencia and the fall of Puerto Cabello (July) proved too much for the patriots. Simón Bolívar's failure, due principally to wholesale desertion, to defend the latter stronghold made further resistance imprudent. The subsequent negotiations resulted in the Capitulation of San Mateo (July 25, 1812) and the early occupation of Caracas by Monteverde.[34]

Miranda attempted flight, but was taken into custody and turned over to the Spaniards. The remainder of his days were spent in Venezuelan and Spanish dungeons. He died at Cádiz on July 14, 1816. Bolívar sailed for the West Indies, and Monteverde assumed undisputed control.[35] The amnesty provisions of the capitulation were straightway disregarded, and Venezuela received the treatment of a conquered province.

[32] The estimates of the number of casualties vary from some 10,000 in Caracas to 30,000 in all Venezuela and the property loss reached $4,000,000 (*ibid.*, II, 147; Bache, *Notes on Colombia*, p. 39, Scott to Monroe, Nov. 16, 1812, Con. Let., La Guayra, I).

[33] Robertson, *Miranda* (1929), II, 145-148.

[34] *Ibid.*, II, 148, 150, 152, 154, 164; Con. Let., La Guayra, I.

[35] Robertson, *Miranda* (1929), II, 178-180.

REVOLUTIONARY CONTAGION PERVADES THE
VICEROYALTY

The development of colonial opposition to the exacting rule of the Spanish regency, doubtless encouraged by the news of the temporary establishment of juntas at Quito and Caracas, inevitably led to a disagreement between the viceroy and certain radical leaders in Bogotá. The viceroy considered the juntas as a disguised movement towards independence, while the colonials felt that his opposition was nothing short of oppression.

In an effort, as he felt, to maintain royal authority and at the same time to alleviate discontent, the viceroy proposed a plan for an American *Cortes* to function in case of Spanish national demise. However, the colonials recognized a catch in the plan. The viceroy and the *audiencia* were to continue in power during the five years necessary for the perfection of the new government. This did not fit into their philosophy:

Sovereignty resides essentially in the majority of the nation. . . . The Monarchy dissolved and Spain lost, we are in the same position as sons who have reached their majority at the death of their father.[36]

However, the news of fresh outbreaks in Pamplona and Socorro and the organization of a junta in Cartagena by the newly arrived regency commissioner (Antonio Villavicencio) himself revived colonial hope. It was felt that he would take similar action in Bogotá; therefore his arrival was anxiously awaited. However, as is often the case, "the excitement hurried events and the storm broke on July 20, 1810."[37]

The initial outbreak—caused by an altercation between a Spanish merchant and some creoles who were preparing for Villavicencio's reception[38]—resulted in the

[36] Henao y Arrubla, *op. cit.*, p. 325.
[37] *Ibid.*, pp. 322, 326.
[38] Blanco, *Documentos*, II, 550-552.

meeting of an open session of the *cabildo* on the same
day. Taking advantage of the favorable situation, the
patriot leaders proceeded to urge the organization of a
junta with the viceroy incumbent as its president. By
dawn of the following day the governmental change had
been completed.[39]

"The Act of July 20th" did not renounce allegiance
to Ferdinand VII, but entrusted the supreme authority
temporarily to the junta while a constitution was being
drawn up and a permanent government established by
and for the provinces. Until then the junta was to surrender its powers to no one except Ferdinand VII, providing that he should come to rule the colony.[40] But the
Regency's authority was denied, and Viceroy Amar was
soon imprisoned, awaiting his sailing for Spain.[41] The
colonials had thus secured complete control of the government.

"La Patria Boba"

At the critical epoch, when a compact union was required to
consolidate what had been conquered, petty details, parochial
rivalries, and what not led to quarrels which spoiled the patriot
cause. Yet the fathers of the country should not be ridiculed
for their acts. They were full of fervor and good faith, but
they lacked experience in government.[42]

This characterizes well the subsequent five years of
New Granadian history. Following the political changes
of July 20 at Bogotá, the provinces of Santa Marta, Antioquia, El Chocó, Socorro, Casanare, Neiva, Pamplona,
and Tunja organized juntas. In answer to invitations
from Bogotá, representatives from five provinces met
there in a *supremo congreso* (December 22, 1810). Since
Cartagena championed the federal system and Bogotá

---

[39] *Ibid.*, II, 554-555; Henao y Arrubla, *op. cit.*, pp. 326-328.
[40] Blanco, *Documentos*, II, 555-559.
[41] Henao y Arrubla, *op. cit.*, pp. 329-335.
[42] *Ibid.*, p. 372.

insisted on a centralized government, the congress did little more than debate, swear allegiance to their king, and deny the authority of the Regency. Disorders in the provinces had now developed into a series of civil wars. Some juntas set about to subjugate others, while counter revolutions were raging along the coast and in the southern portion of the viceroyalty.[43]

Since the other provinces seemed to favor the federal system and had already provided their own governments, the junta of Bogotá assembled, the following February, a *colegio constituyente* to frame a provincial constitution. This document, signed March 30, 1811, renamed the province the "State of Cundinamarca." Ferdinand VII was recognized as king for life "under oath to observe faithfully the constitution." During his absence a president, with two advisers and two secretaries, was to administer affairs. Jorge Tadeo Lozano was chosen as first president.[44]

A spirited Centralist opposition headed by Antonio Nariño soon led to his accession to the presidency and the framing of a new constitution. This one, promulgated in April, 1812, omitted all mention of the king, but did not declare for independence. However, such a declaration was forced upon Cundinamarca (July 16, 1813), because royal troops were attacking its forces as enemies of the Crown.[45]

In the meanwhile, Antioquia, Cartagena, Neiva, Pamplona, and Tunja had established (fall of 1811) a confederation under the name of the "United Provinces of New Granada" and had invited others to join. Cartagena (November 11, 1811) had declared its independence of Spain and assumed the leadership in the Confederation.[46]

Nariño, the advocate of a strong central government,

[43] *Ibid.*, pp. 336-339.　　[44] *Ibid.*, pp. 342-344.
[45] *Ibid.*, pp. 345-346, 378.　　[46] *Ibid.*, pp. 346-348.

refused to join it until he had annexed Margarita, Neiva, Tunja, Socorro, and Pamplona to the State of Cundinamarca—at least three of these were members of the Confederation. This determination on the part of Nariño amounted to a declaration of civil war between the Federalists and Centralists throughout the viceroyalty. The confusion was greatly increased by the alarming reaction against independence in the South and by the struggle between Cartagena and Santa Marta due to the recapture of the latter by the Spanish in 1812.[47] The Federalists and the Centralists were at war with each other and, at the same time, with their common enemies, the reactionaries and the Spaniards—certainly a unique situation.

Bolívar, having left La Guayra after the San Mateo Capitulation (July, 1812), arrived at Cartagena in November and offered his services to the patriot cause. Within sixty days he opened up the Magdalena to navigation. After receiving congressional permission he left Cúcuta (May, 1813) for Venezuela at the head of a small army. Three months later the provinces of Mérida, Trujillo, Barinas, and Caracas had been liberated. Popular enthusiasm rose to a high peak, especially when he marched into the city of Caracas. He was declared captain general and given the title of *Libertador*. However, since the battles of Bárbula and San Mateo had been won only by great sacrifices, the early reverses of Puerta, Aragua, and Urica forced Bolívar to retire and leave Venezuela (1814) again in the hands of the Royalists.[48]

Although his report to Congress was not favorable, Bolívar was chosen to proceed against Bogotá for the purpose of forcing Cundinamarca into the Confederation. His march was unopposed by the towns along the route. Bogotá soon surrendered. And January, 1815, found Congress in session there.[49]

[47] *Ibid.*, pp. 350-360.   [48] *Ibid.*, pp. 362, 369-371, 392-396.
[49] *Ibid.*, pp. 398-400.

THE RECONQUEST OF NEW GRANADA

Seemingly, the period of internal dissension and civil war had ended and early independence might be expected. However, the patriots now found that Popayán, Riohacha, Santa Marta, the Isthmus of Panama, Quito, Guayaquil, and the vast region of Venezuela were still under Spanish control. Bolívar determined to move first against Santa Marta. He re-occupied Ocaña on the way down the Magdalena, but soon realized that he lacked sufficient popular confidence and adequate forces to oppose the invading Spaniards. Therefore he gave up his command and embarked (May 8, 1815) for Jamaica.[50]

The close of the Napoleonic wars in Europe and the restoration of Ferdinand VII made available large Spanish forces for the subjugation of the colonies. Five thousand under General Pablo Morillo took Cartagena on December 6, 1815. Meanwhile, Barranquilla, Soledad, Mompós, and Pamplona had also passed into royalist hands.[51]

Morillo, although offering pardon to those ''who submit[ted] themselves to the mercy of His Majesty,'' imprisoned numerous patriots (rebels), confiscated property, and collected 100,000 pesos of taxes in Cartagena alone. The viceroyalty was declared reorganized, and the Inquisition and the *audiencia* were soon reëstablished in Cartagena.[52]

The Spanish advance towards Bogotá nowhere encountered stout opposition. Their reception at certain points was even enthusiastic. Independence ideas were being discredited, and many were won over by the flattering promises of the reconquering army. The President and Congress fled before the arrival of the Spaniards. Bogotá was occupied on May 6, 1816, *''sin disparar un*

[50] *Ibid.*, pp. 399-400.

[51] *Ibid.*, pp. 400-406; Frederic L. Paxson, *The Independence of the South American Republics*, p. 82.

[52] Henao y Arrubla, *op. cit.*, pp. 406-412.

fusil.''   The patriots were pursued and crushingly defeated on July 10. The Republic of New Granada was now at an end and all of its territory, except Casanare, under Spanish power.[53]

A *"Régimen del Terror"* followed the arrival of Morillo. His officers were warned that they ''should take very few at the end of . . . [any] engagement.'' He refused to accept the festivities prepared for him. The capital was placed under martial law and Antonio María Cassano made military governor. The prisons were filled with rebels. A permanent Council of War, a Council of Purification, and a Board of Sequestrations were established to expedite the procedure of ''pacification.'' Wholesale confiscations and executions followed. Affairs in the other provinces were little better. Thinking that his task was complete, Morillo went to Venezuela in the fall of 1816.[54]

Juan Sámano was left in charge of the pacification of Bogotá. If fewer rebels suffered, it was because there were fewer still alive. The Royal *Audiencia*—overthrown in July, 1810— was re-established by Viceroy Montalvo on March 27, 1817. Early the next year Sámano succeeded Montalvo. So cruel and bitter was he that even the *audiencia* warned the Council of the Indies that his ''harshness and severity'' were producing ''desperation instead of loyalty and confidence in the government'' and that ''the New Kingdom of Granada . . . [was] on its way to extermination. . . . ''[55]

THE TRIUMPH OF PATRIOT ARMS

Morillo made the boast that he had not ''left alive in the Kingdom of New Granada a single individual of sufficient influence or talents to conduct the revolution.''[56] The ''silence of terror'' was considered as ''complete submission.'' However, he was soon to find that colonial

[53] *Ibid.*, pp. 414-421.
[55] Quoted by *ibid.*, p. 436.
[54] *Ibid.*, pp. 422-430.
[56] Paxson, *op. cit.*, p. 82.

loyalty for the Crown had changed to eternal hatred. His ruthless measures produced a colonial solidarity scarcely dreamed of by revolutionary leaders. The ideas of a few now became the conscience of the masses and the passions of the masses created an almost irresistible force for independence.

Since experience had shown the Royalists at an advantage in open fighting, numerous patriot guerrilla bands appeared and began to harass the enemy on all sides. Bolívar, who had left for Jamaica before the arrival of Morillo, led two expeditions into Venezuela in 1816. In the second attempt, with the coöperation of Sir Gregor McGregor, he was able to set up a government at Barcelona, about two hundred miles east of Caracas. But Morillo, with the army he had brought from Bogotá, forced evacuation in April, 1817. The seat of government was then transferred to Santo Tomás de Angostura.[57]

The campaigns of the following year gave slight advantage to either side, but on the whole made the patriot outlook darker, at least until the arrival of a large number of Irish and English troops. Two years previous when all hopes were low, Bolívar had instructed his agent in London, Luis López Méndez, to secure British money, arms, and men.[58] In spite of the British proclamation forbidding such enlistments,[59] Méndez experienced little difficulty in securing volunteers. The government officials merely gave warning and took no action. By the middle of 1818 large numbers of these volunteers began to arrive in Venezuela.[60]

In the spring of 1819 Bolívar was ready to meet Morillo and his ten thousand men as they advanced inland from Caracas. Santander and Mariño were sent to

[57] *Ibid.*, pp. 83-84.
[58] Alfred Hasbrouck, *Foreign Legionaries in the Liberation of Spanish South America*, pp. 28-29.
[59] Nov. 27, 1817, *B. F. S. P.*, IV, 488-489.
[60] Paxson, *op. cit.*, p. 85; Hasbrouck, *op. cit.*, pp. 46-47.

cut off reinforcements, while Bolívar and Páez proceeded against the main column. The move proved a success. Páez was left to drive the crippled Royalists into Maracaibo. Bolívar started (May, 1819) on his famous march across the plains and up the Andes through the Pisba Pass to Bogotá. Joined by Santander, he began the ascent (June 22), five days later took Paya, and forced the Spanish general, Barreiro, back on Tunja. After the indecisive engagement in Vargas Swamp, he won the brilliant victory of Boyacá on August 7 and three days later rode triumphantly into Bogotá.[61]

Bolívar's march during the rainy season—considered impossible by royalist and many patriot leaders—spread havoc in the Royalist ranks. Great confusion followed at Bogotá. The day before Bolívar's arrival there, Viceroy Sámano and other Spanish officials fled. Spanish governors throughout the viceroyalty began to give way before the patriot forces. Within a few days Pamplona, Tunja, Neiva, Margarita, and most of Popayán and Socorro were free of Spanish rule.[62]

By the decree of September 11, 1819, a provisional government was set up, pending the decision of a subsequent congress regarding the form of the permanent one. After the public celebration of the recent victory Bolívar made a hurried return to Angostura, where he had left affairs in the hands of Vice-President Zea. The day following his arrival (December 17, 1819) the Venezuelan congress voted the "Fundamental Law" for the union of Venezuela and New Granada under the title of the "Republic of Colombia." Provision was made for the meeting of a congress at Rosario de Cúcuta in the early part of 1821. After a prolonged debate this Congress promulgated a constitution on August 30, 1821.[63]

Meanwhile, a new revolution had occurred in Spain

---

[61] Paxson, *op. cit.*, pp. 85-86; Henao y Arrubla, *op. cit.*, pp. 447-466.

[62] Henao y Arrubla, *op. cit.*, pp. 467-468.

[63] *Ibid.*, pp. 469-476; Paxson, *op. cit.*, pp. 86-90.

(1820), and Ferdinand VII had been forced to accept the Constitution of 1812. His attitude naturally became more conciliatory towards the colonies. Morillo was instructed to negotiate for peace on the bases of the extension of the Constitution to the colonies and their representation in the Spanish *Cortes*. To these overtures, the Congress of Angostura replied that negotiations could proceed only on the basis of an "absolute acknowledgment of the entire sovereignty and independence of the Republic of Colombia."[64]

However, a truce was arranged on November 25, 1820, and fighting ceased until Bolívar, the following March, declared it at an end and began a new campaign. Negotiations had accomplished little, and it was proving impossible to hold his forces intact except in prospect of immediate fighting. And early news from Spain indicated that Ferdinand was not ready to recognize independence.[65]

While the Congress of Cúcuta was discussing the political fate of the republic, Bolívar administered a crushing defeat to the much reduced Royalist forces of Venezuela in the Battle of Carabobo on June 24, 1821. Caracas, La Guayra, and Cartagena soon fell, leaving only Puerto Cabello and the Isthmus in Spanish hands.[66] The latter —long in sympathy with the patriots, but hesitant on account of the presence of a large Spanish garrison— declared its independence on November 28, 1821, and asked admission into the republic. Bolívar recognized its aspirations and granted the request in the following February.[67]

After the Battle of Boyacá, Bolívar had sent Antonio de Sucre against Guayaquil and Quito. Guayaquil had

[64] Williams, *op. cit.*, p. 301; Paxson, *op. cit.*, pp. 87-88; Henao y Arrubla, *op. cit.*, pp. 480-482.

[65] *Ibid.*, pp. 482-487; Todd to Adams, Feb. 20, 1821, Desp. Col. I.

[66] Paxson, *op. cit.*, pp. 90-91.

[67] From 1550 to 1740 Panama had been attached to the Viceroyalty of Peru, thereafter to the Viceroyalty of New Granada.

declared its independence in the fall of 1820 and, supported by the more or less frequent visits of Cochrane's
fleet and the arrival of troops from San Martín's army
at Lima, had maintained it. Before Bolívar arrived from
his Carabobo victory, Sucre had routed the Spaniards in
the Battle of Pichincha on May 24, 1822. Quito was immediately taken. An assembly of leading citizens approved its incorporation into the Republic of Colombia.
And Guayaquil was soon occupied by the patriots. Bolívar entered Quito on June 16, just three days before the
United States recognized Colombian independence, and
proceeded to Guayaquil for his famous conference with
San Martín in July.[68]

As Bolívar declared in a bulletin of June 8, 1822,
"from the banks of the Orinoco to the Andes of Peru the
liberating army, marching from one triumph to another
. . . [had] covered with its protecting arms the whole of
Colombia . . ."[69]—embracing approximately the territory of present-day Venezuela, Colombia, Ecuador, and
Panama.[70]

[68] Stevenson, *op. cit.*, p. 396; C. R. Enock, *Ecuador*, p. 76; Paxson,
op. cit., pp. 92-94; C. F. Adams, (ed.), *Memoirs of John Quincy Adams*,
VI, 23.

[69] Quoted by Pilling, *op. cit.*, p. 413.

[70] The battles of Junín and Ayacucho in 1824 put an end to organized
Spanish power in South America.

CHAPTER V

SUNDRY REVOLUTIONARY RELATIONS
(1810-1824)

PRIOR to 1783, as already noted, contacts between the North American colonies and the Viceroyalty of New Granada were slight and were made principally through European channels. However, the independence of the "pigmy" republic increased its interests and commercial leadership in the Western Hemisphere. Its motives were both sentimental and ambitious.

The visit of Miranda in 1783-1784 had aroused considerable enthusiasm from Charleston to Boston. He had experienced little difficulty in meeting influential Americans and seemed to feel that he had encountered in Hamilton and Knox spirits akin to his own. Rufus King, the American minister in London, did not hesitate to indicate to his government a decided leaning towards Miranda's scheme. Nor did he withdraw his unofficial counsel when the latter was preparing the expedition of 1806.

Jefferson and Madison had listened attentively to Miranda as he unfolded plans for the emancipation of his country. Although official approval was probably lacking, American vessels, crews, volunteers, arms, and ammunition were used. A government official (Colonel William Smith) and certain American merchants assisted in the recruiting and outfitting; the expedition sailed from an American port; and American citizens were among those executed by the Spanish for participation in the attack.

While Miranda's expedition was on the high seas, the Richmond (Va.) *Enquirer* commented enthusiastically on the possibility of a "United States of South America."[1] The autumn of the same year found Simón Bolívar on a

[1] Chandler, *op. cit.*, p. 44.

visit to the battlefields of Lexington and Concord and the cities of Boston, New York, Philadelphia, Washington, and Charleston.[2] Two years later William Burke, an Englishman, was arguing that, if some other power did not, the United States would emancipate Spanish America.[3]

Evidently this feeling was widespread, for Jefferson wrote President Madison that Napoleon would consent to the United States "receiving Cuba into . . . [the] Union to prevent . . . [American] aid to Mexico and the other provinces."[4]   But no serious negotiations of this nature seem to have been undertaken.

The British felt that the United States had "not swerved from the policy of fomenting the spirit of revolt and even of absolute separation from Spain" and had "offered every aid to French agents [1808-11] who . . . [had] been engaged in the same design."[5]   Gil Fortoul has been quoted as saying that the government of the United States in 1809 actually "suggested to prominent men of the Spanish colonies that, if they proclaimed their independence, the North American Congress would recognize the mission that might be sent and would consider a confederation of all America."[6]   Although such an official promise is improbable, many did feel that early recognition might be expected.[7]

In 1810 revolutionary agents arrived in the United States, and an American commercial agent was dispatched to the port of La Guayra. There were numerous evidences of the influence of the United States. Conscious attempts were made to imitate its institutions.[8] Juan Germán Roscio translated for publication in Car-

---

[2] *Ibid.*, p. 46.   [3] *Ibid.*, p. 52.

[4] Jefferson to Madison, April 27, 1809, Jefferson, *Writings* (Memorial ed.), XII, 274-277.

[5] Quoted by J. Fred Rippy, *Rivalry of the United States and Great Britain over Latin America, 1808-1830*, p. 19.

[6] C. Parra-Pérez, *Bolívar; contribución al estudio de sus ideas políticas*, p. 171.

[7] Hildegrade Angell, *Simón Bolívar*, p. 24.

[8] Lowry to Smith, Oct. 1, 1810, Con. Let., La Guayra, I.

acas Thomas Paine's *The Rights of Man* (1811);[9] W. Burke, in the *Gaceta de Caracas*, stressed the advantages of the American constitution;[10] Miguel de Pombo published at Bogotá *Constitución de los Estados Unidos de América* (1811);[11] and Manuel García de Sena published at Philadelphia *La independencia de la Costa Firma justificada por Thomas Paine trienta años ha, extracto de sus obras traducido del inglés al español* (1811)[12] and *Historia concisa de los Estados Unidos desde el descubrimiento de la América hasta el año de 1807* (1812).[13]

In the midst of the congressional debates Francisco Javier Yañes urged that a declaration of independence from Spain be adopted on July 4—the anniversary of the North American document. On that day Antonio Nicolás Briceño did read the American constitution to congress, but the Declaration of Independence was not approved until July 5. The wording of this document and of the subsequently adopted constitution unmistakably indicates a careful study of the North American instruments.[14]

There were contacts other than personal and political between the young republic of the North and the viceroyalty. By 1797 the flour trade with the Caracas area had reached the volume of 6,000 barrels annually.[15] That very year the port of La Guayra was opened to neutral trade. The order was revoked in 1800, but the port was re-opened by the captain general '(May 20, 1801), and continued thus through the war.[16]

In the meanwhile, the American congress (January 8, 1800) had chosen Augustin Maden as consul to La Guayra.[17] The following year the Philadelphia and New York newspapers carried advertisements of "first

[9] Chandler, *op. cit.*, p. 59.　　　[10] *Ibid.*, p. 58.

[11] Robertson, *Hispanic-American Relations*, pp. 75-77.

[12] *Ibid.*, p. 71.　　　[13] Chandler, *op. cit.*, p. 89.

[14] Angell, *op. cit.*, p. 24; Robertson, *Hispanic-American Relations*, pp. 71-73; Chandler, *op. cit.*, p. 67.

[15] Robertson, *Miranda* (1907), p. 222.

[16] Bache, *op. cit.*, p. 27.　　　[17] *Sen. Ex. Jour.*, I, 332-333.

quality Caracas cocoa"; coffee, cotton, and indigo from
La Guayra; cocoa and tobacco from Puerto Cabello; and
cotton from Cumaná. The papers of Boston, New York,
Philadelphia, Baltimore, and Charleston announced the
frequent arrival of ships from the Spanish Main.[18] This
trade amounted to some $1,500,000 from August, 1810,
to August, 1812.[19]

YANKEES IN THE PATRIOT SERVICE

Since these early contacts were quite numerous and,
in most cases, both beneficial and harmonious, it seems
strange that more Yankees did not fight in the patriot
armies. Those who entered the service did so individ-
ually and not in commands composed of and officered by
fellow-nationals, as did a large portion of the British
volunteers.

However, there are a few examples of meritorious
services rendered by citizens of the United States. Colonel Alexander Macaulay of Baltimore commanded one of
the patriot armies during the early activities around
Quito and Popayán (1810-1811)—was captured and executed two years later near Pasto.[20] José M. Villamil
of the Louisiana Territory also fought in this area.[21]
Colonel Felix Jastran served from Carabobo (1813) to
Ayacucho (1824), and William Robinson, a merchant,
proved of great assistance in furnishing military supplies.[22]

The most outstanding of the naval volunteers was
John Daniel Daniels (Danells) of Baltimore. Daniels,
with two captured Spanish vessels, joined the squadron
of Admiral Brión in 1818. He operated off the coast of

[18] Chandler, *op. cit.*, pp. 24, 31-33, 42, and "United States Commerce
with Latin America at the Promulgation of the Monroe Doctrine," *Quar.
Journal of Economics*, XXXVIII, 470.
 [19] Lowry to Monroe, Dec. 6, 1816, Con. Let., La Guayra, I.
 [20] Hasbrouck, *op. cit.*, pp. 347-348; Chandler, *op. cit.*, p. 114; Pilling,
op. cit., p. 318; Robertson, *Hispanic-American Relations*, p. 63.
 [21] *Ibid.*, p. 63.   [22] Hasbrouck, *op. cit.*, p. 350.

Cumaná and La Guayra and in the blockade of Puerto Cabello until 1822, when he was sent to the United States to purchase a war vessel. The corvette *Hercules* was secured, manned principally from the crew of the United States frigate *Macedonia,* and its name changed to *Bolívar.* Daniels not only presented this corvette as a gift to Colombia but likewise refunded money paid him for the purchase of two brigatines and three schooners, and cancelled the debt due him for munitions furnished in 1818.[23]

Others who served—entering in most cases near the end of the struggle—were Captains Joseph C. Swain and Clement Castell (Calthel); Lieutenants Francis X. Curtis, Thomas Severs, Christie, and Hawley; and Ensigns James Williams and John M. Doyle.[24]

Certainly, this list does not include all Yankees who aided the patriot cause. The Colombian navy of 1820 contained a considerable number among its officers and crews.[25] After the close of the War of 1812 numbers of the idle privateers and crews secured Colombian commissions and began to prey on Spanish commerce. The "imperfections of the [American] law and the prevalence of popular sympathy" even permitted the wholesale distribution of these commissions in the North Atlantic coast towns.[26]

There were numerous complaints of American sailors being impressed into the Colombian navy, either forced to swear allegiance or under intoxication persuaded to do so. In most instances all evidence of American citizenship had been either lost or destroyed. Therefore it

[23] *Ibid.,* pp. 347-348; Chandler, *op. cit.,* p. 135. Daniels was retired in 1844 on one-third of a captain's salary and a bonus of 4,000 pesos by the Venezuelan government. His son, Simón Bolívar Daniel Daniels (Danells), served for years as the Venezuelan consul at Baltimore.

[24] *Ibid.,* p. 137; Hasbrouck, *op. cit.,* pp. 347-350.

[25] Todd to Adams, Desp. Col., I.

[26] Paxson, *op. cit.,* p. 119; A. Curtis Wilgus, "Spanish American Patriot Activity along the Atlantic Seaboard, 1816-1822," *N. C. Hist. Rev.,* IV, 172.

is quite possible that many claimed citizenship merely to escape from the undesirable service. However, in 1824 the release of seventy men was effected. Three years later Secretary Clay instructed the American consul at Puerto Cabello to render assistance to distressed seamen who had served on Colombian privateers and men-of-war.[27]

THE FIRST AMERICAN MISSION : COMMERCIAL AND CHARITABLE

It has been claimed that "the United States had little commerce with South American ports; [that] its sympathies were almost entirely sentimental."[28]   The dearth of early commercial data renders it impossible to disprove this.   However, the fact that Augustin Maden was sent as consul to La Guayra in 1800 and Robert K. Lowry as commercial agent, ten years later, at least indicates an American commercial ambition in that area. Lowry as commercial agent ten years later at least infavor of Great Britain and of supposed British efforts to secure exclusive commercial privileges[29] further indicates that American interest and motives were mixed.   Trade seems to have been a large factor in the American diplomacy.

Although feeling that the colonials preferred a commercial "connection with the United States," Lowry suggested that naval vessels be sent to protect trade and, at the same time, to place the United States "on the same footing" with England.[30]   The lack of knowledge in official circles, he feared, would cause the government to be "wheedled into some great error, by a belief . . . that their political existence . . . [depended] on Great Britain."   The continuance of British vessels off the coast

[27] Lowry to Adams, April 16, Sept. 22, 1822, April 26, 1823, Jan. 24, 1824, Con. Let., La Guayra, I; Clay to Litchfield, Sept. 11, 1827, Inst. to Con., II, 442.
[28] Paxson, *op. cit.*, p. 184.
[29] Lowry to Smith, Sept. 6, 1810, Con Let., La Guayra, I.
[30] *Ibid.*

and the establishment of several commercial houses in La Guayra were not interpreted as favorable to American commerce.[31]

The following year (1811) brought no relief to American trade, since the British still paid one-fourth less duty and the privateers were capturing everything possible except vessels licensed by governors of neighboring British islands. However, Lowry was encouraged by the fact that certain government officials were declaring that their only hope lay with the United States, maintaining that the British were more "their enemies than friends." He felt that attention paid to the Venezuelan agents in the United States might have a savory effect on trade. Both money and arms were necessary for patriot success. "If assistance . . . [was] at all contemplated by the Government of the U[nited] S[tates], it should be prompt and decisive."[32]

Although apparently converted to the idea of inevitable American assistance, Lowry declined the request of the Venezuelan executive to return to the United States for the purpose of securing arms and money. He confined his efforts to protests against the tariff discrimination.[33]

Before a special mission could be sent to Washington, the fateful earthquake of March 26, 1812, occurred. The news of the tragedy brought a suggestion from Alexander Scott, already appointed as an American representative to Caracas but still in Baltimore, that Congress make an appropriation for the relief of the sufferers.[34] The president was authorized (May 4) to expend $50,000 for the purchase of provisions to be presented as a gift to the Venezuelan people. And Scott was soon selected to ad-

[31] Lowry to Smith, Oct. 1, 1810, *ibid.*

[32] Lowry to Monroe, June 9, Aug. 21, Nov. 1, 1811, *ibid.*

[33] Lowry to Monroe, Feb. 2, 1812, *ibid.*

[34] Scott to Monroe, March 26, April 1, 21, 1812, *ibid.;* Spccl. Agts. Ser., Scott.

minister the fund.[35] He was instructed "to intimate in suitable terms" that this relief was "a strong proof of the friendship and interest which the United States . . . [took] in their welfare . . . [and] to explain the mutual advantages of a commerce with the United States. . . ."[36]

Five vessels laden with the relief provisions reached La Guayra on June 27. The gift was well received and, Scott thought, would not soon be forgotten by the people. He strongly suspected, however, that Miranda was acting as a British agent in capitulating to the Spaniards.. Yet he found the new Royalist government under Monteverde even more hostile to the United States. The release of captured American merchantmen and their crews was secured only after repeated remonstrances. He was fully convinced that this government was likewise "in British interest" and that too much ignorance and superstition prevailed to insure stable popular rule.[37]

Royalist attacks on American commerce and the refusal to recognize Lowry as commercial agent seemed to be poor recompense for the 3,000 barrels of the relief flour, which fell into their hands with the patriot capitulation.[38] Moreover, insult was added to injury by the order for the immediate departure of all Yankees from the province of Caracas. Both Scott and Lowry were given notice (January 1) to leave the country within forty-eight hours. Not being permitted by the British governor to land on Curaçao, they returned to Puerto Cabello on the Mainland and thence proceeded to the United States bringing along some ninety destitute American seamen picked up in the West Indies.[39]

[35] Monroe to Telésforo de Orea, May 14, 1812, Notes to Col. Leg., II, 28; Chandler, *op. cit.*, p. 72.

[36] Monroe to Scott, May 14, 1812, Specl. Agts. Ser.

[37] Scott to Monroe, Nov. 7, 1812, *ibid.*, Con. Let., La Guayra, I. Since Scott's departure the United States had declared war on Great Britain. The latter power and Spain had been allies since 1808.

[38] Lowry to Monroe, Nov. 30, 1816, *ibid.*

[39] Scott to Monroe, Dec. 1, 1812, Jan. 1, 4, 1813, Lowry to Monroe, Feb. 17, 1813, Scott to Monroe, Feb. 20, April 5, 17, 1813, *ibid.;* Specl. Agts. Ser., Scott.

Although the Royalist government was still in control, Lowry was planning, in the autumn of 1816, to return to his post. He suggested (November 30) an immediate mission, in order to prevent the British from monopolizing trade; the stationing of American vessels off the coast, regardless of the party in power; and the sending of the American agent on a man-of-war, in order to increase his prestige. All this was necessary, he felt, to place American trade on an equal basis with the British.[40] Lowry resumed his duties at La Guayra in 1821 and served there intermittently until after the United States recognition of Colombian independence, but never succeeded in securing entire equality for American trade.[41]

PRIVATEERS, SEIZURES, AND UNSETTLED CLAIMS

All commercial intercourse was rendered more precarious by the prevalence of both patriot and royalist privateers. Lowry complained (November, 1811) of the capture of two American schooners.[42] However, it was not until the close of the War of 1812 that piracy became so menacing. The West Indian waters were soon swarming with "pirates under the independent flag." Even the northern coasts of Spain were not exempt from their ravages.[43] Many of these vessels were built, outfitted, and manned in North American ports—especially in Baltimore, Norfolk, New York, Philadelphia, Charleston, and New Orleans.[44]

These vessels "rather increased in audacity and violence than diminished." In 1820 one José Almeida,

[40] Scott to Monroe, Jan. 1, 1813, Lowry to Monroe, Nov. 30, Dec. 6, 1816, Con. Let., La Guayra, I.
[41] Lowry to Adams, Jan. 13, March 20, July 9, 1822, *ibid.* Lowry's commission was renewed in Dec., 1815, but he did not return to his post until, at least, late in 1821.
[42] Lowry to Monroe, Nov. 1, 1811, *ibid.*
[43] *Niles' Reg.* (Aug. 1, 1818), XIV, 392; (Oct. 3, 1818), XV, 88.
[44] A. Curtis Wilgus, "Spanish American Patriot Activity along the Atlantic Seaboard, 1816-1822," *N. C. Hist. Rev.*, IV, 172-181; "Spanish American Patriot Activity on the Gulf Coast, 1811-1822," *La. Hist. Quar.*, VIII, 193-215.

a citizen of Baltimore, departed from Norfolk with the *Wilson;* changed the vessel's name to *Bolívar;* plundered a Spanish vessel in American waters of $7,000 of specie belonging to American citizens; and then reappeared off Charleston attempting to secure recruits. Almeida possessed a privateer's license from the Republic of Colombia.[45]

Naturally such flagrant breaches of neutrality by citizens of the United States drew numerous and vigorous protests from the Spanish minister in Washington. These were usually followed by official investigations, but convictions seem to have been rare.[46] The American government insisted (1821) that its authority extended "only to measures of vigilance and precaution and . . . [did] not admit of exercising the power of punishment."[47] Nevertheless, beginning in 1817, several acts were passed by Congress providing for punishment for the outfitting of privateers in American ports and for additional naval forces for the suppression of piracy.[48]

Evidently these laws were ineffectual, since the consular letters from La Guayra continued to urge the presence of American vessels for the protection of commerce.[49] The question was presented to the cabinet on May 13, 1818, but no decision was reached.[50] The first American representative to Bogotá urged that a man-of-war be dispatched to cruise "off the Spanish Main,"

[45] Adams to Todd, Aug. 1, 1820, Inst. to Con., II, 212-213. Todd protested and requested suspension of Almeida's commission, but to no avail. Todd to Adams, Dec. 19, 1820, Desp. Col. I.

[46] Wilgus, *op. cit., N. C. Hist. Rev.*, IV, 176-178; Hilario de Rivas de Salmón to Brent, Sept. 29, 1824, *A. S. P. F. R.*, V, 405-406.

[47] Adams to Joaquín de Anderaga, Nov. 17, 1821, Notes to For. Leg., III, 42.

[48] Acts of March 3, 1817, April 20, 1818, March 3, 1819, May 15, 1820, Dec. 20, 1822, Jan. 20, 1823, *Statutes at Large*, III, 370-371, 447-450, 510-514, 600-601, 720-723; *A. S. P. Naval Affairs*, II, 174, 419.

[49] Lowry to Secy. of State, Sept. 6, Dec. 2, 18, 1810, June 11, 1811, Nov. 30, 1816, April 30, 1818, Sept. 22, 1821, April 16, 1822, Con. Let., La Guayra, I.

[50] Adams, *Memoirs*, IV, 91-92.

since he felt that it was "a more safe and efficient policy to prevent the perpetration of outrages . . . by the appearance of an armed force, rather than to be compelled to recur to the remedial system of diplomatic representation and negotiation."[51]

For some reason the United States pursued the latter course in dealing with both belligerents. Early in 1816, on receiving authentic information of outrages committed against American citizens and property by the Spanish blockade of Cartagena,[52] Christopher Hughes, Jr., was sent to secure the release of the prisoners and the restoration of the property captured. Armed with letters to the governor of Cartagena from both President Madison and the Spanish minister, he "met with a most gracious reception." His demands for the release of the prisoners were promptly granted. But his efforts to recover the property were futile.[53] Three years later the American minister at Madrid was instructed to urge "in a language equally candid and amicable" the liberation of all American citizens then being held without "just cause" in Spanish prisons.[54]

Negotiations with the patriot authorities were equally unsatisfactory. In 1818 Baptis Irvine was sent to Angostura to demand indemnity for two American merchantmen, *Liberty* and *Tiger*, which had been seized by Admiral Brión in July, 1817, and later condemned and sold. The ships and their cargoes were advertised for sale even before a trial by the prize court. Bolívar received Irvine and expressed a warm attachment for the United States, adding that he believed the British looked

[51] Todd to Adams, Dec. 19, 1820, Desp. Col., I.

[52] Lowry (Philadelphia) to Monroe, Jan. 22, 1816, Con. Let., La Guayra, I.

[53] Monroe to Hughes, March 25, 1816, Inst. Col., VIII, 40-42; *idem* to *idem*, March 14, 1816, Inst. to Con., I, 371-372; Monroe to Chevalier de Onis, March 13, to Governor of Cartagena, March 25, 1816, Notes to Col. Leg., II, 132, 135; Hughes to Monroe, March 14, 1816, July 6, 1816, Specl. Agts. Ser., Hughes.

[54] Adams to Forsyth, June 29, 1819, Inst. Sp., VIII, 342-343.

at Spanish America only from the standpoint of their own interest. He talked favorably of indemnity for the seizures, but made no immediate arrangement for payment.[55]

The following year Captain Oliver H. Perry was also sent to Angostura to collect indemnity for two illegal seizures. Vice-President Zea promised to submit the claims to the Venezuelan congress—another method of postponing settlement. Charles O. Handy, who accompanied Perry, noted that the Venezuelan people believed the United States to be indifferent to "their struggle for independence," because it was more strict than Britain in the enforcement of the neutrality laws against enlistments. The arrival of about one hundred British volunteers while Handy was there, he thought, gave much weight to the British propaganda against the United States.[56]

When Charles S. Todd was dispatched as "Confidential Agent" to Bogotá in 1820, his instructions included information on the claims which Irvine and Perry had been unable to collect. He was told "to preserve a tone and manner at once firm and conciliatory—yielding no principle of right and justice, but using no harsh or offensive expressions."[57]

About the same time these claims were also turned over to Dr. Samuel D. Forsyth, an American citizen domiciled in Cúcuta and Angostura but visiting in the United States. Shortly after his return he was instructed to assist in securing payment for some six hundred barrels of flour taken from aboard the American schooner *Betsy-Ann* in May, 1819.[58] He soon informed the State

[55] Adams to Irvine, Jan. 16, 20, 1818, Dom. Let., XVII, 109, 111; *idem* to *idem*, Jan. 31, Dec. 21, 1818, Inst. to Con., II, 93 ff.; Irvine to Adams, Feb. 20, March 11, June 1, July 20, 1818, Feb. 28, June 1, Nov. 27, 1819, Specl. Agts. Ser., Irvine.

[56] Handy to Adams, Sept. 29, 1819, Misc. Let.

[57] Adams to Todd, June 5, 1820, Inst. to Con., II, 180 ff.

[58] Adams to Forsyth, Aug. 1, 1820, Inst. to Con., II, 214-216.

Department that he had secured a promise of the settlement of this claim as soon as there was enough money in the treasury.[59] However, his conferences with Bolívar the following February (1821) and the enormous military expenditures of the year convinced him by October that early collection of any of the claims was impossible.[60] His letters to the State Department ceased.

Lowry continued to report from La Guayra irregular seizures and condemnation of American vessels. His protest, in the case of the *Caravan* captured by Colombian privateers, that free ships made free goods was ignored.[61] In the case of the brig *Mary-Ann* it was denied that he had any jurisdiction, since he was agent for commerce and seamen and not a regularly-appointed consul. The brig *George* was condemned on ex parte evidence, and Lowry was not even notified.[62] These instances illustrate the unsatisfactory relations during the revolutionary period.

[59] Forsyth to Adams, Sept. 22, 1820, Specl. Agts. Ser., Forsyth.

[60] Forsyth to Adams, April 17, June 21, Aug. 31, 1820, Jan. 7, May 24, Sept. 4, Oct. 24, 1821, *ibid.*

[61] Lowry to Soublette, Dec. 3, 1822, Con. Let., La Guayra, I.

[62] Lowry to Adams, Dec. 24, 1822, *ibid.*

CHAPTER VI

THE EVOLUTION OF THE RECOGNITION POLICY OF THE UNITED STATES

(1810-1822)

SOLICITOUS REBELS AND INTERESTED SPECTATORS (1810-1816)

THE establishment of a colonial junta in Caracas (April, 1810) was soon followed by the sending of Juan Vicente Bolívar—brother of the Liberator—and Telésforo de Orea to Washington. Although not officially received on their arrival in June, they presented credentials and made official contacts.[1] A letter from the junta gave an account of the recent governmental changes and expressed a desire for closer friendship and increased commercial relations with the United States.[2] The appointment of Robert K. Lowry as American commercial agent to La Guayra was made the same month, evidently to take advantage of this offer of profitable trade.[3]

Orea soon returned to La Guayra—leaving Baltimore July 10—but Bolívar tarried. Although the latter had 60,000 pesos for the purchase of supplies and ammunition,[4] the Spanish minister in Washington seems to have persuaded him that the Regency would soon recognize the Caracan junta; therefore he secured agricultural machinery instead of military equipment. But both Bolívar and the machinery were later lost in a shipwreck off the coast of Florida.[5]

[1] Pedro A. Zubieta, *Apuntaciones sobre las primeras misiones diplomáticas de Colombia, 1809-1830*, p. 24.

[2] Manning, *Diplomatic Correspondence*, II, 1143.

[3] See *supra*, chap. v.

[4] Lowry (Baltimore) to Smith, July 10, 1810, *ibid.*, II, 1144; Francisco José Urrutia, *Páginas de historia diplomática*, p. 4.

[5] J. Gil Fortoul, *Historia constitucional de Venezuela*, I, 128; Urrutia, *op. cit.*, p. 4; Angell, *op. cit.*, p. 20.

Since "the recent transactions in Spain . . . [had] produced in her American colonies a sensation tending to a change of the old established policy" and the recent Spanish actions in West Florida had made necessary American preparation for its occupancy, Secretary Robert Smith advised Lowry that "the United States could not remain an unconcerned spectator of such important events in . . . [its] own immediate neighborhood. . . ."[6]

Early the following year (1811) Telésforo de Orea returned to Washington, accompanied by José Rafael Ravenga. Along with their credentials was presented another letter from the Caracan junta expressing regret that no reply had been received from the communication of the year previous. Notwithstanding this silence, Lowry had been generously received at La Guayra and a new mission had been sent to the United States for the purpose of convincing it of Venezuelan sincerity and of pointing out "the advantage flowing from an alliance. . . ."[7]

Orea's presentation letter also expressed the desire "to form a lasting [*duradero*] alliance with the United States and commercial treaties useful to both."[8] During the summer of 1811 Lowry (from La Guayra) was urging "the advantages which would probably result to our commerce," if a "little attention" were given to the Caracan representatives.[9] The news of the Venezuelan "Declaration of Independence" (July 5, 1811) gave Orea additional boldness. He then requested recognition of Venezuelan independence and expressed the hope that treaties of friendship and commerce would follow.[10]

To this request Monroe gave a very friendly and conciliatory answer and assured Orea that American repre-

[6] Smith to Lowry, Nov. 6, 1810, Inst. to Con., I, 352.
[7] Manning, *Diplomatic Correspondence*, II, 1148-1149.
[8] Orea to Monroe, May 17, 1811, Col., I, pt. 1.
[9] Lowry to Monroe, June 9, Aug. 21, 1811, Con. Let., La Guayra, I.
[10] Orea to Monroe, Nov. 6, 1811, Col., I, pt. 1.

sentatives at the European courts would exert every
effort towards the securing of recognition. However, he
was too cautious to commit his government to immediate
recognition.[11] In the meanwhile, both France and Russia
had been sounded by the United States,[12] and a special
congressional committee had set forth the American
policy:

[The United States] behold, with friendly interest, the establishment of independent sovereignties by the Spanish provinces
in America . . . as neighbors and inhabitants of the same hemisphere, . . . feel great solicitude for their welfare; and . . .
when those provinces shall have attained the condition of nations, by the just exercise of their rights, [will establish with
them] amicable relations and commercial intercourse.[13]

During 1811 the new government at Bogotá sent
Pedro de la Lastra and Nicolás Mauricio de Omaña to
secure arms and ammunition.[14] A desire "to draw closer
the ties of friendship and political relations"[15] was expressed but seemingly no effort made to secure either
recognition or a formal alliance. Nevertheless the junta
of Bogotá made an appeal to President Madison for
assistance in forming the new government. Great re-
liance must be placed, it declared, "on the powerful aid
of the people who took the lead in American happiness."
It was hoped that, since Madison had "gone over the
road which . . . [they were] about to take," he would guide
them and point out the "precipices to be avoided."[16]

M. Palacio Fajardo, representative of the Cartagena
government, arrived in Washington near the end of 1812.
His unsuccessful efforts to secure North American support and his favorable conferences with the French min-

[11] Monroe to Orea, Dec. 19, 1811, Notes to Col. Leg., II, 17-18.
[12] Manning, *Diplomatic Correspondence*, I, 6-14.
[13] *A. S. P. F. R.*, III, 538-539.
[14] Urrutia, *op. cit.*, p. 25; Rivas, *Relaciones*, p. 9.
[15] Lastra to Monroe [Dec., 1812, or Jan., 1813], Col. I, pt. 1.
[16] Undated note, *ibid.*

ister in Washington carried him to Paris (1813) to seek aid from Napoleon.[17] In answer to his insistent note of December 26, 1812, Monroe replied that the United States could not take any steps which would compromise its neutrality, but assured Palacio Fajardo that it took a "likely interest in the prosperity and welfare" of its southern neighbors.[18]

Still another revolutionary agent, Manuel García de Sena, probably from Caracas, appeared in Washington in March, 1814, and requested a conference with the president. After emphasizing the Spanish hostility towards the United States, he asked permission to export necessary revolutionary material to the patriots. From Edenton, North Carolina, he wrote Monroe (June 10), protesting against the insistence of the government inspector on opening cases which he was shipping. Without stating the contents thereof—the inspector suspected muskets—he asked that the difficulty be removed.[19]

Nearly two years later the arrival of Pedro Gual in New York as New Granadian deputy was reported.[20] It is probable that he was there,[21] but the records do not indicate the presentation of his credentials to the State Department at that time.

During the War of 1812 North American policy changed little. The great demands of the war on national interest and resources and the uncertainty of the colonial struggle itself[22] made for extreme reticence. The

[17] M. Palacio to Secretary of State, Dec. 26, 1812, *ibid.;* M. Palacio to Bolívar, Feb. 7, 1815, Simón B. O'Leary (ed.), *Memorias del General O'Leary,* IX, 403-410.

[18] Monroe to M. Palacio, Dec. 29, 1812, Manning, *Diplomatic Correspondence,* I, 16.

[19] Manuel García de Sena to Monroe, March 29, June 10, 1814, Col. I, pt. 1.

[20] Adams (London) to Monroe, March 30, 1816, Manning, *Diplomatic Correspondence,* III, 1436-1437.

[21] *Appleton's Cyclopaedia of Amer. Biog.,* VI, 8-9; *B. F. S. P.,* VI, 1067.

[22] Quito was back under Spanish rule, New Granada in the midst of civil wars, and Venezuela changing almost annually from patriots to Spaniards and vice versa.

policy as set forth in Scott's instructions of May 14, 1812, was strictly followed:

A principal motive in delaying to recognize in greater form the independence . . . proceeds from a desire to ascertain how far those provinces are competent to its support. . . . If the people are resolved to maintain their independence, their success seems to be inevitable. The United States takes a sincere interest in it from generous sentiments and from a conviction also that in many ways it will prove reciprocally advantageous. Nothing, however, would be more absurd than for the United States to acknowledge their independence in form, until it was evident, that the people themselves were resolved and able to support it. Should a counter-revolution take place after such acknowledgment, the United States would sustain an injury without having rendered any advantage to the people. . . . A friendly communication may, in the meanwhile be preserved, as if their independence had been thus formally acknowledged. . . . Instructions have been already given to their American ministers in Paris, St. Petersburg, and London, to make known to those courts that the United States take an interest in the independence of the Spanish provinces.[23]

RECOGNITION CONSIDERED (1816)

The close of the Napoleonic struggle in Europe and the termination of the war with Great Britain permitted the United States to concern itself again with the affairs of the Western Hemisphere. The territorially aggressive South and West, powerful factors in thrusting the nation into the War of 1812,[24] still cast covetous eyes towards the Floridas and certain lands beyond the Mississippi— possessions of decadent Spain. Privateers, deprived of a profitable business by the making of peace with England, now anxiously sought commissions from the new Spanish American governments. These selfish groups, supported by a sort of republican nationalistic sentiment,

---

[23] Monroe to Scott, May 14, 1812, Con. Let., La Guayra, I.
[24] See Julius W. Pratt, *The Expansionists of 1812;* Walter F. McCaleb, *The Aaron Burr Conspiracy.*

which pervaded the Union following the war, contributed
to a revival of interest in the struggle between Spain and
its colonies[25] and rendered the maintenance of strict neutrality almost impossible.

In the early stages of the struggle Jefferson had
feared that the people were "disqualified . . . for the maintenance or even knowledge of their rights and that much
blood . . . [would] be shed for little improvement in
their condition," since there was no example in history
of "a priest-ridden people maintaining a free civil government."[26] But feeling (1816) that a war was "brew-
ing" between the United States and Spain, he declared
that the colonies had "a right to be free, and we [United
States] a right to aid them, as a strong man . . . [had]
a right to assist a weak one assailed by a robber or mur-
derer." If war should come with Spain, he favored
"joining the South Americans and entering into treaties
of alliance with them."[27]

Secretary of State Monroe had advanced to the point
of considering the struggle "a civil war and not a rebellion."[28] The instructions given (1817) by Secretary
Richard Rush to Joel R. Poinsett and to Caesar Rodney
and John Graham evidenced the same attitude.[29] Monroe
on becoming president held to his earlier view regarding
the nature of the contest.[30] In July of the following year
Monroe requested Secretary Adams to propose to the
British minister Anglo-America coöperation "to pro-

[25] See *Niles' Reg.*, XI, 187; XII, 319; XIII, 61, 266; XV, 78, 89; XIX,
221, 308; XVII, 141, 174, 328, 429; XX, 8, 191, 415; XXI, 21, 109, 127,
175, 223, 257, 290.

[26] Jefferson to Dupont de Nemours, April 15, 1811, to Baron von Hum-
bolt, Dec. 6, 1813, to Lafayette, Nov. 30, 1813, Jefferson, *Writings* (Mem.
ed.), XIII, 37-40; XIV, 20-25.

[27] Jefferson to Monroe, Feb. 4, 1816, *ibid.*, XIV, 432.

[28] Monroe to Christopher Hughes, Jr., March 25, 1816, Inst. Col., VIII,
40-42.

[29] Rush to Poinsett, April 25, 1817, to Rodney and Graham, July 18, 1817,
Inst. to Con., I, 29, 34-35.

[30] Annual message, Dec. 2, 1817.

mote the independence of South America"[31]—a policy far more advanced than that of 1812-1815.

ADAMS ADVISES CAUTION

Secretary Adams considered this "a crude idea," which probably the Richmond (Va.) *Enquirer* had "put ... into his [Monroe's] head," and therefore persuaded the President to abandon it.[32]   Nor was Adams ready for recognition, since it would have been "a departure from that system of neutrality, which the United States . . . [had] adopted, and which . . . [was] believed to be as much the interest of the South Americans themselves as of the United States."   He favored extending "all the advantages of a friendly and commercial intercourse," but feared that recognition, "without benefiting them, [might] entangle us [the United States] in disputes with other powers."[33]

However, Adams warned Russia (June 28, 1818) that, although the United States desired harmony among the powers, it would "not participate in or . . . [could] not approve of any interposition of other powers unless it ... [was] to promote total independence, political and commercial, of the colonies."[34]   Shortly thereafter he inquired of England, France, and Russia as to their attitude towards American recognition, in case it led to a Spanish declaration of war.[35]   The replies were interpreted as being favorable, since all declared that they "could not well move in the affair without the U[nited] States, by which, it was meant, as . . . [was] inferred, against the U[nited] States."[36]

It was learned, however, that when the American

[31] Diarial entry, July 25, 1818, Adams, *Memoirs*, IV, 118.
[32] *Ibid.*
[33] Adams to Baptis Irvine, Jan. 31, 1818, Inst. to Con., II, 98.
[34] Adams to Campbell, June 28, 1818, Inst. Russia, XIII.
[35] Adams to Rush, Gallatin, Campbell, Aug. 20, 1818, Manning, *Diplomatic Correspondence*, I, 74-75.
[36] Monroe, *Writings*, VI, 83-85.

attitude was discussed at the Congress of Aix-la-Chapelle (autumn of 1818) "France and Russia expressed
great disapprobation of the proposed recognition, and
that the Minister of Great Britain, the power most favorable to the colonies, declared that he should consider it as
rash."[37] Furthermore, George W. Campbell wrote from
St. Petersburg that he feared American recognition
would place Russia in case of war on the side of Spain.[38]
The new Russian minister to Washington, Poletica, was
instructed (1819) to exert every effort—even to invite the
United States to join the Holy Alliance—to prevent
recognition of the colonies.[39] Although convinced by
November that Spain could never recover them, Poletica
still argued against recognition. But Adams "hinted to
him that after a reasonable time, if the great powers of
Europe should continue to decline the acknowledgment in
concert with us [United States], we should, perhaps,
adopt the measure ourselves."[40]

This hint, however, was for effect only. The North
American policy already had been set forth by President
Monroe earlier in the year:

Our object is to promote a recognition of their independence
by the Allies [European powers] at the earliest day at which
it may be obtained and we are satisfied that the best mode of
accomplishing it is by moving in concert with the Allies, postponing the recognition on our part until it can be obtained
from them, or until it shall be manifest that it shall at least
do them [colonies] no harm.[41]

There were still weightier factors in the strained relations between the United States and Spain. It was
entirely probable that the unsettled claims of North

[37] *Ibid.*, VI, 96.
[38] J. C. Hildt, "Early Diplomatic Negotiations of the United States
with Russia," *Johns Hopkins Univ. Studies*, XXIV, 124-125.
[39] *Ibid.*, pp. 129-132; Adams, *Memoirs*, IV, 394..
[40] Diarial entry, Nov. 17, 1819, Adams, *Memoirs*, IV, 442-443.
[41] March 24, 1819, Monroe. *Writings*, VI, 97.

Americans for destroyed shipping; the unneutral activities of Spanish agents on the Florida frontier; and the resultant American seizure (1817-1818) of St. Marks, Pensacola, and Amelia Island might cause a rupture between the two nations, irrespective of the recognition policy.[42]

In the midst of British efforts to mediate between the United States and Spain—as it was also attempting to do between Spain and the colonies—Andrew Jackson's execution of two British subjects (Ambrister and Arbuthnot) in the Floridas almost caused a rupture with Great Britain. But the amicable settlement of the affair convinced Spain that it could not expect British support in a war with the United States.[43]

Since the Washington government feared that a break with Spain might cause a complete European rupture, it likewise was anxious for the settlement of the long-standing grievances. Therefore, Adams and Luis de Onís were soon able to agree on a treaty (January 22, 1819) for the settlement of the claims, the cession of the Floridas, and the determination of the Louisiana Purchase boundary.[44] The shrewd two-year delay of the Spanish sovereign in ratifying the treaty, however, forced the United States into an inactive recognition policy. Adams did not doubt ultimate colonial independence and thought that "at the proper time it ought to be acknowledged," but for the time being he felt that the United States "should avoid anything of which Spain might make a handle, and which would dispose France and Russia" against it.[45] Monroe in his annual message of 1819 did little more than note the progress of the colonial struggle, point out the difficulties of enforcing strict neu-

[42] In fact, Adams refused to guarantee not to recognize the colonies as a means of securing an agreement with Spain (*Memoirs*, IV, 209).
[43] J. Fred Rippy, *Rivalry . . . over Spanish America*, pp. 68-69.
[44] *Ibid.*, pp. 69-70.
[45] Diarial entry, Dec. 3, 1819, Adams, *Memoirs*, IV, 461.

trality, and pledge the influence of his government towards a just settlement of the controversy.[46]

CLAY EMBARRASSES THE ADMINISTRATION

In the meanwhile, Henry Clay[47] had become the principal advocate of recognition, partly through "genuine sympathy" and partly because of "his desire to annoy the administration," which, for reasons now obvious, was forced to pursue a guarded course.[48] In January, 1816, Clay opposed a bill for the reduction of certain war taxes, because he felt that the United States might have "to take part with the patriots of South America."[49] When the House was considering (January, 1817) a stricter neutrality bill,[50] recommended by the President to reduce Yankee piratical activity,[51] Clay declared: "For my part, I wish their independence. . . . Let them have free government, if they are capable of enjoying it; but let them have at all events, independence."[52]

Having opposed, under Madison, all measures which might hinder independence, Clay, under Monroe, attempted to force recognition. By the opening of Congress in the fall of 1817, the matter was squarely in politics. Clay soon "mounted his South American great horse [in an effort] to control or overthrow the Executive by swaying the House of Representatives."[53] He secured the acceptance of a resolution (December 3) requesting the committee on the presidential message to determine the prerequisites of belligerent recognition for the revolting colonies.[54]

[46] Monroe, *Writings*, VI, 112-113.
[47] Clay's speeches received wide circulation in New Granada (Paxson, *op. cit.*, p. 132).
[48] See F. E. Chadwick, *The Relations of the United States and Spain*, p. 151; Paxson, *op. cit.*, pp. 127, 174-175; Carl Schurz, *Henry Clay*, I, 147.
[49] Quoted by Chandler, *op. cit.*, p. 150.
[50] *Annals of Cong.* (14.2), p. 477.   [51] *Ibid.*, p. 40.
[52] *Ibid.*, p. 742.
[53] Diarial entry, Dec. 6, 1817, Adams, *Memoirs*, IV, 28.
[54] Chandler, *op. cit.*, p. 150.

The following March his move to provide $18,000 as salary and outfit for a minister to Buenos Aires was defeated by the vote of 115 to 45.[55] But two years later (April 4, 1820) Clay introduced a resolution for an appropriation to send such ministers as the President and Senate might determine. The vote was favorable (80 to 75), but nothing came of it. A similar motion was defeated on February 5, 1821, but deep interest was expressed, and by a large majority vote the president was authorized, "whenever he . . . [might] deem it expedient, to recognize the sovereignty and independence of any of the said provinces."[56] The proclamation of the Spanish treaty (February 22, 1821) made Clay's policy that of the administration. Especially was this true in regard to Colombia, for the year 1821 brought the patriot victory of Carabobo (June), the Congress of Cúcuta (July), and the Constitution of La Gran Colombia (August).

THE PATRIOT AGENTS BLUNDER

Encouraged by military victories and Clay's spectacular advocacy of colonial independence, Venezuela, in 1817, sent José Cortés Madariaga to request recognition and establish "diplomatic arrangements and stipulations."[57]

In July of the following year Bolívar appointed General Lino de Clemente as envoy extraordinary and minister plenipotentiary to the United States to secure recognition, negotiate a treaty, and arrange for military supplies.[58] But Adams advised that the latter's unneutral activity in the recruiting of men and the preparation

[5] Adams, *Memoirs*, IV, 67; Paxson, *op. cit.*, p. 135; H. L. Hoskins, "The Hispanic-American Policy of Henry Clay, 1816-1828," *H. A. H. R.*, VII, 464-466; Chadwick, *op. cit.*, p. 151.

[56] Hoskins, *op. cit.*, pp. 467-468; Paxson, *op. cit.*, pp. 142-144; Adams, *Memoirs*, V, 111.

[57] Pres. of U. S. of Venezuela to Pres. of Rep. of the North, May 21, 1817, Col. I, pt. 1.

[58] Rivas, *op. cit.*, p. 9; Zubieta, *op. cit.*, p. 52.

of expeditions within American jurisdiction rendered him unacceptable. Clemente and Pedro Gual, deputy for New Granada, had signed a privateer's commission for Gregor McGregor to seize East and West Florida; and Clemente, Adams claimed, had sent an "insulting" protest to the American government on account of its seizure of Amelia Island.[59]

The Venezuelan executive, Francisco Antonio Zea, accepted Adams's decision in good grace[60] and proceeded (August, 1819) to approve Don Manuel Torres of Philadelphia as chargé of Venezuela, with full powers to negotiate.[61] The following May, Torres was commissioned chargé for all Colombia.[62]

TORRES AND RECOGNITION

Don Manuel Torres, nephew of the Archbishop-Viceroy Antonio Caballero y Góngora, was forced to flee his native Venezuela in 1796 on account of his *opiniones liberales*. And he soon took up residence in Philadelphia,[63] where he made many influential contacts. Henry Clay and William Duane, editor of *The Aurora,* were among his friends.[64] The reports of his revolutionary zeal and his activities in securing patriot military supplies caused his vast estate in Venezuela to be confiscated. With his last ties thus severed, his every effort was exerted towards securing North American assistance and

---

[59] Clemente to Adams, Dec. 11, 1818, Col. I, pt. 1; Adams to Clemente, Dec. 16, 1818, Manning, *Diplomatic Correspondence,* I, 82; *B. F. S. P.,* VI, 1066-1067. Adams felt that Clay had used Clemente as a tool "against the Administration" (Adams, *Memoirs,* IV, 472).

[60] C. O. Handy, Sept. 29, 1819, Misc. Let.

[61] Urrutia, *op. cit.,* p. 136; García Samudio, *op. cit.,* p. 46.

[62] *A. S. P. F. R.,* IV, 833-834.

[63] Rivas, *op. cit.,* p. 12; *Enciclopedia universal ilustrada Europeo-Americana,* LXII, 1431; *In Honor of the Patriot Don Manuel Torres 1764-1822* (a pamphlet published by the Colombian legation); Pedro Ignacio Cadena, *Anales diplomáticos de Colombia,* pp. 98-150; García Samudio, *op. cit.,* pp. 43-98.

[64] The Congress of Cúcuta (1821) voted "*acciones de gracias*" to both Clay and Duane (Rivas, *op. cit.,* p. 20).

recognition.[65]   The news of his appointment was well
received by Secretary Adams, who expressed great
"pleasure in entertaining relations of friendship and
good understanding" with Torres's country.[66]

Torres was soon able to secure by private contract
4,000 muskets. But deeming this number insufficient, he
applied to the American government for the purchase of
some 20,000 more.[67]   After a special cabinet meeting,
Adams replied (April 30, 1820) that, although former
interest was unabated, the Administration could not thus
depart from its neutrality. Besides, he felt that the
sale would require congressional legislation.[68]

In the meanwhile, Charles S. Todd had been chosen
as "Confidential Agent to Venezuela and New Granada"
for the purpose of obtaining "correct information," promoting and maintaining "relations of friendship and
reciprocal good will," and obtaining "indemnity for
certain . . . claims."[69]   He was instructed to advise, if
he were sounded on the subject, that he was not "authorized to discuss" formal recognition.[70]   Nevertheless the
Administration continued to insist that it would not
forego its right to recognize the colonies in order to secure Spanish ratification of the Treaty of 1819.[71]   Adams
avowed to the Spanish minister that America was of the
opinion "that Spain must shortly recognize" colonial
independence.[72]

Spurred on by these favorable tendencies and by

[65] Duane, *A Visit to Colombia in the Years 1822 and 1823*.

[66] Torres to Adams, Nov. 19, 1819, García Samudio, *op. cit.*, p. 161;
Adams to Torres, Nov. 29, 1819, Notes to Col. Leg., II, 381.

[67] Torres to Adams, March 18, 1820, Manning, *Diplomatic Correspondence*, II, 1185-1189; García Samudio, *op. cit.*, pp. 165-169.

[68] Adams to Torres, April 30, 1820, Notes to Col. Leg., II, 383.

[69] Adams to Todd, Feb. 22, 1820, Inst. to Con., II, 176-177; Todd to
Adams, Desp. Col., I.

[70] *Idem* to *idem*, June 5, 1820, *ibid.*, II, 180 ff.

[71] Presidential message, May 9, 1820, Richardson, *Messages and Papers*,
II, 640.

[72] Diarial entry, May 13, 1820, Adams, *Memoirs*, V, 116.

Clay's advice of the passage of his resolution,[73] Torres approached Adams (May 13, 1820) regarding the formation of "an American system to embrace this whole hemisphere in opposition to that of Europe, and especially in opposition to England." The Colombians, said he, "were jealous of the European Alliance . . . [and] were willing and desirous that the United States should take the lead" in a new system. Adams refused to commit himself on the proposal, but assured Torres that, if it were presented in writing, he would bring it to the President's attention.[74] Even though Adams had shown himself cool on the subject, Torres declared to his government a week later that the United States had "already recognized in substance our [Colombian] political independence."[75]

Todd, on presenting his credentials in August, 1820, declared that North American disposition towards Colombia was "as friendly as . . . [could] be consistent with the obligation of neutrality . . . [and that] the people, as well as the government . . . unite[d] in sincere and unabated wishes for . . . [their] success . . . in the present interesting struggle."[76] During the same month Adams again sounded England, France, and Russia as to their attitude towards American recognition of the colonies.[77] Monroe in his annual message said that nothing was known "to warrant the belief that any of the powers of Europe . . . [would] take part in the contest" and it was felt that a final adjustment would "take place on the basis proposed by the colonies." To such a policy he committed his government.[78]

[73] Clay to Torres, May 11, 1820, García Samudio, *op. cit.*, p. 88.
[74] Adams, *Memoirs*, V, 115-116. But he confided in his diary that he saw "no basis for any such system" (*ibid.*, V, 176).
[75] Quoted in García Samudio, *op. cit.*, pp. 173-179.
[76] Todd to Vice-Pres. of Col., Aug. 2, 1820, Desp. Col., I.
[77] Adams to Rush, Aug. 15; to Gallatin, Aug. 20; to Campbell, Aug. 20, 1820, Inst. to Min., VIII, 247.
[78] Richardson, *Messages and Papers*, II, 646.

During the autumn and winter of 1820-1821 Torres became insistent in his requests for arms, recognition, and a commercial treaty.[79] He called on Adams on October 16, "to renew his old propositions" and the following day "entertained . . . [Adams] again nearly two hours with his demand for recognition and a supply of muskets."[80] These interviews were followed by letters of the same character.[81] On January 20 he "came, as usual, to ask for an acknowledgment of the republic, a loan of money, and a supply of arms."[82] On the very day (February 19) of the Senate's ratification of the Spanish treaty, "Torres came to renew the demand" for recognition;[83] the next day requested it by letter and suggested treaties of navigation and commerce.[84]

The proclamation of the Spanish treaty (February 22) had removed a great obstacle, but it was not until after Bolívar's victory of Carabobo (June) and the promulgation of the Colombian constitution (August) that the Washington government showed any additional interest in the recognition of Colombia. In October Lowry was ordered to return to La Guayra—having been in the United States for some time. Soon after his arrival (December 3) he recommended recognition as the surest means of increasing American at the expense of British trade.[85] Monroe, in his annual message of the same date, noted the extension of Colombian territory and the considerable augmentation of its strength, and added: "It has long been manifest that it would be impossible for

[79] He even intimated the possibility of a treaty granting the United States a monopoly on Colombian carrying trade, if it would head the "American system" (Adams, *Memoirs*, V, 115-116).

[80] Diarial entry, Oct. 16, 17, 1820, *ibid.*, V, 186-187.

[81] Torres to Adams, Dec. 15, 26, 1820, García Samudio, *op. cit.*, pp. 181-183, 185-189; Col., I, pt. 2.

[82] Diarial entry, Jan. 20, 1821, Adams, *Memoirs*, V, 240.

[83] Diarial entry, Feb. 19, 1821, *ibid.*, V, 283.

[84] Torres to Adams, Feb. 20, 1821, Col. I, pt. 2.

[85] Lowry to Adams, Oct. 19, Nov. 23, Dec. 3, 1821, Con. Let., La Guayra, I.

Spain to reduce these colonies by force, and equally so that no condition short of their independence would be satisfactory to them.'' He further expressed the hope that Spain would be ''guided by enlightened and liberal councils'' and settle the differences by granting independence.[86]

A few days prior to the message (November 30) Torres had again requested recognition, pointing out the danger of the establishment of monarchies in South America and the necessity of a coöperative opposition to the Holy Alliance.[87] In another letter of January 2, 1822, he stressed the urgency of recognition. Adams replied that the letters were being referred to the President.[88] Todd—then on leave in the United States—was ordered ten days later ''to resume [his] duties'' at Bogotá instead of at Angostura and was advised that probably ''the formal recognition of the Republic of Colombia . . . [would] ensue at no distant date.''[89]

In complying with the request of the House for documents concerning Spanish America, President Monroe (March 8) communicated his views on recognition and requested those of his Congress:

This contest has now reached such a stage and been attended with such decisive success on the part of the Provinces that it merits the most profound consideration whether their right to the rank of independent nations . . . is not complete. . . . The provinces composing the Republic of Colombia . . . were united by a fundamental law of the 17th of December, 1819. A strong Spanish force occupied at that time certain parts of the territory . . . and waged a destructive war. That force has since been repeatedly defeated, and the whole of it either made prisoners, or destroyed, or expelled from the country, with the exception of an inconsiderable portion only, which is blockaded

[86] Richardson, *Messages and Papers*, II, 674.
[87] Torres to Adams, Nov. 30, 1821, Col. I, pt. 2.
[88] Torres to Adams, Jan. 2, Adams to Torres, Jan. 18, 1822, García Samudio, *op. cit.*, pp. 199-201.
[89] Adams to Todd, Jan. 28, 1822, Inst. to Con., II.

in two fortresses. . . . When we regard, then, the great length
of time which this war has been prosecuted, the complete success which has attended it in favor of the Provinces, the present
condition of the parties, the utter inability of Spain to produce
any change in it, we are compelled to conclude that its fate is
settled, and that the Provinces which have declared their independence and are in the enjoyment of it ought to be recognized.[90]

The following day the Spanish minister vigorously
protested that recognition would *"in no way now, or at
any time, lessen or invalidate in the least the rights of
Spain to said provinces, or to employ whatever means
may be in her power to unite them to the rest of her
dominions."* Adams replied that recognition was not
"intended to invalidate any right of Spain," but merely
to acknowledge "existing facts."[91] On March 19 the
House committee on foreign relations reported favorably on the recognition of Colombia, since it now had "a
well-organized Government, instituted by the free will of
its citizens, and . . . [exercised] all the functions of sovereignty, fearless alike of internal and foreign enemies."
And two months later Congress appropriated $100,000
for such missions as the President thought proper.[92]

Torres was advised (May 23) that the President
would receive him as Colombian chargé as soon as his
health and convenience would permit him to come to
Washington.[93] The reception of June 19, 1822, was
something of a triumph tinged with tragedy. It was to
Torres the reward of a quarter of a century of patriotic
effort, yet it came when he was near the exhaustion of
his physical strength.[94] He had "scarcely life in him to

[90] Richardson, *Messages and Papers*, II, 685-687.

[91] Anduaga to Adams, March 9, Adams to Anduaga, April 6, 1822,
A. S. P. F. R., IV, 845-846.

[92] *Ibid.*, IV, 848; Chadwick, *op. cit.*, p. 155. The news of the appropriation caused a great celebration in Caracas (*National Intelligencer*, July 13,
1822).

[93] Adams to Torres, May 23, 1822, Notes to Col. Leg., III, 104. He
was ill at Hamilton Village, near Philadelphia.

[94] Torres to Adams, June 8, 18, 1822, Col. I, pt. 2. .

DR. ENRIQUE OLAYA HERRERA UNVEILING A TABLET TO THE MEMORY
OF DON MANUEL TORRES, FIRST LATIN AMERICAN DIPLOMATIC REPRE-
SENTATIVE IN THE UNITED STATES, PHILADELPHIA, JULY 20, 1926.

walk alone" and was "deeply affected" by the ceremony.[95] So near the end was he that his death on July 15 was not unexpected. Two days later his remains were interred in the churchyard at St. Mary's, Philadelphia.[96] His grave was rediscovered more than a century later and a tablet was placed in the walls of St. Mary's Church bearing the following inscription:[97]

In memory of
Manuel Torres
1764-1822

A Minister of the Republic of Colombia He was the First Latin American Diplomatic Representative in the United States of America

Tribute from the Government of Colombia and from Philadelphia Descendants of His Friends
July 20, 1926

EUROPE FOLLOWS IN GRANTING RECOGNITION

Since it was feared that the sending of first-grade missions might be interpreted as an effort to influence the organization of the new nations—thereby preventing European recognition[98]—Todd was dispatched to Bogotá as a "Confidential Agent" to advise officially of American recognition.[99] Before leaving the United States he had at least two conferences with Torres.[100] On his arrival in Caracas (October 9, 1822) he was well received, and found all arrangements made beforehand for his accommodations in the towns along the route to Bogotá. His reception there was ultra-enthusiastic.[101] He expressed the same tenor of feeling on behalf of the United States at a banquet given in his honor:

[95] Adams, *Memoirs*, VI, 23.
[96] *Niles' Reg.*, XXII, 347; *The Aurora*, July 18, 1822.
[97] *In Honor of the Patriot Don Manuel Torres*, p. 1.
[98] Monroe to Jonathan Russell, March 12, 1822, Monroe, *Writings*, VI, 211-213.
[99] Adams to Todd, July 2, 1822, Inst. to Con., II, 260.
[100] Todd to Adams, June 6, 13, 1822, Desp. Col., I.
[101] *Idem* to *idem*, Oct. 15, 1822, *ibid.*

The spirit of liberty in the republics of the United States and Colombia—may its march be as irresistible as the streams of the Mississippi and Oronoco [sic]; and the hearts of the people present barriers as formidable against invasion as the Andes and Alleghenies.[102]

Having granted recognition, the United States next sought to secure the same from the European powers. The Dutch ports were soon opened to Colombian commerce,[103] Portugal acknowledged Colombia's independence,[104] and the American ministers in Europe were again instructed to forward the cause at their respective posts.[105] Richard C. Anderson was dispatched (1823) as envoy extraordinary and minister plenipotentiary to Colombia, and José María Salazar was received at Washington in the same capacity.[106]

In Europe the Colombian agents kept in close touch with the American representatives.[107] Zea issued a statement (April 8, 1822) from Paris to the European governments, declaring that Colombian ports were to be closed to those which did not grant recognition.[108] Although the statement was disavowed at Bogotá,[109] it called forth a memorial favoring British recognition from twenty-six leading mercantile firms of London.[110] A banquet given to Zea (July 10) by London merchants was attended by many members of Parliament.[111] The commercial forces were pressing the Cabinet towards recognition.

The early British policy of "moral opposition" to colonial independence and determination to protect the colonies from France was later modified to one of "neu-

[102] *Niles' Reg.* (Dec. 14, 1822), XXIII, 232.
[103] *Ibid.* (Sept. 28, 1822), XXIII, 55.
[104] *Ibid.* (Oct. 5, 1822), XXIII, 70.
[105] Adams to Anderson, May 27, 1823, Inst. Col., IX, 274 ff.; Clay to Salazar, April 11, 1825, Jan. 9, 1827, Notes to Col. Leg., III, 321-322.
[106] Adams to Anderson, Feb. 1, May 27, 1823, Inst. Col., IX, 274 ff.; *Niles' Reg.* (June 21, 1823), XXIV, 246.
[107] *A. S. P. F. R.*, IV, 828-829; V, 1006; Desp. G. B., XXVII.
[108] Alexander Walker, *Colombia*, I, xxvii-xxx; *B. F. S. P.*, IX, 851-854.
[109] *Ibid.*, X, 745.   [110] Walker, *op. cit.*, II, 248.
[111] Rush to Adams, July 26, 1822, Desp. G. B., XXVII.

trality and a willingness to mediate upon a liberal basis."[112] It evolved under Canning to one of recognition in case of restrictions on British trade, or of "foreign interference" (meaning French) between Spain and its colonies.[113] Castlereagh's suggestions of mediation, used to defer American recognition,[114] and Canning's hesitancy in recognizing were swept aside by economic factors and by fear of the prestige which would accrue to the United States in a possible American system.[115]

A commission, headed by Colonel J. P. Hamilton, set out for Colombia in October, 1823.[116] Santander received them on March 8, 1824, but Gual refused to issue exequaturs, since they were accredited to "provinces and dependencies" instead of the Republic of Colombia.[117] Before the end of 1824 Colombia requested Great Britain to mediate between it and Spain in regard to independence. On the last day of the year England decided to recognize the Republic. Instructions for the negotiation of a treaty were drawn up on January 3, 1825. The pact was signed April 18. Ten days later Patrick Campbell was named chargé, and the treaty ratified on November 7.[118] Canning referred to the British recognition of Colombia and Mexico as:

An act which will make a change in the face of the world almost as great as that of the discovery of the continent now set free. The Allies will fret; but they will venture no serious remonstrance. France will fidget; but it will not be with the view of hastening after our example. The Yankees will shout in triumph; but it is they who lose most by our decision.[119]

[112] J. Fred Rippy, *Latin America and World Politics*, p. 40.
[113] Harold W. V. Temperley, *The Foreign Policy of Canning*, pp. 115-118.
[114] C. K. Webster, *The Foreign Policy of Castlereagh, 1815-1822*, pp. 405 ff. [115] Temperley, *op. cit.*, p. 158.
[116] Colonel J. P. Hamilton, *Travels through the Interior Provinces of Colombia*, I, 1. [117] Paxson, *op. cit.*, p. 223.
[118] Temperley, *op. cit.*, pp. 161-165; Paxson, *op. cit.*, pp. 245-252.
[119] Canning to Hookham Frere, Jan. 8, 1825, quoted by E. M. Lloyd, "Canning and Spanish America," *Royal Hist. Soc., Transactions*, XVIII, n. s., 77.

Chapter VII

AN ERA OF TRANSIENT GREATNESS
(1822-1830)

THE Fundamental Law of 1819 provided for the union of Venezuela and New Granada, including Quito, under the title of the Republic of Colombia, and for the convening of a constitutional convention at Rosario de Cúcuta.[1]

LAYING THE CONSTITUTIONAL FOUNDATION

This body met in May, 1821. After words of admonition from the Precursor Antonio Nariño,[2] it set about the consideration of a constitution.[3] The finished document emerged on July 12, after two months of debate. It was similar to the Constitution of the United States in that it provided for the traditional division of powers and contained an analogous "Bill of Rights." It differed, however, in that the government established thereby was much more centralized. The president could, in certain circumstances, practically set aside the constitution; and congress, instead of the supreme court, possessed the power to interpret it. A treaty required the ratification of both houses of congress. Finally, a revision convention was provided for the year 1831.[4]

The Congress proceeded to choose Bolívar as president and Santander as vice-president of the new republic. The latter in his inaugural address (October 3) plainly showed that he realized the great responsibility of being placed at "the helm of a ship which, though pro-

[1] Text of the law, Antonio José Uribe, *Anales diplomáticos y consulares de Colombia* (hereinafter cited as Uribe, *Anales*), III, 1-4.
[2] Henao y Arrubla, *op. cit.*, pp. 488-489.
[3] *Congreso de Cúcuta: Libro de actas* (Bogotá, 1923).
[4] Henao y Arrubla, *op. cit.*, pp. 489-490; *Niles' Reg.* (June 8, 1822), XXII, 230 ff.

tected from the storm of civil strife . . . [was] still floating between the reefs of war and politics.''[5]   In choosing
Pedro Gual, José María del Castillo y Rada, José Manuel Restrepo, and Pedro Briceño Méndez for cabinet positions, the best Colombian talent was brought into the
national service.[6]

The patriot victories at Carabobo (June 24, 1821),
Cartagena (October 1), and Pichincha (May 24, 1822),
and the actual annexation of Panama (requested November 28, 1821) naturally gave the young republic a feeling
of security and importance.

SIGNS OF PROGRESS AND LEADERSHIP

Colombia early seemed destined to assume a leading
rôle among the American republics.   Its first Congress,
besides framing a constitution, declared for the speedy
administration of justice, individual security, economy in
disbursements, sacred fulfillment of engagements contracted with public faith, and liberty of speech and press.

The matter of education had received attention in the
earliest provincial constitutions. Those of Cundinamarca
(1811), Tunja, Antioquia, Cartagena, and Marquita, all
contained provisions for elementary schools.[7]   In 1820
Santander ordered the opening of popularly supported
schools until the government was financially able to
assume the burden.[8] Congress, the following year, desig-
nated certain property of religious orders for educational
purposes and provided that schools for both sexes be
established in every city, village, or parish.[9] Santander
soon (1822) ordered the opening of normal schools. The
English educator, Joseph Lancaster, on the invitation of
Bolívar, came to Bogotá in 1823 and established schools

[5] Henao y Arrubla, *op. cit.*, pp. 491-492.
[6] Cochrane, *op. cit.*, II, 90-97.
[7] Pombo y Guerra, *Constituciones de Colombia;* Henao y Arrubla,
op. cit., p. 343.
[8] *Archivo Santander*, V, 231-234.
[9] Act of July 28, 1821, *Congreso de Cúcuta*, pp. 374-375.

on the mutual teaching or monitor system.[10] Schools were opened for girls. And educational privileges were extended to the native Indians.

According to the reports of early foreign travelers, notable progress was made. Lancasterian schools sprang up throughout the country—in Popayán, Medellín, Tunja, Valencia, Cartagena, and even the remote villages. The University of Antioquia was established; Popayán boasted of a college of grammar and philosophy; a college at Quito had three hundred students in attendance; the University of Caracas made rapid strides; and the capital city, now called Bogotá, contained three colleges and a school of mineralogy.[11]

It was reported that during the year 1824 forty Lancasterian schools, ten colleges, and three universities were founded.[12] Naval schools were opened at Cartagena and Guayaquil,[13] and provision was made for a national museum (1823).[14] The National Library now contained some 14,000 volumes.[15] The "Bible Society of Colombia" was organized with Gual as president and Santander and Castillo as liberal contributors.[16] An official report in 1827 stated that there were fifty-two Lancastrian schools, 434 of the old type, three universities, and twenty colleges in the Republic.[17]

The Congress of Cúcuta abolished the Inquisition.[18] In 1823 the example of the first Venezuelan congress (1811) was followed by the encouraging of emigration to Colombia. Unoccupied land was to be distributed

---

[10] Pedro M. Ibáñez, *Crónicas de Bogotá*, p. 262.

[11] Hamilton, *op. cit.*, I, 222, 254; II, 74, 75, 99; Cochrane, *op. cit.*, I, 23; II, 16, 17, 288, 389, 471; James Thomson, *Letters of the Moral and Religious State of South America*, pp. 244, 258, 288, 289.

[12] *Niles' Reg.* (May 21, 1825), XXVIII, 179.

[13] *Ibid.* (March 19, 1825), XXVIII, 46.

[14] *Gaceta de Colombia*, Nov. 30, 1823.

[15] *Niles' Reg.* (May 21, 1825), XXVIII, 179.

[16] Thomson, *op. cit.*, p. 258.

[17] Summary of report, *Niles' Reg.* (July 21, 1827), XXXII, 345.

[18] Law of Aug. 22, 1821, *N. Amer. Rev.*, XX, 441.

among the colonists and "internal commerce" was opened to foreigners.[19]   Through the influence of Felix Restrepo of Antioquia, a congressional act was passed (1821) giving freedom to children of slaves at birth, prohibiting new importations, and establishing boards to administer the manumission fund provided by a three per cent levy on all inheritances.[20]   Captain Cochrane reported in 1824 that "the emancipation of slaves . . . [had] been very great in Bogotá, and only a few remained."[21]

Provision was made (1824) for the increase of the Colombia army to 50,000,[22] and under the direction of Briceño Méndez the navy was not entirely neglected.   It was officered principally by Yankees and British and, according to the American minister, was decidedly superior to any Spanish squadron in the Caribbean.[23]

THE YANKEE SUSPECTS THE BRITON

Colombia's commercial independence came long before its political freedom.   From the beginning of the revolution foreigners were welcomed and the ports were wide open to commerce.   In fact, as already observed, closer trade relations with the United States had been officially sought since 1810.   However, it was the English merchants who first migrated to Colombia in considerable numbers.[24]   Captain Cochrane (1823) felt that a "decided preference" was given "to everything English."[25]

The North Americans had been jealous of this "decided preference" throughout the revolutionary era and

[19] Anderson to Adams, (15) Aug. 20, 1824, Desp. Col., III; Robertson, *Miranda* (1929), II, 108; Robertson, *Hispanic-American Relations*, p. 281; Cochrane, *op. cit.*, I, 145.

[20] Law of July 19, 1821, Henao y Arrubla, *op. cit.*, p. 491; Cochrane, *op. cit.*, II, 38-39; Anderson to Adams, (8) Feb. 7, 1823, Desp. Col., III.

[21] Cochrane, *op. cit.*, II, 38.

[22] Henao y Arrubla, *op. cit.*, p. 510.

[23] Anderson to Adams, (3) Sept. 4, 1823, (31) Nov. 10, 1825, Desp. Col., III.

[24] See Cochrane, *op. cit.*, I, 2, 8, 49, 59, 76, 89, 118; II, 31, 186, 212, 438; Hamilton, *op. cit.*, I, 116, 134, 234, 259; II, 34, 187, 241, 242.

[25] Cochrane, *op. cit.*, I, 108.

had generally interpreted British commercial gains as the result of anti-Yankee propaganda.[26] This was not entirely true. It seems quite natural that the presence of so many British in the patriot armies and the well-recognized prestige of the "Mistress of the Sea" would impress, at least, the masses with the sincerity and importance of British friendship. Secretary Adams himself felt that "commerce with South America . . . [would] be much more important and useful to Great Britain" than to the United States and that "Great Britain . . . [would] be a power vastly more important to them . . . [since] she had the power of supplying their wants by her manufactures." However, Adams was convinced that Colombian jealousy of England would prevent the granting of "any exclusive advantages to our prejudice."[27]

None the less, the ceaseless efforts of the resident British to gain dominant influence caused American agents and travelers to deduce a contrary conclusion. British merchants resided in all the cities of any consequence; Colonel Mamby was proposing to install gas street lights in Bogotá; Colonel Johnston and Mr. Thompson secured the grant to operate the famous salt mines at Zipaquirá; Rundell, Bridge, and Rundell of London secured exclusive pearl fishing rights; James Hamilton acquired the exclusive right of steam navigation on the Orinoco; Captain Cochrane was endeavoring to secure a canal concession for an Anglo-Colombian company; and British consuls were making themselves conspicuous at the Colombian ports.[28] Moreover, Bolívar had three Britons on his staff, and Santander kept an English aide. It was reported that in Bogotá alone there were thirty

[26] Handy to Secretary of State, Sept. 29, 1819, Misc. Let., LXXI; Con. Let., I.

[27] Adams, *Memoirs*, VI, 25.

[28] Cochrane, *op. cit.*, I, 2; II, 31, 140, 145, 186, 212, 432, 460; Mollien. *op. cit.*, p. 391; Bache, *op. cit.*, p. 97; Koebel, *op. cit.*, p. 241.

English officers in the Colombian service—all with "the common characteristic of English effrontery."[29] The British commissioners and concession hunters spared no expense in entertaining the Colombian officials.[30] Colonel Hamilton, on being received by Santander, assured him that the people of Colombia would "find a firm and constant friend in Great Britain. . . ."[31] Such British activity and such assurances of friendship, in addition to widespread propaganda,[32] seemed quite sufficient to arouse the jealousy, suspicion, and opposition of the commercially minded Yankees.

Todd's suspicion that certain French and Swedish agents had "in view some exclusive commercial advantages" disappeared with Gual's assurance that proposals to that end would be rejected.[33] However, his suspicions of the British could not be dissipated so easily. He seemed to fear that England would soon possess Guiana, as well as Maracaibo, and that Colombia might even become a British colony.[34] Every day Todd became "more confirmed [that] devotion to Great Britain . . . [was] clearly developed."[35] A translation of Gual's report to Congress (1823) was forwarded to London two days before it was delivered. Todd secured a copy much later, only after "often repeated personal and ineffectual attempts."[36] Yet Gual expressed to Todd great apprehension over British actions and insisted that the United States continue to use its good offices in Europe to secure the wholesale recognition of Colombia.[37]

[29] Hamilton, *op. cit.*, I, 234, 270; Watts to Clay, Jan. 5, 1826, Desp. Col., III.

[30] Hamilton, *op. cit.*, I, 203; II, 156. On July 4, 1823, the American minister also became extravagant and spent $560 for a "ball and supper to the public authorities"—quite out of proportion to his office rent of $16 per month (Todd to Adams, July 29, 1823, Desp. Col., II).

[31] *Niles' Reg.* (June 12, 1824), XXVI, 244.

[32] See Rippy, *Rivalry . . . over Latin America*, p. 19.

[33] Todd to Adams, Feb. 28, March 6, 1823, Desp. Col., II.

[34] *Idem* to *idem*, March 29, 1823, *ibid.*

[35] Todd to Adams, (48) April 17, 1823, Desp. Col., II.

[36] *Idem* to *idem*, (49) May 5, 1823, *ibid.*

[37] *Idem* to *idem*, (42) Feb. 5, 1823, *ibid.*

Richard Bache, an American army officer who traveled in Colombia in 1822 and 1823, felt that British influence had not been "idly employed" and that by their "constantly referring everything to England, as a standard of perfection, extolling her power and riches, giving the name English to all goods, whether manufactured in France, Germany, or the East; they . . . [had] produced a belief among the uninformed creoles, that everything not Spanish must be English. . . ."[38] The first American minister to Bogotá, Richard C. Anderson, regretted (1824) that a number of the Colombian newspapers were published "under the auspices and at the expense of Colombian stockholders in London."[39] His successor, Beaufort T. Watts, by January, 1826, was almost ready to despair of American trade, since "English enterprize, English wealth, and intelligence . . . [had] penetrated the passes of the Andes, as well as the Indies, and probably all the passes of the world, where mercantile influence . . . [could] be required."[40]

DEVELOPMENT OF COMMERCIAL CONTACTS

However, the situation was hardly one for despair. American trade was flourishing, in spite of the five per cent tariff discrimination in favor of direct European commerce.[41] The average annual trade of $750,000 ($1,500,000 from August, 1810, to August, 1812)[42] had increased to $3,858,446 (September 30, 1824, to September 30, 1825). Among the Spanish American nations, Colombia ranked first in exports to the United States and second only to Mexico in imports from the United States.[43]

Within two years after recognition Colombia had at least seven commercial agents in North American cities.[44]

[38] Bache, *op. cit.*, p. 95.
[39] Anderson to Adams, (15) Aug. 20, 1824, Desp. Col., III.
[40] Watts to Clay, Jan. 5, 1826, *ibid.*
[41] Lowry to Adams, Jan. 13, March 20, July 9, 1822, Con. Let., La Guayra, I; Anderson to Clay, (33) Feb. 1, 1826, Desp. Col., III.
[42] Lowry to Monroe, Dec. 6, 1816, Con. Let., La Guayra, I.
[43] Robertson, *Hispanic-American Relations*, p. 197.
[44] *Niles' Reg.* (Aug. 7, 1824), XXVI, 369.

Savannah, Baltimore, and Philadelphia seem to have received the first of these. Soon the consular activities were extended to the District of Columbia, Norfolk, New York, Boston, and Charleston. By the end of 1826 a consul-general was stationed in New York and vice-consuls were appointed for Philadelphia, New York, Boston, and Charleston.[45]

Lowry had returned to his post at La Guayra before Colombian recognition. American consuls were soon appointed to Cartagena (1822), Santa Marta (1823), Guayaquil (1824), Puerto Cabello (1824), Angostura (1824), Maracaibo (1825), Bogotá (1825), Panama (1826), and La Guayra[46] (1826)—leaving only eight open ports without Yankee consular service.[47] La Guayra, Cartagena, and Santa Marta were already enjoying considerable Yankee trade.[48] During the year ending June 30, 1825, seventy-three American vessels called at La Guayra and thirty at Puerto Cabello, as compared with seventeen and five British vessels, respectively.[49]

Dr. Forsyth of Virginia and Dr. Litchfield of Baltimore were conducting a successful commission business in Caracas in 1822. The leading hotel of La Guayra was managed by a man from Baltimore. Lowry and another North American were marketing a subdivision—characteristically Yankee—in the village of Maiquitia, just west of La Guayra.[50] Christian L. Manhardt of Pennsylvania proposed (1824) to place steamers on Lake Maracaibo.[51] The following year an American-built steamer was navigating the Magdalena River.[52] The

---

[45] Notes to Col. Leg., III, 154, 233, 278, 279, 315; Notes from Col. Leg., I, pt. 2.

[46] Inst. to Con., II, 264, 294, 317, 322, 323, 327, 344, 351, 385, 388, 415.

[47] Anderson to Clay, (43) May 1, 1826, Desp. Col., III.

[48] Todd to Adams, (61) Oct. 5, 1823, Desp. Col., III; Bache, *op. cit.*, p. 13.

[49] An Officer (late in Colombian service), *The Present State of Colombia*, p. 162.   [50] Bache, *op. cit.*, pp. 17, 23, 97.

[51] *El Colombiano* (Caracas), Sept. 1, 1824.

[52] *Niles' Reg.* (April 9, 1825), XXVIII, 86.

new consul at La Guayra, J. G. A. Williamson, reported
the following as doing a large business in American
goods: I. Bolton, John M. Foster, M. Pascal, E. W. Robinson, and R. W. Taylor.[53]

ILL OMENS

The lack of republican governmental experience or
tradition, the want of education among the masses, the
conflicting ambitions of various *caudillos,* the ecclesiastical opposition to liberalism[54]—more than one-third of
the House of Representatives in 1823 were priests[55]—the
existence of certain natural elements of discord, and the
prolonged absences of Bolívar from Bogotá made unrest
(and possibly disunion) inevitable. Fiscal affairs were
soon in disorder, and congressional disavowal (1823) of
Zea's financial transactions in Europe almost destroyed
the national credit.[56]

Scarcely had the new minister to London, Manuel
José Hurtado, negotiated a favorable loan (1824) when
a new revolt occurred in Pasto, the center of persistent
royalism.[57] The following year the loss of 2,000,000
pesos in a London bank failure further depleted the already fast-diminishing funds in the national treasury.[58]
Instead of dealing with the urgent problems of public
credit, education, the army, and the navy, the Congress
of 1826 turned to the consideration of certain charges
against José Antonio Páez, general commander of the
department of Venezuela. Páez was suspended and ordered to Bogotá for trial.[59]

THE PÁEZ REBELLION (1826)

In August, 1824, Santander had decreed the enforcement of a law of 1821 providing for the enlistment in the

[53] Williamson to Clay, 1827-1828, Con. Let., La Guayra, I, II.
[54] *Niles' Reg.* (May 3, 1823), XXIV, 141.
[55] Todd to Adams, (56) July 20, 1823, Desp. Col., II.
[56] Henao y Arrubla, *op. cit.,* pp. 504-510.
[57] *Ibid.,* p. 511.   [58] *Ibid.,* p. 518.
[59] *Ibid.,* pp. 518-519.

army of all men between the ages of sixteen and fifty. The following year, when troops were needed badly and his calls were unheeded, Páez began to force men into the service. Loud (and probably exaggerated) complaints poured into the capital from Caracas. The latter city, always critical of the Bogotá government, was divided into two groups: Federalists and Constitutional Monarchists. And Bolívar, almost the only symbol of union between the factions and sections, was in Peru. The situation was indeed critical.[60]

The Monarchists dispatched Antonio Leocadio Guzmán to propose a monarchy to Bolívar, and another agent to Bogotá to sound the leaders there. Páez (October 1, 1825) pleaded with Bolívar to return and save Colombia as Napoleon had returned from Egypt and saved France. Bolívar (March, 1826) announced himself as opposed to monarchy and proceeded to Bogotá to take charge of the government and to restore order. In the meanwhile, Páez's preparation for his trip to Bogotá was halted by a riot in Valencia on April 30. Through the influence of Miguel Peña—an impeached, disgruntled national judge —Páez was prevailed upon to resume the office from which Congress had suspended him. Open rebellion was now declared; and other cities, including Caracas, followed the example of Valencia. Santander's appeal (May 12) to Páez's patriotism and revolutionary prestige availed nothing.[61]

Arriving in Bogotá on November 14, Bolívar assumed *"facultades extraordinarias,"* restored temporary harmony, then set out for Venezuela. As he advanced, Páez abandoned the revolution and called on all Venezuelans to recognize Bolívar. The two leaders met on January 4, 1827. Páez was given the title of "Civil and Military

[60] *Ibid.*, pp. 519-520.
[61] *Ibid.*, pp. 521-532; Villanueva, *El imperio de los Andes*, pp. 10-33.

Chief of Venezuela," and they entered Caracas together on January 10.[62]

Meanwhile, opposition to Bolívar—led by Vice-President Santander, Francisco Soto, and Vicente Aznero—was gaining force in Bogotá. The papers *El conductor* and *Gaceta* were violent in their attacks on the *"Libertador."* He had ceased to enjoy "the unlimited and indiscriminate confidence" of a large group, and "some doubts . . . [began] to be entertained of his attachment to Republican principles." In fact, he was openly accused of favoring monarchy.[63]

Chargé Watts thought that the accusation was unjust and that Bolívar's name would take its place in history "as a friend of Freedom with Washington's and Franklin's." His introduction to Bolívar only increased his admiration. He was fully convinced that "the boldness and indignation with which he [Bolívar] met the charge [had] recoiled upon his accusers."[64]

In a letter of resignation, dated February 6, 1827, Bolívar requested that he be left "at liberty to retire to the enjoyment of private life," since the dangers which had forced upon him the duties of "Supreme Head and President of the Republic" no longer existed.[65] Although this, the fourth resignation, was rejected by Congrees at its meetings in May by a vote of fifty to twenty-four, the fact that only four members voted for the dismissal of Santander indicated that the two parties were of about equal strength. The only notable accomplishments of this Congress were the approval of Bolívar's recent actions and the calling of a convention to

[62] Henao y Arrubla, *op. cit.*, pp. 532-534.
[63] *Ibid.*, pp. 534-536; Watts to Clay, (15) Nov. 14, 1826, Desp. Col., IV.
[64] Watts to Ravenga, Nov. 14, 1826, enclosed with Watts to Clay, (18) Nov. 14, 1826, Watts to Clay, (19) Nov. 28, (22) Dec. 27, 1826, (26) March 2, 1827, *ibid.*
[65] Quoted in *Niles' Reg.*, XXXII, 106.

meet the following year at Ocaña for the purpose of amending the Constitution of Cúcuta.[66]

Before the convening of this body (April, 1828), all social intercourse had ceased between Bolívar and Santander. The latter had been almost stripped of his powers by their distribution among the respective departmental heads. Decrees had been approved placing all of the Republic, except Ocaña, under martial law. Grave dangers threatened the Republic, and fears of disunion increased.[67]

According to Bolívar, the convention was to decide "whether the friendly nations should repent having granted recognition and erase our [Colombian] name from the peoples who compose the human species."[68] All eyes were turned towards Ocaña. Sundry proposed amendments came from all groups, factions, and territorial divisions. It was early apparent that intense feeling would prevent the cool consideration of even obvious facts. Naturally, attempts at remodelling the government failed, since the representatives agreed only in their desire to change the old constitution. The withdrawal of the Bolívar group caused the lack of a quorum and the adjournment of the convention in June.[69]

In the meanwhile, Pedro A. Herrán had led in the formation of a group pledged to disregard all results of the convention. Acting on their invitation, Bolívar returned to Bogotá and established a dictatorship, which lasted for the next two years. Since the vice-presidency was thereby suppressed, Santander was more available to the enemies of the Liberator. The unsuccessful plot to assassinate Bolívar on the night of September 25, 1828, was probably known to Santander, but it seems doubtful that he was actually involved. Nevertheless he

[66] Henao y Arrubla, *op. cit.*, pp. 536-537.
[67] *Ibid.*, pp. 537-538; Watts to Clay, (41) Feb. 10, 1828, Desp. Col., IV.
[68] Quoted in Henao y Arrubla, *op. cit.*, p. 538.
[69] *Ibid.*, pp. 539-543.

would have suffered the death penalty with some fourteen others had not Bolívar commuted the sentence to banishment for life.[70]

Partisans of the Cúcuta constitution, under José María Obando and José Hilario López, had already taken up arms against the government in Popayán. Although this revolt was soon crushed, the Peruvians, angered at Colombian interference in Upper Peru (Bolivia), declared war and invaded Colombian territory. And it was not until September 22, 1829, that a final treaty was signed.[71]

In September, also, José María Córdoba declared for the Cúcuta constitution, led an uprising in Antioquia, and appealed to Páez to follow. General O'Leary (British member of Bolívar's staff) soon crushed the movement, but not before open revolt had occurred in Caracas. Páez headed a new government there and requested permission (December, 1829) for Venezuela to withdraw from the Republic. Bolívar was ready to advance against the Venezuelans, but the new Congress opposed the move. Negotiations were preferable. Commissions of the two governments met at Cúcuta, but no agreement was possible, since nothing short of independence would even be considered by the Venezuelans.[72]

Believing that only a monarchy could reconcile the conflicting elements and restore harmony, the council of state (September 3, 1829) had decided to negotiate with England and France to that end. It was proposed that Bolívar serve with the title of *Libertador* until death and that his successor take the title of King. Negotiations were actually undertaken in both Bogotá and the European capitals, but subsequent events and bitter Colombian opposition caused the abandonment of the plan.[73]

[70] *Ibid.*, pp. 544-549.   [71] *Ibid.*, pp. 550-555.
[72] *Ibid.*, pp. 555-558, 560-562.
[73] *Ibid.*, 558-560; J. B. Lockey, *Pan-Americanism: Its Beginnings*, pp. 82-133.

The Congress of 1830 opposed coercion, at least until it had drawn up a new constitution and elected new officers thereunder. The new document differed little in its essential features from the former one, except that it attempted to curb the power of the president.[74] Bolívar continued nominally in power until Congress had approved the constitution. Then he insisted on retiring to private life. Joaquín Mosquera was chosen (May 4) to succeed him as president, with Domingo Caicedo as vice-president.[75]

THE DISSOLUTION OF LA GRAN COLOMBIA[76]

Many, including Caicedo, were convinced that the Republic would not accept this constitution; therefore they favored the formation of a temporary government which would summon a convention later. Subsequent events proved the correctness of the view. Popayán, Tunja, Zipaquirá, Sogamoso, and Neiva expressed opposition to the use of force against Venezuela. General Juan José Flores was effecting the separation of certain provinces in the South. Venezuela, refusing even to negotiate as long as Bolívar remained in Colombia, retained Páez in power. The Bogotá garrison revolted on the eve of Bolívar's departure for Cartagena, and Antonio de Sucre was assassinated (June 4) while en route from Bogotá to Quito.[77]

Mosquera's patriotic appeal to the opposing factions proved of no avail. The new constitution was scarcely anywhere accepted in good grace. Cartagena was not enthusiastic, in spite of the Liberator's arrival there in May. When it was known that Bolívar was to surrender

---

[74] Pombo y Guerra, *Constituciones de Colombia*, II, 829 ff.

[75] Henao y Arrubla, *op. cit.*, pp. 563-564.

[76] E. G. González, ''The Dissolution of Greater Colombia,'' *Inter-America*, VI, 320-323; G. P. Troconis, ''The Dismemberment of Greater Colombia,'' *ibid.*, V, 19-24; G. Silva Herrera, ''The Dissolution of Greater Colombia,'' *ibid.*, VI, 224 ff.

[77] Henao y Arrubla, *op. cit.*, pp. 564-568.

his power, a movement was started to organize the departments of Quito, Guayaquil, and Asuay into a separate government. Flores called a convention on August 10, and a few days afterward the first constitution of Ecuador was drawn up and approved. Six days later (August 16) a convention at Valencia rejected the Colombian constitution and proceeded to promulgate a new one for Venezuela.[78]

Rebel troops administered crushing defeats to the national army at Zipaquirá and Santuario during August. The capital was soon at their mercy. After unsuccessful attempts to continue legitimate government, Mosquera resigned on September 4 and General Rafael Urdaneta assumed the powers of a military dictator—supposedly until Bolívar could be called from retirement.[79]

However, the Liberator was too near death to answer the call. He was removed from Cartagena to Santa Marta on December 1. Doctors Révérend (French) and MacNight (American) readily saw that tuberculosis had so weakened him that the end was a matter of days. He breathed his last on December 17, 1830—the eleventh anniversary of the adoption of the Fundamental Law creating La Gran Colombia, which had just preceded him in dissolution.[80]

[78] *Ibid.*, pp. 573-574.   [79] *Ibid.*, pp. 571-573.
[80] Angell, *op. cit.*, pp. 262-267; T. R. Ybarra, *Bolívar*, pp. 354-357.

Chapter VIII

ON THE MARGIN OF WORLD POLITICS
(1822-1826)

THE privileged geographic position of Colombia, its immense resources, its decisive action in favor of the liberation of its sister republics, the prestige of its men, the consciousness of its power, its plans for the liberation of Cuba, [and] its projects for an American Confederation"[1] gave it temporary preponderance in Latin American affairs, and the recognition of its independence —first granted by the United States—made it an active member of the family of nations.

With few exceptions the early contacts of Colombia with the Republic of the North were cordial. Todd did complain to his chief of Gual's "want of cordiality in his personal intercourse, [and] his notorious unfriendliness towards the United States," which Todd thought was due to the recollections of supposedly unkind treatment accorded him while in the United States. In fact, Todd ceased all official intercourse with him.[2]

Nevertheless the arrival in December, 1823, of Richard C. Anderson as envoy extraordinary and minister plenipotentiary restored the relations to a friendly footing. José María Salazar, Colombian representative of the same rank, some six months earlier, had taken up the work of the late Manuel Torres in the North American capital.[3] The new minister mentioned to Adams the misunderstanding between Todd and Gual, as well as certain offensive letters written by Irvine to Bolívar in

[1] Urrutia, op. cit., p. 269.
[2] Todd to Adams, (52) May 20, (53) May 29, (55) July 4, 1823, Desp. Col., II.
[3] Adams to Salazar, June 10, 1823, Notes to Col. Leg., III, 138; Niles' Reg. (April 13, 1824), XXVI, 23.

1818, but added that he had been instructed to make no complaint. An expression of regret from Adams completely settled the difficulties.[4]

Numerous indications of mutual admiration and friendship were evident. Salazar was elected to membership in the National Institute of Washington and the Historical Society of Boston.[5] A portrait of Henry Clay was presented by Todd and very graciously received at Bogotá.[6] The Washington family forwarded to Bolívar certain relics—Washington's portrait, a lock of his hair, and a medal voted him by the State of Virginia. In 1828 Mrs. Eliza Parke, granddaughter of Mrs. Washington, sent Bolívar a package of letters written by General Washington to his wife during a military campaign.[7]

Fernando Bolívar, nephew and adopted son of the Liberator, resided in Philadelphia some five years, preparing himself to enter the United States Military Academy at West Point. But his admiration for Thomas Jefferson led him instead to the University of Virginia in the spring of 1827.[8] *Niles' Register* had reported in June, 1823, that a number of Colombian youths had come to the United States for their education and that three sons of General Páez had been admitted by special permission to West Point.[9]

THE MONROE DOCTRINE (1823)

Although circumstances had prevented strict adherence to any definite diplomatic course, the North American tradition had been one of isolation from European politics. Washington (1787) hoped that the new states might not form "separate, improper, or indeed any

---

[4] Diarial entry, Nov. 29, 1823, Adams, *Memoirs*, VI, 219.

[5] Rivas, *Relaciones*, p. 37.

[6] Calvin Colton, *Works of Henry Clay*, IV, 76-77.

[7] Rivas, *Relaciones*, p. 37; C. Parra-Pérez, "Bolívar and His Friends Abroad," *Inter-America*, III, 259-264.

[8] Elizabeth R. Shirley, "Fernando Bolívar and the University of Virginia," *B. P. A. U.* (Dec., 1929), pp. 1188-1191.

[9] *Niles' Reg.* (June 7, 14, 1823), XXIV, 209, 236.

connection with European powers.'' In his ''Farewell
Address,'' he advised the young republic ''to steer clear
of permanent alliances with any portion of the foreign
world.'' Jefferson (1792) felt a ''perfect horror at
everything like connecting ourselves with the politics of
Europe''; (1801) rejoiced that nature had ''kindly separated'' the United States from the ''exterminating
havoc'' of the Old World;[10] (1808) considered the interests of the United States and the Spanish colonies (Mexico and Cuba) identical, ''the object of both . . . [be-
ing] to exclude all European influence from this hemisphere'';[11] and (1820) stressed ''the importance of their
[the American nations] coalescing in an American system of policy, totally independent of and unconnected with
that of Europe.''[12]

In a speech before the House of Representatives on
May 10, 1820, Clay advocated that the United States become the center of a system which would constitute the
rallying point against all the despotisms of the Old
World,[13] ''a sort of counterpoise to the Holy Alliance.''[14]
Torres in an interview with Secretary Adams on May 13,
1820, suggested just such ''an American System'' and
expressed the desire that the United States ''take the
lead'' in it.[15] Adams saw ''no basis'' for such a move,
although the Portuguese and Chilean representatives
were pressing the same point.[16] Torres again, on November 30, 1821, pointed out the importance of a policy
for ''maintaining American independence of Europe and
conserving the establishment of free government.''[17]

[10] Quoted by David Y. Thomas, *One Hundred Years of the Monroe Doctrine*, pp. 2, 4, 5.

[11] Letter to Claiborne, Oct. 29, 1808, Jefferson, *Writings* (Mem. ed.), XII, 183. See also I. J. Cox, ''The Pan-American Policy of Jefferson and Wilkinson,'' *Miss. Valley Hist. Rev.*, I, 212-239.

[12] Quoted by Thomas, *op. cit.*, p. 6.

[13] *Annals of Cong.* (16.1), II, 2226-2227.

[14] Speech, Lexington, Ky., July, 1821, *Niles' Reg.*, XX, 301.

[15] Adams, *Memoirs*, V, 115.   [16] *Ibid.*, V, 176.

[17] Torres to Adams, Nov. 30, 1821, García Samudio, *op. cit.*, pp. 193-197.

Early in 1823 Gual was expressing to Todd great apprehension over British actions.[18] Santander (June 17) declared that Colombia was "resolved, and wished the other governments in America to pursue the same policy, not to permit any European Government to obtain a further footing on this continent" and inquired if the United States would join in "a continental confederacy against Europe, of constitutional against anti-constitutional governments."[19]

The idea of a confederation of the former Spanish colonies was not a new one. By 1790 sundry plans of union had been worked out by Espejo and by Miranda, advocated by the Caracas junta in 1810, proposed by Burke in *Gaceta de Caracas* in 1811, and advocated by Bolívar in his Jamaica letter of 1815.[20] The forming of La Gran Colombia was a step in that direction. Colombia, in the fall of 1821, dispatched Joaquín Mosquera to Peru, Chile, and Buenos Aires, and Miguel Santamaría to Mexico to negotiate treaties of perpetual union, league, and confederation. The ones negotiated with Peru and Chile were almost alliances.[21]

However, Adams was not ready to be brought into a confederation with the new republics. The danger of European complications was too great. He advised Anderson that "so far as the proposed Colombian Confederacy . . . [had] for its object a combined system of total and unqualified independence of Europe . . . it . . . [would] have the entire approbation and good wishes of the United States, but . . . [would] require no special agency of theirs to carry it into effect."[22] It seems,

[18] Todd to Adams, (42) Feb. 5, 1823, Desp. Col., II.
[19] Substance of a conference, June 16, 1823, Todd to Adams, (55) July 4, 1823, *ibid.*
[20] Blanco, *Documentos*, V, 331 ff.; Villanueva, *El imperio de los Andes*, p. 138.
[21] Charles W. Hackett, "The Development of John Quincy Adams' Policy with respect to an American Confederation and the Panama Congress, 1822-1825," *H. A. H. R.*, VIII, 496-502.
[22] Adams to Anderson, May 27, 1823, Manning, *Diplomatic Correspondence*, I, 205.

then, that the aims of the two governments were identical —non-interference of the Old World in the affairs of the New—but that the United States had not resolved on a method of preventing interference.

Both feared that Spain, supported by the Neo-Holy Alliance, would make new efforts to subdue the former colonies. Colombia claimed also to fear British aggression. But Adams, realizing that trade and not conquest was uppermost in the British policy, anticipated little danger from that quarter. The menace of French and Russian assistance to Spain was much more real.

Furthermore, the Tsar's ukase of 1821 claiming all territory along the Pacific coast of North America north of the fifty-first parallel, including much of the Oregon Territory, caused Russia to loom large as a factor in the determination of Monroe's policy. The protection of North America from Russian aggression seemed quite as important as the preservation of South America from subjugation by Spain and the Allies.

The commercial interests of Great Britain in the New World and its traditional policy of endeavoring to remain aloof, as far as possible, from continental affairs made expedient a Spanish American policy independent of the Holy Allies and France. British representatives had taken part in the congresses of Vienna (1814-1815) and Aix-la-Chapelle (1818), but, owing largely to the fear of a ''continental police force'' under reactionary control, remained aloof from those of Troppau (1820) and Laibach (1821). The British agent to the Congress of Verona (1822) was instructed against concerted intervention and withdrew (after unheeded protests) when the Congress authorized it.

The subsequent French invasion of the Peninsula, in support of Ferdinand VII against the liberal rebels, increased both the British and American uneasiness in regard to French designs on Spanish America. The revival of the "Family Compact" might do great harm to the commerce of both the United States and Great Britain, for French assistance in the reconquest of the former Spanish colonies would mean French dominance and discrimination against Anglo-American trade in that area. The situation was further aggravated by Spain's refusal to pay certain British claims and its inability to suppress the privateers who were preying on the commerce of both Great Britain and the United States. Of course, the Tsar "favored armed intervention in Spanish America, [but] he did nothing to put it into practice or to urge it on his allies." Nothing was to be feared on his account if the two English-speaking nations could effect a joint policy.[23]

Towards this end, Canning (August 20, 1823) made a declaration of British policy to Minister Rush and added: "If these opinions and feelings are . . . common to your government with ours, why should we hesitate to confide them to each other, and to declare them in the face of the world?"[24] Rush was favorably impressed, but, since he possessed no instructions, communicated the proposal to the State Department and continued his conferences. Because of Canning's insistence on an early decision he agreed to sign the joint declaration on the condition that Great Britain would first recognize the independence of the new republics. This, Canning was not ready to do. He could promise only "future acknowledgment"; therefore Rush was unwilling to proceed.[25]

Canning, foreseeing French victory in Spain, attempted single-handed to eliminate France from Spanish America. If he were successful, Russia would not dare to act alone. The French representative, Polignac, was called into conference on October 3. The results were

[23] Temperley, *The Foreign Policy of Canning*, pp. 99-106.
[24] Canning to Rush, Aug. 20, 1823, Monroe, *Writings*, VI, 365-366.
[25] Temperley, *The Foreign Policy of Canning*, pp. 112-113.

an English threat of recognition of the former colonies, in case of the imposition of trade restrictions by Spain, and French abjuration of ''any design of acting against the Colonies by force of arms.''[26] With France thus committed to the policy of non-intervention, the importance of a joint declaration with the United States decreased, and Rush found Canning growing cool towards the proposition.

The first word of Canning's proposal to Rush reached the State Department on October 9, the last day of the Polignac conferences. Before submitting the matter to his Cabinet, Monroe sought the advice of his predecessors, Jefferson and Madison.[27] Both expressed themselves as favorable to the joint declaration.[28] In the subsequent cabinet meetings Adams, however, showed himself to be unalterably opposed to any coöperative policy.

He felt that Britain was merely trying to secure from the United States a ''public pledge . . . against the acquisition . . . of any part of the Spanish American possessions.'' The United States should not tie itself down ''to any principle which might immediately afterwards be brought to bear'' against it, but should be ''free to act as emergencies . . . [might] arise.'' Besides, the Yankees should not come ''in as a cock-boat in the wake of the British man-of-war.'' Calhoun favored the non-acquisition pledge if Great Britian would commit itself not to seize Cuba or Texas. Monroe was undecided but was certainly opposed to the taking of ''a position subordinate to that of Great Britain.''[29]

The fall of Cádiz into French hands greatly alarmed Monroe and increased his indecision. Calhoun was ''perfectly moon-struck'' by it. Both he and Monroe now

[26] *Ibid.*, pp. 114-121.   [27] Monroe, *Writings*, VI, 323-325.
[28] Jefferson to Monroe, Oct. 24, 1823, Madison to Monroe, Oct. 30, 1823, *ibid.*, VI, 391-395.
[29] Adams, *Memoirs*, VI, 177-179.

favored giving Rush "discretionary powers," but Adams opposed.[30] Wirt "remarked upon the danger of assuming the attitude of menace without meaning to strike." Monroe proposed retreating "to the wall before taking to arms [against the Allies] and . . . [making] sure at every step to put them as much as possible in the wrong." But Adams had no fear of an Allied invasion of Spanish America. British "interest," if not British "principle," might be relied upon to produce coöperation in preventing it.[31] "Hence the United States could safely blow a blast on the republican trumpet, while sheltered behind the shield of England."[32]

Monroe's message of December 2, 1823, contained two very important principles: (1) "The American continents . . . are henceforth not to be considered as subjects for future colonization by any European powers." (2) The United States will "consider any attempt on their part to extend their system to any portion of this hemisphere as dangerous to our peace and safety."[33] Since the first principle obviously referred to Russian aggression, Colombia was interested primarily in the latter.

The message was received enthusiastically in Bogotá. A special edition of the *Gaceta de Colombia* carried the important paragraphs of it, preceded by an article attributed to Vice-President Santander.[34] Some thought that it would dispel the danger of European intervention, while others contemplated actual aid in case Spain should renew the struggle.[35]

Santander, in a message to Congress, characterized

---

[30] *Ibid.*, VI, 185-186, 188, 192-193.
[31] *Ibid.*, VI, 197, 200, 201, 203, 204-205, 226.
[32] Temperley, *The Foreign Policy of Canning*, p. 127. See also Dexter Perkins, "Europe, Spanish America, and the Monroe Doctrine," *A. H. R.*, XXVII, 207-18; W. F. Craven, Jr., "The Risk of the Monroe Doctrine," *H. A. H. R.*, VII, 320-333.
[33] Monroe, *Writings*, VI, 328, 340.
[34] García Samudio, *Capítulos*, p. 128.
[35] Anderson to Adams, (8) Feb. 7, 1824, Desp. Col., III.

the declaration as "an act worthy of the classic land of liberty." "Such a policy," he added, "might secure to Colombia a powerful ally in case her independence and liberty should be menaced by the allied powers." Therefore he was "actively engaged in determining the scope and intent of this policy."[36]

Gual had already been sounding Anderson in regard to an alliance, pointing out that Colombia interpreted the message as implying such.[37] The latter advised that he was not instructed to negotiate on that basis, but Gual continued to speak of some sort of a confederacy.[38] Meanwhile, Salazar (in Washington) was inquiring of Adams: ". . . in what manner the Government of the United States . . . [intended] to resist any interference of [the] Holy Alliance?" To his disappointment, Adams answered that, "by the constitution of the United States, the ultimate decision of this question . . . [belonged] to the Legislative Department of the Government." He did not feel that interference was probable, but, should such a crisis occur, the President would make proper recommendations to Congress.[39] Since the United States was evasive (to the point of refusal) on the subject of entering a Colombian confederacy, more interest was shown in the negotiation of a mere commercial treaty.

THE FIRST TREATY WITH THE UNITED STATES (1824)

Don Manuel Torres had been instructed as early as June, 1820, regarding a commercial treaty with the United States on the basis of *"estricta igualdad y reciprocidad."* Although noting the scarcity of American manufactured articles and fearing the prejudice of the cotton and tobacco growers against Colombian trade,[40]

[36] Quoted in Alejandro Alvarez, *The Monroe Doctrine*, p. 122.
[37] Anderson to Adams, (9) March 18, 1824, Desp. Col., III.
[38] *Idem* to *idem*, Aug. 18, 1824, Manning, *Diplomatic Correspondence*, II, 1283.
[39] Adams to Salazar, Aug. 6, 1824, Notes to Col. Leg., III, 184-186; Salazar to Adams, July 2, 1824, Notes from Col. Leg., II, pt. 2.
[40] García Samudio, *op. cit.*, p. 70.

he approached Adams numerous times even prior to the recognition of Colombia. Two days thereafter Torres again mentioned the subject.[41]

Todd had scarcely returned to Bogotá (December, 1822) with the official announcement of Colombia's recognition when Gual advised him that a treaty project was ready for his perusal. Having no authority to negotiate, Todd agreed to communicate it to Washington;[42] whereupon Gual requested that the negotiations proceed at Bogotá instead, not on account of any distrust of the United States, but in order to set a precedent and thereby protect Colombian agents in London and Paris from "the intrigues and corruption of those courts."[43] Although the request was unusual, Adams very graciously granted it and instructed Minister Anderson, on his departure for Bogotá, to proceed with the negotiations in that capital.[44] Everything awaited his arrival in December, 1823.[45]

Todd had felt that the request was "only another move of procrastination."[46] But Gual's uneasiness over the European situation now made him ready and anxious to proceed,[47] although he was unable to commit Anderson, the new minister, to his interpretation of Monroe's message.[48] He turned to the negotiations in May, 1824.[49]

The entire summer was spent in conversations and in the exchange of notes and projects. The final draft was not agreed upon until September and not signed until October 3. The main difficulty had been Gual's

[41] Adams, *Memoirs*, VI, 27.
[42] Todd to Adams, (40) Jan. 2, 1823, Desp. Col., II.
[43] *Idem* to *idem*, (41) Jan. 8, 1823, *ibid.*
[44] W. C. Ford (ed.), *The Writings of John Quincy Adams*, VII, 441 ff.; Uribe, *Anales*, III, 12.
[45] Salazar and Adams did discuss a treaty draft in Washington, but formal negotiations were conducted only in Bogotá (Adams, *Memoirs*, VI, 219).
[46] Todd to Adams, (57) July 29, 1823, Desp. Col., II.
[47] Anderson to Adams, (4) Dec. 22, (5) 29, 1823, *ibid.*, III.
[48] *Idem* to *idem*, (9) March 18, 1824, *ibid.*
[49] *Idem* to *idem*, (11) May 19, 1824, *ibid.*

insistence on a clause, operative until Colombia's final settlement with Spain, declaring against the principle of "free ships make free goods."[50] But the treaty, as signed, accepted the Yankee maritime views, contained a most-favored-nation clause, and guaranteed religious freedom. It was to remain in force for twelve years.[51]

The treaty was presented to the United States Senate on January 22, 1825, approved March 3, and proclaimed May 31.[52] The British had secured a more favorable one in April, 1825, but protests were soon answered by a decree extending the same advantages to American commerce.[53]

THE CONTEMPLATED INVASION OF CUBA (1823-1826)

The strategic importance of Cuba had long been recognized by the powers of both hemispheres, and a pronounced rivalry had grown up concerning its possession, should decadent Spain prove unable to maintain authority there. Madison as early as 1810 had decided that the United States "could not be a satisfied spectator at its falling under any European Government."[54] Seven years later it was rumored that Great Britain had offered to cancel a £15,000,000 claim in return for Cuba.[55]

The cession of the Floridas to the United States (Treaty of 1819) aroused the London press to advocate British possession of Cuba as an offset.[56] Early in 1822 the French minister, Hyde de Neuville, attempted to in-

---

[50] *Idem* to *idem*, Nos. 12, 14, 15, 16, 17, 18, 19, *ibid.*

[51] For text, see Wm. M. Malloy (ed.), *Treaties, Conventions, International Acts, Protocols, and Agreements Between the United States and Other Powers*, I, 292-301.

[52] *Sen. Ex. Jour.*, III, 416-417, 424. A treaty for the suppression of the African slave trade, presented at the same time, however, was overwhelmingly rejected by the American Senate (*ibid.*, III, 416, 418, 427, 444-446; Unperfected Treaties, Colombia, K).

[53] Uribe, *Anales*, V, 609; VI, 43 ff.; Watts to Clay, May 10, 1825, Jan. 17, 1826, Desp. Col., III.

[54] Madison to Pinckney, Oct. 30, 1810, Madison, *Writings*, VIII, 122.

[55] *Niles' Reg.* (Nov. 8, 1817), XXIII, 174.

[56] Latané, *The United States and Latin America*, p. 85.

crease the American distrust of Great Britain by confiding to Secretary Crawford that the latter power had been negotiating for the last two years for the purchase of the island.[57] Even British official assurance that no designs on it were entertained failed to destroy Yankee suspicion.

However, the proposal of a Cuban secret agent, Señor Sánchez, that the United States concur in a "plan of declaring the island independent of Spain" and of annexing it "as a state into the American Union" was declined by Monroe's Cabinet in September, 1822. It was felt that even encouragement might mean war with Spain, and annexation might cause war with Great Britain. Both results were undesirable and the latter was even to be feared.[58]

The French invasion of Spain (1823) in support of the monarchy accentuated the American uneasiness in regard to the permanency of Spanish rule in Cuba.[59] Adams felt that eventual annexation to the United States would be "indispensable to the continuance and integrity of the Union itself,"[60] but he favored a cautious policy. Calhoun was for war with England if it attempted to take Cuba. The Cabinet discussion of March 15, 1823, grew "almost warm." There was even a suggestion that Congress be called to consider the matter.[61] Luckily, the tension was eased by a mid-summer *rapprochement*—the Canning-Rush conversations. However, the augmentation of the French naval forces in the Caribbean during 1824 and early 1825 again alarmed both the United States and Great Britain.[62]

[57] Adams, *Memoirs*, VI, 112.
[58] *Ibid.*, VI, 70-74. See also J. M. Callahan, *Cuba and International Relations*, pp. 120-165.
[59] William R. Manning, *Early Diplomatic Relations between the United States and Mexico*, p. 94.
[60] Adams to Nelson, April 28, 1823, *B. F. S. P.*, XLIV, 138.
[61] Adams, *Memoirs*, VI, 138.
[62] Temperley, *The Foreign Policy of Canning*, pp. 169-170; Rippy, *Rivalry . . . over Latin America*, p. 85.

Meanwhile, Colombia and Mexico had been discussing plans to revolutionize Cuba and prevent its use as a Spanish base. The project seems to have been initiated by the Colombian minister, Salazar, in Washington,[63] but the discussion was later continued in Bogotá in 1825 by the new Mexican minister, General Bustamante.[64]

The defeat of the Spanish forces on the Mainland by 1824 allowed Colombia to face the sea. Its privateers harassed Spanish commerce, not only in the Caribbean but "snapped up Spanish prizes in the Mediterranean and in sight of Gibraltar."[65] In these circumstances it was quite natural that Cuba should attract more attention. There seems to be little doubt that Bolívar favored some sort of joint action for freeing the island from Spanish rule.[66] On May 15, 1825, he instructed the Peruvian representatives to the Panama Congress to negotiate towards that end, if the Congress thought Cuba and Puerto Rico ought to be independent.[67]

Clay, the new secretary of state, on March 25, 1825, summed up the American policy as follows:

Although the United States has no desire to acquire Cuba, yet, if that island must be attached to any American state, the law of its position demands that it be attached to us. . . . Any effort of Mexico or Colombia to seize it would be regarded with apprehensions, and the attempts at domination by European powers would be just cause for alarm.[68]

The American minister in Madrid was instructed to urge Spanish recognition of the former colonies, since that would probably prevent any attack on Cuba.[69] On

[63] Manning, *Early Diplomatic Relations*, p. 99.
[64] *Ibid.*, pp. 100-101. See also Luis Chávez Orosco, *Un esfuerzo de México por la independencia de Cuba* (Archivo histórico diplomático Mexicano, num. 32).
[65] Temperley, *The Foreign Policy of Canning*, p. 172.
[66] José Antonio Páez, *Memorias*, pp. 449-481.
[67] Alejandro Álvarez, *The Monroe Doctrine*, pp. 149-153.
[68] Clay to Poinsett, March 25, 1825, Inst. Mex., X, 225.
[69] Clay to Everett, April 27, 1825, *A. S. P. F. R.*, V, 866.

May 10 a letter was dispatched to Tsar Alexander requesting that he use his influence to secure colonial recognition on the basis of the Spanish retention of Cuba and Puerto Rico. The Tsar expressed his satisfaction with the present status of the islands, but refused to move except along with his allies and Spain.[70] However, by the end of the year Clay either thought or pretended to think that the Tsar had made some progress towards the securing of Colombian recognition. He advised Salazar to that effect and suggested the postponement of the Cuban expedition then reported to be preparing at Cartagena.[71]

Salazar denied any knowledge of such an expedition and expressed the opinion that the report was ill-founded.[72] Anderson soon wrote from Bogotá that although Colombia felt the independence of Cuba absolutely essential to permanent peace, it disavowed any attempt to annex the island.[73] He perceived no danger of immediate attack, especially after receiving official advice that nothing would be done until a discussion of the matter by the Panama Congress.[74] Suspicion of Mexico and the lack of funds were probably the determining factors in the decision.

THE PANAMA CONGRESS (1826)[75]

The idea of a Pan American confederation was not new in Colombia.[76] In fact, such an organization had been advocated as a means of protection against threatened or feared European movements to force the colonies back under Spanish rule. Within three years after recognition Colombia had signed treaties of perpetual

[70] *Ibid.*, V, 850; Temperley, *The Foreign Policy of Canning*, p. 170.
[71] Clay to Salazar, Dec. 20, 1825, Notes to Col. Leg., III, 245-246.
[72] Salazar to Clay, Dec. 30, 1825, Notes from Col. Leg., II, pt. 2.
[73] Anderson to Clay, (34) Feb. 7, 1826, Desp. Col., III.
[74] *Idem* to *idem*, (39) March 9, (40) 29, 1826, *ibid.*
[75] See Petro A. Zubieta, *Congresos de Panamá y Tacubaya;* F. Verlarde y F. J. Escobar, *El Congreso de Panamá en 1826;* Pablo García de la Parra, *Colombia en las conferencias Panamericanas.*
[76] See *supra*, ''Monroe Doctrine.''

union, league, and confederation with Chili, Peru, Buenos
Aires, Mexico, and Central America. All of these, except
the one with Buenos Aires, provided for a general meeting of plenipotentiaries from those states.[77]

There was advocacy of a general congress of the
Americas in Colombian official circles as early as 1820.[78]
Three years later Gual intimated that shortly the United
States would be "invited to concur in an American Con-
federacy."[79] In fact, Todd thought that Colombia hoped
to use its Latin American alliances to force the United
States into such a confederation, or lose its equal footing
in trade.[80]

Secretary Adams (1823) noted that "floating, undi-
gested purposes of this great American Confederation
. . . [had] been for some time fermenting in the imag-
inations of many speculative statesmen." He felt that
the idea should not be "disdainfully rejected because its
magnitude . . . [might] appal the understandings of
politicians accustomed to the more minute but complicated machinery of a contracted political standard." But
too little was known as yet for the United States to commit itself.[81] Anderson had scarcely arrived at Bogotá
(December, 1823) before Gual suggested that the commercial treaty be followed by a connection of a "more
intimate nature."[82]

After the contents of Monroe's famous message were
known, the discussions in Bogotá seemed to indicate a
wish that the United States might in some way become
connected with a confederation.[83] However, the latter
power was still less interested in the idea, since it had

[77] Alvarez, *The Monroe Doctrine*, pp. 135-141; Uribe, *Anales*, V, 608.
[78] Todd to Adams, Aug. 10, 1820, Desp. Col., I.
[79] *Idem* to *idem*, Jan. 8, 1823, *ibid.*, II.
[80] *Idem* to *idem*, March 21, 1823, *ibid.*, II.
[81] Adams to Anderson, May 27, 1823, Inst. Col., IX, 301.
[82] Anderson to Adams, (5) Dec. 29, 1823, Desp. Col., III.
[83] *Idem* to *idem*, (13) Aug. 18, 1824, *ibid.*, III.

already chosen another more dignified and less self-denying method of opposing the possible European intervention.

Meanwhile, Colombia had been continuing its negotiating with the other republics and preparing for a general congress to meet at Panama. Vice-President Santander, who in 1819 had complained of the indifference of the United States and noted the favorable attitude of Great Britain,[84] now began to look on the former power as a possible ally against Europe. He was enthusiastic over the Monroe Doctrine. Although Adams refused shortly thereafter the suggestion of an alliance, there was probably a close connection between Santander's interpretation of the message and his desire that the United States be represented at the forthcoming Panama Congress.[85]

Salazar was instructed (October 7, 1824) to sound the American attitude towards the Congress with the view of issuing an invitation, if it would be accepted.[86] Two months later Bolívar (from Lima) invited Brazil, Buenos Aires, Chile, La Gran Colombia, Central America, and Mexico, but omitted the United States.[87]

Santander, however, soon wrote Bolívar suggesting that the United States be invited.[88] It seems that Bolívar considered the Monroe Doctrine of "minor importance,"[89] especially since he was already convinced (1820) that the United States, "pursuing its arithmetical round of business . . . [would] avail itself of the opportunity to gain the Floridas, our [Colombian] friendship,

[84] Santander to Bolívar, Feb. 24, 1819, García Samudio, *op. cit.*, p. 108.
[85] *Ibid.*, p. 139; Anderson to Adams, (11) May 19, Aug. 18, 1824, Desp. Col., III.
[86] Gual to Salazar, Oct. 7, 1824, O'Leary, *Memorias*, XXII, 515.
[87] García Samudio, *op. cit.*, p. 136; Robertson, *Hispanic-American Relations*, p. 381.
[88] Santander to Bolívar, Feb. 6, 1825, O'Leary, *Memorias*, XXIV, 255.
[89] Dexter Perkins, "John Quincy Adams," *American Secretaries of State and Their Diplomacy*, IV, 78.

and a great hold on commerce."[90]   He felt that the Congress should be limited to Latin America. If any other power were included, he preferred Great Britain. He feared that an invitation to the United States would compromise Colombia with the former power on account of Anglo-American trade rivalry in that area.[91]

Some think that Bolívar had, even this early, recognized a danger in the ambiguous Monroe Doctrine and was determined to build up a barrier against the imperialistic grip of the United States, thereby saving at least Cuba and Puerto Rico from Yankee as well as from Spanish control. In other words, the aims of the Congress were "to defend their [Spanish American] independence against any attempt of European reconquest and to establish a counterpoise to any excessive ambitions of the United States."[92]   While it is probable that Bolívar did not feel very strongly about it,[93] it is well established that originally he did not intend to invite the United States. In fact, he had characterized (May, 1825) a confederation including that power as *"muy peligrosa."*

Santander seems to have initiated the idea of Yankee representation.[94]   Bolívar very graciously gave in, but objected to the publication of the invitation until its acceptance.[95]

[90] Bolívar to William White, May 1, 1820, quoted by William R. Shepherd, "Bolívar and the United States," *H. A. H. R.*, I, 278.

[91] Carlos Pereyra, *Bolívar y Wáshington: un paralelo imposible*, p. 158; Lockey, *op. cit.*, p. 393; García Samudio, *op. cit.*, p. 131.

[92] Vargas, *Historia del Perú independiente*, III, 69; Gil Fortoul, *Historia constitucional de Venezuela*, I, 386; Henao y Arrubla, *op. cit.*, p. 506; Gilberto Silva Herrera, "The Dissolution of Greater Colombia," *Inter-America*, VI, 224.

[93] See Álvarez, *The Monroe Doctrine*, p. 347.

[94] Bolívar to Santander, May 8, Oct. 27, 1825, *Archivo Santander*, XIII, 254; García Samudio, *op. cit.*, pp. 107, 132; Pereyra, *op. cit.*, pp. 158, 163, 168; Lewis Hanke, "The Attitude of Simón Bolívar toward the Participation of the United States in the Congress of Panama" (paper read before the meeting of the American Historical Association on Dec. 29, 1925).

[95] Bolívar to Heres July 9, 1825, quoted by Shepherd, "Bolívar and the United States," *op. cit.*, pp. 288-289.

Earlier in 1825 both the Colombian and Mexican agents in Washington had talked informally with Clay, and Gual had already sounded Watts at Bogotá in regard to American participation.[96] On November 2 Salazar extended a formal invitation—Mexico had extended a similar one the day before. The subjects to be discussed by the Congress, he advised, were: (1) matters concerning the belligerents exclusively, and (2) matters concerning both belligerents and neutrals. The United States was expected to take part in the discussion of the latter only. It was pointed out that ample opportunity would be afforded thereby for the United States to fix certain principles of international law and to determine the manner of opposing further European colonization and of abolishing African slave trade.[97] Although preferring a more definite statement of the objects to be discussed, Clay accepted the invitation, subject to the advice and consent of Congress.[98] Before the end of the year Adams presented for approval the names of Richard C. Anderson (then in Bogotá) and John Sergeant of Pennsylvania as envoys.[99]

In compliance with a Senate resolution, certain pertinent documents were delivered on January 9. A week later the committee on foreign affairs made an unfavorable report. On March 5 the President suggested to both Houses and appropriation for carrying the appointments into effect. The Lower House, on the same day, requested documents on the subject. The nominations were approved by the Senate on March 14. But the House continued its discussions on the appropriations until April 22.[100]

The debates in both Houses were "earnest and sometimes violent." Both Calhoun and Van Buren were

[96] Lockey, *op. cit.*, p. 394; Watts to Clay, June 30, 1825, Desp. Col., III.
[97] Salazar to Clay, Nov. 2, 1825, Notes from Col. Leg., I, pt. 2.
[98] Clay to Salazar, Nov. 30, 1825, *A. S. P. F. R.*, V, 838.
[99] Richardson, *Messages and Papers*, II, 868, 884-886.
[100] *Ibid.*, II, 887, 894; *A. S. P. F. R.*, V, 857-865.

unalterably opposed to the measure. The latter even pretended to believe that the whole movement had been inspired in Washington.[101] The opposition speeches of Randolph of Roanoke and Berrien of Georgia were seized upon, Watts advised in December, by the English editors of Caracas and Bogotá to show how unfavorable the United States was towards Colombia.[102] In so far as the opposition was sincere, it was "based upon Washington's precept against entangling alliances" and the fear of upsetting the slavery arrangement of the Missouri Compromise of 1820. However, "it was in fact largely factitious, and indicated hostility to the administration much more than disapproval of the idea of coöperation with the new states."[103]

Clay's instructions (May 8, 1826) to Anderson and Sergeant did little more than summarize the Latin American policy of the Adams's administration—refusal to form any alliance or lead any confederation as a means of opposing Europe, but manifestation of a lively interest in the development of republican governments in the new states. He did, however, mention a few important subjects suitable for discussion by the Congress: the removal of all trade discriminations between nations, an interpretation of the maritime rules of trade more favorable to neutrals during warfare, and the possibility of a canal across the Isthmus.[104]

Anderson was ordered on June 6 to proceed to Porto Bello, there to await Sergeant or further word from his government. He was ill upon his arrival at Cartagena, and died there on July 24.[105] According to President

[101] John C. Fitzpatrick (ed.), "Autobiography of Martin Van Buren," *A. H. A. A. R.* (1918), II, 200-202.

[102] Watts to Clay, (20) Dec. 7, 1826, Desp. Col., IV.

[103] Lockey, *op. cit.*, p. 399. A perusal of congressional speeches on the measure substantiates this conclusion.

[104] Clay to Anderson and Sergeant, May 8, 1826, Inst. Col., XI.

[105] Anderson to Clay, (44) June 7, 1826, Robert Anderson to Clay, June [July?] 21, Sept. 1, 1826, Desp. Col., IV.

Adams, "the impediments of the season . . . delayed the departure" of Sergeant, thereby depriving the United States of "the advantage of being represented" at Panama. However, Sergeant was ordered the latter part of the year to proceed to Tacubaya, Mexico, to attend the reconvened session. Joel R. Poinsett, already in Mexico, was to have been the second delegate. But since the Congress never met at Tacubaya, Sergeant returned in 1827,[106] and, as Van Buren remarked, Adams in his message of that year "sang a graceful requiem over the lost project."[107]

Of the other nations invited, only Colombia, Central America, Peru, and Mexico sent official representatives; Great Britain and the Netherlands, non-participating ones.[108] It seems that only Peru and the Caribbean area were at all disposed to coöperate in the plan. In fact, Bolívar (May, 1825) had favored the exclusion of all except these powers, Upper Peru (Bolivia), and Chile.[109]

Before the Congress met, however, Bolívar had evolved a much broader scheme, which included all the American states and Great Britain. Each nation was to be independent, but controlled somewhat in its foreign affairs by a general congress. Spain was expected to make peace, and the Holy Alliance to recognize the new republics. All were to aid any one oppressed by a foreign nation. All race and color prejudices were gradually to disappear. In establishing this code of public law, "England should necessarily take in her hands the beam of the scales." British influence would increase in both Europe and the Americas, and British customs would become so prevalent that "in the advance of the centuries,

[106] Messages of Dec. 5, 1826, Dec. 4, 1827, Richardson, *Messages and Papers*, II, 922, 951.

[107] Fitzpatrick, "Autobiography of Martin Van Buren," *op. cit.*, p. 202.

[108] Henao y Arrubla, *op. cit.*, p. 523; J. L. Andara, "The Bolívar Doctrine," *Inter-America*, IV, 40-46.

[109] Bolívar to Santander, May 30, 1825, quoted by García Samudio, *op. cit.*, p. 132.

there would be, perhaps, one single nation covering the world—a federal union." "These ideas," he thought, ".... [were] in the mind of some Americans of the most prominent class; they ... [were] waiting impatiently the initiation of the project in the Panama Congress, which ... [might] be the occasion of consolidating the union of the new states with the British Empire."[110] On the Isthmus "alone, perhaps, the capital of the world might be set, as Constantine pretended to make of Byzantium the capital of the ancient world."[111]

Bolívar's instructions to the Peruvian delegation, however, contained little of such utopian schemes. They dealt with the actual problems of Spanish recognition of the new republics, the independence of Cuba and Puerto Rico, the suppression of the slave traffic, and the interpretation of international law concerning belligerents and neutrals.[112] In the Peruvian-Colombian conferences, which started on December 17, 1825, all was not harmony. The Mexicans, arriving the following June, however, were more favorable to the Colombian views. Formal meetings of the Congress began June 22 and lasted until July 15, 1826.[113]

Out of the deliberations of these four republics came four treaties: one of perpetual union, league, and confederation; another dealing with armed forces, equipment, etc., to be furnished by each; a third regarding future meetings and qualifications of delegates; and a confidential convention concerning the movement of troops and the organization of the army and navy.[114] Largely because of the merciless climate of the Isthmus, the Congress was adjourned to meet at Tacubaya, Mex-

[110] Simón Bolívar, *Un pensamiento sobre Congreso de Panamá* (Manuscript dated from Lima, Feb., 1826).

[111] Quoted by F. García Calderón, *Latin America; Its Rise and Progress*, p. 77.

[112] Álvarez, *The Monroe Doctrine*, pp. 149-153.

[113] Lockey, *op. cit.*, pp. 333-340.

[114] *Ibid.*, pp. 340-341. For texts, see Uribe, *Anales*, VI, 571-588.

ico.[115] One of the Colombian delegates, Pedro Briceño Méndez, returned to Bogotá with the treaties, and the other, Pedro Gual, proceeded to Mexico, where he remained some two years. But the Congress never reconvened.[116]

Bolívar feared that the removal to Mexico might put the Congress under "the immediate influence of that power, already too preponderant, and also under the influence of the United States."[117] He was not alone in his suspicion of the latter power. Canning's instructions to the English agent, Edward J. Dawkins, indicated a similar lack of faith in Yankee policy. Any "league among the states, lately colonies of Spain, limited to objects growing out of their common relations with Spain" would not be disapproved by England, but "any project for putting the U[nited] S[tates] of North America at the head of an American Confederacy, as against Europe, would be highly displeasing" and an ill return for services already rendered by the British. Dawkins was to avow the wish of his government "that the principles of. Maritime Law, to be adopted by the new States . . . [might] be those which Great Britain . . . [had] always contended to be the true principles . . . and . . . [to] take care to have it duly understood that our [British] determination to act on these principles . . . [had] not been shaken by European Confederacies, [and] . . . [would] not be altered by any Resolution or combination of the States of the New World."[118]

Dawkins was also to point out the contrast in the attitudes of the two powers in regard to a "hostile attack upon Cuba." Great Britain had "uniformly refused to join with the United States in remonstrating with Mex-

[115] Briceño Méndez to Bolívar, July 22, 1826, O'Leary, *Memorias*, VIII, 208-213.
[116] Lockey, *op. cit.*, pp. 347-354. Colombia alone approved the treaties.
[117] Bolívar to Briceño Méndez, quoted by Lockey, *op. cit.*, p. 346.
[118] Quoted by Temperley, *The Foreign Policy of Canning*, p. 179.

ico and Colombia against the supposed intention, or intimating that we [Great Britain] . . . [felt] displeasure at the execution of it.'' On the other hand, the United States had "hardly . . . [disguised] its intention to interfere directly, and by force, to prevent or repress such an operation.''[119]

On these three points, at least, Canning's instructions were anti-American.[120] Since the United States promised no active support to the new republics and no representative appeared at Panama, Dawkins had a free hand in opposing Yankee influence. Apparently, the only discordant note was the publication of certain letters of Alexander Everett, United States minister to Spain, to the effect that England had been only half-hearted in its efforts to secure Spanish recognition of the new states. But Dawkins's free access to Gual and his urbane manner soon restored harmony.[121]

Colombia had already recognized the Yankee interpretation of maritime rights in the Treaty of 1824. And Gual was not opposed to North American membership in the Confederation on condition of a declaration of war on Spain. However, Dawkins thought that Yankee influence was not especially to be feared. "It certainly . . . [existed] in Colombia,'' he admitted, but he felt that it had been "very much weakened even there by their protests against an attack on Cuba, and by the indiscretions . . . committed at Madrid.''[122]

The "Colombians, particularly, were the object of his [Dawkins's] special attention,'' admitted Briceño Méndez, and "Gual received greater consideration than any

[119] *Ibid.*, pp. 175-176.
[120] Adams considered him as ever "an implacable and rancorous enemy of the United States'' (Adams, *Memoirs*, VII, 328).
[121] Temperley, *The Foreign Policy of Canning*, p. 180; Rippy, *Rivalry . . . over Latin America*, p. 243.
[122] Quoted by Rippy, *Rivalry . . . over Latin America*, p. 245; Temperly, *The Foreign Policy of Canning*, p. 180.

of the rest,"[123] However, the favorable attitude of the Colombian leaders towards the United States was changed little thereby. Evidently American influence had not suffered greatly from non-representation at the Panama Congress. It is true that the "tone and tenor" of Clay's instructions to Poinsett and Sergeant, published some three years later, might have caused some "abatement" of Colombian cordiality,[124] but in all probability this was due more to reaction against well-meant, but unwise, activities of American representatives in the internal politics of Colombia.

[123] Briceño Méndez to Secy. of For. Rel., Aug. 15, 1826, quoted by Lockey, *op. cit.*, p. 375.

[124] Moore to Van Buren, (14) Sept. 28, 1829, Desp. Col., VI. These referred to the "ambitious projects and views of Bolívar" (Inst. Colombia, X, 274-277).

Part IV

ANTECEDENTS OF THE TREATY OF 1846

Chapter IX

CLASHES OF TEMPERAMENTS
(1826-1846)

THE year 1827 opened with Bolívar in Venezuela and the separatist movement there temporarily checked. However, unrest was prevalent not only throughout La Gran Colombia but also in Peru and Bolivia. Beaufort T. Watts, the American chargé at Bogotá, expressed grave doubts as to the permanency of these republics, especially since news of Bolívar's resignation of the presidency had just reached the capital and many favored its acceptance. In such an event Watts despaired of "the tranquillity of the nations" Bolívar had emancipated. In spite of "all the calumnies and distrust that different partizans . . . [had] raised" against Bolívar, he saw "an intrinsic moral force in the man, that . . . [awed] the disaffected and [inspired] courage in the patriot."[1]

THE WATTS'S LETTER

Such expressions from Watts on March 14 seem to indicate that his letter (March 15) to the Liberator was caused not by any desire to meddle in Colombian politics but by a sincere interest in the national welfare.[2] "As the Representative of the Republic of Washington," he requested Bolívar to return to Bogotá and save the new republics of Colombia, Peru, and Bolivia. "All is lost without you," he pleaded, "the three nations which you alone have created and rescued from a mass of chaos

[1] Watts to Clay, March 14, 1827, Manning, *Diplomatic Correspondence*, II, 1309.

[2] Urrutia, *Páginas*, pp. 323-337, favorable towards Watts; Rivas, *Relaciones*, pp. 40-42, critical; Moore to Van Buren, (3) Aug. 10, 1829, Desp. Col., VI, Watts was "generally disliked."

will soon have returned to their original darkness without a continuation of your services to sustain.''[3]

Watts was advised by the foreign minister at Caracas, José R. Ravenga, that the Liberator considered the letter as a ''new proof of the interest'' of the United States in the ''prosperity of Colombia'' and therefore had seen fit to publish it.[4] Naturally the knowledge of an official letter so favorable to Bolívar was not relished by the opposition faction at Bogotá. The foreign minister there, José Manuel Restrepo, on the instructions of Vice-President Santander, advised him that an explanation of his action would be requested of Washington.[5]

Somewhat alarmed, Watts almost immediately (June 14) wrote Secretary Clay, attempting to justify himself on the bases of the uncertain conditions throughout Colombia and the fact that he never suspected that the letter would be published.[6] Before the delivery of this despatch, the Department had heard of the incident through the press and had written Watts for an explanation.[7] With statements being demanded by both governments, he was indeed in an embarrassing position. To reinstate himself with his own government, Watts secured a letter from Ravenga to Clay and forwarded it to the Department.[8] This reassurance of Bolívar's favorable view of the matter and a subsequent letter from Bolívar himself to the effect that Watts's conduct had been ''very satisfactory'' saved him from a severe reprimand. Ravenga was advised (January 30, 1828) that although Watts had acted without instructions, the Washington government was ''disposed to overlook it,'' since the letter gave satisfaction to Colombia.[9]

[3] Manning, *Diplomatic Correspondence*, II, 1310.

[4] Ravenga to Watts, April 21, 1827, *ibid.*, II, 1311.

[5] Restrepo to Watts, June 12, 1827, *ibid.*, II, 1314-1315.

[6] Watts to Clay, June 14, 1827, *ibid.*, II, 1315-1318.

[7] Brent to Watts, July 6, 1827, Inst. Col., XI, 368-369.

[8] Ravenga to Clay, Sept. 25, 1827, enclosed with Watts to Clay, Sept. 28, 1827, Desp. Col., IV.

[9] Clay to Ravenga, Jan. 30, 1828, Notes to Col. Leg., III, 421 ff.

In answering Bolívar's letter of November 21—some eleven months later—Clay did not evince much enthusiasm for the Liberator, although the latter had expressed Colombia's "purest gratitude for the incomparable services [Clay] . . . [had] rendered to [Colombians] by sustaining . . . [their] cause with a sublime enthusiasm." Clay wrote that such services had been rendered in the hope that "along with independence would be established free institutions," but he was still "anxiously" looking for this accomplishment. He then proceeded to lecture to the Liberator on the ways of tyrants and the rights of the people. The tenor of the entire letter was one of doubt as to the purity of Bolívar's republican principles.[10] Raimundo Rivas thinks that both Clay and Adams had begun to look on Bolívar *"como un hombre ambicioso."*[11] The following year (1829) Bolívar wrote O'Leary: "I have appointed you Minister to the United States, where my enemies will certainly try their best to tear me to bits, and where I most need some one to defend me."[12] He seemed to realize that the Adams administration did not share Watts's confidence in him.

THE UNFORTUNATE HARRISON MISSION

The month before Watts wrote his letter to Bolívar, Clay began to urge the selection of General W. H. Harrison as minister to Colombia—Watts was only a chargé d'affaires. Soon the Ohio delegation also recommended his appointment. Adams opposed the sending of any minister, and especially Harrison, whom he considered to be a man "of a lively and active, but shallow mind, a political adventurer, not without talents, but self-sufficient, vain, and indiscreet"—certainly not the type for a turbulent post. The nearness of the November presidential elec-

[10] Quoted in Carl Schurz, *Henry Clay*, I, 295; Lockey, *op. cit.*, pp. 129-130.
[11] Rivas, *Relaciones*, p. 71.
[12] Quoted in Shepherd, "Bolívar and the United States," *op. cit.*, p. 297. O'Leary never presented himself in that capacity.

tion, however, made some concessions to the doubtful West necessary; therefore Adams gave in and agreed upon Harrison, not as "the best adapted to the place," but as "the most suitable appointment."[13]

In November, 1828, Harrison set out for his post, accompanied by his son, Carter Bassett, as attaché and Edward Tayloe (formerly with Poinsett in Mexico) as secretary of the legation. Rensselaer van Rensselaer joined the group in June, 1829. They arrived at Bogotá (February 5) in the midst of the war between Colombia and Peru.[14] In spite of Clay's instructions that he should "cautiously abstain from identifying . . . [himself] with either of the contending parties,"[15] Harrison "had formed opinions not very favorable to the existing Government, even before his arrival at Bogotá.[16] Since this was his first trip outside the United States,[17] Colombian conditions were disappointing. He had expected a peaceful and flourishing republic. Instead, he found discontent on all sides; therefore he proved a willing listener to the opponents of Bolívar's rule.[18]

Since the report was soon current that Harrison had been sent to assist in the settlement of the difficulty between Colombia and Peru, he suggested (February 13) that the United States offer to mediate. Within two weeks he was officially approached in regard to the matter. But the new Jackson administration sent him no instructions, and the new minister, Thomas P. Moore, found no need for them, since the differences were practically settled when he arrived.[19]

[13] Adams, *Memoirs*, VII, 223, 530, 547; VIII, 4-5.

[14] Dorothy M. Goebel, *William Henry Harrison*, pp. 253-257. Young Van Rensselaer's letters throw interesting light on the subsequent episode (Catherine van Rensselaer Bonny, *A Legacy of Historical Gleanings*, I, 523-532).

[15] Clay to Harrison, (2) Oct. 13, 1828, Inst. Col., XII.

[16] General W. H. Harrison, *Remarks*, p. 4.

[17] *Ibid.*   [18] Goebel, *op. cit.*, pp. 272-275.

[19] Harrison to Secretary of State, Feb. 13, 27, May 14, 16, Moore to Van Buren, Nov. 7, 1829, Desp. Col., V, VI.

Harrison had been at his post scarcely a month when Jackson decided to recall him.[20] The new minister presented his credentials on September 26. Two days later he reported that it seemed evident that Harrison "had identified himself with the faction . . . [there] inimical to Bolívar" and had restricted his social intercourse to "a few disappointed Americans, English, and German claimants, and to the secret friends of the banished Santander."[21]

This was at least partially true. Harrison's original unfavorable impression of the existing government was intensified (March, 1829) by his belief that Bolívar desired a British prince to follow him in office. By May he became convinced that Bolívar intended to become a monarch, and during the early days of September he began to apprize his government of the secret movements of certain anti-Bolívar factions.[22] He likewise learned of the attempted negotiations of the council of state with England and France in regard to a monarchy and reported it to Van Buren in his code message of September 7.[23] Tayloe's former connection with Poinsett in Mexico marked him as "a petty intriguer" from the time of his arrival.[24] And there seems to be little doubt that Harrison himself had been indiscreet in certain of his actions and words.

On the day following the termination of his duties (September 27) Harrison, along with Tayloe and a Dr. Cheyne, set out for a visit with the British consul-general, Henderson. Two days later Van Rensselaer arrived and advised them of the possibility of governmental action being taken against Henderson, Torrens (Mexican representative), Leidersdorf (banking agent), Harrison, and Harrison's son, on the ground of correspondence

[20] Van Buren to Moore, (1) April 2, 1829, Inst. Col. XIV, 1.
[21] Moore to Van Buren, (3) Sept. 28, 1829, Desp. Col., VI.
[22] Harrison to Van Buren, (6) March 27, (13) May 27, (22) Sept. 14, 1829, *ibid.*
[23] Goebel, *Harrison*, pp. 276-280. [24] *Ibid.*, p. 262.

with the insurgents and knowledge of their intrigues.[25] The party returned to Bogotá to investigate the charges, but were advised that the proofs were "of too secret a nature to be presented." There the matter rested for several days.[26]

Secretary Vergara claimed to believe that Harrison, Henderson, and Albert Gooding (a Yankee jeweler in Bogotá) were planning an insurrection and an attempt on the lives of General Urdaneta, Bresson (French representative), García del Río, Leandro de Miranda, and himself. Harrison was considered as the head of the plot, which had been revealed by "an angel in the form of a man."[27] This "angel" seems to have been a Virginian by the name of Carr,[28] who had visited in Henderson's home and was at that time aide to General O'Leary in the campaign against General Córdoba.[29]

After several days in Bogotá, Harrison and Tayloe (October 13) visited the salt mines of Zipaquirá. The following day word was received of the imprisonment of Gooding on the charge of having given a dinner the preceding Sunday to opponents of the government—meaning Harrison and Tayloe. By standing surety for Gooding's actions, Moore obtained his release. Henderson and Torrens were ordered to leave the country, and Harrison probably saved himself from deportation by leaving Bogotá for Washington on October 19, 1829.[30]

On the previous September 27 Harrison had committed another indiscretion by writing to Bolívar.[31] This letter pointed out to the Liberator the pitfalls in the paths of tyrants and did more than intimate a suspicion

[25] *Ibid.*, p. 283; Harrison, *Remarks*, pp. 8-10.
[26] *Ibid.*, pp. 11-12.
[27] Vergara to Bolívar, Oct. 15, 1829, O'Leary, *Memorias*, VII, 224-225.
[28] Goebel, *Harrison*, p. 284.   [29] Harrison, *Remarks*, p. 12.
[30] *Ibid.*, pp. 12-18; Moore to Van Buren, (6) Oct. 19, 1829, Desp. Col., VI.
[31] The letter was written in August, but not sent to Bolívar in Peru until after Harrison surrendered his post to Moore (Harrison, *Remarks*, pp. 42, 58).

of Bolívar's republican principles—Clay had suspected them in 1828. Harrison pointed out that the Colombians were capable of self-government and would submit to a monarchy only if held in subjection by brute force. He argued that if the Liberator desired to be considered great by posterity, he could do no better than follow the course blazed by Washington, whose fame did not rest "upon his military achievements," but upon his "devotedness to the interest of his country." "The friends of liberty throughout the world, and the people of the United States in particular," concluded Harrison, were anxiously awaiting his decision between military despotism and democracy.[32] When known, this letter was added to the complaints against Harrison.[33]

In presenting these charges Vergara said that Harrison had been viewed "with much dissatisfaction" by the Colombian government for some months before the arrival of Moore and his recall would have been requested if it had not been known that a new minister was soon to be sent. He claimed to possess absolute proof of Harrison's knowledge of and complicity in an insurrectionary movement and of revolutionary expressions tending to arouse the garrison of Bogotá against the Administration. The letter to Bolívar was also resented.[34]

Harrison admitted that he knew of the movements of Córdoba, but insisted that this did not prove complicity "to overthrow the authority of General Bolívar and reestablish the Republic." He denied that he had shown himself to be the "enemy of the Liberator" or that he had attempted to arouse the Bogotá garrison. That certain words of his should be repeated to the government with "trifling alteration" was not sufficient proof of his

[32] Harrison to Bolívar, Sept. 27, 1829, enclosed with Moore to Van Buren, (15) March 27, 1830, Desp. Col., VI.
[33] Vergara to Moore, Jan. 17, 1830, *ibid.*
[34] *Ibid.*

guilt. He confessed that certain hostile letters had passed between Vergara and himself, but claimed that both had withdrawn them when that particular matter (Traver's imprisonment case) had been settled. He felt positive that the charges had originated with General Urdaneta and had received little credence with his official colleagues.[35]

That Harrison was indiscreet can scarcely be denied. His lack of previous foreign contacts, his ultra-republicanism, and his obvious ignorance of diplomatic forms and duties made him ill-fitted for such a post. Under a dictatorship, jealousy and suspicion are always prevalent and spies are ever "eager to catch every incautious word" and to turn "every movement of a suspected person into treason."[36] The English representatives in Bogotá thought that the new Jacksonian minister, Moore, actually encouraged the Colombian suspicion of Harrison for the purpose of discrediting the late Adams administration. This seems entirely probable.[37] In any case, Harrison was given slight chance to defend himself, for the whole affair was soon dropped from the correspondence between the two countries.

TEMPORARY RAPPROCHEMENT

The official denunciation of Bolívar in the Tacubaya instructions and the Harrison affair certainly decreased Colombia's good feeling towards the United States. To offset this, Moore very early pointed out that the Colombian disposition "should not take its character from sentiments expressed by those whom the people [of the United States] . . . [had] divested of executive authority." On being presented to Bolívar, Moore assured him that President Jackson's "confidence in the purity of . . . [his] motives and the rectitude of . . . [his] intentions

[35] Harrison to Van Buren, March 8, 1830, Desp. Col., VI.
[36] Adams, *Memoirs*, VIII, 211.
[37] Rippy, *Rivalry . . . over Latin America*, p. 194.

. . . [had] never been shaken.'' Bolívar, in reply, expressed the greatest admiration for the new president and pointed out certain very close parallels between his and Jackson's careers.[38] Complete official harmony seems to have been restored.[39]

Moore did not yield the ''slightest credence'' to the accusations of monarchical desire leveled against Bolívar on his retirement from the presidency in May, 1830. He was soon convinced, however, that the people were not prepared for ''free institutions'' and that ''the return of Bolívar alone . . . [could] prevent this country from being subdivided into half a dozen petty despotisms, waging war upon each other.''[40] The Urdaneta revolution of September was viewed with alarm, especially since the English openly exulted in the success of these ''conquerors of the constitution.'' The report that Panama had seceded and offered its sovereignty to Great Britain likewise was interpreted as inimical to Yankee interests. Nevertheless Moore was not in despair, even at the death of the Liberator. ''Though I believe,'' he wrote, ''that Genl. Bolívar has not left behind him a man more devoted to the interests of his country than himself, yet it would be uncharitable to suppose, that all others are destitute of public virtue.''[41] The overthrow of Urdaneta in April, 1831, was ''not merely satisfactory but delightful'' to Moore, who believed that the English party was discredited ''forever.''[42]

THE FORMATION OF NEW GRANADA

Although La Gran Colombia had dissolved and both Ecuador and Venezuela had adopted constitutions, the re-

[38] Moore to Van Buren, (11) Jan. 21, 1830, Desp. Col., VI; Lockey, *op. cit.*, p. 132.

[39] Bolívar presented Jackson with a medal. *H. Rep.*, No. 170 (21.1).

[40] Moore to Van Buren, (18) May 21, (20) Aug. 28, 1830, Desp. Col., VI.

[41] Moore to Van Buren, Oct. 21, 1830, Jan. 14, 1831, Manning, *Diplomatic Correspondence*, II, 1363-1364; Desp. Col., VI.

[42] Moore to Van Buren, May 21, 1831, *ibid.*

mainder of the territory continued in disorder through most of 1831. General Domingo Caicedo, who took over the government in May, convened a constitutional convention in October.[43] Moore believed that this body contained "more talent than any other deliberative body of the same number that . . . [had] ever been convened in Colombia." The clergy and the military therein were few. That the convention intended to and would imitate the United States constitution, he had little doubt.[44]

In some respects Moore was correct. The new document (approved February 29, 1832) provided for a president and vice-president elected for a term of four years, a council of state, a bicameral congress, a supreme court, and a large amount of provincial self-government. On the other hand, it differed from the North American constitution in that the president was not eligible for re-election, the cabinet was chosen by congress, and the judges held office for a period of only four years.[45] The old title of *New Granada* was assumed instead of *Columbia*. Santander, then in exile, and José Ignacio de Márquez were chosen president and vice-president, respectively.[46]

THE RETURN OF SANTANDER

Santander, after a sojourn in Europe, had come to make his residence in New York in the fall of 1831. A delegation, composed of Joaquín Acosta and Honorato Rodríguez, was dispatched to advise him of the election and to accompany him to Bogotá. Before his departure he held numerous conferences with Secretary Albert Gallatin in regard to the financial affairs of the new republic. On the recommendation of Minister Moore, the use of a public vessel was offered to convey him to New Granada.

---

[43] Henao y Arrubla, *op. cit.*, pp. 585-586.
[44] Moore to Livingston, Oct. 21, 1831, *H. Doc.*, No. 173 (22.1), p. 6.
[45] Henao y Arrubla, *op. cit.*, p. 588.
[46] *Ibid.*, pp. 589-590; Pombo y Guerra, *op. cit.*, II, 885 ff.

"This act of courtesy,", wrote Moore, produced "the happiest results" at Bogotá. However, for some reason Santander chose to return on a merchant vessel instead.[47] The reason given by him for declining the offer was that his ill health would not permit the long land or water trip to Pensacola, whence the vessel was to sail.[48] Moore felt, however, that the New York enemies of the Jackson administration had persuaded him that the offer was made "in bad faith and intended for mere compliment."[49] His subsequent attitude towards Moore's attempt to negotiate a commercial treaty might indicate that he did partake of some party bias while in New York.[50] Of course, the anti-Bolívar press had been doing its bit also to prejudice the new government against Moore and the Jackson administration. It does seem, however, that the offering of a vessel so far from New York might be interpreted, if not as a "mere compliment," at least as indifference.[51] To offset the Colombian prejudice in regard to the affair, Moore's successor recommended (September, 1833) that Jackson include in his annual message some compliment to Santander. This was not done.[52] The Washington liberals seem to have had little faith in those of New Granada.

NATIONAL RENAISSANCE

Santander was enthusiastically welcomed at Bogotá.[53] He assumed his official duties on October 7, 1832, and was

[47] García Samudio, *op. cit.*, p. 155; Moore to Livingston, (42) March 14, (52) July 30, 1832, Desp. Col., VII; Livingston to Santander, May 19, 1832, Notes to Col. Leg., I, pt. 2.

[48] Santander to Livingston, May 22, 1832, Notes from Col. Leg., I, pt. 2.

[49] Moore to Livingston, (53) Aug. 21, 1832, Desp. Col., VII.

[50] See *infra*, chap. x.

[51] Livingston explained (May 19) the smallness of the navy would not permit the vessel to await Santander's orders "at any port" (Notes to Col. Leg., V).

[52] McAfee to McLane, Sept. 24, 1833, Desp. Col., VIII.

[53] *Niles' Reg.* (Dec. 1, 1832), XL, 217.

formally inaugurated on the first of the following April.[54] Under the administration of the "Man of the Laws,"[55] insurrectionary plots were quickly suppressed and the nation was soon enjoying comparative peace and prosperity.

The National Academy was re-established. Public support was given to the National Museum now under the direction of Joaquín Acosta.[56] A renaissance in education was almost immediate. During the period of 1833-1837 the number of schools increased from 378 with 10,500 pupils to 1,052 with 25,577. In 1837 there were three universities, nineteen colleges, and six "houses of education" with 3,102 students.[57] Treaties for the settlement of boundaries and the liquidation of the debts of La Gran Colombia were negotiated.[58] And diplomatic representation was resumed in the United States.[59]

However, the correspondence between the New Granadian Legation and the State Department was slight. The Treaty of 1824 had been negotiated at Bogotá, and such matters as claims and commerce continued to be dealt with there. Since the Colombian (New Granadian) representatives evidently steered clear of internal politics and few of their nationals became involved with American authorities, friction was conspicuously lacking in Washington.[60]

Santander's administration, at least outside of Washington governmental circles, was considered "eminently successful." Although a military man himself, he made the army "the servant, not the master of the government." It was thought by some that he was "perhaps

[54] Henao y Arrubla, *op. cit.*, pp. 591-593.

[55] "El hombre de las leyes," Bolívar to Santander, *Archivo Santander*, XII, 245.

[56] Henao y Arrubla, *op. cit.*, pp. 594-595.

[57] G. Arboleda, *Historia contemporánea de Colombia*, I, 285, 315.

[58] Henao y Arrubla, *op. cit.*, pp. 594-595.

[59] Notes from Col. Leg., I, pt. 2; Uribe, *Anales*, III, 60-61. The last chargé had departed in May, 1828.

[60] In fact, the chargé resided principally in New York.

the only man who . . . [had] been at the head of any of the new Spanish-American republics, who . . . [had] been equally the friend of law as well as liberty and who . . . [might] be considered a democrat of the true school."[61]

In Bogotá, however, the delay in the settlement of certain long-standing claims and in the removal of discriminating duties[62] and Yankee persistence in becoming involved in local politics caused irritation to an embarrassing degree. The four years (1837-1841) of political agitation and civil war made negotiations almost impossible and increased the chances of misunderstanding.

José Ignacio de Márquez, a moderate, was elected to the presidency in 1837. Santander then proceeded to lead the anti-administration forces until his death in May, 1840. Agitation over amending the Constitution of 1832 and the suppression of certain convents in Pasto led to armed revolts in 1839-1840. And it was not until the summer of 1841 that Pedro A. Herrán and Tomás C. Mosquera were able to restore peace. Meanwhile, Herrán had been chosen president.[63]

THE ABRUPT DEPARTURE OF CHARGÉ SEMPLE

Edward Leoni, a citizen of the United States, was imprisoned for alleged participation in the Pasto revolt. After unsuccessful attempts to secure what he considered justice in the case, Chargé James Semple demanded his passport and returned to the United States.[64] This seems to have been viewed with alarm by the Herrán administration. Joaquín Acosta was dispatched posthaste to Washington. Fearing that some one unfriendly to New Granada—probably meaning Semple—might prejudice Secretary Webster before all the facts were presented, he wrote from Cartagena advising of his ap-

[61] *Niles' Reg.*, (April 1, 1837), LII, 69; (June 13, 1840), LVIII, 226.
[62] See *infra*, chap. x.   [63] Henao y Arrubla, *op. cit.*, pp. 597-612.
[64] Semple to Webster, (47) March 4, 1842, Blackford to Calhoun, (27) Nov. 1, 1844, Desp. Co., IX, X; Rivas, *Relaciones*, pp. 92-93.

pointment. This "sudden and purely temporary" mission, explained Acosta on arrival, was for the purpose of explaining matters in connection with Semple's departure and of "soliciting the appointment of an impartial representative" of the United States. The guilt of Leoni was beyond question, Acosta held; therefore justice must be meted out. However, New Granada desired close relations with the United States, and was anxious to settle all the outstanding claims.[65]

Webster advised Acosta that the Department had anticipated the desire for Semple's recall and had already appointed W. M. Blackford as his successor."[66] Acosta then set out for Bogotá in November, 1842. And New Granada remained unrepresented in the United States, except for a consul-general in New York, until 1847. Blackford, on his arrival at Bogotá, proceeded "as if nothing unpleasant had occurred," and was received in the same manner. Acosta's pleasing account of his reception in the United States and his appointment as secretary of foreign affairs caused Blackford to hope for early adjustments in regard to claims and commerce.[67]

The enlightened administrations of Pedro A. Herrán (1841-1845) and Tomás C. de Mosquera (1845-1849), under the revised Constitution of 1843, made for not only internal peace and economic development but international harmony and understanding. Blackford and his successor, Benjamin A. Bidlack, found negotiations at Bogotá much more satisfactory than formerly. In 1847 the former President Herrán came to Washington as envoy extraordinary and minister plenipotentiary. Such able administration and foreign representation naturally tended towards more consonant relations.

[65] Acosta to Webster, April 29, June 16, Aug. 23, 1842, Notes from Col. Leg., II. Leoni was pardoned after six months in prison. New Granadian Foreign Secretary to Bidlack, Feb. 20, 1846, Desp. Col., X.

[66] Rivas, *Relaciones*, p. 93.

[67] Blackford to Webster, (1) Sept. 15, (2) 30, 1842, (8) Feb. 17, (16) Oct. 20, 1843, Desp. Col., X.

Chapter X

CLAIMS AND COMMERCE

(1822-1848)

THE early North American claims against Colombia grew out of alleged illegal seizures of ships and cargoes during the revolutionary era. Baptis Irvine, Captain Oliver H. Perry, Dr. S. D. Forsyth, and Robert K. Lowry, were all unsuccessful in making collections.[1] Todd (1823) received the impression from Gual that a "speedy settlement of claims" was not probable.[2] However, the following year Gual declared to Anderson that he was not unfriendly towards the United States and promised to go into the matter.[3]

UNSUCCESSFUL CLAIMS NEGOTIATIONS

On March, 1825, Anderson advised that he had secured settlement for all claims, except one, for seizures made before the formation of the republic. Of course, other more recent ones were still pending.[4] But President Adams, in his annual message of 1825, expressed "great satisfaction" at the "liberal spirit with which the Republic of Colombia . . . [had] made satisfaction."[5]

Harrison, even before reaching Bogotá, was unfavorably impressed with the political conditions and the chances of claim adjustments.[6] The near bankruptcy of the treasury made settlements improbable. During his short service he was able to make only one collection.[7]

[1] See *supra*, chap. v.
[2] Todd to Adams, (46) March 21, 1823, Desp. Col., II.
[3] Anderson to Adams, (6) Jan. 4, 1824, *ibid.*, III.
[4] Anderson to Clay, (28) March 18, 1825, *ibid.*, III.
[5] Richardson, *Messages and Papers*, II, 868.
[6] Harrison (Maracaibo) to Clay, (1) Dec. 23, 1828, Desp. Col., V.
[7] Harrison to Van Buren, (18) July 28, 1829, *ibid.*; Goebel, *Harrison*, p. 274.

Moore made greater progress. He negotiated a convention (November 25, 1829) recognizing certain Yankee claims.[8] However, he scored the methods of American citizens in applying for redress of grievances. The utterance of " a philippic against this Government, its organs, and its measures," he argued, was the worst course that could be "pursued and of all others, the least calculated to promote the views of the petitioner or memorialist."[9]

Naturally the dissolution of La Gran Colombia in 1830 prevented the early execution of the convention of the previous year. After more than two years with little apparent effort at adjustment, Secretary Livingston instructed Moore to "state seriously but amicably, that the President . . . [made] it a point of honor, as well as duty to leave no national demand that . . . [was] founded on justice, unsettled during his administration."[10] Although no tangible results came from this, Jackson was anxious to keep Moore near the Colombian government to urge the claims.[11]

Three years later Chargé McAfee estimated the amount due Yankee claimants at $500,000 and thought that if the Department did not "speak plainly," the sum would never be paid.[12]

The New Granadian congress voted in 1837 for the payment of one half of the claims included in the convention of 1829—by an agreement with Ecuador and Venezuela this was the Granadian share.[13] Van Buren, in his first annual message, complained that many of these long-standing claims were still pending, but "hoped our citizens . . . [would] ere long receive full compensation."[14]

[8] Moore to Van Buren, (12) Feb. 6, 1830, Desp. Col., VI.
[9] *Idem* to *idem*, (9) Nov. 28, 1829, *ibid.*
[10] Livingston to Moore, (18) Feb. 16, 1832, Inst. Col., XIV, 250.
[11] Livingston to Jackson, March 16, 1832, *B. F. S. P.*, XXIV, 374-376.
[12] McAfee to Forsyth, (26) June 5, 1835, Desp. Col., VIII.
[13] *Idem* to *idem*, (43) June 12, 1837, *ibid.*
[14] Richardson, *Messages and Papers*, IV, 1594.

The new chargé, James Semple, was instructed (1838) to present the claims immediately on his arrival at Bogotá. A list of some eleven was given him.[15] He appeared personally before the board of plenipotentiaries of New Granada, Ecuador, and Venezuela meeting at Bogotá in 1838, but he concluded that if the United States did not demand settlement, none would be made by any of the three republics.[16] He proceeded to make such a demand, but with no success.[17]

Forsyth's new instructions of October, 1839, took on a much firmer tone,[18] yet New Granada refused to pay any claim not passed upon by the board of plenipotentiaries.[19] Van Buren's renewal of his complaint against the delay seemingly passed unheeded.[20] Early in 1841 Semple urged that the Department issue a "positive demand of payment" or, at least, recognition of the claims, and suggested that a threat to sever diplomatic relations might be effective.[21] But Forsyth hesitated to take such vigorous action. He seemed to prefer letting the new Harrison administration settle the knotty problem.

Secretary Webster was likewise slow in using forceful measures and left Semple without definite instructions. However, the latter made a "formal and positive demand" for immediate settlement.[22] When this was not forthcoming and justice (as he considered it) in the Leoni case denied, Semple demanded his passport and returned to the United States.[23]

His successor, W. M. Blackford, was instructed that it was "far from the intention of . . . [his] government to

[15] Forsyth to Semple, (3) Jan. 9, 1838, Inst. Col., XV, 43 ff.
[16] Semple to Forsyth, (10) Sept. 28, (11) Nov. 16, 1838, Desp. Col., IX.
[17] Semple to Herrán, May 18, 1839, enclosed with Semple to Forsyth, (19) May 28, 1839, *ibid.*
[18] Forsyth to Semple, (10) Oct. 20, 1839, Inst. Col., XV, 69 ff.
[19] Semple to Forsyth, (27) July 17, 1840, Desp. Col., IX.
[20] Richardson, *Messages and Papers*, IV, 1822.
[21] Semple to Forsyth, (32) March 26, 1841, Desp. Col., IX.
[22] Semple to Webster, (46) March 3, 1842, *ibid.*
[23] See *supra*, chap. ix.

abandon those claims.'' They must at least be acknowledged. A short time, however, might be allowed for their
payment.[24] Blackford soon concluded that unless he was
authorized to threaten a naval demonstration, he could
accomplish no more than his predecessors. He felt that
New Granada mistook the ''motives and . . . [did] not
appreciate the forbearance hitherto displayed by the
United States.'' In January, 1843, he requested instructions approaching ''as near to intimidation as . . .
[might] be consistent'' with Yankee character.[25]

A naval demonstration was again suggested in June,
1844. So much forbearance had been exercised, Blackford argued, that New Granada had begun to feel itself
the injured party when the matter of claims was approached.[26] Secretary Calhoun advised him that he did
not doubt the effectiveness of the suggested remedy but
that it would have to receive the sanction of Congress.
He thought, however, that some of the fleet might call at
New Granadian ports after the hurricane season.[27] But
no demonstration was made. Blackford turned his attention towards the negotiation of a commercial treaty
and soon returned to the United States, having settled
only five claims.[28]

The new chargé, Benjamin A. Bidlack, was told that
claims ''constituted the principle pending business of . . .
[his] mission.'' The list furnished him contained ten.
Of this number, seven had appeared in Semple's instructions of 1838 and six, with the Leoni claim, were later
disallowed under the Claim Treaties of 1857 and 1864.[29]
This might indicate, then, that the clashes over claims

[24] Webster to Blackford, (2) May 20, 1842, Inst. Col., XV, 79 ff.
[25] Blackford to Webster, (5) Dec. 23, 1842, (7) Jan. 20, 1843, Desp.
Col., X.
[26] Blackford to Calhoun, (25) June 14, (26) July 26, 1844, *ibid.*
[27] Calhoun to Blackford, (19) Ang. 15, 1844, Inst. Col., XV, 89.
[28] Blackford to Secretary of State, Nos. 8, 27, 28, 29, Desp. Col., IX.
[29] Buchanan to Bidlack, June 23, 1845, Inst. Col., XV, 93; John Bassett
Moore (ed.), *Works of James Buchanan*, VI, 175.

were owing largely to New Granadian procrastination
and Yankee misrepresentation.

THE REMOVAL OF EARLY COMMERCIAL DISCRIMINATION

All commerce during the revolutionary era was subject not only to the privateer hazard, but also to rather
precarious port regulations. These varied with the
parties in power and even with ports under the same
authority. On the eve of American recognition of Colombia, European direct commerce to La Guayra was paying
five per cent lower duties than the North American.[30]

Don Manuel Torres, two days after recognition, promised to investigate the matter, but his early death prevented it.[31] Naturally, Todd attributed the discrimination to British influence.[32] Watts, writing from Caracas
in 1824, held the same view.[33] The following year Anderson, just before his return to Bogotá, was authorized
to negotiate a treaty for the ''equalization of import and
tonnage duties.''[34] On his arrival in January, 1826, he
experienced little difficulty in securing an executive order
placing the United States on the same basis as Great
Britain.[35]

ADVERSE LEGISLATION : COMMERCE ON THE WANE

For the next three years unsettled internal affairs
made trade conditions very uncertain.[36] The United
States shipping to La Guayra decreased nearly fifty per
cent from November, 1826, to June, 1829.[37] The consul
there continued to insist that a small naval force be sta-

[30] Lowry to Graham, March 20, 1822, Con. Let., La Guayra, I.
[31] Adams, *Memoirs*, VI, 27.
[32] Todd to Adams, (53) May 29, 1823, Desp. Col., II.
[33] Watts to Adams, Sept. 4, 1824, *ibid.*, III.
[34] Clay to Anderson, Sept. 16, 1825, Inst. Col., IX, 380 ff.; Anderson to
Clay, (30) Oct. 16, 1825, Desp. Col., III.
[35] Anderson to Clay, (32) Jan. 26, (33) Feb. 1, 1826, *ibid.*
[36] From the Páez rebellion to the dissolution of La Gran Colombia.
[37] Con. Let., La Guayra, I, II.

tioned off the coast to protect commerce and to insure an equal footing with the British. And in 1829 Ministers Harrison and Moore joined in this request.[38]

Bolívar's decree of May 8, 1829, caused still greater decrease in trade between the two nations. A new tariff schedule based on it was issued on June 21. The duty on flour, the principle import from the United States, was increased from $3 to $8 per barrel, and a five per cent additional import tax placed on all products not of the growth or manufacture of the shipping country.[39] Since much of the United States trade was in articles of European manufacture, the new schedule operated as a discrimination in favor of the British, who possessed both the products and the merchant marine.

The United States protested under the most-favored-nation clause of the Treaty of 1824 and demanded that Article XI of the treaty between New Granada and Central America[40] be extended to apply to its trade. New Granada contended, on the other hand, that Article XI had been granted to Central America in return for an alliance and was not subject to the most-favored-nation interpretation.[41]

The fall of the Urdaneta government in May, 1831, made it possible, however, for Moore to secure (November 21) the repeal of the recent tariff schedule and the restoration of the Tariff Act of 1826, which placed the United States on an equal footing with Great Britain. Moore exulted over the change and noted that an "undisguised partiality" was being shown North American citizens in Bogotá.[42] But he warned that their interests

[38] *Ibid.;* Desp. Col., VI.

[39] Rivas, *Relaciones*, p. 76; Goebel, *Harrison*, p. 274; Harrison to Van Buren, (15) June 27, 1829, Desp. Col., V.

[40] See Uribe, *Anales*, VI, 40.　　　[41] Rivas, *Relaciones*, pp. 77-78.

[42] Moore to Secretary of State, (29) May 7, (private) May 21, (30) June 7, (31) June 28, (37) Nov. 21, 1831, Desp. Col., VI; *B. F. S. P.*, XXIV, 371-372, 378 ff.

must be "vigilantly guarded," since the English were "not less industrious than formerly."[43] The early repeal of the decree of November 21, on the ground that the President had exceeded his constitutional powers, was attributed by Moore to Dutch protests and to British intrigues. He said that England seemed "as much offended as if this Government had not the right to regulate its own concerns." In spite of this, however, Moore felt (May, 1832) that the time was ripe for a favorable commercial arrangement.[44] He was instructed some five months later to offer the placing of coffee and cocoa on the American free list and the admission of indigo at fifteen per cent ad valorem in return for the equivalent of the decree of November 21, 1831.[45]

PROLONGED NEGOTIATIONS FOR AN EQUAL TRADE FOOTING

Meanwhile, the United States congress had passed an act (May 19) placing New Granadian direct shipping on the same basis as that of nationals and also providing for the removal of the "restriction of coming direct" whenever New Granada removed the same.[46] Moore then argued that since the United States had enacted this legislation on the basis of the decree of 1831, its repeal was "an injurious breach of contract." Besides, the in terpretation of Article II of the Treaty of 1824, in the light of the Central American treaty, guaranteed equality of trade. However, in order to avoid "an unpleasant collision with a sister republic . . . and to place their commercial relations on a permanent foundation," the Washington government would make certain tariff concessions.[47]

[43] Moore to Livingston, (38) Jan. 19, 1832, Desp. Col., VII.
[44] Moore to Livingston, (47) May 21, (48) June 7, (50) 21, 1832, Desp. Col., VII; Forsyth to McAfee, (25) May 1, 1835, Inst. Col., XV, 15.
[45] Livingston to Moore, (21) Oct. 31, 1832, *ibid.*, XV, 269 ff.
[46] *Statutes at Large*, IV, 515-516.
[47] Moore to Livingston, (62) March 7, 1833, Desp. Col., VI.

Such arguments seemingly had little effect. Moore felt that the officials realized how much the United States would benefit by the suggested arrangement and were "disposed to exact a corresponding price." Santander, he feared, had partaken of party bias while in the United States and preferred not to negotiate with the Jackson administration. Since a treaty, then, was impossible, Moore soon returned to the United States, leaving J. C. Pickett as chargé ad interim.[48]

On arrival at Bogotá, Chargé McAfee attempted to renew the negotiations, but Secretary Mosquera wanted to postpone these until matters were settled with Venezuela and Ecuador.[49] By December, 1833, McAfee thought that affairs had taken "a favorable turn" and proposed a new treaty.[50] However, his letters soon assumed the usual discouraged tone. He complained of the indifference or neglect of his own government and the unceasing activity of the British and French agents.[51] Before the end of the first year at his post, however, this despair had changed into a feeling of the necessity of retaliation. "Too much forbearance" had been shown, he felt, during the four years already spent in "remonstrating against the imposition of discriminating duties." The time had arrived for "not only asking what is right but promptly enforcing our rights. . . ." If the government would support him, he added, little more time would be wasted in "vain remonstrances."[52] But such support was not forthcoming.

Early in 1835 a project and counter-proposal passed with the usual procrastination following. Since New Granada already enjoyed the full benefit of the North American tariff of 1832 and did not expect a change in

---

[48] Moore to Livingston, (63) April 10, 1833, *ibid.*, VII.
[49] McAfee to McLane, July 17, 1833, *ibid.*, VIII.
[50] *Idem* to *idem*, (private) Dec. 2, 1833, *ibid.*
[51] *Idem* to *idem*, Jan. 24, April 4, 1834, *ibid.*
[52] *Idem* to *idem*, June 18, 1834, *ibid.*

it until 1842, there was no special reason for favoring a new treaty. And McAfee soon concluded that none was to be expected until the expiration of the existing one— May, 1837.[53] A measure to abolish the discriminating duties was defeated in the Granadian lower house in 1836. By September of that year McAfee's patience was again exhausted. If the United States did not wish to continue negotiating for another seven years, he felt that it must ''resort to prompt and effectual retaliation by the imposition of countervailing duties.''[54]

Soon, however, public opinion had reacted favorably towards the United States, principally because of the exorbitant British demands in regard to the imprisonment of Vice-Consul Russell at Panama.[55] McAfee noted a fear that Great Britain would seize the Isthmus and a Granadian tendency to look to Washington for protection, since North Americans were most interested in the opening of a communication between the two oceans.[56]

In March, 1837, Secretary Pombo referred the matter to Congress.[57] The defeat of the resultant bill by the vote of thirty to twenty-nine set the question ''at rest, at least for several years,'' thought McAfee, since the United States could ''not consistently with self-respect ask it again.'' Retaliation, he concluded, was the only remedy and might prove very effective, since the Liberals (anti-administration) were rather favorable towards the United States.[58]

Instead of resorting to retaliation Secretary Forsyth merely instructed the next chargé, James Semple, to

[53] McAfee to Forsyth, (24) Feb. 23, Pombo to McAfee, Jan. 9, McAfee to Forsyth, (28) Sept. 25, Pombo to McAfee, Sept. 19, 1835, *ibid.;* Uribe, *Anales,* III, 86.

[54] McAfee to Forsyth, (32) April 2, (33) June 3, (35) Sept. 2, 1836, Desp. Col., VIII.

[55] See McAfee to Forsyth, (38) Dec. 9, 1836, *ibid.*

[56] McAfee to Forsyth, (38) Dec. 9, 1836, *ibid.*

[57] Uribe, *Anales,* III, 111.

[58] McAfee to Forsyth, (43) June 12, 1837, Desp. Col., VIII.

negotiate a treaty, in case New Granada should change its attitude.[59]

On Semple's arrival at Bogotá, the matter of a treaty was mentioned in a conference with Pombo, but no proposal was made by either.[60] With the new foreign secretary, Pedro Herrán, Semple assumed an air of indifference, pointing out that a recent favorable convention with Venezuela made one with New Granada less important.   Herrán first asked for a copy of the Venezuelan treaty; then he appointed Domingo Acosta to negotiate with Semple. A few conferences, however, plainly showed that an agreement was impossible.[61]

To Semple's complaint against the granting of equal privileges to Spain, Herrán rather resentfully replied that New Granada had a right to legislate for its own interest without foreign interference.[62] Naturally, the negotiations made no headway and were finally dropped in October, 1840.[63]

The *customary full powers* of negotiations were given to Blackford.[64] In February, 1843, President Herrán empowered Lino de Pombo to treat with the North American representative.[65] The matter of discriminating duties again halted the negotiations, this time on account of the known congressional delusion of a great future merchant marine. The probability of an immediate British naval demonstration, Blackford considered, "particularly fortunate."[66] Favorable legislation was soon introduced into the Colombian congress. The Senate, however, by a "decided vote" adhered to the old policy; therefore negotiations again temporarily ceased.[67]

[59] Forsyth to Semple, (3) Jan. 9, 1838, Inst. Col., XV, 42 ff.
[60] Semple to Forsyth, (9) Sept. 12, 1838, Desp. Col., IX.
[61] *Idem* to *idem*, (13) Feb. 20, (16) March 20, 1839, *ibid.*
[62] *Idem* to *idem*, (18) May 16, 1839, *ibid.*
[63] Semple to Secretary of State, (34) May 20, 1841, *ibid.*
[64] Webster to Blackford, (2) May 20, 1842, Inst. Col., XV, 77 ff.
[65] Memoria de 1843—Ospina, Uribe, *Anales*, III, 141.
[66] Blackford to Webster, (9) March 18, 1843, Desp. Col., X.
[67] Blackford to Webster, (10) April 21, (11) June 3, 1843, *ibid.*

Secretary Upshur thought this reluctance was due to "the counsels, the insinuations, or suggestions of other governments" and saw no reason for making any treaty unless these duties were removed.[68] Early in 1844 Blackford felt that certain trade advantages might be secured and urged the Department to send fuller instructions. Acosta assured him that the next Congress would remove the discrimination. Nevertheless a bill to that effect, after passing the Lower House, was defeated in the Senate by the vote of fourteen to thirteen, and Pombo resigned his commission to negotiate.[69]

In the meanwhile, negotiations for a postal convention had been more successful. It was signed on March 6, 1844, and ratifications were exchanged at Bogotá on December 20.[70]

On the latter date Blackford also secured a treaty of peace, friendship, commerce, and navigation. But since this did not abolish the discriminating duties, it was quite natural that the United States would not be enthusiastic about its ratification. President Tyler submitted it to the Senate on February 21, but no action had been taken on it two years later when Polk presented the new treaty of December 12, 1846,[71] which *for a consideration* did remove all discriminations.[72]

THE YANKEE DEFECTIVE CONSULAR SYSTEM

In the meanwhile, commerce between the two nations had not enjoyed a healthy growth. The principal deterring factors were the discriminating duties, the numerous internal disturbances of New Granada, and the defective American consular system.

[68] Upshur to Blackford, (17) Nov. 9, 1843, Inst. Col., XV, 85 ff.

[69] Blackford to Upshur, Nos. 20, 21, 22, 23, 24, 26, (1844), Desp. Col., X.

[70] For text, see Uribe, *Anales*, VI, 123 ff.

[71] Richardson, *Messages and Papers*, V, 2217; *Sen. Ex. Jour.*, VI, 399, 453; VII, 40, 103, 167, 168, 180.

[72] See *infra*, chap. xii.

Minister Moore complained of the small income of Yankee consuls as compared with the British. Not one of the former was receiving more than $400 per year, while the highest paid of the latter drew $30,000.[73] Mc-Afee noted the general lack of respect accorded the American consular agents. H. E. Fudger had been murdered at Bogotá (1826), J. G. A. Williamson imprisoned at La Guayra (1829), and J. M. McPherson imprisoned at Cartagena (1829). Yet the United States tamely submitted to such treatment, while the British and French agents had demanded and received respect.[74]

With one exception (McPherson at Cartagena) every consular agent of the United States in 1837 was either an English or a French subject. This was particularly unfortunate at this time in the light of Granadian prejudice against these nationalities arising from the Russell and Barrot affairs. Semple, the following year, insisted that all ''consuls be citizens of the United States, if possible; and if not, then appoint citizens of this country, but never Europeans.'' Experience with New Granadian appointees, however, was not always fortunate.[76] It is evident that the smallness of the compensation made it practically impossible to secure competent consular representation. Naturally, trade suffered accordingly.

THE VOLUME OF TRADE

Unfortunately, the available statistics for this commerce are principally for years when New Granada was suffering from internal disorder and therefore do not present a fair estimate.[77] The $3,858,446 trade between La Gran Colombia and the United States in 1825 was

[73] Moore to Livingston, (38) Jan. 19, (47) May 21, 1832, Desp. Col., VII.
[74] McAfee to McLane, Nov. 15, 1833, *ibid.*, VIII.
[76] McAfee to Forsyth, (41) Feb. 10, 1837, *ibid.*
[76] Semple to Forsyth, (9) Sept. 12, 1838, *ibid.*, IX; Acosta to Forsyth, April 9, 1838, Notes from Col. Leg., II.
[77] Based on Robertson, *Hispanic-American Relations*, pp. 197, 204, 419, 420.

reduced to $1,201,999 in 1830. After the dissolution of La Gran Colombia, the trade of New Granada increased to $2,364,811 in 1835, only to drop to $223,761 in 1840. The figures for 1845 decreased still more to $203,510, while those for the United States and Venezuela reached $1,812,920—largely the result of better trade relations with the latter. With the removal of the discriminating duties (Treaty of 1846), the volume again passed the million mark ($1,145,173) by 1850 and enjoyed a decided growth thereafter.

CHAPTER XI

THE GROWTH OF THE CANAL IDEA
(1500-1842)

THE search for a shorter route to the Orient led Columbus to encounter quite accidentally the lands of another hemisphere. In his wake Rodrigo de Bastidas and Juan de la Cosa set out from Cádiz in October, 1499, and seem to have been the first Europeans to touch the Isthmus of Panama. During the winter of 1502-1503 Columbus himself skirted the coast from the Bay of Porto Bello to the Gulf of Urabá (Darién).[1]

"THE SECRET OF THE STRAIT"

The discovery of the Pacific, indicating that still another ocean must be traversed before the Orient could be reached, was followed by numerous efforts to find a suspected passageway between the two oceans. Before the middle of the sixteenth century the Spaniards had explored most of the coastline of the two Americas and were familiar with every river valley as far north as the St. Lawrence on the east and (almost to) the Columbia on the west.

INITIAL SPANISH INTEREST

As early as 1523 Charles V, doubtful of the existence of a strait, had adopted the idea of a canal.[2] Hernando de la Serna was ordered (1527) to explore the Chagres and Río Grande.[3] Two years later Alvaro de Saavedra Cerón, after a study of twelve years, prepared a plan for the construction of an artificial waterway, but death pre-

[1] W. F. Johnson, *Four Centuries of the Panama Canal*, pp. 14, 19.
[2] C. H. Haring, *Trade and Navigation between Spain and the Indies*, p. 192.
[3] Rudolf J. Taussig, "The American Inter-Oceanic Canal: An Historical Sketch of the Canal Idea," *The Pacific Ocean in History*, p. 118.

vented his submitting it to the King. In 1534 the governor of Costa Firma was directed to survey and report on the Chagres route.[4]

Antonio Galvoa, a Portuguese historian, published a book (1550) showing the possibility of canals by the Panama, Darién, Nicaragua, and Tehuantepec routes. These were pointed out also by López de Gomara in *Historia general de las Indias* (1552), and action was urged.[5] After an unfavorable report of the Antonelli survey of the Nicaragua route (1567), the Spanish king, Phillip II, changed his policy entirely. He feared that a canal might prove advantageous to the British, whose rising sea power already appeared a menace to Spanish dominance in the New World.[6]

Nothing came of the Velasco survey of the Atrato-Darién route of 1616, ordered by Phillip III. The idea of a canal does not seem to have been involved in the buccaneering operations of Henry Morgan (British) on the Isthmus (1671) or in the planting of the Scotch colony on Darién (1698) by William Patterson. However, the activities of the buccaneers and freebooters and the publication of Patterson's *Central America in 1701* kept European attention somewhat centered on the Isthmus.[7]

There are numerous accounts of the early existence of a short canal connecting the headwaters of the Atrato and the San Juan rivers. One is that four hundred filibusters in eighteen large canoes passed through it in 1680 from one ocean to the other.[8] Another says that this—the Raspadura Canal—was constructed in 1745 by a priest with Indian assistance and that the remains of

[4] Johnson, *op. cit.*, pp. 31-33; Haring, *op. cit.*, p. 192.

[5] *Ibid.*

[6] Johnson, *op. cit.*, p. 33; Haring, *op. cit.*, p. 193.

[7] Johnson, *op. cit.*, pp. 34-37; Haring, *op. cit.*, p. 194; Taussig, *op. cit.*, p. 124.

[8] Anthony de Gogorza, "Problem of Inter-Oceanic Communication by way of the American Isthmus," *Jour. Amer. Geog. Soc.* (1889), XXI, 526-529.

the canal were still visible in 1837-1838.[9] Still another story has it that a *padre* with the aid of his Indian converts cut the ditch in 1788 and during the rainy season actually made their way through it.[10] More recent surveys, however, indicate that all these accounts were ill-founded.

THE IDEA BECOMES INTERNATIONAL

The French Academy of Science discussed the possibility of canal construction in 1735 and again in 1785. During the latter year the report of M. de la Nauerre was considered by the Council of the Indies and referred to the Viceroy of New Granada. A plan was later discussed (1787) by D. Manuel Gijón y León (of Quito) before the *Sociedad de los amigos de Madrid*. That very year, however, Charles III ordered the postponement of all canal projects.[11]

Thomas Jefferson, then representing the United States in Paris, thought that a canal across the Isthmus would be "a work much less difficult than some even of the inferior canals of France," since a small opening would soon be widened by the tropical currents.[12] He proceeded to inquire for copies of plans and surveys already made by the Spaniards.[13] The instructions of the Revolutionary Junta (Paris, December 22, 1797) to Miranda included a proposal for a canal across Panama, with free transit to both Great Britain and the United States.[14]

The French Revolution and subsequent wars naturally diverted attention elsewhere. Nevertheless interest was somewhat revived by the publication of Baron von

[9] John M. Niles, *History of South America and Mexico*, II, 6.
[10] Bedford Pim, *The Gate of the Pacific* (1863), p. 183.
[11] Haring, *op. cit.*, pp. 195-197.
[12] Jefferson to M. Le Roy de L'Académie des Sciences, Nov. 13, 1786, Jefferson, *Writings* (Mem. ed.), V, 471.
[13] Jefferson to William Carmichael, Dec. 11, 1787, May 27, 1788, *ibid.*, VI, 382-383; VII, 27.
[14] Moses, *Spain's Declining Power*, p. 327.

Humboldt's works in which some nine routes were discussed.[15] In 1814 the Spanish *cortes* passed a measure favoring a canal and authorizing the formation of a company to execute the work, but the colonial revolt made definite action impossible.[16]

LA GRAN COLOMBIA CONSIDERS A CANAL

Even before Colombian recognition, Antonio Zea is reported to have secured the guarantee of 60,000,000 *pesos duros* for the opening of a canal.[17] In 1821 an application for a concession, perhaps from a North American, was opposed by Bolívar because of the possible use of the canal by the Spaniards in reconquering Colombia.[18] Nevertheless interest grew apace with the probability of the maintenance of independence.[19]

Many felt that the construction of a canal would be a "matter of no great difficulty," since at least "nine easy communications" were known to exist.[20] William Duane, backed by Yankee capitalists, made a proposal for a concession in 1822-1823.[21] His stepson, Richard Bache, thought (1822) that a canal by the Atrato route would "ere long" be opened.[22] Captain Charles S. Cochrane (1823) found the canal "perfectly practicable" and formed a company in Bogotá to lay a proposal before the next Congress.[23] In 1825 Wellwood Hislop of Jamaica requested an exclusive privilege to construct either a canal or a railroad.[24]

By this time the activities of the Central Americans

[15] Alexandre de Humboldt, *Essai politique sur le Royaume de la Nouvelle-Espagne*, I, 11-28.

[16] Haring, *op. cit.*, p. 197.   [17] Rivas, *Relaciones*, p. 50.

[18] Niles, *op. cit.*, II, 6.

[19] See *Niles' Reg.*, XVI, 416; XXIII, 49; XXV, 43; XXVII, 219; XXVIII, 198.

[20] Walker, *Colombia* (1822), I, xv.

[21] Duane, *A Visit to Colombia*, preface.

[22] Bache, *Notes on Colombia*, p. 64.

[23] Cochrane, *Journal of a Residence*, II, 140, 432; Watts to Adams, Sept. 4, 1824, Desp. Col., III.

[24] *Niles' Reg.* (May 28, 1825), XXVIII, 198.

regarding the Nicaragua route and the interest manifested in that area by both North American and British capitalists aroused the leaders of the new republic.[25] Although insisting that national interest required "that a Colombian corporation take over the enterprise instead of a foreign company," Vice-President Santander reminded Congress of the danger of being outstripped by the possessors of other routes. A project for the construction of either a canal or railroad at the calculated cost of 10,000,000 pesos was seriously considered. It contemplated the securing of foreign capital and American engineers.[26] The Colombian minister to London protested (1826) against the building of a canal through Central America (Nicaragua route) on account of the Colombian claim to the Mosquito Coast.[27] In November, 1827, Bolívar commissioned John A. Lloyd (British) and a Swede named Falcmar to survey the Isthmus. The report was favorable,[28] but the early dissolution of La Gran Colombia and Bolívar's death prevented definite action.

THE YANKEES MANIFEST AN INTEREST

Scarcely had Colombian independence been recognized before North American capitalists and statesmen became interested in an interoceanic canal. Three years after Duane's proposal,[29] William Wheelright of Massachusetts made at least a casual inspection of the Isthmus.[30] As early as August, 1826, William Radcliff and associates of New York were making inquiries in regard to the construction of either a canal or railroad across

[25] In 1825 a concession was granted to the "United States Atlantic and Pacific Canal Company" for a communication by the Nicaragua route. *Sen. Misc. Doc.*, No. 80 (30.1).

[26] Henao y Arrubla, *op. cit.*, p. 517.

[27] Rivas, *Relaciones*, p. 50.

[28] John A. Lloyd, *An Account of Levellings across the Isthmus of Panama* (London, 1830).

[29] See *supra*, p. 181.

[30] William Wheelright, *Observations on the Isthmus of Panama*, p. 4.

Panama. Permission to make a survey and a promise of the necessary concession were secured.[31] It must be remembered also that a group of Yankee capitalists were interested in the Nicaragua route at the same time.

Secretary Clay expressed "deep interest" in any canal undertaking. He instructed the United States representatives to the Panama Congress that an interoceanic canal would "form a proper subject for consideration."[32] In 1827 the House committee on naval affairs recommended the establishment of a steamer line to the Isthmus.[33] As a prophecy of the North American course when interest was thoroughly aroused, Goethe's words of February 21, 1827, hold interest: "I would be surprised if the United States would miss the opportunity of getting such a work into its own hands. . . . It is absolutely necessary for the United States to build the interoceanic canal and I am sure it will do so."[34]

Although far from advocating a canal as a governmental project, North American representatives at Bogotá were ever suspicious of British designs on the Isthmus. Todd (1823) reminded his chief of the danger of British aggression both at Panama and on the Mosquito Coast.[35] Moore felt greatly relieved when the rebellion of 1830 on the Isthmus was crushed, since it had been rumored that Panama had offered to surrender its sovereignty to Great Britain for protection against the Bogotá government.[36]

The revival of general confidence and prosperity under Santander (1833-1837) marked the beginning of a more active interest in an Isthmian communication. Less

[31] Watts to Clay, (41) Feb. 10, 1828, Desp. Col. IV.

[32] *Moore's Digest*, III, 2.   [33] *H. Doc.*, No. 56 (19.2).

[34] Johann Peter Eckermann, *Gespräche mit Goethe in den letzten Jahren seines Lebens*, III, 83-84.

[35] Todd to Adams, (47) March 29, 1823, Desp. Col., II.

[36] Moore to Van Buren, (23) Oct. 21, 1830, to Livingston, (35) Oct. 14, 1831, *ibid.*, VI.

than a week after his inaugural (April 6, 1833) he recommended to Congress the urgent necessity of opening a road across the Isthmus.[37] A congressional decree of May 25, 1834, authorized him to enter into a contract for the construction of a highway, railroad, or canal.[38] McAfee, although questioning as to "how far an incorporated company ought to have control of so important a point or whether such a united company alone would be able to accomplish it," expressed to Secretary Pombo the belief that "the combined energies and means of all the Governments of the two Americas could be brought to bear upon it, should New Granada deem it advisable to call upon them in convention for that purpose"[39]— almost a proposal for a Pan American treaty.

Santander's subsequent decree (May 27) was published throughout New Granada and also in the United States.[40] The Central American congress was likewise urging the North Americans to construct a canal.[41] William Radcliff had returned to Washington and was lobbying in favor of canal negotiations with both New Granada and Central America. He argued that both the Panama and Nicaragua routes were practicable; the cost would not exceed $20,000,000; the profit on the invested capital would be at least ten per cent; and the canal should be constructed by individuals under the patronage of their respective governments. He felt that it was the duty of the United States to initiate the enterprise and sug-

[37] See El Vijía del Istmo (Panamá), July 13, 1834; Gaceta de la Nueva Granada, June 14, 1835; Comercio libre (Panamá), Dec. 29, 1833; Los amigos del país (Panamá), Aug. 1, Dec. 15, 1835.

[38] For text, see El Vijía del Istmo, July 13, 1834; Codificación nacional, V, 313-314.

[39] McAfee to Pombo, May 31, 1834, enclosed with McAfee to McLane, June 18, 1834, Desp. Col., VIII.

[40] Rivas, Relaciones, p. 51.

[41] Arias says that an offer of prior rights to the United States by the Congress of Central America was behind the Senate resolution of 1835 (Harmodio Arias, The Panama Canal: A Study in International Law and Diplomacy, pp. 12-13).

gested that it treat with the European nations regarding an ample guarantee of the work.[42]

On March 3, 1835, the Senate passed a resolution, introduced by Senator Clayton, requesting the President "to consider the expediency of opening negotiations with the governments of other nations and particularly with the governments of Central America and New Granada" for the protection of "such individuals or companies as might undertake" a canal and for the purpose of securing forever the "free and equal right" of its use by all nations on the payment of "reasonable tolls."[43] To carry this into effect, President Jackson chose Charles A. Biddle.

Before the arrival of Biddle, the New Granadian congress passed a decree (May 25, 1835) opening the cantons of Porto Bello and Panama to the trade of all nations, free of all import and export duties on goods crossing the Isthmus, and suppressing the custom houses at Porto Bello, Chagres, and Panama. The decree was to be effective for a period of twenty years from the date of the opening of an interoceanic communication across these two cantons.[44] A few days later a canal concession was granted to Baron de Thierry on a very liberal basis.[45]

THE BIDDLE MISSION

Secretary Forsyth's instructions directed Biddle to proceed first to Nicaragua; after an investigation, to Guatemala; thence to Panama; and finally, to Bogotá.[46]

[42] These arguments and suggestions were shown in manuscript to Senator John M. Clayton, who suggested that they be published. William Radcliff, *Considerations of a Communication between the Atlantic and Pacific Oceans* (Georgetown, 1836). Radcliff takes much credit to himself for the Resolution of 1835.

[43] *Moore's Digest*, III, 2; *Sen. Jour.* (23.2), p. 238.

[44] For text of decree, see *Los amigos del país* (Panamá), Aug. 1, 1835; *H. Rep.*, No. 145 (30.2), p. 294; *Codificación nacional*, V, 463-465.

[45] Decree of May 29, 1835, Uribe, *Anales*, V, 611. For text of grant, see *Codificación nacional*, V, 481-483.

[46] Forsyth to Biddle, May 1, 1835, Inst., Specl. Missions, I, 126-128.

Instead of following the prescribed route, however, he proceeded directly to Panama and never visited Nicaragua.[47] Arriving at Panama on December 1, Biddle noted a general lack of confidence in the Thierry project. He started correspondence with *La sociedad de los amigos del país,* which soon published a pamphlet containing available documents regarding a canal.[48] Through the close coöperation of this society, a large amount of data was collected and a genuine enthusiasm aroused during Biddle's stay of about a month and a half.[49]

Biddle was thoroughly convinced that New Granada would soon be dismembered, owing to diverse interests and the tendency of the central government to restrict the provinces. The recent decree opening the ports of the Isthmus to free trade on the completion of an interoceanic communication would only cause dissatisfaction in the other provinces. It was "tolerably well understood," he added, "that overtures . . . [had] already been privately made by influential men to place the Isthmus under the protection of the British Government, and that such a course . . . [had] been declined by the English from an apprehension of giving offense to the United States." That the people of the Isthmus preferred attachment to almost any other government than Bogotá, he felt positive. Therefore, since the Thierry grant was already considered a dead letter, he saw no special reason for the United States to negotiate for a concession— merely to keep its eye focused on that area.[50]

Leaving Panama (January 19) in company with the members of Congress from that province,[51] Biddle ar-

[47] Biddle to Forsyth, Dec. 14, 1836, Specl. Agts. Ser.

[48] Biddle to Forsyth, undated, *ibid.; Documentos importantes, sobre la apertura de un canal fluvial entre océanos Atlántico y Pacífico por el istmo de Panamá.*

[49] Biddle to *La sociedad de los amigos del país,* Dec. 7, 1835, Specl. Agts. Ser.

[50] Biddle to Forsyth, Dec. 7, 1835, *ibid.*

[51] *Idem* to *idem,* Jan. 18, 1836, *ibid.*

rived at Bogotá (March 13), met Pombo (March 15) and Santander (March 16), and was soon negotiating for a concession.[52] McAfee had been instructed to render every aid possible to this "special agent appointed by the President to make observations and inquiries in respect to the projects" for communications across the Isthmus[53]—no mention of negotiations of any sort.

A decree of grant passed both Houses on May 18 and went to the President, who had already promised his support. In the meanwhile, however, a group of citizens of Bogotá had petitioned for a concession and offered better terms than Biddle. The latter was advised of the new proposal and invited to an interview. Santander returned the decree of May 18 to Congress and requested the passage of a law granting the concession to the party or parties offering the most favorable terms. This naturally forced Biddle to come to terms with the local company.[54]

Santander soon received the requested authorization and by an executive decree of June 22 gave the concession to Biddle, Aznero and Company.[55] The ill-feeling engendered during the long negotiations were forgotten in the midst of a banquet given in Biddle's honor by the New Granadian members of the company. Santander wrote a personal letter of congratulation to Biddle, and the latter soon departed for home, arriving in New York in September, 1836.[56]

The concession as granted provided for the construction of a trans-isthmian communication by means of a macadamized road, or a railway, and the steam naviga-

[52] McAfee to Forsyth, (31) March 21, 1836, Desp. Col., VIII.

[53] Forsyth to McAfee, (24) May 1, 1835, Inst. Col., XII, 12-13.

[54] Biddle to Forsyth, undated, Chief Clerk New Granadian Foreign Office to Biddle, May 19, 1836, Specl. Agt. Ser. See also *Gaceta de la Nueva Granada*, May 29, June 26, 1836.

[55] Uribe, *Anales*, V, 611; Specl. Agts. Ser., Biddle; Rivas, *Relaciones*, p. 61; *Codificación nacional*, VI, 168-173, 220-222.

[56] Banquet Committee to Biddle, Santander to Biddle, June 28, Biddle to Forsyth, Sept. 25, 1836, Specl. Agts. Ser.

tion of the Chagres—not a canal grant, although it did nullify the Thierry concession.[57] Two-thirds of the stock was to be held by Charles Biddle and his associates in the United States and one-third by the New Granadian group. The directorates were to be distributed on the same basis, and the office of the company was to be located in Philadelphia. The "preponderating influence," as Biddle expressed it, was in the hands of North American citizens. Then, since "an exclusive grant for the only practicable mode of communication between the two oceans . . . [was] now vested in citizens of the United States," he advised Forsyth that it appeared unnecessary "to enter into negotiations with foreign nations upon the subject."[58]

Both Forsyth and Jackson were infuriated by Biddle's use of a governmental mission to secure a private concession. The rumor of such action (July, 1836) caused a request for a full report. Since none came, either then or immediately on his return to the States, the request was repeated on September 26. Near the middle of November, Biddle made the desired report.[59] His early death (December 21)[60] probably saved him from the most violent of Jacksonian reprimands. In the meanwhile, McAfee had been instructed to "disclaim all connection with the project on the part of . . . [his] government."[61]

Jackson's message to the Senate of January 9, 1837, closed the affair and committed the United States government to temporary inactivity. Although admitting that Biddle's information was "not as full as could have been desired," Jackson felt that it was "sufficient to

[57] *Codificación nacional*, VI, 168-173, 220-222.
[58] Biddle to Forsyth, undated, Specl. Agts. Ser.
[59] Forsyth to Biddle, July 19, Sept. 26, 1836; Biddle to Forsyth, undated (recd. Nov. 15, 1836), *ibid.*
[60] Hopkinson to Forsyth, Dec. 21, 1836, *ibid.*
[61] Forsyth to McAfee, Sept. 23, 1836, Feb. 18, 1837, Inst. Col., XV, 37-39.

show that the probability of an early execution of the projects which . . . [had] been set on foot . . . [was] not so great as to render it expedient to open a negotiation at present with any foreign government upon the subject.''[62]

THE PROVERBIAL YANKEE PERSISTENCE

North American capitalists were not content to dismiss the subject so lightly. A year later certain citizens of New York and Philadelphia presented to the House a memorial recommending negotiations with Central America, New Granada, Great Britain, France, Holland, and Russia in regard to a canal and the choosing of competent engineers to make an immediate survey.[63] In reply to the House's request of February 17 for documents concerning a trans-isthmian canal, President Van Buren gave the desired information, but did not commit himself on the recommendations of the memorial. The result was merely a non-committal resolution (1839) expressing an interest in the project and recommending that the President negotiate with other nations to ascertain its practicability and to secure free and equal navigation rights therein for all nations.[64]

In 1839 John L. Stephens was dispatched to Central America to secure the information that Biddle had failed to get. He contended that a canal by the Nicaragua route was practicable and that its cost would not exceed $25,000,000, but suggested that conditions there were too unsettled to risk so much capital.[65] In the spring of the same year Radcliff was again corresponding with the United States representative at Bogotá. It was rumored there that he was organizing a company in New York and would soon send an agent to New Granada.[66]

[62] Richardson, *Messages and Papers*, IV, 1492.
[63] *H. Rep.*, No. 145 (30.2), II, 237-239.
[64] *Ibid.*, No. 322 (25.3); Johnson, *Four Centuries of the Panama Canal*, pp. 47-48.
[65] *Ibid.*; *Sen. Ex. Doc.*, No. 80 (30.1).
[66] Semple to Forsyth, (17) April 15, 1839, Desp. Col., IX.

Through Senator Clayton certain citizens of Delaware memorialized the Senate (March, 1840) to unite with other nations in the survey of Darién route and to co-operate in construction, if a canal should be found practicable.[67] The following year a meeting of Yankee merchants in Rio de Janeiro resolved that "as the whole credit of this enterprise ought to belong to the United States, they should undertake it without delay, before other nations interfere[d] to snatch from them the profit and credit of so great an enterprise."[68] Although nothing definite directly resulted from these efforts to secure official action, they did indicate an ever growing commercial interest in an interoceanic communication.

THE SECOND SECESSION OF THE ISTHMUS

Although Bolívar's influence had brought the Isthmus back under Colombian authority after its secession in 1830, the separation sentiment there was revived with each sign, either real or fancied, of national neglect or disregard of Isthmian welfare. Biddle thought (1836) that it would secede within two years.[69] In 1838 Radcliff pointed out that Panama had long desired to be independent of New Granada and under the protection of some strong power.[70] The disorder incident to the New Granadian civil war of 1839-1841 naturally gave impetus to the independence idea, especially since the Isthmus had become more cognizant of its international importance and a rumor was astir that the Bogotá government anticipated its transfer to Great Britain in payment of certain long-standing debts.[71] Therefore, in November, 1840, the provinces of Panama and Veragua, under the title of the "State of the Isthmus," declared themselves independent. President Van Buren was notified by the new state of its "reassuming for the time

[67] *Niles' Reg.*, LVIII, 58, 123.   [68] *Ibid.*, LX, 160.
[69] *Supra.*
[70] Radcliff to Charles Mercer, Oct. 5, 1838, *H. Rep.*, No. 145 (30.2).
[71] Semple to Forsyth, (28) Oct. 2, 1840, Desp. Col., IX.

. . . [its] sovereignty . . . until New Granada . . . [should] have been reorganized under a Federal Government.''⁷² The following June a constitution was adopted, and Tomás Herrera was elected president.⁷³

Six months later William Radcliff informed Secretary Webster that he (Radcliff) had been chosen by the new state to initiate "international relations" with the United States. He argued that the dissolution of La Gran Colombia in 1830 was a recognition of the right of secession and that the weakness, instability, maladministration, and neglect of the Bogotá government and the geographic position of the Isthmus were sufficient reasons for the exercise of that right. It was to the interest of the United States to recognize the State of the Isthmus, Radcliff urged, since it held the only feasible canal route and was both willing and anxious to negotiate a treaty for the accomplishment of the work, on the basis of an American guarantee of the perpetual neutrality of the territory. The despatch closed with the suggestion that trade with *"our own territory on the Pacific"* would be greatly benefitted by the taking of proper steps to secure a canal right of way across the Isthmus and the warning that other nations might secure advantages detrimental to the United States, if quick action were not taken.⁷⁴

After due conference with the President, Webster advised:

Although the President does not doubt that the facts mentioned in it [letter of December 31] are substantially correct, the shortness of time which has elapsed since the declaration of independence referred to was made, the duty of this government to avoid doing anything which might give just cause of offence to the Republic of New Granada, with which it has

⁷² Tomás Herrera to the President of the United States, Dec. 5, 1840, Notes from Col. Leg., II.

⁷³ Arosemena to Webster, July 3, 23, 1841, *ibid.;* Radcliff to Webster, Dec. 31, 1841, Specl. Agts. Ser., Ingraham.

⁷⁴ Radcliff to Webster, Dec. 18, 31, 1841, *ibid.* (Italics are mine.)

hitherto maintained pacific and friendly relations, and that wise yet generous Caution which have heretofore marked its steps in similar cases, all admonish that there is no occasion in this instance to deviate from the usual course by acknowledging the State of the Isthmus upon information less authentic and satisfactory than in other cases.[75]

However, immediate measures to ascertain the ability of the new state to maintain its independence and "assume the obligations and discharge the duties of an independent power" were promised.[76] J. H. Ingraham was chosen to proceed to the Isthmus to report on these factors, but before he set out the consul at Cartagena notified the Department that the two provinces had rejoined New Granada on December 31.[77]

Although this absorption of his adopted nation deprived him of any claim to diplomatic standing, Radcliff took advantage of his close contacts with the Administration to present "some ideas and views of . . . [his] own, as a citizen of the United States." He stressed the importance of a "free, safe, and convenient passage," its possible effect on Yankee trade, and the danger of the route remaining subject to the "will and pleasure or caprice or cupidity" of other nations. He argued that the canal should be built by a concert of nations for the use of all on the basis of free and equal navigation rights.[78] The time had arrived, he concluded, for the United States "to take the subject into serious consideration, and the lead in initiating the measures prelim-

[75] Webster to Radcliff, Jan. 28, 1842, Inst. Specl. Missions, I. This "caution" is quite in contrast with the "haste" of 1903.

[76] *Ibid.*

[77] Sánchez to Webster, (19) Jan. 20, 1842, Con. Let., Cartagena, IV; Webster to Ingraham, Feb. 11, 1842, Dom. Let., XXXII, 198; Specl. Agts., Index cards.

[78] Stewart, the British chargé at Bogotá, "frankly admitted" in the fall of 1842 that he had written his government suggesting the independence of the Isthmus and the placing of it under the protection of Great Britain, France, and the United States (Blackford to Webster, [3] Oct. 20, 1842, Desp. Col., X).

inary to the undertaking."[79] It is quite clear, however, that the North American commercialists were far in advance of their government in the formation of a definite canal policy.

[79] Radcliff to Webster, Feb. 19, 1842, Specl. Agts. Ser., Ingraham.

CHAPTER XII

THE ISTHMUS GUARANTEED; DISCRIMINATION ABOLISHED
(1842-1848)

SINCE the conditions of the concession of 1836 were never fulfilled by Biddle and his associates, it was declared void two years later and a new privilege granted to Augusto Salomón and Company—a Franco-Granadian concern.[1] And a vigorous reaffirmation of New Granada's claim to the Mosquito Coast, which commanded the Nicaragua route, soon followed. The Bogotá government seemed to have had "much at heart the making of a canal or railroad over the Isthmus of Panama."[2]

NEW GRANADA SEEKS A FOREIGN GUARANTEE

Those interested in the project had begun to press the government to secure a guarantee of the Isthmus by treaties with more powerful nations. In November, 1839, Manuel M. Mosquera, representative at London, was instructed to sound Great Britain on the matter. Also the signatures of France and the United States to treaties of guarantee were to be sought. A conference with Lord Palmerston, however, was sufficient to convince Mosquera that the time was not opportune. Since there was no precedent for such a guarantee, Palmerston feared the consequences. Besides, the moment of New Granada's protest against British activities on the Mosquito Coast was hardly the time to seek a favorable treaty arrangement.[3]

The civil war of 1839-1841 and the secession of the

[1] *Codificación nacional*, VIII, 187-190.
[2] *B. F. S. P.*, XI, 816; Semple to Forsyth, (13) Feb. 20, 1839, Desp. Col., IX.
[3] Rivas, *Relaciones*, pp. 105-109.

Isthmus naturally prevented further negotiations.[4] With the coming of peace and the re-incorporation of Panama, however, the Pedro A. Herrán administration ardently turned to the new course, which had been initiated in 1839. Congress (1842) declared *caducados* all privileges granted under the decrees of 1835 and 1836 and set forth the bases for new propositions.[5] The following year the Salomón concession was specifically voided, over the protest of the French chargé, and the President was authorized to negotiate a new contract.[6]

Manuel Mosquera, still in London, was instructed (September, 1843) to conclude a treaty with Great Britain, France, the United States, Holland, and Spain,[7] "with a view to realizing this great undertaking [canal]; the Governments charging themselves with the execution of the work, and guaranteeing the inter-oceanic line of communication, and the fulfillment of the conditions upon which its execution . . . [was] stipulated." Secretary Upshur was advised that an appropriate person would be appointed to begin negotiations with the United States, if it should see fit to coöperate.[8]

Mosquera's instructions stipulated that the treaty must reserve to New Granada "the jurisdiction over the line of communication . . . [and] a certain per cent of the produce of the tolls until the cost of the canal . . . [was] reimbursed; after which the whole of the tolls." If the work was to be accomplished by a private corporation, the treaty was to be limited "to those governments which . . . [would] guarantee the neutrality of the canal . . . as well as the sovereignty of New Granada

[4] *Supra*, chap. xi.
[5] Decree of June 1, 1842, *Codificación nacional*, IX, 390-391.
[6] Decrees of June 24, July 15, 1843, Uribe, *Anales*, V, 611; Rivas, *Relaciones*, p. 112.
[7] Antonio José Uribe, *La reforma administrativa*, p. 279; Rivas, *Relaciones*, p. 107. Holland and Spain were to be approached only in case the other three would not sign treaties.
[8] Ospina to Upshur, Sept. 30, 1843, enclosed with Blackford to Upshur, (16) Oct. 20, 1843, Desp. Col., X.

over the canal'' and its environs and the fulfillment of the conditions on which the grant was made to the corporation. Only Granadian troops could be used to protect the work, but these must be paid by the contractors. The work must start within two years after the signing of the treaty.[9]

EUROPEAN NEGOTIATIONS FAIL

By November, 1843, Mosquera was in Paris conferring with M. Guizot, who had already become interested in the canal project through his contacts with Salomón and had discussed it before the French chamber of deputies the previous June. Guizot favored construction by either a private corporation or by the governments of France, Great Britain, and New Granada—the United States not included. But since he had no confidence in the previous surveys, he would do nothing until a new one was made.[10] For that purpose M. Napoleón Garella was sent to the Isthmus.[11]

On his return to London, Mosquera talked with Lord Aberdeen, the French ambassador, and the United States minister. Aberdeen appeared to be favorably inclined toward the canal project, but pointed out that the British government could furnish no funds and, if a treaty were made, British capitalists must finance the scheme. Both M. de Saint Aulaire and Edward Everett insisted that they had no instructions on the subject. The latter, however, frankly admitted that he did not believe the United States would make such a treaty, not only because his government opposed the investing of capital in national property outside of its own territory, but also because the Democratic party denied that the government had the

[9] Abstract of the instructions, enclosed with Blackford to Upshur, (17) Nov. 3, 1843, *ibid.*

[10] Rivas, *Relaciones*, p. 109; Johnson, *Four Centuries of the Panama Canal*, p. 48.

[11] M. Napoleón Garella, *Projet d'un canal de junction . . . à travers l'Isthme de Panamá* (Paris, 1845).

right to undertake new works or even preserve old ones within its own boundaries.[12]

Aberdeen's hesitancy and the continued activity of his agents on the Mosquito Coast revived at Bogotá the fear of British aggression. The Herrán administration, originally pro-English, now despaired of securing either the treaty or a satisfactory explanation of the "disguised invasion." Mosquera protested more strongly against this British disregard of New Granada's claim to Mosquitia. Secretary Acosta desired to interest the United States in the matter, thinking that the Monroe Doctrine might thereby be made applicable.[13]

Meanwhile, Aberdeen and Guizot postponed committing themselves on the proposed canal treaty. Both were probably awaiting the report on the Garella survey, and the former was also attempting to exact a postal convention on a reciprocal franking basis as a prerequisite to a definite answer in regard to the canal negotiations.[14] Naturally, Mosquera contended that there was no connection between the two matters and refused to negotiate on that basis.[15]

By this time the indecision of the European governments and capitalists had been increased by the fast developing rivalry between the various canal routes. During 1842-1843 there were made at least four surveys —Wheelright (Yankee), Hellert or Ellet (French), Lloyd (English), and Garella (French)—of the Panama route.[16] Signor Graetano Moro (1842-1843) made a survey also by way of Tehuantepec. And it was soon reported that the Mexican capitalist, Don José de Garay, was to undertake the construction of a canal.[17] In 1844 Francisco Castellón

[12] Rivas, *Relaciones*, pp. 110-111. A search of the official instructions sent the American representative at London from April 16, 1840, to July 21, 1849, fails to reveal any specific instructions regarding such a treaty.
[13] *Ibid.*, pp. 115-119.   [14] *Ibid.*, p. 121.   [15] *Ibid.*, p. 122.
[16] Charles T. Bidwell, *The Isthmus of Panama*, p. 96; Wheelright, *Observations on the Isthmus of Panama; Niles' Reg.*, LXIV, 208.
[17] *H. Rep.*, No. 145 (30.2), II, 78 ff.; Rivas, *Relaciones*, p. 122.

of Nicaragua appeared in Paris, attempting to induce Louis Philippe to establish a protectorate over his country and build a canal by the Lake Nicaragua route. The French monarch manifested little interest, but contact was made with Louis Napoleon, who (then imprisoned at Ham) began working towards the organization of a company to construct *Le Canal Napoleón de Nicaragua.*[18] Although Mosquera found out that Garella favored the Panama route, he realized that France would not make any treaty until all the routes were thoroughly surveyed.[19]

The French and United States representatives in London continued to say that they possessed no instructions for the negotiation of the desired treaty. And Lord Aberdeen (July 14, 1844) destroyed the remainder of Mosquera's hopes by advising that the board of trade considered the treaty of too unusual a nature for England to sign, and since the practicability of the canal had not yet been shown, he could not discuss the matter further. A still more emphatic refusal to negotiate was given on February 6, 1845. Great Britain would take no part in the project and would guarantee neither the neutrality and sovereignty of the Isthmus nor the fulfillment of the conditions of any concession. Aberdeen added that the ruler of Egypt had not attempted to secure such a guarantee for the Suez route, and he did not think one necessary for the Panama.[20] Since it was evident that Great Britain would not negotiate, Mosquera was ordered to protest more vigorously against English aggressions in Mosquitia.[21]

The Tomás C. de Mosquera administration (1845-1849) gave new instructions to Manuel Mosquera for the forwarding of the negotiations with France. The President in a confidential note to Secretary Gómez advised a

[18] Johnson, *Four Centuries of the Panama Canal*, pp. 49-50.
[19] Rivas, *Relaciones*, p. 122.   [20] *Ibid.*, pp. 123-125.
[21] *Ibid.*, p. 127.

radical procedure in dealing with Great Britain. If it did not answer the remonstrances of the New Granadian agent, he was to present his letter of recall, protest *con el tono emfático* against British conduct, and publish all the pertinent documents. Although New Granada weakened on such an extreme policy, Pedro Fernández Madrid of the Bogotá foreign office, with his pamphlet *Nuestras costas incultas,* aroused public opinion to a high pitch against the British. Their activities in Mosquitia were pictured as an invasion of New Granadian territory, and all true patriots were called upon to unite in defending the national rights.[22]

Meanwhile, Salomón and Company were insisting that their concession was still in force, and were attempting to secure capital in Paris and London. Since neither France nor England would negotiate a treaty of guarantee, Mosquera feared that such a concession with the resultant planting of nationally supported French and British colonies on the Isthmus would be dangerous. Therefore, he refused to negotiate with the company. About the same time (1845) Captain W. B. Liot of the Royal Mail Company surveyed the Panama route, and on the strength of his report an English company was organized. However, with the British refusal to guarantee the neutrality of the route the company failed. The project seems to have been actually discouraged by the Foreign Office.[23]

The Franco-Granadian company then became more active. In December, 1845, it was decided to send M.

[22] *Ibid.,* pp. 128-139.

[23] *Ibid.,* pp. 141-144; W. B. Liot, *Panama, Nicaragua and Tehuantepec* (London, 1849); M. G. Mulhall, *The English in South America,* p. 625; W. H. Koebel, *British Exploits in South America,* p. 515. It is claimed that Colonel Edward MacGeachy also made a survey of the Isthmus in 1845 looking towards the construction of either a canal or a railroad. In 1844 he was sufficiently assured of the British semi-official sanction to use his own funds for the survey, expecting to be reimbursed. He was to be disappointed, however, by the total withdrawal of his government's support. The plans were then turned over to Louis Napoleon and later to De Lesseps (Charles Edward A. MacGeachy, *Who Started the Panama Canal and Its Railroad?* New York, 1915).

Mateo Klein to Bogotá to secure a definite contract. The congressional laws of May 7, 1845, and June 9, 1846, gave the President sufficient powers to negotiate. Juan de Francisco Martín was appointed to treat with Klein, but no agreement was reached. Klein returned to Paris during the summer of 1846. After being advised (September, 1846) that the company was ready to negotiate on the New Granadian basis, Mosquera was authorized (November) to deal with the matter in Paris and at the same time to urge on Guizot the necessity for the treaty of guarantee.[24]

The negative character of the British policy and the indecision of the French caused President Mosquera to turn towards the United States. New Granada wished a canal, yet it was felt necessary to neutralize the possible French power on the Isthmus and to obstruct British territorial ambitions on the Mosquito Coast. A treaty with the United States was calculated to accomplish these two ends, since that power above all others was interested in preventing the European nations from securing footholds in Central America.[25]

In the midst of the violent anti-British agitation and a growing doubt as to French aims, the new Yankee chargé, Benjamin A. Bidlack, arrived at Bogotá on December 1, 1845.

WASHINGTON ASSUMES A DEFENSIVE ATTITUDE

North American interest in a canal had grown apace with the European activity. Secretary Webster (1842) urged a favorable treaty of commerce with New Granada, since he felt that such might "serve to prevent a grant . . . to any other foreign government, company, or individuals of a special privilege in regard to the communication." He added that it was of great importance to the United States that a railroad or canal be constructed and that all nations should be on the same basis in its

[24] Rivas, *Relaciones*, pp. 144-145.   [25] *Ibid.*, p. 146.

use.[26] Various rumors in regard to surveys and canal projects were afloat in the press.[27] The House of Representatives (December 15, 1843) requested of the President all papers "relative to the formation of a juncture between the Atlantic and Pacific Oceans."[28]

Secretary Buchanan instructed Bidlack as follows:

The United States have strong motives for viewing with interest any project which may be designed to facilitate the intercourse between the Atlantic and Pacific Oceans . . . as it is important to us that no other nation should obtain either an exclusive privilege or advantage in regard to such a communication. . . . You will lose no time in transmitting any information upon the subject. . . . You will also use your influence, should this become necessary, with the Government of New Granada, to prevent it from granting privileges to any other nation which might prove injurious to the United States.[29]

Bidlack soon reported from Bogotá the activities of a British company as well as a rumor that the United States had offered to loan New Granada 1,500,000 pesos to build a road across the Isthmus on the condition "that it be a national business." A favorable attitude towards the United States was everywhere apparent, likewise a fear of British and French ambitions.[30] During the first half of 1846 Bidlack and Secretary Mallarino held frequent conferences in regard to the canal projects then before the government. The former seems to have been kept fully advised in each case.[31]

Meanwhile, the American minister to Prussia, Henry Wheaton, had forwarded (December, 1845) to the Department a lengthy canal treatise advocating that the United States government take the initiative in making

[26] Webster to Blackford, (2) May 20, 1842, Inst. Col., XV, 79.
[27] *Niles' Reg.*, LXIV, 176, 208, 302, 303.
[28] Richardson, *Messages and Papers*, V, 2128.
[29] Buchanan to Bidlack, (2) June 23, 1845, Inst. Col., XV, 99-100.
[30] Bidlack to Buchanan, July 27, (1) Dec. 4, (2) 28, 1845, Desp. Col., XI.
[31] *Idem* to *idem*, (16) May 13, 1846, Pardo to Bidlack, July 16, 1846, *ibid.*

surveys of both the Panama and Nicaragua routes. In the execution of the work he recommended the coöperation of all the great powers.[32] In compliance with the Senate resolution (February 24, 1846) requesting all available documents "on the subject of a ship canal across the Isthmus of Panama," Wheaton's exposition and sundry correspondence were submitted. But Polk in no way committed the administration.[33] On April 20 James Semple, former chargé to New Granada, in a report for the Senate committee on post offices and post roads, stressed the Pacific trade and pointed out the enormous commercial advantages of a canal.[34]

Justo Arosemena of Panama, by this time, had become convinced that there was no probability of the great powers constructing a canal. Great Britain preferred a railroad, France was interested only from a scientific standpoint, and the United States would not undertake such a work outside of its own territory. Besides, he felt that sufficient scientific data had not been secured and that ample capital would not be subscribed to any individual company. Therefore he suggested that New Granada itself should construct a macadamized road across the Isthmus.[35]

THE TREATY OF 1846

President Mosquera, however, seemed more interested in the securing of a guarantee of the canal or railroad route. Since nothing of this nature was to be expected from Great Britain or France, he began to sound Bidlack on the question of a North American treaty. For some twenty years agents of the United States had been attempting to secure favorable commercial arrangements, but New Granada had consistently refused

[32] Wheaton to Buchanan, (278) Dec. 17, 1845, Desp. Prussia, III.
[33] Buchanan, *Works*, VI, 474-475; *Sen. Doc.*, No. 339 (29.1).
[34] *Ibid.*, No. 306 (29.1), p. 1-47.
[35] Justo Arosemena, *Examen sobre la franca comunicación entre los dos océanos* (Bogotá, 1846).

to abolish certain discriminating duties, contending that these were necessary in order to build up a large national merchant marine. Public opinion now, however, favored the removal of the discrimination. Mosquera, therefore, was able to interest Bidlack in the negotiating of a treaty.[36]

After numerous "free conferences" between the two, Bidlack (October 2, 1846) requested the authority to negotiate. On November 20 he urged the Department to rush his instructions, since New Granada had agreed to abolish the discriminating duties. A week later he was "anxiously awaiting authority and instructions" and fearing that the Bogotá government might change its views. He considered it "important that a treaty should *immediately* be made . . . securing to the Government of the United States the right of way across the Isthmus of Panama" and thought that he had prepared the way for such a treaty.[37]

The early part of December found Bidlack "every day in conference with the Secretary of Foreign Relations and sometimes with the President himself endeavoring to arrange" the text of the convention. His suggestion of a separate Isthmian treaty was opposed by Mallarino on the basis that if the removal of the discriminating duties was not shown as a condition of the guarantee of the Isthmus, the same commercial arrangement might be claimed by Great Britain under the most-favored-nation clause of its treaty. Since he possessed no instructions—Mallarino and Mosquera were cognizant of this fact—Bidlack felt "a deep responsibility in acting"; yet he feared that "by refusing to act, the opportunity of securing important rights on the Isthmus and the removal of differential duties . . . [might] be lost." The daily conferences, therefore, continued but always

[36] Rivas, *Relaciones*, pp. 146-148.
[37] Bidlack to Buchanan, (26) Oct. 2, (27) Nov. 20, (28) 27, 1846, Desp. Col., XI.

in such manner and place as not to arouse British suspicion.[38]

An additional factor entered the negotiations at this point. It was reported that General Juan José Flores, with English and Spanish assistance, was about to invade Ecuador and Peru. Bidlack was asked whether the United States "would adhere to the declared policy [Monroe Doctrine] of not silently permitting the interference of European Governments to change the Governments of the South American Republics against the wishes of the people of those Republics?" To this, he replied that his government "would no doubt act in good faith in the redemption of any pledges which she had made to any of the governments of the world and that she would not change her policy 'for any light or trifling causes'." (Note, however, he did not commit himself on the applicability of the Monroe Doctrine.) To the Department, he wrote that "the eyes of the Government and the people of New Granada seem[ed] to be turned toward the United States for protection in this threatened emergency."[39]

The activities of Flores gave Mallarino an opportunity to play up to Bidlack the danger of British aggression. He pointed out their conduct in the Argentine Republic in regard to extraterritoriality, their activity on the Orinoco in Venezuela, and their encroachments on the Mosquito Coast in Central America. All these cases, he contended, unveiled "a preconceived and long meditated intention of grasping the most mercantile spots of America, putting the competition of the United States out of the question, and dictating her will as a law in all matters concerning the consumption of foreign commodities." If the Isthmus should be added to these encroachments, it would be in the "hands of the only nation that

[38] *Idem* to *idem*, (29) Dec. 9, 1846, *ibid.*
[39] *Idem* to *idem*, (30) Dec. 10, (31) 11, 1846, *ibid.*

the United States . . . [could] consider as a badly disposed rival."[40]

Moreover, the protecting mediation of the United States, claimed Mallarino, was necessary for the safety of all the American republics. However, it should have "an entirely peaceful and conventional origin" and not be introduced in such a manner as to awaken international jealousies. The incidental introduction of the Isthmian guarantee into a commercial treaty would accomplish just that. Furthermore, the glory and affection of South America to be gained by such a move would assist the North American mercantile interests, and the Yankee privileged position would not be lost by another nation's acquisition of too strong a foothold in the Americas.[41]

With such arguments as these, it was not difficult to overcome Bidlack's rather weakly advanced objection to the guarantee clause as being too near an alliance. The treaty was signed on December 12 and forwarded to the Department two days later. It conceded to the United States the abolition of all discriminating duties (Articles IV, V, VI); secured the largest possible liberty "with regard to the right of transit and free passage over the Isthmus (which appeared to me [Bidlack] to be becoming more and more important every day)"; and extended the guarantee (Article XXXV) only to the Isthmus, thereby avoiding "anything like a general alliance." Bidlack, therefore, did not expect very bitter opposition in the United States senate. He urged early action on their part, since he knew the incumbent New Granadian congress was favorable, but could make "no calculations" on the next one.[42]

[40] Memo., Dec. 10, 1846, enclosed with Bidlack to Buchanan, (32) Dec. 14, 1846, *ibid.*
[41] *Ibid.*
[42] Bidlack to Buchanan, (32) Dec. 14, 1846, *ibid.;* W. M. Malloy, *Treaties, Convention* . . . , I, 302-314. With the exception of one document of Dec. 1, the New Granadian archives contain none of the prelimi-

Since he feared that the British legation would create some opposition to the treaty at Bogotá, Bidlack set about bringing the New Granadian legislators around to "the same conclusion . . . to which . . . [he had been] so fortunate to bring the Granadian Executive and his Cabinet."[43] The treaty was reported favorably in May by Lino de Pombo and Juan M. Gómez and, after several days' debate, was ratified by both Houses.[44]

However, it was not to fare so well in the United States senate. The opposition there developed principally around Article XXXV, which read in part as follows:

The United States of America and the Republic of New Granada, desiring to make as durable as possible the relations which are to be established between the two parties by virtue of this treaty, have declared solemnly, and do agree to the following points: . . . For the better understanding of the preceding articles, it is and has been stipulated between the high contracting parties, that the citizens, vessels and merchandise of the United States shall enjoy in the ports of New Granada, including those of the part of the Granadian territory generally denominated Isthmus of Panama, from its southernmost extremity until the boundary of Costa Rica, all the exemptions, privileges and immunities concerning commerce and navigation, which are now or may hereafter be enjoyed by Granadian citizens, their vessels and merchandise; and that this equality of favors shall be made to extend to the passengers, correspondence and merchandise of the United States, in their transit across the said territory, from one sea to the other. *The Government of New Granada guarantees to the Government of the United States that the right of way or transit across the Isthmus of Panama* upon any modes of communication that now exist, or that may be hereafter constructed, *shall be open and free to the government and citizens of the United States,* and for

_____

naries to the treaty. It was arranged by private conferences (Rivas, *Relaciones*, p. 153).

[43] Bidlack to Buchanan, (41) Jan. 20, 1847, Desp. Col., XI.

[44] Bidlack to Buchanan, Nos. 47-49, *ibid.;* Rivas, *Relaciones*, pp. 160-161.

the transportation of any articles of produce, manufactures or merchandise, of lawful commerce, belonging to the citizens of the United States; that no other tolls or charges shall be levied or collected upon the citizens of the United States, or their said merchandise thus passing *over any road, or canal that may be made by the government of New Granada, or by the authority of the same,* than is, under like circumstances, levied upon and collected from the Granadian citizens; that any lawful produce, manufactures or merchandise, belonging to citizens of the United States, thus passing from one sea to the other, in either direction, for the purpose of exportation to any other foreign country, shall not be liable to any import-duties whatever; or, having paid such duties, they shall be entitled to drawback upon their exportation; nor shall the citizens of the United States be liable to any duties, tolls or charges of any kind, to which native citizens are not subjected for thus passing the said Isthmus. And, in order to secure to themselves the tranquil and constant enjoyment of these advantages, and as an especial compensation for the said advantages, and for the favors they have acquired by the 4th, 5th, and 6th articles of this treaty, *the United States guarantee, positively and efficaciously, to New Granada,* by the present stipulation, *the perfect neutrality of the before-mentioned Isthmus, with the view that the free transit from the one to the other sea may not be interrupted or embarrassed in any future time while this treaty exists;* and, in consequence, *the United States also guarantee,* in the same manner, *the rights of sovereignty and property which New Granada has and possesses over the said territory.*[45]

AMERICAN HESITANCY: GRANADIAN ANXIETY

President Polk, being undecided as to the advisability of submitting the treaty for Senate ratification, first consulted his Cabinet, which he found to entertain "serious doubts . . . whether this stipulation [Article XXXV] was consistent with our [United States] long settled policy to cultivate friendship with all nations, entangling

[45] Malloy, *op. cit.,* I, 312. The italics are inserted here to emphasize the portions which have since been the subject of almost endless discussion and conflicting interpretations.

alliances with none."[46]　Nevertheless after "mature consideration" he submitted it on February 10, 1847.

Polk recommended its ratification on the grounds that (1) the United States had not been asked to guarantee a territory in which it had no common interest with New Granada; (2) the guarantee was confined to the Isthmus of Panama; (3) the treaty would "constitute no alliance for any political object but for a purely commercial purpose, in which all navigating nations of the world . . . [had] a common interest"; (4) neither the United States nor New Granada had any "narrow or exclusive views" in making the agreement; (5) Great Britain and France were expected to make a similar convention; (6) "such a guarantee . . . [was] almost indispensable to the construction of a railroad or canal across the territory."[47]

Despite these recommendations, little enthusiasm for the treaty was evinced by either the President,[48] often accused of imperialistic inclinations, or by the Senate. Apparently they did not agree with Bidlack that it was "dangerous to let the golden opportunity pass."[49]　The instructions for which Bidlack had been clamoring since October 2 had not been forwarded until January.[50]　He complained (January 24) of his "mortification" at having to inquire at the British legation for the latest news from the United States.[51]　The receipt of the treaty draft was not even acknowledged until March 25, a month and a half after its submission for ratification.[52]　The Senate (March 3) postponed its consideration until the Decem-

[46] Diarial entry, Jan. 30, 1847, Milo Milton Quaife (ed.), *The Diary of James K. Polk*, II, 363.

[47] Richardson, *Messages and Papers*, V, 2361-2363.

[48] There is no further reference to the treaty in Polk's *Diary* until its ratification. Even then no comment is made.

[49] Bidlack to Buchanan, (34) Dec. 14, 1846, Desp. Col., XI.

[50] Buchanan to Bidlack, (14) Jan. 2, 1847, Inst. Col., XV, 107.

[51] Bidlack to Buchanan, Jan. 24, 1847, marked "Please read this," Desp. Col., XI.

[52] Buchanan to Bidlack, (15) March 25, 1847, Inst. Col., XV.

ber session,[53] because of the "pressure and urgency of important business." Notwithstanding the delay, Sevier, chairman of the foreign relations committee, thought that it would be ratified at the next session.[54]

President Mosquera decided to dispatch former President Pedro Herrán as envoy extraordinary and minister plenipotentiary to Washington—no diplomatic representative had resided there since 1842. Herrán presented his credentials on December 7, 1847, the very day of Polk's annual message to the new Congress.[55]

According to Dr. Rivas, the main object of the Herrán mission was to secure the Senate ratification of the treaty.[56] The methods adopted to accomplish this end indicate the diplomatic astuteness of the new minister. An impressive legation was established at Washington— former representatives had resided principally in New York.[57] He remained in the capital until after the treaty was ratified.[58] Instead of flooding the Department with long argumentative notes pointing out the advantages of the treaty,[59] he chose to work quietly through conferences —the method used by Bidlack in his lobbying at Bogotá.

Herrán soon discovered that the main obstacles to ratification were (1) the Senate's fear of the alliance characteristics of Article XXXV, (2) the nearly equal strength of the two political parties in the body (two-thirds majority was necessary for ratification), (3) the active British and French lobbying among the senators. In an effort to overcome these, he urged the necessity of the United States sending settlers to its new possessions on the Pacific and pointed out the advantages of the

[53] *Sen. Ex. Jour.*, VII, 191-193, 235.

[54] Buchanan to Bidlack, (15) March 25, 1847, Inst. Col., XV.

[55] Rivas, *Relaciones*, pp. 177 ff.   [56] *Ibid.*, p. 199.

[57] The personnel of the legation totalled fifteen, including the wife of President Mosquera (Herrán to Buchanan, Dec. 7, 1847, Notes from Col. Leg., II).

[58] *Idem* to *idem*, July 3, 1848, *ibid.*

[59] The appropriate volumes in the archives of the State Department contain no letter from him regarding the treaty ratification.

Isthmian route over the transcontinental. Likewise, he did not fail to mention the British aggressions, especially in Mosquitia, and warned of the dire consequences these might have on North American trade and prestige.[60]

The treaty came up again in the Senate on January 3, 1848. On the motion of Chairman Sevier, it was referred to his committee and ordered printed in confidence. It was reported without amendments and ordered (June 2) to lie on the table. The following day Senator Hannegan, new chairman of the foreign relations committee, moved its consideration. After less than a day's debate it was ratified (June 3) by a vote of twenty-nine to seven.[61] The ratifications were exchanged on June 10 and the treaty proclaimed on June 12[62]—exactly one year and a half after its signing at Bogotá and nearly five years after the United States was apprized of New Granada's desire for a foreign guarantee of the Isthmus.

Out of the negotiations of the 1840's there naturally arise certain puzzling questions: (1) Why did New Granada urge a treaty in Europe some three years before it discussed the matter seriously with the United States?[63] (2) In the light of repeatedly manifested interest (both congressional and private) in a canal,[64] why was the Washington government so hesitant in favoring a guarantee obviously necessary for the success of any project? (3) What drove Bidlack to negotiate the Treaty of 1846 without instructions from Washington? (4) Why was New Granada willing and even anxious to treat with him, knowing that he did not possess proper authorization? (5) What caused the postponement of the ratification of

[60] Rivas, *Relaciones*, pp. 199-205.
[61] *Sen. Ex. Jour.*, VII, 278, 423, 424.
[62] Malloy, *Treaties, Conventions* . . . , I, 302.
[63] New Granada did not even maintain representation in Washington from 1842 to 1847.
[64] Jefferson, 1787; Clay, 1825-1826; Radcliff, 1826-1842; Senate Resolution, 1835; Biddle Mission, 1835-1836; numerous memorials, 1839-1842; House Resolution, 1839; various instructions to representatives at Bogotá, 1842-1845; the Wheaton treatise, 1845; Senate Resolution, 1846, etc.

the treaty by the United States senate? (6) If it was due to the thirty-fifth article, what factor overcame or removed this objection?

These questions will not admit of definite answers, but some tentative deductions concerning them seem possible. The greater power and prestige of France, and especially of Great Britain, made a European guarantee desirable as a protection against the aggressions not only of other nations but of these nations themselves. If such a guarantee could be secured, the acquiescence of the United States was of only secondary importance, since it would not dare encroach on the Isthmus in defiance of the guarantee and could already be counted upon to assist in resisting European encroachments. North American adherence to such a guarantee could almost be forced and, if secured, would have the effect of an acceptance of a self-denying provision to the Monroe Doctrine as far as the Isthmus was concerned. Then, since the Washington government had evinced no enthusiasm when notified of New Granada's intentions, whereas Guizot and Aberdeen had been at least encouraging in their conferences, it was natural that the European negotiations should be pushed with more vigor.

However, when both Great Britain and France refused to make the guarantee, it was inevitable that New Granada should turn to the United States. The fact that both private and congressional interest in an Isthmian communication had been evident there for some twenty years seemed encouraging. Yet since no Yankee company capable of executing the work had appeared and Congress had limited itself to general resolutions, the lack of North American enthusiasm for this treaty of guarantee is quite understandable. Besides, the Washington tradition of avoiding anything of the nature of an alliance was still the policy of both political parties. It is little wonder, then, that Bidlack was given no information regarding the failure of the European negotiations and no instructions for the making of such a treaty.

Since he possessed no authorization, why did he assume the responsibility of the negotiations? Some think that British territorial aggression in the Caribbean area was "the impelling cause of Bidlack's action."[65] The fear of French influence on the Isthmus, in case of canal construction by Salomón and Company, also might have been a contributing factor. However, the more important reason, as expressed by Bidlack himself, for his signing such a treaty seems to have been his fear that "important rights on the Isthmus and removal of differential duties" might be lost, if he permitted this "golden opportunity" to pass.[66] Therefore, he was not only willing but seemingly anxious to negotiate the guarantee.

But why was New Granada willing to negotiate knowing that Bidlack possessed no powers? The important factors seem to have been: (1) the feeling that some sort of a foreign guarantee of the Isthmus was necessary; (2) the failure of the negotiations in Europe; (3) the fear of British encroachments in the Caribbean area and assistance to the rumored Flores invasion of Peru and Ecuador. It is entirely possible that Mallarino consciously played up British aggressive activities in an effort to arouse Bidlack's suspicion and thereby forward the negotiations. However, "exaggerated or not," thinks Rivas, the British menace was of an alarming character, and New Granada felt itself greatly in need of protection. Therefore it was willing to remove the differential duties in order to secure a guarantee.[67]

When the treaty arrived in Washington, the country was in the midst of the Mexican War. "Misgivings respecting the thirty-fifth article and the pressure of other business caused a postponement of action until the next

[65] Howard C. Hill, *Roosevelt and the Caribbean*, p. 40.
[66] See *supra*, pp. 201 ff.
[67] Rivas, *Relaciones*, p. 165.

session of Congress."[68]   By that time the ratification of the treaty with Mexico (March, 1848), the expansionist sentiment then prevalent, and the anti-British lobbyists —including Herrán—soon brought the treaty before the Senate for debate. Since the debate lasted less than one day and the treaty passed by a nice majority, opposition to the thirty-fifth article must have been only slight.

Yankee agents in New Granada had always been jealous of British influence there, and many times had warned their government of supposed British attempts to secure territorial footholds. However, for two decades after the Monroe Doctrine the "United States Government took . . . [no] special interest in British encroachments on the American Isthmus . . . [and] made . . . [no] active attempts to check them."[69]   The British activities in Texas (1838-1842),[70] the annexation of that area (1845), the settlement of the Oregon question (1846), and the acquisition of vast regions from Mexico (1846-1848) aroused the Washington government to a realization of the necessity of a free route across the Isthmus and to a determination to oppose Great Britain whenever and wherever the latter power attempted to stand in the way. It seems, then, that the British menace might have caused the Senate to forget its objection to the thirty-fifth article.

At any rate, Secretary Buchanan soon congratulated Bidlack "upon the association of your [his] name with this Instrument," advised him that it had been "most favorably received by the public," and prophesied that it would be of "great and lasting advantage to both countries."[71]   On hearing of its ratification, the joy at Bogotá was *"tan grande como sincero."*[72]

[68] Eugene I. McCormac, *James K. Polk: A Political Biography*, p. 710.

[69] Mary Wilhelmine Williams, *Anglo-American Isthmian Diplomacy, 1815-1915*, p. 29.

[70] See Ephriam D. Adams, *British Interests and Activities in Texas, 1838-1846*.

[71] Buchanan to Bidlack, (20) July 20, 1848, Inst. Col., XV, 117.

[72] Rivas, *Relaciones*, p. 206; Uribe, *Anales*, III, 216.

SUSPICION AND REACTION

Nevertheless both nations were still anxious to secure European adherence to a similar guarantee. On September 17, 1847, Manuel Mosquera had been instructed to include such a guarantee in treaties which he was negotiating with Belgium and the Hanseatic cities.[73] Two years later Rafael Rivas was writing to Secretary Paredes that it was not Great Britain that New Granada ought to fear but the United States and that it was then necessary to seek a defense against that power as had been done against England by the Treaty of 1846.[74] The same year (1849) Secretary Clayton (October 20) expressed a willingness to share the guarantee and its benefits with Great Britain, (October 31) invited that power to join in the guarantee, and (December 14) instructed Minister Lawrence to assist the Granadian representative in securing an English guarantee similar to the Treaty of 1846.[75]

The new administration in Washington not only wanted European coöperation in protecting Panama but was unwilling to extend similar protection to other canal routes. The minister to Mexico was instructed that the United States was "not willing to incur the risks or bear the burdens which it would entail." In fact, the policy of the former administration was roundly denounced:

The guarantee in the treaty with New Granada is a conspicuous exception to our usual cautious and wise policy. That treaty was concluded without instructions from this department. There is reason to believe that it was reluctantly submitted to the Senate. It was approved by that body without full ex-

[73] Rivas, *Relaciones*, p. 173.

[74] Rivas to Paredes, Nov. 25, 1849, *ibid.*, p. 286.

[75] Clayton to Lawrence, (4) Oct. 20, (informal) 31, Dec. 14, 1849, Inst. G. B., XVI, 60-70; Sullivan and Cromwell, *Compilation of Executive Documents and Diplomatic Correspondence Relative to a Trans-Isthmian Canal in Central America*, I, 529.

amination and passed at the very close of the session of 1848. It cannot be deemed a safe precedent.[76]

The fear that Great Britain might seize Panama in payment of New Granadian debts caused Clayton, in instructing the new chargé,[77] Thomas M. Foote, to give to the treaty its first official interpretation:

Hence the obligations which we have incurred give us a right to offer, unasked, such advice to the New Granadian Government in regard to its relations with other powers, as might tend to avert from that Republic a rupture with any nation which might covet the Isthmus of Panama.[78]

[76] Clayton to Letcher, Sept. 18, 1849, *Sen. Ex. Doc.*, No. 97 (32.1), pp. 11-13.

[77] Bidlack died at Bogotá on Feb. 6, 1849.

[78] Clayton to Foote, (1) July 19, 1849, Inst. Col., XV, 123.

PART V

RELATIONS UNDER THE TREATY OF 1846

CHAPTER XIII

ISTHMIAN DISTURBANCES AND AMERICAN
INTERVENTIONS
(1846-1903)

ACCORDING to President Theodore Roosevelt, the Isthmus experienced fifty-three revolutions, rebellions, riots, and outbreaks between 1846 and 1903.[1] Although this figure could be only approximate, it is certain that Colombia suffered numerous civil wars, which either spread to the Isthmus or necessitated the withdrawal of garrisons, making possible serious disturbances there against the constituted authorities. And there were many local outbreaks which had no counterparts on the mainland. Some forty chief magistrates exercised authority over the area between 1855 and 1903.[2] Further evidence of Isthmian disorderliness is the fact that American military forces were landed eight times at Panama, six at Colón, and twice at Bocas del Toro—thirteen *distinct* interventions.[3]

EXPLOSIVE POSSIBILITIES (1849-1856)

The hosts of North Americans crossing the Isthmus on their way to the California gold fields and the great influx of foreign laborers to build the Panama railroad[4] added to the existing unrest.[5] The blustering manner of

[1] Richardson, *Messages and Papers*, XIV, 6812.
[2] See list, Tracy Robinson, *Panama: A Personal Narrative of Forty-Six Years, 1861-1907*, appendix.
[3] Panama, 1856, 1860, 1865, 1873, 1873, 1885, 1901, 1902; Colón, 1868, 1885, 1885, 1901, 1902, 1903; Bocas del Toro, 1895, 1902, Milton Offutt, *The Protection of Citizens Abroad by the Armed Forces of the United States*, pp. 37, 42, 48, 52, 60-61, 66-67, 79, 89, 92, 94, 96.
[4] See *infra*, chap. xvii.
[5] It had already seceded from Colombia twice—1830 and 1840—besides having shared in various general New Granadian disorders since independence.

the "Forty-Niners" and their contempt for the native blacks, who both feared and disliked them, produced a feeling of uneasiness. One American, who had recently crossed the Isthmus, warned (1849) his fellow country-men not to parade themselves before the "simple and timid Isthmians, armed to the teeth, and sweating under a mule-load of rifles, pistols, and bowie-knives." Such "ludicrously formidable and bombastic displays" were no more wanted on the Isthmus, he said, than a "toad . . . [had] need of a caudicular extension of the dorsal vertebrae."[6]

The reported storming of a Panama jail by an American mob bent on releasing a fellow countryman, caused Chargé Foote to fear (1850) for the continuance of cordial relations. The friendliness and common sense of President López and Governor Obaldía, he hoped, would prevent an open clash.[7] However, the attitude of Consul Ward at Panama (1855) brought a protest from Minister Herrán, who complained that Ward had shown a lack of respect for the Panama authorities and had attempted to defeat justice in the trials of certain lawless Americans.[8]

Secretary Marcy realized (1856) that many of the Yankees crossing the Isthmus were not inclined to submit to the "apparently exacting and arbitrary control" of New Granada. He feared they might become involved through "ignorant or perverse disregard of law" and then make unfounded demands for "protection and redress."[9] The arrogance of these travelers and their antipathy for the Isthmians; the latter's fear that every

[6] J. Carrington, *The Passage of the Isthmus or Practical Hints to Persons about to Cross the Isthmus of Panama* (New York, 1849), pp. 5, 13.
[7] Foote to Clayton, (11) April 25, (15) July 5, 1850, Desp. Col., XII.
[8] Herrán to Marcy, Oct. 18, 1855, Notes from Col. Leg., II. On account of his "wayward and ungovernable character," New Granada requested Ward's recall (Herrán to Marcy, Feb. 27, 1856, Notes from Col. Leg., II).
[9] Marcy to Bowlin, (17) Jan. 16, 1856, Inst. Col., XV, 213.

Yankee was a "potential filibuster";[10] and the presence of many ignorant lawless Negro laborers, who lacked adequate means of livelihood since the completion of the Panama railroad,[11] indeed, created a situation with violent possibilities. The Panama Riot was but the explosion of antipathies and jealousies long pent up.

THE PANAMA RIOT (1856)

On the morning of April 15, 1856, the steamer *Illinois* sailed into the Colón harbor with some 940 passengers aboard—about one-fourth being women and children.[12] By 4:30 P.M. a majority of them had been transferred by train across the Isthmus to Panama City. The crowd soon became scattered. Some were registering for passage on the *John L. Stephens;* some were already on board the small boat *Taboga* waiting for high tide to carry them out to their steamer; others were at the various hotels and stores; the remainder were wandering about the streets.

One Jack Oliver—reported to have been intoxicated —became embroiled with José Manuel Luna, a Negro fruit vendor, over a ten-cent piece of watermelon. It seems that the latter drew a knife, whereupon the former drew his revolver. Two fellow passengers stepped up, persuaded Oliver to put away his weapon, and paid for the melon. But another native, Miguel Habrahan

[10] Yankee filibusters were active in Nicaragua (William Walker) and Mexico, and had designs on Cuba. Besides, the Mexican War of the 1840's was still remembered. See W. O. Scroggs, *Filibusters and Financiers,* and "William Walker's Designs on Cuba," *Miss. Valley Hist. Rev.,* I, 198-211.

[11] The railroad was completed in 1855.

[12] Unless otherwise indicated this account is taken from *The Panama Massacre: A Collection of Principal Evidence and Other Documents, Including the Report of Amos B. Corwine, Esq., United States Commissioner, the Official Statement of the Governor and the Depositions Taken before the Authorities, Relative to the Massacre of American Citizens at the Panama Railway Station, on the 15th of April, 1856* (Panama, 1857). Besides Corwine's report, this publication contains some thirty-four depositions.

(or Habraan) grabbed the revolver, fired at a passenger,[13] and then fled towards the native huts. He soon returned with a considerable mob at his heels. Upon the tolling of the bells of Santa Ana,[14] still others joined the mob until it numbered possibly six hundred. The McFarland Hotel, Pacific House, Ocean House, and McAllaster's Store were attacked and pillaged. Then the mob opened fire on the railway station, where many had taken refuge.[15]

Available police, some twenty-five, under Manuel María Garrido, were called out but soon joined the mob in the attack.[16] Governor Francisco de Fábrega, on arrival at the scene, ordered a charge on the station, since the Yankees there were firing on the police. Certain Americans denied this, but it is entirely probable that they did fire, since many were undoubtedly armed and it was impossible to distinguish between the mob and the police.

After the smoke had cleared from the scene, it was found that eighteen (some say fifteen) passengers and two natives had been killed, and sixteen of the former and thirteen of the latter injured.[17]

General Totten of the Panama Railroad Company protested against what he termed "an indiscriminate massacre and pillage of defenseless strangers, and helpless women and children, which would disgrace the most

[13] Habrahan claimed that the passenger fired first. However, evidence seems to indicate otherwise (*ibid.*, p. 64).

[14] It was claimed that the tolling of the bells was a signal for a premeditated attack. New Granada, however, contended that a cry of "Fire" was heard at the church—in the midst of a funeral service—and, as was the custom, the bells were rung (Memoria de 1857—Pombo, Uribe, *Anales*, III, 390).

[15] Some women of the latter group reported that "their persons had been violated by colored men" (*The Panama Massacre*, p. 44).

[16] Garrido is reported to have advanced crying, "*Muerte a todos los Americanos*" (*ibid.*, pp. 40-41).

[17] These figures indicate that the natives were probably much better armed than the passengers, especially since the latter were barricaded in the railway station.

savage country on earth.''[18] Commander Bailey of the U. S. S. *St. Marys* added his protest and inquired regarding the punishment of the guilty, including Garrido. Fábrega attempted a defense, but was advised that action and not sophistry was desired and that the matter would be laid before the Washington government.[19]

Governor Fábrega reported to Bogotá that the passengers themselves had started the commotion by firing on the natives. He saw no one robbed, but realized that the presence of many "perverse fellows of different nations" made it impossible to prevent pilfering. Many of the natives thought that the passengers were filibusters. And the police had charged the station, he said, only after the refugees there had fired on them.[20]

On receipt of the news at Washington, Secretary Marcy felt that the evidence "directly and deeply . . . [implicated] not only the people but the civil authorities of Panama."[21] Amos B. Corwine was chosen to proceed to the Isthmus and make a thorough survey. In his report of July 18 he concluded that the whole affair was premeditated and for the purpose of robbery and plunder, at the same time satisfying a desire for revenge for imagined wrongs; and that the Panama authorities knew of and encouraged the plot.[22] This seemed to confirm the Department's initial judgment. Therefore, since it was felt that New Granada was neglecting to punish those guilty of the outrage and to provide properly for future protection, Isaac E. Morse was dispatched as special commissioner to assist Minister Bowlin at Bogotá in

[18] Totten to Fábrega, April 18, 1856, *The Panama Massacre*, pp. 49-50.

[19] Bailey to Fábrega, April 24, 25, Fábrega to Bailey, April 23, 1856, *ibid.*, pp. 51-54.

[20] Fábrega to Minister of Foreign Affairs, April 22, 1856, *ibid.*, p. 56.

[21] Marcy to Bowlin, (19) May 3, 1856, Inst. Col., XV, 216 ff.. For newspaper presentation of Colombia's side of the question, see *Gaceta de Nueva Granada*, Nos. 1977, 1990, 2003, 2007, 2039, 2073, 2090, 2091, 2098, 2404, 2570.

[22] *The Panama Massacre* . . . ; Specl. Missions, III; Specl. Agt. Ser., Amos B. Corwine; Con. Let., Panamá, IV, V.

securing some agreement on these matters and also indemnity for the losses already suffered.[23] The progress of the negotiations will be discussed in subsequent chapters of this study.[24]

NORTH AMERICAN FORCES INTERVENE (1856-1860)

Although no North American forces were available to land during the riot, the ships *Independence* and *St. Marys* were rushed to Panama City. It was well, too, since a disturbance in the state legislative assembly soon threatened to cause a civil war. On the afternoon of September 19, 1856, one hundred and sixty men under Commodore William Mervine landed and occupied the railway station. When the expected fight did not occur— probably due to the presence of these troops—they reembarked on September 22.[25] Four years later (September 27, 1860), when some six white inhabitants of Panama City had been killed and three others wounded by stray bullets from a local clash just outside the city, Commander W. D. Porter of the *St. Marys* again landed troops. The following day the Governor turned the city over to American and British forces. The insurrection had subsided sufficiently, however, by October 7 for the troops to re-embark.[26]

THE ISTHMIANS TALK SECESSION (1860-1873)

On two former occasions (1830 and 1840) the Isthmus had seceded from the Bogotá government, but had been persuaded to return. By a constitutional amendment of 1855 it was made a federal state[27] with considerable local autonomy. The unsettled conditions on the mainland following the election of 1857 permitted the Isthmus to en-

---

[23] Marcy to Morse, Oct., 30, 1856, Specl. Missions, III, 81-82.
[24] See *infra*, chaps. xviii, xix.
[25] Consul Sabla to Marcy, Oct. 2, 1856, *Sen. Doc.*, No. 143 (58.2), p. 4; Offutt, *op. cit.*, pp. 37-38.
[26] *Ibid.*, p. 42.
[27] Herrán to Marcy, Aug. 18, 1855, Notes from Col. Leg., II.

joy temporary independence.[28]   A cry for secession arose.[29]   Soon a plenipotentiary was appointed at Bogotá to secure Panama's adhesion to the new central government.[30]   The Isthmus agreed to remain loyal on condition that it become one of the sovereign states of the United States of New Granada with independent courts, that it be considered neutral in all wars between other states, and that national forces should never be landed as long as local troops protected the Isthmus.[31]

In spite of this agreement, secession agitation continued.   Minister Burton was approached (1862) regarding American attitude towards the independence of Panama and its establishment as a protectorate under the United States, Great Britain, and France.   It was hoped at least to secure "quiet sympathy."[32]   The intendent general of Panama and the Granadian minister at Washington were appealing (1861-1862) to the United States for intervention to protect the Isthmus from the domination of the new Mosquera government.   Recognition of Mosquera was postponed, but no intervention took place.[33]   A civil war at home was quite enough for the Washington government.

There was a fear (1865) that the states of Panama, Bolívar, Magdalena, and Cauca might secede and form an independent confederation.   In 1866 Burton reported that the prospect of separation still existed.[34]   Rumors

[28] Some claim that it was actually independent from 1857 to 1863 (Hill, *Roosevelt and the Caribbean*, p. 38).

[29] Pombo to Seward, May 14, 1861, Notes from Col. Leg., III.

[30] Convention of Sept. 6, 1861, Jones to Seward, (60) Oct. 14, 1861, Desp. Col., XV.

[31] Jones to Seward, (62) Nov. 4, 1861, *ibid.*

[32] Burton to Seward, (47) July 29, 1862, Desp. Col., XVII.   The New Granadian legation "invoked the coöperation of the United States to preserve the neutrality of the Isthmus" (*Sen. Doc.*, No. 143 [58.2], pp. 2 ff.).

[33] Seward to Burton, (43) Oct. 28, 1862, Inst. Col., XVI, 52.

[34] Burton to Seward, (private) Dec. 17, 1865, (217) Feb. 6, (277) Oct. 3, 1866, Sullivan to Fish, (134) May 31, 1869, Desp. Col., XXI, XXII, XXIV, XXVII.

of a revolt were current. Burton thought that such a movement was "likely to make good," since nine-tenths of the people favored independence and these were aroused by the rumored sale of Colombia's share in the railroad.[35] The consul at Panama reported a "growing desire" for independence, but felt that it would amount to nothing in consequence of "the want of men and money to carry it into effect."[36]

Meanwhile, the Liberals had gained control at Bogotá and had promulgated another constitution (1863), under which the central government was forbidden to intervene in Isthmian local revolts. This left the transit route and Yankee lives and property at the mercy of Isthmian political and military factions. A rather unexpected revolution on the afternoon of March 9, 1865, resulted in the landing of a small detachment of troops by Captain Middleton of the *St. Marys.* The consulate was occupied overnight. But the following day brought peace and the re-embarkation of the troops.[37]

Three years later the absence of the Aspinwall (Colón) garrison in Chiriquí and the presence of rather boisterous groups in the streets caused alarm for the safety of the passengers and treasure crossing the Isthmus. Two officers and twelve men under the command of Acting Master Thomas Nelson landed (April 7, 1868) from the *Penobscot.* When the danger disappeared, they returned to the ship.[38] The following year, while canal treaty negotiations were in progress[39] between the United States and Colombia, it was feared by some at Bogotá that Panama would secede and make the treaty itself.[40]

[35] Burton to Seward, (275) Sept. 15, (277) Oct. 3, 1866, *ibid.,* XXIV. There is reason to believe that the Panama Railroad Company and the *Panama Star and Herald* were influential in the support of the movement.
[36] Little to Seward, Sept. 18, 1866, *Sen. Doc.,* No. 143 (58.2), p. 44.
[37] *Sen. Doc.,* No. 143 (58.2), pp. 25-26.
[38] Report of Secretary of Navy, 1868, *H. Ex. Doc.,* No. 1 (40.3), p. xiii.
[39] See *infra,* chap. xxi.
[40] Sullivan to Fish, (134) May 31, 1869, Desp. Col., XXVII.

Clashes between local Isthmian factions necessitated the landing of American forces twice during 1873. One hundred men from the *Tuscarora*—the *Pensacola* was also in the harbor—went ashore (May 7) and occupied the Panama station of the railroad. The following morning still another hundred were placed in the city for the protection of foreign citizens and property. Considerable native fighting took place, but the American forces did not become involved. All had returned to their vessel by May 22.[41] The continuance of the struggle and the prospect of another violent clash brought a notice from the Governor of Panama that he was unable to furnish needed protection, whereupon Admiral John J. Almy landed (September 24) one hundred and fifty men from the *Benecia* and *Pensacola* to protect the railroad property and guard the trains in transit. When affairs became more disorderly that night, forty more men were sent ashore. With the restoration of peace all except thirty had re-embarked by October 6.[42]

THE IDEA OF A YANKEE PROTECTORATE (1862-1885)

Secretary Seward manifested no interest (1862) when Minister Burton reported that he had been approached regarding an Isthmian protectorate under the United States, Great Britain, and France. Secretary Fish (1869) feared that this might prove "a source of future trouble."[43] Burton, however, was not unimpressed. And Minister Scruggs, fearing that the possible defeat of Rafael Núñez for the presidency (1875) might mean the secession of the coastal states, suggested that, should the United States adopt the policy of an independent Isthmus under its protection or the "ultimate acquisition" of the area, there were "seldom wanting, under the constantly

[41] *Sen. Doc.*, No. 143 (58.2), pp. 2 ff.; Offutt, *op. cit.*, pp. 60-61.

[42] *H. Ex. Doc.*, No. 1 (43.1), pp. 263-264; *Sen. Doc.*, No. 143 (58.2), pp. 44-51, 97-103.

[43] Seward to Burton, (43) Oct. 28, 1862, Fish to Hurlbut, (6) Sept. 4, 1869, Inst. Col., XVI, 52, 365-367.

changing and unsettled political conditions of this country [Colombia], opportunities favorable to the initiation
of such a movement."[44]

Minister Dichman, writing from Colón in 1878, pointed
out the importance of the Isthmus and the need of the
extension of the "watchful care" of his government to
it, and noted that the Isthmians were not satisfied with
their $25,000 share of the $250,000 annual rental paid
Colombia by the Panama Railroad Company.[45] The following year, when the very existence of the Bogotá government was threatened by chronic revolution, he noted
the "ever present danger of the secession of the State of
Panama" and pointed out that "the idea of political
connection with the United States" had been "a feature
of more of less importance" for the last fifteen years.
He felt quite sure that union with Colombia was "a question entirely dependent upon the will of the people" of
the Isthmus.[46]

The necessity of affording protection for the operations of the French Panama Canal Company[47] caused
the passage of a law (1881), making it the duty of the
Bogotá government to defend the legal authorities of
Panama against hostile attacks—the Constitution of 1863
had enforced neutrality in such contests—and to increase
the Isthmian garrison to one thousand men.[48] But comparative quiet seems to have existed there until 1884.
Even before the inauguration (August, 1884) of the new
president, Rafael Núñez, there were "serious disturbances" on the Isthmus. Minister Scruggs soon requested
the stationing of a vessel nearby to afford protection.
The violence of the revolution in the interior states

[44] Scruggs to Fish, (101) May 17, 1875, Desp. Col., XXX.
[45] Dichman to Evarts, Aug. 20, 1874, Desp. Col., XXXII.
[46] Dichman to Evarts, (94) June 10, (98) 18, July 19, Aug. 1, 1879,
Desp. Col., XXXIII; *For. Rel.* (1879), pp. 292, 296.
[47] See *infra*, chaps. xxii, xxiii.
[48] Becarra to Bayard, April 2, 1885, Notes from Col. Leg., VII; *For.
Rel.* (1885), pp. 239 ff.

caused the withdrawal of the Isthmian garrisons, thereby making it possible for "professional politicians" to attempt the overthrow of the legal authorities. The Colombian minister intimated (April 3, 1885) the advisability of American forces being nearby.[49] But fighting had begun and the marines were already on hand.

On January 18 the new Panama executive, General Ramón Santo Domingo Vila, announced that he was unable to protect the Panama railroad property and asked for United States intervention. A contingent of twelve marines landed at Colón for the night, then re-embarked.[50] Some two months later a general revolt broke out during the absence of most of the Colombian forces in Buenaventura and the State of Bolívar. Soon a triangular fight developed between General Gónima (commander of government troops), General Aizpuru (former Liberal president of Panama), and Prestán (a Haitian Negro leader of the Radical group). The Bogotá government hastened to request (April 14, 1885) the United States intervention "to the end that, pending the arrival there of the national troops," the Americans would "undertake to maintain the right and authority of the Colombian government in the State of Panama."[51]

The Atlantic squadron under Acting Rear Admiral James E. Jouett had already been ordered to Aspinwall (Colón). Other forces under Commander Bowman H. McCalla were dispatched to the scene of disorder. When the Prestán and Aizpuru forces set fire to Colón, a small fire and rescue party went ashore (March 30-April 1). On arrival at Colón (April 10) Rear Admiral Jouett found that the commander of the *Shenandoah* had also landed troops at Panama City. Commander McCalla

[49] *Ibid.*
[50] Commander Clark (Colón) to Chandler (Panama), (tel.) Jan. 18, 1885, *For. Rel.* (1885), p. 203; Offutt, *op. cit.*, pp. 66-67.
[51] Restrepo to Scruggs, April 14, 1885, *For. Rel.* (1885), p. 210; Scruggs to Bayard, (tel.) April 14, 1885, Desp. Col., XXXIX.

and his force of seven hundred and fifty arrived at Colón on April 11 and 15.[52]

Additional troops were landed (April 10), both Colón and Panama were occupied, and McCalla placed in command of all the forces. Still others came ashore from the *Iroquois* at Panama on April 24. Four days later Colombian troops under Colonels Montoya and Reyes began to arrive at Panama from Buenaventura. A clash was avoided by Jouett's mediation. Aizpuru surrendered on April 29[53] and peace was soon restored. The American forces from the *Shenandoah, Swatara, Alliance, Tennessee, Galena,* and *Iroquois* were all withdrawn by May 25.[54]

During the disturbance Aizpuru hinted to Consul Adamson that "he would declare the secession of the Sovereign State of Panama from the Union and place it under the protection of the United States," if he could be assured of the acceptance of the proposal and of the governorship of Panama for himself."[55] Later in the year Adamson reported also that numerous "men of exceptionally high character" had attempted to sound him regarding an American protectorate.[56] But such a policy does not seem to have been considered by the Cleveland administration, which had intervened only "in aid of the sovereignty of Colombia."

THE ISTHMUS AS A FEDERAL DEPARTMENT (1886–1903)

The necessity of more adequate protection on the Isthmus was quite evident. To prevent the repetition of the regrettable affair of 1885, President Núñez thought it wise to deprive Panama of its statehood and give it the status of a department. Article CCI of the new Constitu-

[52] Offutt, *op. cit.,* pp. 67-70.
[53] Prestán was soon captured and hanged.
[54] Report of Commander McCalla upon the naval expedition to the Isthmus of Panama, April, 1885, *Sen. Doc.,* No. 143 (58.2); Report of Secretary of Navy, 1885, *H. Ex. Doc.,* No. 1; Offutt, *op. cit.,* pp. 67-70.
[55] Adamson to Hunter, April 18, 1885, *Sen. Doc.,* No. 143 (58.2), p. 67.
[56] Adamson to Porter, (192) Nov. 14, 1885, Con. Let., Panama, XVII.

tion of 1886 provided that the "Department of Panama
. . . [should] be subject to the direct authority of the
government, and it . . . [should] be administered by
laws especially enacted therefor."[57] In the determining
of its new status Panama had no voice. Even its representatives at the "National Council of Delegates," which
drew up the constitution, were residents of Bogotá and
appointed by Núñez, instead of being elected by the
Isthmians.[58]

Such treatment did not tend to increase their loyalty,
but the presence of a considerable military force—
ostensibly to protect the transit route—made successful
revolt impossible as long as peace was maintained on the
Mainland. Comparative quiet reigned until the Liberal
revolt of 1894-1895, when American troops were ordered
to be in readiness to protect the canal route.[59] The rumor
that García, a Mexican filibuster, and a small force were
marching on Bocas del Toro sent Captain B. J. Cromwell and the *Atlanta* hurrying from Colón to the threatened area. On arrival (March 7) it was felt that the
native force of fifty-eight was sufficient to afford protection. The *Atlanta,* therefore, left shore for target practice, only to find on return (afternoon of March 8) that
García had attacked the town. He and four others had
been killed and the entire force repulsed. But fearing
that the filibusters might return and set fire to the city,
Captain Cromwell sent ashore some seventy men until
noon of the following day.[60]

During the Colombian civil war of 1899-1903 it was
again necessary to land troops at Bocas del Toro. Commander Henry McCrea of the *Machias,* fearing a Liberal
attack on the city, landed a small force on April 16, 1902.

[57] For text, see *For. Rel.* (1886), pp. 179-206.
[58] T. C. Dawson, *The South American Republics,* II, 481-484.
[59] Gresham to General Newton, (tel.), Feb. 1, 1895, *Moore's Digest,* III,
43 ff.
[60] *Sen. Doc.,* No. 143 (58.2), pp. 160-164.

Through Commander McCrea's mediation, an agreement was reached (April 17) for the peaceful surrender of the city to the Liberals. The arrival of National reinforcements soon reversed the situation, and the Liberals marched out of the city on April 21. At the request of General Gómez of the National forces McCrea took charge of the city for the night. The following morning the Americans returned to their ship, leaving the lawful authorities in control.[61]

It had been necessary during the autumn of 1901 to use American troops at both Panama City and Colón for the protection of property and the safety of traffic over the railroad. McCrea sent a force ashore at Colón (November 20) and Captain Thomas Perry landed two hundred and forty-eight troops at Panama (November 24). The line of transit was soon opened, and the trains under heavy guard were running on schedule. McCrea, whose cleverness and tact later cleared the situation at Bocas del Toro, assisted in securing an agreement for the withdrawal of the Liberals in favor of the National troops. The transfer took place without disorder, the train guard was reduced, and the National troops were again allowed the free use of the railroad. By December 5 the last of the American forces had returned to their respective vessels—*Machias, Iowa, Marietta,* and *Concord.*[62]

Less than a year later, however, local disorders necessitated the same procedure. Troops from the *Cincinnati* went ashore at Colón (September 17, 1902) and from the *Ranger* at Panama City. The *Panther* and *Wisconsin* raced to the scene of danger with reinforcements. The use of the railroad was denied both the contending parties. By November 12 American interests and interoceanic traffic were sufficiently safe to warrant the gradual withdrawal of the forces. A treaty (November 21)

[61] *Ibid.*, pp. 254-258.   [62] *Ibid.*, pp. 69-73, 201-222.

between Generals Víctor M. Salazar and Lucas Caballero soon ended the civil war.[63]

With the return of peace on the Mainland the national garrisons were able to keep the Isthmians in subjection. However, American interest in the construction of a canal gave the inhabitants an exaggerated idea of the importance of the area and tended to increase their resentment of Colombian rule. The volume of Yankee investments and the presence of Yankee agents on the Isthmus naturally encouraged the secession idea. The failure of the Colombian congress to ratify the Hay-Herrán Treaty (1903), which would have made possible the construction of a canal by the United States, proved too much for the Isthmians. The resulting revolution of November 3, 1903, necessitated the landing of troops again at Colón.[64]

In anticipation of the uprising President Roosevelt had already ordered vessels to the Isthmus. On November 3 the commanders of certain American vessels were instructed to protect the transit route by whatever means necessary and to preclude the landing of "any armed force with hostile intent, either government or insurgent" near the scene of action. Some four hundred Colombian troops had already been permitted to land at Colón. When Commander John Hubbard, after receiving the above instructions, went ashore (November 4) to prevent these troops from proceeding to Panama City, he found that the revolution had occurred the previous night. To prevent an attack on the Americans and their property in Colón by Colonel Torres of the Colombian forces, troops were landed on November 4 and 5. But the decision of Colonel Torres to return with his forces to Cartagena cleared the situation, and the last of the Americans withdrew on November 6.[65]

With one exception, the independence of Panama

[63] *Ibid.*, pp. 73-76, 285-290, 317-321, 326-330.
[64] See *infra*, chap. xxv.
[65] *For. Rel.* (1903), pp. 266-271; Offutt, *op. cit.*, pp. 96-99.

ended the period of American intervention in that area
—none had ever taken place on the Mainland.[66] The numerous disturbances and resulting interventions naturally affected the Colombian guarantee of an open and
free transit, the American guarantee of the neutrality of
the Isthmus, the growth of commerce between the two nations, Yankee economic adventures in Colombia, and the
American policy of protection of citizens and property
abroad.[67]

[66] Nov., 1904, Offutt, *op. cit.*, pp. 101-102.
[67] These topics will be discussed in the succeeding chapters of this study.

CHAPTER XIV

THE GUARANTEE OF AN OPEN AND FREE TRANSIT
(1848-1903)

''The Government of New Granada [Colombia] guarantees to the Government of the United States that the right of way or transit across the Isthmus of Panama . . . shall be open and free to the Government and citizens of the United States, and for the transportation of any articles of produce, manufactures or merchandise, of lawful commerce, belonging to the citizens of the United States; [and that such commerce] . . . shall not be liable to any import duties whatever. . . .''—Article XXXV, Treaty of 1846.

IT HAS been noted already that the Treaty of 1846 was unpopular with both of the new administrations of 1849 —José Hilario López and Zachary Taylor. Bogotá feared Yankee aggression, as it had feared British aggression prior to the treaty, while Washington thought the treaty ''a conspicuous exception to our usual cautious and wise policy'' and not to be considered ''a safe precedent.''

PASSENGER, TONNAGE, AND MAIL TAXES (1849-1886)

The first issue to arise under this treaty grew out of New Granada's attempt to tax passengers, vessels, and mails entering the Isthmian harbors. The riotous national election of 1849, the subsequent political agitation, the promulgation (1853) and nullification (1854) of a new liberal constitution, and the Melo revolt and dictatorship (1854) permitted and caused considerable disorder on the Isthmus. The hordes of California immigrants and the foreign laborers imported to construct the Panama railroad likewise added greatly to the confusion.[1]

Either for the purpose of exploiting the unprecedented traffic across the Isthmus or of providing money to preserve order along the line of transit, the Panama

[1] Henao y Arrubla, *op. cit.*, pp. 620-652.

[235]

legislature levied (1849) a tax on the steamship companies of $2 per passenger transported. The American minister was instructed to protest against such a tax as contrary to the spirit of the Treaty of 1846. He was advised, however, by the Bogotá government that it could not interfere.[2] The consul at Panama complained also of a tax of $125 per month being levied on the American commercial houses of that city. He had experienced some difficulty in securing the release of one F. J. Folger, who had been arrested for non-payment. "Worse consequences" were feared if the laws were not repealed.[3]

The occupation tax was soon suspended, but the passenger tax continued to be paid under protest for at least three years—the Pacific Mail Steamship Company paying $121,000.[4] In 1853 the tax was raised to $10 per passenger, an estimate of ten per cent of the steamship company's profit, but later it was lowered to $2, and Minister Green reported the tax practically suspended by August, 1854. The New Granadian supreme court on April 23, 1855, declared the levy null and void. Washington thought this was done on the basis of the Treaty of 1846. Bogotá later claimed, however, that it was because such legislation was beyond the powers of the Panama assembly. In any case, the Granadian congress soon (May 22) passed an act empowering the president to withdraw exequaturs from consuls who protected foreigners in their resistance to such taxes.[5]

[2] Clayton to Foote, (14) Jan. 9, 1850, Cass to Jones, (2) April 30, 1859, Inst. Col., XV.

[3] Corwine to Clayton, Feb. 23, March 22, Aug. 26, Sept. 9, 1850, *Sen. Ex. Doc.*, No. 40 (31.2), pp. 2 ff.

[4] Since a large portion of this amount had been collected from passengers and an agreement on the interpretation of Article XXXV had not been reached, the umpire of a claims commission (1866) rejected the company's plea for recovery (John Bassett Moore, *History and Digest of International Arbitrations*, II, 1412-1415).

[5] Marcy to Green, (13) Feb. 16, 1854, Marcy to Bowlin, (10) July 31, 1855, Cass to Jones, (2) April 30, 1859, Inst. Col., XV, 139, 177, 205; Green to Marcy, (7) April 22, (11) Sept. 25, 1854, Desp. Col., XIII.

Even before the passage of this act (May 22, 1855) was known in Washington, Secretary Marcy advised Minister Bowlin that it was "not improbable that a vessel of war . . . [might] be stationed at Aspinwall [Colón] and Panama, and, if necessary, be authorized to protect . . . [American] vessels and citizens from the threatened exaction." He was instructed to remonstrate orally and informally but to avoid "anything like a threat." Bowlin's protests were effective and the passenger tax was abandoned, but the refund of money collected was refused.[6]

Meanwhile, the State of Panama had discovered a new method of taxation. An act of August 27, 1855, levied a tonnage duty of twenty cents on steamers and forty cents on sailing vessels entering Panama harbors. Secretary Marcy contended that this act also was at variance with the Treaty of 1846 and warned the Bogotá government that it would be held "accountable for any exactions" made on American vessels.[7] The New Granadian minister, Pedro A. Herrán, argued that importation duties were forbidden by the treaty, but not tonnage dues.[8] However, an executive resolution of October 11 (14?) exempted Panama and Aspinwall (Colón) from the law.[9]

The Panama Riot (April 15, 1856)[10] and the subsequent mutual ill-feeling made a settlement of the Isthmian tax question difficult, if not impossible. The Bogotá government, on hearing the news of the riot, issued (April 25) a congressional decree (effective September 1) providing that all mails must cross the Isthmus under the supervision and care of Granadian postal authorities and that

---

[6] Marcy to Bowlin, (11) Aug. 31, (14) Dec. 17, 1855, Inst. Col., XV; Bowlin to Marcy, (27) Dec. 5, 1856, Desp. Col., XIII.
[7] Marcy to Herrán, Oct. 23, Nov. 17, 1855, Notes to Col. Leg., VI.
[8] Herrán to Marcy, Oct. 26, 1855, Notes from Col. Leg., II.
[9] Bowlin to Marcy, (9) Oct. 18, 1855, Desp. Col., XIII; Uribe, *Anales*, V, 559.
[10] See *supra*, chap. xiii.

a toll of $3.20 per pound be charged on all closed bags of nations with which no postal convention existed.[11] The Post Office Department estimated that such a tax would cost the United States $2,000,000 per annum, in addition to the amount (nineteen cents per pound) already being paid to the Panama Railroad Company. Besides, Washington was determined not to pay the tax, even if no postal convention existed, since the Treaty of 1846 mentioned mails specifically and Articles XXVIII, XXIX, XXX of the Panama railroad concession gave it the power to contract with the United States for the transportation of mails. Bowlin was ordered to return from the Isthmus to Bogotá and press the matter.[12]

Meanwhile, the tonnage tax had been revived (June 25). Bowlin felt that such a "scheme of plunder" might be expected until the New Granadians were "taught in a manner not susceptible to doubt, to respect their obligations—[and] to preserve the freedom of the Isthmus."[13] Evidently, the Washington government agreed, since Commodore William Mervine of the Pacific squadron was ordered "to resist by force, if necessary, the collection of the tonnage taxes" and his threat of forceful resistance was later approved by Marcy. At any rate, his threat was effective enough to cause the abandonment of efforts to collect the tax, and Pombo advised Bowlin that the matter would be presented to the next Congress before enforcement would be attempted.[14]

Both Pombo (at Bogotá) and Herrán (at Washing-

[11] Bowlin to Marcy, (18) May 14, 1856, Desp. Col., XIII; Cass to Jones (2) April 30, 1859, Inst. Col., XV. New Granada had already (1852) given notice of its annulment of the Convention of 1844 (Paredes to Clayton, June 18, 1852, Notes from Col. Leg., II).

[12] Marcy to Bowlin, (21 and confidential) July 3, 1856, Inst. Col., XV.

[13] Richardson, *Messages and Papers*, VI, 2948; Herrán to Marcy, Dec. 8, 1856, Notes from Col. Leg., II; Bowlin to Marcy, (18) May 14, Sept. 17, 1856, Desp. Col., XIII.

[14] Seward to Burton, (21) Feb. 27, 1862, Inst. Col., XVI, 30; Bowlin to Marcy, (21) Oct. 3, 1856, Desp. Col., XIII; Marcy to Herrán, Dec. 22, 1856, Notes to Col. Leg., VI.

ton) argued that additional revenue was needed to protect the transit route from the greatly increased lawless element there, and that neither the tonnage dues nor the mail tax was contrary to the Treaty of 1846 or to the Panama railroad contract. The former added that "in no controversy therewith [could he] permit the intervention of the Government of the United States."[15]

Nevertheless Pombo did suggest negotiations and Herrán presented a project to the State Department. The proposed adjustment provided that the United States should pay the same postage as Granadian nationals and a duty equal to one-eighth of the amount paid the Panama railroad for the transportation of mails across the Isthmus. New Granada agreed in turn never to charge more than forty cents tonnage on the first hundred tons and twenty cents on each thereafter, all exemptions to remain the same as then existed.[16]

The opening of the Panama railroad (1855) with its enormous traffic had greatly increased the administrative expenditures on the Isthmus, Herrán argued. Furthermore, the loss of life during the riot (April 15, 1856) indicated that a still greater outlay was necessary to preserve order along the transit route. Since the United States was the chief benefactor by this increased expense, he saw no reason why it should object to paying certain taxes, which New Granada had a perfect right to levy. He questioned the justice of New Granada's being held responsible for the acts of April 15, 1856, yet being refused its lawful right to raise the money to prevent

[15] Herrán to Marcy, Dec. 8, 1856, Notes from Col. Leg., II; Bowlin to Marcy, (22) Oct. 9, Bowlin to Pombo, Nov. 10, Pombo to Bowlin, Nov. 14, 1856, Desp. Col., XIII. Meanwhile, Marcy had again threatened the use of force to prevent collection (Marcy to Bowlin, [29] Dec. 31, 1856, Inst. Col., XV, 246-249). Herrán, on the other hand, contended that the railroad's acknowledged right to contract for the transportation of mails did not deprive Colombia of the right to charge for a permit to send them across (Herrán to Marcy, Dec. 8, 1856, Notes from Col. Leg., II).

[16] Herrán to Cass, Aug. 10, 1857, Notes from Col. Leg., II.

such in the future.[17]   Sound as these arguments may have seemed to Herrán, the Washington government was unmoved.

The passage of an act by the Granadian lower house (May, 1858) to repeal the decree of May 25, 1835,[18] drew another protest from Washington. Secretary Cass held that this would amount to the confiscation of American property, since the railroad had been constructed under its protection. The Granadian answer that national ships paid as much as American was held non-valid, since there were few, if any, of the former trading in the Isthmian harbors. The renewed threat to use force[19] brought a counter-protest from Herrán. He argued that Americans were not being discriminated against; that the decree of 1835 was "purely domestic," foreign nations having "no right of interference"; and that the United States was the only power which considered it as a pledge. Besides, it had been invalidated by the acts of April 5, 1848, and June 2, 1849. Therefore it could not have induced subsequent foreign investments. And Colombian failure to collect duties since Mervine's threat of 1856 was not to be interpreted as a forfeiture of this right.[20]

Herrán, realizing the ineffectiveness of his past efforts, then proposed new bases of settlement. New Granada would surrender its right to tax passengers, merchandise, and mails and waive all claims to unpaid dues if the United States would pay the damages

[17] *Idem* to *idem*, Dec. 11, 1857, *ibid.*, II.

[18] This decree declared the ports of the cantons of Porto Bello and Panama free for the period of twenty years from the date of the opening of an interoceanic communication.

[19] Cass to Herrán, June 4, 1858, Notes to Col. Leg., VI, 82; Cass to Jones, (2) April 30, 1859, Inst. Col., XV, 269 ff.

[20] Herrán to Cass, Aug. 23, 1858, Notes from Col. Leg., III. Herrán was probably in error here, since an executive decree of Oct., 1855, had considered the decree of 1835 as valid and a congressional resolution of 1865 declared it still in force (Notes on Herrán's letter [by Bowlin], Notes from Col. Leg., III; Burton to Seward, [149] Feb. 10, 1865, Desp. Col., XX).

awarded under the Treaty of 1857.[21] When no results
came from these new proposals, he made claim for the
mail and tonnage dues uncollected since September, 1856.
But Cass dismissed the whole matter by refusing to discuss it until Colombia had ratified the pending treaty.[22]

The unsettled conditions at Bogotá forced Herrán to
return home early in 1860. The election of Mariano
Ospina (Conservative) over Manuel Murillo (Liberal)
and Tomás de Mosquera (Nationalist) had led to the
promulgation of a new constitution (1858), reorganizing
the government under the title of "Granadine Confederation." Mosquera then led a revolution. Bogotá was
captured in 1861, Mosquera made "Provisional President," the name of the country changed to "United
States of Colombia," and a state sovereignty constitution issued (1863) by the Liberal convention of Río
Negro.[23]

On returning to Washington, Herrán (April, 1862)
again approached the State Department regarding the
payment of the long due mail and tonnage duties and
insisted on satisfaction for the "grave offenses" of Minister Bowlin, Commodore Mervine, former Consul Ward,
and Commissioner Corwine—all of these having been involved either in the tax controversy or the negotiation
of the Treaty of 1857 or both. Six months later when
reminded that this letter had not been answered,[24] Secretary Seward promised to consider the complaints. Later
when he advised that nothing could be done until full
awards had been made under the Treaty of 1857,[25] the
matter was dropped.

[21] Herrán to Cass, Oct. 9, 28, 1858, March 14, 1859, Notes from Col.
Leg., III. This treaty provided for the settlement of American claims,
especially those growing out of the Panama Riot of 1856—not ratified by
Colombia until 1860.

[22] Cass to Herrán, March 31, 1859, Notes to Col. Leg., VI, 89.

[23] Henao y Arrubla, *op. cit.*, pp. 651-672.

[24] Herrán to Seward, April 17, Oct. 27, 1862, Notes from Col. Leg., III.

[25] Seward to Herrán, Oct. 28, Dec. 16, 1862, Notes to Col. Leg., VI.

Meanwhile, the almost continual disorder on the Isthmus (1857-1863) had brought the imposition of new taxes by the state assembly. When Americans at Colón complained of a commercial tax,[26] they were advised not to pay it and to make reclamation for any already paid under protest. The Navy Department was requested to be in readiness to resist with force, if necessary, the collection of this tax.[27] "Numerous and considerable" claims began to pour into the State Department. Prominent among those involved were the Panama Railroad Company, the Pacific Mail Steamship Company, and Cornelius Vanderbilt.[28]

The return of peace did not remove this irritation. Panama City attempted to levy an occupation tax. Minister Burton was assured at Bogotá that Colombia's tax policy was being considerably modified. But he was not convinced of the government's ability to force its will on the Isthmus, since the new constitution had strengthened the states at the expense of the central government. Therefore he suggested the use of force, and Seward requested the Navy Department to station vessels in the ports to protect American citizens against "any undue and unwarranted exactions."[29]

Although the Colombian government accepted Burton's views regarding the freedom of the Isthmian ports by declaring the decree of May 25, 1835, still in force; nevertheless, when certain reclamations[30] were pressed, it unconditionally asserted the right of Panama to levy such taxes. Burton thought that the only remedy was "a

[26] Jones to Cass, Aug. 12, 1860, Desp. Col., XVI.
[27] Seward to Burton, (21) Feb. 27, (32) Aug. 28, 1862, Inst. Col., XVI, 30, 43; Burton to Seward, (169) May 9, 1865, Desp. Col., XX.
[28] Burton to Seward, (84) May 27, (95) Sept. 20, 1863, (125) Oct. 17, 1864, Desp. Col., XVIII.
[29] Burton to Seward, (107) April 21, (126) Oct. 22, (137) Dec. 2, 1864, Desp. Col., XIX; Seward to Burton, (119) Feb. 10, (125) July 13, 1865, Inst. Col., XVI.
[30] Cornelius Vanderbilt, Panama Railroad Company, and Pacific Mail Steamship Company.

little plain talk," accompanied by "prompt, firm, and energetic measures, [and] tempered with a little rigor."[31] Nevertheless he realized that the pressure must be put on Panama instead of Colombia, since the latter feared to protect foreigners on the Isthmus, on account of the growing sentiment of secession there.[32]

The year 1866 brought complaints of tax exactions from Cartagena and the State of Bolívar, also a national decree attempting to establish tonnage dues on the vessels of all nations not having postal conventions with Colombia.[33] Meanwhile, Minister Salgar had been attempting to negotiate such a convention at Washington. Seward held that the decree (August 17, 1866) could not apply to American vessels, since the Postal Convention of 1844 was still in force, yet he felt that a new arrangement might be desirable and was willing to treat on the subject. But Salgar withdrew before any agreement was reached. The question was again raised in 1876, but dismissed on the ground that the old convention was still in effect.[34]

When it seemed that "prompt, firm, and energetic measures" would be used on the Isthmus and after Burton, thoroughly discouraged and disgusted, had broken

[31] Burton to Seward, (149) Feb. 10, (180) June 14, (188) Aug. 9, (190) Aug. 11, 1865, Desp. Col., XX, XXI.

[32] The Isthmian threats of secession probably made Colombia hesitant in questioning the local taxing power.

[33] Burton to Seward, (229) March 16, (237) May 31, (confidential) Dec. 16, (291) Dec. 21, 1866, Desp. Col., XXIII, XXV; Seward to Burton, (163) Nov. 12, 1866, Inst. Col., XVI, 207.

[34] Salgar to Seward, July 13, 1865, Dec. 16, 1866, June 10, Aug. 12, 1867, Notes from Col. Leg., IV; Seward to Salgar, July 18, 25, 1865, Dec. 6, 1866, June 29, 1867, Notes to Col. Leg., VI, 187, 189, 210, 226; Seward to Burton, [163] Nov. 12, 1866, Fish to Scruggs, [114] June 3, 1876, Inst. Col., XVI, 207; XVII, 21-23. Colombia did not consider the treaty in force (Memoria de 1853—José María Plata, Uribe, *Anales*, III, 309) and had instructed its minister to negotiate a new one (Herrán to Marcy, Nov. 22, 1856, Notes from Col. Leg., II), but the United States used both this convention and the Treaty of 1846 as arguments against the decree of Aug. 17, 1866. At any rate, this treaty was superseded by the Universal Postal Union Convention of 1878 to which both nations became parties.

off relations with the Bogotá officials, three modifying decrees were issued and all attempts at collection of the contested taxes ceased. So complete was the surrender to the American interpretation that Burton felt that the whole project might "be considered as abandoned . . . at least for the present."[35]

The State Department, however, never ceased to warn that it would never acquiesce in the revival of the mail and tonnage dues. It likewise continued to protest against too heavy exactions for military purposes, although the Americans paid no higher rates than Colombians.[36]

During the Revolution of 1885 President Núñez made the last major attempt to levy taxes on Isthmian commerce. Executive Decree No. 636 did not establish mail and tonnage dues, but provided that after December 1, 1885, all merchandise entering the ports of Panama and Colón must pay import duties at the rate of sixty per cent of that paid in the other national ports. Naturally, such a measure aroused the Yankee merchants and the State Department. After an unsuccessful effort to compromise with those affected, Núñez abandoned the project without having tried to enforce it.[37] Thus the American interpretation of a "free" transit route was accepted.[38]

[35] Burton to Seward, (291) Dec. 21, 1866, Desp. Col., XXV.

[36] Seward to Sullivan, (4) June 13, 1867, Fish to Scruggs, (106) March 14, 1876, Inst. Col., XVI, XVII; Sullivan to Seward, (49) Jan. 1, 1868, Dichman to Evarts, (96) June 14, 1879, Scruggs to Fish, (145) Jan. 27, 1876, Desp. Col., XXVI, XXXI, XXXIII.

[37] Scruggs to Bayard, (239) Oct. 2, (240) 3, Jacob to Bayard, (8) Feb. 22, 1886, Desp. Col., XXXIX; Bayard to Jacob, (2) Nov. 3, to Scruggs, (72) 17, (74) 19, 1885, Inst. Col., XVII, 483-489; Adamson (Panama) to Porter, (187) Oct. 10, (192) Nov. 14, 1885, Jan. 20, 1886, Con. Let., Panama, XVII, XVIII; *Panama Star and Herald*, Oct. 10, 1885. The Isthmian secession movement might have affected the Colombian decision. It is known that Consul Adamson was approached by seemingly responsible parties regarding an American protectorate over the area.

[38] This does not mean, however, that during subsequent disorders Americans were not temporarily subjected to irregular exactions by both local Panama authorities and insurgents, nor that Colombia admitted the levying of custom duties to be contrary to the Treaty of 1846 (Uribe, *Anales*, IV, 381 ff.), but merely that efforts to collect such duties ceased.

THE PASSAGE OF AMERICAN TROOPS ACROSS THE
ISTHMUS (1852-1865)

The transporting of some six hundred troops in July, 1852, across the Isthmus, without the consent of either the Panama or Bogotá governments, made a bad impression in Colombia, and was followed by a request for an explanation of such an unseemly procedure.[39] Secretary Marcy replied that the measure had not been adopted "without due consideration." The right was "deemed obvious from the words of the treaty itself," and New Granada had received "ample equivalent for any sacrifices she may have made. . . ."[40]

Chargé Paredes differed with this interpretation. He denied that the Treaty of 1846 was ever intended to be construed in such a manner and therefore contended that a new agreement was necessary.[41] After some three months of delay Marcy restated his position and added that the United States expected "no unnecessary impediment" to the enjoyment of a right so clearly implied in the existing treaty. The ineffectual attempt of Paredes to secure the submission of the matter to the decision of a friendly power temporarily closed the discussion.[42]

However, press reports (December, 1855) that more American troops had been ordered to the Pacific by way of the Isthmus brought a new request for some arrangement. Herrán claimed to fear such a precedent, since other powers might claim the same under the most-favored-nation clause of their treaties.[43] He declared that Colombia had "no particular cause for objecting" and no desire "to impose unnecessary restrictions"; but, since no such right of passage could be claimed under the Treaty of 1846, he felt that, as an "act of courtesy to

[39] Paredes to Marcy, June 6, 1853, Notes from Col. Leg., II.
[40] Marcy to Paredes, June 20, 1853, Notes to Col. Leg., VI, 35-38.
[41] Paredes to Marcy, July 19, 1853, Notes from Col. Leg., II.
[42] Marcy to Paredes, Oct. 12, 1853, Notes to Col. Leg., VI, 43-46; Paredes to Marcy, April 8, 1854, Notes from Col. Leg., II.
[43] Herrán to Marcy, Dec. 9, 1855, *ibid.*

[the] sovereign of territory," permission should be asked and notification given by the United States prior to the dispatching of each contingent of troops across the Isthmus. He presented the bases of a special convention and secured Marcy's verbal approval of it,[44] but the Panama Riot (1856) and the subsequent negotiations turned the excited diplomatic minds to other questions.

In 1858 Herrán attempted to open the discussion again and connect it with the settlement of the Isthmian tax question, but nothing came of it.[45]

During the American Civil War the Panama authorities were instructed (December 10, 1864) to refuse passage to all foreign troops. The application of this ruling to Admiral Pearson on his way from the West Coast to New York was quickly followed by a special mission to Panama and Bogotá. Seward argued that the obligation to protect obviously implied the right of unimpeded troop movements, otherwise protection would be impossible. If American rights were not recognized, Congress might be asked to authorize the adoption of "other measures to maintain and secure them."[46]

On arrival at Panama, the special mission, headed by Major General D. E. Sickles, was advised that Colombia's policy had been due to its desire to observe strict neutrality in the North American struggle and to the fear of having to grant the same transit privileges to European nations. The reason given at Bogotá was Washington's silence regarding its action in case Spain sought to send troops across the Isthmus to make an attack on Peru. But after being assured that Spain had been duly warned, the American views were "frankly and without reservation conceded." Sickles advised Seward that there was "no longer any misunderstanding" on the mat-

---

[44] Herrán to Marcy, Jan. 24, 1856, to Cass, July 21, 1858, *ibid.*, II, III.
[45] Herrán to Cass, July 21, Oct. 9, 1858, *ibid.*, III.
[46] Burton to Seward, (119) June 30, 1864, Desp. Col., XIX; Seward to Sickles, (1) Jan. 6, 1865, Specl. Missions, II, 29-33.

ter,''[47] and Minister Salgar accepted Article XXXV as permitting the passage of American troops across the Isthmus ''whenever they . . . [were] sent on the service of the American Union, and not destined to commit hostilities upon another nation.''[48] By this time, however, the restoration of peace in the United States caused the question to lose ''much of its immediate interest.''[49]

THE TRANSPORTING OF PRISONERS ACROSS THE ISTHMUS (1865-1890)

On the suggestion of Minister Hurlbut,[50] an extradition treaty was signed at Bogotá on March 30, 1872. It was forwarded to Washington[51] but never presented to the Senate for approval.[52] In 1878 Minister Dichman expressed his belief to the Department that recognition of the American right to transport prisoners across the Isthmus ought to be secured.[53] The release of one C. I. Scrafford (captured in Peru and wanted for forgery in Kansas) by the Panama officials, even after an American vessel had been sent to convey him home, made the matter of extreme importance. Therefore Dichman was instructed to secure the Colombian views.[54] The result was a protocol (February 22, 1879) granting the desired right, on condition that the prisoners be placed in the custody of Isthmian officials during the passage.[55]

[47] Sickles to Seward, Jan. 26, Feb. 5, 23, April 17, 1865, Desp. Col., XX.

[48] Salgar still thought, however, that the matter should be covered by a definite agreement, apart from the Treaty of 1846. Salgar to Seward, March 27, May 29, 1865, Notes from Col. Leg., IV.

[49] Seward to Burton, (124) June 13, 1865, Inst. Col., XVI, 130-131.

[50] Hurlbut to Fish, (49) Feb. 15, (53) May 23, 1871, Desp. Col., XXVIII; Fish to Hurlbut, (36) March 29, (39) April 11, 1871, Inst. Col., XVI, 387-390.

[51] Hurlbut (N. Y.) to Fish, May 4, 1872, Desp. Col., XXVIII.

[52] Note on copy: ''Directed *not* to be sent to the Senate for ratification. March 10, 1873.'' Unperfected Treaties, Col., L.

[53] Dichman to Evarts, (17) Oct. 30, 1878, Desp. Col., XXXII.

[54] Evarts to Dichman, (12) Nov. 12, 1878, Inst. Col., XVII, 54; Uribe, *Anales*, IV, 11-13, 37-38.

[55] Dichman to Evarts, (58) March 17, 1879, Desp. Col., XXXII. Dichman found that Colombia had already recognized this right, along with the

Dichman's efforts to work out a final agreement on the subject were handicapped by the early dissolution of the Colombian congress and the resignation of the minister of foreign affairs.[56] When it was again taken up, disagreement developed around the points of capital punishment and the custody of the prisoners during the passage.[57] An additional protocol of October 23, 1879, accepted the American view on the latter point.[58] A treaty of extradition followed on November 1. But the Senate's opposition to certain of its clauses was so well known that the treaty was withheld and Dichman instructed to reopen negotiations.[59]

These were more successful. Another convention was signed on January 3, 1881, and approved by the American senate and Colombian congress on May 5 and June 25, respectively. But an amendment by the latter providing that extradited persons should not be subject to "capital punishment or to corporal punishment of a permanent character" proved unacceptable to the United States.[60] Here the matter rested for six years. It was Colombia which reopened negotiations. One Foyer, a former conductor on the Panama railroad, under a nine-year sentence for the murder of a Colombian, had escaped and was supposed to be living in Arkansas. Secretary Bayard refused extradition papers on the ground that no treaty on the subject existed between the two nations. He called attention to the Scrafford case of 1878 and expressed regret that so much time had been lost in mak-

---

right of passage of American troops across the Isthmus (Antonio Del Real to the Panama government, May 15, 1865). For text of the protocol, see Uribe, *Anales,* VI, 295-296.

[56] Dichman to Evarts, (89) May 18, 1879, Desp. Col., XXXIII.

[57] *Idem* to *idem,* (148) Oct. 6, 1879, *ibid.*

[58] For text, see Uribe, *Anales,* VI, 296.

[59] Dichman to Evarts, (159) Nov. 9, 1879, Desp. Col., XXXIV; Evarts to Dichman, (101) March 8, 1880, Inst. Col., XVII, 138-144.

[60] Evarts to Dichman, (157) Feb. 25, (166) May 9, Blaine to Dichman, (181) Aug. 29, 1881, *ibid.,* pp. 236, 251, 271; Unperfected Treaties, Col., M.; *Sen. Ex. Jour.,* XXIII, 30, 67, 68.

ing the needed treaty.[61] The subsequent negotiations produced the Extradition Convention of May 7, 1888, which became effective late in 1890.[62]

THE USE OF AMERICAN TROOPS TO MAINTAIN AN OPEN TRANSIT (1850-1903)

Although New Granada (Colombia) was bound by treaty to keep open the transit route for passengers and commerce, circumstances often proved to be stronger than the government. The numerous revolts and the persistent secession sentiment on the Isthmus made necessary the stationing of strong national garrisons there. But since these disturbances were often mere local manifestations of national discontent, the Bogotá government, fighting for its own existence, was sometimes unable to furnish sufficient troops to maintain peace along the transit. Therefore the landing of American forces was often necessary to prevent the obstruction of traffic by the contending national and revolutionary armies.

These interventions were made at the suggestion, or request, or with the permission and sanction of the Panama authorities. Since they resulted from disturbances on the Isthmus already discussed, the relating of details at this point is unnecessary. It is sufficient to point out that Colombia accepted American proffered assistance in fulfilling its obligation to keep open the transit for world commerce.

[61] Bayard to Becerra, July 8, 1887, Notes to Col. Leg., VII, 116 ff.; Uribe, *Anales*, IV, 382-383.

[62] Blaine to Maury, (142) April 12, 1889, Inst. Col., XVII, 120; *Sen. Ex. Jour.*, XXVI, 303, 464; XXVII, 17, 36, 42; Uribe, *Anales*, VI, 336-340.

CHAPTER XV

THE GUARANTEE OF ISTHMIAN NEUTRALITY
(1848-1903)

"... the United States guarantee, positively and efficaciously, to New Granada, ... the perfect neutrality of the ... isthmus, with the view that the free transit ... may not be interrupted or embarrassed in any future time while this treaty exists; and, ... also guarantee, in the same manner, the rights of sovereignty and property which New Granada has and possesses over the said territory."—Article XXXV, Treaty of 1846.

THE fear of Yankee aggression on the Isthmus was concomitant not with the degree of Yankee activity there but with the probability of hostile attacks from other sources, foreign or domestic.

THE THREATENED FLORES EXPEDITION (1852)

The rumor that General Flores, with the support of Spain and possibly Peru, was contemplating a hostile attack on Ecuador caused Chargé Paredes (1852) to suggest an American condemnatory demonstration and to express his opinion that Washington was called upon to take "an active part" in favor of the endangered republics.[1] From Bogotá came a request that a vessel be placed near the Isthmus, since Flores might attack there if repulsed from the Mainland.[2] But the State Department did not believe extreme danger imminent. At all events, it did not feel that the circumstances called for its interposition. However, an investigation of a report that California filibusters were assisting Flores was promised.[3] The failure of the expedition to materialize

[1] Paredes to Webster, June 20, 1852, Notes from Col. Leg., II.
[2] Plata to King, July 1, 1852, forwarded with King to Webster, (9), Desp. Col., XII.
[3] Conrad to Paredes, Oct. 5, 1852, Everett to Paredes, Feb. 14, 1853, Notes to Col. Leg., VI, 24-28.

made a definite interpretation of the guarantee obligation unnecessary.

THE PERIOD OF MUTUAL STORM AND STRESS
(1860-1865)

As previously noted, Isthmian disorders made necessary the landing of American forces in October, 1856, and September, 1860.[4] By the latter date the control of Bogotá over the area was slight.[5]

Nevertheless General Mosquera, as "Supreme Dictator of War," determined to bring Panama under his authority. Since neither the local intendant-general nor the chargé at Washington recognized the Mosquera government as legal, both appealed to the United States. Chargé Pombo declared that he did "not mean to insinuate that the United States should interfere in the political contest . . . but . . . [believed] that the time . . . [had] arrived . . . to coöperate with the Granadian Confederacy to prevent the closing of the interoceanic route. . . ."[6] News came from Bogotá, however, that the United States was considered responsible for Isthmian "subjection and obedience and for the domination" of Granada over it.[7] But Seward would not be drawn into a discussion. He merely advised Pombo that the Navy Department had been requested to issue proper orders for "affording adequate protection to American interests and insuring the tranquillity of the Isthmus."[8] To the protest of the Mosquera government, Minister Jones replied that the United States would, "in no event, interfere between the contending parties. . . ."[9]

[4] Report of Secretary of State, Jan. 30, 1904, *Sen. Doc.*, No. 143 (58.2) p. 2.

[5] Howard C. Hill, *Roosevelt and the Caribbean*, p. 38, claims that Panama was actually independent from 1857 to 1863.

[6] *Sen. Doc.*, No. 143 (58.2), p. 10; Pombo to Seward, May 29, 1861, Notes from Col. Leg., III.

[7] Pardo to Jones, June 12, 1860, forwarded with Jones to Cass, Aug. 12, 1860, Desp. Col., XIV.

[8] Seward to Pombo, May 30, 1861, Notes to Col. Leg., VI, 110.

[9] Jones to Seward, (59) Sept. 17, 1861, Desp. Col., XV.

Meanwhile, Civil War had broken out in the Northern republic. Jones, who had written a confidential note to President Calvo giving much gratuitous advice and pointing with pride to the government of the "Mother Republic,"[10] was "made daily to blush for shame, when asked . . . as to the progress of the war in the model republic."[11] While he was trying to mediate in the Granadian civil war,[12] strife had begun in his own country. Herrán soon returned to Washington, after a temporary leave, expecting to offer his mediatory services to Presidents Lincoln and Davis.[13] And Mosquera dispatched notes to each of them.[14] While Americans were attempting to reclaim Isthmian taxes forcibly collected, Manuel Murillo, representative of the new Mosquera government, was complaining of forced taxes in New York and of the drafting of his secretary into military service. But these matters were soon settled.[15]

Although Herrán had returned to Washington as a Mosquera appointee,[16] he soon grew hostile to his father-in-law's dictatorship[17] and appealed (June, 1862) to the State Department to save the Isthmus from his "mob of armed men." He argued that since the legitimate Granadian government could not "by itself alone answer for the safety of the interoceanic transit," the case had arisen when it must call upon its "ally," who had "guaranteed the neutrality of the Isthmus against the

---

[10] Jones to Calvo, March 31, 1861, forwarded with Jones to Cass, (47) April 14, 1861, Desp. Col., XV. This was very similar to the letters of Watts (1826) and Harrison (1829).

[11] Jones to Seward, (60) Oct. 14, 1861, Desp. Col., XV.

[12] *Idem* to *idem*, (52) June 22, 1861, *ibid.*

[13] *Idem* to *idem*, (59) Sept. 17, 1861, *ibid.*

[14] For copies of these, see *ibid.* and Pombo to Seward, July 25, 1863, Notes from Col. Leg., IV.

[15] Seward to Murillo, Oct. 2, 13, 1863, Notes to Col. Leg., VI, 150-151.

[16] Herrán to Garrido, Aug. 6, 1861, enclosed with Jones to Seward, (59) Desp. Col., XV.

[17] See Pedro A. Herrán, *Protesta . . . contra la dictadura del titulado "Presidente de los Estados Unidos de Colombia,"* Tomás C. de Mosquera (dated June 14, 1862).

assaults, and military operations of any force,'' except those of the national government.[18] The expedition against Panama, he contended, was under the order of the "self-styled Provisional President of the so-called United States of Colombia,'' and therefore was a "wanton act committed against the people" thereof. It was a violation of Isthmian neutrality, since the "United States of Colombia" was not the name of a political faction but "a new member in the family of nations" which certain groups in New Granada were attempting to create for the purpose of dominating "all, or any part, of the territory of the former Republic of Colombia.''[19] Therefore, the Isthmus was being attacked by foreign forces and American coöperation was expected.[20] When no assistance was immediately forthcoming, the appeal was renewed in September.[21]

Since the Civil War was in progress and the recognition of the Confederacy was being strongly advocated in Europe, Seward feared to formulate any definite policy without first consulting England and France. He wanted advice as to whether the United States should intervene with British and French acquiescence; if so, to what extent; and whether these two powers would join in the guarantee. England saw no reason for interposition; but, if such a need arose, agreed to coöperate. France held somewhat the same view and suggested that Herrán did not represent the real government at Bogotá.[22] Naturally, no aid was given the opponents of the Mosquera government.

However, Washington was slow to recognize this new

[18] Herrán to Seward, June 26, 1862, Notes from Col. Leg., III.
[19] Mosquera had talked with the American minister regarding the restoration of La Gran Colombia.
[20] Memo., June 27, 1862, Notes from Col. Leg., III. In conference Herrán suggested not only a naval force but also 300 cavalrymen (Seward to Adams, [296] July 11, 1862, *Moore's Digest*, III, 13).
[21] Herrán to Seward, Sept. 18, 1862, Notes from Col. Leg., IV.
[22] Seward to Adams (296), to Dayton (180), Adams to Seward (201), Dayton to Seward (185), *Moore's Digest*, III, 13 ff.

government. Mosquera expressed surprise that Minister
Burton did not present his credentials on arrival in November, 1861, especially since his immediate predecessor,
Jones, had been so kindly disposed towards the revolutionary movement.[23]   Sentiment at Bogotá was rather
hostile to the United States. Many would have welcomed
the success of the Confederacy, since there was no assurance that the victorious Union army and navy might not
be used for conquest.[24] Gradually, however, public opinion changed with the establishment of the Liberal government (1863) and the presentation of Burton's credentials on March 9, 1864.[25]

Meanwhile, Murillo was making every effort in the
United States to secure recognition. In *El continental*
(New York, January 1, 1863) he published Seward's letters to England and France and interpreted them as
meaning that the United States had renounced the Monroe Doctrine by thus inviting European interference.[26]
The effect of Murillo's propaganda is not known.[27] But
he was officially received on July 21, 1863,[28] and President
Lincoln (1864) acknowledged "the directness, frankness,
and cordiality" of the new régime.[29]

ARTICLE XXXV INTERPRETED (1864-1866)

Out of the Colombian fear (1864) that Spain might
send troops across Panama to fight Peru, again emerged
the question of treaty interpretation.[30] The matter was

[23] Jones to Seward, (62) Nov. 4, 1861, Desp. Col., XV.
[24] Burton to Seward, (42) July 22, 1862, *ibid.*, XVII.
[25] *Idem* to *idem*, (103) March 9, 1864, *ibid.*, XIX. Burton had been at
Bogotá for more than two years.
[26] Seward to Herrán, Sept. 5, 1862, Notes to Col. Leg., VI, 132; Romero
to Mexican Minister of Foreign Affairs, Jan. 8, 1863, *Correspondencia de la
legación Mexicana*, III, 86.
[27] Herrán (still representing the old government) sent a copy of the
article to Seward and requested a public reply, but Seward refused to take
any notice whatsoever of it (Seward to Herrán, Jan. 12, 1863, Notes to
Col. Leg., VI, 141).
[28] Seward to Murillo, July 20, 1863, *ibid.*, p. 147.
[29] Dec. 6, 1864, Richardson, *Messages and Papers*, VII, 3444.
[30] Burton to Seward, (119) June 30, 1864, Desp. Col., XIX.

referred to the American attorney general,[31] but the dissipation of this fear made an immediate pronouncement unnecessary.

However, the landing of a small contingent of American forces in March, 1865, was necessitated by Isthmian disorders.[32] This was unopposed. But the unauthorized landing of a band and marine guard in September to take part in the funeral of Consul Alex R. McKee aroused the ire of the Panama executive. He refused to attend the services, since his presence might be construed as an approval of the American action. In the subsequent exchange of notes Admiral Pearson raised no objection to asking permission to land troops, but insisted that he did not consider such a request in any way essential.[33]

Less than two months later Bogotá called upon American forces to prevent the landing of certain armed men, reported to have been sailing from Buenaventura. Minister Burton, temporarily accepting the Herrán interpretation of the treaty guarantee, advised the consuls and naval commanders of the movement.[34]

He argued with Seward that since the various Colombian states were constitutionally "sovereign and independent of each other" and the United States was treaty bound to protect Colombia's "rights of sovereignty and property" over the State of Panama, it was obligated to defend the Isthmus from invasion by the other Colombian states.[35] Before this despatch had reached Washington, however, Seward had forwarded the opinion of

[31] Seward to Burton, (101) Aug. 20, 1864, Inst. Col., XVI, 108-109.
[32] *Sen. Doc.*, No. 143 (58.2), p. 25.
[33] Pearson to Colunje, Sept. 8, 1865, *For. Rel.* (1866-1867), p. 460. While admitting that Pearson should have asked permission, Seward felt that, under the "peculiar circumstances," criticism was "uncalled for and unkind" (Seward to Burton, [139], April 30, 1866, Inst. Col., XVI, 168-189).
[34] Burton to Seward, (199) Nov. 5, 1865, Desp. Col., XXI. The Bogotá government was constitutionally bound not to intervene in interstate struggles as long as national forces and property were not involved.
[35] *Ibid.*

the attorney general on that very question.[36] Burton later admitted his mistake, but insisted that his interpretation was the one held by Colombia prior to 1862,[37] when Herrán had appealed for assistance against Mosquera.

Meanwhile, Burton had been officially advised of the rumor of a contemplated secession uprising on the Isthmus, supposedly instigated by the agents of the Panama railroad.[38] But the movement failed without American intervention becoming necessary.[39]

This exchange of notes tended to clarify the views of each government. The American interpretation emerged as follows:

The thirty-fifth article of the Treaty of 1846 with New Granada [Colombia] binds the United States absolutely to guarantee the perfect neutrality of the Isthmus of Panama, on the demand of the proper party; and this obligation must be performed by any and all means which may be found lawful and expedient.[40]

But this article does not obligate this government to protect the Isthmus of Panama from invasion by a body of insurgents from the United States of Colombia.[41]

In the case, however, that the transit trade across the Isthmus should suffer from an invasion from either domestic or foreign disturbances of the peace . . . the United States will hold themselves ready to protect the same.[42]

---

[36] Seward to Burton, (134) Nov. 9, 1865, Inst. Col., XVI, 144-145.

[37] Burton to Seward, (277) Oct. 10, 1866, Desp. Col., XXIV.

[38] Garrido to Burton, Sept. 3, 1866, *For. Rel.* (1866-1867), p. 572; *Moore's Digest*, III, 38.

[39] Owing to the mistaking of rockets discharged during a religious celebration for a signal from the consul, troops were landed on July 15, 1866, but soon re-embarked (Burton to Seward, [271] Sept. 11, 1866, Desp. Col., XXIV).

[40] Decision of Atty. Gen. Bates (1864), *Wharton's Digest*, II, 111.

[41] Decision of Atty. Gen. Speed (1865), *ibid.*

[42] Seward to Burton, (156) Oct. 9, 1866, Inst. Col., XVI, 202-203; *Sen. Doc.*, No. 143 (58.2), p. 43.

[However,] the treaty and the law of nations must regulate the actions of both governments should such an emergency unhappily arise.[43]

The Colombian view seems to have been as follows:

The Colombian Government declares that it does not feel itself authorized by the treaty to require the aid of the United States for the suppression of any insurrection, rebellion or other disturbances on the Isthmus on the part of Colombian citizens, not even an invasion by another Colombian State, unless such movement be intended to detach the State of Panama from the Colombian Union and to annex it to a foreign power.[44]

... the use ... of the [American] forces ... for the preservation of order and the maintenance of the sovereignty of Colombia over the Isthmus has to be determined by the Colombian authorities, and not by the chiefs of those forces.[45]

Apparently the two interpretations differed little, except Colombia insisted on determining when intervention should take place, while the United States chose to leave such to "the treaty and the law of nations."

AMERICAN INTERVENTION—NOT A DUTY BUT A RIGHT (1868-1903)

While the Panama police and troops were suppressing a revolt in Chiriquí, a small American force was landed, April, 1868, as a precautionary measure.[46] Five years later, when the meager Colombian forces were unable to crush a revolt on the Isthmus, others were landed at the request of the local authorities.[47] The failure on the part

---

[43] Seward to Burton, (139) April 30, 1866, Inst. Col., XVI, 189.

[44] Burton to Seward, (277) Oct. 3, 1866, Desp. Col., XXIV; *Sen. Doc.*, No. 143 (58.2), p. 35. Burton felt sure that, if this attitude were generally known on the Isthmus, a successful secession movement would be initiated there.

[45] Pérez to Burton, Oct. 16, 1865, *For. Rel.* (1866-1867), p. 459.

[46] Report of the Secretary of Navy, *H. Ex. Doc.*, No. 1 (40.3).

[47] *Sen. Doc.*, No. 143 (58.2), pp. 2 ff. It was reported that there were "only a few policemen to attend to the town duties" at Colón and "no national troops" at Panama (*For. Rel.* [1874], pp. 364-365).

of Colombia to afford proper protection brought a restatement of the American position by Secretary Fish:

This engagement [to guarantee the neutrality of the Isthmus]
. . . has never been acknowledged to embrace the duty of protecting the road across it from the violence of local factions;
but it is regarded as the undoubted duty of the Colombian
Government to protect it against attacks from local insurgents.
. . . The discharge of this duty will be insisted on.[48]

In response to the request that more troops be stationed on the Isthmus, the Colombian president decreed
(December 15, 1873) that henceforth at least two hundred would remain there permanently. And Secretary
Jil Colunje declared to Minister Scruggs:

The Colombian Government has considered, and will always
consider as its exclusive function and duty to give that protection; a protection which this government has never refused,
although it may have appeared inadequate during the late
disturbances. . . .[49]

Thus the matter stood until the Revolution of 1885.
The inauguration of President Rafael Núñez (1884) was
followed almost immediately by an expected Liberal revolt. Scruggs reported the country in the "most deplorable condition; worse, perhaps, than it . . . [had] been at
any time since its independence. . . ." The rights of
private property were almost "wholly disregarded, and
what one faction . . . [failed] to take in the form of forced
loans, the other usually . . . [took] by force of arms."[50]

Panama had experienced "serious disturbances, even
before the inauguration." Scruggs, unable to keep in

[48] Fish to Scruggs, (15) Oct. 29, 1873, Inst. Col., XVI, 448.
[49] Colunje to Scruggs, Dec. 26, 1873, enclosed with Scruggs to Seward,
(27) Jan. 7, 1874, Desp. Col., XXIX.
[50] Scruggs to Frelinghuysen, Jan. 20, 1885, *For. Rel.* (1885), p. 203 ff.
Conditions were such that this letter did not reach the Department until
May 11.

touch with affairs there, requested (December, 1884, and January, 1885) a naval vessel. The request was certainly well timed, since things were soon happening with startling rapidity. During the disturbance Colón was burned by the insurgents.[51]

Minister Becerra claimed that there was no connection between these "unprincipled agitators on the Isthmus" and the "political rebels of the interior"; therefore the United States was treaty bound to suppress the former. He even intimated that the failure of the American forces to render proper assistance to the Panama authorities made it possible for this lawless element to burn Colón.[52] Secretary Bayard did not argue the point, but merely explained how difficult it was at such times to determine just who were the lawful authorities.[53]

Colombia seemed temporarily to waver from its former treaty interpretation. The United States remained theoretically consistent, but actually favored the national government against the insurgents. Scruggs was told that American operations would be restricted to the transit route, since the guarantee was of "international neutrality [and] not intervention with local strife."[54] But President Cleveland later advised Congress that although the military intervention had "involved police control where the local authority was temporarily powerless," it had been "always in aid of the sovereignty of Colombia."[55] The charge of American laxity in the enforcement of neutrality laws seems ill-founded, for not only were earnest efforts made in this direction, but actual loans of arms and ammunition were made to the

---

[51] Scruggs to Bayard, (tel.) April 21, 1885, Desp. Col. XXXIX.
[52] Becerra to Bayard, April 3, 4, 1885, Notes from Col. Leg., VII.
[53] The explanation was accepted as satisfactory. Becerra to Bayard, April 8, 1885, Notes from Col. Leg., VII.
[54] Bayard to Scruggs, (tel.) April 29, 1885, Inst. Col., XVII.
[55] Richardson, *Messages and Papers*, X, 4911.

national government.[56] Besides, the landing of troops had meant, in effect, intervention in favor of Bogotá.

The Revolution of 1885 brought to a close the Liberal régime and ushered in an era of comparative peace under a strongly centralized Conservative constitution.[57] Only two major disturbances occurred prior to 1903, while some forty clashes had marred the peace of the Liberal era.[58]

During the first of these disorders (1893-1895) Secretary Gresham called upon Colombia to keep the "transit free and open and afford needed protection"[59] and instructed American naval officers to furnish this protection, if Colombia failed. When local forces seemed inadequate at Bocas del Toro, American troops were landed in March, 1895, for the protection of life and property.[60] Colombia soon assured the State Department that it was sufficiently prepared to furnish the promised protection.[61] But, again, during the Revolution of 1899-1903 American military intervention became necessary: once at Bocas del Toro, twice at Panama City, and three times at Colón.[62]

By this time mere notification of intention to intervene with force was considered by the United States as sufficient permission therefor. Gradually the Department had expanded Article XXXV by interpretation to suit the protection of Yankee vested interests and the transit route. In 1901 national troops were restricted in their use of the railroad, in 1902 both national and insurrectionary forces were denied its use, and in 1903 the

[56] See correspondence from March to Sept., 1885, Notes from Col. Leg., VII; to Col. Leg., VI; *For. Rel.* (1885), p. 231 ff.

[57] This constitution changed the name of the nation to the "Republic of Colombia." With subsequent amendments it is still in force.

[58] Henao y Arrubla, *op. cit.*, pp. 713-760.

[59] Gresham to McKinney, (tel.) Feb. 1, 1895, Inst. Col., XVIII.

[60] *Moore's Digest*, III, 43.

[61] Rengifo conferences, July 25, 29, 1895, Notes from Col. Leg., IX.

[62] *Sen. Doc.*, No. 143 (58.2), pp. 2 ff.

armies of neither—affecting only the national government—were permitted to land within fifty miles of the transit route. This last prohibition naturally prevented the suppression of the revolt of November, 1903, and thereby deprived Colombia of its "rights of sovereignty and property," which the Treaty of 1846 was supposed to have guaranteed.

CHAPTER XVI

THE GROWTH OF COMMERCE
(1845-1903)

ECONOMIC relations assumed an unprecedented importance on the ratification of the Treaty of 1846. The removal of discriminating duties by New Granada[1] proved an open sesame to trade development, while the guarantee of the Isthmus by the United States[2] afforded the needed protection for the investment of Yankee capital in that area. Other factors contributing to this economic acceleration were the American annexation of Texas (1845), "reoccupation" of Oregon (1846), acquisition of a large territory from Mexico (1848), and the discovery of gold in California (1849). These made imperative the establishment of interoceanic communications between the Eastern ports and the Great West. Since Panama proved the most practical and popular route, traffic, commerce, and investments grew there and, in turn, gave impetus to Granadian economic life.

TRADE PROSPERS (1845-1875)

Even before the Treaty of 1846 became effective, New Granada not only repealed the discriminating duties but actually reduced the tariff on certain American staples as much as fifty per cent.[3] The establishment of steamship lines between New York and Chagres, Panama and San Francisco;[4] and the negotiation of a consular convention (1850)[5] likewise contributed to mutual prosperity.

[1] Articles IV, V, VI.   [2] Article XXXV.
[3] Bidlack to Buchanan, (49) Sept. 4, 1847, Desp. Col., XI.
[4] Clayton to Foote, (1) July 19, 1849, Inst. Col., XV, 123.
[5] This was provided for by Article XXXIV of the Treaty of 1846, signed at Washington May 4, 1850, and ratifications exchanged Oct. 10,

The volume of trade between the two nations had declined during the decade preceding 1845 from $2,364,811 to $203,510, because of discriminations and Granadian internal disorder. The volume increased, however, during the next five years to $1,145,172. This amount expanded to $2,108,910 (1855), $4,345,930 (1860), $8,666,584 (1865), $8,666,878 (1870), and $16,717,030 (1875).[6] In other words, New Granada, among the Latin American nations, advanced from seventh to second place in exports to, and from seventh to third place in imports from, the United States during the period of 1845 to 1875—Brazil alone enjoying a more favorable balance.[7]

DANGERS ENCOUNTERED (1870-1884)

As was usual in all Latin American countries, however, Colombian trade continued very largely in European hands, especially English. More fleet and frequent steamship communication with the Old World, the European long-credit and low-interest system of sales, and the American protective tariff policy certainly operated to the advantage of the Europeans—so much so that Minister Hurlbut (1870) suggested a drastic reduction of tariff on Colombian products and a five-year government subsidy for needed steamship lines.[8]

During the 1870's the latter policy received considerable attention at both Washington and Bogotá, but commercial pressure was not sufficient to secure its approval at either place.[9] Meanwhile, the Atlas Steamship Com-

---

1851. An additional protocol was signed Jan. 7, 1879. *Sen. Ex. Jour.*, VIII, 173, 246; Rivas, *Relaciones*, p. 282; King to Webster, (2) Oct. 31, 1851, Desp. Col., XII; *Diario oficial* (Bogotá) No. 4343; Uribe, *Anales*, VI, 167-172, 293-295.

[6] Robertson, *Hispanic-American Relations*, pp. 204, 210, 420-428.

[7] The figures for Cuba are not considered since it was still a Spanish colony.

[8] Hurlbut to Fish, (39) Oct. 31, 1870, Desp. Col., XXVIII.

[9] Pérez to Fish, May 3, 1871, Notes from Col. Leg., VI; Fish to Pérez, May 11, 1871, Notes to Col. Leg., VI, 271; Hurlbut to Fish, (45) Feb. 1, 1871, Dichman to Evarts, (23) Nov. 29, 1878, (89) May 18, 1879, Desp. Col., XXVIII, XXXII, XXXIII. James G. Blaine, later Secretary of State, spoke before Congress in favor of such a subsidy.

pany (British owned) enjoyed a profitable carrying trade between New York and Colombia, and a new British subsidized line was soon initiated between the same points.[10] It would seem, then, that the Britons were not only enjoying a larger volume of business with Colombia but were actually curtailing the Yankee carrying trade.

The preponderance of the European nations in Colombian trade was not due entirely to preference for their products but rather to "self-interest." This is evidenced by Colombia's persistent efforts to secure a reciprocity agreement with the United States.   In 1878, when it was suggested that the duty would be removed on American beer and reduced by twenty-five per cent on cotton goods in return for a substantial reduction on Colombian tobacco,[11] Minister Dichman recommended to the Department a change from the policy of a general tariff to one of a "conventional or treaty tariff adapted to the different commercial wants and interests."[12]   But Evarts clung to the traditional view that the matter could be handled better by appropriate action on the part of Congress.[13]

PRESIDENT ARTHUR ADVOCATES RECIPROCITY

The Arthur administration favored both legislation and negotiation in determining tariff levels.   Although Congress refused to make operative a reciprocal convention signed with Mexico (1883),[14] its interest was sufficiently aroused to provide for a trade commission to

[10] Scruggs to Fish, (41) June 27, 1874, *ibid.*, XXIX; Smith to Frelinghuysen, Aug. 15, 1884, *Con. Rep.* (1884), p. 42.

[11] Dichman to Evarts, (18) Nov. 7, 1878, Desp. Col., XXXII.   The Department merely acknowledged this note.   A bill removing all duties on flour, petroleum, mining and agricultural machinery, and reducing certain other duties failed of passage in 1879, because of the sudden dissolution of the Colombian congress (Dichman to Evarts, [89] May 18, 1879, Desp. Col., XXXII).

[12] Dichman to Evarts, (60) March 24, 1879, *ibid.*

[13] Memo. for file, Dec. 11, 1879, Notes from Col. Leg., VII.

[14] *Sen. Ex. Jour.*, XXIV, 210, 211; XXV, 687, 688.

South America.[15] This commission was instructed to ascertain "the best.modes of securing more intimate international and commercial relations" with the American republics. It was pointed out that foreign competition was "especially felt" in Colombia, but a "closer commercial alliance" should be easily obtainable.[16] After hearings in several of the North American commercial centers, some twelve of the Latin American states were visited. The itinerary included Panama, but the Revolution of 1885 prevented a visit to Bogotá.[17]

On the eve of the commission's departure for Mexico, President Arthur, after advising Congress of his securing another reciprocity agreement with the Dominican Republic, set forth his general policy. Since governmental income was already in excess of immediate needs, he felt that a policy might be evolved which would assist the growth of a healthy merchant marine and increase sales abroad, without affecting adversely the wages and living standards of the American workmen. To accomplish this, he suggested a "series of reciprocal commercial treaties" with the Latin American nations, the placing of the consular service on a salary basis, the passage of laws favoring the construction of a greater merchant marine, and the Pan American adoption of a uniform currency system.[18]

Almost immediately the new Colombian minister, Ricardo Becerra,[19] advised Secretary Frelinghuysen that his country was willing and anxious to negotiate an agreement similar to the ones signed with Mexico and the Dominican Republic. Correspondence and confer-

[15] Act of July 7, 1884. The idea was not new (Carlos Butterfield [N. Y.] to Seward, Sept. 25, 1868, Misc. Let., 1868).

[16] Inst. to Specl. Com. to Central and South American States, Aug. 27, 1884, Specl. Missions, III, 352-359.

[17] Report of the commission, Specl. Agts., I, II.

[18] Dec. 1, 1884, Richardson, *Messages and Papers*, X, 4838-4839.

[19] Colombia had lacked representation at Washington from Feb. 15, 1881, to Oct. 18, 1884.

ences followed and a text was agreed upon. But before Becerra could secure full powers from Bogotá, it became evident that the other two treaties would not be approved by the Senate.²⁰ It was not until the Harrison administration that reciprocity agreements were again attempted.

Meanwhile, the volume of trade between the two nations had rapidly decreased. The $16,717,030 total of 1875 shrank to $13,779,286 (1880), $7,925,446 (1885), and $6,161,081 (1890)—even below the level of 1865.²¹ European competition, mutual high tariffs,²² and Colombian political uncertainties were playing havoc with a once profitable trade.

This did not mean, however, that Yankee commercial houses and manufacturers were not seeking opportunities in Colombia.²³ Consul Smith (Cartagena) expressed gratification (1880) with the interest shown and noted a steady shift of trade from European to American hands. But he felt that Americans would profit greatly by adapting themselves "to the tastes of the people," studying and catering to their wants, adopting European sales methods, and making a "direct and forcible effort to drum up" trade.²⁴

But Minister Abbott (1889) was not so optimistic. He was amazed at the American ignorance of Colombian trade conditions, especially since he saw on all sides a general inclination to trade with the Yankee merchants. The Europeans, "instead of sending price-lists in an un-

---

²⁰ Unperfected Treaties, Col. N; Becerra to Frelinghuysen, Dec. 5, 15, 23, 1884. Notes from Col. Leg., VII; Frelinghuysen to Becerra, Dec. 8, 1884, Notes to Col. Leg., VI, 371 ff. Justo Arosemena had suggested a similar agreement—the balancing of coffee and tobacco against cotton goods (Memo. for file, Dec. 11, 1879, Notes from Col. Leg., VII).

²¹ Robertson, *Hispanic-American Relations*, pp. 420-428.

²² Colombia, by Law 88 of Dec. 20, 1886, increased its tariff schedule by 25% (King to Bayard), [105] Jan. 6, 1887, Desp. Col., XL).

²³ The legation at Bogotá was "constantly in receipt" of trade inquiries (Dichman to Evarts, [90] May 19, 1879; *ibid.*, XXXIII).

²⁴ Smith to Hunter, Dec. 31, 1880, Con. Let., Cartagena, VIII.

known tongue to consuls and ministers," sent active representatives, who lived among the people, learned their language, studied their mode of life, opened stores, displayed samples, and sought in every possible way to cater to the wishes and needs of their customers. On the other hand, the American merchant seemed "to act upon the theory that the Colombian . . . [was] only waiting to learn his name to give him an order." Abbott's conclusion was that, if the Yankee merchant wished to trade with Colombia, he "must at least take as much pains to introduce his goods to these people as he . . . [did] to sell to the country merchants at home."[25] The Yankees seemed not to realize that circular letters were poor substitutes for personal contacts and that it might prove more profitable to create products suitable for the Colombian market than to create a demand there for standard American goods.

RETALIATORY RECIPROCITY (1890-1894)

The trade enthusiasts of the Pan American Conference of 1889 revived the idea of reciprocity. Argentina was quick to suggest negotiations on that basis. Secretary Blaine made capital of this agitation to secure a reciprocity clause in the McKinley Tariff Act of 1890.[26]

This act empowered the president to remove sugar, molasses, coffee, tea, and hides from the free list, whenever he was convinced that the duties on American products in the ports of nations exporting these enumerated articles were "reciprocally unjust and unequal."[27] Since these articles and practically all others from Colombia already entered duty free,[28] this law, in effect, empowered the president to retaliate by placing a tariff on them, should that power refuse to reduce or

[25] Report of Sept. 4, 1889, *H. Misc. Doc.*, No. 232 (51.1) XXV, 201-206.

[26] Robertson, *Hispanic-American Relations*, pp. 214-215.

[27] *Ibid.*, pp. 215-216; *Statutes at Large*, XXVI, 612.

[28] W. E. Curtis, *Trade and Transportation between the United States and Spanish America*, p. 40.

abolish its duties on certain American goods—hence, retaliatory reciprocity.

Agreements were soon negotiated with Brazil, the Dominican Republic, Salvador, Nicaragua, Honduras, and Guatemala,[29] but Colombia hesitated. When more than a year had passed without the Colombian minister being empowered to treat on the subject, Blaine dispatched instructions to Bogotá. He reminded Minister Abbott that the desired convention was in line with Colombia's proposals of 1884 and argued that since no European nation could offer the same exemptions, such an agreement could not be at variance with any most-favored-nation clause.[30]

In January, 1892, Blaine wrote Abbott that the proclamation making effective the reciprocity clause against Colombia would be withheld, if success was imminent at Bogotá;[31] but he advised Minister Hurtado that an agreement must be reached by March 15. He considered it "reciprocally unequal and unreasonable" that practically all Colombian products were on the free list, while American goods still paid duties in Colombian ports.[32]

Hurtado complained of the short time allowed, since only the Colombian congress could alter tariff rates and it did not convene until July 20. He proceeded to point out that forty per cent of the imports from the United States already entered free. On certain other articles no profit would accrue from reduction of rates, since Yankees already enjoyed a monopoly in them. He also

[29] Robertson, *Hispanic-American Relations*, p. 218.

[30] Blaine to Abbott, (129) Dec. 4, 1890, (217) Oct. 12, 1891, Inst. Col., XVIII, 222-225, 281 ff.; Unperfected Treaties, Col., N.

[31] Blaine to Abbott, (235) Jan. 12, 1892, Inst. Col., XVII. See also Abbott's Nos. 274, 278, 284, 285, 289, 292, 298, 312, 337, 339, 372, 394, 395, 397, 404.

[32] Blaine to Hurtado, Jan. 7, 1892, Notes to Col. Leg., VII, 184-186. Acting Secretary Wharton estimated (1891) that only two-fifths of one per cent of Colombian products paid duties in American ports, while at least 80% of Yankee products paid in Colombian ports. He advised the Senate that the same condition had existed for years and pointed out an unfavorable trade balance of $1,582,710 (*Sen. Ex. Doc.*, No. 68 [52.1]).

reminded the State Department of Colombia's liberal policy in exempting Isthmian commerce from "tonnage and other dues."[33] To Blaine's show of impatience at the delay,[34] Hurtado argued that Colombia had already conceded enough in the Treaty of 1846. Besides, he saw no reason why his country could not deal with the matter legislatively as the United States had done. Colombia was willing to coöperate, but preferred to choose its own method. He assured Blaine, however, that the matter of the extension of the free list would be presented to the next Congress; therefore he hoped that American retaliatory action would be postponed.[35]

After the passing of eighteen months without an acceptable proposal from Colombia,[36] President Harrison issued a proclamation (March 15, 1892) placing duties on Colombian coffee, sugar, and hides.[37] Hurtado protested on the basis of "discrimination against Colombian produce, in favor of goods of like character from other countries," declared it "contrary to the spirit and express stipulations of the Treaty of 1846," and gave notice of the reservation of all Colombian treaty rights.[38] This note was ignored by the Department, and a subsequent one expressly requesting tariff exemption for coffee and hides[39] was not answered for two months— then, merely to advise that the President did not consider his policy as a treaty violation.[40]

After failure to convince the new secretary of state, John W. Foster, of the validity of the Colombian arguments, Hurtado demanded reparations for injury to his country's commerce, caused by American violation of

[33] Hurtado to Blaine, Feb. 25, 1892, Notes from Col. Leg., VIII.
[34] Blaine to Hurtado, March 7, 1892, Notes to Col. Leg., VII, 186.
[35] Hurtado to Blaine, March 12, 1892, Notes from Col. Leg., VIII.
[36] Blaine to Hurtado, March 14, 1892, Notes to Col. Leg., VII.
[37] Richardson, *Messages and Papers*, XIV, 5700.
[38] Hurtado to Blaine, March 23, 1892, Notes from Col. Leg., VIII. This letter was not acknowledged.
[39] Hurtado to Blaine, March 25, 1892, *ibid.*
[40] Blaine to Hurtado, May 31, 1892, Notes to Col. Leg., VII.

Articles II, III, and V of the Treaty of 1846.[41] Still getting no action—not even replies to his notes—he secured a conference with Foster, only to find the latter greatly concerned over the "grave charges" made against the United States.[42]

Soon, however, new instructions arrived from Bogotá, and Hurtado softened his language considerably. The Colombian president had decided to request Congress to remove the duties on certain American products —previously agreed to by Foster and Hurtado—and requested the suspension of Harrison's proclamation, as soon as such action was taken.[43] Foster would promise nothing, but felt that a settlement was possible in case of favorable congressional action at Bogotá.[44] Hurtado hastened to assure him that the tenor of his former note had been misinterpreted.[45] But evidently such an explanation was not acceptable, since Foster wired Abbott that the Colombian minister still appeared "quite unfriendly."[46] Protests from the Colombian legation continued,[47] but the Department remained adamant, and the Congress at Bogotá failed to pass the promised legislation.

IMPROVED TRADE RELATIONS (1894-1905)

The Democratic victory in the United States naturally brought a change in policy. The Wilson Tariff Act of 1894 terminated the reciprocal arrangements made under the former law. Three days after its passage Secretary Gresham wired Bogotá: "Colombian coffee and hides on

[41] Hurtado to Foster, July 5, 25, 1892, Notes from Col. Leg., VIII. See also Uribe, *Anales*, IV, 598-602, 650-653.

[42] Memo. of Hurtado interview, Aug. 24, 1892, Notes from Col. Leg., VIII.

[43] Hurtado to Foster, Sept. 5, 1892, *ibid.*

[44] Foster to Hurtado, Sept. 8, 1892, Notes to Col. Leg., VII, 203.

[45] Hurtado to Foster, Sept. 14, 1892, Notes from Col. Leg., VIII.

[46] Foster to Abbott, (tel.) Sept. 21, 1892, Inst. Col., XVIII, 327.

[47] Rengifo to Gresham, June 16, Hurtado to Gresham, Oct. 5, 31, 1893, Notes from Col. Leg., VIII.

free list since Monday midnight.''[48] American politics had availed where Colombian protests had failed.

On returning to power the Republicans again incorporated the reciprocal principle in the new Dingley Tariff Act of 1897. This provided for trade agreements somewhat similar to those negotiated under the McKinley Act—except sugar and hides were dutiable in any case—and for formal reciprocity treaties, under certain conditions. But Colombia made no move to negotiate a convention of either type.[49] Although Secretary Sherman would not admit Colombian exemption under the Treaty of 1846,[50] severe pressure was never exerted to enforce conformity. It seems that Minister Hart practically assured the Bogotá authorities that the law would never be applied in a manner detrimental to the existing commercial relations.[51]

In spite of considerable uncertainty concerning tariff schedules, the American war with Spain, a Colombian civil war, and the secession of Panama, commerce between the two nations steadily increased after 1890. The $6,161,081 of that year grew to $6,309,984 (1895), $7,018,502 (1900), and $9,994,582 (1905). Even this figure had more than trebled by 1916.[52]

[48] Gresham to McKinney, (tel.) Aug. 30, 1894, Inst. Col., XVIII; Robertson, *Hispanic-American Relations*, p. 218.

[49] In fact, only four nations—Germany, France, Italy, and Portugal—made agreements and none made formal treaties under this act. The reciprocity provisions were repealed in 1909 (F. W. Taussig, *The Tariff History of the United States*, pp. 353-354, 407; D. R. Dewey, *Financial History of the United States*, p. 465).

[50] Sherman to Hart, (41) Nov. 26, 1897, Inst. Col. XVIII, 625-626.

[51] Informe de 1898—Restrepo, Uribe, *Anales*, IV, 760-761.

[52] Robertson, *Hispanic-American Relations*, pp. 420-428.

CHAPTER XVII

YANKEE ECONOMIC ADVENTURES IN COLOMBIA
(1846-1903)

SINCE the demand for Isthmian transportation facilities was already pronounced, the Treaty of 1846
inspired sufficient confidence to enlist North American
capital. Even before ratification, mail contracts had been
made with five vessels plying between New York and
Chagres and three between Panama and Oregon.[1]

THE PANAMA RAILROAD COMPANY

In December, 1848, John L. Stephens, William H.
Aspinwall, and Henry Chauncey concluded a contract
with Minister Herrán for the construction of a railroad
across the Isthmus. The following year the Panama
Railroad Company was chartered by the New York legislature. Its concession—somewhat altered, but still quite
liberal—was approved at Bogotá on June 4, 1850. A
forty-nine-year exclusive privilege for constructing and
operating the railroad was granted in return for three
per cent of the net annual profits and the reversion of
the property at the end of the period to Colombia.[2]

Work was soon begun and the road was opened to
traffic on January 27, 1855. Its construction was accomplished at the enormous cost of some $8,000,000, six
thousand lives, and untold suffering.[3] From the beginning, however, the monetary returns were substantial.

[1] Richardson, *Messages and Papers*, V, 2411.
[2] Herrán to Clayton, July 24, 1849, Notes from Col. Leg., II; *Sen. Doc.*,
No. 264 (57.1), pp. 203-211.
[3] *Report of John L. Bristow, Special Panama Railroad Commission, to
the Secretary of War* (Washington, 1905), also published as *Sen. Doc.*,
No. 429 (59.1); Forbes Lindsay, *Panama and the Canal Today*, pp. 41 ff.;
Rippy, *The Capitalists and Colombia*, pp. 39-43; Robertson, *Hispanic-
American Relations*, pp. 252-256.

The lowest annual dividend prior to 1885 was three per cent (1871) and the highest was forty-four per cent (1868)—exclusive of stock dividends of ten per cent in 1853 and forty per cent in 1865. The total dividends paid on a capital stock never exceeding $7,000,000 (increased to this amount by the stock dividends of 1885) reached the enormous figure of $37,798,840.12 during the period from 1853 to 1905.[4]

The financial success of the project and a growing interest in a canal, on the one hand, and the virtual bankruptcy of the Colombian treasury, on the other, made a new contract desirable by 1867. The concession was extended for ninety-nine years, and Colombia was to receive therefor $1,000,000 in cash and $250,000 annuity. The reversionary rights in the road were retained, as well as one half of the indemnity, which might be demanded from any corporation undertaking the construction of a canal by the same route.[5]

Later the French Panama Canal Company deprived Colombia of any share in this indemnity by purchasing 68,534 of the 70,000 shares of the railroad stock. But American investors profited handsomely by the sale, since they secured some $291 per share—$250 contract price plus the division of the cash and surplus on hand—for stock, which had already paid more than four hundred per cent on par valuation. The remaining shares later came into the hands of the United States government.[6]

THE CHIRIQUÍ IMPROVEMENT COMPANY

Work had scarcely begun on the Panama railroad before advocates appeared for a road between the Chiriquí

[4] *Bristow Report*, pp. 336 ff.

[5] Text of contract, *Sen. Doc.*, No. 264 (57.1), pp. 211-218; Sullivan to Seward, (17) Aug. 16, 1867, Desp. Col., XXVI.

[6] *Bristow Report*, pp. 336 ff.; Tracy Robinson, *Panama: A Personal Record*, p. 112; Lindsay, *Panama*, pp. 46 ff.; Rippy, *The Capitalists and Colombia*, pp. 43-44. For the indemnity controversy, see. Barlow and Coudert to Blaine, May 10, 1889, *Sen. Doc.*, No. 264 (57.1), pp. 196-232.

Lagoon and the town of David.[7]   In February, 1854, the provincial legislature granted a sixty-year exclusive concession (including 120,000 acres of land) to Ambrose W. Thompson. The grant was soon transferred to the Chiriquí Improvement Company, which secured a Pennsylvania charter. The validity of the concession seems to have been admitted by the Granadian attorney-general in 1855 and by Minister Herrán in 1859.[8]

For strategic reasons President Buchanan was interested in the grant.[9]   After conferences and title examination the Navy Department (May, 1859) signed an agreement with the company for the use of the harbors and five thousand acres of land on each side of the Isthmus for naval stations and depots, and for the right to traverse the company's highway and to secure coal from its mines.[10]

This contract naturally required congressional ratification. The House committee on naval affairs reported favorably and recommended the appropriation of the $300,000 purchase price. The bill failed of passage, but the sum of $10,000 was provided for more accurate surveys. In January, 1861, Buchanan transmitted to the House a favorable report of the surveys.[11]   But Congress soon adjourned without action, and Buchanan turned the reigns of government over to Lincoln, who was forced to direct his efforts towards saving the Union.

[7] B. Franklin Jackson (ed.), *A Brief Description of the Facilities and Advantages* . . . (Philadelphia, 1852). This contains five favorable survey reports and a representation from the inhabitants of David.

[8] William W. Warden and Charles A. Eldridge, *The Chiriquí and Golfito Naval Stations Matter*, p. 6; *Report of Hon. F. H. Morse . . . from the Committee of Naval Affairs, House of Representatives, in Relation to the Contract . . . for Coal and Other Privileges on the Isthmus of Chiriquí*, also printed as *H. Rep.*, No. 568 (36.1), pp. 14-35.

[9] It has been claimed that Herrán brought Thompson and the Administration together (Warden and Eldridge, *op. cit.*, p. 6).

[10] *H. Rep.*, No. 568 (36.1).

[11] A minority report expressed doubt of the right to convey (*ibid.*, pp. 1-13; *H. Ex. Doc.*, No. 41 [36.2], pp. 1-56).

Meanwhile, Thompson's application for the privilege to construct a railroad between Bocas del Toro and David had been unanimously rejected by the Granadian senate. Fear of too much Yankee influence and the Panama railroad's opposition seem to have been the determining factors.[12]   The Bogotá government not only expressed surprise that Washington would contract with the Chiriquí Improvement Company without its consent, but protested vigorously against the transference of the privilege.   The Granadian supreme court (1860) even declared the contract void.[13]

Although considering the grant valid, Secretary Cass questioned whether it included the right to build a railroad.   Buchanan had no doubts on this point and thought the traffic sufficient for two roads.[14]   But New Granada's refusal of Thompson's application made the project impossible.

Thompson, ever on the alert to realize on his property, lost little time in securing a contract with the Lincoln cabinet after Congress had made $600,000 available for the colonization of freed Negroes.[15]   The Cabinet even discussed the plan of sending the Negroes to Chiriquí to mine coal for the navy.   Senator Pomeroy suggested that he go along as government agent and carry a cargo of Negroes with him.   Lincoln, however, insisted on formal treaty arrangements before any colonization began.[16]

[12] Jones to Cass, (19) Jan. 28, (21) Feb. 28, 1860, Desp. Col., XXIV.

[13] Enclosures with Jones to Cass, No. 27 and Dec. 11, 1860, *ibid.;* Pombo to Black, Feb. 27, 1861, Notes from Col. Leg., III.

[14] Cass to Jones, (18) May 4, 1860, Inst. Col., XV, 303-308. See also Thomas F. Meagher, ''The New Route through Chiriquí,'' *Harper's Monthly Magazine* (June, 1861), XXII, 198-209. The *Panama Star and Herald* (Feb. 8, 1860) reported several Texans on their way to settle in Chiriquí.

[15] John George Nicolay and John Hay, *Abraham Lincoln*, VI, 357-358; Warden and Eldridge, *op. cit.*, pp. 10-11.

[16] J. T. Morse, Jr. (ed.), *Diary of Gideon Welles*, I, 123, 150-153, 162. In a pamphlet, *Information for Persons Proposing to Join the Free Colored Colony of Central America*, Pomeroy set the date of departure at Oct. 1, 1862. See also Andrew N. Cleven, ''Some Plans for Colonizing Liberated Slaves in Hispanic America,'' *The Southwestern Pol. and Soc. Sci. Quar.*, VI, 151-166.

But the new Bogotá government had not been recognized, and the European powers possessing tropical lands evinced no interest when approached regarding negotiations.[17]

Meanwhile, Thompson was attempting to secure Colombian permission for the settlement of his grant with Negro colonists. He elaborated the plans to Señor F. Párraga, fiscal agent at New York. Five hundred Negroes were to sail in the fall of 1862. The American government was to finance the project and receive its pay in coal. Besides Colombian approval of this project, he desired the exclusive grant of 3,000,000 acres of unoccupied land along the Magdalena River for 50,000 more Negroes.[18] Párraga, after a conference with Minister Murillo,[19] advised Thompson that he had no instructions on the matter, but could give an idea of Colombia's attitude. If proper provisions for the physical care of the emigrants during the first year were made and the colonists became Colombian citizens (thereby renouncing all claim to foreign protection), Colombia would "not only consent, but . . . [would] see with satisfaction, and . . . [would] encourage" the emigration of even more than fifty thousand.[20]

However, the protests of the Central American states[21] and the Administration's decision to enlist the freed Negroes in the Federal army brought disappointment to both Thompson and Pomeroy.[22] But the former

[17] Seward to Adams, Sept. 30, 1862, Inst. G. B., XVIII; Seward to Dayton, Sept. 30, 1862, Inst. Fr., XVI; Adams to Seward, (253), Oct. 30, 1862, *For. Rel.* (1862), pp. 227-228.

[18] Thompson to Párraga, Sept. 20, 1862, published in *Panama Star and Herald*, Oct. 30, 1862.

[19] Murillo represented the Mosquera government, which was not recognized until 1863.

[20] Párraga to Thompson, Sept. 26, 1862, *Panama Star and Herald*, Oct. 30, 1862.

[21] These states did not object to the Negroes, but feared subsequent United States intervention and also possible Confederate attack.

[22] Benjamin P. Poore, *Reminiscences of Sixty Years in the National Metropolis*, II, 107; Cleven, *op. cit.*, pp. 154-155; Warden and Eldridge,

did not remain inactive. In March, 1866, he signed a contract in London with Tomás C. de Mosquera (then minister to Great Britain, but soon to return as Colombian president) for the construction of a communication across Chiriquí. The contract received congressional approval, but was never executed.[23]

The attention of President Grant was called to the possibilities of the Chiriquí concession,[24] but little governmental interest was shown until 1880. A House resolution of February 7 recommended the acquisition of suitable locations for coaling stations in the Chiriquí area.[25] In spite of Colombian protests and Isthmian excitement, two vessels were sent to make surveys and soundings. The Department still considered Thompson's grant valid. It did intend to request Colombia's consent to the transfer, but expected to make no compensation therefor.[26]

Coal was actually deposited at two ports,[27] and President Hayes (February 2, 1881) recommended the appropriation of $200,000 for the establishment of the stations.[28] It seems, however, that congressional doubt

---

op. cit., p. 11. This did not mean, however, that the scheme was forgotten. Minister Burton forwarded the Department a ninety-three-page report by John May, a civil engineer, on the practicability of settling the freed Negroes in Colombia (March 24, 1863, Desp. Col., XVIII). It was reported in Panama (1865) that General Sickles had been sent there to arrange for a Negro colony. The *Mercantile Chronicle* (Panama) published the rumor that the United States had paid $1,000,000 for the privilege and that 30,000 colonists would soon arrive. Some Colombians feared that it would be another case of Texas, while others thought that the Negroes would be more peaceful and submissive than Texans (Sickles to Seward, Feb. 23, 1865, Desp. Col., XX).

[23] *Diario oficial*, Nos. 646, 676; Burton to Seward, (249) June 30, 1866, Desp. Col., XXIV.

[24] Warden and Eldridge, *op. cit.*, p. 12.

[25] *H. Rep.*, No. 390 (46.3), II, 7. It was reported that the English were casting about for likely coaling stations in the area.

[26] Arosemena to Evarts, Feb. 13, April 1, 15, 1880, Notes from Col. Leg., VII; Evarts to Dichman, April 19, 1880, Inst. Col., XVII, 147-153.

[27] Report of Secretary of Navy, Nov. 30, 1880, *H. Rep.*, No. 390 (46.3), II, 7.

[28] Richardson, *Messages and Papers*, X, 4586; Warden and Eldridge, *op. cit.*, p. 12.

regarding the validity of the grant[29] caused the matter to be dropped.[30]

OTHER ISTHMIAN TRANSPORTATION ADVENTURES

The interest and activities of William Duane, William Wheelwright, Charles Biddle, and William Radcliff regarding an interoceanic communication have already been discussed.[31] In this connection at least three other Yankees deserve mention. Joseph Gooding[32] secured a contract in 1855 to construct a road across the Province of Chocó,[33] but was unable to execute it.

More important was Frederick M. Kelley, "a mystical and imaginative New York capitalist," who became interested in a canal as early as 1851. He made seven surveys at his own expense, helped to secure three governmental surveys, and spent some $125,000 attempting to realize his dream. Although never securing a formal concession or organizing a construction company, he spent some thirty years promoting the canal idea.[34]

The third, Anthony de Gogorza,[35] manifested an interest around 1864. Unlike Kelley, he was convinced of the existence of a natural passage between the two oceans. He made a partial survey and then conferred with members of the Grant administration. Securing no encouragement, he presented his project to the International Geographical Congresses of 1871 and 1875. The enthusiastic reception there of his plan sent him to Bogotá to

[29] See reports of Secretary of Navy (Nov. 28, 1881) and House committee on naval affairs (July 31, 1882).

[30] Warden and Eldridge, *op. cit.*, pp. 12-13. An effort to revive the project in 1898 proved futile (Confidential report of the Navy Department, filed, Feb. 12, 1900, Misc. Let.).

[31] See *supra*, chap. xi.

[32] Evidently the Goodings had lived long in Colombia, since Albert Gooding had been involved with Harrison in 1829.

[33] Uribe, *Anales*, V, 616.

[34] Frederick M. Kelley, *The Union of the Oceans by Ship-Canal without Locks via the Atrato Valley; H. Misc. Doc.*, No. 16 (46.3); Rippy, *The Capitalists and Colombia*, pp. 45-49.

[35] An American by birth but long a resident of Colombia.

secure a concession and back to Europe to organize a company. His project, however, soon merged with the French Panama Canal Company, and Gogorza disappeared from the scene.[36]

SUNDRY INVESTMENTS ON THE ISTHMUS

Other activities interested the Yankees on the Isthmus. The *Panama Star and Herald,* published by A. B. Boyd, made its appearance in 1852.[37] The property at his death passed to his children by a Colombian wife. Evidently fearing that the transfer had destroyed the American character of the property, the heirs secured a New York charter in 1883. Although this "pretended change in nationality" was not recognized by Colombia,[38] it served admirably in securing State Department support in the collection of a claim for the paper's temporary suppression in 1885.

Around 1866 the Boston Ice Company was engaged in an ice, lumber, and general merchandise business in Panama and Colón. The investment must have been considerable, since its estimated loss during the Colón fire of 1885 amounted to $194,356[39] (business at Panama City unaffected) and the Colombian effort in 1887 to establish a national monopoly on ice brought the full force of the State Department to the support of the company.[40] By 1871 H. Shuber and Brother were not only

[36] Washburn (Paris) to Fish, (1369) Sept. 13, 1876, *For. Rel.* (1877), pp. 125-126. A letter from Gogorza to President Grant was enclosed.

[37] The *Panama Star* appeared around 1849, the *Herald* a little later. The two were combined in 1852 (Tracy Robinson, *op. cit.,* p. 253; Chas. T. Bidwell, *op. cit.,* p. 261).

[38] Blaine to Hurtado, Jan. 31, 1890, Notes to Col. Leg., VII, 168; Rengifo to Hay, Nov. 26, 1898, Notes from Col. Leg., IX. James Boyd, a brother, was also connected with the paper from 1863 to 1882 (*The Athenæum,* June 10, 1882).

[39] See *infra,* chap. xix.

[40] Protest of the Boston Ice Company, Aug. 27, 1885, *Sen. Doc.,* No. 264 (57.1), pp. 46-47; Inst. Col., XVIII. The claim for damages included: lumber, $84,700; merchandise, $30,126; ice, $16,000; buildings, furniture, and fixtures, $33,530; business interruption, $30,000.

trading in Panama but operating a steamer between certain Isthmian ports.[41]

Under a concession of 1867 the International Ocean Telegraph Company of New York had laid a cable between New York and Colón. The Central and South American Telegraph Company of New York constructed a line between San Juan del Sur and Panama, also between Panama and Colón.[42] The Pacific Mail Steamship Company, chartered in New York in 1848, had seventeen vessels in service by 1889.[43]

It was reported in 1856 that former Consul Nelson and an American steamship company owned practically all of a group of islands near the Panama harbor. The award of some $195,500 for damages caused by the Panama Riot of 1856 indicated a substantial beginning for Yankee investments in that city, while claims to the amount of some $3,750,000 growing out of the Colón fire of 1885 clearly evidenced the presence of much North American capital in Colón business and real estate. Even investments at Bocas del Toro were sufficient to call for naval protection in 1895.[44]

ADVENTURES ON THE MAINLAND

Yankees early realized the importance of the Magdalena River in Colombian economic development. An American-built steamer was plying its waters as early as 1825.[45] Colonel George H. Totten (later connected with the Panama railroad) contracted in 1844 to reopen the old canal *(el dique)* from above Cartagena to the sea.[46] When it again became obstructed (1855), Henry Ven-

[41] See ''Montijo Claim,'' *infra*, chap. xix.
[42] Sullivan to Seward, (29) Sept. 26, 1867, Desp. Col., XXVI; Bayard to Scruggs, (49) June 24, 1885, Inst. Col., XVII, 458-460; Robertson, *Hispanic-American Relations*, pp. 260-261.
[43] *Ibid.*, pp. 238-239.
[44] Morse to Marcy, Dec. 22, 1856, Secret Service, pp. 649 ff.; *Sen. Doc.*, No. 264 (57.1); *Sen. Doc.*, No. 143 (58.2), pp. 160-164.
[45] *Niles' Reg.* (April 9, 1825), XXVIII, 86.
[46] This canal had been dug by the Spaniards, but had become obstructed.

dryes (British) secured a concession to clear and exclusively navigate it for a sixty-year period. This
privilege was soon acquired by the New Granada Canal
and Steam Navigation Company of New York, in which
some $2,000,000 of Yankee capital were invested.[47] Later
the Atlas Steamship Company of London took over the
project and established a steamer line inland to Honda
through the canal. But the enterprise failed and the
canal was closed to steamers by 1893.[48]

In the early 1820's a German citizen (Elbers) secured
a twenty-year exclusive privilege for the steam navigation of the Magdalena.[49] Around 1846 the United Magdalena Steam Navigation Company was organized in
Europe. Gradually North Americans purchased $162,500
of the $360,000 capital stock and moved the business
offices to New York. Alexander Weckbecker (Yankee)
was also operating steamers on the river by 1858. However, competition and seizures during civil wars prevented expected returns on the investments.[50] John
Bidlake of New Jersey failed to execute his contract
(1902) to place boats on the Caquetá and Putumayo rivers, but the American Transport Line was operating four
steamers and one gasoline launch between the Caribbean
ports and Quibdó on the Atrato in 1903.[51]

Americans likewise interested themselves in railroad-
building on the Mainland. Charles S. Brown obtained a
contract (1875) to construct one through the Cauca Valley.[52] Although this project failed, the New York and
South American Contract Company (1878) was awarded
a contract on one hundred and ten miles from Cali to the

[47] New Granada Canal and Steam Navigation Company, *Remarks on the Canal or "Dique" of Cartagena . . .* (New York, 1885).

[48] *Con. Rep.*, Sept., 1884; *Monthly Con. and Trade Rep.*, Aug., 1908, pp. 60-61.

[49] Cochrane, *op. cit.*, II, 477.

[50] Rippy, *The Capitalists and Colombia*, pp. 52-53; Scruggs to Fish, (166) May 18, 1876, Desp. Col., XXXI; *For. Rel.* (1866-1867), pp. 552 ff.

[51] *Monthly Con. Rep.* (1904), LXXV, 43 ff.

[52] Scruggs to Fish, (80) Jan. 6, (126) Oct. 17, 1875, Desp. Col., XXIX.

Pacific Coast.[53] After the failure of certain Illinois and Colombian engineers, Francisco J. Cisneros (Cuban born, but a naturalized American) took charge. But a revolution soon prevented operations. In 1891 James Cherry of California secured a new contract, and West Virginia chartered the Cauca Company to complete the work. However, internal disorder and lack of funds prevented the completion of the road until 1914.[54]

Meanwhile, Cisneros had begun the construction of the Antioquia railway between Puerto Berrío and Medellín. He turned the project over to the State of Antioquia in 1885 (not completed until 1929) and started work (1881) on a road between Girardot and Bogotá. Later he assisted on the line between Puerto Colombia and Barranquilla and, at the time of his death, was on the eve of joining Barranquilla with the Cartagena-Calamar system. Numerous American engineers were associated with Cisneros in these adventures.[55]

The Cartagena-Calamar road had been constructed under a contract granted to S. S. McConnico in 1889. During the 1890's he organized at Boston the Cartagena Terminal and Improvement Company, the Cartagena-Magdalena Railway Company, and the Compañía Fluvial de Cartagena. By August, 1894, the Cartagena wharfs and sixty-seven miles of railroad had been completed. In spite of the civil war of 1899-1903, the work seems to have progressed. It was turned over to British capitalists in 1906.[56]

At least three other concessions were granted to Americans: Santa Lucía-Medellín road to J. T. O'Bryan and C. L. Wright (1903), Gulf of Urabá-Medellín to Henry Granger (1905), and Buenaventura-Palmira-Bogotá to A. B. and E. H. Mason (1906). Although none of these lines were completed as expected,[57] the Bogotá

[53] Evarts to Dichman, (20) Dec. 13, 1878, Inst. Col., XVII.
[54] Rippy, *The Capitalists and Colombia*, p. 54.
[55] *Ibid.*, pp. 54-55. [56] *Ibid.*, p. 56-57. [57] *Ibid.*, p. 56.

Street Railway Company of New York was more successful. After the transference of the original concession of 1882 from W. W. Randall to this company, the road was soon in operation. But the ill-repair of the roadbed and the poor service rendered the public caused the Bogotá city government to take over the company in 1911.[58]

Mining and agriculture likewise attracted American capital. Boston and Philadelphia interests put some $500,000 in the mines of Chocó, and a considerable amount was invested in the Antioquia area.[59] Yankees acquired numerous coffee, sugar, and banana plantations. The Eder family have made enormous contributions to the agricultural development of the Cauca Valley since 1862. The Snyder Banana Company of New Jersey controlled considerable acreage near Bocas del Toro, and Minor C. Keith was rapidly acquiring control of the Colombian Land Company (British) in the Santa Marta district by 1895. Four years later the United Fruit entered. It purchased the interests of both the above companies and increased its acreage from 13,035 in 1900 to 32,826 improved and 49,177 unimproved by 1913—exclusive of the Bocas del Toro holdings. By 1916 the United Fruit investments probably totalled $3,000,000.[60]

Information concerning lumber operations is meager. But it is known that the Boston Ice Company was trading in that commodity on the Isthmus around 1866,[61] the Vroomans of Philadelphia and the Emerys of Boston were logging in Chocó before 1900, and two American sawmills and one woodworking plant were operating on the Atrato in 1903.[62] Yankee urban investments were considerable, even outside of Panama and Colón, but

[58] Abbott to Blaine, (134) Sept. 16, (163) Dec. 8, 1890, Desp. Col., XLV; *For. Rel.* (1904), p. 227; Uribe, *Anales*, V, 96-97.
[59] Rippy, *The Capitalists and Colombia*, p. 58.
[60] *Ibid.*, pp. 58-59; F. M. Halsey, *Investments in Latin America and the West Indies*, p. 281.
[61] Bayard to Walker, (63) March 6, 1888, Inst. Col., XVIII, 39-44.
[62] *Monthly Con. Rep.* (1904), LXXV, 43 ff.

were made in such small amounts that accurate figures are unavailable.

A few investors also made loans. In 1880 the Panama Railroad Company advanced the Núñez government $3,000,000 to be deducted from the regular annuities due under the railroad concession.[63] Substantial loans were also made annually by the United Fruit Company and certain coffee traders to the native growers—probably amounting to $500,000.[64] However, other official negotiations in 1900 proved unsuccessful.[65]

It is estimated that Yankee interests in Colombia reached the peak in 1881, with the total of $14,000,000: Panama Railroad, $8,000,000; loans, $3,500,000; urban real estate, $1,000,000;[66] miscellaneous, $1,500,000.[67] The passing of the railroad into French hands (1881), the destruction of the Colón fire (1885), the civil war (1899-1903), and the secession of Panama (1903) greatly reduced the above total. The low level came probably in 1913, when estimates vary from $2,000,000 to $4,000,000.[68]

[63] Dichman to Evarts, (99) June 19, 1879, (196) Aug. 11, (235) Dec. 20, 1880, Desp. Col., XXXIII, XXXIV, XXXV; J. T. DuBois, ''Colombia's Claims and Rights,'' *Cong. Rec.*, appendix (63.2), LI, 779.

[64] Rippy, *The Capitalists and Colombia*, p. 60.

[65] ''Have seen your friend. The President thinks no legal authority to make or guarantee such a loan'' (Hay to Hart, [tel.] July 2, 1900, Inst. Col., XIX, 107).

[66] The fact that some $3,750,000 were claimed as damages caused by the Colón fire of 1885 might indicate that this figure is too low.

[67] Rippy, *The Capitalists and Colombia*, p. 61.

[68] *Ibid.*, p. 62.

Chapter XVIII

THE PROTECTION OF UNITED STATES CITIZENS AND INTERESTS

(1845-1861)

CONTINUED disturbances on the Isthmus naturally endangered life and property, but did not prevent Yankees from acquiring considerable interests there. These investors invariably retained their American citizenship[1] and called upon the State Department for protection in time of danger and diplomatic pressure for indemnity after the occurrence of losses. On thirteen different and distinct occasions (1856-1903) American troops were employed to render this protection and to maintain an open transit route.

The strategic position of the Isthmus undoubtedly caused Washington to give these citizens and investments consideration quite out of proportion to their number and value. An open transit was considered essential for the proper development of the West Coast. Besides, if chronic disorders should prevent peaceful Isthmian traffic, powerful European nations might seize the area, thereby endangering American security and prestige and making void the Monroe Doctrine.

CONTINUED EFFORTS TO ADJUST CLAIMS (1845-1856)

Chargé Bidlack's instructions (1845) gave information on some ten outstanding claims originating between 1813 and 1841.[2] But with negotiations soon in progress for the removal of the discriminating tariffs on American goods, the time proved inopportune to urge them. The Treaty of 1846 made no claims adjustment. The

[1] In fact, many Europeans stopped in the United States just long enough to be naturalized before proceeding to the Isthmus.

[2] Buchanan to Bidlack, June 23, 1845, Inst. Col., XV, 93.

unsettled conditions following the elections of 1849 convinced Chargé King that "a different appeal, one to their fears, should be made, experience having demonstrated that an appeal to their sense of justice . . . [was] in vain."[3]

His successor requested (1854) the stationing of naval forces near the Isthmus and along the Mainland coast to protect life and property and to assist in the collection of claims. But the Department was unwilling to go to such limits, at least until the Bogotá government was better organized.[4] In 1855 Minister Bowlin was instructed to negotiate for the settlement of claims,[5] but little progress was made. The following year Commodore William Mervine prevented the inception of possible claims by threatening "forcible resistance" to the collection of tonnage duties on American vessels in the Panama harbor.[6] It would seem then that Washington was unwilling to use force for the collection of claims, but not averse to such action for their prevention.

A FIRMER POLICY (1856-1860)

The Panama Riot[7] caused a general stiffening of American policy, almost to the point of using duress to secure reparation for Yankee losses. The news of the riot threw the inhabitants of San Francisco into a frenzy. The early restoration of peace on the Isthmus alone prevented the dispatching of volunteers to the area.[8] American naval forces were rushed to both Panama and Colón.

Minister Herrán claimed that these were sent "for the purpose of taking possession of the Isthmus," but

[3] King to Webster, (10) Oct. 1, 1852, Desp. Col., XII.
[4] Green to Marcy, (7) April 22, (9) May 23, 1854, *ibid.*, XIII; Marcy to Green, (19) June 19, 1854, Inst. Col., XV.
[5] Marcy to Bowlin, (4) Jan. 30, 1855, *ibid.*, XV, 194 ff.
[6] Marcy to Herrán, Dec. 22, 1856, Notes to Col. Leg., VI, 62.
[7] See *supra*, chap. xiii.
[8] *San Francisco Daily Herald*, May 4, 7, 11, 18, 1856.

that the orders were revoked and negotiations agreed to.[9]
This is quite improbable. Yet it is known that some
favored the acquisition of the area. Special investigator
A. B. Corwine argued that the Isthmus "must sooner or
later fall into the hands of the United States" and, since
"the fruit . . . [was already] ripe—we need only come
and take it."[10] Such an aggressive move was undoubtedly feared not only by New Granada but by other Latin
American states. At a Bogotá celebration (July 20, 1856)
Señor Arosemena suggested a great Southern Confederacy—*Colombianos* v. *Americanos*—as the only effective
remedy.[11] The Washington representatives of New Granada, Mexico, Guatemala, Salvador, Costa Rica, Peru, and
Venezuela (November, 1856) discussed a "union for the
common defense against possible foreign aggressions,
which then seemed imminent." A pact was signed but
never ratified by their governments.[12]

Although the seizure of the Isthmus seems not to have
been officially contemplated, President Pierce recommended that naval forces remain near at hand until New
Granada had made adequate protective arrangements.[13]
The Democratic Platform of 1856 declared for "a timely
and efficient exertion of the control which we [the United
States] have the right to claim" over the Isthmian transit, and against the surrender of "preponderence in the
adjustment of all questions arising out of it."[14]

[9] Herrán to Secretary Garrido, Aug. 6, 1861, enclosed with Jones, No. 59,
Desp. Col., XV.

[10] Corwine to Jefferson Davis, Dec. 31, 1857, Dunbar Rowland (ed.),
Jefferson Davis: Constitutionalist . . . , III, 128. Corwine, after investigat-
ing the riot, had been appointed consul to Panama (Marcy to Bowlin, [26]
Sept. 19, 1856, Inst. Col., XV, 230).

[11] *Harper's Magazine* (Nov., 1856), XIII, 841. Justo Arosemena, how-
ever, was reported to have opposed the Treaty of 1857 for the reason that
New Granada's failure to ratify would mean American seizure of the
Isthmus and, in turn, an increase in the value of his vast estates there
(Jones to Cass, [6] July 12, 1859, Desp. Col., XIV).

[12] Pablo García de la Parra, *Colombia en las conferencias Panamericanas*,
p. 84; Uribe, *Anales*, VI, 619-622.

[13] Dec. 2, 1856, Richardson, *Messages and Papers*, VI, 2949.

[14] Kirk A. Porter (compiler), *National Party Platforms*, p. 46.

The new Democratic president, James Buchanan, however, doubted his possession of the constitutional power
"to employ the land and naval forces" to maintain this
declared predominance and protect properly the endangered lives and interests of Americans. On four different occasions he recommended that Congress so authorize
him.[15] Although the suggested legislation was never
passed, Buchanan ordered the landing of troops twice
(1856 and 1860) on his own authority[16] and attempted
(1859) to secure naval bases near the Panama route.[17]
Henceforth the presidential power to use troops for the
protection of Yankee interests on the Isthmus seems to
have been recognized.

THE TREATIES OF 1857 AND 1864

On receipt of the first news of the Panama Riot, Secretary Marcy was convinced that not only "the people
but the civil authorities of Panama . . . [were] directly
and deeply" implicated. Minister Bowlin was ordered
from Bogotá to the Isthmus; a special investigator, A. B.
Corwine, was dispatched to the scene of the riot; Consul
Ward, already on the ground, was instructed to begin an
inquiry; and naval forces were rushed to Panama and
Colón.[18] When New Granada appeared dilatory in making investigations, punishing the guilty, and providing
indemnity for the losses, Marcy (June 4) instructed
Bowlin to present the whole matter firmly at Bogotá.[19]

Bowlin almost immediately demanded[20] the punishment of "the guilty perpetrators of this heart rending
massacre" and "ample provisions for indemnifying

[15] Dec. 8, 1857, Dec. 6, 1858, Feb. 18, Dec. 19, 1859, Richardson, *Messages
and Papers*, VI, 2978; VII, 3047, 3070, 3100.

[16] See *supra*, chap. xiii.

[17] Chiriquí Improvement Company contract, never ratified by Congress.

[18] Marcy to Bowlin, (19) May 3, 1856, Inst. Col., XV, 216 ff.; Marcy to
Corwine, May 12, 1856, Specl. Missions, III, 74-77.

[19] Marcy to Bowlin, (20) June 4, 1856, Inst. Col., XV, 218 ff.

[20] Since Washington had already been advised, Bowlin had made no move
at Bogotá until specifically instructed.

promptly the sufferers by wounds and robbery, and a reckless destruction of property.'' He insisted that the testimony of more than forty witnesses was at variance with the report of the Panama governor, that the known facts indicated premeditation on the part of the mob, and that the police ''committed their violences, murdering by wholesale, under the express directions of the Governor and his commanding officer.''[21]

Foreign Minister Pombo answered this explosive note in a very conciliatory tone. Several of the guilty had been imprisoned and many stolen articles returned. Besides, he added, New Granada was ''ready to make reparation and mete justice to whomsoever they . . . [should] be due,'' the Governor of Panama not excepted. Yet certain observations seemed in order. He questioned Consul Ward's jurisdiction in gathering evidence, declared the charge of premeditation unfair, and called attention to the race antipathy on the Isthmus and the presence of filibusters among those allegedly attacked. The deficiency of the Panama government was admitted, but defended on the grounds that foreigners objected to the tax levies[22] necessary to maintain a better one. The situation might be improved, Pombo concluded, if there were fewer fire arms, less drunkenness and insolence among railway passengers, and more moral countenance given to the Panama authorities.[23]

Bowlin soon set out for Panama, where he found that the thorough two months' work of Corwine left little for him to do. He was fully convinced that the Panama government would make no efforts to punish the guilty or indemnify for losses and that Bogotá was powerless to compel it. Therefore the seizure of the Isthmus might

[21] Bowlin to Pombo, June 23, 1856, enclosed with Bowlin to Marcy, June 27, 1856, Desp. Col., XIII.

[22] In 1856 Commodore Mervine actually threatened the use of force to prevent collection of the tonnage tax.

[23] Pombo to Bowlin, June 28, 1856, enclosed with Bowlin to Marcy, Aug. 1, 1856, Desp. Col., XIII.

eventually prove necessary for the proper protection of life and property.[24] On returning to Bogotá, Bowlin noted a prevalent belief that the rivalry and jealousy between the United States, Great Britain, and France would prevent any pressure on New Granada.[25] It was hoped that a threatened British blockade to collect the "MacIntosh Loan" would dissipate this idea.[26] But its failure to materialize left Bogotá obdurate—even refusing to consider testimony collected by Consul Ward.[27]

Meanwhile, Herrán[28] had been called in for a conference at Washington,[29] but was found to possess no powers to negotiate on the subject. He expressed the "genuine regret and horror" of his country at the "outrages committed," but said that its liberal Isthmian policy did not yield adequate revenue to furnish the needed protection.[30] Naturally this effort to condition the Granadian obligation to protect foreign lives and property on American payment of taxes in Isthmian ports was not acceptable to a temporarily bellicose State Department.

In October it was decided to dispatch Isaac E. Morse to assist with the negotiations at Bogotá.[31] On December 2 President Pierce told Congress that "complete responsibility" for the "violent and outrageous attack" lay with New Granada and advised that he had "demanded" punishment for the guilty and indemnity for the losses.[32] But the instructions given to Morse the next day went far beyond this. These complained of the failure to take precautionary measures prior to the riot

[24] Bowlin to Marcy, Aug. 1, 1856, *ibid.*
[25] *Idem* to *idem*, Sept. 25, 1856, *ibid.*
[26] See *idem* to *idem*, Oct. 9, 11, 1856 and enclosures, *ibid.*
[27] *Idem* to *idem*, Sept. 17, 1856, *ibid.*
[28] He spent from March to July in Costa Rica, Panama, and possibly Bogotá (Herrán to Cass, July 21, 1856, Notes from Col. Leg., II).
[29] Letter of Sept. 1 and telegram of Sept. 2, 1856, Notes to Col. Leg., VI, 55-56.
[30] Herrán to Marcy, Oct. 10, 1856, Notes from Col. Leg., II.
[31] Marcy to Morse, Oct. 30, 1856, Specl. Missions, III, 81-82.
[32] Richardson, *Messages and Papers*, VI, 2949.

in the face of "well-founded fears of serious disturbance," as well as to punish the wrongdoers and return
the goods stolen; and attributed such delinquency to the
inability "to afford the proper protection." Then, assuming this inability, it was felt that New Granada was
"bound to agree to any fair arrangement to accomplish
these objects."[33]

An accompanying treaty draft more clearly indicated
what was considered a "fair arrangement." Although
insisting that no exclusive rights were sought, Marcy
proposed that: Colón and Panama be made free ports
with semi-independent municipal governments, including
within the jurisdiction of each a twenty-mile strip of territory extending to the center of the Isthmus; New Granada retain sovereignty over the area, but be restricted
in its exercise; American forces be authorized to intervene whenever local police proved inadequate to assure
the needed protection; other nations be invited to join in
the guarantee of the neutrality of the transit route; New
Granada transfer to the United States its interest in and
control over the Panama railroad and also a cluster of
islands in the Bay of Panama, and receive as compensation therefor not over $1,800,000, less $400,000 for damages resulting from the Panama Riot.[34]

Marcy thought the money payment offered was adequate, especially since the cost of protecting the railroad
would far exceed any annuity that New Granada might
receive therefrom and the United States could no longer
be "satisfied with bare assurances of future protection."
However, if the former asked for a larger amount, Morse
and Bowlin were to "remind her that the route through
Nicaragua . . . [was] only temporarily embarrassed" and

[33] Marcy to Morse and Bowlin, (28) Dec. 3, 1856, Inst. Col., XV, 232-
246; *Sen. Doc.*, No. 237 (56.1), p. 26.

[34] *Ibid.; Moore's Digest*, III, 19 ff.; *Nueva Granada y los Estados
Unidos—final controversia diplomática con relación a los sucesos Panamá
del día 15 de abril de 1856*, pp. 2 ff. (Hereinafter cited as *Final controversia.*)

possessed considerable advantages over Panama in the development of California, Oregon, and Washington.[35]

The instructions concluded by saying that naval stations were "a powerful motive in favor of the arrangement," therefore failure to secure the islands "ought perhaps to be regarded as a failure of the entire object of the negotiations." However, if assurance could be secured that they would never be ceded to or controlled by "any other power, without United States consent," this provision might be eliminated from the treaty draft.[36]

On the way to Bogotá, Morse heard it rumored that Great Britain was attempting to secure a naval base on one of the desired islands. But since former Consul Nelson and an American steamship company owned a large interest in them, he expected little difficulty in acquiring full sovereignty for the United States.[37] In reaching this judgment, however, he had evidently overlooked the hostile atmosphere of Bogotá. On arrival there, the latter part of January, 1857, he found the newspapers attacking President Pierce's message and glorying in the belief that the persistent Bowlin had been recalled. The presence of an English fleet off the coast (in connection with the MacIntosh Loan settlement) was interpreted by many as meaning that the British were watching Isthmian affairs and would not permit American pressure.[38]

Although making "every effort, consistent with diplomatic ceremony," Morse was unable to confer with Minister Pombo before the convening of Congress on February 1. The reports of the Governor of Panama and the French consul—the latter admitting that he was not an eye-witness to the riot—were the only documents

---

[35] Morse to Marcy, Dec. 18, 22, 1856, Secret Service, pp. 694 ff.
[36] *Ibid.*
[37] Morse to Marcy, Dec. 18, 22, 1856, Secret Service, pp. 694 ff.
[38] Bowlin to Marcy, (32) Jan. 29, 1857, Desp. Col., XIII.

obtainable.[39] The Administration seemed determined not to modify its views. This might have been justified in the light of Pierce's message, but it undoubtedly made an early and amicable settlement more difficult.

President Mallarino claimed that the riot had its origin in an "unjustifiable act" of one Jack Oliver, that it became general only when the passengers brought their revolvers into play against what they considered an inferior people, and that officials had succeeded in stopping the native firing until fresh volleys came from the barricaded passengers. Therefore New Granada was not responsible for the damages.[40]

Secretary Pombo was equally firm in his convictions and more violent in expression. He insisted that thorough investigation of the riot had been made,[41] but nothing found to implicate the Panama officials. He was fully convinced that

... a drunken and quarrelsome North American by brutally firing a pistol shot upon a native, produced the alarm and popular excitement; that the armed support rendered to that barbarian by his countrymen, in order to prevent his arrest, caused the riot to augment quickly and to infuriate the people; that the North Americans fired upon the Governor and upon their own consul; that the Station-House of the Railroad was one of the spots from which they kept up a sharp fire; that the number and fury of the contending parties, rendered it impossible to calm the violent tempest and avoid many of the fatal consequences, although the zeal of the disproportionately small police force, aided by not a few natives and foreigners, and the spirited cooperation of the generality of the inhabitants of Panama, saved many lives and much property; that the four buildings in which the popular inroad was productive of damage and depredations had all of them served as offensive and defensive posts to the North Americans. . . .[42]

[39] Morse to Marcy, Feb. 5, 1857, Secret Service, pp. 770 ff.
[40] Mensaje de 1857—Mallarino, Uribe, *Anales*, III, 372 ff.
[41] For copies of investigation orders, see *Gaceta del estado* (Panamá), July 31, 1856.
[42] Uribe, *Anales*, III, 387 ff.; *Final controversia*, pp. 69 ff.

These conclusions were confirmed, Pombo said, by the reports of the consuls of England, France, and Ecuador. If the Yankees were hated on the Isthmus, they had only themselves to blame;[43] if murders and robberies were committed during the riot, the chief perpetrators were the blacks brought there by the Yankees to build the railroad and then left to starve. However, he did favor legislation necessary to provide adequate protection.[44]

The *memoria* ended with the intimation that foreigners were not always safe in the United States, especially in California.[45] If Americans "accustomed to respect nothing, to abuse the revolver and the bowie knife, commit excesses and attacks upon private persons, it . . . [was] not to be wondered at, that those persons carried away by a feeling of indignation should repress and punish them in their own defense, before the authorities . . . [could] interfere."[46]

The tone of this document and Pombo's refusal to confer with Morse before thus giving vent to his emotions and prejudices certainly did not augur a kind reception for Marcy's treaty draft. But it was presented on February 4.[47] Eight days later the Foreign Office advised that the proposals were unacceptable, since they implied "in reality a cession to the United States, as complete and gratuitous as it would be unconstitutional and disgraceful." New Granada denied responsibility for a riot, which "sprang from the brutal act" of an Amer-

[43] At this point he reports an incident of the Governor of Panama talking with the American consul, when another American approached and knocked off the Governor's hat, saying: "Our consul is not to be spoken to with your hat on."

[44] On May 27, 1856, Pombo had recommended such legislation. He had also reprimanded the Governor of Panama for his "feeble and tardy intervention." See *Gaceta oficial*, May 31, 1856.

[45] He also mentioned the *New York Herald* account of a Baltimore election in which one man was killed and some eighty wounded.

[46] Uribe, *Anales*, III, 387 ff.; *Final controversia*, pp. 73 ff.

[47] Bowlin to Marcy, (33) Feb. 6, 1857, Desp. Col., XIII; *Final controversia*, pp. 2-18.

ican, nor would it consent to the United States "award-
ing conclusively on the responsibility," even if impartial
data were overlooked. The propositions submitted,
therefore, were impossible as grounds for negotiations,
yet New Granada was willing to treat on the basis of the
recognition of territorial sovereignty and international
freedom of the transit route.[48]

Morse and Bowlin (February 13) expressed regret
that the messages of both Mallarino and Pombo had exhibited "such a decided opinion against the claims" and
a fear that this attitude had "once for all closed the door
against any amicable arrangement." The thoroughness
of the American investigation was again stressed and
much of the Granadian evidence characterized as hear-
say. The "irresistible conclusion," they claimed, was
that "the attack, murder, and plunder of the passengers"
were premeditated. Since New Granada refused to make
reparations for the butchery of the citizens of the United
States and destruction of their property, it had forced
upon Washington "the alternate either to stand degraded
before the world and its own fellow-citizens as unable
or unwilling to protect their lives and property—or to
take into their own hands the adjustment of the indemnity, the means and measures of redress, and to provide
for the safety of her citizens on the transit of the
Isthmus."[49]

Pombo replied that President Pierce's decided position regarding guilt and liability[50] had forced upon President Mallarino the duty to present "conclusive and un-
impeachable" evidence in support of New Granada's
position. Responsibility for the riot was again attributed to the Yankee filibusters, "dreaded passengers," and

[48] Pombo and González to Morse and Bowlin, Feb. 12, 1857, *ibid.*, pp.
18-22.
[49] Morse and Bowlin to Pombo and González, Feb. 13, 1857, *ibid.*, pp.
22-32.
[50] Annual message of Dec. 2, 1856.

"savages" who outraged the Isthmians. "The hour for retaliation, fixed by providence, sounded, without New Granada being at all to blame." But better treatment by the Americans could scarcely have been expected, since Chileans and Mexicans were "hanged, hunted down like wild beasts in California, without safeguard or reparation; [and] American citizens who have seized the reins of power, after the manner of Conquerers, shoot, confiscate property, and level even to their foundations the cities of Nicaragua."[51]

However, New Granada did not refuse to treat regarding the proper protection of the transit route. In fact, it proposed an agreement for the permanent stationing of an American vessel in Panama Bay empowered to intervene at the request of the governor; moderate taxes on Isthmian business to support the administration of efficient government there; and negotiations with the United States, Great Britain, and France for an international guarantee.[52] These proposals were rejected by the American commissioners on the ground that they possessed no instructions to negotiate on bases permitting European nations "to decide what guarantees . . . [were] sufficient for the safety of the property and lives" of American citizens. New Granada had already given "every possible guarantee," but was "either unable or unwilling" to enforce any. Henceforth "something more tangible than paper pledges and written contracts" was essential. Therefore the $400,000 indemnity for the riot damages must be paid immediately.[53]

The demand was repeated on February 27.[54] Pombo countered by not only denying liability for the $400,000 damages but claiming $150,000 for the loss of lives and

[51] Pombo and González to Morse and Bowlin, Feb. 23, 1857, Desp. Col., XIII; *Final controversia*, pp. 34-48.

[52] *Ibid.*, p. 48.

[53] Morse and Bowlin to Pombo and González, Feb. 26, 1857, *ibid.*, pp. 54-55; Desp. Col., XIII.

[54] *Idem* to *idem*, Feb. 27, 1857; *ibid.*; *Final controversia*, p. 56.

property of the natives and unoffending foreigners. Furthermore, reparations were claimed for the insulting protests of Consul Ward (April 21, 1856) and Commander Bailey (April 24, 25, 26) and demand made for the unpaid mail and tonnage dues.[55] Obviously no early settlement was possible.

Morse soon left for Washington. Bowlin remained hoping to arrange matters with the new administration, which would assume control on April 1.[56] Meanwhile, the Buchanan administration had come into power at Washington. Secretary Cass wrote Bowlin only once and then to instruct him to demand his passport and return home unless there was a change in the Granadian attitude.[57] Buchanan lost his patience early.[58]

On March 17 the Granadian house of representatives formally approved the policy of the Foreign Office and appropriated $500,000 for defense. Bowlin expressed astonishment at "their moderation in not making it five million," since the whole affair was mere "bravado, without sense or reason, [and] without money or credit to raise a dollar."[59] He was convinced that force was the only method of dealing with a nation that could "bluster in heroics and plead insignificance in the same breath." When the new administration made no move towards settlement, Bowlin set out for Washington (May, 1857), leaving the United States unrepresented at Bogotá for more than two years.[60]

This brought the desired results. Minister Herrán had all along appeared coöperative, but his government had left him without definite instructions on the matter until the return of his secretary, Rafael Pombo, in May,

[55] Pombo to Morse and Bowlin, Feb. 28, 1857, *ibid.*, pp. 58-60.
[56] Bowlin to Marcy, (35) March 6, 1857, Desp. Col., XIII.
[57] Cass to Bowlin, (31) April 17, 1857, Inst. Col., XV.
[58] See *supra*, "A Firmer Policy."
[59] Bowlin to Marcy, (36) March 20, (37) 27, 1857, Desp. Col., XIII.
[60] *Idem* to *idem*, (39) April 17, (40) 24, (41) May 1, 1857, *ibid.* He received Cass's instructions at Cartagena after leaving for home.

1857.[61]   Almost immediately he requested a conference, and soon negotiations were in progress at Washington.[62]

On June 18 President Ospina was empowered not only to conclude a treaty but also "to carry it into effect without posterior approbation of congress being necessary; with the only limitation [that the treaty was] not to affect the rights of national sovereignty . . . nor . . . of property." Arbitration was suggested but not made obligatory. Herrán forwarded a copy of this law to Cass and advised him that he possessed full powers to negotiate.[63]

A conference was arranged for July 23. From this point the State Department records are almost silent. On August 27 Cass forwarded a treaty draft to Herrán and on September 9 set the following day for the attaching of signatures. He acknowledged Herrán's "fair and candid manner" during the negotiations,[64] and Herrán, in turn, the "friendly disposition" of General Cass.[65] Three months later President Buchanan advised Congress that the recent difficulties were "in a fair train of settlement in a manner just and honorable to both parties."[66]

These expressions of mutual good feeling and satisfaction, however, give little idea of the tenseness behind the scenes, the determined attitude of Washington, and the ill-concealed reluctance of Bogotá. Appeals to France and England brought Herrán only the advice to settle on the American terms. Lord Napier, British represent-

[61] Herrán to Marcy, Nov. 28, 1856, to Cass, March 24, 28, April 14, 1857, Notes from Col. Leg., II. Pombo had been sent to Bogotá the previous December "on special business" (Herrán to Marcy, Dec. 8, 1856, to Cass, May 16, 1857, *ibid.*).

[62] Herrán to Cass, May 20, 1857, *ibid.*

[63] *Idem* to *idem*, July 21, 1857, *ibid.;* Cass to Herrán, July 21, 1857, Notes to Col. Leg., VI, 68-69.

[64] Cass to Herrán, Aug. 27, Sept. 9, 10, 1857, *ibid.*, VI, 70-71.

[65] Herrán to Cass, Sept. 11, 1857, Notes from Col. Leg., II.

[66] Dec. 8, 1857, Richardson, *Messages and Papers*, VII, 2978.

ative at Washington, recommended this, even at the sacrifice of honor, since a war would mean not only Granadian defeat but the harmonizing of Yankee domestic quarrels.[67] No reasonable alternative appearing, Herrán signed.

The Cass-Herrán Treaty,[68] although falling far short of Washington's expectations, contained provisions not authorized by the Granadian law of June 18; therefore Ospina submitted it for congressional approval.[69] On July 8 it was ratified with certain modifications: a refusal to approve the coaling stations clause and a declaration that the acknowledgment of liability for the late Panama Riot was not to be considered a precedent.[70] The treaty with these modifications was transmitted to the American senate on December 23 and was soon ratified with a few unimportant amendments.[71] The loss of the treaty draft in a Magdalena River wreck[72] prevented its presentation at Bogotá until the following February.[73] But before the end of the month Minister Jones reported its approval with minor changes. To these the American senate unanimously agreed, and ratifications were exchanged on November 5, 1860.[74]

The treaty provided for the settlement of all claims of Americans against New Granada filed prior to September 1, 1859, and "especially those for damages which

[67] Posada e Ibáñez, *Vida de Herrán*, pp. 157-159.

[68] Malloy, *Treaties*, I, 319-321; Uribe, *Anales*, VI, 229-233.

[69] Mensaje de 1858—Ospina, *ibid.*, III, 407.

[70] *Ibid.*, VI, 232; Herrán to Cass, Aug. 16, 1858, Notes from Col. Leg., III.

[71] *Sen. Ex. Jour.*, XI, 33, 37, 75, 76, 89-91.

[72] American press reports had it that the treaty had been "drowned in the Magdalena river" (Herrán to Cass, May 17, 1859, Notes from Col. Leg., III).

[73] Mensaje de 1860—Ospina, Uribe, *Anales*, III, 459.

[74] Jones to Cass, (21) Feb. 28, 1860, Desp. Col., XIV; *Sen. Ex. Jour.*, XI, 182-184. Meanwhile, Cass refused to discuss any other grievances until the treaty was ratified (Cass to Herrán, March 31, 1859, Notes to Col. Leg., VI, 89).

were caused by the riot of Panama . . . for which the
Government of New Granada . . . [acknowledged] its
liability.'' A claims commission was provided and a
limit of nine months from the date of its first meeting
set for completing its work.[75] The commissioners, J. M. Hurtado[76] and E. W. Leav-
enworth, met on June 10, 1861, but did not agree on the
umpire, N. G. Upham of New Hampshire, until October
1. The remainder of the allotted time proved insufficient
to pass on the two hundred and sixty-two claims furnished by the State Department.[77] On March 11 Leaven-
worth reported that two hundred and eighteen had been
entered on the calendar, of which only one hundred and
eleven had been settled. Of these cases seventy-three
had been allowed and thirty-eight denied. The total
awards on the seventy-three claims were $496,635.47.[78]
But Herrán refused to accept the umpire's ruling on five
old claims amounting to $333,888.04.[79] This reduced the
awards to $162,747.43, including $135,410.22 for Panama
Riot damages.[80]

The Mosquera revolution prevented an early extension of time for claims settlement. Both Hurtado and
Herrán were hostile to the new government,[81] and two
years passed before the United States recognized it. In

[75] For text, see Malloy, *Treaties*, I, 319-321.

[76] Although Hurtado's government was overthrown by Mosquera and a
new appointment seemingly made, the personnel of the commission was
not altered. See Uribe, *Anales*, V, 618.

[77] On March 5 the United States senate agreed to a six months' extension, but the change of government at Bogotá complicated matters.

[78] J. B. Moore, *History and Digest of International Arbitrations*, II,
1384-1386.

[79] *La Constantia*, $146,508.50 (1818); *Good Return*, $44,291.78 (1818-
1819); *Medea*, $43,347.49 (1818-1819); R. W. Gibbes, $6,952.60 (on early
Colombian bond); John Daniels (Danels), $92,787.67. Herrán claimed
that these ''had already been decided by competent tribunals.''

[80] Moore, *History and Digest*, II, 1393; Herrán to Cass, March 20, 1862,
Notes from Col. Leg., III.

[81] Herrán even asked American intervention to protect the Isthmus from
his father-in-law.

September, 1863, Secretary Seward requested a statement from Minister Murillo regarding the five claims denied by Hurtado.[82] Murillo admitted Colombian liability under the Treaty of 1857 and expressed a readiness to reopen negotiations, but insisted that the disputed claims be resubmitted.[83] On February 10, 1864, a new convention was signed, providing for another commission and a nine months' extension of time for the settlement of the claims.[84] Ratifications followed and the treaty was proclaimed on August 19, 1865.[85]

The new commission was composed of Thomas Biddle and Eustorgio Salgar, with Sir F. W. A. Bruce (British minister) as umpire. Although Seward had formerly refused the resubmittal of the five disputed claims,[86] Bruce considered and disallowed four of them. The fifth (Gibbes) was stricken from the calendar, when the claimant's counsel protested and refused to appear before the commission.[87] Some one hundred and eighty-five cases were submitted but only thirty-three allowed—one hundred and fifty-one being denied and the Gibbes claim not passed upon.[88] However, the State Department considered the Gibbes award valid, compensated the claimant, and demanded the amount in 1874 before the issuance of a final receipt.[89] The total award on the thirty-three claims was $90,781.09, including approximately $60,000 for Panama Riot damages.[90] Under the Treaties of 1857

[82] Seward to Murillo, Sept. 5, 1863, Jan. 9, 1864, Notes to Col. Leg., VI, 148, 155.

[83] Murillo to Seward, Jan. 12, Feb. 6, 9, 1864, Notes from Col. Leg., IV.

[84] For text, see Uribe, *Anales*, VI, 251 ff.

[85] *Ibid.*, V, 618; Hunter to Salgar, Aug. 18, 1865, Notes to Col. Leg., VI, 191-192.

[86] Atty. Gen. Speed (Nov. 18, 1865) gave the opinion that the new commission was competent to decide what claims were to be considered (Claims Ser., Col.).

[87] *Ibid.;* Moore, *History and Digest*, II, 1409-1415.

[88] *Ibid.*, II, 1415-1420.

[89] Fish to Martín, Jan. 8, 1873, July 23, 29, 1874, Notes to Col. Leg., VI, 307, 317, 319; Martín to Fish, Oct. 31, 1872, Notes from Col. Leg., VI.

[90] Claims Ser., Col.; Moore, *History and Digest*, II, 1415-1420.

and 1864, Colombia paid into the American treasury $412,393.95 for losses of Yankee lives and property.[91]

[91] Martín to Fish, Oct. 31, 1872, Notes from Col. Leg., VI.

Under Treaty of 1857	$162,747.43
Under Treaty of 1864	90,781.09
Gibbes claim	6,952.00
Total awards	$260,480.52
Commission expense	9,276.70
Total principal	$269,757.22
Interest	142,636.73
Total paid by Colombia	$412,393.95

CHAPTER XIX

THE PROTECTION OF UNITED STATES CITIZENS
AND INTERESTS *(continued)*
(1861-1903)

A VIGOROUS protection policy abroad was possible—
perhaps advisable—as long as peace reigned within
the United States. But the outbreak of the Civil War in
1861 placed the matter in a far different setting.

CIRCUMSTANCES COMPEL CONSISTENCY (1861-1865)

The destruction of alien property by Federal campaigns into the Southern states and the fear that certain
European powers would bring diplomatic pressure for
reclamations led Seward to announce (1862) a much modified policy towards Colombia:

Citizens of the United States, no matter how they acquire that
title, who have gone to New Granada [Colombia], become domiciled there, and are pursuing business or otherwise living there,
without definite and manifest intentions of returning to this
country,[1] are subject to all the laws of New Granada affecting
property and material rights exactly the same as citizens of
New Granada.[2]

The actual presentation of claims growing out of military operations brought to President Lincoln's attention
"the uncertain state of international questions touching
the rights of foreigners in this country and of United
States citizens abroad." Treaties with some nations
partially defined these rights. But he contended that it
had never been agreed

. . . that in the event of civil war a foreigner residing in this
country within the lines of a belligerent . . . [was] to be exempt

[1] There were many Americans of this type in Colombia.
[2] Seward to Burton, (12) Jan. 12, 1862, Inst. Col., XIV, 20-22.

from the rule which classes him as a belligerent, in whose behalf the Government of his country can not expect any privileges or immunities distinct from that character.[3]

After reading Lincoln's message Minister Murillo suggested a convention on the subject. Nevertheless an exchange of notes failed to reconcile existing differences, and Seward seems to have dismissed the matter by promising to forward full powers to Minister Burton.[4] Murillo soon returned to Bogotá to assume the presidency. His administration (January, 1865) advocated the indemnification of foreign residents for losses suffered during the Colombian civil war (1858-1863) and for their future exemption from "any war tax, expropriation, forced loan, military service or other requisitions, provided, they maintain[ed] a true neutrality. . . ."[5] But such a liberal policy was not adopted.

COLOMBIA'S GROWING INDEPENDENCE

The re-establishment of stable governments in both nations naturally meant that Bogotá insisted strenuously on the retention of Seward's announced policy, while Washington desired a return to its ante-bellum one. Under a Colombian congressional resolution of April 19, 1865, foreigners found themselves on the same basis as nationals—war taxes, forced loans, and military service excepted.[6] The British and French protested. And the State Department instructed Minister Burton to advise Colombia that such a measure, if contrary to treaty rights, was not to be considered applicable to American citizens.[7]

---

[3] Dec. 8, 1863, Richardson, *Messages and Papers*, VII, 3381.
[4] Murillo to Seward, Jan. 6, 1864, Notes from Col. Leg., IV; Seward to Murillo, Jan. 9, Feb. 3, 8, 1864, Notes to Col. Leg., VI, 154, 161, 162.
[5] Burton to Seward, (154) Feb. 15, 1865, Desp. Col., XX.
[6] Repealed June 21, 1866, Burton to Seward, (248) June 29, 1866, *ibid.*, XXIII.
[7] Burton to Seward, (176) May 16, 1865, *ibid.*, XX; Seward to Burton, (129) Sept. 14, 1865, Inst. Col., XVI, 138.

An act of May 2 made it compulsory for foreigners to establish their claims before Colombian courts within a year. Burton wanted to consider this law void.[8] He estimated the forced loans and confiscations at $2,000,000, but doubted that the next congress would appropriate more than $100,000 for their payment. In the latter prediction he was correct. Congress insisted that the claims first be legally established.[9]

Seward acquiesced. It was felt necessary, in spite of the well-known "delay and inefficiency of the courts," to "continue to repose confidence in their independence and integrity," or consider Colombia "outside the pale" of civilization. Regarding Yankee investors he added:

The people who go to these regions and encounter great risks in the hope of great rewards, must be regarded as taking all the circumstances into consideration, and cannot with reason ask their government to complain that they stand on a common footing with native subjects in respect to the alleged want of an able, prompt, and conscientious judiciary. We cannot undertake to supervise the arrangements of the whole world for litigation, because American citizens voluntarily expose themselves to be concerned in their deficiencies.[10]

Some claims were accordingly established and paid,[11] but many others received little or no attention. In fact, this neglect was the major cause of Burton's break with the Bogotá government in December, 1866.[12] However, all this indicated "on the part of Colombia a growing disposition to require all claimants to submit themselves to the courts of the country."[13]

[8] Burton to Seward, (202) Nov. 8, 1865, Desp. Col., XXI.

[9] *Idem* to *idem*, (204) Dec. 21, 1865, (227) March 14, 1866, *ibid.*, XXII.

[10] Seward to Burton, (137) April 27, 1866, *For. Rel.* (1866-1867), p. 522.

[11] United Magdalena Steam Navigation Company, $100,000; John Capela, $10,137; and Harmony and López, $758.01 (Burton to Seward, [238] June 2, [239] 3, 1866, Desp. Col., XXIII).

[12] He left some sixteen claims unsettled (Burton to Seward [confidential], Dec. 16, 1866, *ibid.;* also despatches Nos. 240, 272, 279, 287, 294, 301-311, 316).

[13] Hurlbut to Fish, (59) Sept. 12, 1871, *ibid.*, XXVIII.

There are two incidents which are especially indicative of this growing spirit of independence—the Cartagena Riot and the *Montijo* arbitration.

THE CARTAGENA RIOT

On September 1, 1867, a Cartagena mob attacked four Americans; two were killed, and the others narrowly escaped. Minister Sullivan began an investigation and requested an explanation from the Bogotá government. Certain individuals were arrested and tried, but acquitted.[14] Sullivan, considering the procedure a mere "mock trial of the murderers of American citizens," demanded indemnity. Colombian indignation rose, but he remained firm.[15] A repetition of the Panama Riot pressure negotiations seemed entirely probable.

However, the tension was temporarily lessened by President Mosquera's promise to request his Congress to authorize indemnity for the relatives of the victims and by the transfer of the discussions to Washington. An investigation showed that the four men had deserted the United States navy to join the Confederate forces and had never resubmitted themselves to the Washington government.[16] Early in 1867 they had enlisted in New York as officers on the *R. R. Cuyler* or *Rayo*.[17] Since this action was illegal under the neutrality laws, they had thereby become a part of the forces of a foreign government. By their services as such they became obnoxious to certain Cartagenians and for that reason were attacked. Since the victims were not American citizens— by this process of reasoning—Seward accepted this ex-

[14] Sullivan to Seward, (29) Sept. 26, (33) Oct. 12, 1867, (52) Feb. 15, 1868, *ibid.*, XXVI; Seward to Sullivan, (14) Sept. 23, 1867, Inst. Col., XVI, 234-236.

[15] Sullivan to Seward, (52) Feb. 15, 1868, (59), Desp. Col., XXVI.

[61] *Idem* to *idem*, (65) May 13, 1868; *ibid.;* Seward to Sullivan, (47) June 30, 1868, Inst. Col., XVI, 279.

[17] A ship purchased by Mosquera, presumably for the Colombian navy but actually, for the service of Peru in its war with Spain.

planation as "entirely satisfactory."[18] The Colombian courts had won another victory.[19]

THE MONTIJO ARBITRATION (1871-1875)

The second incident was hardly a judicial triumph, but did indicate a determined mood. During an Isthmian revolution (April, 1871) the steamer *Montijo,* property of H. Shuber and Brother, was commandeered by certain rebels. It was later returned by the Panama government, but no compensation was made for the loss. On December 1 Minister Hurlbut filed a claim in the amount of $94,465.[20] An attempt at Panama to convict the guilty on a charge of piracy failed, and the decision was upheld by the national supreme court.[21]

When Colombia formally denied liability, Hurlbut proposed to his chief (1871) a threat to terminate the Treaty of 1846. He was convinced that since this treaty alone prevented a successful Isthmian revolution, Colombia would of necessity agree to any terms demanded.[22] Secretary Fish approved such a threat, but suggested first an inquiry to determine whether other nations had guaranteed the Panama route.[23]

Because of Hurlbut's return to Washington the discussions were temporarily suspended. But the new minister, William L. Scruggs, was instructed (1873) to secure a settlement of the claim. Colombia suggested arbitration. The claimants agreed, and Scruggs signed a convention on August 17, 1874. A commission—com-

[18] Seward to Sullivan, (72) Feb. 4, 1869, Inst. Col., XVI, 345 ff.; Seward to Acosta, Feb. 11, 1869, Notes to Col. Leg., VI, 243.

[19] Seward's acceptance of this inconsistent citizenship argument was probably due to his desire for a liberal canal treaty (then in process of negotiation) and his lack of interest in the fate of four ex-Confederates.

[20] Hurlbut to Fish, (73) Jan. 6, 1872, Desp. Col., XXVIII. See also Moore, *History and Digest,* II, 1420-1447.

[21] *Ibid.,* II, 1424.

[22] Hurlbut to Fish, (69) Nov. 17, 1871, Desp. Col., XXVIII.

[23] Fish to Hurlbut, (55) Dec. 19, 1871, (59) Feb. 20, 1872, Inst. Col., XVI, 407, 411.

posed of Mariano Tanco, Bendix Koppel, and Robert Bunch (umpire)—made a decision, by the vote of the umpire, favorable to the claimants and awarded the sum of $33,401.[24] It was true that Colombian court decisions had not been upheld, but the question of liability had been decided by an arbitration commission and not by the State Department.

THE COLÓN FIRE CLAIM

During the Revolution of 1885[25] Colombia not only requested and accepted Yankee intervention[26] but complained that its tardiness permitted the rebel forces to burn Colón.[27] The United States, on the other hand, contended that protective intervention was its treaty right but not its duty. This policy was acquiesced in, if not accepted, by Colombia and was followed until the secession of Panama in 1903.[28]

However, the losses suffered at the hands of rebel forces were a different matter. Since Yankee investments on the Isthmus were considerable, the Colón Fire[29] claims began to pour into the State Department. The tenor of the accompanying notes indicated that the claimants anticipated the same vigorous policy asserted to collect the Panama Riot losses.

Isaacs and Asch expected the United States to compel the restoration of their property and payment for merchandise destroyed.[30] Tracy Robinson felt that the only

[24] Scruggs to Fish, (43) June 27, 1874, (115) Aug. 3, 1875, Desp. Col., XXIX; Fish to Scruggs, (24) Jan. 27, (28) Feb. 26, 1874, Inst. Col., XVI, 457, 460; Moore, *History and Digest*, II, 1427 ff.; Uribe, *Anales*, III, 776.

[25] See *supra* chap. xiii.

[26] Forces had already been landed in 1856, 1860, 1865, 1868, 1873.

[27] Becerra to Bayard, April 3, 4, 1885, Notes from Col. Leg., VII.

[28] Other armed interventions occurred in 1885, 1895, 1901, 1902, 1903.

[29] There were some thirty-three of these claims: Panama Railroad Company, $1,706,627.81; Isaacs and Asch, $486,811.86; W. J. Field, et. al., $345,000; Boston Ice Company, $194,356; Aepli, Ebenbach and Salmon, $180,000; James and Company, $155,000; Tracy Robinson, $120,000; L. W. Rathbun, $100,000; and twenty-five others; ranging from $1,380 upward—totalling around $3,750,000 (*Sen. Doc.*, No. 264 [57.1], pp. 5-196).

[30] *Ibid.*, p. 5.

hope of recovering the losses was the interference of Washington, and desired to see the Isthmus under American protection.[31] Henry Noble requested and demanded "prompt and efficient measures . . . to the end that . . . [he] be promptly and fully reimbursed"; suggested that Colombia be forced to set aside its Panama railroad annuities as a guarantee for the payment of the claims; and advocated a neutral Isthmus under the protection of the United States, Great Britain, and France.[32]

The Panama Railroad attorney was still more determined:

For all this loss and damage the Panama Railroad Company will at the proper time make a formal claim against the United States of Colombia and against the State of Panama, and in the meanwhile this company desires to secure from the Government of the United States such good offices and assistance as may be properly asked under the existing treaty . . . ; and the *railroad company desires also to reserve all its right to claim restitution for all the aforesaid losses and damages from the Government of the United States for the failure to fulfill its treaty obligations* to keep the transit . . . open for commercial intercourse . . . , and it now gives this notice of such claim so that the Government of the United States may, in such form and manner as it may deem proper . . . be enabled to save itself from the liability aforesaid.[33]

Secretary Bayard's answers to such demands clearly indicate the Department's attitude. The railroad attorney was advised:

The notification . . . of the reservation . . . to claim restitution from the Government of the United States for all the losses and damages recited . . . under the allegation of a failure . . . to perform its treaty stipulations . . . will receive due consid-

---

[31] *Ibid.*, p. 9.　　　　　　[32] *Ibid.*, pp. 11-12.

[33] *Ibid.*, pp. 13-14. (Italics are mine.) The fact that some sixty-eight seventieths of the railroad stock was owned by the Panama Canal Company (a French corporation) was claimed not to affect the right to protection, since the original investment represented "undoubtedly American capital" (*ibid.*, pp. 232-233).

eration should the company you represent see fit ever seriously and actually to present it.[34]

Benjamin Howard's Sons, agents for the Boston Ice Company, were told that the government was under no "obligations to make good the losses of its citizens who establish[ed] themselves in foreign lands," since the risks arising out of internal disorder and "defective administration" must be "foreseen and borne like any other risks of foreign trade."[35] And to Tracy Robinson, Bayard wrote:

As a general rule of international law, a government is not responsible for the consequences of acts of rebellion against its authority, and no special case of exception may be determined in advance of the establishment of some competent governmental authority in Colombia.[36]

However, Colombia, not knowing of this liberal policy but remembering its bitter Panama Riot experience, was obviously nervous. Minister Becerra (April, 1885) sought assurance that the forces rushed to the Isthmus would not be used to seize it.[37] President Núñez is reported to have expressed the fear that the "Panama canal . . . [would] be snatched away from us [Colombia] by the Yankees. . . ."[38] The Colombian minister in Paris approached his South American colleagues regarding a protective league against United States aggression.[39]

But Colombia soon recognized its liability for losses of foreigners during revolutions and suggested the submission of claims to an international mixed commission.[40] A decree of August 19, 1885, expressed a willingness to negotiate, but proposed as an alternate the submission

[34] *Ibid.*, pp. 15-16.   [35] *Ibid.*, p. 9.
[36] *Ibid.*, pp. 9, 11.
[37] Becerra to Bayard, April 4, 1885, *Sen. Doc.*, No. 143 (58.2), pp. 61-64.
[38] M. A. Nieto, *Recuerdos de la regeneración*, pp. 311-312.
[39] *Archivo histórico diplomático Mexicano*, num. 19, pp. 215-219.
[40] Scruggs to Bayard, (216) June 25, 1885, Desp. Col., XXXIX.

of the claims to the Colombian courts.[41] Bayard favored negotiations, but would not instruct Scruggs until Colombia made known the bases.[42] President Cleveland interpreted the decree as including the Colón Fire losses,[43] which represented the principal Yankee claims. But the matter was not to be settled so easily. A new decree of February 17, 1886, set forth the minute formalities to be observed in filing claims and limited the time for action to March 31. Minister Jacob's protest accomplished nothing.[44] In fact, the National Council of Delegates, called to prepare a new constitution, passed a resolution repudiating the claims entirely.[45]

Furthermore, to the Panama Railroad's claim of $1,706,627.81 for Colón Fire damages, Colombia offered a counter claim for its share of the indemnity due from the Panama Canal Company.[46] Jacob (March 19) protested in favor of the company, but Bayard disapproved his action, since the treaty relations with Colombia were ''incompatible with [the] appearance of advocacy of pecuniary interests of [the] Railroad Company.'' The matter grew out of a contract, and therefore was not one for diplomatic interference.[47] The withdrawal of this protest was interpreted at Bogotá, Jacob thought, as the renunciation of all Colón Fire claims.[48] At any rate, it was intimated to him that the negotiations were being transferred to Washington.[49] On June 14, J. M. Hurtado

[41] *Idem* to *idem*, (243) Oct. 10, 1885, *ibid.; Sen. Doc.*, No. 264 (57.1), pp. 48, 72.
[42] Bayard to Scruggs, (60) Aug. 20, 1885, *ibid.*, p. 43; Inst. Col. XVII.
[43] Dec. 8, 1885, Richardson, *Messages and Papers*, X, 4912.
[44] Jacob to Bayard, (20) March 23, 1886, Desp. Col., XXXIX; *Sen. Doc.*, No. 264 (57.1), p. 80.
[45] *Ibid.*, p. 81.
[46] The canal company had attempted to escape the paying of indemnity by purchasing some 6,800 of the 7,000 shares of stock.
[47] Jacob to Bayard, (23) March 25, 1886, Desp. Col., XXXIX; Bayard to Jacob, (tel.) April 23, (28) May 10, 1886, Inst. Col., XVII, 512, 518.
[48] Jacob to Bayard, (28) May 4, 1886, Desp. Col., XXXIX.
[49] *Idem* to *idem*, (29) May 4, 1886, *ibid.*

presented himself there as a special commissioner to arrange the settlement of all revolutionary claims.[50]

COLOMBIA'S SUCCESSFUL DENIAL OF LIABILITY FOR COLÓN CLAIMS

It seems that Hurtado's instructions were based on the American acceptance of the arbitration of "the principle of responsibility," as well as the amount of the awards.[51] On this basis he presented (October, 1886) a convention draft providing for the adjudication of the claims by a joint commission. Two months later Bayard submitted a counter draft, including the Colombian admission of responsibility.[52]

While waiting for new instructions, Hurtado attempted to show that Colombia was not liable for the damages under the Treaty of 1846, since it referred "solely and exclusively to persons and things in transit across the Isthmus." Paragraph IV[53] of Article XXXV actually exonerated Colombia of all liability. Certainly the capture and execution of the culprit, Prestán, had given "vindicatory satisfaction,"[54] all that the treaty required. He saw no similarity between the Panama Riot

[50] Hurtado to Bayard, June 14, 1886, Notes from Col. Leg., VIII. This special mission was probably due to Jacob's inability to remain on friendly terms with the Bogotá officials. Becerra had complained of his bitter and indecorous language and Bayard had promised to call him home for investigation (Bayard to Becerra, May 28, 1886, Notes to Col. Leg., VII).

[51] Becerra claimed that he had understood Bayard to agree to this during his conference in March, 1886 (Becerra to Bayard, March 1, 1887, Notes from Col. Leg., VIII).

[52] Hurtado to Bayard, Oct. 22, 1886, *ibid.;* Bayard to Hurtado, Dec. 20, 1886, Notes to Col. Leg., VII. With the former is filed a thirty-two page "confidential exposition" on Colombian liability, by John Bassett Moore, dated Dec. 15, 1886.

[53] "If any one or more of the citizens of either party shall infringe any of the articles of this treaty, such citizens shall be held personally responsible for the same. . . ."

[54] Bayard's marginal note: "Vindicatory satisfaction is a new and aetherial satisfaction—transubstantiation—*crede quod habes—et habes*—a photograph of our marines and war vessels would have complied with the guarantee of the United States."

and the Colón Fire.[55] Colombia had been "compelled to accept the responsibility" in the first case because it could not well refute the United States argument that forces to quell the riot were available and should have restored order, but, instead, joined the mob in attacking the passengers. Even so, the Treaty of 1857 had been ratified by New Granada (Colombia) with the understanding that the admission of liability therein was not to be considered a precedent.[56]

To this argument Secretary Bayard (March 2, 1887) merely expressed the hope that Hurtado did not intend "to convert the negotiations . . . into a fruitless and unhappy controversy."[57] The latter soon set out for Europe, and negotiations were dropped until near the end of 1887.[58]

Hurtado's memorandum of December 22 clearly indicated a more determined attitude on the part of Colombia. He insisted that his government could not surrender its right to determine proper claims for damages inflicted by its own officials, yet would agree to their decision by a commission. "But as for claims arising out of injuries or losses caused by the act or acts of persons not public officers, or not acting with the sanction or consent of the legitimate authorities, the Government of Colombia . . . [refused] to recognize their validity against itself," because under Colombian law it was "not possible to transfer the individual responsibility to the Government, unless the person . . . [was] a public official acting within his legal functions." Furthermore, Hurtado would admit no distinction between claims in Panama and the rest of Colombia, nor between American and Colombian claim-

[55] Bayard's marginal note: "The grounds of the responsibility of the Panama Riot are found in the Treaty of 1846. The responsibility of Panama in 1856 and 1885 are [*sic*] the same in law and fact."

[56] Hurtado to Bayard, Feb. 21, 1887, Notes from Col. Leg., VIII; Uribe, *Anales*, VI, 232.

[57] Bayard to Hurtado, March 2, 1887, Notes to Col. Leg., VII.

[58] Hurtado to Bayard, June 4, Dec. 8, 1887, Notes from Col. Leg., VIII.

ants.[59] This strong position again halted negotiations. The next note to Hurtado was dated February 11, 1889.[60]

Meanwhile, the Bogotá government, while declaring itself "not . . . absolutely responsible for the damages and exactions suffered by foreigners on account of the rebels," had provided for the consideration of claims presented. The president and the foreign minister had been empowered to settle all claims of proven "alien and neutral character," arising out of acts of either national officials or a "regular force of insurgents under the command of a known chief" and presented within a specific time limit.[61]

But this was not interpreted at Bogotá as covering the Colón Fire losses. The denial of liability for these claims received encouragement by the refusal of the British minister to support one for a fellow countryman. Minister Maury was soon convinced that all foreign representatives there concurred in the view that the burning of Colón was not sufficiently due to any default of Colombia to justify a demand for compensation.[62] On November 3, 1887, he received official denial of liability for the fire losses.[63] Since the United States had been guided by the principle of governmental non-liability for unauthorized destructive acts of its citizens during its recent Civil War, surely it could not consistently object to the same policy now upheld by Colombia, especially in view of the Treaty of 1846.[64]

In spite of this consistent denial of liability, Bayard still entertained hopes of securing a settlement to pre-

[59] Hurtado Memo., Dec. 22, 1887, *ibid.*

[60] Notes to Col. Leg., VII. It is quite probable, however, that occasional conferences took place, since the Department continued to advise claimants that negotiations were in progress.

[61] Law 10 of Aug. 31, 1886; Ex. Decree, No. 602 of Sept. 11, 1886; Decree, No. 132 of Feb. 15, 1887, King to Bayard, (70) Sept. 11, (83) Oct. 27, 1886, Desp. Col., XL; *Sen. Doc.*, No. 264 (57.1), p. 125.

[62] Maury to Bayard, (61 and enclosure) Oct. 31, 1887, *ibid.*, p. 163.

[63] Angulo to Maury, Nov. 3, 1887, *ibid.*, p. 164.

[64] Informe de 1888—Restrepo, Uribe, *Anales*, IV, 470-474.

sent to the Senate before the Cleveland administration closed.[65] For this purpose he called Hurtado into conference early in February.[66] As usual, the latter had a new argument ready. He observed that differences over claims could arise only from non-observance of the Treaty of 1846, which provided (Paragraph IV of Article XXXV) that only those violating it were responsible, not their governments. He suggested, therefore, the incorporation of this paragraph in the convention. Bayard preferred that the commission be permitted to determine its own procedure and to examine each case in accordance with international law and the treaties existing between the two nations.[67]

Bayard's amendment incorporating this arrangement was returned by Hurtado, along with a request for another conference for March 1. The latter now claimed that "the protection of the transit route was incumbent on both the United States and Colombia, and under certain conditions, it became the special duty of the United States; that such was precisely the case when the burning of Colón took place in 1885; [and] that [the] city then was under the sole guardianship of the United States naval forces." Therefore any claim based upon insufficient protection would raise the question as to which nation failed in its duty. Then, under a settlement by arbitration, Colombian citizens might also make claims.[68] Naturally this stand was not acceptable to Bayard.

The new secretary of state, James G. Blaine, was too enthusiastic about the contemplated meeting of the International Congress of American Republics to antagonize Colombia by pressing doubtful claims. But when Bogotá hesitated to sign the general arbitration conven-

[65] *Sen. Doc.*, No 264 (57.1), p. 192.
[66] Bayard to Hurtado, Feb. 11, 1889, Notes to Col. Leg., VII.
[67] Hurtado to Bayard, State Dept. Memo., Feb. 13, 1889, Notes from Col. Leg., VIII.
[68] Report of interview of March 1, 1889, *ibid.*

tion drawn up by this congress, Minister Abbott was instructed (October, 1890) to press the claims again.[69]

Meanwhile, various claimants were harassing the Department,[70] and Abbott was clamoring for specific instructions.[71] On receipt of Blaine's note he sought conferences with the Bogotá officials, only to be assured that new and more inclusive instructions would immediately go forward to the legation at Washington.[72] He soon returned home on leave, and the Colombian foreign minister frantically set about to secure official declarations from France and England renouncing their Colón Fire claims. The minister was assured that such claims would not be supported, unless Colombia should first pay those of other nationals[73]—meaning, of course, the Yankees.

On return to Bogotá, Abbott recommended the complete abandonment of the claims, because he considered them of a "most doubtful nature" and saw clearly that an arbitral decision favorable to the United States would likewise fix Colombian liability to France and England. In such case, the probable $5,000,000 indemnity could be collected only by the seizure of the custom houses, which, in turn, would completely bankrupt the entire nation. Surely, the United States did not desire to bring "so serious a result upon this little Republic . . . even supposing that . . . [it] had the right to do so."[74]

Evidently the expediency of Abbott's argument was recognized by the Department, since for the time being negotiations for the settlement of the fire claims ceased

[69] Blaine to Abbott, (120) Oct. 24, 1890, Inst. Col., XVIII, 215.
[70] *Sen. Doc.*, No. 264 (57.1), pp. 186, 191, 192, 195, 246, 251, 253.
[71] Abbott to Blaine, (15) July 31, (28) Sept. 4, 1889, Desp. Col., XLV.
[72] *Idem* to *idem*, (177 and enclosures) Jan. 20, 1891, *Sen. Doc.*, No. 264, (57.1), pp. 258-264.
[73] Abbott to Wharton, July 14, 1891, *ibid.*, p. 266.
[74] Abbott to Under-Secy. Curtis, Aug. 16, 1891, *ibid.*, pp. 266-267. Curtis was asked to present the matter to Blaine "in the most sure and unostentatious way" and to convince him that his subordinates had little faith in "the justice of the claims."

and the Colombian reaffirmation (1892) of its non-liability for them[75] passed unchallenged. This did not mean, however, that American claimants gave up hope of recovery,[76] nor that the State Department would not press the claims at any future opportune time. But, in effect, it ended all serious attempt to hold Colombia responsible for the destruction of American property by Isthmian revolutionary chieftains.[77]

CONTINUED DIPLOMATIC AND MILITARY INTERVENTION

Although expediency forced the abandonment of the Colón Fire claims, vigorous diplomatic support was given claims of the *Panama Star and Herald* and the *Estrella de Panamá*. In 1886 these papers were suspended for sixty days by order of General Ramón Santo Domingo Vila. Since the company, publishing both of these, was incorporated in New York (1883) and maintained offices there, its nationality was not questioned by the Department. Minister Jacob was instructed to insist on official disavowal of the suspension order and the punishment of the officer, or the "assumption of responsibility for his acts."[78]

When the efforts at Bogotá roved futile, Secretary Blaine presented the matter to Minister Hurtado,[79] who claimed to have understood from Bayard that the reclamation would not be supported until the Colombian courts had determined whether the officer had acted "within the scope of his legal authority." Since the action had now been disavowed by Colombia, Hurtado argued, the only way of securing redress was to proceed

---

[75] Uribe, *Anales*, IV, 605-606.

[76] List of claimant letters, 1892-1899, *Sen. Doc.*, No. 264 (57.1), p. 5.

[77] For subsequent correspondence regarding the claims, see *Sen. Doc.*, Nos. 199 (58.2); 405 (63.2), pp. 1-115. Efforts to secure their deduction from the amounts due Panama under the Hay-Bunau-Varilla Treaty (1903) and Colombia under the Thomson-Urrutia Treaty (1914) failed.

[78] Bayard to Jacob, (31) May 15, 1886, Inst. Col., XVII, 526-538.

[79] Blaine to Hurtado, Jan. 31, 1890, Notes to Col. Leg., VII, 168.

against General Santo Domingo Vila personally before the national courts.[80]

Here the matter seems to have rested for a season. But it was urged quite vigorously by Secretaries Gresham (1895) and Olney (1895-1897).[81] When the Colombian representative at Washington received no powers to treat,[82] Olney instructed Minister McKinney to present the claim again at Bogotá and urge a final answer. The claimants were now willing to accept an immediate settlement for $30,000—less than one-third of the original amount.[83]

It was not until the stern hand of Secretary Hay intervened that a settlement was effected. He instructed Minister Hart to press for "immediate payment" of the $30,000.[84] In Washington, Minister Rengifo denied the responsibility of his government for the unauthorized action of Santo Domingo Vila and questioned the nationality of the newspapers, claiming that they were owned by Colombian citizens (sons of an American and a native woman) and were chartered in New York merely to secure American protection. Furthermore, the papers had continued publication, under the suspension, as *The Evening Telegram* and *El telegrama*, using the same equipment and serving the same subscribers. He thought also that even a $30,000 claim was absurd, since the entire property of the papers had been sold in 1893 for some $13,000 in American gold—or $26,270 Colombian silver.[85]

Hay, unaffected by this pleading, still maintained that Colombia was "responsible for the acts of its higher military and civil officials—whether done by its authority or

[80] Hurtado to Blaine, May 9, 1890, Notes from Col. Leg., VIII.
[81] Gresham to Rengifo, Feb. 11, 1895, Olney to Rengifo, Feb. 25, April 21, 1896, Notes to Col. Leg., VII, 225, 241, 243.
[82] Rengifo to Olney, June 11, Sept. 9, 1895, Feb. 27, April 23, 1896, Notes from Col. Leg., IX.
[83] Olney to McKinney, (259) Feb. 24, 1897, Inst. Col., XVIII, 279-285.
[84] Hay to Hart, (111) Aug. 20, (tel.) Oct. 3, (tel.) Nov. 1, 1898, *ibid.*, XVIII, 682, 690; XIX, 1.
[85] Rengifo to Hay, Nov. 26, 1898, Notes from Col. Leg., IX.

not''—and could not be relieved of the consequences by mere disavowal. The New York charter was considered sufficient to establish the nationality of the claimants, and the subsequent sale of the papers could not be permitted to affect the claim.[86] On January 9, 1899, he again urged Hart to press for payment and two weeks later congratulated him on his successful settlement of it for $30,000.[87]

Although the European attitude had made it inadvisable to use pressure for the collection of the Colón Fire claims, the full force of the American government was still available for the protection of life and property. In fact, the affording of such protection was a powerful factor in the armed interventions on the Isthmus in 1895, 1901, 1902, and 1903.[88]

[86] Hay to Rengifo, Dec. 17, 1898, Notes to Col. Leg., VII, 287. See also Uribe, *Anales*, IV, 506, 696, 758.

[87] Hay to Hart, (tel.) Jan. 9, 23, 1899, Inst. Col., XIX, 22.

[88] See *supra*, chap. xiii.

Part VI

THE EVOLUTION OF THE AMERICAN
CANAL POLICY

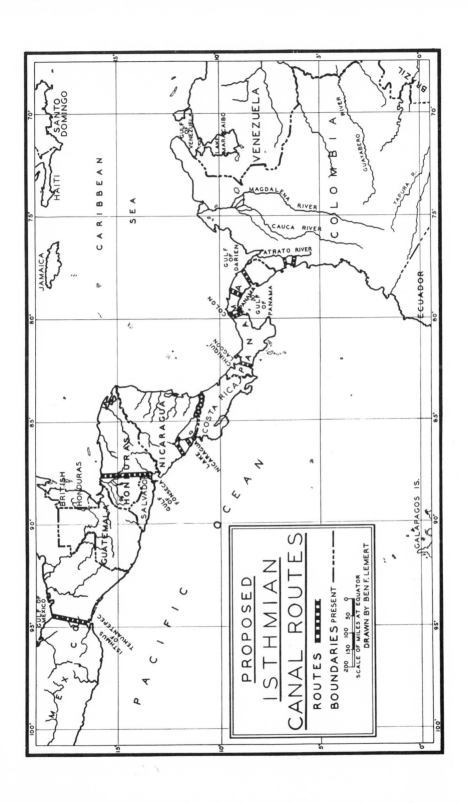

PROPOSED
ISTHMIAN
CANAL ROUTES

ROUTES ▪▪▪▪▪▪
BOUNDARIES PRESENT — — — —

SCALE OF MILES AT EQUATOR
200 150 100 50 0

DRAWN BY BEN F. LEMERT

CHAPTER XX

NATIONAL SELF-INTEREST CONDITIONED BY INTERNATIONAL EXPEDIENCY (1848-1866)

> It is our policy to encourage every practicable route across the isthmus . . . either by railroad or canal, which the energy and enterprise of our citizens may induce them to complete. . . . [However,] should such a work [proposed Nicaragua canal] be constructed under the common protection of all nations, for equal benefits to all, it would be neither just nor expedient that any great maritime state [Great Britain] should command the communication.—PRESIDENT TAYLOR.

THE settlement of the Oregon question, the successful termination of the Mexican War, and the acquisition of vast undeveloped territory on the Pacific Coast made the subject of an interoceanic communication a "matter of utmost practical importance."[2] The subsequent migration to the newly discovered California gold fields created a governmental problem for Washington but an economic opportunity for American citizens.[3] Secretary Clayton viewed a canal as essential to the future maintenance of government over the area.[4] Yankee merchants and capitalists were not slow to realize the possibilities of the situation.

, THE YANKEES SCAN THE ENTIRE ISTHMUS (1848-1850)

In keeping with the "Manifest Destiny" philosophy of the period, Americans attempted to dominate all three of the major interoceanic routes—Panama, Nicaragua, and Tehuantepec. But competition proved keen.

[1] Dec. 4, 1849, Richardson, *Messages and Papers*, VI, 2554-2555.
[2] Rockwell Report, Feb. 20, 1849, *H. Rep.*, No. 145 (30.2), p. 1.
[3] See C. D. Griswold, *The Isthmus of Panama and What I Saw There;* Wolford Nelson, *Five Years at Panama;* Benjamin C. Wright, *San Francisco's Ocean Trade, Past and Present.*
[4] Clayton to Lawrence, (4) Oct. 20, 1849, Inst. G. B., XVI, 60-70.

[323]

Even before the Senate ratification of the Treaty of 1846, Mathew Klein, for an Anglo-French company, had secured an exclusive ninety-nine-year railroad concession across Panama.[5] But Minister Herrán, fearing that the United States would construct a communication by some other route,[6] favored the cancellation of this contract and the making of a new one with the Panama Railroad Company of New York. A monetary crisis in Great Britain and political disturbances in France played into the hands of the American concern. The Klein concession was voided, and Herrán was authorized to treat in New York.[7]

Meanwhile, John P. Adams, who already held certain navigation privileges on the Orinoco River, was attempting to secure exclusive rights over the Panama route. Both Adams and the Panama Railroad Company sought aid for the enterprise from the United States government.[8] But before the attitude of the American congress was known, Herrán had closed a contract with the Panama Railroad Company. With certain alterations this received official approval at Bogotá on June 4, 1850.[9]

Other routes were also receiving the attention of Americans. The Polk administration (1847) offered $5,000,000 for the right of "free passage" across the Isthmus of Tehuantepec.[10] Although Mexico spurned

[5] Dated May 10, 1847, and ratified June 6, 1848. Herrán to Buchanan, Oct. 2, 1848, Notes from Col. Leg., II; Rivas, *Relaciones*, pp. 184-198. The United States was assured, however, that no European government was connected with the project (Bidlack to Buchanan, [41] Jan. 20, 1847, Desp. Col., XI).

[6] Some seven other Atlantic-Pacific railroad routes were being discussed (*DeBow's Rev.*, VII, 1 ff.).

[7] Rivas, *Relaciones*, pp. 229-231.

[8] *Ibid.*, pp. 231-234; Robertson, *Hispanic-American Relations*, pp. 252 ff.; *H. Rep.*, No. 26 (30.2), pp. 1-46. Naturally, the Democrats, who opposed federal appropriations for even internal improvements, refused the Panama Railroad's request for $250,000 per annum aid. The petition of Adams seems to have received little or no attention. For debates, see *Cong. Globe* (30.2), pp. 20, 40, 49, 59, 68, 78, 130, 268, 382, 457, 626.

[9] Rivas, *Relaciones*, pp. 232-239, 264-275; Uribe, *Anales*, V, 614-615.

[10] *Polk's Diary*, II, 473-475.

this, the grant of José de Garay (1842) was purchased in 1849 by Peter A. Hargous, who later transferred it to certain citizens of New Orleans. However, surveys of the route were halted the following year by the official cancellation of the concession.[11]

In 1848 Elijah Hise was dispatched from Washington to Central America to determine the extent of British aggressions there and to encourage united action to resist them. He found Salvador, Honduras, and Nicaragua friendly, owing to English encroachments on the Mosquito Coast; but Guatemala and Costa Rica were antagonistic. Becoming alarmed regarding British intentions, he negotiated a treaty (June 21, 1849) with Nicaragua securing for the United States or its citizens the exclusive right and privilege to construct and fortify a canal across its territory.[12]

But the new Whig administration, which assumed control March 4, 1849, recalled Hise and sent Ephriam G. Squier with more definite instructions. Meanwhile, Commodore Vanderbilt and his American Atlantic and Pacific Ship-Canal Company of New York had acquired a concession.[13] Squier then secured a new treaty providing for the protection of the enterprise and the guarantee of the neutrality of the route. Other powers were to be permitted to join in the guarantee.[14]

Thus the spring of 1850 found Yankees in control of exclusive concessions at Panama, Tehuantepec, and Nicaragua. However, the British seizure of San Juan (1848)

[11] See *Sen. Rep.*, No. 355 (32.1); *Sen. Doc.*, No. 231 (56.2), IV, 81 ff.; Richardson, *Messages and Papers*, VI, 2693; J. J. Williams, *The Isthmus of Tehuantepec*; C. A. Duniway, ''Daniel Webster,'' *American Secretaries of State and Their Diplomacy*, VI, 97-99.

[12] M. W. Williams, *Anglo-American Isthmian Diplomacy*, pp. 54-58.

[13] Vanderbilt opened a transit by boat and wagons in 1852, likewise had the route surveyed (O. W. Childs, *Report of the Survey of a Route for the Proposed Nicaragua Ship-Canal*, 1852; William Ludlow, ''The Trans-Isthmian Canal Problem,'' *Harper's New Monthly Mag.*, XCVI, 837-846).

[14] M. W. Williams, *Anglo-American Isthmian Diplomacy*, pp. 60-66; E. G. Squier, *Notes on Central America*; J. L. Stephens, *Incidents of Travel in Central America*.

and Tigre Island (1849)[15] made futile the efforts of Hise and Squier and shifted negotiations to London and Washington. The result was the Clayton-Bulwer Treaty, which crystallized the American canal policy for the first half of the century but proved a hindrance to its subsequent development.

THE CLAYTON-BULWER TREATY (1850)

The British had never neglected an opportunity to increase their commercial power and influence in the Caribbean area. The unsuccessful negotiations with the Spanish American patriots (1790-1805) had included commercial privileges and the right to the free use of any canal constructed. Many Englishmen, who fought in the independence struggle, remained to enjoy the fruits of economic development. And British merchants and capitalists almost monopolized the commerce of the area.

Large English loans had been endangered by the dissolution of the Central American Republic (1838). Insistent demands on the small bankrupt individual states for payment merely led to more active British participation in their internal political affairs, which, in turn, resulted in economic exploitation and gradual territorial encroachment. Yankee aggressiveness on the Pacific Coast aroused the British to a fear of rivalry in Central America. Therefore the rather uncertain seventeenth-century claims to the Mosquito Coast, the Bay Islands, and Belize (British Honduras) were resurrected and reaffirmed. San Juan and Tigre Island were then seized to prevent American monopoly of the canal route and dominance of the Pacific trade.[16]

[15] Both the Atlantic and Pacific termini of the proposed canal.

[16] But President Taylor denied that the United States desired to secure ''any monopoly or exclusive advantage in the use of the canal'' (Richardson, *Messages and Papers*, VI, 2577).

The Caribbean countries early noticed and feared the ever increasing British encroachments. Nicaragua began to plead for American interposition. New Granada used it effectively to persuade Bidlack to negotiate the Treaty of 1846 without official instructions.[17] After the ratification of the treaty Herrán turned to the question of Mosquitia, since New Granada still claimed a large portion of that area. He endeavored to secure: (1) a new convention defining the limits of Panama as guaranteed by the Treaty of 1846; (2) a congressional denunciation of British aggression; and (3) an American company to construct a railroad across Panama. In 1848 he also circularized the Central American states regarding a territorial guarantee by alliance. His successor, Rafael Rivas, was authorized to spend three hundred pesos annually for press propaganda stressing the British menace and its violation of the Monroe Doctrine.[18]

When the Taylor administration took office, it found Great Britain in possession of San Juan and seemingly attempting to monopolize the Nicaragua canal route, yet no official remonstrances had been made.[19] Although unwilling to extend the Panama guarantee to Tehuantepec and roundly denouncing Polk's foreign policies,[20] the new government was forced to take a vigorous stand in Nicaragua. To the United States it was an immediate "problem of transportation involving industrial advantages"; to Great Britain it was "a factor of future strategic importance that touched . . . her foreign policy."

[17] See *supra* chap. xii; Clayton to Bancroft, (55) May 2, 1849, Inst. G. B., XV, 386.

[18] Raimundo Rivas, *Relaciones*, pp. 206-211, 260, 293.

[19] Richardson, *Messages and Papers*, VI, 2575. Suspicion of British aggression on Panama and the Mosquito Coast was voiced by American representatives at Bogotá as early as 1823 (Todd to Adams, [47] March 29, 1823, Desp. Col., II).

[20] Clayton to Letcher, Sept., 1849, *Sen. Ex. Doc.*, No. 97 (32.1), pp. 11-13.

The course of the negotiations, then, lay "between the immediate economic needs of the one party and the ultimate political demands of the other."[21]

Negotiations, opening in London, were soon transferred to Washington, where the Clayton-Bulwer Treaty was signed on April 19, 1850.[22] Article I forbade that either power should "obtain or maintain for itself any exclusive control over the said ship canal"; Article VI, that all friendly states be invited to join in the neutrality guarantee; Article VIII, that the protection be extended to include "any other practicable communication."[23]

Both powers denied any desire to secure a monopoly on any interoceanic route, but maintained that their respective policies were to prevent the other from acquiring exclusive advantage.[24] If this be true, they succeeded admirably. Great Britain reluctantly gave up the Bay Islands, renounced its protectorate over Mosquitia, and settled the boundaries of Belize by treaties. But more than once during the next half century amicable relations were disturbed by contradictory interpretations of the treaty.

[21] L. M. Keasbey, The Terms and Tenor of the Clayton-Bulwer Treaty, pp. 7-17; Richard Olney, The Clayton-Bulwer Treaty; Memorandum, pp. 3-4.

[22] Text, Sen. Doc., No. 237 (56.1), pp. 134 ff. For thorough discussions, see M. W. Williams, Anglo-American Isthmian Diplomacy, chap. iii; R. B. Mowat, The Diplomatic Relations of Great Britain and the United States; John Bigelow, Breaches in Anglo-American Treaties.

[23] Buchanan contended that the treaty "altogether . . . [reversed] the Monroe Doctrine" and would "some day cost us a bloody war with Great Britain." Stephen A. Douglas called it a "practical negation and repudiation" of the Monroe Doctrine. Recent writers are inclined to agree with this view (Buchanan to McClernand, April 2, 1850, Amer. Hist. Rev., V, 101-102; Douglas, The Monroe Doctrine [reprint of a speech, Feb. 14, 1853]; Scruggs, The Colombian and Venezuelan Republics, p. 264; W. W. Pierson, Jr., "Political Influence of an Inter-Oceanic Canal, 1826-1926," H. A. H. R., VI, 212; George Morgan, The Life of James Monroe, p. 409; M. W. Williams, Anglo-American Isthmian Diplomacy, p. 323).

[24] Mowat, op. cit., p. 150; Richardson, Messages and Papers, VI, 2577-2580; John M. Clayton, The Central American Treaty (reprints of speeches, 1853, 1856).

AMERICAN SELF-INTEREST DEPENDENT ON TEMPORARY
SELF-DENIAL

Clayton had secured a British guarantee of the Panama route by Article VIII.[25] He felt that this was "necessary for the security of capital to be invested in the railroad."[26] However, this feeling was probably intensified by the fear that Great Britain might seize Panama in payment of Granadian debts or that the area might be sold to any power willing to assume this indebtedness.[27] On the other hand, Rafael Rivas maintained that his conferences with Bulwer were responsible for the inclusion of the extended guarantee. He confided to his government that this guarantee would free New Granada from the fear of both Yankee annexation and British usurpation.[28]

At any rate, the Clayton-Bulwer Treaty was a literal crystallization of the vague American policy as expressed in the congressional resolutions of 1835 and 1839 and advocated by numerous interested nationals.[29] But the policy had begun to be tempered by a feeling of the necessity of national defense. Buchanan (1845) had instructed Chargé Bidlack to prevent New Granada "from granting privileges to any other nation which might prove injurious to the United States."[30] It also seems evident that Clayton's effort (1849) to secure an Anglo-Granadian guarantee of Panama grew out of the acknowledged

[25] Clayton to Lawrence, (4) Oct. 20, (informal) 31, Dec. 14, 1849, Inst. G. B., XVI, 60-70; Sullivan and Cromwell, *op. cit.*, I, 529; Joseph P. Comegys, *Memoirs of John M. Clayton*, p. 191.

[26] Clayton to Foote, Dec. 15, 1849, *Moore's Digest*, III, 11.

[27] *Idem* to *idem*, (1) July 19, 1849, Inst. Col., XV, 123; Foote to Clayton, (11) April 25, 1850, King to Webster, (5) March 9, 1852, Desp. Col., XII.

[28] Rivas, *Relaciones*, p. 299. He had earlier expressed a greater fear of the United States than of Great Britain (Rivas to Paredes, Nov. 25, 1849, *ibid.*, p. 286).

[29] William Radcliff (1836), New York and Philadelphia petition (1838), Delaware petition (1840), Wheaton's treatise (1845), Ruggles (1846), Palmer's memoir (1848), Niles' plan (1849).

[30] Buchanan to Bidlack, (2) June 23, 1845, Inst. Col., XV, 99-100.

necessity of protecting American interests. Undoubtedly
Washington was resentful of London's interference in
regions so vitally connected with its national life and
development. But since England had rudely intruded,
it was hoped that France and Russia would soon accede
to the Clayton-Bulwer Treaty,[31] thereby checking British
ambitions. After all, it was American, and not European, capital and commerce that were to be made secure.
Necessity alone brought agreement to a British guarantee of the canal routes. Thus uncontrollable circumstances had made self-interest dependent on self-denial.

GRANADA INTERNALLY WEAK : AMERICA AGGRESSIVE

The fear that British capitalists were on the verge of
purchasing the Granadian "right of redemption" in the
Panama railroad caused Minister Green (1854) to advocate a canal by the Atrato route "under the control of
the United States."[32] The Democratic Platform of 1856
declared that a free communication between the two
oceans "should be secured by a timely and efficient exertion of the control which we [United States] . . . [had]
the right to claim over it, and no power on earth should
be suffered to impede or clog its progress by any interference with the relations it . . . [might] suit our policy
to establish. . . . We . . . [could], under no circumstances,
surrender our preponderance in the adjustment of all
questions arising out of it."[33]

The destruction of American lives and property in
the Panama Riot,[34] the passenger and tonnage tax controversy,[35] and the continual fear of Granada's rights in

---

[31] Richardson, *Messages and Papers*, VI, 2582.
[32] Green to Marcy, (11) Sept. 25, 1854, Desp. Col., XIII. Some Americans had already advocated such a policy (Resolution of the Yankee merchants at Rio de Janeiro [1841], *Niles' Reg.*, LX, 160; Col. George W.
Hughes, *Letter in Answer to the Hon. John M. Clayton on Inter-marine
Communication*, Washington, 1850).
[33] Kirk H. Porter (compiler), *National Party Platforms*, p. 46.
[34] See *supra*, chap. xiii.   [35] See *supra*, chap. xiv.

the railroad falling into European hands[36] led to official efforts to dominate the Isthmus and even to the advocacy by some of outright seizure. The State Department demanded not only indemnity for the riot losses but the establishment at Panama and Colón of semi-independent governments with jurisdiction over the communication route, the authorization of American intervention in times of disorder, and the transfer of Granadian interest in and control over the Panama railroad to the United States. Thus the formal recognition of Granadian sovereignty over the territory would have been reduced to a nullity. Naturally such demands were rejected, and Washington was forced to content itself with the adjustment of claims.[37]

Minister Bowlin recommended the seizure and retention of the Isthmus, at least until Bogotá came to its senses.[38] Corwine was convinced that it "must sooner or later fall into the hands of the United States. . . . The fruit . . . [was] ripe—we need[ed] only [to] come and take it."[39]

AMERICAN POLICY TEMPORARILY EMBARRASSED

Meanwhile, a controversy was raging over the interpretation of the Clayton-Bulwer Treaty. President Buchanan (1857) favored mutual abrogation. England would agree to this only on the *status quo ante* basis, which certainly was not desired at Washington. The State Department negotiated the Cass-Yrisarri Treaty with Nicaragua guaranteeing the canal route, but it was never ratified by the congress of the latter. Therefore, when Great Britain made treaties with Honduras (1859) and Nicaragua (1860) recognizing the Bay Islands as possessions of the former and relinquishing the Mosquito pro-

[36] Bowlin to Marcy, (37) March 27, 1857, Desp. Col., XIII.
[37] See *supra*, chap. xviii.
[38] Bowlin to Marcy, Aug. 1, 1856, (34) Feb. 20, 1857, Desp. Col., XIII.
[39] Corwine to Davis, Dec. 31, 1857, Dunbar Rowland (ed.), *Jefferson Davis*, III, 128.

tectorate to the latter, Buchanan declared the interpretation controversy "amicably and honorably adjusted."[40]

The American policy of 1857—a semi-independent
Isthmus, an American-owned and -controlled railroad, and
an abrogated Clayton-Bulwer Treaty—was modified by
Granada's refusal to negotiate, except regarding claims,
and by Britain's new treaties with Honduras and Nicaragua. The outbreak of the American Civil War and
the attendant expectation of more vigorous European
policies in the Caribbean softened Washington's attitude
still more. In 1862, when Herrán requested forceful
intervention to protect the Isthmus from Mosquera's
troops, Secretary Seward first inquired regarding the
views held at Paris and London. He declared that America had "no interest in the matter different from that of
other maritime powers"; therefore he desired European
coöperation if the landing of forces became necessary.[41]
This invitation for Old World intervention in acknowledged American affairs was occasioned by the unprecedented insecurity of the Union. And this seems to have
been the only instance where such a division of responsibility was proposed by Washington.

PANAMA IN THE LIMELIGHT (1848-1866)
Cleave America asunder
This is worthy work for thee.
Hark! The seas roll up imploring
Make the oceans free.
—Francis Lieber.[42]

While the American official policy was vicissitudinous
—but always defensive—Panama was gradually gaining
in popularity among the canal enthusiasts whose ardor
had not been dampened by the completion of the Panama

[40] *Sen. Ex. Doc.*, No. 194 (47.1), pp. 117, 126, 138, 151; Richardson,
Messages and Papers, VI, 2975; VII, 3170.
[41] See *supra*, chap. xv; *Moore's Digest*, III, 13 ff.
[42] "The Ship Canal from the Atlantic to the Pacific," *Hunt's Merchants
Mag.*, XIX, 676; B. E. Stevenson (ed.), *Poems of American History*, pp.
374-375.

railroad. Chargé Foote (1850) and Minister Green (1854) recommended a canal by the Atrato Valley.[43] From 1850 to 1855 American, British, and French surveys were made and transit concessions were granted by New Granada for four different routes to as many companies— Manuel Cárdenas and Florentino González (1851); Ricardo de la Parra and Benjamin Blagge (1851); Edward Cullen, Patrick Wilson, Charles Fox, James Henderson, and Thomas Brassy (1852); and Joseph Gooding and Ricardo Vanegas (1855).[44]

Dr. Edward Cullen, M.D., F.R.G.S., of Dublin, Ireland. In 1850 Dr. Cullen presented a paper on the Caledonia Bay-Gulf of San Miguel route before the Royal Geographical Society of London. In spite of British official indifference, a concession was secured in 1852, the Atlantic and Pacific Junction Company organized, Lionel Gisborne sent to make a more thorough survey, and Dr. Black of Kentucky dispatched (1853) to Washington to urge a governmental survey of the Darién routes. Gisborne reported favorably on the Cullen route, but Lieutenant Strain, U. S. N., declared it impracticable.[45]

Cullen continued his investigations in 1854, 1859, and 1862; renewed his concession in 1859; and visited Washington in 1863. But with the Civil War still raging, he was unable to arouse any interest in his project. After the return of peace, however, he flooded the State Department with plans, maps, and surveys. Since his concession had lapsed, he sought employment with the American government in making a new and more thorough survey. He assured Seward that Colombia "would be glad to sell the Isthmus" and stressed how vitally impor-

[43] Foote to Webster, Dec. 19, 1850, Desp. Col., XII.
[44] Uribe, *Anales*, V, 615-616; Scruggs to Fish, (14) July 17, 1875, Dichman to Evarts, (151) Oct. 17, 1879, Desp. Col., XXX, XXXIII.
[45] Edward Cullen, *The Isthmus of Darien Ship Canal; H. Ex. Doc.*, No. 107 (47.2), XXIII, 45; Johnson, *Four Centuries of the Panama Canal*, pp. 68-70; William Ludlow, "The Trans-Isthmian Canal Problem," *Harper's New Monthly Mag.*, XCVI, 837-846; Lionel Gisborne, *The Isthmus of Darien in 1852.*

tant its possession was to the United States.[46]   Although Cullen was not employed, his information and ideas were valued by the Department and undoubtedly influenced the negotiations of 1868-1870 and subsequent governmental surveys.

Frederick M. Kelley.   This New York capitalist, aroused by his boyhood reading of Baron von Humboldt's legend of the Raspadura Canal, sent T. C. Trautwine to survey the Atrato Valley in 1851-1852.   He financed two other surveys (1853) by Lane and Porter and still another (1854) by Captain William Kennish.   Convinced of the practicability of the Atrato-Truando route, he set out (1855) for Europe, where he presented his plans to the engineering and geographical societies of London and Paris, and Berlin; Baron von Humboldt; and the British and French governments.   When little success crowned his efforts, he returned to Washington to advocate a governmental survey in coöperation with Great Britain and France.[47]

In 1859 Kelley estimated the cost of a sea-level canal at $75,000,000 and suggested a government guaranteed loan as a means of raising that amount.   It was believed that Great Britain and France would coöperate in such a project; but, if not, the United States should proceed alone.[48]   He sent two more expeditions to the Isthmus in 1863-1864.   These estimated the cost of a canal by the San Blas route at $105,000,000 to $135,000,000.   But nothing came of these projects.   Although Kelley seems never

[46] West to Seward, (160) April 26, (172) Nov. 29, 1867, (192) Feb. 19, (216) Aug. 1, 1868, to Washburne, (257, 258), Con. Let., Dublin (Ireland), V, VII.   With these were enclosed letters and material from Cullen.

[47] *H. Misc. Doc.*, No. 16 (46.3); pp. 87-88; *Proceedings of the Royal Geographical Society of London, 1856; The Practicability and Importance of a Ship Canal to Connect the Atlantic and Pacific Oceans . . .* (N. Y., 1855) ; F. M. Kelley, *The Union of the Oceans by Ship-Canal without Locks via the Atrato Valley* (N. Y., 1859) ; Johnson, *Four Centuries of the Panama Canal,* pp. 68-70; José Carlos Rodríguez, *The Panama Canal; . . . Its Political Aspects, and Financial Difficulties,* pp. 5-12.

[48] Kelley, *op. cit.,* pp. 14-15; *Cong. Globe* (35.2), appendix, pp. 125-128.

to have organized a construction company, he spent some thirty years of his life and $125,000 of his private fortune in the financing of seven expeditions and securing three American governmental surveys.[49]

Ambrose W. Thompson. The provincial legislature of Chiriquí granted (1854) to Thompson an exclusive privilege of constructing a road from the Chiriquí Lagoon to the town of David. Preliminary surveys were later made by the Chiriquí Improvement Company, and American official surveys were made in 1860 and 1880, when contracts were under consideration for the use of parts of the grant for naval and coaling stations.[50]

President James Buchanan. The activities of Dr. Cullen had caused Buchanan, then minister to Great Britain, to urge some action on the part of his government. In 1854 Lieutenant Isaac C. Strain was dispatched to investigate the Cullen route. The expedition, joined by two Colombians,[51] encountered Gisborne and also a French party. Strain reported in favor of the Panama-Colón route.[52] Colombia evinced sufficient interest to make legal provisions for an official survey under General Codazzi and to invite negotiations for canal concessions[53]—four had already been granted since 1850.

Buchanan was still in London when Kelley arrived with a letter of introduction from Secretary Marcy. Lord Palmerston in a "private and unofficial conversation" intimated (1856) his approval of a joint survey. But Buchanan doubted American willingness to unite with

[49] *H. Misc. Doc.*, No. 16 (46.3), pp. 87 ff.; Rodríguez, *op. cit.*, p. 13; *Engineering News*, VI, 378.

[50] See *supra*, chap. xvii.

[51] Ramón Castello Rada and Bernado Polanco—both lost their lives in the Isthmian jungle.

[52] Lieut. I. C. Strain, *History and Prospects of Interoceanic Communication by the American Isthmus* (1856); *Sen. Ex. Doc.*, No. 1 (33.2), II, 417-427. For a vivid account of the hardships and horrors of the expedition, see *Harper's Monthly Mag.*, X, 433-458, 600-615, 745-764.

[53] Report of J. M. Quijano Otero to Colombian Congress, 1875, enclosed with Scruggs to Fish, (114) July 17, 1875; Dichman to Evarts, (151) Oct. 17, 1879, Desp. Col., XXX, XXXIII.

Great Britain in such an undertaking, on account of the latter's claims in Central America.[54]

In the year that Buchanan became president he secured an appropriation of $25,000 and the authority to use army and navy officers to survey the Darién routes. For the work he chose Lieutenants Nathaniel Michler, U. S. A., and T. A. Craven, U. S. N. The former reported favorably on a canal at an estimated cost of $134,000,000, but the latter considered the scheme impracticable.[55] Nothing definite resulted from the investigation. In 1859-1860 Buchanan also had the termini of the Chiriquí route surveyed, looking towards the establishment of naval and coaling stations. He favored the construction of a railroad by this route, but New Granada considered such a privilege a violation of the exclusive Panama railroad contract.[56]

Some felt that these adverse reports "would probably put an end to all efforts to explore the Isthmus with the view of the construction of a ship canal," since the enterprise seemed impracticable.[57] Minister Bowlin was equally positive that a canal would soon be undertaken.[58] Both prophesies were wrong.

The Granadian president was given enlarged powers (Law of May 6, 1859) regarding Isthmian exploration and concessions.[59] In 1860 Charles Caudest, agent for New York capitalists, appeared at Bogotá seeking a canal privilege,[60] and the following year Theodore Moore opened negotiations with General Mosquera.[61] But the

[54] Buchanan to Marcy, Feb. 22, 1856, Moore, *Works of James Buchanan*, X, 58.

[55] *H. Ex. Doc.*, Nos. 63 (46.2), 107 (47.2), p. 67; *Sen. Ex. Doc.*, No. 51 (34.3), pp. 1-20; Johnson, *Four Centuries of the Panama Canal*, pp. 68-70.

[56] *Ibid.*, p. 71; see *supra*, chap. xvii.

[57] *Harper's Mag.* (May, 1854), VIII, 834.

[58] Bowlin to Marcy, (3) May 10, 1855, Desp. Col., XIII.

[59] Uribe, *Anales*, V, 617.

[60] Jones to Cass, (20) Feb. 12, 1860, Desp. Col., XIV.

[61] Burton to Seward, (5) Dec. 10, 1861, *ibid.*, XVI.

outbreak of the American Civil War soon directed attention back home.

The French, however, became all the more active. Soon five separate and distinct surveys were under way.[62] The initial success of Ferdinand de Lesseps at Suez had thrown Panama in the limelight. Some three or four canal companies were in process of organization in Paris, and one was especially active in securing funds to colonize and canalize the Isthmus. José M. Samper, Colombian chargé in Paris, stated that Colombia would assist any reasonable enterprise, but warned against those then appealing to the public for support, since none of them possessed a legal concession.[63]

American agents at Bogotá continued active in preventing grants prejudicial to their government or nationals. In 1864 Minister Burton reported that Colombia had declined a 600,000 franc offer for a canal concession, fearing that the French government was back of the company, and had "assured" him that it would make such a grant to "an American company, but to no other."[64] The following year President Murillo convinced Major General D. E. Sickles that none of the European proposals was acceptable, since he considered "the enterprise as yet, premature."[65]

[62] Johnson, *Four Centuries of the Panama Canal*, pp. 70-71.

[63] José M. Samper, *Note sur les sociétés ou enterprises fondées à Paris pour la colonisation ou la canalisation de l'isthme de Darién* (Paris, 1862); M. Henry Bionne, *La question de percement de l'isthme de Panama devant un congrès international* (Paris, 1864).

[64] Burton to Seward, (133) Nov. 6, 1864, Desp. Col., XIX.

[65] Seward to Sickles, (1) Jan. 6, 1865, Specl. Missions, II, 29-33; Sickles to Seward, (4) April 17, 1865, Desp. Col., XX.

CHAPTER XXI

WASHINGTON ENTHUSIASTIC: BOGOTÁ
RETICENT
(1866-1872)

I regard it as of vast political importance to this country that no European Government should hold such a work. For this reason I have endeavored for the last year to get such a thorough survey . . . through the territory of Colombia, as would fully determine whether such a project is feasible, not doubting but that on the presentation of such feasibility American capital and an American company, under some treaty that could be easily arranged . . . would undertake it.—U. S. GRANT.

. . . time will sooner or later satisfy the Colombian Government, as it has already satisfied us, that the Darién canal must be an American work, and can in no case become a distant work.— PRESIDENT JOHNSON.[1]

THE close of the American Civil War ushered in an era of expansion. The destruction of the institution of slavery dissipated Northern opposition to the acquisition of new territory. The "Manifest Destiny" of the late forties, temporarily arrested by the internal conflict, now sought still greater triumphs. The French were curtly ordered out of Mexico, the Alaska Territory was acquired from Russia, an attempt was made to purchase the Danish West Indies, and a proposal entertained to annex Santo Domingo.

Secretary Seward, who had been an arch-expansionist at least since 1846,[2] favored (1866) the purchase of

[1] Grant to Chas. H. Davis, June 7, 1866, *H. Ex. Doc.*, No. 107 (47.2), p. 29; quoted by Seward to Sullivan, (57) Sept. 17, 1868, Inst. Col., XVI, 287-290.

[2] Seward was convinced (1846) ". . . that the popular passion for territorial aggrandizement is irresistible. . . . Our population is destined to roll its resistless waves to the ice barriers of the North and to encounter Oriental civilizations on the shores of the Pacific. The Monarchs of Europe are to have no rest, while they have a colony remaining on this continent . . . We must dare our destiny." (1852) The shadow of our institutions "stretches beyond the valley of Mexico, reaches even to the plains of

Tigre Island (Pacific terminus of the Nicaragua route), although this was forbidden by the Clayton-Bulwer Treaty;[3] and advocated a strong hand in the Isthmian tax controversy, since "forceful and successful resistance" to the taxes might strengthen the party on the Isthmus desirous of annexation to the United States.[4]

GENERAL REVIVAL OF CANAL INTEREST

The Colombian congress, after rejecting the proposals of Daniel W. Teller (American) and Henry Duesbury (English), empowered the president to negotiate with applicants for canal concessions and ordered the bases therefor published in the leading periodicals of Europe and North America.[5] Numerous proposals were received during 1867-1868, but none was acceptable.[6] Even the government of Peru (1869) expressed a readiness to purchase a large block of stock in any reputable canal company.

Washington was now becoming officially aroused regarding the importance of a canal. In compliance with a

Central America . . .'' (1860) ''Resistance to our ambition daily grows more and more impossible . . .'' (1860) ''It has been the result of my best conjecture that the seat of power for North America would yet be found in the valley of Mexico; that the glories of the Aztec capital would be renewed; and that city would become ultimately the capital of the United States of America'' (George E. Baker, ed., *The Works of William H. Seward*, III, 10, 409; IV, 311-312; H. Addington Bruce, *The Romance of Expansion*, p. 172).

[3] Seward to Adams (England), April 25, 1866, *Sen. Doc.*, No. 237 (56.1).

[4] J. T. Morse, Jr. (ed.), *Diary of Gideon Welles*, III, 106-107. Welles considered Seward as ''crazy on the subject of obtaining territory.''

[5] Law No. 60 of June 27, 1866, Uribe, *La reforma administrativa*, pp. 279-280; *Anales*, V, 619; Burton to Seward, (232) May 4, (252) July 3, 1866, Desp. Col., XXIII, XXIV; *Canal interoceánico: colección de artículos editoriales de "El Tiempo" de Bogotá* (Bogotá, 1866). Similar editorials in the *Diario oficial* and *La unión* indicate a growing interest in a canal.

[6] Page, Kappel, Marshall, and Webb of London; Chevey, Rochn, Ragon, and Villelieux of Paris; Lucian de Puydt of Paris; Ayrian (French); and Count Gleichen, reputed relative of the English royal family (*Documentos relativos al canal interoceánico*, Bogotá, 1870; Report of J. M. Quijano Otero to Congress in 1875, enclosed with Scruggs, No. 114, Desp. Col., XXX).

Senate resolution of March 19, 1866, Charles H. Davis, superintendent of the Naval Observatory, reported on the "various proposed lines for interoceanic canals and railroads." Although admitting that sufficient data for an intelligent decision did not exist, he favored the Darién route advocated by Kelley.[7] On July 28 an appropriation of $40,000 was made for the survey of this route.[8] The following year the House requested information regarding measures taken by foreign governments or capitalists to get control of Central American transit routes.[9] In support of American capitalists the State Department negotiated the Dickinson-Ayón Treaty (1867) with Nicaragua—canal privilege in return for neutrality guarantee—and assisted the Panama Railroad Company in securing a new contract at Bogotá.

MOSQUERA AND THE BRITISH

Acting-President Garrido's fear of American cancellation of the Treaty of 1846 and the Colombian need of ready cash appeared to clear the way for negotiations.[10] But rumor soon had it that Mosquera, president-elect, had already sold Colombia's interest in the railroad to English capitalists. Although Mosquera openly expressed his pro-British feelings, Burton was not inclined to take the rumor too seriously. However, he did urge upon his government "timely and judicious action," in order to secure "advantageous terms" and prevent the railroad and the canal route from falling into "unfriendly hands."[11] When the Colombian congress approved an English loan contract for $7,500,000, Burton became frightened lest the United States should lose control of the Isthmus to the English.[12] Congressional rejection of Mosquera's sale contract

[7] *Sen. Ex. Doc.*, No. 62 (39.1).   [8] *H. Ex. Doc.*, No. 81 (41.2).
[9] *H. Misc. Doc.*, No. 24 (40.1).
[10] Burton to Seward, (232) May 4, 1866, *For. Rel.* (1866-1867), p. 532.
[11] *Idem* to *idem*, (235) May 30, (244) June 8, 1866, Desp. Col., XXIII.
[12] *Idem* to *idem*, (250) July 1, 1866, *ibid.*, XXIV.

with William Henry Cotterill (English) relieved the tension. But Burton was fully convinced that Mosquera belonged "body, soul, and breeches to British capitalists." There seems little doubt that he did prefer selling the Colombian interest in the railroad to the English. At the same time, however, he wished to renew the treaty of guarantee with the United States—negotiations had already been initiated in Washington.[13] In this double play he was unsuccessful. Cotterill's renewed proposal (fall of 1866) was likewise rejected by Congress,[14] and the Panama Railroad Company secured a new contract in 1867, thereby saving the Isthmus from the English.[15]

LONDON REFUSES A GUARANTEE: WASHINGTON APPROACHED

Meanwhile, Minister Salgar (March, 1866) made certain unsolicited exclusive proposals at Washington. Colombia would permit and would coöperate in an American financed survey, if made within three years, and give preference to United States citizens wishing to secure a canal concession. Johnson and Seward lost little time in giving their approval, on condition that Colombia would sanction the arrangement by the "requisite treaty stipulations."[16] Here the matter rested for more than a year, Salgar pleading lack of further instructions.[17] Next he called attention to the numerous canal proposals recently received at Bogotá[18] and expressed, in the name

[13] *Idem* to *idem*, (253) July 4, (273) Sept. 13, (295) Oct. 26, 1866, *ibid.*, XXIV, XXV.

[14] *Idem* to *idem*, (confidential) Feb. 7, 1867, *ibid.*, XXV. It is possible that rumors of Isthmian secession and Burton's abrupt break with the government (Dec., 1866) had considerable effect.

[15] See *supra*, chap. xvii. Mosquera's business failure as commission merchant in New York (1854) and the persistence of his creditors seem to have created in him "an inveterate hatred" of all things North American (Burton to Seward, [37] Nov. 1, [39] 14, 1867, Desp. Col., XXVI).

[16] Salgar's Memo., March 16, 1866, Notes from Col. Leg., IV; Seward to Salgar, March 19, 1866, Notes to Col. Leg., VI, 200.

[17] Salgar to Seward, Nov. 26, 1866, Notes from Col. Leg., IV.

[18] Proposals had been invited by Law No. 60 of June 27, 1866.

of President Mosquera, a wish that the United States might be associated with any canal project; likewise he inquired whether that government would "make any offer similar or better for Colombian interests" than those under consideration.[19]

Two factors probably prompted this move: failure to secure British and French guarantees in 1865-1866 and the fear of American termination of the Treaty of 1846.[20] Salgar had already approached the State Department regarding the renewal of this convention and on April 23, 1867, submitted a project. But negotiations stopped here—apparently without even a conference. Before the end of the year Mosquera was exiled, Salgar recalled, and former President Murillo sent to Washington on a "special mission of salutation and felicitation."[21] Negotiations then shifted to Bogotá.

SEWARD ENTHUSIASTIC, BUT TO NO AVAIL

In September, 1867, Seward forwarded to Minister Sullivan a copy of a letter that he had received from Dr. Edward Cullen of Dublin and instructed him "on any suitable occasion to recommend a careful survey" of the Darién route.[22] When approached, Colombia was not only receptive but seemingly anxious. In December a convention project was submitted to Sullivan. It provided for an exclusive grant for the construction of a canal by the American government, a canal zone twelve miles in width, free terminal ports, joint defense of the completed work, the same neutrality guarantee as in the Treaty of 1846, and arbitration for the settlement of disagreement over interpretation. Sullivan recommended

[19] Salgar to Seward, April 27, 1867, Notes from Col. Leg., IV.

[20] Published correspondence enclosed with Dichman to Evarts, (247) Jan. 28, 1881, Desp. Col., XXXV. The Treaty of 1846 could be terminated by proper notice from either party after June, 1868.

[21] Salgar to Seward, Jan. 23, April 23, Oct. 18, 1867, Carlos Martín to Seward, Sept. 10, 1867, Notes from Col. Leg., V.

[22] Seward to Sullivan, (12) Sept. 5, 1867, Inst. Col., XVI, 232.

this to the Department as a good basis for negotiations, and added:

Should you prefer this mode of acquiring a foothold on the Isthmus of Darién, you can, I believe, succeed by spending a good deal of secret service money in engineering the treaty through the Colombian Congress. . . . Should you choose to acquire the desirable privilege, otherwise than by treaty, you will have to push the Cartagena murders [see *supra,* chap. xix] to the wall, muster up all the existing claims against this government, nurse both complaints for a reasonable time, and then make a bold and decisive demand for redress, which can not be given. In that case, you will have a good pretext for seizing upon Colombian property as indemnity for the said wrongs and injuries.[23]

In March, 1868, full powers and a counter project were forwarded to Sullivan. Seward advocated first of all a survey,[24] since the feasibility of such a canal was "not yet established in the popular mind, or even in the financial circles of the nation." He regretted that congressional consent to undertake the work "on the national account" could not be secured. Therefore the terms of the new convention must be very general. President Johnson favored something "more definite and decisive," but feared that some time would be required to familiarize the public mind with the enormous cost of such an enterprise.[25]

Disagreement in the negotiations centered around three main points: first, money consideration; second, use of the canal by other nations; third, agent of construction. Colombia demanded ten per cent of the gross profits for ten years after completion of the work until the builder had been reimbursed, and twenty-five per cent thereafter. It insisted that the canal be open to all nations in times of peace and war alike. Operation by a

[23] Sullivan to Seward, (45) Dec. 18, 1867, Desp. Col., XXVI.
[24] Funds for the survey had already been appropriated.
[25] Seward to Sullivan, (34) March 2, 1868, Inst. Col., XVI, 263-268.

private corporation was permissible, but the canal must be constructed by the United States government.[26] These provisions were obviously beyond Sullivan's instructions. He desired to return to Washington for conferences, especially since both English and French proposals were under consideration at Bogotá and a Prussian man-of-war was reported to be making a survey of the Bay of Limón.[27] But he was ordered to remain at his post, since Johnson was convinced that "time . . . [would] sooner or later satisfy the Colombian Government, as it . . . [had] already satisfied us, that the Darién canal must be an American work. . . ."[28]

Seward prepared a new draft with slight modifications. It was not until he had requested and secured a conference with certain "enlightened capitalists" of New York, however, that he became really enthusiastic. On October 24 he rushed new instructions to Bogotá. It had been a pleasant surprise to him to find that the canal idea had "manifestly gained favor" recently. He entertained "no doubt that, if a proper treaty . . . [could] be concluded, the necessary capital . . . [would] be immediately secured. . . ."[29] Minister Acosta was consulted, and Caleb Cushing hastened to Bogotá with still more liberal instructions. If Colombia could not otherwise be won to the American view, Sullivan and Cushing were "authorized and directed to abate from any part, and if absolutely necessary the whole, of the points of difference heretofore insisted upon by the United States." Seward

[26] Sullivan to Seward, (82) Aug. 12, 1868, Desp. Col., XXVII.

[27] *Idem* to *idem*, (80) July 23, (81) 30, 1868, *ibid.*

[28] Seward to Sullivan, (57) Sept. 17, 1868, Inst. Col., XVI, 287-290.

[29] Cooper to Seward, (tel.) Oct. 17, 1868, Seward to Sullivan, (58) Sept. 27, (59) Oct. 24, 1868, Inst. Col., XVI, 290-330. On Sept. 24 the New York legislature had chartered the "Isthmus Canal Company," composed of such men as Frederick Kelley, Peter Cooper, William M. Evarts, William H. Vanderbilt, William H. Seward, Jr., Charles A. Dana, William C. Fargo, et al. (Seward to Cooper, Sept. 28, 1868, Misc. Let., LXXIX, 361-362).

hoped by this means to present the treaty to the Senate the following February.[30]

Johnson, in his last annual message, advised Congress of the pending negotiations,[31] and Seward continued his conferences with Acosta, who now began to advocate an international convention of guarantee. Seward emphasized the American traditional fear of entangling alliances and branded the belief that European nations would make such a treaty as "impracticable and visionary."[32]

Meanwhile, Sullivan had made no progress at Bogotá. In fact, the fierce political, even military, struggle between the Liberals and Conservatives and the anti-American influence of the resident Anglo-French group caused him to despair of any early treaty.[33] Then Cushing arrived on the scene, and negotiations were reopened on January 7, 1869. One week later a treaty, "considerably within the limits" of Seward's instructions, was signed.[34]

The Washington government or any company to which it might transfer the contract agreed to make a survey and construct a canal with a one-hundred-year exclusive privilege to operate it. The treaty draft provided for a twenty-mile strip of territory under American control but Colombian sovereignty; afforded protection by American troops under joint orders; freed transit commerce and persons from tolls or duties; opened the canal to the peaceful commerce of all nations at all times; and compensated Colombia with ten per cent of the net earnings until the builders had been reimbursed

[30] Seward to Cushing, Nov. 25, 1868, Inst. Col., XVI, 332.

[31] Richardson, *Messages and Papers*, VIII, 3885.

[32] Memo. of conference of Jan. 14, 1869, Acosta to Seward, Jan. 15, 1869, Notes from Col. Leg., V; Seward to Acosta, Jan. 18, 1869, Notes to Col. Leg., VI, 240-242.

[33] Sullivan to Seward, (94) Oct. 10, (99) Nov. 16, (100) 20, (103) 30, 1868, Jan. 2, 1869, Desp. Col., XXVII.

[34] Cushing to Sullivan, Jan. 3, 14, 1869, *ibid.*; Claude M. Fuess, *The Life of Caleb Cushing*, II, 301-302.

for the cost of the work, and twenty-five per cent thereafter. Other nations were to be invited to guarantee the Isthmian neutrality.[35]

Cushing raced back to Washington with the treaty, and Johnson hastened to submit it to the Senate,[36] but the Administration lacked sufficient strength to secure ratification before it surrendered the reins of power. It was soon reported from Bogotá that the treaty had been rejected by the Colombian senate by the vote of sixteen to eight. In the American senate its consideration was postponed until April 15, and then the treaty was dropped without a vote.[37]

President Johnson's gracious address on receiving Santos Acosta (September, 1868),[38] Seward's speech before the New York capitalists (October, 1868), and Cushing's special mission convinced many Colombians that still better terms were possible. Besides, the Anglo-French element at Bogotá was not inactive. Sullivan again suggested the use of money to secure the ratification of the treaty.[39]

But there were signs of Colombian moderation. Congress requested the President to renew the negotiations, and Sullivan conferred with the Colombian senate committee on foreign relations before he returned to Washington in June.[40] It is quite probable that Panama's threatened secession[41] and the argument of Galindo (late chargé to London and Paris) that only the United States

[35] *Sen. Doc.*, No. 237 (56.1), pp. 45-51.

[36] Richardson, *Messages and Papers*, VIII, 3900.

[37] *Sen. Ex. Jour.*, XVI, 476, 501; XVII, 7, 10, 136, 163, 174; Sullivan to Dept., (116) March 1, (119) 15, 1869, Desp. Col., XXVII.

[38] Notes to Col. Leg., V.

[39] Sullivan to Seward, (116) March 1, 1869, Desp. Col., XXVII. The British legation had a copy of the treaty before Cushing left Bogotá. Sullivan intimated that he had been ''forced'' to sign it, in order to prevent an Anglo-Colombian agreement (Cushing to Seward, Feb. 4, 1869, Sullivan to Fish, [134] May 31, [135] June 17, 1869, *ibid.*).

[40] Sullivan to Washburne, (128) April 24, to Fish, (131) May 19, 1869, *ibid.*

[41] See *supra*, chap. xiii.

could build the canal[42] might have affected congressional opinion. In Washington, Acosta became fearful that the United States would turn to another route. M. Felix Belly of Paris was claiming the promise of American patronage and listing among his active supporters such men as Cyrus Field, Peter Cooper, General Dix, Commodore Maury, Senator Sprague, Charles A. Dana *(New York Sun)*, Horace Greeley *(New York Tribune)*, and Henry J. Raymond *(New York Times)*.[43]

GRANT'S FUTILE EFFORTS

President Grant's interest in a canal was of long standing. He had been impressed with the need of one in 1852, when he crossed the Isthmus with troops enroute to California.[44] At the close of the Civil War he set about to secure a thorough governmental survey to deter mine the feasibility of the project.[45] A Senate resolution soon followed. Then came the Davis report on canal routes, an appropriation for a survey, and Seward's negotiations with Colombia.

General Stephen A. Hurlbut, a clever Illinois lawyer, soon replaced Sullivan at Bogotá. After conferences in Washington with Acosta and Cushing he requested (August, 1869) a "special allowance" of $5,000 for his legation. Cushing was to inform the Department of "reasons in his knowledge" for such a procedure. The requested amount was granted from the secret service fund, and Hurlbut set out for Bogotá. Soon after arrival he secured "the good will and services of . . . [the] owner and publisher of the *Diario oficial, El liberal,* and *La*

[42] Aníbal Galindo, *El tratado de 14 de enero de 1869 para la escavación del canal de Darién* (Bogotá, 1869), enclosed with Sullivan, No. 132, Desp. Col., XXVII.

[43] Acosta to Fish, Sept. 8, 1869, Notes from Col. Leg., VI; M. Felix Belly, *Canal intérocéanique de Nicaragua* (Paris, 1869).

[44] William R. Scott, *The Americans in Panama*, p. 47.

[45] Grant to C. H. Davis, *H. Ex. Doc.*, No. 107 (47.2), p. 29.

revista de Colombia.'' These papers were to publish from time to time articles regarding ''the canal and the duties of this Republic to that work.'' Of course, Hurlbut reserved the right to revise them before publication[46]—the work of a lawyer, not a general.

The new minister had quite positive ideas regarding a canal. Since the English, French, and Prussian interests would probably prevent the securing of an exclusive grant, he recommended that a corporation be created by congressional enactment with offices in the United States and boards in the three countries named. The stock was to be allotted to the capitalists of each nation and a five per cent income on investment guaranteed by the four powers. In any case, he was convinced that within fifty years the canal would ''of necessity'' belong to Americans.[47] But Grant feared that ''such a joint protectorate would be a source of future trouble.'' Besides, he regarded the canal ''as an American enterprise . . . to be undertaken under American auspices. . . .'' If it were executed by an international group, more than fifty per cent of the stock must be American.[48]

Hurlbut, overruled by the Administration, reopened negotiations for an exclusive contract in November, 1869. The following January he signed another treaty. The principal advantages of this one over the former were the free use of the canal by American men-of-war at all times and the right to maintain docks and repair yards in both terminal harbors. A disadvantage was a more specific provision for the payment of equitable damages to the Panama Railroad Company as provided by its contract of 1867. The clause inviting the European nations

[46] Hurlbut to Fish, Aug. 11, 18, (5) Nov. 29, 1869, Desp. Col., XXVIII. An article already published in *La revista de Colombia* was enclosed with the November despatch.

[47] Hurlbut's memo., Aug. 29, 1869, *ibid.*

[48] Fish to Hurlbut, (6) Sept. 4, 1869, Inst. Col., XVI, 365-367.

to join in the guarantee was retained for "home consumption" at Bogotá.[49]

Hurlbut set about canvassing the Colombian senators and thought that he had a sufficient number committed to the approval of the treaty. But the presence at Bogotá of representatives of European capitalists—Lanauze (English),[50] Guillermo Martín (Cullen's company),[51] Chevalier Barrot (French); the activities of the British chargé, Robert Bunch;[52] and the American failure to recognize Cuban independence made matters rather uncertain.[53] Hurlbut regretted that a rich American company was not prepared to take the charter and "disburse handsomely to the doubtful members of either House."[54] Meanwhile, he was arguing that the Treaty of 1846 had expired, and giving out as his opinion that the present treaty must be ratified to secure the renewal of the Isthmian guarantee.[55] But the temporary opposition to the treaty was too great; therefore he suggested that money be made available for use during the session of 1871[56]—

[49] Hurlbut to Fish, (5) Nov. 29, 1869, (7) Jan. 5, (8) Feb. 1, 1870, Desp. Col., XXVIII; *Sen. Doc.*, No. 237 (56.1), pp. 51-61.

[50] He first came to Washington for support, but Fish advised him that it was preferred that the work be done by American capitalists. He then set out for Bogotá, where he published an anti-American pamphlet (Fish to Hurlbut, [private] March 19, 1870, Inst. Col., XVI, 373; Hurlbut to Fish, [28] June 10, 1870, Desp. Col., XXVIII).

[51] A brother of Dr. Carlos Martín, who bitterly fought the treaty, Hurlbut to Fish, Nos. 9, 12, 21, *ibid.*

[52] He was former British consul at Charleston, S. C., but was "by order of President Lincoln, dismissed in disgrace. . . ." His brother-in-law, Enrique Cortés, was secretary to the Colombian legation in Washington (Sullivan to Seward, [unofficial] July 13, 1868, [115] Feb. 22, 1869, *ibid.*, XXVII).

[53] Hurlbut to Fish, (9) March 4, (12) 16, (19) April 17, (21) May 6, (22) 16, (28) June 10, 1870, *ibid.*, XXVIII.

[54] Hurlbut said that some of the senators "understood the commercial value of their positions well enough to qualify for Albany" (Hurlbut to Fish, [20] April 26, [27] June 6, 1870, *ibid.*).

[55] Hurlbut to Fish, (8) Feb. 1, 1870, *ibid.* This question arose in 1871, when it was agreed that the Treaty of 1846 was still in force (Fish to Pérez, Feb. 8, May 27, 1871, Notes to Col. Let., VI, 265, 272; Pérez to Fish, April 15, 1871, Notes from Col. Leg., VI).

[56] Hurlbut to Fish, (31) June 29, 1870, Desp. Col., XXVIII.

evidently thinking that North American post-war lobby methods might prove effective. However, the treaty with some seventeen amendments was approved on July 8, 1870.[57]

In Washington, Grant had enthusiastically advised Congress of the negotiations[58] and on April 1 had submitted the treaty for Senate approval. It was reported out of committee (July 13) unamended and its passage recommended, but it seems never to have come to a vote.[59] The Colombian amendments had made it wholly unacceptable. Grant proposed a year's extension of time for the exchange of ratifications,[60] but his next Congress never so much as considered the treaty.

Hurlbut continued his efforts to secure favorable action at Bogotá. He advised his government (October, 1871) that the desired grant might be secured gratis, if the United States would guarantee the construction and maintenance of a railroad from Bogotá to the Lower Magdalena.[61] The nullification of a federal internal revenue act by Cauca and Antioquia, destroying all chance of Colombian private capital building the road, and actual fighting on the Isthmus made the time seem "propitious for final and decisive negotiations."[62] But Washington had reasons for delay.

[57] *Idem* to *idem*, (33) July 13, 1870, *ibid.; Sen. Doc.*, No. 237 (56.1), pp. 105-113.

[58] Richardson, *Messages and Papers*, VIII, 3987.

[59] *Sen. Ex. Jour.*, XVII, 415.

[60] Fish to Hurlbut, (40) April 11, 1871, Inst. Col., XVI, 391-392.

[61] The matter was referred to Senator Cameron and the senate committee on foreign affairs (Hurlbut to Fish, [61] Oct. 3, [65] 17, 1871, Desp. Col., XXVIII; Fish to Hurlbut, [52] Nov. 9, [53] Dec. 5, 1871, Inst. Col., XVI; Misc. Let., Nov. 19, 1871).

[62] Hurlbut to Fish, (69) Nov. 17, 1871, Desp. Col., XXVIII. Fish was willing to threaten the termination of the Treaty of 1846 to secure the payment of a claim, but not to force a favorable canal treaty (Fish to Hurlbut, [55] Dec. 19, 1871, [59] Feb. 20, 1872, Inst. Col., XVI, 407-408, 411-412).

CHAPTER XXII

WASHINGTON RETICENT: BOGOTÁ ANXIOUS
(1872-1880)

DURING the recent negotiations President Grant had secured permission from Colombia to survey the various routes. In 1870-1871 Commander T. O. Selfridge examined four of them,[1] but recommended only the Atrato-Napipi route as practicable. Grant created an interoceanic canal commission[2] and obtained surveys of some ten routes, eight through Colombian territory, between 1872 and 1876.[3] After considering all the collected data, the canal commission (February 7, 1876) reported unanimously in favor of the Nicaragua route.[4]

The surveys had scarcely begun before Minister Carlos Martín, who had bitterly opposed the ratification of the late treaty, notified the Department that he was authorized to negotiate a pact that would meet with Senate approval. Secretary Fish was courteous but not enthusiastic. He promised to consider any convention draft submitted, but pointed out that the official surveys were as yet incomplete.[5] The new proposals of Feb-

[1] Caledonia Bay, San Blas, Atrato-Tuyra, and Atrato-Napipi routes.

[2] General A. A. Humphreys, chief of army engineers; Captain C. P. Patterson, superintendent of coast survey; and Rear Admiral Daniel Ammen.

[3] Surveys made by Major Walter McFarland; Captains R. W. Shufeldt, Chester Hatfield, E. P. Lull, W. H. Heuer; Lieutenants A. G. Menocal, Frederick Collins; and Professor Henry Mitchell.

[4] Hurlbut to Fish, (4) Nov. 27, 1869, Desp. Col., XXVIII; Selfridge report, H. Misc. Doc., No. 113 (43.3); Report of commission, Sen. Ex. Doc., No. 15 (46.1); Johnson, Four Centuries of the Panama Canal, pp. 71-75; Daniel Ammen, "American Isthmian Canal Routes," Jour. Franklin Institute (Dec., 1889); Frederick Collins, "The Isthmus of Darien and the Valley of the Atrato Considered with Reference to the Practicability of an Interoceanic Ship-Canal," Amer. Geog. Soc., Transactions (1873), V, 138-165.

[5] Martín to Fish, Nov. 4, 1872, Notes from Col. Leg., VI; Fish to Martín, Dec. 6, 1872, Notes to Col. Leg., VI, 303; Uribe, Anales, III, 703, 748.

[351]

ruary, 1873, provided for a ninety-nine-year exclusive concession and the grant of 100,000 hectares of land; the closing of the canal to nations at war with either party; a loan of $6,000,000 to Colombia, to be deducted from its twenty-five per cent of the canal earnings; the renewal of the neutrality guarantee of the Treaty of 1846; and an invitation for other nations (except those permitting slavery) to make a similar guarantee. The United States was to pledge itself either to construct the canal as a national work or assure its completion by interested capitalists. If no treaty resulted from these liberal bases, Martín reserved "perfect liberty to make other arrangements."[6]

Secretary Fish, nearly four months later, refused to pledge his government to execute the work, unless it proved to be "practicable at a reasonable price." He doubled the size of the land grant, reduced Colombia's share of the earnings from twenty-five to seven per cent, eliminated the neutrality guarantee clause of the Treaty of 1846, but retained the provision for an international guarantee.[7] Martín felt that "the definite obligation to construct the canal . . . [should] be a necessary basis of the negotiations." He also insisted on a requirement for joint defense of the canal, in case Colombia was forced to close it against an American enemy, and on retaining the old guarantee of absolute neutrality. Furthermore, he contended, Colombia was not willing to sell such a valuable concession for "a mere mess of pottage."[8] But probably the United States was no longer interested.

When forced to accept this "irresistible truth," Martín advised that he was leaving for Europe in August"[9]—

[6] Martín to Fish, Feb. 13, 1873, Notes from Col. Leg., VI.
[7] Fish to Martín, June 7, 1873, Notes to Col. Leg., VI, 311.
[8] Martín to Fish, July 11, 1873, Notes from Col. Leg., VI.
[9] *Idem* to *idem*, July 29, 1873, *ibid.*

evidently "to make other arrangements." He did not fail, however, to show his anxiety by reiterating his desire for conferences on the subject and assuring the Department that he would return to Washington whenever notified of a favorable decision.[10] Fish answered that it was doubtful whether the United States would decide regarding a route before his contemplated return or whether it would assume a "positive obligation to construct the canal" at all.[11]

In May, 1874, Martín returned to Washington to find Fish still apathetic, and soon resigned his post. Three months later Felipe Zapata stopped long enough in the United States to send in his letter of credence, then sailed for Great Britain and France, never to assume his duties at Washington. More than two years passed without official Colombian representation in the American capital.[12]

Meanwhile, disturbances on the Isthmus necessitated (September, 1873) the landing of American troops,[13] and Minister Scruggs noted a growing public sentiment at Bogotá to consider Panama "only a source of weakness and expense to the general government." Therefore he thought that the safety of the interoceanic transit probably depended on American acquisition of sovereignty over the area.[14] In 1874 Bogotá was expressing "some anxiety" over the Nicaragua surveys, and President Pérez was regretting that the late treaty with the United States had not been ratified. Scruggs thought that the time was opportune for a reasonable canal arrangement. In view of Fish's verbal instructions, however, he gave little or no encouragement to anxious Colombians.[15] Fish

[10] See his letters cited in footnotes 5, 6, 8, 9.
[11] Fish to Martín, Aug. 1, 8, 1873, Notes to Col. Leg., VI, 313, 314.
[12] Martín to Fish, May 22, July 25, 1874, Dept. Memo., Sept. 7, 1874, Notes from Col. Leg., VI; Fish to Martín, May 26, 1874, to Pérez, Oct. 16, 1876, Notes to Col. Leg., VI, 315, 323.
[13] See *supra* chap. xiii.
[14] Scruggs to Fish, (19) Nov. 17, 1873, Desp. Col., XXIX.
[15] *Idem* to *idem*, (74) Nov. 17, 1874, *ibid.*

saw no reason to attempt negotiations until the interoceanic canal commission had made its report.[16]
The activities of the Nicaraguan legation in Washington caused alarm at Bogotá. The minister of foreign
affairs suggested to the Colombian congress (February
1, 1875) that the time had arrived to encourage the
formation of a canal company and added that if the
United States saw fit to initiate new negotiations, an
agreement could be arranged on the bases approved by
the American senate in 1870.[17] The appearance of one
Anthony de Gogorza with the fantastic scheme of reopening the legendary Raspadura canal further aroused
the Colombians.[18] Exploration of this route was contemplated, but the old Liberal-Conservative struggle prevented any definite action.[19] And American interest had
shifted elsewhere.

UNSUCCESSFUL NICARAGUAN NEGOTIATIONS

In 1872, when a House resolution requested the President to "ascertain the views of European governments
in regard to international coöperation" for the construction of a canal, Secretary Fish answered:

It has not been the policy of this government to complicate the
practical question of the construction of such a canal by encouraging discussions or negotiations . . . but rather to foster
the development of the enterprise, when the most practicable
and economical route shall have been determined upon, as an
undertaking which is peculiarly the duty of the American nations to carry forward to a successful completion.[20]

This seems a mere restatement of Grant's policy.
However, the Fish-Martín negotiations (1872-1873) might
have indicated a willingness, even a desire, to supplant

[16] Fish to Scruggs, (60) Dec. 15, 1874, Inst. Col., XVI, 484.
[17] Memoria de 1875—Sánchez, Uribe, *Anales*, III, 748-749.
[18] See *infra*.
[19] Scruggs to Fish, Nos. 105, 114, 116, 118, 119, 123, Desp. Col., XXX.
[20] *H. Misc. Doc.*, No. 219 (42.2), pp. 1-2.

Article XXXV of the Treaty of 1846 by an international guarantee. The completion of the transcontinental railroads had obviously lessened American interest in a canal. Besides, negotiations were considered useless until the most practicable route had been determined.

When the canal commission (1876) reported unanimously in favor of the Nicaraguan route, Fish opened negotiations with Señor Adán Cárdenas. The proposed treaty draft contained none of the special privileges inserted in the recently defeated conventions with Colombia, but was designed to secure "a guaranty of the neutrality of the work by the chief maritime powers, and by grants from Nicaragua such as would be sufficient to tempt the cupidity and inspire the confidence of capital." President Grant was convinced that these were necessary for the immediate success of the enterprise. However, Nicaragua's "undue apprehension of designs upon her sovereignty" defeated his aims. And Cárdenas withdrew.[21]

On the failure of the negotiations Fish dispatched (February 28, 1877) identic notes to the United States representatives abroad, enclosing copies of the proposed treaty and his correspondence with Cárdenas. He also pointed out how the Administration's aim to secure an international guarantee necessary for the immediate construction of the canal had been thwarted by Nicaragua's unreasonable attitude.[22]

This valedictory might well have been, however, an attempt to explain Grant's failure to secure anticipated canal arrangements and to assure the world of the purity

[21] Fish to Cárdenas, Oct. 30, 1876, Feb. 6, 16, 17, 1877, Notes to Nic. Leg., II, 32, 35 ff.; Cárdenas to Fish, Jan. 25, Feb. 6, 9, 1877, Notes from Nic. Leg., V; Joseph B. Fuller, "Hamilton Fish," *American Secretaries of State and Their Diplomacy*, VII, 208-209.

[22] (112) Inst. G. B., XXIV, 525; (883) France, XIX, 450; (328) Germany, XVI, 289; (564) Italy, II, 11; (518) Spain, XVIII, 123; (23) Austria, II, 441; (60) Argentina, XVI; (195) Brazil, XVII, 48; (269) Central America, XVII, 312; (244) Costa Rica, XV, 164; no legation at Bogotá; (277) Japan, II, 378.

of American intentions. So important did Grant consider a canal that he was willing, under seeming necessity, to sacrifice his "American enterprise . . . under American auspices" for an international project. Soon, however, French activities at Panama led his successor to return to a nationalistic policy.

AN AMERICAN DELIVERS PANAMA TO THE FRENCH

Anthony de Gogorza, a United States citizen[23] residing in Colombia, made a partial survey of the Isthmus in 1866, proceeded to Washington, and presented a report to a group of statesmen and financiers.[24] Assistance in securing a resurvey was promised but never given.[25] He conferred with Admiral Daniel Ammen and one of Grant's staff officers. Ammen was shown partial maps but not given the secret of a claimed low-level route. Gogorza later wrote Ammen urging haste, lest his information fall into European hands, but the latter refused to deal further with him.[26] When American support failed to materialize, Gogorza went to Paris. He was organizing a company there, when it was reported that the United States had decided to make official surveys. Grant soon requested the use of his maps for that purpose.[27]

The first International Geographical Congress (1871) approved Gogorza's plan, and the second (Paris, 1875) manifested still greater interest. A committee, including Ferdinand de Lesseps, was appointed to investigate the

[23] His father was naturalized in 1796.

[24] Senator Sprague, General Benjamin Butler, Oakes Ames, Captain Patterson for Fred Billings, J. A. Raynor, E. Hoyt, W. E. Dodge, J. H. Griswold, and M. Ketchum.

[25] Gogorza, "Problem of Inter-oceanic Communication by way of the American Isthmus: Proposed Unique Solution. . . ," *Jour. Amer. Geog. Soc.*, XX, 502-513.

[26] Daniel Ammen, "M. de Lesseps and His Canal," *N. Amer. Rev.*, CXXX, 134-135.

[27] Gogorza, *op. cit.*, pp. 504-505.

project.[28] The spring of 1876 found Gogorza back in Bogotá claiming to represent a French company prepared to construct the canal. He insisted also that he possessed proof from the Spanish archives that a natural passage between the oceans had existed as late as 1680. By this low-level route the project would require a minimum of energy and capital.[29]

Since the United States had definitely turned to Nicaragua, Colombia was naturally attentive to any European proposal. Besides, Gogorza's revival of the old Raspadura canal legend lent romance to his project. On May 26 the Colombian congress empowered the President to contract for the survey and construction of a canal. Two days later a concession was granted to Gogorza and General Étienne Türr.[30]

On Gogorza's return to Paris *La sociétè civile internationale du canal-interoceánique* began to take form under the leadership of General Türr and Lieutenant Lucien Napoleon Bonaparte Wyse. Minister Felipe Zapata and Dr. Joaquín Sarmiento, director of the Bank of Bogotá, were on hand to assist. De Lesseps requested the American minister to call his government's attention to the matter. Gogorza forwarded through him a pamphlet setting forth the canal plan. Both Gogorza and Türr then appealed directly to President Grant.[31]

After a mere glance at the pamphlet Ammen pointed

---

[28] Washburne to Fish, (1369) Sept. 13, 1876, *For. Rel.* (1877), pp. 125-126.

[29] Scruggs to Fish, (163) May 7, 1876, Desp. Col., XXXI. Both J. M. Quijano Otero and Colonel Farrand, former American consul to Callao, supported the Raspadura legend. Scruggs, Nos. 114, 183, *ibid.*, XXX, XXXI. Johnson, *Four Centuries of the Panama Canal*, p. 75, states that during the winter of 1874-1875 Gogorza told the Colombian congress that he himself had crossed the Isthmus by boat in 1868.

[30] Scruggs to Fish, (170) June 6, 1876, Desp. Col., XXXI; Uribe, *Anales*, V, 623.

[31] Washburne to Fish, (1369) Sept. 13, 1876, *For. Rel.* (1877), pp. 125-126; Johnson, *Four Centuries of the Panama Canal*, p. 76; Gogorza to Grant, Sept. 7, Türr to Grant, Sept. 15, 1876, Misc. Let.

out to the Department the fallacy of Gogorza's claims.[32] It is little wonder, then, that Secretary Fish evinced no enthusiasm when Minister Pérez inquired regarding American coöperation in making a resurvey. The former merely asked whether any European government had approved the plan.[33]

FERDINAND DE LESSEPS

Meanwhile, Lieutenant Wyse had set out for the Isthmus. He found the Gogorza route impracticable, as predicted by Ammen, but was favorably impressed with the Panama-Colón route. Early 1878 found him at Bogotá, where he soon secured a revised concession.[34] He then proceeded to Nicaragua, to prevent the granting of a contract to a rival French company; to New York, to deal with the Panama Railroad Company; and to Paris (August, 1878), to lay his plans before De Lesseps and the canal company.[35]

The next step was to submit the project to the International Scientific Congress called to meet at Paris in May, 1879.[36] One hundred and thirty-six delegates were in attendance. Of this number, seventy-four were French and eleven were American;[37] forty-two engineers and geographers; and ninety-four "politicians, financiers, speculators, and promoters." When division of opinion regarding the best route arose, many withdrew, leaving only ninety-eight to vote. Seventy-five favored a sea-level canal via Panama, but only nineteen of these were engineers and only one had ever set foot on the Isthmus.

[32] Ammen, "M. de Lesseps and His Canal," *N. Amer. Rev.*, CXXX, 134-135.

[33] Fish to Pérez, Dec. 20, 1876, Notes to Col. Leg., VI, 328.

[34] *Sen. Doc.*, No. 237 (56.1), pp. 113-120; Uribe, *Anales*, I, apéndice, pp. vii-xx.

[35] Johnson, *Four Centuries of the Panama Canal*, pp. 76-77.

[36] Also known as "International Engineering Congress," "Interoceanic Canal Congress," and "Paris Canal Congress."

[37] Among the American delegates were Nathan Appleton, T. O. Selfridge, Daniel Ammen, A. G. Menocal, W. E. Johnston.

Most of the American delegates suspected a "packed body."[38]

With this approval of the project the canal company effected a permanent organization and dispatched De Lesseps to the Isthmus. He later came to New York, where he gave a grand banquet (March 1, 1880) at Delmonico's (six hundred invitations) and conferred with interested capitalists. Washington received him well. The House committee on interoceanic canals permitted him to testify before it. But official approval of his project was neither given nor promised.[39] On his return to France, however, the Parisian press so garbled American official utterances as to give the impression of unqualified approval. French capital began to pour into the company's coffers, and De Lesseps felt positive of being able to allay American opposition. Therefore work on the canal began on February 1, 1881. To add a touch of the dramatic to the occasion, Sarah Bernhardt went to Panama and rendered Verdi's "Aïda."[40]

AMERICAN OPPOSITION AROUSED

French initial success naturally revived American interest, which had suffered somewhat from the failure of the Colombian (1868-1870) and Nicaraguan (1877) negotiations. Although Washington had officially declared for the Nicaraguan route, the merits of others were ably defended by American engineers. Daniel Ammen and A. G. Menocal favored Nicaragua; Nathan Appleton

[38] A. G. Menocal, "Intrigues at the Paris Canal Congress," *N. Amer. Rev.*, CXXIX, 288-293; Daniel Ammen, "Report of Proceedings . . . ," *Jour. Amer. Geog. Soc.*, XI, 153-160; T. O. Selfridge to Justice Daly, Jan. 14, 1880, *ibid.*, p. 293; "Views of Walton W. Evans on the Proposed Canal. . . . ," *ibid.*, pp. 161-171; George C. Hurlbut, "The Panama Canal from Within," *Forum*, IV, 279-289; W. E. Johnston, *The True History of the Panama Canal Scheme*, pp. 1-14; Johnson, *Four Centuries of the Panama Canal*, pp. 78-80.

[39] *Ibid.*, pp. 80-81; *New York World*, March 4, 9, 1880.

[40] Johnson, *Four Centuries of the Panama Canal*, p. 94; Johnston, *op. cit.*, pp. 14 ff.

(De Lesseps's "right bower"), Panama; Frederick M. Kelley and Walton W. Evans, San Blas; Captain James B. Eads and H. H. Hall, Tehuantepec. An international guarantee of construction bonds was advocated by Evans. But there was a strong undercurrent for American leadership.[41]

Former President Grant headed a Nicaragua canal company. Menocal secured a new concession in 1880—the old one had been granted in 1869. Captain Eads revived interest in Tehuantepec by his proposal to build there an interoceanic ship railway. And the American public was warned against De Lesseps's "hastily-conceived, ill-matured, stock-jobbing scheme," which he had foisted upon the public through his "packed Paris Congress."[42]

Within a month of Colombia's approval of the Wyse contract Ernest Dichman was sent to reopen the American legation at Bogotá which had been closed for some two years.[43] The Department was obviously disturbed. Its instructions were to investigate and report every detail of the concession.[44] As might be expected, Dichman soon noted numerous defects and advised Washington that the whole scheme "ought to be discouraged by all proper means," even to the cancellation of the Treaty of 1846. He contended that the success of the company would mean "nothing less than the planting of a French colony on the Isthmus." Besides, the magnitude of the project and the habitual disturbances on the Isthmus made necessary the support of some powerful govern-

[41] *Jour. Amer. Geog, Soc.,* XI, 113-300.

[42] Johnson, *Four Centuries of the Panama Canal,* pp. 80, 86; *Engineering News,* VI, 273; J. M. Goodwin, *The Panama Ship Canal and the Interoceanic Ship Railway* (Cleveland, O., 1880); Joseph Nimmo, Jr., *The Proposed American Interoceanic Canal in Its Commercial Aspects* (Washington, 1880).

[43] Owing to a general cut in expense, the United States was not represented at Bogotá from Nov. 21, 1876, to Dichman's arrival on Sept. 29, 1878. Colombia lacked representation at Washington from April 27, 1877, to Oct. 27, 1879. Notes to Col. Leg., VI; Inst. Col., XVII; Desp. Col., XXXI.

[44] Inst. Col., XVII.

ment or governments. The Monroe Doctrine would exclude European powers, except by American consent; therefore an official notice from the United States that it would neither support nor guarantee the present scheme would cause its failure. Then Colombia, of necessity, would turn to Washington.[45]

Meanwhile, Congress was showing concern. Information was requested by both houses.[46] Senator Burnside raised the question of the applicability of the Monroe Doctrine by his resolution (June 25, 1879) declaring that the attempt of any European government to establish under its protection and domination an interoceanic canal "could not be regarded in any other light than as the manifestation of an unfriendly disposition toward the United States."[47] The resolution was withdrawn (December 2), but two days later Senator Eaton requested all canal correspondence since 1869, and two weeks later the House created a special committee on interoceanic canals. This body heard testimony on all the various routes, but committed itself to none. Even De Lesseps appeared before it.[48] It seems significant, however, that on the very day that he testified[49] President Hayes declared for an American canal under American control.

[45] Dichman to Evarts, (112) July 19, (118) Aug. 1, (144) Sept. 28, (151) Oct. 17, 1879, Desp. Col., XXXIII.

[46] Sen. Res. of April 15 and H. Res. of May 29, 1879, *Sen. Ex. Doc.*, No. 15 (46.1); *H. Ex. Doc.*, No. 10 (46.1).

[47] *Cong. Rec.* (46.1), p. 2312.

[48] *Ibid.* (46.2), p. 12; *Sen. Misc. Doc.*, No. 9 (46.2); *H. Misc. Doc.*, No. 16 (46.3). Congressional interest is evidenced by H. Res. Nos. 146, 171, 236, 250; Bills Nos. 2794, 4051, 3662, 6609; Eaton and Morgan Res. in the Senate. *H. Rep.*, Nos. 224, 390 (46.3); *Sen. Misc. Doc.*, No. 42 (46.3); *Sen. Jour.* (46.3), p. 479. But none of these had sufficient support to pass.

[49] *H. Misc. Doc.*, No. 16 (46.3), p. 50.

Chapter XXIII

POLICY OF AMERICAN CONTROL ADOPTED AND ABANDONED
(1880-1888)

> The true policy of the United States as to a canal across any part of the Isthmus is either a canal under American control, or no canal.—President Hayes.[1]
>
> Whatever highway may be constructed . . . must be for the world's benefit—a trust for mankind, to be removed from the chance of domination by any single power. . . .—President Cleveland.[2]

THE strategic importance of an isthmian canal was fully recognized by President Hayes. Control of such a work was considered "essential for national defense"; therefore it must not pass to "any hostile nation." In January, 1880, he ordered two vessels to Chiriquí, looking towards the establishment there of naval and coaling stations. If Congress should see fit to purchase the holdings of the Chiriquí Improvement Company, Hayes felt that the United States would thereby gain "a foothold which . . . [would] be of vast service in controlling the passage from ocean to ocean either at Panama or at Nicaragua Lake."[3]

The President then hastened to assert his determined stand:

The policy of this country is a canal under American control. . . . If existing treaties between the United States and other nations . . . stand in the way of this policy . . . suitable steps

---

[1] Diarial entry, Feb. 20, 1880, Charles R. Williams (ed.), *Diary and Letters of Rutherford Birchard Hayes*, III, 589.

[2] Dec. 8, 1885, Richardson, *Messages and Papers*, X, 4912.

[3] C. R. Williams, *op. cit.*, III, 583, 587. Colombia protested, the vessels withdrew after a cursory survey, and Congress failed to ratify the contract. But Colombia was warned against granting any naval station concessions to any European power, "looking to·a surveillance and possible strategic control" of the Isthmus (Evarts to Dichman, [122] July 31, 1880, Inst. Col., XVII, 180-182).

should be taken by just and liberal negotiations to promote and establish the American policy.[4]

It is the right and duty of the United States to assert and maintain such supervision and authority over any interoceanic canal across the Isthmus . . . as will protect our national interests.[5]

DE LESSEPS FAILS TO CONVERT THE AMERICANS

De Lesseps cabled Paris that the President's message of March 8 assured the "political security of the canal." To this the *Pittsburg Post* retorted: "That's so. It secures American control, or no canal. Dog in the manger policy it may be, but not unnatural under the circumstances."[6] But the subsidized French press was claiming American conversion to the project and predicting a mad scramble for stock.[7] The American public, however, did not succumb so easily to De Lesseps's popular and pleasing personality, nor to his propaganda.[8] He delivered addresses in the principal cities and not only used the press freely himself but spent considerable money for press advocacy. But the Nicaragua group just as enthusiastically pointed out numerous alleged errors and misrepresentations and freely prophesied the utter failure of the scheme.[9]

De Lesseps then conceived the plan of grafting an American advisory board on to his organization. The chairmanship of this was offered to former President

[4] March 8, 1880, Richardson, *Messages and Papers*, X, 4537-4538.

[5] Dec. 6, 1880, *ibid.*, X, 4563.

[6] Elizabeth B. White, *American Opinion of France* . . . , p. 228.

[7] W. E. Johnston, *op. cit.*, p. 15. This author, an American resident of Paris, claimed that a "perfect embargo on truth" was maintained and the propaganda methods were more like those used in "the launching of a patent churn company."

[8] The Colombian minister also turned propagandist, Justo Arosemena, *The Panama Canal in the Light of American Interests* (Washington, 1880).

[9] M. de Lesseps, "The Interoceanic Canal," "The Panama Canal," *N. Amer. Rev.*, CXXX, 1-15, CXXXI, 75-78; Daniel Ammen, "M. de Lesseps and His Canal," "The Nicaragua Canal and the Pacific," *ibid.*, CXXX, 130-141, CXXXI, 440-446. The *N. Y. Herald* (Jan. 17, 1880) thought it "better to have the Panama canal constructed than the Nicaragua canal merely talked about."

Grant, who was already head of the rival Nicaragua company.[10] Upon his refusal the same proposition was made to Hayes's secretary of navy, R. W. Thompson, who accepted at the annual salary of $25,000. When this became known, Hayes accepted his resignation—which had not been presented.[11] American financial agents were chosen,[12] and some $1,500,000 were spent for the promotion of the company through bankers, politicians, and editors,[13] but to little avail. Even assurances from the French representatives at both Bogotá and Washington that their government would strictly adhere to a policy of non-interference and the preservation of the "absolute private and international character" of the enterprise[14] failed to draw very many into the scheme. Some were interested in Nicaragua or Tehuantepec, others favored American governmental construction, and the remainder were either indifferent or antagonistic to all projects.[15]

THE PROTOCOL OF 1881

To Secretary Evarts, the De Lesseps's concession presented "an occasion for a deliberate indication by the Government of the United States of its relations to enterprises of this nature both in its position as an American power and under its specific treaty rights and obligations towards the United States of Colombia."[16] The former

[10] Grant ("The Nicaragua Canal," *N. Amer. Rev.*, CXXXII, 107-116) was now opposed to the Panama canal, which he estimated would cost $400,000,000 against $52,577,718 by Nicaragua, likewise to permitting Europe any voice in the control of the canal.

[11] H. J. Eckenrode, *Rutherford B. Hayes: Statesman of Reunion*, p. 303; C. R. Williams, *op. cit.*, II, 224; *Sen. Rep.*, No. 1 (57.1), p. 66.

[12] J. and W. Seligman; Drexel, Morgan and Co.; Winslow, Lanier and Co.

[13] Johnson, *Four Centuries of the Panama Canal*, pp. 84-86.

[14] Max Outrey to Evarts, March 22, 25, 1880, March 7, 1881, *For. Rel.* (1880-1881), pp. 385-86, (1881-1882), p. 440; Dichman to Evarts, (226) Nov. 6, 1880, Desp. Col., XXXV.

[15] There is evidence indicating the opposition of the transcontinental railroad interests (*Popular Sci. Monthly*, XVI, 842-849, April, 1880).

[16] Rep. to Congress, March 8, 1880, *Sen. Doc.*, No. 194 (56.1), p. 165.

would require either a modification or abrogation of the Clayton-Bulwer Treaty, the latter would necessitate an additional understanding with Colombia—and seemed more important.[17]

The guarantee of Isthmian neutrality and Colombian sovereignty over the area was "one thing while the Isthmus . . . [remained] in its natural and unpeopled state and quite another when . . . opened to the interests, the cupidities, and the ambitions of the great commercial nations and occupied by populations of foreign allegiance and discordant habits."[18] Since the United States was the only power making such a guarantee, Colombia must necessarily look to it for protection.[19] Then it did not seem unreasonable to expect "timely information" concerning and "joint consideration" of proposed concessions before their approval at Bogotá. Therefore Secretary Evarts concluded:

This Government cannot consider itself excluded by any arrangement between other powers or individuals to which it is not a party, from a direct interest, and if necessary, a positive supervision and interposition in the execution of any project, which by completing an interoceanic connection . . . would materially affect its commercial interests, change the territorial relations of its own sovereignty and impose upon it the necessity of a foreign policy, which . . . has been hitherto sedulously avoided.[20]

[17] Dichman's reports of French activities on the Isthmus seemed to make new agreements imperative.

[18] *Sen. Doc.*, No. 194 (56.1), p. 166.

[19] Efforts to secure European guarantees had been made in 1843 (*supra*, chap. xii), 1856-1857 (Rivas, *Relaciones*, p. 175), and 1865-1866 (published correspondence enclosed with Dichman to Evarts, 247, Jan. 28, 1881, Desp. Col., XXXV).

[20] Evarts to Dichman, (107) April 19, 1880, Inst. Col., XVII, 153-165. This was not so far in advance of Secretary Clayton's almost forgotten claim of American "right to offer, unasked, such advice to the New Granadian Government, in regard to its relations with other powers, as might tend to avert . . . a rupture with any nation which might covet the Isthmus of Panama" (Clayton to Foote, [1] July 19, 1849, Inst. Col., XV, 123).

Furthermore there were obvious conflicts between the De Lesseps contract and the Treaty of 1846. The former provided for the passage, without charge, of Colombian vessels, troops, and ammunition through the canal, but gave no such exemption to American. In fact, the passage of foreign troops was forbidden, except by Colombian congressional consent.[21] These provisions might easily be interpreted to permit a charge for the transportation of American troops landed to protect the Isthmus or even to forbid their passage over a territory which their government was treaty bound to protect.

Naturally a more specific agreement regarding the rights, privileges, and obligations contained in Article XXXV of the Treaty of 1846 was desirable. But the proposal of Minister Arosemena was unacceptable.[22] And Dichman reported a "strong feeling of resentment" at Bogotá against the United States, because of President Hayes's message, his move to establish naval stations on the Isthmus of Chiriquí, and the hostile tone of the American press. The minister still believed, however, that the desired agreement could be secured if the United States would guarantee bonds for the construction of a railroad from Bogotá to the coast[23]—rather a pet idea with Dichman.

The new minister in Washington, General Santo Domingo Vila, was impressed with the necessity of possessing "in the United States, if not an ally, at least a decided friend,"[24] and therefore expressed his country's "readiness to make the necessary amplifications in support of the Monroe Doctrine." Conferences began on January 7, 1881. The Colombian protocol draft specifically included the entire State of Panama within the

---

[21] Amended Articles V and VI, *Sen. Doc.*, No. 237 (56.1), pp. 121-122.

[22] *Ibid.*, p. 489. For provisions of the Arosemena protocol, see Dichman to Blaine, (272) May 13, 1881, Desp. Col., XXXV.

[23] Dichman to Evarts, (183) July 3, (210) Sept. 25, 1880, *ibid.*, XXXIV.

[24] *Sen. Doc.*, No. 237 (56.1), p. 491.

guarantee of sovereignty. The United States was obligated to protect this area from both foreign conquest or usurpation and Panama secession intrigues "employed by a foreign power." Joint works of defense and coaling stations could be occupied temporarily by American troops, if necessary, but Colombia promised to maintain sufficient forces there to protect the transit from "internal political disorder." Except in case of war between the two nations, the passage was to be open at all times for American troops (without arms), vessels, and supplies.[25]

Evart's counter proposal made American consent imperative for the granting or modifying of any canal concession and its approval necessary before any authorized work could be undertaken. It also reserved the right to fortify and occupy vantage points deemed essential for the fulfillment of the guarantee.[26] The Colombian minister considered the first provision a "direct derogation of the very sovereignty which it . . . [was] proposed to guarantee." Colombia adhered to the Monroe Doctrine, he insisted, but this could not be applied here "without disregarding the fraternal idea which constitutes its essence." He would agree to "permanent fortifications, but only to temporary occupancy."[27]

When no agreement seemed possible, General Santo Domingo returned to New York, expecting to leave soon for Bogotá. But before he could sail, Evarts rushed W. H. Trescot to him with a modified protocol. This one (signed February 17, 1881) recognized that the completion of a canal would increase American treaty obligations and that it was Colombia's duty to concur in the maintenance of Isthmian neutrality. The use of the

[25] *Ibid.*, pp. 480-482; Santo Domingo Vila to Evarts, Dec. 1, 30, 1880, Jan. 10, Feb. 3, 5, 8, 1881, Notes from Col. Leg., VII.

[26] *Sen. Doc.*, No. 237 (56.1), pp. 482-484.

[27] Santo Domingo Vila to Evarts, Feb. 10, 11, memo. of Feb. 12, 1881, Notes from Col. Leg., VII.

canal was to be on the same basis for both, except in case of war between the two; points of vantage were to be fortified and occupied jointly in times of emergency, but only by Colombian troops during peace.[28]

This was considered by the signers merely the basis for a subsequent treaty. As such the Department accepted it, but the Colombian senate rejected it. Foreign Minister Becerra pointed out that since the canal was for world commerce, its construction should not extend the obligations or increase the expenses of either the United States or Colombia. He hoped, however, that negotiations would be reopened at Washington.[29] A commission—Carlos Holguín, Santos Acosta, and Eustorjio Salgar—was soon chosen for that purpose, but internal political conditions prevented its departure. In fact, no Colombian representative resided in Washington again until October, 1884.[30]

On returning to Bogotá, General Santo Domingo was serenaded by the army bands and then was discredited by the government that had appointed him.[31] Soon the public was "highly excited." Posters appeared calling on all parties to arise and protect "the honor and future of the country," and the Senate solicited the President to "consider the propriety and convenience of promoting the annulment" of the Treaty of 1846. So hyper-sensitive were many that they interpreted any negotiations regarding the Isthmus as "a covert attack upon Colombian rights of sovereignty, with the ultimate object of the acquisition of that territory by the United States."[32] President Garfield's inaugural message was "subjected

[28] *Sen. Doc.*, No. 237 (56.1), pp. 477-478.

[29] Santo Domingo Vila to Evarts, Feb. 18, 1881, Becerra to Evarts, May 7, 1881, Notes from Col. Leg., VII.

[30] Dichman to Blaine, (285) June 29, (304) Aug. 15, 1881, Desp. Col., XXXV.

[31] *Idem* to *idem*, (284) June 19, 1881, *ibid.* He defended his actions in *Negociación; Santo Domingo Vila-Trescot* (Bogotá, 1881).

[32] Dichman to Blaine, April 29, May 6, 1881, Desp. Col., XXXV.

to a fire of unfavorable criticism" and a long senatorial debate. The Bogotá press claimed that the American-assumed superintendency of any canal construction and attempted predominance on the Isthmus were merely efforts to destroy the French company and to despoil Colombian sovereignty "under the pretext of guaranteeing same."[33]

Besides, Minister Dichman was apparently guilty of certain indiscretions. It was alleged that he announced, "upon a festive occasion, that in case Colombia should ultimately refuse to enter into such a treaty as we desired, respecting the Isthmian canal transit, the United States would treat with Panama, one of the constituent states of the Colombian union." When his recall was reported, still more serious charges were brought: "indiscreet participation in internal affairs"; giving of "unsolicited advice"; "severe and even clamorous" criticism of men and affairs; suggestion of a plan "to promote . . . the downfall of the federal authorities"; and attempts to corrupt "the morality of some public men of the Isthmus, in order to free that territory from the domination and sovereignty of its legitimate owner." Dichman countered that the charges had "their origin solely in the disordered imagination of Señor Ricardo Becerra," minister of foreign affairs. Be that as it may, the effect of it all was to exaggerate the belief that the United States had "sinister designs on the Isthmus" and to lessen the chances of securing the desired treaty.[34]

WASHINGTON'S FEAR OF A EUROPEAN GUARANTEE

The new minister, George Maney, was instructed merely "to cultivate friendly relations and prevent Euro-

[33] *Idem* to *idem,* April 29, May 11, 19, 1881, and enclosed newspapers, *ibid.*

[34] Memoria de 1881—Becerra, Uribe, *Anales,* IV, 134-135; Becerra to Evarts, April 29, 1881, Notes from Col. Leg., VII; Dichman to Blaine, (305) Aug. 23, 1881, Scruggs to Frelinghuysen, (18) Aug. 23, 1882, Desp. Col., XXXVI.

pean guarantees" of the contemplated canal.[35] The failure of the protocol and the subsequent hostile feeling at Bogotá clearly showed the futility of further negotiations there. The scene of diplomatic action shifted to Europe.

The State Department was aroused by the news that copies of this document had been sent to Colombian agents in London and Paris, with instructions to point out "its unusual pretentions" and to approach England, France, Germany, Spain, and Italy regarding a joint guarantee.[36] Such a guarantee might mean the termination of the Treaty of 1846[37]—only twelve months' notice required—and European control over the entire project, or it might necessitate a vigorous assertion of the Monroe Doctrine. Secretary Blaine had already prepared circular instructions[38] to the United States representatives at the European capitals.[39] If they had reason to believe that Colombia might succeed in securing the joint guarantee, they were to acquaint the powers with the President's views that the American guarantee required no "reënforcement, or accession, or assent, from any

[35] Maney to Freylinghuysen, (16) May 28, 1882, *Sen. Doc.*, No. 237 (56.1), p. 433.

[36] Dichman to Blaine, (269) May 9, (306) Aug. 27, 1881, Desp. Col., XXXVI. It is known that Santo Domingo Vila and Ricardo Becerra favored a European guarantee, and the former was appointed minister to France in 1881.

[37] Termination of the treaty was actually advocated in the Colombian congress (1881-1882), but, since no other guarantee existed, it was considered necessary as a protection against both Europe and the United States (Maney to Frelinghuysen, [16] May 28, Scruggs to Frelinghuysen, Aug. 23, 1882, Desp. Col., XXXVI). It is claimed that De Lesseps tried to secure its termination at both Bogotá and Washington (Johnson, *Four Centuries of the Panama Canal*, pp. 81, 85). The rumor (1883) that Spain had promised to guarantee and to use influence in securing joint European action caused considerable alarm at Washington, but proved to be without foundation (Scruggs to Frelinghuysen, Jan. 29, March 3, June 19, 1883, Desp. Col., XXXVII; Reed to Frelinghuysen, March 28, 1883, Desp. Spain, CV).

[38] Blaine to Dichman, (175) June 24, 1881, Inst. Col. XVII, 265.

[39] Great Britain, France, Germany, Austria, Italy, Belgium, Netherlands, Portugal, Russia, Sweden, Spain, Turkey.

other power." Minister Lowell was also to intimate to Great Britain that such a procedure "would necessarily be regarded by this Government as an uncalled-for intrusion into a field where the local and general interests of the United States . . . must be considered before those of other powers," save those of Colombia.[40] These views were to be elucidated "with some detail to the end that no uncertainty . . . [should] subsist as to the integrity of our motives or the distinctness of our aims." In time of peace, no exclusive privileges were desired. But in time of war the use of the canal by hostile ships could no more be permitted than the use of the transcontinental railroads which European money and energy had aided in constructing.[41]

Replies from the European capitals were to the effect that the respective governments had not been approached, but, in case they were, the interests of the United States would be properly considered.[42] In accordance with Blaine's suggestion,[43] a copy of the circular instructions was left with the British foreign secretary on July 24. It was not until November 10 that Lord Granville re-

---

[40] The lack of just such a guarantee had been used by Evarts as an argument in favor of American supervision of any canal arrangement.

[41] Blaine to Lowell, (187) June 24, 1881, Inst. G. B., XXVI, 162-175. Formerly, the United States had been favorable towards a European guarantee; sometimes enthusiastically, other times passively. Appropriate clauses were included in the following treaties: Treaty of 1846, Clay-Colindres (1864) with Honduras, Clayton-Bulwer (1850), Dickinson-Ayón (1867) with Nicaragua; unratified treaties: Cass-Yrisarri (1857) with Nicaragua, treaties of 1869 and 1870 with Colombia, Fish-Cárdenas (1877) with Nicaragua. The United States urged, at both Bogotá and London, a supplementary guarantee in 1849-1850 (Clayton to Lawrence, Dec. 14, 1849, Sullivan and Cromwell, *op. cit.*, I, 529; Foote to Clayton, [7] Feb. 8, 1850, Desp. Col., XII); approved a similar English and French guarantee in 1857, but did not choose to make a joint one (Cass to Lord Napier, Sept. 10, 1857, *Moore's Digest*, III, 12); approached both England and France before considering Colombia's request for intervention in 1862 (*supra*, chap. xv); and advocated (1877) an international guarantee as the only method of securing sufficient capital to construct the Nicaragua canal (*supra*, chap. xxii).

[42] For the replies, see Sullivan and Cromwell, *op. cit.*, III, 1603-1622.

[43] Blaine to Lowell, (188) June 25, 1881, Inst. G. B., XXVI.

plied, and then only to point out that the position of the two powers towards any canal was set forth in the Clayton-Bulwer Treaty and that Great Britain relied "with confidence upon the observance of all engagements" contained therein.[44]

EFFORTS TO MODIFY THE CLAYTON-BULWER TREATY

Blaine, certain of considerable official support,[45] was ready to question the applicability of this treaty. He contended that it had been made "more than thirty years ago, under exceptional and extraordinary conditions, which . . . [had] long ceased to exist" and suggested that modifications were necessary. The prohibition of the maintenance of American troops in the canal zone and the increasing superiority of the British navy had created an unanticipated inequality, while the "self-protection of her own interests" and the "long established claim of priority on this continent" gave to the United States the "right to control the Isthmus transit." Therefore it was "the fixed purpose of the United States to confine it strictly and solely as an American question, to be dealt with and decided" accordingly. The prior Treaty of 1846 with Colombia required release from the "unequal and unequitable obligations" of the "vague, and, as yet, unperfected" Clayton-Bulwer Treaty.[46]

In reply Lord Granville (January 7, 14, 1882) intimated that Blaine's arguments were based on principles "novel in International law" and then suggested that other powers be invited to adhere to the Convention of 1850. Article VIII of this treaty, he continued, extended joint protection to the Panama route, in order "not only to accomplish a particular object, but also to establish a general principle." The earlier differences in interpre-

[44] Granville to Hoppin, Nov. 10, 1881, *Sen. Doc.*, No. 237 (56.1), p. 388.

[45] Richardson, *Messages and Papers*, X, 4628; *H. Rep.*, Nos. 1121 (46.2), 390 (46.3); *Sen. Misc. Doc.*, No. 42 (46.3); *Sen. Jour.* (46.3), p. 479.

[46] Blaine to Lowell, Nov. 19, 29, 1881, *Sen. Doc.*, No. 237 (56.1), pp. 384-396.

tation had not concerned the Isthmian transit, nor had the United States before contended for exclusive rights. Great Britain had proposed abrogation of the treaty in 1858, but the United States had not taken advantage of the opportunity to rid itself of the now obnoxious pro visions. Therefore it must have been the intention of the latter to extend the "general principle" of guarantee to all Isthmian routes.[47]

Secretary Frelinghuysen—Blaine had withdrawn from the cabinet—replied (May 8) that the President considered it "unnecessary and unwise" to invite other powers "to guarantee the neutrality of the Isthmus, or to give their navies a pretext for assembling in waters contiguous to our shores. . . ." Furthermore the Clayton-Bulwer Treaty was in conflict with the Monroe Doctrine. Therefore, since the particular object of the treaty (the construction of the Nicaragua canal) had not been accomplished and Great Britain had violated and continued to violate the treaty, it was, "of course, voidable at the pleasure of the United States." Besides, Article VIII anticipated further treaty stipulations, which required the consent of both the United States and Colombia. And a British guarantee was not now considered necessary.[48]

Granville, in his belated note of December 30, declared that the meaning and effect of Article VIII were "not open to any doubt." He denied that Great Britain had committed invalidating acts, pointed out that President Buchanan (1860) had accepted as satisfactory the settlement of interpretation difficulties, and insisted that his government did not deem modification necessary.[49]

[47] Granville to West, Jan. 7, 14, 1882, *ibid.*, pp. 397-409.

[48] Frelinghuysen to Lowell, May 8, 1882, *ibid.*, pp. 219-231. It was rumored during the summer that Chile, backed by England, Brazil, and Ecuador, intended to occupy the Isthmus and control the canal route, but this proved to be unfounded (Frelinghuysen to Scruggs, [9] Aug. 7, 1882, Inst. Col., XVII, 294-297).

[49] Granville to West, Dec. 30, 1882, *Sen. Doc.*, No. 237 (56.1), pp. 411-417.

Frelinghuysen's letter of May 5, 1883, merely restated previous arguments and added that Article VIII was only a "declaration of intention . . . to take up, at some subsequent period, the negotiation of a treaty on a particular subject."[50]

Granville (August 17) refused to accept this interpretation, pointing out that no time limit had been set for the accomplishments of the particular object and that the American ratification of the treaty was sufficient proof of its harmony with the Monroe Doctrine.[51] Frelinghuysen's reply of November 22 closed the correspondence.[52]

The Department's arguments had been forced and far from convincing and, some thought, "very uncourteous and even menacing in tone" to the point of unnecessary offensiveness to British self-respect.[53] At any rate, it was clear that a more opportune time must be awaited for successful negotiations.

This temporary failure, however, did not prevent the signing of the Frelinghuysen-Zavala Treaty (1884) with Nicaragua, providing for an exclusive canal grant—contrary in spirit, if not in text, to the Clayton-Bulwer Treaty.[54]

CLEVELAND TURNS PROVINCIAL

Meanwhile, operations had begun in Panama. Minister Scruggs became alarmed at the ill-concealed intention of the canal company to settle its large land grant there with French colonists. This policy, he feared, would necessitate American intervention, especially if

[50] Frelinghuysen to Lowell, May 5, 1883, *ibid.*, pp. 417-421.

[51] Granville to West, Aug. 17, 1883, *ibid.*, pp. 421-423.

[52] Frelinghuysen to Lowell, Nov. 22, 1883, *ibid.*, pp. 423-425. The Senate was kept informed regarding the negotiations (*Sen. Jour.* [47.1], pp. 95, 968, [48.1], p. 95; *Sen. Ex. Doc.*, Nos. 16, 78, 194 [47.1], No. 26 [48.1]).

[53] Editorials, *Nation*, XXXIV, 93, 200; Grotius (Benjamin J. Darneille), *A Review of the Monroe Doctrine and the American Theory of the Panama Canal* (Washington, 1882).

[54] See Latané, *The United States and Latin America*, p. 177.

active French governmental support became essential for the completion of the project. The situation held dire possibilities.[55]

Cleveland had scarcely assumed the presidency when rebel activities on the Isthmus threatened the safety of the transit. American troops were landed during March and April, 1885. Jorge Holguín was sent to Washington to solicit intervention under the Treaty of 1846. President Núñez justified the move as protection against the "apprehended purpose on the part of an European power to jeopardize Colombia's sovereignty" over the area. Scruggs felt that Holguín would first attempt to secure a loan from De Lesseps. If he succeeded, he would then request an American protectorate over Panama; if not, he would probably make a proposition equal to the sale of the area. Now was the long sought "opportune moment" for the treaty, unless the Department contemplated "the abandonment of its traditional policy of exclusive control of the Isthmian transit."[56]

Although Holguín made no favorable propositions at Washington, Núñez indirectly sounded Scruggs regarding the renewal of the Treaty of 1846, including provisions for an offensive and defensive alliance and settlement of subsequent differences by arbitration. Scruggs was assured that Colombia had given up the idea of a European guarantee. But he feared that the financial straits of the government in the midst of a civil war might force it to make some arrangements with Europe, unless Washington acted quickly. Núñez, at least temporarily favorable to the United States,[57] rec-

[55] Scruggs to Frelinghuysen, (131) Jan. 12, (156) May 12, (176) Nov. 29, 1884, Desp. Col., XXXVIII. Captain Bedford T. Pim of the British Navy ("Nicaragua vs. Panama," *The National Republican*, Jan. 20, 1885) even expressed fear of Panama secession and a French protectorate.

[56] Holguín's mission lasted from July 2 to Sept. 11, 1885. Troops had been landed on the Isthmus before his departure from Bogotá (Scruggs to Bayard, [202] April 20, [203] 23, 1885, Desp. Col., XXXIX; Notes to Col. Leg., VIII).

[57] See Rafael Núñez, *Colección de artículos publicados* (Bogotá, 1885).

ommended to the Constitutional Convention of 1885 that
"opportune concessions" be granted to that power to
insure Colombian sovereignty over the Isthmus.[58]

Evidently the new Cleveland administration did not
share Scruggs's enthusiasm, since his letters were merely
marked "File," and remained unanswered.[59] The emergency pro-Americanism of Núñez was unconvincing. Nor
did the information that a large Isthmian group favored
secession and an American protectorate[60] convert Cleveland to the so-called "traditional policy." He did not
hesitate to fulfill treaty obligations by landing troops on
the Isthmus "in aid of the sovereignty of Colombia," but
was unalterably opposed to the assuming of additional
liabilities.

The Frelinghuysen-Zavala Treaty with Nicaragua
was withdrawn from the Senate before its ratification.
Cleveland announced that he opposed the "policy of
acquisition of new and distant territory or the incorporation of remote interests with our own," and therefore
could not "recommend propositions involving paramount
privileges of ownership or right outside of our own territory, when coupled with absolute and unlimited engagements to defend the territorial integrity of the state
where such interests lie." He was not antagonistic to a
canal—he spoke favorably of Tehuantepec and promised
the Senate copies of the latest Nicaraguan survey—but
was convinced that a canal constructed, owned, and operated by the United States government would be inconsistent with its "dedication to universal and neutral
use."[61]

[58] Scruggs to Bayard, (214) June 13, (248) Oct. 23, (251) Nov. 6,
1885, Desp. Col., XXXIX.

[59] Between Maury's letters of Dec. 12, 1886, and Jan. 11, 1887, there is
also filed a copy of a twenty-five year extension of the Treaty of 1846 (Desp.
Col., XL).

[60] Adamson to State Dept., April 18, Nov. 14, 1885, *Sen. Doc.*, No. 143
(58.2), p. 167; Con. Let., Panama, XVII.

[61] Dec. 8, 1885, Richardson, *Messages and Papers*, X, 4912-4913. That
Cleveland's aversion for assuming new foreign obligations did not affect

THE BANKRUPTCY OF THE FRENCH CANAL COMPANY

The temporary reversal of official policy did not necessarily reflect a lack of individual interest in the French Panama canal project,[62] nor a unanimous desire for its failure. In fact, the reports of John Bigelow (1886)[63] and Lieutenant Charles C. Rogers (1887) were enthusiastically favorable. Rogers felt that the main opposition to the work came from Americans and a few Englishmen, and was due to "either ignorance of the facts or else malice against the company."[64] American opinion ran the scale from rabid nationalism with its "dog-in-the-manger" policy to an enthusiasm for any scheme that promised the completion of a canal.

Before the end of 1887, however, there was a general belief that De Lesseps would never be able to complete the work.[65] This proved to be true. The crash came the next year. Unanticipated engineering difficulties, disease, mismanagement, waste, fraud, and corruption forced the company into bankruptcy and receivership, after having spent approximately $400,000,000 and having completed only two-fifths of the work.[66]

his defense of American interests abroad, however, is evidenced by his firm stand in the Colombia-Costa Rica boundary dispute and the Cerruti claim against Colombia (Notes from Col. Leg., VIII, IX; *Moore's Digest*, III, 29 ff.; *Sen. Doc.*, No. 237 [56.1], pp. 521 ff.).

[62] Morgan Res., 1884, *Sen. Jour.* (48.1), p. 297; Rep. of Rogers and Cooper, 1884, *Sen. Ex. Doc.*, No. 123 (48.1); Rep. of Kimball and Capps, 1886, *H. Misc. Doc.*, No. 395 (49.1).

[63] *Report of Hon. John Bigelow* . . . (New York, 1886). He was sent by the New York Chamber of Commerce, at the request and expense of De Lesseps.

[64] *H. Misc. Doc.*, No. 599 (50.1), p. 57.

[65] *Nation* (Nov. 10, 1887), XLV, 367.

[66] Johnson, *Four Centuries of the Panama Canal*, p. 96.

CHAPTER XXIV

THE POLICY OF GOVERNMENTAL CONSTRUCTION AND CONTROL (1889-1903)

> I would be surprised if the United States would miss the opportunity of getting such a work into its own hands. . . . It is absolutely necessary for the United States to build the interoceanic canal and I am sure it will do so.—PROPHECY OF GOETHE, February 21, 1827.[1]

THE bankruptcy of the De Lesseps scheme revived the American fear of active French governmental intervention and increased the determination to prevent it. A congressional resolution of March 2, 1889, declared that the American government would

. . . look with serious concern and disapproval upon any connection of any European Government with the construction or control of any ship-canal across the Isthmus of Darién or across Central America, and must regard any such connection or control as injurious to the just rights and interests of the United States and as a menace to their welfare.[2]

Even early assurances that France contemplated no such intervention[3] failed to allay all fears. But the anticipated failure of the French company made the Nicaragua advocates more enthusiastic and bold.

NICARAGUA TO THE FORE

The company organized (1880) to construct a canal by this route had failed (1882) to secure congressional aid and had suffered an additional reverse by Cleveland's

---

[1] Johann Peter Eckermann, *Gespräche mit Goethe in den letzten Jahren seines Lebens*, III, 83-84.

[2] This was very similar to the resolutions of Burnside (1879), Crapo (1880), and Morgan (1881), *H. Rep.*, No. 4167 (50.2).

[3] McLane to Blaine, (tel.) March 8, (781) April 11, 1889, Desp. France CII.

withdrawal of the Frelinghuysen-Zavala Treaty of 1884. Early in 1887, however, A. G. Menocal secured a new concession. The Nicaragua Canal Construction Company was organized and chartered by the state of Colorado. The concession was soon taken over by the Colorado Construction Company, which was later (February 20, 1889) given an American congressional charter as the Maritime Canal Company of Nicaragua.[4]

Actual operations began in 1890, but lack of funds soon necessitated another appeal for governmental assistance—a three-per-cent guarantee on $100,000,000. Many favored this measure as a means of protecting the project from European control. But sufficient support could not be mustered to pass the bill, and the panic of 1893 forced the complete cessation of operations after the expenditure of some $6,000,000.[5]

OPPOSITION TO EXTENSION OF PANAMA CONCESSION

Meanwhile, the French concession had been extended to October 31, 1894.[6] The route had been examined by other engineers, and the New Panama Canal Company (French) was in the process of organization.[7]

This unexpected activity of a defunct concern aroused both interest and uneasiness at Washington. Secretary Foster, after calling Colombia's attention to the "peculiarly close and friendly relations" existing between the two nations and the major rôle played by Yankee capital and energy in Colombian economic development, remonstrated against any extension of the concession beyond

[4] *Sen. Rep.*, Nos. 368 (47.1), 952 (47.2), 1628 (49.2), 221 (50.1), 1944 (51.2); *Sen. Doc.*, No. 231 (56.2), pp. 107, 135, 139, 141, 187 ff.; Sidney Webster, "The Diplomacy and Law of the Isthmian Canals," *Harper's New Monthly Mag.* (Sept., 1893), LXXXVII, 602-608.

[5] *Sen. Rep.*, Nos. 2234 (51.2), 1142 (52.2), 1262 (52.2); *Sen. Doc.*, No. 231 (56.2), pp. 402, 410, 415; Johnson, *Four Centuries of the Panama Canal*, pp. 111-112.

[6] *Ibid.*, p. 108; Uribe, *Anales*, I, apéndice, pp. xxi-xxvi.

[7] Henry L. Abbot, *Problems of the Panama Canal*, pp. 1-5. General Abbot was on the technical committee of the new company.

1893. He argued that the company was hopelessly bankrupt and "discredited in the eyes of the French people"; its assets valueless, except for the Panama railroad. Since there was no chance of completing the work, he could not consider the application as bona fide. Therefore immediate liquidation of the old company and the resultant reversion of the railroad to its original owners were much preferred.[8]

Although Colombia placed little faith in the new company, it could not overlook certain monetary considerations—especially the liquidation of a 4,000,000 franc debt owed the old company—since there were no other immediate bids for the concession. Minister Abbott reminded the Department that only a definite proposition from either the American government or a reliable company could prevent still other grants to Europeans.[9] Americans must construct the canal, or Europeans would continue their attempts. Abbott's prophecy proved correct. The French concession was further extended to 1904 and later to 1910.[10]

However, the New Panama Canal Company could expect even less support in the United States than De Lesseps. "The word Panama," recorded *The Nation*, "now suggests so universally a huge scandal that its association with an actual isthmus seems only a figure of speech."[11] And the House of Representatives (1893) assured the company's permanent discredit by "airing" the questionable operations of its American agents.[12]

"CANAL INSANITY (FUROR CANALIENSIS)"[13]

By 1894 little was heard of Captain Eads's ship-railway across Tehuantepec, but various Panama schemes

[8] Foster to Coughlin, (323) Dec. 22, 1892, Inst. Col., XVIII, 348-353.
[9] Abbott to Foster, (459) Feb. 22, to Gresham, (493) April 15, 1893, *Sen. Doc.*, No. 237 (56.1), pp. 535-545.
[10] For texts of extensions, see Uribe, *Anales*, I, apéndice.
[11] *Nation* (March 30, 1893), LVI, 229.
[12] *H. Rep.*, No. 2615 (52.2).
[13] *Nation* (Nov. 28, 1895), LXI, 382.

were being "ventilated from time to time," anticipatory of French failure; and "renewed attention" was being directed towards Nicaragua.[14] Senator Morgan of the foreign relations committee reported favorably on a bill to guarantee three per cent on $70,000,000 of Nicaragua canal bonds.[15] Although this failed to pass, an appropriation was voted for a board of engineers to investigate.[16] This board reported (February 7, 1896) that existing data were inadequate for any decision and therefore recommended another appropriation and a resurvey. The money was provided on June 4, 1897, and a new commission was appointed.[17] An act of March 3, 1899, enlarged this commission and instructed it to consider also the Panama route.[18]

Meanwhile, Nicaragua partisans were active both in and out of Congress. " 'I believe in the Nicaragua canal' ... [was] chanted vociferously by press and public, legislators and voters, as the first article of a new national creed." Propagandists substituted prejudice for argument and "rhetorical invective" for accurate facts and figures. They were "princes in enthusiasm and paupers in fact."[19] To many, the belief in the Nicaragua canal became "a thing almost sacred, and he who [questioned]

[14] *Engineering Mag.* (Aug., 1894), VII, 750. Captain Eads had died in 1887.

[15] *Sen. Rep.*, No. 331 (53.2); *Sen. Doc.*, No. 231 (56.2), p. 457.

[16] *Jour. Amer. Geog. Soc.* (1895), XXVII, p. 317. Members of commission: Major Wm. Ludlow, U. S. A.; Commander M. T. Endicott, U. S. N.; and Alfred Noble, civilian.

[17] David Turpie, "Projects for an Isthmian Canal," *Harper's New Monthly Mag.* (1898), XCVI, 351-358; *Jour. Amer. Geog. Soc.* (1897), XXIX, 435. Members of new commission: Colonel Peter C. Hains, U. S. A.; Rear Admiral John G. Walker, U. S. N.; Lewis M. Haupt, civilian.

[18] The following members were added: Alfred Noble, Samuel Pasco, George S. Morison, William H. Burr, Prof. Emory R. Johnson, and Lieut. Col. Oswald H. Ernst, U. S. A. (Abbot, *Problems of the Panama Canal*, p. 10).

[19] Charles B. Going, "The Absence of Facts about the Nicaragua Canal," *Engineering Mag.* (June, 1896), XI, 416-417; W. Henry Hunter, "The American Isthmus and the Interoceanic Canal," *ibid.* (Feb., 1899), XVI, 713.

it thereby . . . [put] himself beyond the pale of regard or influence."[20] The public was told that the Panama project was not even a possibility, and was led to believe that all work there had ceased.

Some of the better informed, however, appealed to American patriotism for assistance in completing the Nicaragua canal before the French could construct theirs.[21] Support of the Nicaraguan project became "one of the first articles in the creed of American patriotism." The strong and persistent influence of the Nicaraguan lobbyists[22] naturally reflected itself in the proposal of numerous favorable measures in Congress.[23] But these failed of passage, largely because of public indifference, opposition of the transcontinental railroads,[24] and the traditional Democratic policy (second Cleveland administration) regarding federal aid for improvements.

NICARAGUA VS. PANAMA

In January, 1897, Señor Rodríguez, minister of the Greater Republic of Central America, suggested to Secretary Olney that certain pending congressional bills were at variance with the Nicaragua concession of 1887. Therefore he recommended the negotiation of a convention similar to the unratified Frelinghuysen-Zavala Treaty of 1884, especially since governmental aid seemed essential for the completion of any canal.[25]

Press rumors of the success of these negotiations aroused Señor Rengifo, Colombian representative, who had utmost confidence in the New Panama Canal Com-

[20] Editorial, "The Common Sense of the Isthmian Decision," *ibid.* (Aug., 1902), XXIII, 653-659; W. J. Curtis, *The History of the Purchase by the United States of the Panama Canal*, p. 8.

[21] Richard Harding Davis, *Three Gringoes in Venezuela and Central America*, p. 211.

[22] *Engineering Mag.* (April, 1900; Aug., 1902), XIX, 107; XXIII, 653.

[23] H. Bills: Mahon, Dec. 3, 1895; Doolittle, Dec. 6, 1895; Barbour, Dec. 6, 1895. Sen. Bills: Perkins, Dec. 30, 1895; Morgan, June 1, 1896.

[24] Emory R. Johnson, "The Nicaragua Canal and the Economic Development of the United States," *Annals* . . . (Jan., 1896), VII, 38-48.

[25] Rodríguez to Olney, Jan. 15, 1897, *Sen. Doc.*, No. 78 (54.2), pp. 1-4.

pany and considerable doubt regarding the practicability of the Nicaraguan route. He felt that America's pronounced interest in a canal was being fully satisfied by the work at Panama and pointed out that "very serious injury would be done to Colombia" by American governmental support of a Nicaragua canal "to the prejudice of that of Panama."[26]

Rengifo seems to have sensed the trend in Washington. With the McKinley administration came a revival of the idea of a Nicaraguan canal, constructed and controlled by the United States government.[27] The war with Spain, especially the forced cruise of the *Oregon* around Cape Horn and the acquisition of the Philippines in the Pacific, clearly showed the strategic importance of a canal. McKinley, therefore, urged definite congressional action.[28]

Meanwhile, the New Panama Canal Company was in still more difficult financial straits. Director-General Hutin, before the House committee on rivers and harbors, expressed a willingness to reincorporate the company under American laws, if the Panama route were preferred. But the Senate seemed to favor an immediate appropriation for the construction of the Nicaragua canal. To this the House objected, and on March 3, 1899, a compromise was effected by a provision for a canal commission to examine and report on both routes.[29]

[26] Rengifo to Sherman, May 15, 1897, Notes from Col. Leg., IX; *Sen. Doc.*, No. 237 (56.1), pp. 545, 548. The note was merely acknowledged.

[27] J. G. Whiteley, "The Diplomacy of the United States in regard to Central American Canals," *N. Amer. Rev.* (Sept., 1897), CLXV, 378 A. S. Crowninshield, "The Dream of Navigators," *ibid.*, (Dec., 1897). This was advocated by leading papers and men of both parties: *Kansas City Times* (D.), *Cincinnati Enquirer* (D.), *Seattle Post-Intelligencer* (R.), *San Francisco Call* (R.), *Current Opinion*, XVI, 521; *Jour. Amer. Geog. Soc.*, XXVI, 277; *Harper's New Monthly Mag.*, XCVI, 358.

[28] Dec. 5, 1898, Richardson, *Messages and Papers*, XIII, 6326-6327.

[29] Abbot, *Problems of the Panama Canal*, pp. 9-10; Curtis, *The History of the Purchase . . .* , pp. 10-12; Hay to Hart, (175) Dec. 29, 1898, Inst. Col., XIX, 20. A New Jersey charter for the New Panama Canal Company was later secured.

Various advocates exerted all possible influence to determine the governmental choice. Even the San Blas route was resurrected.[30] Naturally Nicaragua supporters were not lacking. But engineering opinion by this time seems definitely to have shifted towards Panama. The *Engineering Magazine* had been, ''from the outset, an outspoken advocate'' of a canal by this route as the ''most servicable to commerce, the most economical in operation, the greatest in potential traffic capacity, and most adaptable to the rapidly increasing demands of navigation.'' The Nicaragua route, it contended, had never received ''the endorsement of any engineering talent even approaching in character that which . . . [had] completely approved the Panama route.'' The former, therefore, was ''devoid of authoritative engineering endorsement, [and] incapable of inspiring financial backing.''[31]

A thorough examination of the leading engineering and geographical publications of the period clearly indicates that while politicians and jingoes were invoking patriotism in support of the Nicaragua route, the more sane engineers were being converted to the Panama.[32] The rivalry of two companies—Grace, Eyre, Cragin Syndicate and the Maritime Canal Company—for the renewal of the Nicaragua concession and unprecedented Panama lobbying likewise argued for the latter route.[33]

[30] William W. Redfield, ''Sea Level Canal across the Isthmus of San Blas,'' *Jour. Assn. Engineering Soc.* (May, 1900). This route, originally advocated by Frederick Kelley and Walton W. Evans, had continued to attract some attention (S. F. Weld, ''The Isthmus Canal and Our Government,'' *Atlantic Monthly*, March, 1889). See also Amos G. Hull, ''The San Blas Ship-Canal Project,'' *Engineering News* (June 22, 1893), XXIX, 580-582.

[31] *Engineering Mag.*, XIX, 107; XXII, 485-487.

[32] *Engineering Mag.; Engineering News; American Soc. Civil Engineers, Transactions; Jour. Assn. Engineering Soc.; Jour. Amer. Geog. Soc.; Jour. Franklin Institute.*

[33] Richardson, *Messages and Papers*, XIII, 6366; Johnson, *Four Centuries of the Panama Canal*, p. 116. Representatives of the New Panama

GREAT BRITAIN AGREES TO AMERICAN CONTROL

The efforts of Blaine and Frelinghuysen (1881-1883) to secure release from the Clayton-Bulwer Treaty had proved futile. In 1896 Secretary Olney tried new tactics. He admitted that the convention was still "in full force and vigor," but suggested that since

. . . changed conditions now make stipulations, which were once deemed advantageous, either inapplicable or injurious, the true remedy is not in ingenious attempts to deny the existence of the treaty or to explain away its provisions, but in a direct and straightforward application to Great Britain for a reconsideration of the whole matter.[34]

Instead of clinging to his party's view that the treaty was void or voidable, McKinley chose to adopt the policy of his Democratic predecessor. The British ambassador was assured that the convention would not be ignored, but also was impressed that in the light of recent developments appropriate modifications were desired in order to permit American governmental construction and control of a canal.[35]

British political isolation in Europe[36] suggested the advisability of more cordial relations with the United States. Since this was possible only by admitting the predominance of the latter in Central America, Lord Pauncefote, British ambassador, promised (January, 1899) consideration of Hay's draft of a new convention. Washington's firm stand regarding the Alaskan-Canadian boundary dispute prevented the immediate con-

Canal Co. landed in New York in Nov., 1898. John Bigelow used his influence with Secretary Hay; Lieutenant Commander Asher Baker with Speakers Cannon and Reed; and Bunau-Varilla with Morison, Burr, and Ernst of the canal commission (Bunau-Varilla, *Panama, the Creation, Destruction, Resurrection*, pp. 156, 160, 161, 166).

[34] Olney Memo., *Moore's Digest*, III, 209.

[35] M. W. Williams, *Anglo-American Isthmian Diplomacy*, pp. 301-302; M. W. Hazeltine, "The Clayton-Bulwer Treaty," *N. Amer. Rev.*, CLXV, 452-459.

[36] In 1898 Great Britain made unsuccessful overtures to both Germany (Triple Alliance) and Russia (Dual Entente).

clusion of the negotiations. But the strong probability of some congressional move regarding the canal forced action in order to prevent embarrassment.[37]

The treaty was signed on February 5, 1900. It permitted American governmental construction, regulation, and management of the canal; set forth certain general rules of neutralization; and provided for the adhesion of other powers to the pact. The Senate, however, insisted on a declaration that this agreement superseded the Clayton-Bulwer Treaty, more liberal provisions for American defense of the work, and the exclusion of other nations from the pact. Great Britain refused to accept these amendments. The Senate seemed on the eve of abrogating the old treaty and proceeding with the canal.[38] Hay hastened to prepare a new draft, which included the first and third of the Senate amendments but a modification of the second in England's favor. This was accepted and signed by Pauncefote on November 18, 1901, and later ratified by both governments.[39] Freedom of action had now been secured. And Washington turned to the selection of a route.

THE PANAMA ROUTE CHOSEN

Meanwhile, Nicaragua had refused to reconsider the voiding of the Maritime Canal Company's grant for alleged non-execution, had cancelled the Grace-Eyre-Cragin option because of nonpayment of the stipulated advance, and had made overtures to the United States government. A protocol providing the bases for a new treaty was signed on December 1, 1901.[40]

The Isthmian Canal Commission had reported (No-

[37] M. W. Williams, *op. cit.*, p. 302; C. W. Dilke, ''The Future Relations of Great Britain and the United States,'' *Forum* (Jan., 1899), XXVI, 521-528.

[38] M. W. Williams, *op. cit.*, pp. 302-306.

[39] *Ibid.*, pp. 307-309.

[40] Richardson, *Messages and Papers*, XIV, 6433; Hay to Hepburn, May 15, 1902, *H. Doc.*, No. 611 (57.1), p. 1.

vember 16) in favor of the Nicaragua route. This time, however, the decision was not so much on the ground of its superior merits as the seeming inability to secure the unfinished Panama work at a reasonable price. The possible advantages of the latter route were suggested, in case the interests of the New Panama Canal Company (valued at some $109,000,000) could be purchased for $40,000,000. This suggestion brought a cable (January 4, 1902) offering to accept the latter figure. On January 18 the commission made a supplementary report recommending the Panama route to Congress.[41]

However, before the French offer was generally known, the House (Hepburn Bill, January 8) had authorized the President to secure a Nicaragua concession and to proceed with the construction of a canal. An initial appropriation of $10,000,000 was provided.[42] An amendment leaving the choice of routes to the President was defeated. A long and bitter debate followed in the Senate. Senator Morgan led the Nicaragua forces and Mark Hanna[43] those of Panama, while the transcontinental railroad lobby opposed both.[44] The result was the Spooner Act (approved June 28, 1902) which authorized the President ''to acquire from the Republic of Colombia . . . upon such terms as he may deem reasonable, perpetual control of a strip of land . . . [and] the right to perpetually maintain and operate'' a canal. But if a satisfactory title could not be secured from the French interests on the Isthmus and the necessary arrangements made with Colombia, ''within a reasonable time and upon

[41] Johnson, *Four Centuries of the Panama Canal*, pp. 121-125; Abbot, *Problems of the Panama Canal*, pp. 14-15; Curtis, *The History of the Purchase*, pp. 12-20.

[42] *Statutes at Large*, XXXII, 483.

[43] It is probable that the donation of $60,000 by the New Panama Canal Co. to the Republican campaign of 1900 influenced many of the solons. See *The Story of Panama*, pp. 72, 157.

[44] Johnson, *Four Centuries of the Panama Canal*, pp. 126-127; S. A. Thompson, ''The Effect of Waterways on Railway Transportation,'' *Engineering Mag.* (July, 1902), XXIII, 583-590.

reasonable terms," the President might then turn to the Nicaragua route.[45]

On October 25 the federal attorney-general pronounced the French title good, and on February 17, 1903, the deal was closed, subject to an appropriate treaty with Colombia.[46]

NEGOTIATIONS WITH COLOMBIA

Early in 1901 the Colombian minister of foreign affairs, Carlos Martínez Silva, arrived in Washington.[47] Hay was assured (March 27) that the transfer of the concession would be permitted if an agreement could be reached regarding the construction and operation of the canal. The new minister exerted himself to secure the sale of the French interests to the United States. He pointed out (December 7) that the $109,141,500 was not the company's final figure, but merely one mentioned to open negotiations, and expressed the hope that misunderstandings might not cause the United States to choose the more expensive and less adaptable route.[48]

Early in 1902 Martínez Silva was replaced by José Vicente Concha.[49] The latter soon presented new bases for a concessionary treaty. He announced that Colombia would greatly enlarge on former concessions by renouncing all reversionary rights, granting the use of a more extensive zone, extending the facilities of its ports to aid the construction work, relinquishing its rights in the Panama railroad, and limiting its share of profits to

[45] *Statutes at Large*, XXXII, 481-482.

[46] Curtis, *The History of the Purchase*, p. 21.

[47] Martínez Silva to Hay, Feb. 19, 1901, Notes from Col. Leg., X. Owing to a Liberal revolution, the Colombian legation had been discontinued in Dec., 1900. Both Liberals and Conservatives had maintained representatives at Washington during a part of that year.

[48] Hay to Beaupré, April 28, 1903, Inst. Col., XIX; Martínez Silva to Hay, Dec. 7, 1901, Notes from Col. Leg., X. The Colombian representatives at the company's board of directors meetings (Dec. 21, 23, 1901) also approved the sale.

[49] Notes from Col. Leg., X.

a reasonable annuity. The convention, he assured, would "not be hampered by pecuniary considerations."[50]

The Department advised Concha that it would be ready to sign the "proposed convention" as soon as congressional authorization had been provided and the validity of the company's title investigated.[51] Meanwhile, the House's consideration of a bill regarding Nicaragua brought forth a protest, in so far as such a project affected Colombian sovereignty over the long-claimed Mosquito Coast. This note was merely acknowledged.[52]

After the passage of the Spooner Act, Hay (July 18) presented certain modifications to the original Colombian draft.[53] In the subsequent negotiations the principal controversial subjects were: (1) proper respect of Colombian sovereignty over the Isthmus, (2) adequate protection of investments and traffic, and (3) the monetary consideration due Colombia—the last being the most persistent. Colombia desired $7,000,000 cash and an annuity after fourteen years, the amount to be determined later by the two powers or by a non-partisan commission. Hay suggested $7,000,000 with $100,000 annuity.[54]

On September 9 Concha was instructed to sign the modified treaty. However, before the instructions reached him, American troops had landed on the Isthmus, and the use of the railroad there had been temporarily denied both the national and revolutionary forces. Concha, therefore, contended that changed conditions made it impossible for him to sign the convention. Hay attempted in vain to convince him that no new interpretation of the Treaty of 1846 was intended, and then warned him that

[50] Concha to Hay, March 31, April 18, 1902, *ibid.; H. Doc.*, No. 611 (57.1), pp. 1-16; *Sen. Doc.*, No. 474 (63.2), p. 252.

[51] Hay to Concha, April 21, 1902, Notes to Col. Leg., VII, 339.

[52] Concha to Hay, April 8, 1902, Notes from Col. Leg., X; *Sen. Doc.*, No. 474 (63.2), pp. 250-252. Somewhat similar protests had been made in 1825, 1838, 1890, 1892, 1894.

[53] Hay to Concha, July 18, 1902, Notes to Col. Leg., VII, 340.

[54] *Sen. Doc.*, No. 474 (63.2), pp. 253-270.

delay in securing the new pact might mean the president's turning to the Nicaragua route.[55]

Hay next ordered the matter pressed at Bogotá. Minister Hart was to convince the proper officials that "all possible concessions" had been made and it was "incumbent on Colombia now to say whether they want[ed] the canal or not." Unless Concha was soon instructed to sign, the President was duty bound to turn to Nicaragua, which offered a "perfectly satisfactory treaty."[56]

Meanwhile, Concha began to raise new questions, especially regarding the interpretation of the Treaty of 1846. No early agreement seemed possible. He soon left for New York and advised the Department that ill-health necessitated his return to Bogotá. Tomás Herrán, secretary of the legation and former American consul at Medellín, remained as chargé ad interim.[57]

On December 10 Secretary Hay wired Hart: "Please let us know whether or not Herrán is to receive full powers. Time is critical." The following day President Marroquín properly empowered him.[58] Hay now increased his offer to $10,000,000 cash with a $100,000 annuity. But Herrán's instructions called for $600,000 annuity. Before he could secure new advice from Bogotá, there was a movement in Congress for the adoption of the Nicaragua route. Hay's warnings merely brought assurances from Herrán that new instructions

[55] Concha to Hay, Oct. 26, 1902, Notes from Col. Leg., X; Hay to Concha, Oct. 28, 1902, Notes to Col. Leg., VII, 342 ff.; *Sen. Doc.*, No. 474 (63.2), pp. 255-256.

[56] Hay to Hart, (tel.) Oct. 27, Nov. 22, 25, 1902, Inst. Col., XIX, 209, 213. These indicate a decided preference for the Panama route. Nicaragua had already presented (May 14, 1902) a satisfactory treaty—$6,000,000 with annuity of $25,000—and Costa Rica was favorably disposed for the sum of $1,500,000 (*H. Doc.*, No. 611 [57.1], pp. 16-25).

[57] Concha to Hay, Nov. 11, 22, 1902, Notes from Col. Leg., X; Hay to Concha, Nov. 18, Dec. 12, 1902, Notes to Col. Leg., VII, 346 ff., 352; *Sen. Doc.*, No. 474 (63.2), pp. 257-269.

[58] Hay to Hart, Dec. 10, 1902, Inst. Col., XIX, 215; Notes from Col. Leg., X.

were expected daily.[59] Almost in desperation, Hay (January 16) wired Bogotá: "If Colombian Government persists in present attitude, it renders further negotiations impossible." On January 21 Herrán was notified that the "reasonable time" provided in the Spooner Act had expired and could not be extended. Therefore immediate action was necessary. The President had agreed to increase the annuity to $250,000, but had not authorized the consideration or discussion of "any other change whatever."[60]

This ultimatum brought the desired results. On January 22, 1903, the Hay-Herrán Treaty was signed. Colombia agreed to the transfer of the French concession to the United States government, made it exclusive for one hundred years and renewable at the "absolute and sole option" of the latter, and renounced its annuities and reversionary rights under the Panama Railroad Company contract. In return, the United States was to pay $10,000,000 in cash and $250,000 annual rental beginning nine years from the date of treaty approval. The grant included a zone of ten kilometers in width and certain properties in the cities of Panama and Colón. Although Colombian sovereignty over the area was guaranteed, actual control was placed in American hands, and troops might be landed for protection without the consent of the former.[61]

The treaty was ratified by the American senate on March 17, but was unanimously rejected by the Colombian senate on August 12.[62] The adjournment of the latter body without further consideration of the document was followed by the Panama Revolution of November 3, 1903.

[59] Hay to Hart, (tel.) Dec. 30, 1902, Inst. Col., XIX, 224; Hay to Herrán, Dec. 30, 1902, Notes to Col. Leg., VII, 353; Herrán to Hay, Dec. 31, 1902, Notes from Col. Leg., X.

[60] Hay to Hart, (tel.) Jan. 16, 1903, Inst. Col., XIX, 220; Hay to Herrán, Jan. 16, 21, 1903, Notes to Col. Leg., VII, 354.

[61] Text of treaty, *Sen. Doc.*, No. 474 (63.2), pp. 277-288.

[62] Unperfected Treaties, Col. D-4.

PART VII

THE PANAMA REVOLUTION AND ITS
AFTERMATH

CHAPTER XXV

A CASE IN INTERNATIONAL MORALITY

... I took the Canal Zone. ... .—PRESIDENT ROOSEVELT.[1]

Every action taken was not merely proper, but was carried out in accordance with the highest, finest, and nicest standards of public and governmental ethics.—PRESIDENT ROOSEVELT.[2]

... every act of the President in this wretched Panama business has been a flagrant violation of law. ... .—SENATOR CARMACK.[3]

[Roosevelt obtained a] ... pretended claim there by the methods of a sneak thief and then defended it by the attitude of a bully.—SENATOR TILLMAN.[4]

Even the buccaneers who sailed the Spanish Main would have found it too much for them.—*The Nation*.[5]

The only comfort that one gathers from the shameful and sordid story is that it finds no precedent in our history.—SENATOR THOMAS.[6]

[But,] ... the "damned spot" will still persist.—L. T. CHAMBERLAIN.[7]

THE policy of the United States during the Panama Episode of 1903 has evoked much lengthy and vehement discussion. It has been defended as "studiously correct"; "full duty, nothing more"; "a bit of honest statecraft"; and the "only possible" course. On the other hand, it has been characterized as a "lamentable outrage," "rough-riding assault," "territorial buccaneering," "clear act of spoilation," "international lawlessness," "quite unexampled instance of foul play," and "in every respect ... nefarious." Discussion of the

[1] Speech at Berkeley, Calif., March 23, 1911, *Cong. Rec.* (67.1), LXI, 234.

[2] "How the United States Acquired the Right to Dig the Panama Canal," *Outlook* (Oct. 7, 1911), XCIX, 314-318.

[3] *Cong. Rec.* (58.2), XXXVIII, 704.

[4] *Ibid.*, p. 801.

[5] Nov. 12, 1903.

[6] *Cong. Rec.* (66.3), LX, 879.

[7] "A Chapter of National Dishonor," *N. Amer. Rev.* (Feb., 1912), CXCV, 172.

American policy, then, must lead into the realm of international morals.

Since relevant published material is so voluminous, the purpose of this chapter is twofold: first, to relate merely the essential facts; second, to set forth concisely the arguments advanced regarding the legality and morality of the American policy.

I. THE ESSENTIAL FACTS

A. *Colombia Rejects the Hay-Herrán Treaty.* This convention, approved by the American senate on March 17, 1903, was taken up by the Colombian congress in extra session on June 20 and unanimously rejected by it on August 12.[8] But a Senate committee (August 29) recommended bases for new negotiations: (1) the payment of $10,000,000 by the New Panama Canal Company for the transfer of its concession; (2) the payment of $20,000,000, plus $150,000 annuity up to 1967 and $400,000 thereafter by the United States; and (3) the renewal of the contract every one hundred years with a twenty-five per cent increase in the annual rentals.[9]

These bases were referred to another committee, which presented its recommendations on October 14, after the time allowed for ratification of the treaty had expired. This report questioned the validity of the extension of the French concession to 1910 because it had been granted without congressional approval. If this extension were not valid, the old concession would revert to Colombia on October 31, 1904, and thereby make possible new negotiations on more advantageous footing. But the committee refused to declare definitely against the extension, merely recommending it to the consideration of the next Congress.[10]

On October 30 the Senate, without committing itself

[8] Unperfected Treaties, Col., D-4.
[9] Mensaje de 1904—Marroquín, Uribe, *Anales*, IV, 801-867; *Cong. Rec.* (58.2), XXXVIII, 1661-1662.
[10] *Ibid.; Sen. Doc.*, No. 474 (63.2), pp. 459-462.

on this report, agreed unanimously to postpone action on the treaty, but expressed itself as favorable to the renewal of negotiations. Congress adjourned the following day, and an executive manifesto (November 1) declared that Bogotá was open for new proposals.[11]   But it was too late.

B. *Panama Plans Secession.*   The separatist idea was almost a tradition on the Isthmus. On three former occasions (1830, 1841, 1861) persuasion and concessions had proved necessary to secure Panama's re-adhesion to the Bogotá government. The persistent danger of subsequent secessions (especially evident in 1862, 1866, 1874-1875, 1879, 1885-1886) had continued to cause much official uneasiness.[12]

Even before the submission of the Hay-Herrán Treaty to the Colombian congress, the possibility of secession and American intervention had been discussed by Manuel Amador Guerrero, José A. Arango, and Tomás Arias.[13] The protracted consideration of the treaty at Bogotá and the fear of American negotiations with Nicaragua soon brought others into the plot.[14]   And Colonel J. S. Shaler, Captain J. R. Beers, H. G. Prescott,[15] Colonel William Black,[16] and General Herbert O. Jeffries[17]—presumably American citizens—were kept fully advised of the progress of the conspiracy.[18]

José Gabriel Duque (Cuban by birth but an American

[11] Beaupré to Hay, Nov. 2, 1903, *ibid.*, p. 468; Uribe, *Anales*, IV, 846-848.

[12] See *supra*, chap. xiii.

[13] Amador and Arango were, or had been, employees of the railroad; Arias, the owner of a valuable electric light concession.

[14] Federico Boyd, Constantino Arosemena, Ricardo Arias, Manuel Espinosa, and Nicanor A. de Obarrio.

[15] All three were Panama Railroad officials.

[16] United States Army engineer.

[17] Either was or had been a Colombian general and later became a Panamanian admiral.

[18] Reports of special correspondents of *New York Evening Post*, Dec. 8, 1903, *New York Tribune*, Jan. 2, 1904; Federico Boyd, *The Secession of Panama*, p. 26.

by naturalization)[19] set out for Washington. He claimed to have conferred with both Roosevelt and Hay. Although no promise of assistance and recognition was forthcoming, Duque's impression was that a Panama revolution would not be entirely disagreeable to the Administration. The separatists were assured by Captain Beers, who also had gone to Washington, that American support was certain. Dr. Amador was then dispatched to the United States to confirm these reports. He hoped, owing probably to the encouragement of William Nelson Cromwell,[20] that he might secure $6,000,000 from Roosevelt's "secret fund" to finance the revolt; therefore he was much surprised and discouraged when Washington officials refused to receive him.[21]

Cromwell then began to avoid Amador. The latter was on the point of departing for Panama, when M. Phillipe Bunau-Varilla arrived in New York. These two would-be revolutionists were brought together by M. Lindo, formerly of the Isthmus. Bunau-Varilla, as a French engineer and large investor in the New Panama Canal Company, could gain the attention of official ears denied to Amador. His acquaintance with many men of influence made him a valuable asset to the separatist cause.

Through his friend, Professor William H. Burr of Columbia University, Bunau-Varilla learned that John Bassett Moore held the same views regarding Panama secession and the resulting American policy as those he

[19] Proprietor of the *Panama Star and Herald* and former American vice-consul at Panama.

[20] Senator Thomas of Colorado characterized Cromwell as "the archplotter of his time, the manipulator of legislation, the adviser of home and foreign ministers, the designer of successful revolutions, the master of intrigue, [and] the betrayer of his country's honor among the nations" (*Cong. Rec.* [66.3], LX, 886). Duque claimed that Cromwell offered him the presidency of Panama if he would raise sufficient troops for the revolution (*The Roosevelt Panama Libel Case*, p. 15).

[21] *New York Evening Post*, Dec. 8, 1903; Alvaro Rebolledo, *Reseña histórico-político de la comunicación interoceánica*, pp. 207-210. Rebolledo claims that Beers was sent to Washington by the separatists.

had recently expressed in *Le Matin.* The discovery that
Moore had lately visited President Roosevelt at Oyster
Bay led Bunau-Varilla to suspect that the two agreed on
policy. He therefore secured a conference with the
President on October 9. After subsequent interviews
with Hay and Loomis, Bunau-Varilla was convinced that
the American determination to protect the transit route
would sufficiently insure the success of the secessionists
and even make extensive military preparations unnecessary. In fact, he quotes Hay as saying that the revolution would not catch the United States "napping," since
naval forces were already sailing towards the Isthmus.[22]

With Bunau-Varilla's assurance that American protection was "as certain as if a contract had been signed,"
Amador returned to Panama. There he experienced some
difficulty in convincing his followers of the certainty of
this support. They wanted to see the vessels in the harbors before acting. It was rumored that the Bogotá government had become cognizant of the Isthmian unrest and
was sending additional garrisons. Amador cabled frantically for a warship. After a conference with Loomis
(October 30) Bunau-Varilla wired that a vessel would
arrive at Colón within two and a half days and another
at Panama within four.[23] Roosevelt had already ordered
certain vessels to ports nearer the scene of the anticipated revolt and others to be in readiness.[24] On receipt
of the news of the movement of Colombian troops, the
Nashville was directed (October 30) to hasten to Colón.

C. *The Revolution Is Staged.* The adjournment of
the Colombian congress without favorable action on the
treaty made revolution on the Isthmus almost inevitable.
And the anticipated arrival of new government troops
argued for immediate precautionary measures. On No-

[22] Bunau-Varilla, *Panama, the Creation* . . . , pp. 289-318.
[23] Federico Boyd, *op. cit.,* p. 28; Rebolledo, *op. cit.,* pp. 217-218; Rippy,
The Capitalists and Colombia, pp. 94-96.
[24] W. R. Thayer, *The Life of John Hay,* II, 316.

vember 2 the *Nashville* (already at Colón) and the *Dixie* (at Kingston, Jamaica) were instructed by Roosevelt as follows: "Maintain free and uninterrupted transit. If interruption threatened by armed force, occupy the line of railroad. Prevent landing of any armed force with hostile intent, either Government or insurgent, either at Colón, Porto Bello, or other point . . . Government force reported approaching the Isthmus in vessels. Prevent their landing if in your judgement this would precipitate a conflict." On the same day the *Marblehead* (at Acapulco, Mexico) was ordered to "proceed with all possible dispatch" and prevent any hostile armed force from landing "at any point within fifty miles of Panama."[25]

The stage was set and the American forces were on hand to play their rôles, but no revolution materialized. The situation possessed embarrassing possibilities, and Washington was obviously nervous. A mere press rumor sped a cable (3:40 P.M., November 3) to the Panama and Colón consulates: "Uprising on Isthmus reported. Keep department promptly and fully informed." At 8:15 P.M. a reply from Panama was received: "No uprising yet. Reported will be in the night. Situation is critical." The suspense was somewhat relieved at 9:50 P.M. by Consul Felix Ehrman's second cable: "Uprising occurred tonight, 6:00 no bloodshed . . . order prevails so far. Situation serious. Four hundred soldiers landed Colón today [from] Barranquilla."[26]

Unfortunately the *Nashville* had received its instructions too late to prevent the Colombian troops from landing. But new orders went forward to detain them at Colón.[27] These orders proved unnecessary, however, since the railroad officials had already refused to transport any of the troops, except their commanding officers,

[25] *Sen. Doc.*, No. 474 (63.2), pp. 362-363. The *Concord, Atlanta, Wyoming, Boston,* and *Maine* soon appeared on the scene.
[26] *Ibid.*, pp. 345-346.   [27] *Ibid.*, pp. 346, 351, 363.

Juan B. Tovar and Ramón G. Amaya. The forces were left at Colón under Colonel Torres.[28]

At Panama City the revolution was quite easily accomplished. The rebels seemed to have been permitted to draw on the Colombian bank account, and therefore experienced little difficulty in making conversions to their cause. It was reported that Commanders Huertas of the garrison and Varon of the navy received $25,000 each; the chief engineer and the chief of artillery, $10,000 each; while proportionately smaller sums were judiciously given or promised to the common soldiers.[29] Of course, Tovar and Amaya were arrested after their arrival at Panama as were also Governor Obaldía, General Castro, and Commander Tovar of the gunboat *Bogotá*. With the support of a "good size company of Benedict Arnolds" and the Panama fire department, the secessionists then set about forming a new and independent government.[30]

On receipt of the news of the Panama revolt Colonel Torres threatened hostilities against Americans at Colón, but was persuaded (November 5) for a consideration (reported to have been $8,000) to return with his troops to the Mainland.[31] And the morning of November 6 found the Isthmus free of hostile Colombian forces.[32]

D. *The Independence of Panama Is Recognized.* On November 4 the provisional government, composed of José A. Arango, Federico Boyd, and Tomás Arias, ad-

[28] Rebolledo, *op. cit.*, p. 220.

[29] *New York Evening Post*, Dec. 8, *New York Tribune*, Dec. 21, 1903. Other estimates give Varon $35,000 Colombian silver; Huertas $30,000 silver plus a subsequent payment of $50,000 American gold; lesser officers from $6,000 to $10,000; and privates $50. It is also claimed that the confiscated treasury was not adequate to pay all of the "bonuses"; therefore many promises were redeemed out of a $300,000 loan granted the new republic by J. P. Morgan and Co. See *The Story of Panama*, pp. 382, 446, 462; *Cong. Rec.* (58.2), p. 369.

[30] Rebolledo, *op. cit.*, pp. 221-222. The gunboat *Bogotá* fired a few shells on Panama on the night of Nov. 3, killing one Chinese; but it soon withdrew.

[31] *New York Evening Post*, Dec. 8, 1903.

[32] *Sen. Doc.*, No. 474 (63.2), pp. 348, 352.

vised Washington of the "popular and spontaneous movement" for independence and requested recognition for the new Republic of Panama. Two days later Hay was assured from the same source that "all the towns of the Isthmus . . . [had] adhered to the declaration of independence." Two hours and eleven minutes after the receipt of this information, he cabled Consul Ehrman to enter into relations with the new state whenever he was "satisfied that a *de facto* government, republican in form, and without substantial opposition from the people" had been established. Hay then advised Bogotá of the Administration's decision and recommended "the peaceful and equitable settlement of all questions at issue" between Colombia and Panama.[33]

On November 7 Bunau-Varilla notified the Department of his appointment as envoy extraordinary and minister plenipotentiary for Panama and expressed the appreciation of his adopted country for the "protecting wings" of the American Eagle. He was officially received by Roosevelt on November 13. Five days later the Hay-Bunau-Varilla Treaty was signed, giving the United States the right to dig the Panama canal.[34] Although Hay knew that Federico Boyd, Amador Guerrero, and Pablo Arosemena were en route to Washington to assist in the negotiations, he chose to arrange the treaty with the Frenchman before their arrival.[35]

E. *Colombia Is Prevented from Suppressing the Revolt.* Naturally Chargé Hèrrán (November 7) lodged a "solemn protest" against the American policy as injurious to Colombian rights and at variance with the Treaty of 1846.[36] When the Bogotá government heard

[33] *Ibid.*, pp. 348, 353-356.

[34] *Ibid.*, pp. 295-303, 354-355, 361-362.

[35] Ehrman to Hay, (tel.) Nov. 10, 1903, *ibid.*, pp. 349-350. See also Jorge E. Boyd, *Refutation of Bunau-Varilla's Book.* This is a severe attack on the treaty and an attempt to show that Bunau-Varilla had other motives than the interest of Panama for signing before the mission reached Washington.

[36] Herrán to Hay, Nov. 7, 1903, *Sen. Doc.*, No. 474 (63.2), p. 359.

(November 5)[37] through its Quito legation of the actual revolt, it appealed to the presidents of all the Latin American republics.[38]   Troops were prepared to proceed to the Isthmus.   Minister Beaupré was approached regarding American intentions.   On November 6 General Rafael Reyes promised that if the United States would use its forces to restore Panama, martial law would be declared in Colombia and the Hay-Herrán Treaty ratified by executive decree, or, if preferable, a new congress of friendly personnel called to ratify it.[39]   The following day the minister of foreign affairs inquired whether Colombia would be permitted to land troops to suppress the revolt, but was hesitant about confirming Reyes's promise.[40]

It mattered little any way, since *de facto* recognition had already been granted Panama and the subsequent American policy decided upon. On November 11 Hay cabled that it was ''not thought desirable to permit the landing of Colombian troops on the Isthmus, as such a course would precipitate civil war and disturb for an indefinite period the free transit which we [the United States] . . . [were] pledged to protect.''[41]

F. *Washington Refuses Arbitration.* Since the American attitude made coercion of the revolutionists impossible, General Reyes led a mission[42] to Washington to protest against the injuries and damages suffered by Colombia and to secure either a direct agreement or the submission of the entire question to The Hague Tribunal. He soon found, however, the differences too great for negotiations and the State Department too adamant for

[37] See *ibid.*, p. 355.
[38] Mensaje de 1904—Marroquín, Uribe, *Anales*, IV, 852-856.
[39] Beaupré to Hay, Nov. 6, 1903, *Sen. Doc.*, No. 474 (63.2), p. 356.
[40] *Idem* to *idem* (tel.), Nov. 7, 1903, *ibid.*, p. 357.
[41] Hay to Beaupré, (tel.) Nov. 11, 1903, *ibid.*, p. 358; Uribe, *Anales*, IV, 859.
[42] The other members were Pedro Nel Ospina, Lucas Caballero, and Jorge Holguín.

arbitration.[43]   Settlement, therefore, was left to plague subsequent relations for almost two decades.

The legality and morality of the American course during the entire Panama Affair have been attacked and defended with almost equal vehemence. It may prove of interest to consider the preceding facts in the light of the following: first, international law and equity; second, American "interests and safety"; third, the interests of "collective civilization."

II. INTERNATIONAL LAW AND EQUITY

The formal rules of international law are but declarations of what is just and right in the generality of cases. But where the application of such a general rule would impair the just rights or imperil the existence of neighboring states or unduly threaten the peace of a continent or would injuriously affect the general interests of mankind, it has always been the practice of civilized nations to deny the application of the formal rule and compel conformity to the principles of justice upon which all rules depend.—Elihu Root.[44]

Although the general rules of international law recognize neither the right of one sovereign state to interfere in the internal affairs of another nor the right of the strong to impose its will upon the weak, there may be exceptions "growing out of circumstances and founded in those circumstances." Weakness is no more a "charter to license" than strength is a "charter to oppression." If a nation desires justice, it must act in an equitable manner.

Since both Colombia and the United States admit that the circumstances surrounding the American acquisition of the canal route were exceptional and each contends that the other took advantage of these circumstances to further its selfish ends, it is not enough that the policies

---

[43] Reyes to Hay, Dec. 23, 1903, Jan. 6, 11, 1904, Hay to Reyes, Jan. 5, 9, 13, 1904, *Sen. Doc.*, No. 474 (63.2), pp. 481-511.

[44] Elihu Root, *Addresses on International Subjects*, p. 180.

connected therewith be considered in the light of law only; they must be regarded also in the light of equity.

A. *The Equality*[44a] *of Sovereign States under International Law.* International law recognizes the legal equality of sovereign states. But it would be absurd to contend that this principle is always maintained. Strong powers often impose their wills upon the weak and the victors upon the vanquished. The right of equal consideration and respect might even be forfeited by the disregard of the rights of others or the failure to fulfil obligations.

On this basis it is argued that even if the governments of Colombia and Central America had been "administered with more regard to the just demands of other nations," they should not be permitted "to close the gates of intercourse on the great highways of the world, and justify the act by the pretension that these avenues of trade and travel belong to them and that they chose to shut them, or, what is almost equivalent, to encumber them with such unjust regulations as would prevent their general use."[45] It would follow that states deserve treatment as equals only when they act in harmony with the interests of the whole family of nations.

But what agent has the power or right to pass upon the morality of a state's conduct? Certainly, if the stronger state acts as a judge, even the semblance of legal equality disappears and the sovereignty of the weaker is endangered. Yet the United States attempted to sit in judgment on Colombia's actions and violated the latter's sovereignty without compunction.

By the Treaty of 1846 the United States both recognized Colombian sovereignty over the Isthmus and guar-

---

[44a] The term "equality" is used here to denote equality before the law—not equality in ability to protect substantive rights, nor equality in determining new rules of international law.

[45] Statement of Secretary Cass, 1858, quoted by Roosevelt in his message of Jan. 7, 1904, *Moore's Digest*, III, 47.

anteed it against foreign aggression. The destruction of this sovereignty by internal forces, however, was made possible by the American refusal to permit Colombia to land troops. The fact that Washington had never interpreted the treaty to include protection from secessionists hardly seems to justify the preventing of Colombia from suppressing a revolt within its own domain. It appears, therefore, that the United States not only refused to protect Colombian sovereignty but actually violated it, thereby nullifying the principle of the legal equality of sovereign states. The contention that the circumstances were such as to make inapplicable "the formal rule [of international law] and compel conformity to the principles of justice upon which all rules depend" lacks a firm basis in fact.

B. *Treaty-Making Powers and Duties of Sovereign States.* Colombia undoubtedly initiated the treaty negotiations. Minister Martínez Silva (1901) assured Secretary Hay that his government would permit the transfer of the canal concession to the United States. Minister José Vicente Concha (1902) promised that Colombia would "not place any obstacle whatever in the way"; in fact, it would "enlarge those concessions."[46] This illustrates the friendly spirit and sincere coöperation evidenced while the American congress was wrangling over the choice of routes.

However, with the passage of the Spooner Act indicating a preference for the Panama route, Concha grew, to say the least, indifferent. He was instructed (September 9, 1902) to sign the prepared treaty draft, but refused, except on new instructions, because of the activities of the American forces, which landed in the meantime on the Isthmus. Evidently new powers were not forthcoming. Concha soon withdrew, leaving the legation in charge of Tomás Herrán. The latter signed the more

[46] Concha to Hay, March 31, 1902, *H. Doc.*, No. 611 (58.1), p. 2.

liberal treaty only after receiving an ultimatum from
Secretary Hay. Before the news reached Bogotá, Herrán
was cabled (January 24) not to conclude an agreement
until the arrival of new instructions. President Marroquín felt that since the long civil war had been successfully terminated, Colombia was in a position to demand
less reduction in its sovereignty over the Isthmus and
much larger monetary considerations.[47]

The restoration of peace in Colombia meant that an
elected congress assumed much of the power formerly
exercised by Marroquín as dictator. Although friends of
his administration seemed to dominate this body,[48] Marroquín submitted the treaty without definitely committing
himself.[49] He refused to sign it before presentation, but
in conference with leaders urged its ratification.[50] Of
course, he could have approved it without congressional
action, as General Reyes is reported to have suggested
to Beaupré. It is obvious, however, that the terms were
not entirely satisfactory to Marroquín. Besides, the continuation of dictatorship after the restoration of peace
might have proved difficult to defend. But, even if continued, could Marroquín have utterly disregarded public
opinion? The despatches of Minister Beaupré contain
abundant evidence that popular opposition was very pronounced even before Congress met.[51]

The press teemed with articles "rancorous in en-
mity" to the treaty. These were often as exaggerated as
bitter. One Bogotá lawyer insisted that the United
States would profit by at least $1,186,537,377 during
merely the first term of the concession. Others stressed
the impairment of Colombian sovereignty. Only one
Colombian of prominence, Enrique Cortés, dared support

[47] See *supra*, chap. xxiv; Uribe, *Anales*, IV, 840-481.
[48] Beaupré to Hay, June 23, Aug. 15, 1903, *Sen. Doc.*, No. 474 (63.2),
pp. 401, 428.
[49] Mensaje de 1904—Marroquín, Uribe, *Anales*, IV, 793-794.
[50] Beaupré to Hay, July 2, 1903, *Sen. Doc.*, No. 474 (63.2), p. 404.
[51] *Ibid.*, pp. 379, 380, 388, 390.

the treaty before the people.[52] It would seem, then, that rejection was in accordance with popular desire.

The question arises, however, did not Colombian initiation of the negotiations and Herrán's signing of the treaty morally bind the Bogotá government to ratify? The American senate has never considered itself so bound. It rejected, or modified so as to render unacceptable, the treaty of 1869 with Colombia and the first Hay-Pauncefote Treaty with England, after the State Department had initiated negotiations in each case. Besides, did not the Hay-Herrán Treaty itself condition its operation on ratification "in conformity with the laws of the respective countries"? In Colombia congressional approval was required, although the executive had authorized the signing of the treaty. The refusal to ratify, in the face of an uncompromising popular opposition, could hardly be termed an international offense, especially when Colombia publicly announced its willingness to reopen negotiations.[53] Neither should the postponement of consideration until the next Congress have been considered unfriendly, since it took the American senate eighteen months to ratify the Treaty of 1846.[54]

Furthermore, it might be contended that Herrán signed the treaty under the pressure of Hay's ultimatum[55]—either sign on these terms or we will turn to Nicaragua. It seems certain, however, that Herrán was less apprehensive of the shift of negotiations than of the American seizure of the Isthmus. Roosevelt was known to be a decided partisan of the Panama route. There was some agitation for a direct understanding with the New

[52] *Ibid.*, pp. 388, 416-418, 440.

[53] The Spooner Act, by providing for negotiations with Nicaragua, recognized Colombia's right to reject any agreement.

[54] Later, the United States senate postponed the ratification of the Thomson-Urrutia Treaty for more than seven years.

[55] Herrán wired Bogotá, Jan. 22, 1903: "Treaty signed today accepting *ultimatum* ten million and two hundred fifty thousand dollars annuity" (Uribe, *Anales*, IV, 833).

Panama Canal Company and the expropriation of the territory "on the ground of universal public utility"— Colombian compensation to be determined later. This plan, Herrán advised his government, was favored by Senator Stone of the foreign relations committee and might not prove "distasteful" to the "impetuous and violent disposition" of Roosevelt.[56]

General Reyes believed, however, that the treaty would have received Colombian approval, with certain reasonable amendments, had not Minister Beaupré assumed such an obnoxious attitude.[57] This seems doubtful, since congressional fear of an aroused public opinion and the Liberal Party's concerted and determined effort to embarrass Marroquín were probably sufficient to defeat it. Beaupré early noted the force of these two factors and suggested a "strong intimation" against unnecessary delays.[58] The subsequent "intimations" undoubtedly solidified the opposition and hastened the inevitable rejection of the treaty.

When amendments were suggested, Hay argued that they would be in violation of the Spooner Act, not making it plain just how Colombian legislation could transgress an American statute. Beaupré was instructed (June 9) to warn the Bogotá officials that rejection or undue delay of ratification would so seriously compromise the relations between the two nations "that action might be taken by Congress next winter which every friend of Colombia would regret."[59] The reading of this admonition before a secret session of the Colombian senate created considerable sensation, since it was inter-

[56] Herrán to Colombian government, eight days after assuming duties, quoted by Senator Thomas, *Cong. Rec.* (66.3), LX, 880-881. See also Uribe, *Anales*, IV, 831.

[57] Reyes to Hay, Dec. 23, 1903, *Sen. Doc.*, No. 474 (63.2), pp. 481-491.

[58] Beaupré to Hay, July 11, 1903, *ibid.*, p. 410.

[59] Hay to Beaupré, April 7, June 9, 1903, *ibid.*, pp. 379, 392. Could this have meant the forceful expropriation feared by Herrán? No congressional action was necessary to turn to Nicaragua.

preted by many "as a threat of direct retaliation."
Beaupré thought that this warning and a current rumor
that Panama would secede, in case of rejection, would
hasten ratification.[60] But he was mistaken. Even the
repetition of his warnings (August 5) failed to prevent
the unanimous disapproval of the treaty (August 12)
and the subsequent adjournment of Congress without
serious reconsideration.[61]

Although Congress was amazed and indignant at the
American attitude, the Conservative-Liberal struggle
shoved the treaty into the background. Generals who
had recently faced each other on the battlefield were now
contending for political dominance. Internal politics
alone was sufficient to have defeated the treaty.[62]

The grounds given for non-ratification, however, were
as follows: impairment of sovereignty, absence of previous arrangement by the New Panama Canal Company
for the transfer of the concession, and the American refusal to consider reasonable amendments.[63] But the limited congressional debates centered around the issues of
diminished sovereignty and additional monetary remu-
neration.

Possibly Colombia was unduly sensitive regarding its
sovereignty[64]—not an uncommon characteristic of weaker
nations—but the perpetuity of the concession granted
and the most recent American interpretation of the
Treaty of 1846 certainly argued caution. Hays's refusal
to consider amendments, his threats of subsequent congressional action, and his warning of the uselessness of

---

[60] Beaupré to Hay, July 5, 1903, *ibid.*, p. 405.

[61] *Ibid.*, pp. 423, 426-427.

[62] Beaupré admitted that not more than four or five days were spent by
Congress in discussing the treaty prior to Oct. 10 (*ibid.*, p. 456). See also
J. T. Du Bois in *New York Times*, July 20, 1913.

[63] Herrán to Hay, Aug. 22, 1903, Notes from Col. Leg., X.

[64] Subsequent disputes between the United States and Panama under the
Hay-Bunau-Varilla Treaty probably indicate the opposite.

reopening negotiations, all lack diplomatic precedent.[65] The United States most assuredly would have resented these from Great Britain during the consideration of the first Hay-Pauncefote Treaty.

In regard to permission for the transfer of the concession, Minister Martínez Silva (1901) had assured that this could be arranged, but made no mention of a monetary consideration. On January 27, 1902, however, he was instructed to secure, if possible, $20,000,000 from the New Panama Canal Company for the privilege.[66] The company itself was later (December 24) promised consent for the transfer, but was advised that a subsequently determined sum of money would be demanded. Again, before the treaty was submitted for ratification, the canal agent at Bogotá was officially informed that $10,000,000 would probably be necessary to secure approval, since the amount provided in the treaty was considered insufficient by many.[67]

Because of this insistence on greater compensation from both the canal company and the United States, the Colombians have been characterized as "blackmailers." It must be remembered, however, that the ratification of the treaty meant much more than the mere transfer of the old concession. It meant the loss of (1) $16,000,000 in rentals from the Panama Railroad Company; (2) the reversionary ownership of the railroad in 1967 (estimated value of $16,446,000 in 1906); (3) canal annuities and the canal itself at the end of ninety-nine years, if completed under the old concession. Even Senator Lodge (1921) accepted $50,146,942.75 as the probable loss to Colombia.[68] Of course, this figure could be only approximate, but it was sufficiently accurate to indicate that

[65] See *Sen. Doc.*, No. 474 (63.2), pp. 462, 465, 467, 468, 472; Herrán to Hay, Sept. 16, 1903, Notes from Col. Leg., X.

[66] Uribe, *Anales*, IV, 810.

[67] José Ramón Lago to New Panama Canal Co., Dec. 24, 1902, Beaupré to Hay, June 10, 1903, *Sen. Doc.*, No. 474 (63.2), pp. 387, 396.

[68] *Cong. Rec.* (67.1), LXI, 160.

$10,000,000 cash and the perpetual annuity of $250,000 might properly be considered inadequate compensation.

Furthermore, whether Colombia seriously contemplated the voiding of the concession extension and the seizure of the French company's property is quite doubtful. The Senate report, usually cited in support of this theory, did not declare against the validity of the extension, but merely suggested that the matter be considered by the next Congress; nor was the report itself adopted by the Senate. Colombian statesmen realized the inexpediency of declaring the extension void. It would have necessitated the payment of loans of 5,000,000 francs to the canal company and $600,000 to the railroad company. And Colombia was already near bankruptcy. Besides, the continued French control of the Panama railroad, unaffected by the lapse of the canal concession, would have made futile any further negotiations with the United States for a canal by the Panama-Colón route.

It would appear, then, that the charge of blackmail was unfounded and that Colombia was justified in rejecting the Hay-Herrán Treaty on any one or all of the grounds advanced.

C. *Mutual Rights and Obligations under the Treaty of 1846.* President Roosevelt defended himself as follows:

The great design of the article [XXXV] was to assure the dedication of the Isthmus to the purposes of free and unobstructed interoceanic transit, the consummation of which would be found in an interoceanic canal. . . . The treaty vested in the United States a substantial property right carved out of the rights of sovereignty and property which New Granada [Colombia] then had and possessed over said territory.[69]

I feel we are certainly justified in morals, and therefore justified in law, under the Treaty of 1846, in interfering summarily and

[69] *Moore's Digest*, III, 47, 72.

saying that the canal is to be built and that they must not stop it.[70]

Admittedly, the United States was treaty bound to protect all transit routes across the Colombian Isthmus from foreign aggressors. Did not such a guarantee of the peaceful enjoyment of all modes of communication bind Colombia to grant reasonable concessions for the construction of the most efficient and valuable mode—a canal? If true, then, when it became evident that no corporation of individuals could complete the work and no European nation was willing to attempt it—or even to guarantee its neutrality[71]—was not Colombia morally, if not legally, obligated to grant a liberal contract to the United States?

Colombia was willing enough, if not anxious, to negotiate regarding a canal, but denied any obligation to give special privileges. It was true that the United States had assumed the guarantee of the Isthmus, but not with an eye to future governmental canal construction, nor as a benefit to Colombia. The protection of trade and the commercial provisions of Articles IV, V, and VI of the Treaty of 1846 had been the motivating factors. Evidently the advantages of an unobstructed transit and the commercial benefits bestowed by these articles had proved sufficient compensation for the effective fulfillment of Article XXXV, since the required twelve months' notice of a desire to terminate the treaty had never been given.

In regard to American "property right carved out of the rights of sovereignty and property" which Colombia had on the Isthmus, this could not have possessed a

[70] Roosevelt to Hanna, Oct. 5, 1903, J. B. Bishop, *Theodore Roosevelt and His Time*, I, 278.

[71] Martínez Silva was instructed (Jan. 22, 1902) to approach the British and French representatives at Washington regarding an international guarantee. If secured, the Treaty of 1846 was to be terminated. But nothing resulted from the move (Uribe, *Anales*, IV, 809-810).

great degree of permanency under a treaty of such uncertain tenure. It seems more reasonable to assume that Article XXXV imposed the duty to protect Colombian property rights, instead of conferring these rights on the United States. Yet the latter power not only failed to protect Colombian property and sovereignty but refused to permit the landing of Colombian troops to do this.

It is argued that on the secession of Panama Colombia ceased to own any property on or to exercise sovereignty over the Isthmus. The Treaty of 1846 was no longer with Colombia but with Panama. In other words, the "covenant ran with the land," and it was of minor importance whether the latter was a part of the republic or independent. Therefore, on the recognition of the independence of Panama, the United States became treaty bound to protect the property and sovereignty of the new state against foreign aggressors— including Colombia.

This argument may be legally valid, but certainly the Administration's use of it lacked sincerity. Roosevelt wrote Oscar S. Strauss: "Your 'covenant running with the land' idea worked admirably. I congratulate you on it." John Bassett Moore wrote Strauss: "So you had a finger in the pie! I find a great deal of amusement in reflecting on the end reached from the premise of my memorandum and almost as much on the conclusion reached from your suggestion. Perhaps, however, it is only a question of words, that is to say, it is, indifferently, a question of the 'covenant running with the land' or a question of the 'covenant running (away!) with the land'!!"[72]

Moore's memorandum (August, 1903) for Roosevelt had defended the view that the Treaty of 1846 furnished sufficient basis for proceeding with the construction of

[72] Oscar Strauss, *Under Four Administrations*, pp. 175-176.

a canal without Colombian consent. This led to Moore's visit to Oyster Bay early in September and seemingly to the definite formation of the Administration policy.[73] However, if Panama had not revolted, Roosevelt later admitted, or boasted: "I should have recommended Congress to take possession of the Isthmus by force of arms . . . I had actually written the first draft of my Message to this effect."[74]

This policy had as its base the same political philosophy as that of the Ostend Manifesto (1854), which the Democrats dared not endorse and the Republicans specifically denounced as "in every respect unworthy of American diplomacy." It assumed Colombian obligation to make a new canal arrangement whenever and on whatever terms the United States desired. The rejection of the Hay-Herrán Treaty, according to this assumption, constituted a breach of the Treaty of 1846 and justified the forceful seizure of the Isthmus, if necessary, and the construction of the canal without Colombian approval.

D. *American Actions during the Panama Revolution.* Concerning official complicity in the movement, Roosevelt said

. . . that no one connected with this Government had any part in preparing, inciting, or encouraging the late revolution . . . and that save for the reports of our military and naval officers . . . no one connected with this Government had any previous knowledge of the revolution except such as was accessible to any person of ordinary intelligence who read the newspapers and kept up a current acquaintance with current affairs.[75]

[73] Hill, *Roosevelt and the Caribbean*, pp. 57-59. Based on the Roosevelt papers.

[74] Roosevelt to Thayer, July 2, 1915, Thayer, *The Life and Letters of John Hay*, II, 328. G. F. W. Holls (to Roosevelt, Jan. 20, 1903) advocated a deliberate annexation campaign and "the right kind of diplomacy" at Bogotá to accomplish that end (N. W. Stephenson, *Nelson W. Aldrich*, p. 458).

[75] Message of Jan. 4, 1904, *Moore's Digest*, III, 71.

There was no need for an outsider. . . . There were dozens of leaders on the Isthmus already doing their best to excite revolution.[76]

I simply ceased to stamp out the different revolutionary fuses that were already burning.[77]

This contention was defended by Secretary Hay and Bunau-Varilla,[78] and has never been successfully refuted. No doubt Roosevelt desired Panama secession, but he "cast aside the proposition" to foment the movement.[79] It is equally certain, however, that Bunau-Varilla's conference with Roosevelt, Hay, and Loomis permitted him to make "a very accurate guess" as to the movements of the American naval forces and the official attitude towards the contemplated revolt, and to advise his fellow-conspirators accordingly. In fact, the President admitted "he would have been a very dull man, had he been unable to make such a guess."[80] But this could hardly be construed as complicity in the plot.

The subsequent intervention was justified by Roosevelt on the following bases: (1) Colombia's utter inability to maintain order on the Isthmus, (2) the long and persistent efforts of Panama for independence, and (3) Washington's unwillingness to continue its assistance in the subjugation of the area—especially for "an irresponsible dictator." In order to end such a state of affairs, it was necessary to prevent Colombian troops from coercing Panama.[81] But the President failed to mention

---

[76] "How the United States Acquired the Right to Dig the Panama Canal," *Outlook* (Oct. 7, 1911), XCIX, 314-318.

[77] T. R. Roosevelt, *Autobiography*, p. 567.

[78] Hay to Reyes, Jan. 5, 1904, *Sen. Doc.*, No. 474 (63.2), p. 492; Bunau-Varilla, *The Great Adventure of Panama*, p. 162.

[79] Roosevelt to Albert Shaw, Oct. 10, 1903, Bishop, *op. cit.*, I, 279.

[80] Roosevelt to John Bigelow, Jan. 6, 1904, *ibid.*, p. 295.

[81] Dec. 7, 1903, Richardson, *Messages and Papers*, XIV, 6807 ff. Whitelaw Reid characterized the intervention as a right under the Monroe Doctrine; Senator Lodge, as an act to prevent war; Dr. Theodore Woolsey, as an act of war (*Cong. Rec.* [67.1], p. 158; Royal Cortissoz, *The Life of Whitelaw Reid*, II, 292; *Outlook*, Jan. 30, 1904, LXXVI, 248, 249).

the fact that Washington became aroused over the subjection of the Isthmians only when their independence contributed to the success of the American policy.[82]

The orders issued to the naval forces, Roosevelt maintained, were precisely the same as those issued on numerous former occasions and in harmony with the accepted American policy.[83] This statement can certainly be questioned. To be sure, former instructions had denied the use of the railroad for the transportation of troops and supplies of both the Bogotá government (although such a right had been reserved in the railroad concession) and the insurgents, in case such use interfered with the freedom of transit. Roosevelt, however, refused Colombia the right even to land troops "either at Colón, Porto Bello, or other point" on the Atlantic or "at any point within 50 miles of Panama" on the Pacific side of the Isthmus. These instructions surely indicate an extremely liberal, if not unwarranted, interpretation of the Treaty of 1846 and entirely lack precedent in American diplomacy.

Colombia held that, except to keep open the transit route and protect American interests, the United States had no more right to intervene on the Isthmus than on the British Isles. Did not the guarantee against foreign powers also exclude an American invasion? A treaty guaranteeing sovereignty would hardly confer on the guarantor the right to intervene in behalf of its destruction. However, suppose that Washington possessed such a right, would not Colombian self-preservation take precedence over any treaty stipulation?

Of course, it might be contended that the United States did not actively engage in the revolution, but merely performed its treaty obligation to protect the transit. If true, such an interpretation was new and had never been advanced to or accepted by Colombia. Be-

[82] See *supra*, chap. xiii.
[83] Dec. 7, 1903, Richardson, *Messages and Papers*, XIV, 6813.

sides, it can hardly be denied that the favorable attitude of Washington towards secession was well known on the Isthmus and was the determining factor in winning converts to the cause. Many believe that a group of resolute policemen could have crushed the movement if the American forces had not been on hand. Dr. Amador is quoted as saying to his "subsidized battalion": "President Roosevelt has made good, for there, you know, are the cruisers which defend us and prevent any action by Colombia."[84]

Although official complicity in the plot lacks substantial proof, the activities of certain American nationals are suspect. William Nelson Cromwell was of service to the revolutionists as an advisor and possibly as intermediary between them and Washington. American employees of the railroad—Colonel Shaler, Captain Beers, and Mr. Prescott—were probably cognizant of the conspiracy from its inception. Captain Beers and José G. Duque reported encouraging Washington conferences to the revolutionists. An American bank in Panama City, in which Consul Felix Ehrman was an active director and large stockholder, is reported to have permitted the rebels to draw on Colombian deposits and to have made them a loan voluntarily on the day following secession. The $8,000 paid Torres to withdraw the Colombian reinforcements seemed to have been advanced by Colonel Shaler from railroad funds, on the promise of repayment from the Colombian bank account at Panama. The bribe was accepted after Shaler's assurance that five thousand American troops were en route to the Isthmus. And the agent for the steamship company later testified that Colonel Shaler and Commander Hubbard signed a guarantee for the payment of the passage of troops to Cartagena.[85]

[84] Senator Thomas, Jan. 3, 1921, *Cong. Rec.* (66.3), LX, 884.
[85] *New York Evening Post*, Dec. 8, 1903; *New York Tribune*, Dec. 21, 1903; Jorge E. Boyd, *op. cit.*, p. 20; *The Story of Panama*, pp. 456-457.

Large shipments of ammunition went from Andreas and Company of New York to A. Arias F., later a member of the council of the provisional government.[86] The declaration of independence was prepared and the first Panama flag made in New York. And Colonel William Black, "an American officer, in the uniform of the United States Army, raised the flag of the new Republic" before one per cent of the inhabitants knew of the revolt.[87]

The close connection of so many Yankees with the plot; the fact that José A. Arango and Manuel Amador Guerrero (both among the conspirators and later members of the new government) were, or had been, in the employ of the French-owned Panama railroad; and the activities of Bunau-Varilla in the United States might be considered as having given the revolution a sufficient Franco-American color to justify a demand from Colombia for the protection of the Isthmus (under the Treaty of 1846) from foreign aggression. Most assuredly, the plot was not strictly native.

E. *Recognition of the New Republic.* The traditional American policy had been to recognize revolutionary states at

. . . that stage when independence is established as a matter of fact so as to leave the chances of the opposite party to recover their domination utterly desperate. . . .[88]

. . . when the new government is in possession of [the] machinery of administration, maintaining order, executing the laws . . . with general assent of the people, and responsibly fulfilling international obligations. . . .[89]

. . . [and to] insist that a nation that recognizes a revolutionary state, with a view to aid in effecting its sovereignty and inde-

[86] Hay to Herrán, Oct. 12, 1903, Notes to Col. Leg., VII, 360; *Sen. Doc.*, No. 474 (63.2), p. 375.

[87] J. T. Du Bois, "Colombia's Claims and Rights," *Cong. Rec.* (63.2), LI, appendix, p. 778.

[88] Adams to Monroe, Aug. 24, 1818, *Moore's Digest*, I, 78.

[89] Assistant Secretary Hill to Hart, Sept. 8, 1900, Inst. Col., XIX, 112.

pendence, commits a great wrong against the nation whose integrity is invaded, and makes itself responsible for a just and ample redress.[90]

Did Panama possess the prerequisites under this traditional American policy for recognition? On the morning of November 6 the state was entirely free of hostile Colombian forces. Since the United States refused to permit others to land, undoubtedly Colombia's chance to recover the Isthmus was "utterly desperate" and its independence "established as a matter of fact." Although few persons, even in Colón, knew of the revolt until November 4, all the isthmian towns had adhered to the declaration of independence by November 6, and the provisional government had no organized internal opposition. Foreign powers also were assured of adequate protection of their interests. It would seem, therefore, that the *de facto* recognition of November 6 was not premature.

This argument might be valid if Roosevelt's interpretation of the Treaty of 1846 were accepted. It is obvious, however, that the stability, even the existence, of the new state depended on American protection, since it possessed no efficient army, no navy, no courts, and no financial credit.

Yet should Roosevelt be condemned merely because the precautions taken to protect the transit operated in Panama's favor? There was no treaty obligation to defend Colombian sovereignty against Isthmian revolts, only against foreign aggression. It mattered little, except as it concerned the future peace and justice to an oppressed people, which power controlled the area. Both Colombia and Panama now expressed a willingness to approve a favorable canal treaty. Therefore it was merely a choice between a friendly Panama and a disgruntled Colombia. Justice and expedience argued in

[90] Seward to Adams, April 10, 1861, Inst. G. B., XVII, 392.

favor of the former. If Panama was justified in seceding and Roosevelt's actions were the mere fulfillment of treaty obligation to protect the transit, was it a crime to recognize the new status promptly? Instead of a case of "indecent haste," it seems one of the arrival of the hour and the man at the same time.

However, many question Roosevelt's right to prevent a sovereign state from suppressing rebellion within its own borders, regardless of any interpretation of treaty stipulations. Such interference was an infringement on the sovereignty of a sister republic. Who was to judge when and how Colombia should be dismembered? Did not the United States, when itself in danger of dismemberment, protest against possible recognition of the Confederacy by Great Britain? And there was no probability of British restrictions of Federal troop movements. If British recognition had been granted three days after the firing on Fort Sumter, it would have undoubtedly been interpreted as an act of intervention for the purpose of assisting the rebels in effecting their independence and have resulted in a claim for "just and ample redress."

When Colombia merely requested permission from a foreign power to crush a revolt within its own territory, the reply was a recognition of the rebels and a stinging denunciation of its rule over the area. Although the Isthmians had continually advanced charges of neglect, exploitation, and oppression, never before had Washington been so stirred with compassion. In November, 1840, the "State of the Isthmus" had declared its independence; in the following June adopted a constitution and elected a president; and in December requested American recognition. But the Department advised (January, 1842) that the shortness of time since the declaration (some fourteen months) and the existing friendly relations with New Granada made the usual caution expedient. And before proper investigation could be made, it was learned that Colombia had negotiated for the return of the seceded state.[91]   At two other times during the century (1830 and 1861) Colombian-Panamanian differences had been settled by negotiations.   Possibly this method might have proved successful in 1903, except for Roosevelt's impatience.   He chose rather to recognize the new state.

Prior to 1903 American troops landing on the Isthmus had meticulously avoided assisting the insurgents.   In fact, more than once American actions had materially contributed to the maintenance of Colombian sovereignty. It was not until an American-owned canal seemed at stake that Washington grew interested in the plight of the long-oppressed Isthmians and recognized the new state without requiring evidence of its ability to maintain itself.

The recognition of Panama was purely an act of intervention,[92] granted "with a view to aid in effecting its sovereignty and independence" and in expectation, if not assurance, of a favorable canal treaty.   Recognition came before a real nation existed.   The child was adopted before it was born.   Roosevelt "safeguarded its puny, puling infancy" and by certifying its legitimacy gained for it world-wide recognition."[93]

F. *American Refusal to Arbitrate.*   When permission to coerce the Isthmus was refused, Colombia requested the submission of the entire affair to The Hague Tribunal and agreed to make no aggressive moves in the meantime.[94]   This request apparently was ignored, since the independence of Panama was soon guaranteed in the Hay-Bunau-Varilla Treaty.   General Reyes again suggested arbitration in December, only to be advised that

[91] See *supra*, chap. xi.

[92] Julius Goebel, Jr., *The Recognition Policy of the United States*, p. 217.

[93] Leander T. Chamberlain, "A Chapter of National Dishonor," *N. Amer. Rev.*, CXCV, 145 ff.

[94] Beaupré to Hay, (tel.) Nov. 14, 1903 (rec'd. Nov. 17), *Sen. Doc.*, No. 474 (63.2), p. 478.

the matter was one touching American foreign policy, therefore political and not a fit subject for arbitration. Although adamant on this point, Hay did suggest the arbitration of the Colombian claims against Panama.[95] But the Roosevelt administration objected to being brought to trial for the recognition of a state now accepted by some seventeen other sovereign nations.

However, there is another phase worthy of consideration. As stated above, the presence of American forces, the issuance of unprecedented naval orders, and the refusal to permit the coercion of rebel Panama were defended by the Administration as the fulfillment of treaty obligations. Since it can scarcely be denied that this intervention alone made possible the success of the revolution, and therefore recognition, it follows that even recognition itself rested upon treaty interpretation, which has often been considered a proper subject for arbitration.

It is true that the Treaty of 1846 did not provide for arbitration. But the subsequent Colombo-American treaties of 1857 and 1864, the unratified canal treaties of 1869 and 1870, the Cotesworth and Powell Claims Convention of 1872, the *Montijo* Convention of 1874, and the Hay-Herrán Treaty of 1903 did recognize the principle of arbitration. Moreover, the United States had agreed to such a mode of settlement in the Panama-Costa Rica boundary dispute, and the President had served as an arbiter in adjusting the Cerruti claim against Colombia.[96]

Yet the United States, advocate of this peaceful method of international settlement, rejected it when there appeared a strong possibility of loss and embarrassment.

III. AMERICAN "INTERESTS AND SAFETY"

President Roosevelt maintained that the "interests and safety" of the American people demanded the policy

[95] Reyes-Hay correspondence, *ibid.*, pp. 481-511.
[96] Moore, *History and Digest*, V, 4694 ff.

which he adopted.[97] These interests could have been only commercial and strategic. Undoubtedly the immediate construction of a canal would have resulted in untold benefits to American commerce. And possibly national safety dictated American domination of the work. But could not these ends have been accomplished by other and less controversial means?

The Spooner Act provided for negotiations with Nicaragua, in case a satisfactory agreement could not be secured with Colombia within a "reasonable time." Colombia's adverse action should have caused only slight delay in the execution of American canal plans, since Nicaragua proffered inviting treaty terms. And the latter route offered equal protection to American commercial and strategic interests. Moreover, the fact that the rejected Hay-Herrán Treaty permitted a maximum of thirty-six years for the completion of a canal indicates that its construction was not considered an immediate necessity.[98]

The United States was at peace with all nations. France had consistently refused to give support to the New Panama Canal Company, and Great Britain by the Hay-Pauncefote Treaty had recognized American supremacy in the Isthmian area. No European nation had guaranteed the neutrality of either the Nicaragua or the Panama route, and none showed any intention of attempting the construction of a canal. Therefore there was no reason to believe that American "interests and safety" demanded Roosevelt's hasty and unprecedented policy.

IV. THE INTERESTS OF "COLLECTIVE CIVILIZATION"

The case of the administration was set forth by Roosevelt and Root:

The possession of a territory fraught with such peculiar capacities as the Isthmus in question carries with it obligations to

[97] "How the United States Acquired the Right to Dig the Panama Canal," *Outlook* (Oct. 7, 1911), XCIX, 314-318.

[98] Article XXIV, text in *Sen. Doc.*, No. 474 (63.2), pp. 286-287.

mankind. The course of events has shown that this canal cannot be built by private enterprise, or by any other nation than our own; therefore it must be built by the United States.[99]

If ever a government could be said to have received a mandate from civilization to effect an object the accomplishment of which was demanded in the interest of mankind, the United States holds that position with regard to the interoceanic canal.[100]

. . . the sovereignty of Colombia over the Isthmus of Panama was qualified and limited by the right of other civilized nations of the earth to have the canal constructed across the Isthmus and to have it maintained for their free and unobstructed passage.[101]

This defense approaches the doctrine of eminent domain (unrecognized in international law) and presupposes the existence of an authority superior to sovereign states. Otherwise the weak would be placed at the mercy of the territorial greed of the strong, the legal equality of sovereignties destroyed, and international law supplanted by force.

For the sake of argument, admit this dangerous doctrine and its applicability to the case in hand. What constituted the president's power-of-attorney for civilization? No international congress or plebiscite, nor any diplomatic agreements so empowered him. How, then, could he claim that the United States possessed a "mandate from civilization" to construct an interoceanic canal on terms unacceptable to the owner of the route? Besides, did the world at large particularly object to the Nicaragua route? Congress had instructed Roosevelt to turn to this route if he failed to secure an agreement with Colombia after a "reasonable time." In Nicaragua no armed intervention would have been necessary, since it was already independent and was even anxious to nego-

[99] Roosevelt's Message, Dec. 7, 1903, *Moore's Digest*, III, 53.
[100] Roosevelt's Message, Jan. 4, 1904, *ibid.*, III, 75.
[101] Root, *Addresses on International Subjects*, p. 181.

tiate. However, the Administration chose instead to secure the Panama route by a "devious finesse."

But grant that "collective civilization" did demand
the Panama route, should not international etiquette—if
not treaty obligations—have dictated the formal presentation of the case to Colombia with arguments, persuasion,
entreaty, and even the suggestion of arbitration (in short,
the exhaustion of all peaceful methods) before the resort
to forceful intervention? No demands in the name of
civilization were ever made of Colombia. It seems strange
that this state was not advised of civilization's grievances
before summary justice was called down upon it.

The admission of Roosevelt's mandate for civilization
and of Colombia's obligation to grant a reasonable concession still would not whitewash the Administration. Colombia as owner of the expropriated territory possessed
certain rights in determining its value. Yet these were
essentially denied by Washington's refusal to accept
any amendments to the Hay-Herrán Treaty, by Hay's
"threats" of congressional retaliation and warnings of
the uselessness of new negotiations, and by Roosevelt's
prevention of Colombia's coercion of Panama. It was a
matter of either accepting the amount offered or taking
the consequences. Even where eminent domain is admittedly applicable, the determining of the value of
expropriated property is not so arbitrary a process.

Of all Roosevelt's *ex post facto* logic his "collective
civilization" argument is probably the most far-fetched
and erroneous. It assumes the existence of a doctrine of
international eminent domain (in truth non-existent)
under which he was directly empowered not only to
choose between the canal routes but also to determine
the value of the route chosen and to proceed with the
construction of a canal. Such assumptions lack substan-
tiation in the facts and clearly indicate an effort to defend
a policy previously determined upon and already executed.

CHAPTER XXVI

CIRCUITOUS INDEMNITY VS. ARBITRATION
(1903-1913)

THE vigorous and unswerving policy of the Administration naturally fell under the condemnation of the Democratic minority—also, of a few independent Republicans—in the Senate and produced numerous resolutions to discredit Roosevelt and defeat the Hay-Bunau-Varilla Treaty with Panama. Senator Hoar requested an inquiry into American activities during the revolution;[1] Morgan declared that only Congress possessed power to use American forces on foreign territory;[2] Gorman desired a complete account of the past use of American troops in Colombia;[3] Hale suggested that the President use his good offices in securing an adjustment between Colombia and Panama;[4] Bacon favored either new negotiations with Colombia or arbitration of the entire Panama question;[5] Newlands advocated negotiations for Colombian rights on the Isthmus and arbitration of the compensation due therefor;[6] while Daniel[7] and Culberson[8] requested that all pertinent correspondence and documents be submitted for the Senate's consideration.

The presentation of this material,[9] Roosevelt's de-

[1] Res., Dec. 9, 1903 (debated), *Cong. Rec.* (58.2), XXXVIII, 65, 93, 316, 363.

[2] Res., Dec. 18, 1903 (debated), *ibid.*, pp. 361, 399, 425, 459, 487, 516.

[3] Res., Jan. 5, 1904 (debated and passed), *ibid.*, pp. 473, 703, 752, 795, 827, 865, 912, 958, 1023.

[4] Res., Jan. 13, 1904 (debated and referred), *ibid.*, pp. 702, 912, 1103, 1247.

[5] Res., Jan. 12, 1904 (debated), *ibid.*, pp. 614, 1103, 1242, 1366, 1367, 1467, 1501, 1661, 1702, 1728, 1763, 1823, 2015, 2120, 2191, 2244.

[6] Res., Jan. 22, 1904 (debated and referred), *ibid.*, pp. 1033, 1247, 1302.

[7] Res., Jan. 12, 1904 (debated), *ibid.*, pp. 613, 1103, 1243.

[8] Res., Jan. 25, 1904 (debated and passed), *ibid.*, pp. 1101, 1176, 1247, 1303, 1361.

[9] *Sen. Doc.*, Nos. 51, 95, 143 (58.2).

fense messages,[10] and Hay's correspondence with General Reyes[11] further agitated senatorial minds, but failed to alter materially the result. Roosevelt was ready to stake his political fortunes on his Panama record and possessed sufficient support to secure Senate approval, while the Democrats continued their bitter denunciations —some on moral grounds, others merely to embarrass the Administration. Such international legal authorities as John Bassett Moore and Elihu Root defended the Rooseveltian policy. However, public opinion probably veered towards the view held by Dr. Theodore S. Woolsey, Yale law professor, that American actions had been aggressive, illegal, hasty, and withal unjustified.

The Colombian view evidently was anticipated at Washington. Hay wired Beaupré (October 31, 1903) permission to take a previously authorized leave; (November 15) authority to close the legation, in case Colombia suggested his retirement; and (December 14) information that a war vessel would call at Cartagena for him.[12] On January 16, 1904, Assistant Secretary Loomis inquired of Chargé Snyder whether there was "serious talk of hostilities" at Bogotá.[13] But there was no change in the Administration's policy.[14]

Bogotá was as acrimonious as Washington was determined. The executive's advisory council voted ten to one for handing Beaupré his passport.[15] Although the Government was deterred from this by its fear of open hostilities, the severance of diplomatic relations continued under discussion.[16] Snyder reported on January 2 that "the bitter feeling against Americans . . . [had]

[10] Dec. 7, 1903, and Jan. 4, 1904.
[11] Dec. 23, 1903, to Jan. 13, 1904, *Sen. Doc.*, No. 474 (63.2), pp. 480-511.
[12] Hay to Beaupré, (tel.) Oct. 30, Nov. 15, Dec. 14, 1903, Inst. Col., XIX, 277, 281, 284.
[13] Loomis to Snyder, Jan. 16, 1904, *ibid.*, XIX, 287.
[14] *Idem* to *idem*, Jan. 29, 1904, *For. Rel.*, (1904-1905), p. 204.
[15] Beaupré to Hay, Nov. 14, 1903, *Sen. Doc.*, No. 474 (63.2), p. 478.
[16] Snyder to Hay, Feb. 28, 1904, *For. Rel.* (1904-1905), p. 204.

not abated one particle.'' Economic boycott petitions were ''widely circulated and enthusiastically signed by the merchants'' of Bogotá.[17] Clifford Smythe, former consul at Caragena, wrote: ''In all my experience in Colombia, I have never seen the people of this country so fully aroused. That they want war is beyond argument. . . .''[18]

But it was obvious that such an unequal struggle would be suicidal. The Government, therefore, contented itself with the unequivocal presentation of Colombia's case at Washington and a formal denial of the validity of the transfer of the canal concession to the United States.[19] Public opinion soon became less heated, but remained ever ready to burst into flame at the least provocation.

EARLY RECONCILIATION EFFORTS OF REYES

The new president, Rafael Reyes, early showed signs of desiring good relations with the power that he dared not fight. Minister Russell was easily ''convinced that the only thing necessary to bring about cordial relations . . . and restore American prestige would be some sort of a treaty arrangement with the United States and Panama by which Colombia could obtain . . . some of the advantages'' lost by its recent policy.[20] Reyes proposed American consent to a Panama independence plebiscite and the settlement of the differences between Colombia and Panama by means of a formal treaty and arbitration. Although this was in line with Hay's proposals of January, 1904, the Department now rejected the idea of a plebiscite, which was considered necessary as a

[17] *Idem* to *idem*, Jan. 2, 1904, *ibid.*, p. 204.

[18] Smythe to *Washington Post*, quoted in *Cong. Rec.* (58.2), XXXVIII, 614.

[19] Reyes-Hay correspondence, *Sen. Doc.*, No. 474 (63.2), pp. 480-511; Mensaje de 1904—Marroquín, Uribe, *Anales*, IV, 803-867; Rico to Snyder, April 12, 14, 1904, *For. Rel.* (1904-1905), pp. 206-225.

[20] Russell to Hay, Dec. 20, 1904, *Sen. Doc.*, No. 474 (63.2), p. 110.

"matter of form and a salve to [Colombia's] national honor."[21]

Unperturbed by this, however, Reyes dispatched Diego Mendoza Pérez to Washington to treat concerning the pending questions[22] and assured his Congress that arrangements entirely in harmony with national honor and dignity were possible.[23] Enrique Cortés, former minister of foreign affairs and one of the few friends of the Hay-Herrán Treaty, soon went as confidential agent to Panama, then to Washington to assist Mendoza. Even Presidents Reyes and Roosevelt were drawn closer together by direct correspondence and by the interviews of one Alfred Bishop Mason.[24] Settlement seemed imminent during the summer of 1905.

Unfortunately, however, Mendoza either failed to share the views of his chief or lacked sufficient tact to present them. In October, when the newly appointed minister, William W. Russell, advised him that the Department desired a conference, he asked for a postponement and added that if it was regarding negotiations with the Panama minister, he must refuse anyway, since he had "no questions to discuss with Panama or its agents until after formal settlements of all pending matters with the United States."[25] In a rather strong note he then set forth his grievances. No doubt was entertained that the Washington officials had promised the Panama rebels that Colombian troops would not be permitted to land and that the American war vessels were dispatched to fulfil that promise. Hence, the well-known attitude of the United States was the determining factor of the revolution—

[21] *Idem* to *idem*, (tel.) Jan. 7, 1905, *For. Rel.* (1905), p. 239; *idem* to *idem*, (17) Jan. 13, 1905, Loomis to Russell, Jan. 9, 1905, *Sen. Doc.*, No. 474 (63.2), pp. 110-111.

[22] Notes to Col. Leg., VII; Notes from Col. Leg., X; Uribe, *Anales*, V, 35-37.

[23] Mensaje de 1905, Uribe, *Anales*, V, 2.

[24] Russell to Hay, May 8, 1905, *Sen. Doc.*, No. 474 (63.2), p. 111; Reyes to Roosevelt, May 6, 1905, Notes from Col. Leg., X.

[25] Mendoza to Root, Oct. 11, 1905, *ibid.*

therefore in violation of the Treaty of 1846. Furthermore the hasty recognition and subsequent armed protection of the Isthmus were not in accord with international law. Since American denial of these contentions
was expected, he suggested arbitration to determine "the
exact interpretation of the Treaty of 1846" and the
"correct meaning of the law of nations."[26]

This objectionable note remained unanswered for almost three months. Secretary Root then denied official
complicity in the revolution, insisted that the arguments
presented had already been ably answered in the Hay-
Reyes correspondence, and rejected the suggestion of
arbitration.[27] Press reports had it that this firm response
had so aroused Colombian displeasure as to make a
definite break inevitable. But Reyes warned Mendoza
against any hasty action.[28] Therefore the latter's note
of April 6 lacked the earlier "objectionable features"
and, the Department thought, bore "internal evidence"
of having been prepared at Bogotá and "put into English by a less intemperate adviser." It was not answered, however, because of the receipt of advice that
Mendoza's mission had been disavowed.[29] He was soon
recalled, and the legation was intrusted to Cortés, already
in Washington.[30]

Meanwhile, Minister Barrett noted a "gradual growth
of a new friendly feeling" towards the United States.
Although admitting there was "still much bitterness
among a certain element of political leaders and among
the masses," he added that the press abounded with
kindly references and there had not been "one complaint
lodged by Americans in this legation of unkind treat-

[26] *Idem* to *idem*, Oct. 21, 1905, *ibid.; For. Rel.* (1906-1907), pp. 412 ff.

[27] Root to Mendoza, Feb. 10, 1906, Notes to Col. Leg., VII, 410-412.

[28] Barrett to Root, April 7, 1906, *Sen. Doc.*, No. 474 (63.2), p. 112.

[29] Departmental note, April 6, 1906, Notes from Col. Leg., X.

[30] After his recall Mendoza made public in New York certain confidential
correspondence, for which he was declared traitor (Resolution of Aug. 17,
1906, *Sen. Doc.*, No. 474 [63.2], pp. 598-602).

ment by Colombians due to any political or anti-American feeling.'' Regarding the economic resources and possibilities of the country, Barrett was convinced that it possessed ''a latent capacity of development second only to that of Mexico'' among the Latin American republics. New Yankee investments would prove profitable.[31]

It was quite natural, then, that Barrett would be in a receptive mood when Reyes made his next move. On May 23, 1906, he was invited to spend the day on the President's estate, Madrid, where matters having ''*most important* bearing'' on the relations between the two nations were informally discussed. Reyes expressed regret that Mendoza's unseemly attitude had made futile the negotiations at Washington and showed how this failure had given impetus to an existing movement to merge ''Panama, the Atlantic coast of Colombia, and the Departments of Antioquia and Cauca'' into a new ''Interoceanic Republic.'' He assured Barrett that he rejected the widespread rumor of American secret aid to this plan and its intention to recognize the new republic, but emphasized the possibility of this rumor being used at the forthcoming Pan American Conference to the great embarrassment of the United States. Therefore Reyes thought it to their mutual advantage to reopen negotiations for the settlement of the Panama question.[32]

TEMPORARY RENUNCIATION OF ARBITRATION AND INDEMNITY

The Colombian president declared that he had abandoned the idea of arbitration or indemnity and suggested the following general bases of agreement: a new convention of peace and commerce to replace the Treaty of 1846, including practically the same canal privileges as now enjoyed by Panama; Colombian recognition of Pan-

[31] Barrett to Root, April 14, 1906, *For. Rel.* (1906-1907), pp. 443-450. He enclosed for publication an article, ''Colombia, A Land of Great Possibilities.''

[32] *Idem* to *idem*, May 23, 1906, *Sen. Doc.*, No. 474 (63.2), pp. 112-120.

ama and the latter's assumption of its proportional share of the national debt; American private arrangement with Panama to send a negotiator to Bogotá; and the signing of a protocol before the official reception of such representative. It was understood that actual negotiations would have to be postponed until after Secretary Root had returned from the Pan American Conference at Rio de Janeiro, but immediate acceptance of the proposed bases was urged.[33]

The State Department was "favorably impressed."[34] Reyes was so much pleased with this attitude that he recalled Mendoza; instructed Valencia, delegate to the Conference at Rio, to confer with Root on common matters; and requested a public announcement from Washington of the reopening of negotiations and the early appointment of Cortés as minister.[35] He likewise suggested the advisability of Root's visiting Colombia, at least Cartagena, and began deliberate propaganda to develop a friendly sentiment and convince Colombians of the impossibility of arbitration and indemnity.[36]

Minister Barrett was enthusiastic, especially since he possessed "unsought assurance of aid" from Archbishop Bernardo and Monsignor Ragonesi, the papal nuncio. He appealed for the liberal treatment of Colombia. Special concessions to its commerce, he felt, would destroy the "deep-seated feeling" against the United States and thereby insure Yankee leadership in the development of this potentially wealthy area. The friendship of the commercially important coast provinces, which had favored the Hay-Herrán Treaty, was desirable in time of peace and essential for canal protection in time of war.[37]

[33] *Ibid.*, pp. 115-116.
[34] Root to Barrett, (tel.) June 2, 1906, Inst. Col., XIX, 358.
[35] Barrett to Root, June 7, 30, 1906, *For. Rel.* (1906-1907), pp. 434-435.
[36] *Idem* to *idem*, June 13, 1906, *Sen. Doc.*, No. 474 (63.2), pp. 121-122. "Pecuniary indemnification," Reyes said, "would stain the national honor" (*ibid.*, pp. 125-128).   [37] *Ibid.*, pp. 121-122.

On September 24, 1906, Secretary Root, returning from Rio de Janeiro, stopped for a few hours at Cartagena, where he conferred with Barrett and A. Vásquez Cobo, Colombian minister of foreign affairs.[38] Negotiations were soon under way at Washington. Cortés preferred tripartite treaties dealing solely with the Panama question, the more debatable commercial clauses to be settled later.[39] With the Department's assistance he secured (August 17, 1907) a protocol with Panama providing for (1) the recognition of the latter's independence, (2) the acknowledgment of Colombia's title to the disputed 50,000 shares of the New Panama Canal Company stock, and (3) the payment to Colombia of Panama's first ten annuities ($2,500,000) under the Hay-Bunau-Varilla Treaty. On the same day a protocol between the United States and Panama approved this arrangement.[40]

The concluding of permanent treaties, however, was held up by a disagreement over the Panama-Colombia boundary. Although Root accepted the Colombian view, as established by the law of June 9, 1855,[41] and refused to support Panama in its occupation of the Jurado district, the latter power held firm for all territory under its administration at the time of secession.[42] Cortés found it an "absolute impossibility" to accept such a view, whereupon Minister Arango (Panama) agreed to arbitration.[43] Since arbitration would indefinitely suspend negotiations, Cortés finally agreed "to proceed on the basis of no mention being made of the boundaries in

[38] For texts of formal speeches, see *For. Rel.* (1906-1907), pp. 441-442; Colombian minister's account of the conference, *Sen. Doc.*, No. 474 (63.2), pp. 131-133; Uribe, *Anales*, V, 6-7.

[39] Memo., Jan. 3, March 4, 1907, *Sen. Doc.*, No. 474 (63.2), pp. 134-146.

[40] Texts of protocols, *ibid.*, pp. 152-156. The 50,000 shares were originally issued to Colombia but were claimed by Panama upon secession.

[41] Root to Cortés, Aug. 26, 1907, *ibid.*, p. 157.

[42] *Ibid.*, pp. 158-170.

[43] Cortés to Root, Jan. 26, Root to Cortés, Feb. 18, 1908, *ibid.*, pp. 168-170.

the treaty."[44] But through the mediation of Secretary Root and William Nelson Cromwell a partial line was determined upon, leaving the nationality of Jurado to be decided later by arbitration.[45]

With this boundary agreement incorporated, the Cortés-Arosemena Treaty was signed on January 9, 1909.[46] The United States immediately approved the convention and guaranteed the payment of the money involved by signing the Root-Arosemena and the Root-Cortés treaties. The latter granted Colombia considerable privileges in the use of the canal.[47]

Before the end of January, Panama had ratified its two of the tripartite treaties.[48] The American senate did likewise before Roosevelt surrendered the presidency.[49] Meanwhile, Minister Thomas C. Dawson had been dispatched to Bogotá with the treaties. On arrival (February 13) he found Congress called to meet on February 22 and the Reyes-inspired press high in its praise of the conventions. Unanimous ratification was expected. But stiff Liberal and student opposition soon put a new face on the situation. Some conscientiously objected to the treaty stipulations, some were still bitter against the United States, and many others considered opposition an effective means of overthrowing the Reyes dictatorship. Mobs thronged the streets and stoned the homes

[44] Cortés to Root, March 21, 1908, *ibid.*, pp. 173-174.

[45] Root to Córtes, Dec. 29, 1908, *ibid.*, p. 175.

[46] For text, see *ibid.*, pp. 321-325. Besides this $2,500,000 from Panama, Colombia had already received $800,000 from its 50,000 shares of canal stock (Cromwell to Taft, March 17, 1908, *ibid.*, p. 172); some $150,000 deposited in London under the concession of 1878, not claimed by the United States (Root to Cortés, March 17, 1908, *ibid.*, p. 173); and some $600,000 of the $3,000,000 loan of 1880 from the Panama Railroad, never demanded by the United States (J. T. Du Bois, "Colombia's Claims and Rights," *Cong. Rec.*, [63.2], LI, appendix, p. 779)—total approximately $4,000,000.

[47] For texts, see *Sen. Doc.*, No. 474 (63.2), pp. 314-320.

[48] Arosemena to Root, undated (received, Jan. 31, 1909), *ibid.*, p. 190.

[49] *Ibid.*, p. 314.

of public officials. The American legation was placed
under guard. Only the declaration of martial law brought
peace again.[50]

Threats of assassination received by members of Congress and the danger of a general civil war made it unwise for Reyes to attempt the immediate ratification of
the treaty.[51] Congress was dissolved and a new one
called for July 20. But before it met, Reyes had resigned
and fled from the country. And with him went all hopes
of ratification. The new government expressed a desire
to reopen negotiations at Bogotá, but would have nothing
to do with the old treaties.[52] The United States, however, refused to cast these aside and "enter upon a separate negotiation with Colombia alone," since there was
no need for this except in connection with a Panama-
Colombia convention.[53] The three treaties must rise or
fall together. Washington now assumed an air of indifference and instructed its legation to "maintain an im-
passive and dignified attitude."[54]

Rarely had Colombian public opinion asserted itself
so forcibly as in the defeat of these treaties. Among the
masses, American actions during the Panama episode of
1903 were still a "burning issue" and through all discussion of them ran a "vein of bitterness." The school
children were still taught that Panama had been seized
in "violation of a sacred treaty." Reyes was forced into
exile and Cortés not permitted to return home.[55] The
Reyes administration and the commercial coastal prov-

[50] Dawson to Dept., Feb. 17, March 1, 10, 14, 27, 1909, *ibid.*, pp. 193-228.

[51] *Ibid.*, p. 228.

[52] Northcott to Dept., Oct. 1, 1909, *ibid.*, p. 239; Henao y Arrubla, *op. cit.*, pp. 768-770.

[53] Northcott to Calderón, Oct. 26, 1909, *Sen. Doc.*, No. 474 (63.2), pp. 245-246.

[54] Dept. to Northcott, (tel.) June 11, 1909, March 24, 1910, *ibid.*, pp. 237, 248.

[55] Earl Harding, "In Justice to Colombia," *World's Work*, XXVI, 674-680.

inces, but certainly not the majority of the Colombians were willing to renounce indemnity and arbitration.

The reorganization of the Colombian government (1910) and the popular election of Carlos E. Restrepo to the presidency ushered in an era of peace, prosperity, and liberal reforms; and with it came a return to the old policy of arbitration of the Panama question.[56]

Nevertheless Colombia's immediate representation at Washington was unfortunate. Former President Roosevelt's "I-took-the-Canal-Zone" speech of March 23, 1911, so aroused Minister Francisco de Paul Borda that he demanded satisfaction on the basis of this confession. His post was soon filled by Pedro Nel Ospina—member of the Reyes mission of 1903-1904—who urged (November, 1911) arbitration before The Hague Tribunal, but personally remained rather aloof from the Department and was known to be anti-American. When it was suggested that the Secretary of State include Colombia on a contemplated Caribbean cruise, Ospina replied that this was "inopportune." He was finally recalled on complaint of the Department, and a more conciliatory minister, Julio Betancourt, was sent in June, 1912.[57]

Meanwhile, Taft had dispatched James T. Du Bois to Bogotá—formally received November 18, 1911. The new minister frankly admitted his "sincere sympathies for Colombia," but was advised that these were no bar to the mission, since good relations were greatly desired. On contact and investigation these sympathies were confirmed. Du Bois found the Colombian officials not "blackmailers" and "bandits" but comparable "with the public men of other countries in intelligence and respectability," and the social life of the capital "refined

[56] Henao y Arrubla, *op. cit.*, pp. 773-774; Memo., Nov. 30, 1910, *H. Doc.*, No. 1444 (62.3), p. 6.

[57] Memoria de 1912—González Valencia, Uribe, *Anales*, V, 156-159.

and cultured.'' However, his instructions were ''drawn with so much regard for Colonel Roosevelt's feelings'' that he almost despaired of any success.[58]

After a careful study of the situation and a visit to Washington for conferences, Du Bois actively launched negotiations in January, 1913. He offered $10,000,000 for the ratification of the tripartite treaties, a canal option by the Atrato route, and a perpetual lease on the Islands of San Andrés and Providencia. Colombia was also to receive certain preferential canal privileges and assistance in settling its differences with Panama. The question of reversionary rights under the railroad and canal concessions might even be submitted to arbitration. Restrepo would not consider the tripartite treaties, nor would he discuss the Atrato option, the leases of the islands, and the arbitration suggestion. The elimination of the unratified treaties from the discussion and the substitution of coaling stations for leases still did not make the proposals acceptable. Du Bois was soon convinced that Colombia had no intention of treating until the views of the new Democratic administration could be ascertained. But he continued his efforts.[59]

In subsequent conferences Du Bois set forth the advantages of an Atrato canal and the proposed privileges in the use of the Panama canal. He argued that there was a possibility of Colombia's receiving as much as $49,946,000[60] under the arbitration clause, exclusive of the $10,000,000 cash payment. His memorandum of February 15 went a step further. It declared that ''the Gov-

[58] Du Bois, ''Colombia's Claims and Rights,'' *Cong. Rec.* (63.2), LI, appendix, pp. 778-779.

[59] Knox to Taft, Feb. 20, 1913, *H. Doc.*, No. 1444 (62.3), pp. 9-11; Memoria de 1913—Urrutia, Uribe, *Anales*, V, 233-237. Du Bois quotes Restrepo as saying: ''President Roosevelt took Panama, our richest asset, and now you are sent to take our islands, and the only canal route that we have left. Is there anything else that the northern Colossus would like to separate us from'' (*Cong. Rec.* [63.2], LI, appendix, p. 778).

[60] Value of railroad (1906), $16,446,000; unpaid railroad annuities, $16,-000,000; unpaid canal annuities under old concession, $17,500,000.

ernment and the people of the United States honestly regret [*lamentan sinceramente*] anything should have occurred to mar in any way, the long and sincere friendship" between the two nations. But he found Colombia unwilling to consider anything less than either the arbitration of the entire Panama question or an unconditional offer of adequate "moral and material reparations." The $10,000,000 proposal was considered insufficient. The mention of even $25,000,000 failed to arouse enthusiasm.[61]

This almost eleventh-hour effort at reconciliation proved abortive, but not through lack of zeal on the part of Du Bois. The failure must be attributed to the "tender regard" shown for Roosevelt in the instructions and the unbounded faith of Colombia in the Democratic Party's sense of justice.

De Bois was ordered to drop the matter. The proposals were withdrawn, and the American congress was fully advised (March 1) of Colombia's unwillingness to negotiate.[62]

[61] Memoria de 1913—Urrutia, Uribe, *Anales*, V, 237-241; Knox to Taft, Feb. 20, 1913, *H. Doc.*, No. 1444 (62.3), pp. 11-12; Du Bois to Knox, Feb. 5, 28, 1913, *For. Rel.* (1913), pp. 287-296. Du Bois later claimed that the "regret clause" was presented on his own initiative to feel the Colombian pulse (*New York Times*, June 26, 1914, p. 9).

[62] *Cong. Rec.* (62.3), XLIX, 4407, 4470. See also Rafael Reyes, "Go Slow with Latin America," *New York Times*, Sept. 21, 1913; *The Two Americas* (New York, 1914).

CHAPTER XXVII

OIL AND IDEALS

(1913-1921)

COLOMBIA was correct in assuming that at least a large minority in the United States favored the reopening and just settlement of the old Panama controversy. Many saw the "inconsistency and hypocrisy" of negotiating arbitration treaties with powerful nations, while "complacently and contemptuously" ignoring the Colombian arbitration demands.[1] And others were willing to confess a temporary lapse and to make adequate monetary atonement. When Minister Betancourt, encouraged by the Hitchcock and Rainey resolutions,[2] again (May 3, 1913) requested arbitration, he found that the new Wilson administration held the latter view.[3]

DEMOCRATIC PENANCE FOR ROOSEVELTIAN SINS

The change of administrations in Washington brought the appointment of Thaddeus A. Thomson to the Bogotá post—formally received on August 30, 1913. In subsequent conferences Colombia still insisted on arbitration, but agreed to negotiation. The former proposals for the Atrato canal option, the coaling stations, and the arbitration of certain reversionary rights were declared untenable by both powers. Instead, Thomson expressed a sincere desire "that everything that may have marred or seemed to interrupt the close and long-established friendship . . . should be cleared away and forgotten," suggested the cession of certain special privileges to

[1] *Cong. Rec.* (62.2), XLVIII, 2653-2656; *Sen. Doc.*, No. 693 (62.2), pp. 1-2.

[2] *Cong. Rec.* (63. spec.), L, 196, 357, 367; *Sen. Doc.*, No. 259 (63.2), pp. 1-2; *New York Times*, Dec. 31, 1913, p. 6.

[3] Betancourt to Bryan, May 3, 1913, *For. Rel.* (1913), pp. 309-316.

[440]

Colombia in the use of the Panama Canal, and offered $20,000,000 for the termination of all pending claims and differences.[4]

Colombia insisted upon an expression of "sincere regret" and the payment of $50,000,000,[5] probably remembering the Du Bois estimates. Secretary Bryan agreed to the "sincere regret" clause, but refused to increase the indemnity, whereupon Urrutia, minister of foreign affairs, proposed $30,000,000 and $250,000 annuity for one hundred years. After personal conferences in Washington,[6] Thomson raised the American offer to $25,000,000. Urrutia then agreed to accept $30,000,000, fifty annuities of $250,000, and equal rights for the Colombian merchant marine in the use of the canal. When Thomson held firm, Urrutia first reduced his demands to $30,000,000 (the extra $5,000,000 to be used for sanitation work in the ports of Cartagena and Buenaventura), then finally accepted the American offer of $25,000,000. The treaty was signed on April 6, 1914.[7]

Although Minister Betancourt frankly admitted to Bryan that the convention did not measure up to his hopes, the Colombian congress lost little time in ratifying it unamended.[8] But its history in Washington is not so quickly told.

AMERICAN RECEPTION OF THE NEW TREATY

After Colombian ratification Wilson submitted the Thomson-Urrutia Treaty to the Senate.[9] But immediate

---

[4] Thomson to Urrutia, Oct. 1, 1913, Uribe, *Anales,* V, 324; *Cong. Rec.* (63.3), LII, 17; Bryan to Thomson, Sept. 29, 1913, *For. Rel.* (1913), p. 321.

[5] Thomson to Bryan, Oct. 23, 1913, *ibid.,* pp. 324-325.

[6] Owing to the illness of his wife, Thomson left Bogotá in Nov., 1913, and returned the following February or March.

[7] Memoria de 1914—Urrutia, Uribe, *Anales,* V, 322-326; *For. Rel.* (1913), pp. 287-309, 327, 329; *Cong. Rec.* (63.3), LII, 6, 17, 18.

[8] Betancourt to Bryan, April 9, 1914, Thomson to Bryan, (tel.) June 8, 1914, *For. Rel.* (1914), pp. 155, 162; Urrutia to Thomson, June 10, 1914, *Sen. Doc.,* No. 64 (68.1), p. 6.

[9] *For. Rel.* (1914), p. 162.

and determined opposition prevented the foreign relations committee from even reporting it during the session.

Former President Roosevelt—from Pará, Brazil—cabled his opposition[10] and later requested a hearing before the committee. To Chairman Stone he wrote: "I had full knowledge of everything of importance that was done in regard thereto [Panama Revolution] by any agent of the Government, and I am solely responsible for what was done."[11] Bryan did not consider a discussion of this episode as "material to the present settlement"[12] and Stone "remarked that he did not want any horse play in the committee room, [therefore] . . . suggested that Roosevelt should write out what he wanted to say, or should put it in a speech delivered on the steps of the capitol." Later, however, Roosevelt was given a hearing.[13]

Although Democratic accession to power had deprived Du Bois of the chance to conclude favorable negotiations, he unequivocally supported the treaty. In July, 1913, he advocated full arbitration of the great wrong done Colombia. In the following March, before the Colombian Commercial Club of New York, he proposed a plan of settlement almost identical with that of the subsequent treaty. When Roosevelt (June 25) publicly denounced the treaty as "merely the belated payment of blackmail with an apology to the blackmailers," Du Bois retorted that the Colonel was "badly informed." The expression of "sincere regret," he held, was not an apology but a "chivalrous act." He was amazed that Americans could get so aroused over the German disregard of treaty stipulations in the invasion of Belgium,

[11] Quoted in *ibid* (Aug. 3, 1914), LXXIX, 154.

[12] Bryan to Thomson, (tel.) Sept. 5, 1914, *For. Rel.* (1914), p. 168.

[13] *Independent* (Aug. 3, 1914), LXXIX, 154; James C. Malin, *The United States after the World War*, p. 404.

yet remain "unmoved and voiceless at the grim tragedy
of 1903." Surely the United States was "not too proud
to be just."[14]

Public opinion on the treaty naturally varied, but in
circles not suffering from Rooseveltmania, obviously
veered towards approval. Even the American *Review
of Reviews* favored doing "anything in reason to assure
Colombia of our good will," although feeling that the
treaty should contain "reciprocal expressions [of regret]
on the part of Colombia."[15] Many considered it "an act
of justice," the "fair and honorable" thing to do, and
well calculated to "establish a formal peace, if not cordial relations." It was felt that Colombia certainly
ought to be placated before the formal opening of the
Panama Canal. Others supported the treaty, expecting
great commercial and petroleum exploitation opportunities and the destruction of "the monopoly plans of the
British interests in Colombia." The formal expression
of regret meant little or nothing, since it was thought to
be due Colombia or implied in the money payment. The
opposition centered around the "sincere regret" or "vindication by confession" clause, thereby attempting to
make it a moral issue. Some even preferred arbitration
to the payment of "hush money." Others favored a
settlement out of court and were willing to purchase
Colombian friendship, but not to apologize for the acts of
the Roosevelt administration.[16]

---

[14] *New York Times*, July 20, 1913, p. 10, March 30, p. 5, June 23, p. 3,
June 25, p. 2, June 26, p. 9, July 2, 1914, p. 8, Feb. 23, 1916, p. 12, April
22, 1917, p. 1. Even party efforts to prevent his advocacy of the treaty and
a two-hour conference with Roosevelt failed to halt this veteran, who placed
"love of justice" above party interests.

[15] *Review of Reviews* (March, May, June, 1914), XLIX, 264-265, 528-
529, 682-684.

[16] *Nation* (April 21, 1914), XCVIII, 416; *Outlook* (Feb. 7, 1914), CVI,
295; *Review of Reviews* (March, 1914), XLIX, 263-266; L. Ames Brown,
"A New Era of Good Feeling," *Atlantic Monthly* (Jan., 1915), CXV,
99. For the attitude of some fifty leading newspapers, see "Our Panama
Regrets," *Literary Digest* (May 2, 1914), XLVIII, 1035 ff.

FORCES BEHIND THE TREATY

The idealism of Wilson and Bryan was sufficient to account for their desire to do justice to a lesser power. And certainly they can not be accused of consciously promoting the interests of big business dangerous to constitutional power in their own country, yet their Colombian policy favored and received the support of the American commercial and, oil groups. Business interests[17] probably shared little of the Administration's idealism, but cared still less for the Rooseveltian theory of "belated payment of blackmail." Great prizes were to be had in Colombian commerce and concessions, if only this old wound might be healed.

In the midst of the treaty negotiations it had been learned that Lord Cowdray—representing S. Pearson and Son, Limited, of London—was attempting to extend his operations beyond Mexico by securing executive approval of valuable oil concessions in Costa Rica, Ecuador, and Colombia.[18] This company's support of the anti-Wilson group in Mexico had already proved exasperating. Besides, the Colombian concession permitted not only the exploitation of large "virgin oil fields" but granted "the necessary rights for building railways, docks, quays, and canals, [and] installing telephone and telegraph systems . . . ," and the lands might be chosen *anywhere within the republic.*[19] It was rumored also that English capitalists, through Lord Cowdray, might furnish Colombia money to construct a rival Atrato Canal, thereby evading the Monroe Doctrine.[20] And it was not unreasonable to believe that the British company, by the

[17] Twenty-six New York importing firms petitioned for ratification (*New York Times*, Feb. 25, 1915, p. 9).

[18] This company had constructed a railroad from Honda to Beltrán in 1905-1907 (A. C. Veatch, *Quito to Bogotá*, p. 273). American, German, and Canadian companies were also trying to secure oil concessions (*New York Times*, Dec. 30, 31, 1913).

[19] Summary of contract, dated April 24, 1913, *New York Times*, Dec. 13, 1913.

[20] *New York Times*, Sept. 27, 1913, p. 1, quoting *The Standard* (London).

judicious choice of its lands along the Atrato River and near the termini of the Panama Canal, might not itself attempt to construct a rival canal and possibly prove a real menace to the security of the American work. All this, considered in the light of well-known British resentment of the already determined policy of the United States to exempt its own coastwise vessels from Panama Canal tolls,[21] made Colombian friendship all the more valuable.

However, for reasons never fully explained at Bogotá, Washington, or London, the Pearson contract was withdrawn before the Colombian congress acted upon it. Ambassador Page at London claimed much credit. On January 8, 1914, he wrote: "They [British cabinet] took up the dangers that lurked in the Government's contract with Cowdray for oil;[22] and they pulled Cowdray out of Colombia and Costa Rica—granting the application of the Monroe Doctrine to concessions that might imperil a country's autonomy." Page likewise busied himself with the Central and South American representatives in London, "loading them up" on the dangers of such concessions.[23] *The Independent* quoted Lord Cowdray as saying that the contract was withdrawn, because it was being used to arouse hostility to the Pearson interests elsewhere. But this periodical intimated that Washington disapproved, and recalled that Cowdray had recently requested American protection of his Mexican interests.[24]

Lord Murray, the Cowdray representative at Bogotá, refused to discuss the matter on account of "international involvements." The *London Times* stated that

[21] See *Sen. Doc.*, No. 474 (63.2), pp. 85-102.

[22] Evidently meant a contract to furnish fuel oil for the British navy. See *Independent* (Dec. 4, 1913), LXXVI, 433.

[23] B. J. Hendrick, *The Life and Letters of Walter Hines Page*, I, 212, 251; III, 112-113.

[24] *Independent* (Dec. 4, 1913), LXXVI, 433; *Review of Reviews* (Jan., 1914), p. 23; *Literary Digest* (Dec. 6, 1913), XLVII, 1098; Veatch, *Quito to Bogotá*, pp. 272-273.

Washington officially intimated that the grant of such a concession to a "British or European firm would prejudice" the Thomson-Urrutia negotiations. And the Washington correspondent of the *London Morning Post* was convinced that Great Britain had been "made to realize the serious consequences" of the ratification of the Pearson contract—not by the exchange of notes but had been "simply made to feel the sentiment existing" against it.[25] It is probable, also, that European politics made American friendship quite as valuable as Yankee economics made Colombian good will.

THE TREATY BEFORE THE SENATE

However, the interests responsible for the treaty were not powerful enough to secure its early ratification. With the outbreak of the World War, American idealism spent itself in denouncing the reported German atrocities in Belgium and quite forgot "the grim tragedy of 1903." British rivalry in Colombia was no longer to be feared. And American official attention was soon occupied with the problems of neutrality.

Minister Betancourt and a small group of propagandists attempted in vain to keep public interest centered on the treaty.[26] The European armies were scarcely on the march before American ratification was being urged on the basis of "the necessity and convenience to unify the interests of all America around the United States."[27] Betancourt was assured that Wilson had lost none of his interest and the treaty would be pressed. When the long delay exhausted his patience and he threatened withdrawal from the Pan American Union, he was reassured (December, 1915) of the Administration's de-

---

[25] *New York Times*, Nov. 29, p. 1, Dec. 30, p. 2:2, Dec. 31, 1913, p. 6:2.
[26] *Washington Post*, June 19, 20, 21, 1914; Memoria de 1915—Suárez, Uribe, *Anales*, V, 454.
[27] Betancourt to Bryan, Aug. 3, 1915, *Sen. Doc.*, No. 64 (68.1), p. 17.

sire for early ratification. Thomson was also having
some difficulty in convincing the Bogotá officials of American sincerity.[28]

Early in 1916 the treaty was reported out of the foreign relations committee with recommendations to make
the expression of regret mutual and to reduce the indemnity to $15,000,000. Naturally Colombia protested. And
Yankee concession hunters were advised by Betancourt
that negotiations could not proceed until the treaty was
ratified.[29] But economics again succumbed to party
spirit, and the treaty was postponed. This created new
press attacks at Bogotá. The withdrawal of Colombian
ratification was advocated on the basis that American
procrastination had made it appear ridiculous and that
unsettled world conditions might make possible better
terms. Resentment ran so high that Bogotá officials asked
for a public statement to calm the furor. Secretary Lansing (February 28, 1917) sought to assure them of the
Administration's constant efforts and advised that the
treaty was one of the subjects to be considered by the
special session of Congress called for March 5.[30]

Betancourt now made his final fight for the treaty.
He pressed the importance of Pan American solidarity,
emphasized Yankee commercial approval, and pleaded
for simple justice to Colombia.[31] Suggestions of possible
Colombian withdrawal from the Pan American Union
were again heard and even urged upon President Concha
as the only method of preserving national honor and

[28] *Idem* to *idem*, Nov. 29, Dec. 2, 1915, Bryan to Betancourt, March 4,
1915, Lansing to Betancourt, Dec. 21, 1915, Thomson to Suárez, Jan. 31,
1916, *ibid.*, pp. 18-27.

[29] *Independent* (Feb. 14, 28, 1916), LXXXV, 222, 298; *New York Times*,
Jan. 27, Feb. 3, 4, 6, 12, 15, 23, 1916; Betancourt to Lansing, Feb. 11,
1916, Associated Press interviews of Feb. 3, 14, 1916, *Sen. Doc.*, No. 64
(68.1), pp. 30-33, 42.

[30] Chargé Belden to Lansing, Feb. 26, 27, 1917, Lansing to Belden,
Feb. 28, 1917, *For. Rel.* (1917), pp. 292-295.

[31] Betancourt to Lansing, March 7, 12, 1917, *Sen. Doc.*, No. 64 (68.1),
pp. 33-34, 36-37.

prestige.[32]   Also an uneasiness was evident in Washington regarding Colombian—and South American—attitude towards the approaching struggle with Germany.   Dire rumors were afloat about a disgruntled Colombia's making an agreement with the enemy.   Wilson's anxiety over the treaty was perfectly understandable, but persistent partisan opposition again made his efforts futile.[33]

The treaty was again reported from the foreign relations committee on March 14, 1917, with certain suggested amendments.   At the same time Senators Lodge, McCumber, Borah, Brandegee, and Fall submitted a minority report of the following tenor:

. . . our conduct in securing an agreement from Panama was just and proper in every respect and . . . the Colombian Government has no just or equitable claim against this nation for any act on our part in connection therewith. . . We can not afford to purchase cordial relations with any country.   We can not afford to answer a blackmail demand.   Once respond to such a demand and we shall be held up for every fancied wrong by other countries. . . . If we believed that we had wronged the Colombian Government, we should be quick to repair that wrong. As we believe we have done that country no injustice, we earnestly protest against the purchase of her friendship.[34]

When Chairman Stone realized how formidable the opposition was, he referred the treaty back to his own committee.   On March 16 Congress adjourned for a month. The pact was called up for consideration when the Senate reconvened, but was again postponed.[35]   This long delay caused "deep resentment" at Bogotá.   But after the fear of Colombian aid to Germany had proved un-

[32] Cablegram from Colombian newspapers to Associated Press, *New York Times*, March 2, 1917, p. 20; Antonio Llano, ''A Colombian View of the Treaty,'' *ibid.*, March 13, 1917, p. 10.

[33] Possible alliance with Germany was vehemently denied by Colombia (*ibid.*; Suárez to Belden, May 24, 1917, *Sen. Doc.*, No. 64 [68.1], p. 38).

[34] *Cong. Rec.* (67.1), LXI, 202.

[35] *New York Times*, March 17, 1917, p. 12, April 21, 1921.

warranted, the treaty was almost forgotten amid the more pressing problems of warfare.

On the return of peace, however, President Wilson (December 2, 1918) urged "an early and favorable action on that vital matter."[36] The following February, Minister Hoffman Philip obtained Colombian executive approval of the elimination of the "sincere regret" clause and of certain other minor changes suggested by the committee on foreign affairs.[37] The revised treaty was then reported favorably by that committee on July 29 and ordered printed.[38] But, when its ratification seemed assured, oil entered diplomacy.

OIL ENTERS DIPLOMACY

Despatches from Bogotá reported the issuance of a decree (June 20, 1919) declaring governmental ownership of all hydrocarbons beneath the soil of the entire republic.[39] This was interpreted as a confiscation of oil deposits already purchased by American operators. Lodge secured the recommittal of the treaty on the basis of this information. It was then referred to a subcommittee composed of McCumber, Smith of Arizona, and Fall, who were to coöperate with the Department in subsequent negotiations.[40]

Philip was instructed to indicate the implications of the decree and suggest confidentially a treaty amendment protecting American interests against such measures.[41]

[36] Richardson, *Messages and Papers*, XVIII, 8640.

[37] Philip to Molina, Molina to Philip, Feb. 27, 1919, *Sen. Doc.*, No. 64 (68.1), pp. 45-47.

[38] For text, see *Sen. Doc.*, No. 64 (66.1), pp. 1-7.

[39] This had been the status of most subsoil wealth under the Spanish Crown and under the Republic until 1858, when such treasures supposedly passed to the owners of the surface lands. After 1873, however, the government retained title to the subsoil wealth of public lands subsequently alienated (Rippy, *The Capitalists and Colombia*, pp. 123-124).

[40] *Cong. Rec.* (66.1), LVIII, 3668-3669, (67.1), LXI, 159.

[41] Lansing to Philip, (tel.) Aug. 9, 1919, *Sen. Doc.*, No. 64 (68.1), pp. 48-49.

Colombia preferred a separate protocol to deal with the petroleum issue, since its Congress had yet to pass on the question of subsoil wealth.[42] It was pointed out that the decree had already been suspended and American interests would naturally be adequately protected by the anticipated legislation. In fact, Colombia was "disposed to give . . . full guarantees" on that point, but feared that the inclusion of these in the treaty would prevent ratification.[43]

Nevertheless the foreign relations committee insisted on an article binding each party never to nullify the rights of the citizens of the other, before it would report the treaty to the Senate. Copies of an amendment incorporating this idea were forwarded to Bogotá. But the Colombian congress was then occupied in framing a petroleum law, and negotiations had to await the result.[44]

A judicial confirmation of the constitutionality of the American concessions and the enactment of a fairly satisfactory oil law (December 29, 1919) restored a feeling of security, if not optimism.[45] However, in conference, President Suárez received the impression that the United States was attempting to premise treaty ratification on Colombian approval of contracts sought by certain Americans, and suggested that fulfillment of obligation should not be dependent on the granting of favors.[46] Minister Philip denied that this was the intention of the Washington government, but expressed as his personal opinion that the celebration of certain contracts with American citizens would undoubtedly create public opinion favorable to the treaty.[47]

The committee on foreign relations, now convinced of

[42] Philip to Lansing, (confidential) Aug. 15, 1919, *ibid.*, pp. 47-48.
[43] Holguín y Caro to Philip, Aug. 19, 1919, *ibid.*, pp. 49-51.
[44] Lansing to Philip, (tel.) Aug. 28, Oct. 10, 1919, Philip to Guzmán, Oct. 20, Guzmán to Philip, Oct. 28, 1919, *ibid.*, pp. 51-56.
[45] Summary of petroleum act, *ibid.*, pp. 56-57.
[46] Presidential memo., Jan. 9, 1920, *ibid.*, pp. 57-58.
[47] Philip to President Suárez, Jan. 20, 1920, *ibid.*, pp. 59-60.

A GREAT CONSCIENCE AWAKENER
HARPER IN THE BIRMINGHAM AGE

the security of American oil investments, again reported the treaty favorably on June 3, 1920. But the nearness of adjournment caused postponement until the following winter.[48] The opening gun in the final campaign for ratification seems to have been fired (January 3, 1921) by Senator Thomas of Colorado. He argued for amends for past actions or for arbitration to convince the world of American innocence.[49] His reference to Roosevelt brought Senator Kellogg to the floor, with the declaration: "I can not sit in the Senate of the United States and listen to reflections upon the character and statesmanship of Theodore Roosevelt without expressing my protest." The securing of the Panama Canal, he continued, was "one of the great acts of a great president in a great era of American history."[50] This incident somewhat foreshadows the nature and bitterness of the subsequent ratification debates.

"A SMELL OF OIL IN THE AUGUST CHAMBER"

The return to power of the Republicans brought a presidential message (March 9) urging the approval of the seven-year-old treaty.[51] When the actual debates began (April 12) the ratification strategist was none other than Senator Lodge. Of the five Republicans signing the 1917 minority report, only Borah remained unconverted. Lodge led the fight; Fall, now in the Cabinet, furnished ammunition in the form of Roosevelt letters and petroleum facts, while McCumber and Brandegee supported the treaty, which they all had once characterized as a "plea of guilty" and the payment of "exemplary damages" in answer to a "blackmail demand."

The principal arguments of the ratification advocates were as follows: (1) the American policy of 1903 was morally correct, but commercial and petroleum interests now make a settlement desirable and Colombian friend-

[48] *Cong. Rec.* (67.1), LXI, 159. [49] *Ibid.* (66.3), LX, 878.
[50] *Ibid.*, p. 887. [51] *Ibid.* (67.1), LXI, 157.

ship essential; (2) Washington committed no wrong, but did acquire valuable property at Colombian expense, and therefore should make proper compensation; (3) Roosevelt sinned grievously, and the United States was fortunate to escape making an apology. The opposition held that the treaty was a reflection on Roosevelt, an admission of guilt, a futile effort to purchase friendship, and an indirect subsidy to the oil interests.[52]

Senator Lodge, conscious of the Roosevelt influence in his party, extolled the acquiring of the Panama Canal as "one of the greatest public services ever rendered by any president of the United States," but hastened to add that the present treaty in no way reflected on Roosevelt's good name; its substance had been virtually approved by him in 1917.[53] This was supported by certain Roosevelt-Fall correspondence, which did indicate the former's desire for a "new and proper treaty," but not for one reflecting on his actions or failing to provide for the following: the cession of certain islands near the canal termini, an option on the Atrato route, the closing of the Isthmian ports to the enemies of both powers in time of war, and the mutual defense of the canal. But Fall insisted that he had "every assurance . . . short of an actual written agreement, that the present Colombian Government, and prominent Colombians, favoring this policy, . . . [would] immediately, upon ratification of the present treaty, of their own motion, or upon a mere suggestion from us, enter into a supplemental treaty embracing the identical suggestions" agreed to by Roosevelt.[54]

The Colombian loss under treaties and concessions made prior to 1903, Lodge accepted as $50,146,942.75. Since the United States had innocently become beneficiary of this, he could not interpret the payment of the

[52] *Ibid.*, pp. 157-482.   [53] *Ibid.*, pp. 158-159.
[54] Fall to Lodge, March 21, 1921, *ibid.*, pp. 162-166.

$25,000,000 as "exemplary damages or a confession of wrongdoing."[55]

He next turned to the *"larger aspects of the question,"*[56] namely, the effect of a satisfactory settlement on the good will of the South American states and, in turn, on the security of the Panama Canal; and the promotion of American trade and investments, especially in oil. The Senate was advised: "We have received every assurance short of a written treaty that this treaty now pending before us will be followed by a treaty of amity and commerce . . . which will rid us . . . of the old Grenadine [*sic*] treaty of 1846."[57]

The post-war decline of exports to Europe made imperative the extension of markets in South America and the Far East. Since trade now followed investments (instead of the flag) and certain European governments were investing in Colombian oil, American nationals were finding themselves in competition not only with individuals and corporations but with governments. An adequate supply of oil is vital to "every great maritime nation"; therefore the United States "must stand behind . . . [its] own people" wherever they invest. Lodge then presented lists and charts to show how the British governmentally controlled Royal Dutch-Shell Combine was making inroads into Colombia and Venezuela, and warned that American companies already there would soon pass into foreign hands, unless governmental protection of their investments was assured. Only the new treaty of amity and commerce, which was to follow the ratification of this treaty, would furnish adequate security to American capital.[58]

Lodge insisted, however, that "no one interested in the production of oil" had approached him regarding the treaty under consideration. On the floor he could

[55] *Ibid.*, p. 160.
[57] *Cong. Rec.* (67.1), LXI, 160.
[56] Italics are mine.
[58] *Ibid.*, pp. 161-166.

recall the name of only one of the American companies interested in Colombia, although a subsequent list furnished by him contained twenty-one.[59]

Senator McCumber had always opposed the "sincere regret" clause, but, with its elimination, was willing "to stake $25,000,000 . . . on the effort of the President to secure without additional donation a supplemental agreement that . . . [would] be worth . . . many times that sum." Private assurances had been given him that the Administration hoped to secure a treaty along the lines approved by Roosevelt in 1917.[60]

Senator Knox considered Roosevelt's actions "studiously correct," but felt that since great benefits had accrued to the United States through the Colombian loss of the Isthmus, there was a moral obligation "to compensate Colombia, not for what she lost, but for what we gained."[61] Sterling agreed that there was "no proof of duplicity or international wrongdoing," but he was convinced that since Colombian loss had been American gain, a liberal settlement might well be made to advance American prestige "in that part of the world where it . . . [was] most needed."[62]

An argument of expediency was advanced by Senator New. He was unable to determine "just where exact justice" lay, but realized the importance of friendship in the rivalry for South American commerce and noted how the failure to settle with Colombia had been "employed to such adverse account" against the United States. Although this was not a "case of purchasing good will . . . that it . . . [affected] good will . . . [was] perfectly reasonable and perfectly certain."[63] Shortridge likewise disregarded any moral issue and supported the treaty on the basis of future friendship and commerce.[64]

But the Democrats refused either to defend or ignore

[59] *Ibid.*, pp. 161, 167; 446.
[61] *Ibid.*, p. 242.
[63] *Ibid.*, pp. 391-392.
[60] *Ibid.*, pp. 442-443.
[62] *Ibid.*, pp. 479-480.
[64] *Ibid.*, pp. 425-428.

the moral factor. Pomerene found it difficult to justify "doing the right thing in the wrong way";[65] Wolcott was convinced that Colombia had a "just grievance";[66] and Smith agreed that "the ends did not justify the means,"[67] while Williams concluded: "I was mighty glad when we did not have any apology in the treaty, although we owed one. I was mighty glad to escape that."[68]

On the other hand, Senator Borah (R.) characterized the treaty as a "fine imposed after a plea of guilty" to a theft charge.[69] Kellogg (R.) agreed that it was an "acknowledgement of guilt" and questioned whether the good will and friendship" of nations could be purchased in international markets.[70] Reed (D.) added that if Colombian good will had been lost by doing a "perfectly proper act" and now $25,000,000 were necessary to recover it, this good will could not possess much permanent value. Besides, the assurance that "some one told somebody else in confidence" of the advantages Colombia would sometime bestow on the United States was hardly acceptable as a "good and valid consideration in view of our experiences with Colombia." In conclusion, he intimated that oil propaganda might have caused "a number of gentlemen to about face on this question."[71]

Senator Johnson (R.) could not understand the "marvelous mutations" in the opinions of certain Senators, how "blackmail for 17 years [had] ripened now into honest obligation," nor "the idea that an act of wickedness under a Democratic administration became an act of virtue . . . under some other."[72] Kenyon (R.) recalled how the Republican campaign speeches of 1918 had "denounced the Colombian treaty as the crowning infamy in the attempt of Woodrow Wilson to slur the life and character of Theodore Roosevelt" and thought it most extra-

---

[65] *Ibid.*, p. 226.
[67] *Ibid.*, p. 482.
[69] *Ibid.*, p. 447.
[71] *Ibid.*, pp. 443-446.

[66] *Ibid.*, p. 449.
[68] *Ibid.*, p. 395.
[70] *Ibid.*, p. 191.
[72] *Ibid.*, pp. 305-307.

ordinary that an "infamous crime" then had now become
"a very divine proceeding."[73]   It was noted by Norris
(R.) that the senatorial conversions had been at the request of Harding, but not until Roosevelt had passed
on.[74]

Senator Watson (D.) felt that the change was due
to "an oil proposition that Secretary Fall had pipe-
lined into this treaty" and saw in the payment of the
$25,000,000 "an indirect subsidy to the oil interests."[75]
But the Colombian oil, Norris (R.) was convinced, would
never reach the United States Treasury. "It is doubtful," he concluded, "if that will ever get beyond Wall
Street, and if the oil interests of this country are anxious
to develop that country and it is necessary to pay
[therefor] . . . let the oil, rather than the Treasury . . .
pay for the smiles we are trying to get."[76]   Besides,
Borah ventured, this treaty did not settle the oil question; in fact, it did not purport to deal with it.[77]

Although the opposition was loud and acrimonious,
the treaty was ratified on April 20 by a vote of sixty-nine
to nineteen.[78]   Enough commercially-minded Republicans
and conscious-stricken Democrats were mustered to defeat
the Roosevelt-worshipping Republicans and the anti-Wall
Street Democrats. The approval was effected, however,
not by "Wilsonian autocracy" but rather by a "steam-
rolled execution of a closed corporation machine,"[79] leaving the "colored gentlemen in the Colombian cordwood"
unrevealed. That Washington desired pledges regarding
a subsequent commercial treaty seems quite certain, but
the nature of these, if given, can only be surmised.[80]

[73] *Ibid.*, p. 472.   [74] *Ibid,*, p. 468.
[75] *Ibid.*, pp. 313-314.   [76] *Ibid.*, p. 468.
[77] *Ibid.*, p. 468.
[78] *Ibid.*, p. 487. Yeas, 40 Republicans and 29 Democrats; Nays, 15
Republicans and 4 Democrats.
[79] "The Colombian Treaty; A Poll of the Press," *Outlook* (May 4,
1921), CXXVIII, 13-15.
[80] The conclusion of the *Chicago Tribune* representative, who was given
access to the official records at Bogotá, was that Colombia did "not obligate

The amended convention, stripped of the "sincere regret" clause and somewhat reducing Colombia's rights in the use of the canal, then went to the Colombian congress for consideration. Former President José Vicente Concha returned from Rome to fight the treaty, and Minister Carlos A. Urueta from Washington to support it. The defense was led by Enrique Olaya Herrera[81] and Antonio José Uribe.[82] Approval was secured in the midst of a financial crisis and after President Marco Fidel Suárez had been forced to resign. Ratifications were exchanged on March 1, 1922.[83]

---

itself to the oil interests" and if a slush fund existed, it was handled at Washington (*New York Times*, April 21, 1924, p. 7).

[81] Rebolledo, *op. cit.*, pp. 306-307; Rippy, *The Capitalists and Colombia*, p. 118.

[82] See *Informe de la comisión de relaciones exteriores del Senado, sobre el proyecto de ley "que aprueba las modificaciones introducidas por el senado norteamericano al tratado de 6 de abril de 1914"* . . . (1915); Uribe, *Las modificaciones al tratado entre Colombia y los Estados Unidos, cuestiones internacionales, economicas, políticas, sociales.*

[83] Henao y Arrubla, *op. cit.*, p. 776; *Sen. Doc.*, No. 64 (68.1), p. 71.

Part VIII

RAPPROCHEMENT

Chapter XXVIII

RECENT RELATIONS[1]
(1922-1934)

THE desire on the part of the United States for a share in the development of Colombian natural resources and the need on the part of Colombia for American capital and skill in the fulfillment of an acknowledged national destiny seem to have been the determining factors, on the one hand, in the payment of the $25,000,000 with the expectation of subsequent favors and, on the other, in the acceptance of mere money as compensation for an alleged moral injury. At any rate, the Americans were anxious to exploit, and the Colombians were not adverse to granting favorable concessions and contracts.

COLOMBIAN ECONOMIC RENAISSANCE

One American described Colombia as "a giant about to burst its bonds."[2] This was scarcely an exaggeration. It possessed enormous potential wealth and certainly exhibited signs of new activity.

Agriculture, the chief occupation of the people, received much attention. Coffee alone represented two-thirds of the total exports. By 1924 there were 13,398 plantations, containing 95,500 acres with 6,814,714 producing trees. Coffee exports increased from approximately 36,000,000 pesos in 1921 to 92,283,862 in 1926, with Colombia ranking second to Brazil in the sale of this product to the United States. The National Federation of Coffee Growers employed production experts, estab-

---

[1] Since the principal phases of this period have been thoroughly treated by Professor Rippy in *The Capitalists and Colombia,* this chapter is intended merely as a general survey.

[2] Earl Harding, "Economic and Industrial Renaissance of Colombia," *B. P. A. U.*, LV, 341; William McFee, "Hale Colombia," *World's Work* (Oct., 1924), XLVIII, 622-629.

lished model plantations and experiment stations, maintained stores to furnish (free from duty) implements and fertilizer to producers, organized the Central Coffee Experiment School near Esperanza with two full years of instruction, published a monthly magazine, and supported propaganda agents abroad. All this brought results. Exports in 1928 reached 351,000,000 pounds, some 420% over those of 1906, and prices leaped from 13.6 cents in 1918 to 26 cents in 1925.[3]

Extensive areas, especially around Santa Marta, were being planted in bananas. The export of these grew from 3,603,400 pesos in 1923 to 5,724,824 in 1927, and 8,989,000 in 1929.[4] At Santa Marta a tobacco factory was established in 1926, and plans were laid for growing the leaf locally. The following year Colombia took second prize at the International Exposition of Tobacco held at London.[5]

Besides native cotton production, a Franco-Belgian company was growing large quantities (1923) in the Department of Santander. British experts requested (1926) permission to establish large plantations in the Cauca Valley. In 1927 the national government appropriated a maximum of 300,000 pesos for the development of the cotton industry and later gave 100,000 pesos for a cotton school and experiment stations in Cauca.[6] By 1924 the Colombian Silk Company had some 80,000 mulberry trees and a silk mill near Sasaima.[7] All agriculture benefited by the governmental decree of June 4, 1927, establishing the Bureau of Agriculture and Zoötechnology. In 1928 the minister of industry estimated the annual value of crops at 628,000,000 pesos.[8]

[3] *B. P. A. U.*, LIV, 174; LVIII, 933; LXI, 1026; LXIII, 276, 817, 818, 1037; Chester Lloyd Jones, *Caribbean Backgrounds and Prospects*, p. 119; *New York Times*, Feb. 20, 1927, VIII, 4:6.

[4] *B. P. A. U.*, LIX, 721; LXII, 617; LXIII, 827; LXIV, 1052.

[5] *Ibid.*, LX, 1130; LXI, 916.

[6] *Ibid.*, LVI, 605; LX, 1024; LXI, 173; LXII, 1049.

[7] *Ibid.*, LV, 606; LVI, 180; LVIII, 1253.

[8] *Ibid.*, LXI, 916; LXII, 1264.

In addition to these commodities, considerable maize, sugar cane, barley, potatoes, and yucca were produced for home consumption.[9] Nor was stock-raising neglected. It is estimated that Colombian pasture lands were supporting some 10,590,000 head of livestock in 1926. More valuable than these, however, were the subsoil products. Between 1913 and 1923 platinum production increased from 17,635 troy ounces to 40,676 and gold from 143,757 to 275,738,[10] while petroleum production leaped from 323,000 barrels in 1922 to 20,384,000 in 1929.[11]

Industry likewise enjoyed a phenomenal growth. Silk, woolen, and sugar mills; building material, match, and tobacco factories; and meat-packing and hydro-electric power plants sprang up on all sides.[12] The principal cities spent millions of pesos on paving, sanitation, telephone installation, electric light and water plants, and other modern public works.

The Marconi Company opened wireless stations (1922) in Bogotá, Barranquilla, Cúcuta, and Medellín. Inter-departmental telephone service was soon available. The *Sociedad Colombo-Alemana de Transportes Aéreos* or *Scadta,* which had established fortnightly air transportation between Barranquilla and Girardot up the Magdalena in 1919, soon extended its lines to Medellín, Cali, Cartagena, Buenaventura, and even to Guayaquil, Colón, and Panama.[13]

This competition, however, failed to prevent an increase in the Magdalena River traffic. The year 1928 found one hundred and nine boats plying its waters.[14] Transportation was facilitated still further by the national and departmental governments' use of their newly

[9] *Ibid.*, LXII, 1264.
[10] Rippy, *The Capitalists and Colombia*, pp. 28-29.
[11] *B. P. A. U.*, LXIII, 1052.
[12] *Ibid.*, LIV, 284; LV, 177, 287; LVI, 180, 492, 506, 605; LXI, 172.
[13] *Ibid.*, LV, 74; LVIII, 77; LXIV, 188; *Current Hist.*, XVIII, 1060; XIX, 676; XX, 305.
[14] *B. P. A. U.*, LXII, 616.

acquired foreign credit for the construction of new highways and railroads.[15] During 1927 alone, 233 kilometers of highway were built, 324 more surveyed, and 1,216 maintained and improved.[16] Between 1921 and 1927 railroad trackage increased 66.6%, number of passengers 67.7%, tons of freight hauled 43.5%, and gross receipts from operation 80.4%.[17]

More adequate connections were also made available with Europe and North America. The Hamburg-American Line renewed its direct service in 1922, a Norwegian company established lines from Antwerp and Montreal in 1924, and American ships rendered more efficient and profitable service.[18]

COLOMBO-AMERICAN RAPPROCHEMENT

Political and business leaders in both countries seemed to sense the opening of an era of prosperity and to realize that their futures were "fatefully correlated." Each nation furnished the best markets for the products of the other. American capital and energy demanded new fields of activity, while Colombia needed just these to insure its economic development.

President-elect Pedro Nel Ospina visited the United States during the summer of 1922. His reception was quite in contrast with that of 1903. He was met at the Washington railway terminal by the Secretary of State, by General John J. Pershing, and by a cavalry escort, and was banquetted at the White House, instead of arriving unnoticed and begging for an unwelcomed interview with an adamant president. Before the New York Chamber of Commerce he pleaded for American capital and talent, not for simple justice in the adjustment of the Panama affair.[19]

[15] President Méndez planned to borrow $100,000,000 for that purpose in 1927 (*Current Hist.*, Oct., 1926, XXV, 124).

[16] *B. P. A. U.*, LXII, 616.   [17] *Ibid.*, LXII, 1273.

[18] *Ibid.*, LIV, 174; LVIII, 185.

[19] *Ibid.*, LIV, 325-327; LV, 98-99; *Current Hist.*, XVI, 540; *New York Times*, June 2, 1922, p. 23:2.

The new president was a graduate of the University of California. Numerous other prominent Colombians held degrees from Harvard, Cornell, and Columbia; and Miguel López, president of the Bogotá Chamber of Commerce, had attended universities in both the United States and Europe.[20] Naturally these joined the leaders of the commercially minded coastal departments in encouraging cordial relations with the United States.

The work of Yankee traveling salesmen was facilitated by a most favorable treaty in 1922.[21] The American and Bogotá chambers of commerce agreed in 1923 to arbitrate subsequently arising private differences.[22] The United States added a commercial attaché to its Bogotá legation.[23] A Colombian law of 1922 provided for the establishment of commercial offices in New York, London, Paris, Hamburg, and Barcelona to exhibit products, maintain libraries, and publish commercial propaganda periodicals.[24] Motion pictures depicting Colombian progress were made for home and foreign showing.[25] A Colombo-American chamber of commerce was established in New York, and the ministry of industry at Bogotá was expanded to include an information and propaganda bureau,[26] which soon began the publication of the *Colombian Review* at New York.

Naturally such determined efforts bore fruit and expelled the economic and financial gloom of 1920-1921.[27] Exports to the United States alone in 1923 were greater than the entire national trade of 1913. The total volume of $50,000,000 of the latter year reached $273,688,701 by 1928. Of the latter amount, approximately eighty per cent

[20] Earl Harding, ''Economic and Industrial Renaissance of Colombia,'' *B. P. A. U.*, LV, 340-355.

[21] Text, *Cong. Rec.* (67.4), LXIV, 1303.

[22] *B. P. A. U.*, LVI, 605.   [23] *Ibid.*, LVII, 184.

[24] *Ibid.*, LVI, 284-85.   [25] *Ibid.*, LIX, 286; LXI, 59.

[26] *Ibid.*, LXII, 509; *New York Times*, Sept. 24, 1927.

[27] *New York Times*, Oct. 22, 31, Nov. 7, Dec. 5, 1920; Henao y Arrubla, *op. cit.*, p. 776.

of the exports came to, and forty-five per cent of the imports came from, the United States.[28]

The ratification of the Thomson-Urrutia Treaty made possible almost a "weekly procession" of Yankee geologists, engineers, contractors, industrialists, and capitalists into the new land of opportunity. The geologists were soon cutting their way through the tropical jungles in search of "liquid gold"; engineers were advising the national, departmental, and municipal governments regarding the construction of streets, highways, railroads, electric and water plants, and telephone systems; contractors were spending the loans which American capitalists vied with each other to grant; and technical experts were rendering valuable service in matters of finance, industry, transportation, and oil.[29]

The principal American investments were made in petroleum development and loans. But some $18,000,000 went into gold, silver, platinum, and emerald mining; meat packing; production of coffee, bananas, and sugar; and public utilities, such as electric, telephone, and telegraph services. Individual real and personal property investments were not very great.[30]

YANKEE *PETROLEROS* ENTER COLOMBIA

It will be remembered that the British application for an oil concession in 1913 was an argument for the negotiation of the Thomson-Urrutia Treaty, and the American desire to exploit Colombian oil areas was a potent factor in its ratification in 1921.

Local interest in petroleum production in Colombia

[28] Jones, *Caribbean Backgrounds and Prospects*, p. 218; *B. P. A. U.*, LXII, 82.

[29] *B. P. A. U.*, LIV, 287; LV, 288; LVII, 184; LIX, 391; LX, 285; LXI, 389; LXII, 297, 947; LXIII, 372, 623. The principal construction companies: American International Corporation, Uhlen and Company, Raymond Concrete Pile Company, Parrish and Company, Foundation Company, R. W. Hebbard and Company (*ibid.*, LIX, 391; *Current Hist.*, XXI, 446; XXII, 981; Rippy, *The Capitalists and Colombia*, p. 174).

[30] Rippy, *op. cit.*, pp. 172-176.

was early apparent, Diego Martínez y Compañía secured
a concession in the Sinú River territory as early as 1905.
Soon two wells were bored, but oil was not found in paying quantities. Around 1914 this grant and the property
of the Cartagena Oil Refining Company (using imported
crude) came into the hands of the Standard Oil Company. New prospecting followed but with little more
promising results. And the concession was abandoned in
1916.[31]

Even prior to 1900 the Armella-De Mares Company
of Barranquilla was granted the right to exploit an area
southwest of that city and east of Cartagena. A Canadian
concern acquired this concession in 1907 and finally
drilled two wells, but the World War halted their none-
too-profitable operations. Roberto de Mares had a grant
also in the Department of Santander del Sur. His early
attempts to interest foreign capital in it proved futile,
owing to the civil war of 1898-1903. However, he secured
renewals in 1905 and 1916. The Tropical Oil Company
of Pittsburgh became interested and later brought in
producing wells there. In 1920 a subsidiary of the Standard Oil acquired the holdings.[32]

Probably the best-known concession is the one granted
(1905) to Virgilión de Barco of Cúcuta. This was located
in the Department of Santander del Norte near Cúcuta
and just opposite the Maracaibo oil fields of Venezuela.
In 1918 Colombia approved the transfer of the property
to the American-owned Carib Syndicate. The following
year it passed to the Colombian Petroleum Company,
owned by the Doherty group of Pittsburgh;[33] and later a
controlling interest to the Gulf Oil Company, owned by
the Mellon group. The status of this one concession was
to plague good relations between Washington and Bogotá for almost a decade.

[31] P. L. Bell, *Colombia: A Commercial and Industrial Handbook*, pp. 126-127.

[32] *Ibid.*, pp. 127-130.   [33] *Ibid.*, pp. 130-131.

Although the Colombian legislation of December, 1919, was not considered entirely satisfactory, "some twenty-four Yankee and about ten British oil companies" had experts on the ground by March, 1921.[34] One American concern had three-producing wells and a refinery near Barranca Bermeja and seven stations along the Magdalena to furnish oil for the railway and river traffic.[35] In the following year production throughout the nation amounted to 323,000 barrels. But with the opening of the three hundred and sixty-five mile pipe-line of the Andean National Corporation in 1926, this amount increased to 6,444,000 barrels.[36]

UNEXPECTED COMPLICATIONS

In February, 1926, the Colombian minister of industries declared the De Barco concession void, because of an alleged failure to develop it according to contract terms. The Gulf Oil Company requested a hearing. But the new Méndez administration (assumed control in August, 1926) was slow to act; in fact, it even seemed inclined towards the policy of nationalization of petroleum deposits. New British rivalry also loomed in the missions of Colonel Henry Yates and Lieutenant-Colonel Sir Arnold T. Wilson, representing the Anglo-Persian Oil Company. They sought to explore and exploit areas in the Urabá-Atrato region and were seemingly successful in winning Méndez and his cabinet. Naturally, protests poured into both Bogotá and Washington. Not only were Yankee vested interests endangered, but American supremacy on the Isthmus appeared at stake if a British partially government-owned company secured a large concession near the termini of the canal.[37]

The oil interests and legally minded Colombians (the

[34] Rippy, *The Capitalists and Colombia*, p. 135.
[35] *B. P. A. U.*, LIV, 287.
[36] *Ibid.*, LX, 1181 ff.; LXIII, 1052.
[37] Rippy, *The Capitalists and Colombia*, pp. 137-138; Ludwell Denny, *We Fight for Oil*, pp. 121-130.

constitution prohibited such a grant to a foreign government) aroused public opinion and effected the defeat of the concession. But the emergency petroleum law of November, 1927, prepared the way for additional complaints. It required oil operators to furnish the minister of industries within six months the proof of ownership and lease contracts on all lands being explored or exploited by them, under pain of heavy fines or forfeiture of rights. It also indefinitely postponed the consideration of all concession applications and doubled the government tax on the production on private lands. Executive Regulation Number 150 of January 28, 1928, reduced this six months' period to thirty days, required drilling permits, and deprived those affected of any appeal to the courts from the decision of the minister of industries.[38]

Yankee protests were met with the retort that the furor might indicate that certain parties knew they were operating on lands with questionable titles.[39] Such a charge seems hardly justifiable, however, in the light of the admitted imperfections of private land-titles in Colombia. In many cases adequate surveys had never been made; in few cases, were land records complete. And correct maps of the oil areas were non-existent. In any event, available records could hardly have been collected and presented within the allotted thirty-day period. The *petroleros* were indeed in a sorry plight.

THE STATE DEPARTMENT TO THE RESCUE

While rumors of an official protest against the granting of the Yates concession considerably aroused the Bogotá press, new reports of possible diplomatic intervention in behalf of the *petroleros* fanned it to white heat. Both governments denied that the protest was made. And the instructions to Minister Samuel H. Piles

[38] Rippy, *The Capitalists and Colombia*, pp. 139-142.
[39] *Current Hist.*, XXVIII, 126-127.

have never been made public. It is known, however, that
the executive regulation of January, 1928, was voided on
June 3, thereby suspending the petroleum act of 1927.[40]

Meanwhile, the Gulf Oil Company, irritated at the
judicial delay in determining the status of the De Barco
concession, appealed to the Department. Piles presented
the matter to the Colombian minister of foreign affairs,
only to be advised that Washington had "committed an
error in initiating this intervention," this was purely
a Colombian judicial question. But Piles contended that
American ownership of ninety-five per cent of the concession was sufficient for his action.[41]

At any rate, the cancellation of the concession was
confirmed on August 4, 1928, this time on different and
more immediate grounds. Piles then requested the allowance of thirty days for the company to prepare a
defense, but was advised that official intervention could
not be permitted in such matters. On new instructions
he insisted (September 22) on a more definite answer to
his request and defended the American right to protect
the property of its nationals abroad.[42]

Minister Uribe made public the correspondence and
thereby lashed into fury the Colombian press, which
agreed that until the Supreme Court had reviewed the
case and refused justice, there were certainly no grounds
for American intervention.[43] Evidently, the disagreement created a greater furor than either government
desired. Secretary Kellogg advised the American public
that his only aim had been to secure the grant of a few
days for the preparation of a memorial by the conces-
sionaries. He regretted that Colombia had misunder-
stood his actions, but promised that he would follow
closely the judicial disposition of the case. President

[40] *New York Times,* Feb. 20, 22, 25, 28, 1928; Denny, *op. cit.,* p. 136;
Rippy, *The Capitalists and Colombia,* pp. 142-143.
[41] Rippy, *op. cit.,* pp. 143-144.   [42] *Ibid.,* pp. 144-146.
[43] *Ibid.,* p. 146.

Méndez calmed a student demonstration by assuring them that Piles had merely requested information and had not intervened in any manner.[44] Here the De Barco question rested for a season.

Meanwhile, most of the American companies, except the Tropical Oil and the Andean National Corporation, adopted a policy of watchful waiting. The status of oil holdings was very precarious. To remedy the situation, Colombia now employed a commission of foreign experts, including H. Foster Bain and J. W. Steele from the United States, to prepare new petroleum legislation. A more favorable law was introduced into Congress in July, 1929, but presidential politics so occupied the attention of the solons that adjournment came without its passage.[45] This likewise had to await solution by a new administration.

Strangely enough, all these difficulties were not sufficient to prevent an enormous increase in oil production and investments in Colombia. The 1929 petroleum output reached 20,384,000 barrels, as compared with 6,444,000 in 1926 and 323,000 in 1923. Professor Rippy estimates American oil investments in Colombia at $45,000,000 by the close of 1929.[46] Another estimate places them at $100,000,000 by July, 1931.[47] The exact figures, of course, are not available.

EXTENSIVE LOANS

Prior to the ratification of the Thomson-Urrutia Treaty, Colombia was accustomed to borrow in Europe, especially in England. However, European post-war financial conditions made a shift to the American money market essential.

[44] *New York Times*, Aug. 7, Sept. 23, 26, 1928.

[45] *Current Hist.*, XXX, 927, 1142; XXXI, 585, 786; *B. P. A. U.*, LXIII, 1041.

[46] *Revista del banco de la república* (Bogotá, Je., 1930), quoted in *B. P. A. U.*, LXIII, 1052; Rippy, *The Capitalists and Colombia*, p. 136.

[47] Max Borse, "Colombia's Oil," *Chile Pan-Am.* (July, 1931), XI, 7.

Large loans were needed by the national, departmental, and municipal governments to carry out their public improvement programs. But Colombia's debt record was not very attractive. From 1820 to 1904 defaults had been frequent. Although none had occurred since the latter date, the country was just emerging from a severe post-war slump. All this argued caution.

In order to establish the desired confidence in the Colombian financial structure, President Pedro Nel Ospina invited an American commission, headed by Professor E. W. Kemmerer, to investigate and to suggest means of strengthening it. This led to the establishment of a national bank and the reorganization of the treasury and revenue systems. Meanwhile, the Colombian congress let it be known that a loan of $100,000,000 was desired for a public works program.[48]

However, American bankers were still hesitant. Small sums had been loaned in 1920 and two slightly larger amounts in 1922. Government bonds to the amount of $9,000,000 were bought in New York in 1924 and $8,000,000 in 1925. But it was not until near the end of 1926 that issues were accepted with such reckless regularity.[49] During that year loans amounted to $34,000,000 and in 1927 to $67,464,000. The peak was reached during the first half of 1928, when $79,235,000 worth of Colombian securities were sold to American investors.[50] The bureau of foreign and domestic commerce estimated that loans secured in the United States up to September 26, 1928, amounted to $235,800,577, representing new capital of some $215,324,557.[51]

With the exception of some six per cent loans to the

[48] *B. P. A. U.*, LVI, 528, LXII, 1065, LXIII, 293, 628; *Current Hist.*, XVII, 1055; XVIII, 1060; XIX, 350. The Colombian bank deposits grew approximately 800% from 1924 to 1928, the National City Bank entered the country in 1928, and the Bogotá Stock Exchange appeared in 1929.

[49] Rippy, *The Capitalists and Colombia*, pp. 121-122; *B. P. A. U.*, LV, 510; LVIII, 403; *Current Hist.*, XVII, 528.

[50] *B. P. A. U.*, LX, 295, 615, 716; LXIII, 89.

[51] Quoted by Rippy, *The Capitalists and Colombia*, pp. 153-159.

national government, most of this amount carried seven per cent interest and was sold to New York bankers at discounts ranging from six and one-half to seventeen per cent.[52] This was rather expensive financing, yet the rates were no higher than formerly paid British capitalists.

During 1928 both countries reacted against excessive flotations. A Colombian law of June 5 required national approval of all subsequent departmental and municipal loans, while the finance and investment division of the United States bureau of domestic and foreign commerce (*Special Circular,* No. 305) intimated that Colombian credit had possibly become "endangered." This official statement was resented at Bogotá, and efforts to borrow were continued. The 1929 national budget provided for a flotation of 34,453,000 pesos. However, before the negotiations could be consummated, the New York stock market suffered its greatest crash. Further loans were out of the question.[53]

THE NEW RÉGIME

The presidential elections of 1930 brought into power Dr. Enrique Olaya Herrera and broke the Conservative domination of forty-four years. The president-elect, who had represented his country at Washington for the past eight years, returned to the United States before his inaugural. He was well received by both the financial group in New York and the official circle in Washington.

Colombia was obviously in financial straits. The price of coffee had greatly declined, the oil industry was inactive, and foreign borrowings had been curtailed by the stock crash. Olaya faced the situation with tact and determination. He declared that it was his "purpose to find an equitable formula" to protect Colombian rights, yet "at the same time stimulate the investment of foreign

[52] *Ibid.*, pp. 162-163; *B. P. A. U.*, LXI, 179, 289, 400, 925, 1036, 1137; LXII, 731-732.

[53] Rippy, *The Capitalists and Colombia*, pp. 166-171; *Current Hist.*, XXX, 696.

capital in the development of the enormous oil resources''
of his country. His policy was to be one of coöperation,
not of litigation. He proposed to secure a large loan in
the United States, settle the oil controversy, freely employ American experts in economic and financial matters, develop Colombian agriculture, and proceed with its
railway and highway construction.[54]

While in New York, he dined with the president of the
United Press, Governor Harrison of the Federal Reserve
Bank of New York, the Colombian-American Chamber
of Commerce, and the Pan American Society; and broad-
casted over the WJZ radio station.[55] He thus made the
influential contacts necessary for the furtherance of his
program.

A loan of $20,000,000 was promised by the National
City Bank, et al.,[56] on the following conditions: a balanced budget, the flotation of an internal loan of 6,000,000
pesos, and the revision of the financial and customs systems. Sufficient reform progress was soon made—thanks
to the second mission of Professor Kemmerer—for the
advance of $3,000,000. In October some $9,000,000 more
were released. But before the next payment of $4,000,000
in March, 1931, additional conditions were imposed: legislative authority for the loan, a debt-limit law, and the
readjustment of the administration of the railroads. The
final $4,000,000 was held up on the ground of an alleged
unbalanced current budget. Olaya claimed that the budget was balanced and charged the bankers with being
unduly technical. He consulted the American minister,
who, in turn, cabled the State Department. Secretary
Stimson called in person on the National City Bank regarding the matter. And the balance was turned over
on June 30, 1931.[57]

[54] *New York Times,* April 21, 1930, p. 5.

[55] *Ibid.,* April 21, 22, 23, 1930.

[56] For a list of these banks, see *ibid.,* Dec. 16, 1930.

[57] Testimony of Vice-President Victor Schoepperle of the National City
Bank, Jan., 1932, *New York Times,* Jan. 13, 1932, pp. 1, 16. See also the
New York Times for Oct. 19, 1930.

According to his announced program, Olaya urged (September 15, 1930) his Congress to pass favorable oil legislation.[58] Obviously, this was necessary, since the Tropical Oil Company alone was producing; and was desirable, since seven other American companies were on the ground awaiting proper security.[59] George Rublee, former petroleum adviser to Ambassador Morrow in Mexico, was called to Bogotá (arrived October 24) to assist in framing the bill.[60] The new law soon passed and received the signature of the President on March 4, 1931. It declared the entire oil industry a public utility; gave preferment to Colombian nationals, when qualified; made all disputes subject to settlement in the Colombian courts; abolished all petroleum export duties for the first thirty years of exploitation; limited concessions to any one person to 50,000 hectares of land; and forbade the transfer of grants to foreign governments.[61] Concessionaires were ordered to prove title to their lands (difficult, if not impossible, in some cases). The royalty to be paid the Colombian government ranged from two to eleven per cent on public and from one to eight per cent on private lands. And the operation of all wells at one-fourth capacity was made compulsory on penalty of the payment of royalty.[62]

The Texas Company considered the law too restrictive and impracticable, and announced the cessation of the development of its 800,000 acres. The Sinclair Exploration Company advised the President that it could not continue under the new arrangement. But the Standard Oil Company of New Jersey thought it satisfactory. Rublee declared it "workable" in normal times and therefore felt that the world-wide depressed petroleum conditions might have caused the Texas and Sinclair withdrawals.[63] In

[58] *Ibid.*, Dec. 16, 1930, p. 2.   [59] *Ibid.*, Oct. 26, 1930.
[60] *Ibid.*, Oct. 11, 1930, p. 29; *Current Hist.*, XXXIII, 929.
[61] *B. P. A. U.*, LXV, 642-643.
[62] *New York Times*, May 3, 1931, II, 9:4.
[63] *Ibid.*, April 7, 29, May 3, 1931.

any case, it seemed quite probable that increased world production and the low price of petroleum, considered with Venezuela's more favorable legislation, might make still greater Colombian inducements necessary.

On March 4, 1931, President Olaya signed a contract with the Gulf Oil Company settling the De Barco dispute. It provided for an exclusive grant of 500,000 acres of the original concession; a royalty of ten per cent on the field or six per cent on the coast; and the construction of a refinery at Cúcuta, when daily production reached 28,000 barrels.[64] Olaya urged congressional approval of the contract as the best means (1) of removing an old embarrassment, (2) eliminating international friction by destroying foreign criticism, (3) securing much needed financial aid, and (4) creating both internal and foreign harmony.[65] Public antagonism again became aroused,[66] but the President's support was sufficient to push the measure through. Final approval came on June 20.

Ten days later the National City Bank released the final $4,000,000 of the Olaya loan, after conferences with Secretary Stimson and other Department officials. It has been freely charged—but not proved—that this balance was deliberately withheld to coerce Colombia into approving the De Barco contract and that Andrew W. Mellon, secretary of the treasury and large stockholder in the Gulf Oil Company, had made it plain to Olaya that proper petroleum arrangements would aid materially in securing the financial assistance needed. However, the State Department denies any connection between the two transactions, and the National City Bank denies the exertion of any influence by the former on its payment of the $4,000,000. Both Mellon and Olaya contend that their conversation was general and contained nothing regarding the settlement of oil difficulties as a means of estab-

[64] "Bogotá Clears Way for Big Oil Trade," *ibid.*, March 5, 1931, p. 10.
[65] *Ibid.*, April 9, 1931, p. 9.
[66] *Ibid.*, April 29, 1931, p. 2, June 17, 1931, p. 16.

lishing future credit. Mellon also maintains that he never talked with Olaya, the State Department, or any bankers about the loan or that any use was made of his official influence in either matter.[67]

That the Department served as a sort of "go-between" for Colombia, on the one hand, and the oil interests and bankers, on the other, seems evident. It likewise appears certain that Minister Caffery in at least one telegram to the Department mentions the approval of the De Barco contract as an additional argument for the advancement of the loan.[68] However, Rublee, who remained in Colombia until April, 1931, insists that he "never heard the remotest suggestion of any connection between the two transactions. . . ."[69] Lawrence Dennis agrees that they were "two unconnected pieces of business," but feels that the Department "acted improperly in connection with both."[70] However that may be, it would be difficult to establish any connection between the two matters—even if one were so inclined—until certain pertinent papers are made public. For the present, at least, official denials must be accepted at their face value.

AMERICA'S INTEREST IN COLOMBIA'S FUTURE

1. Colombia possesses a possible rival canal route.[71] The United States certainly would never permit European domination of this. Suspected British attempts to acquire rights near the termini of the Panama canal in 1913 and 1927 aroused serious opposition in Wash-

[67] *Ibid.*, Jan. 13, pp. 1, 16, Jan. 15, pp. 1, 2, Jan. 16, p. 3, Jan. 20, p. 4, Jan. 21, pp. 15, 20, Jan. 27, p. 8, Jan. 28, 1932, p. 13; *Nation* (Jan. 27, 1932), CXXXIV, 93.

[68] *New York Times*, Jan. 15, 1932, pp. 1, 2.

[69] George Rublee, "The American Government and Colombia," *New Republic* (Feb. 17, 1932), LXX, 21-22.

[70] Lawrence Dennis, "Colombia and the State Department," *ibid.* (March 2, 1932), LXX, 70.

[71] In 1929 Rear Admiral Colby M. Chester urged the construction of a canal by the Urabá-Atrato route, but more recent surveys indicate an American preference for the Nicaragua route (*New York Times*, Nov. 12, 1929, p. 64, April 5, 1931).

ington. But protection of American canal interests will depend on either the most cordial relations with Colombia or the use of drastic measures. And the latter course would not be in harmony with President F. D. Roosevelt's "good neighbor" policy. Also, it would react unfavorably against Yankee trade throughout Latin America and endanger enormous investments in Colombia.

2. It is estimated that these investments already amount to some $301,692,000—only five Latin American nations having more Yankee capital. Since approximately fifty-seven per cent of this amount is in government securities—Brazil alone having sold more in the United States—the burden on the national, departmental, and municipal treasuries has been heavy.[72]

Colombia has not escaped the blighting hand of the world depression. The reduction of its gold reserve from 64,658,000 pesos in December, 1928, to 14,000,000 pesos in September, 1931, caused alarm. President Olaya was granted emergency financial powers—decrees of September 24 and November 16, 1931. Under these, he required the deposit of all metallic reserves in the Bank of the Republic and the registration of all individual deposits abroad amounting to more than 1,000 pesos, created an office of control to regulate exports and exchange, and issued a high tariff schedule on all luxuries.[73]

The new Exchange Control Board then refused to sell exchange for debt service. Interest and instalments due from the departments and municipalities were accepted at the Bank of the Republic and credited to foreign bondholders. Interest-bearing national scrip was issued to the foreign creditors, and the money was reloaned to the departments and municipalities. Deter-

[72] William O. Scroggs, ''The American Investments in Latin America,'' *For. Affairs* (April, 1932), X, 502-504; *B. P. A. U.* (Oct., 1931), LXV, 1069.

[73] *B. P. A. U.* (Oct., 1932), LXVI, 727-732.

mined opposition to this plan, however, caused its abandonment in May, 1932, and subsequently the return of the deposits to the debtors.[74]

Nevertheless, Colombia seems to have exerted every possible effort to pay the interest on national, departmental, municipal, and Agricultural Mortgage Bank bonds—some $6,472,000 annually. The increase of internal gold production, the large volume of coffee exports to the United States, and the rigid restrictions on imports made this possible for a time. National interest charges due October 1, 1932, were met on schedule.[75] However, numerous banks, departments, and municipalities defaulted before the end of the year, largely because of exchange restrictions imposed at Bogotá. These were considered necessary to protect the gold reserve behind the Colombian currency.

But American creditors had already become uneasy.[76] Even before President Olaya approved a private debt moratorium (November 25, 1932),[77] they had begun the organization of the Independent Bondholders Committee for the Republic of Colombia.[78] The departments and municipalities have continued in default. Until April 1, 1933, however, the national government had defaulted only in sinking fund requirements.[79]

This bondholders committee maintained that the rise in coffee and gold prices and the favorable balance of trade with the United States made possible regular payments on debt service. Colombia, on the other hand, insisted that its total trade was unfavorable and that further payments for the year 1933 must be abandoned. A decree issued late in March suspended all cash payments on Colombian obligations after April 1. This applied

[74] *Ibid.* (Nov., 1932), LXVI, 809-810.
[75] *New York Times,* Sept. 3, p. 20:1, Oct. 16, 1932, IV, 4:8.
[76] *Ibid.,* Dec. 4, 1932. [77] *Ibid.,* Nov. 27, 1932, p. 29:4.
[78] *Ibid.,* Nov. 10, p. 31:2, Nov. 17, p. 30:1, Dec. 4, 15, 1932.
[79] *Current History,* May, 1933, pp. 220-221.

even to the Olaya $20,000,000 short-term loan of 1930.[80] Just what debt arrangements, if any, President-elect Alfonso López made on his good will visit to Washington, the latter part of June, 1934,[81] have not been announced. It is to be hoped that Colombia's economic recovery will soon be sufficient to make resumption of debt payments possible.

3. The Colombo-American reciprocal trade agreement of December 15, 1933, many believe, will effect the desired recovery. This convention is especially significant as the first of the Roosevelt-Hull new commercial series, designed to place trade on treaty, rather than the traditional legislative log-rolling, tariff basis.[82] The text of the new treaty has not been published. However, those cognizant of its provisions hail it as a boon to commerce and a practical example of Pan American "neighborliness."[83]

In the past the products of each nation have found only slight, if any, domestic competition with the products of the other. Approximately eighty-five per cent of Colombian coffee comes to the United States. Only Argentina and Brazil of the South American states are better customers for Yankee manufactures. In most cases, trade between Colombia and the United States means the exchange of respective surpluses. Economically, the two nations complement each other.

The retirement of Dr. Enrique Olaya Herrera (August, 1934) elevates to the presidency Dr. Alfonso López, an enlightened statesman and an ardent advocate of the "good neighbor" policy.

[80] *Ibid., New York Times*, Oct. 5, 20, 22, Nov. 2, 1933, Feb. 11, April 15, 24, 1934.

[81] *Ibid.*, June 25, 1934.

[82] E. Taylor Parks, "The Colombian Treaty: A Triumph for Mr. Hull," *World Affairs* (March, 1934), XCVII, 48-50.

[83] On September 5, 1934, the State Department announced intention to negotiate a new agreement with Colombia, since this one could not be brought into force under the Trade Agreements Act of June 12, 1934. The negotiations are still pending.

PRESIDENT-ELECT ALFONSO LOPEZ, OF COLOMBIA, AND SECRETARY OF STATE HULL

APPENDICES

APPENDIX A

COLOMBIAN (NEW GRANADIAN) CHRONOLOGY[1]

1470-1538—Chibcha Empire
1538-1564—The Conquest
1564-1718—Presidency of New Granada
1718-1724—Viceroyalty of New Granada
1724-1740—Presidency of New Granada
1740-1810—Viceroyalty of New Granada
1811-1816—United Provinces of New Granada
1816-1819—Viceroyalty of New Granada
1819-1832—Republic of Colombia (State of New Granada)
1832-1857—Republic of New Granada
1857-1862—Granadine Confederacy
1862-1863—United States of New Granada
1863-1886—United States of Colombia
1886   —Republic of Colombia

APPENDIX B

COLOMBIAN CHIEF EXECUTIVES[1]

Republic of Colombia

1819-30 —Simón Bolívar
1830   —Domingo Caicedo
1830   —Joaquín Mosquera
1830-31 —Rafael Urdaneta
1831   —Domingo Caicedo
1831-32 —José Mariá Obando

Republic of New Granada

1832   —José Ignacio Márquez
1832-37 —Franciso de P. Santander

[1] José Manuel Pérez Sarmiento, *Manual diplomático y consular Colombiano* (Bogotá, 1927).

1837-40	—José Ignacio Márquez
1840	—Domingo Caicedo
1840-41	—José Ignacio Márquez
1841	—Domingo Caicedo
1841	—Pedro A. Herrán
1841	—Juan de Dios Aranzazu
1841-42	—Domingo Caicedo
1842	—Pedro A. Herrán
1842	—Domingo Caicedo
1842-45	—Pedro A. Herrán
1845-47	—Tomás C. de Mosquera
1847	—Rufino Cuervo
1847-49	—Tomás C. de Mosquera
1849-51	—José Hilario López
1851-52	—José de Obaldía
1852-53	—José Hilario López
1853-54	—José María Obando
1854	—José María Melo
1854	—Tomás Herrera
1854-55	—José de Obaldía
1855-57	—Manuel María Mallarino

Granadine Confederacy

1857-61	—Mariano Ospina Rodríguez
1861-62	—Bartolomé Calvo

United States of New Granada

1862-63	—Tomás C. de Mosquera

United States of Colombia

1863	—Interregnum
1863-64	—Tomás C. de Mosquera
1864	—José Augustín Uricoechea
1864	—Tomás C. de Mosquera
1864-66	—Manuel Murillo Toro
1866	—José María Garrido
1866-67	—Tomás C. de Mosquera
1867-68	—Santos Acosta
1868	—Santos Gutiérrez
1868-69	—Salvador Camacho Roldán

1869   —Santos Gutiérrez
1869   —Santiago Pérez
1869-70   —Santos Gutiérrez
1870   —Eustorgio Salgar
1870   —Julián Trujillo
1870-72   —Eustorgio Salgar
1872-74   —Manuel Murillo Toro
1874-76   —Santiago Pérez
1876-77   —Aquileo Parra
1877   —Sergio Camargo
1877-78   —Aquileo Parra
1878-80   —Julián Trujillo
1880-82   —Rafael Núñez
1882   —Francisco Javier Zaldúa
1882   —Clímaco Calderón
1882-84   —José Eusebio Otálora
1884   —Ezequiel Hurtado
1884-86   —Rafael Núñez

Republic of Colombia

1886-87   —José María Campo Serrano
1887   —Eliseo Payán
1887-88   —Rafael Núñez
1888-92   —Carlos Holguín
1892-96   —Miguel Antonio Caro
1896   —Guillermo Quintero Calderón
1896-98   —Miguel Antonio Caro
1898   —José Manuel Marroquín
1898-1900—Manuel A. Sanclemente
1900-04   —José Manuel Marroquín
1904-08   —Rafael Reyes
1908   —Euclides de Angulo
1908-09   —Rafael Reyes
1909   —Jorge Holguín
1909   —Rafael Reyes
1909   —Jorge Holguín
1909-10   —Ramón González Valencia
1910-14   —Carlos E. Restrepo
1914-18   —José Vicente Concha

1918-21	—Marco Fidel Suárez
1921-22	—Jorge Holguín
1922-26	—Pedro Nel Ospina
1926-30	—Miguel Abadía Méndez
1930-34	—Enrique Olaya Herrera
1934	—Alfonso López

APPENDIX C

COLOMBIAN REPRESENTATIVES AT WASHINGTON

1820	—Manuel Torres
1823	—José María Salazar
1827	—Alejandro Vélez
1828-32	—No representative
1832	—Domingo Acosta
1842	—Joaquín Acosta
1842-47	—No representative
1847	—Pedro A. Herrán
1849	—Rafael Rivas
1850-52	—No representative
1852	—Victoriano de Paredes
1855	—Pedro A. Herrán
1860	—Rafael Pombo
1861	—Pedro A. Herrán
1863	—J. M. Hurtado
1863	—Manuel Murillo
1864	—Eustorgio Salgar
1867	—Manuel Murillo
1868	—Santos Acosta
1870	—Enrique Cortés
1870	—Santiago Pérez
1872	—Rafael Pombo
1872	—Carlos Martín
1874	—Felipe Zapata
1874-76	—No representative
1876	—Santiago Pérez
1877-79	—No representative
1879	—Justo Arosemena
1880	—Ramón Santo Domingo Vila

1881-84 —No representative
1884 —Ricardo Becerra
1887 —J. M. Hurtado
1896 —Julio Rengifo
1897-99 —No representative
1899-1900—Clímaco Calderón
1901 —Carlos Martínez Silva
1902 —José Vicente Concha
1903 —Tomás Herrán
1904 —No representative
1905 —Eduardo Pérez Triana
1905 —Diego Mendoza
1906 —Enrique Cortés
1906 —Pomponio Guzmán
1907 —Enrique Cortés
1908-09 —Pomponio Guzmán
1910 —Francisco P. de Borda
1911 —Pedro Nel Ospina
1912 —Julio Betancourt
1917 —Carlos Adolfo Urueta
1921 —Carlos Uribe, Jr.
1922 —Enrique Olaya Herrera
1930 —José A. Coronado
1931 —Fabio Lozano

APPENDIX D

UNITED STATES REPRESENTATIVES AT BOGOTÁ

1820 —Charles S. Todd
1823• —Richard C. Anderson
1826 —Beaufort T. Watts
1828 —William H. Harrison
1829 —Thomas P. Moore
1833 —J. C. Pickett
1833 —Robert B. McAfee
1837 —James Semple
1842 —William M. Blackford
1845 —Benjamin A. Bidlack
1849 —Thomas M. Foote

1851	—Yelverton P. King
1853	—James S. Green
1854	—James B. Bowlin
1857-59	—No representative
1859	—George W. Jones
1861	—Allan A. Burton
1867	—Peter I. Sullivan
1869	—Stephen A. Hurlbut
1873	—William L. Scruggs
1876-78	—No representative
1878	—Ernest Dichman
1881	—George Maney
1882	—William L. Scruggs
1885	—Charles D. Jacob
1886	—Dabney H. Maury
1889	—John T. Abbott
1893	—Luther F. McKinney
1897	—Charles B. Hart
1903	—Arthur M. Beaupré
1904	—William W. Russell
1905	—John Barrett
1907	—Thomas C. Dawson
1909	—Elliott Northcott
1911	—James T. DuBois
1913	—Thaddeus A. Thomson
1917	—Hoffman Philip
1922	—Samuel H. Piles
1928	—Jefferson Caffery
1933	—Sheldon Whitehouse

APPENDIX E

Relevant Clauses of the Treaty of 1846

. . . .

ARTICLE II

The United States of America and the Republic of New Granada, desiring to live in peace and harmony with all the nations of the earth, by means of a policy frank and equally friendly with all, engage mutually not to grant any particular favor to other nations, in respect of commerce and navigation, which shall not immediately become common to the other party, who shall enjoy the same freely, if the concession was freely made, or on allowing the same compensation, if the concession was conditional.

ARTICLE III

The two high contracting parties, being likewise desirous of placing the commerce and navigation of their respective countries on the liberal basis of perfect equality and reciprocity, mutually agree that the citizens of each may frequent all the coasts and countries of the other, and reside and trade there, in all kinds of produce, manufactures and merchandise; and that they shall enjoy all the rights, privileges and exemptions, in navigation and commerce, which native citizens do or shall enjoy, submitting themselves to the laws, decrees, and usages there established, to which native citizens are subjected. But it is understood that this article does not include the coasting trade of either country, the regulation of which is reserved by the parties, respectively, according to their own separate laws.

ARTICLE IV

They likewise agree that whatever kind of produce, manufacture or merchandise of any foreign country can be, from time to time, lawfully imported into the United States in their own vessels, may be also imported in vessels of the Republic of New Granada; and that no higher or other duties upon the tonnage of the vessel and her cargo shall be levied and collected, whether the importation be made in vessels of the one country or of the other. And, in like manner, that whatever kind of produce, manufactures or merchandise of any foreign country can be[,] from time to time[,] lawfully imported into the Republic of New Granada in its own vessels, may be also imported in vessels of the United States; and that no higher or other duties upon the tonnage of the vessel and her cargo shall be levied or collected, whether the importation be made in vessels of the one country or [of] the other.

And they further agree, that whatever may be lawfully exported or re-exported from the one country in its own vessels to any foreign country, may in like manner be exported or re-exported in the vessels of the other country; and the same bounties, duties, and drawbacks shall be allowed and collected, whether such exportation or re-exportation be made in vessels of the United States or of the Republic of New Granada.

ARTICLE V

No higher or other duties shall be imposed on the importation into the United States of any articles the produce or manufacture[s] of the Republic of New Granada, and no higher or other duties shall be imposed on the importation into the Republic of New Granada of any articles the produce or manufactures of the United States, than are or shall be payable on the like articles, being the produce or manufactures of any other foreign country; nor shall any higher or other duties or charges be imposed, in either of the two countries, on the exportation of any articles to the United States or to the Republic of New Granada, respectively, than such as are payable on the exportation of the like articles to any other foreign country; nor shall any prohibition be imposed on the exportation or importation of any articles the produce or manufactures of the United States or of the Republic of New Granada, to or from the territories of the United States or to or from the territories of the Republic of New Granada, which shall not equally extend to all other nations.

ARTICLE VI

In order to prevent the possibility of any misunderstanding, it is hereby declared that the stipulations contained in the three preceding articles are to their full extent applicable to the vessels of the United States and their cargoes arriving in the ports of New Granada, and reciprocally to the vessels of the said Republic of New Granada and their cargoes arriving in the ports of the United States, whether they proceed from the ports of the country to which they respectively belong, or from the ports of any other foreign country; and in either case, no discriminating duty shall be imposed or collected in the ports of either country on said vessels or their cargoes, whether the same shall be of native or foreign produce or manufacture.

ARTICLE XXXV

The United States of America and the Republic of New Granada, desiring to make as durable as possible the relations which are to be established between the two parties by virtue of this treaty, have declared solemnly, and do agree to the following points:

1st. For the better understanding of the preceding articles, it is and has been stipulated between the high contracting parties, that the citizens, vessels and merchandise of the United States shall enjoy in the ports of New Granada, including those of the part of the Granadian territory generally denominated Isthmus of Panama, from its southernmost extremity until the boundary of Costa Rica, all the exemptions, privileges and immunities concerning commerce and navigation, which are now or may hereafter be enjoyed by Granadian citizens, their vessels and merchandise; and that this equality of favors shall be made to extend to the passengers, correspondence and merchandise of the United States, in their transit across the said territory, from one sea to the other. The Government of New Granada guarantees to the Government of the United States that the right of way or transit across the Isthmus of Panama upon any modes of communication that now exist, or that may be hereafter constructed, shall be open and free to the Government and citizens of the United States, and for the transportation of any articles of produce, manufactures or merchandise, of lawful commerce, belonging to the citizens of the United States; that no other tolls or charges shall be levied or collected upon the citizens of the United States, or their said merchandise thus passing over any road or canal that may be made by the Government of New Granada, or by the authority of the same, than is, under like circumstances, levied upon and collected from the Granadian citizens; that any lawful produce, manufactures or merchandise, belonging to citizens of the United States, thus passing from one sea to the other, in either direction, for the purpose of exportation to any other foreign country, shall not be liable to any import-duties whatever; or, having paid such duties, they shall be entitled to drawback upon their exportation; nor shall the citizens of the United States be liable to any duties, tolls or charges of any kind, to which native citizens are not subjected for thus passing the said Isthmus. And, in order to secure to themselves the tranquil and constant enjoyment of these advantages, and as an especial compensation for the said advantages, and for the favors they have acquired by the 4th, 5th, and 6th articles of this treaty, the United States guarantee, positively and efficaciously, to New Granada, by the present stipulation, the perfect neutrality of the before-mentioned isthmus, with the view that the free transit from the one to the other sea may not be interrupted or embarrassed in any future time while this treaty exists; and, in consequence, the United States also guarantee, in the same manner, the rights of sovereignty and property which New Granada has and possesses over the said territory.

2d.   The present treaty shall remain in full force and vigor for the term of twenty years from the day of the exchange of the ratifications; and from the same day the treaty that was concluded between the United States and Colombia, on the thirteenth of October, 1824, shall cease to have effect, notwithstanding what was disposed in the first point of its 31st article.

3d.   Notwithstanding the foregoing, if neither party notifies to the other its intention of reforming any of, or all, the articles of this treaty twelve months before the expiration of the twenty years stipulated above, the said treaty shall continue binding on both parties beyond the said twenty years, until twelve months from the time that one of the parties notifies its intention of proceeding to a reform.

4th.   If any one or more of the citizens of either party shall infringe any of the articles of this treaty, such citizens shall be held personally responsible for the same, and the harmony and good correspondence between the nations shall not be interrupted thereby; each party engaging in no way to protect the offender, or sanction such violation.

5th.   If unfortunately any of the articles contained in this treaty should be violated or infringed in any way whatever, it is expressly stipulated that neither of the two contracting parties shall ordain or authorize any acts of reprisal, nor shall declare war against the other on complaints of injuries or damages, until the said party considering itself offended shall have laid before the other a statement of such injuries or damages, verified by competent proofs, demanding justice and satisfaction, and the same .shall have been denied, in violation of the laws and of international right.

6th. Any special or remarkable advantage that one or the other power may enjoy from the foregoing stipulation, are and ought to be always understood in virtue and as in compensation of the obligations they have just contracted, and which have been specified in the first number of this article.

BIBLIOGRAPHY

I. Manuscripts

A. Archives of the State Department of the United States

Bureau of Appointment Records (principally cards giving personal data on diplomatic agents).

Claims Series: Colombia.

Consular Letters (Despatches from Consuls)

La Guayra, 1810-1832; Cartagena, Vols. IV, VIII; Dublin (Ireland), V, VII; Panama, IV, V, XVII, XVIII.

Despatches from Ministers

Colombia, 1820-1906 (64 vols.); France, Vol. CII; Great Britain, XXVII; Mexico, I; Prussia, III; Spain, CV.

Domestic Letters, 1870-1906.

Instructions to Consuls

La Guayra, 1810-1828.

Instructions to Ministers

Colombia, 1820-1906 (19 vols.)

Argentina, Vol. XVI; Austria, II; Brazil, XVII; Central America, XVII; Costa Rica, XV; France, XVI, XIX; Germany, XVI; Great Britain, XV, XVI, XVII, XVIII, XXIV, XXVI; Italy, II; Japan, II; Mexico, I, X; Russia. XIII; Spain, VIII, XVIII.

Instructions to Special Missions

Charles Biddle; William Radcliff.

Miscellaneous Letters, 1870-1906.

Notes from Foreign Legations

Agents of Colombia
Colombia Legation   1811-1906 (10 vols.).
Nicaragua, Vol. V.

Notes to Foreign Legations

Agents of Colombia }
Colombian Legation } 1811-1906 (7 vols.)
Nicaragua, Vol. II.

Report Books, Vol. VII.

Secret Service, 1849-1862.

Special Agents Series

Biddle; Corwine; Forsyth; Hughes; Ingraham; Irvine; Prevost; Scott; Sickles.

Special Missions; Instructions, 4 vols.

Unperfected Treaty Series: Colombia.

B. MISCELLANEOUS

Watts (Beaufort T.) Papers—deposited in the Library of the University of South Carolina.

II. GOVERNMENT AND SEMI-OFFICIAL PUBLICATIONS

A. UNITED STATES

American State Papers: Foreign Relations, 6 vols., Washington, 1832, 1859.

American Historical Association, *Annual Reports*, Washington, 1894—.

Annals of Congress, Washington, 1834-1856.

Bell, P. L., *Colombia: A Commercial and Industrial Handbook*, Washington, 1921.

Congressional Documents (figures in parentheses represent the congress and session)

House Documents

Nos. 56 (19.2), 173 (22.1), 132 (54.1), 201 (55.2), 611 (57.1), 8 (58.1), 1444 (62.3).

House Executive Documents

Nos. 77 (28.1), 1 (40.3), 81 (41.2), 113 (41.2), 1 (43.1), 10 (46.1), 63 (46.2), 107 (47.2), 82 (52.2).

House Miscellaneous Documents

Nos. 24 (40.1), 219 (42.2), 113 (42.3), 16 (46.3), 395 (49.1), 599 (50.1), 232 (51.1).

House Reports

Nos. 170 (12.1), 322 (25.3), 26 (30.2), 145 (30.2), 568 (36.1), 1121 (46.2), 224 (46.3), 390 (46.3), 4167 (50.2), 2615 (52.2), 2375 (52.2).

Senate Documents

Nos. 244 (26.1), 306 (29.1), 339 (29.1), 78 (54.2), 41 (55.3), 59 (56.1), 194 (56.1), 237 (56.1), 231 (56.2), 264 (57.1), 17 (58.1), 102 (58.2), 143 (58.2), 429 (59.1),

357 (61.2), 693 (62.2), 259 (63.2), 474 (63.2), 64 (66.1), 272 (66.2), 37 (67.1), 64 (68.1).

Senate Executive Documents
Nos. 40 (31.2), 97 (32.1), 1 (33.2), 51 (34.3), 62 (39.1), 75 (45.3), 15 (46.1), 112 (46.2), 16 (47.1), 78 (47.1), 194 (47.1), 26 (48.1), 123 (48.1), 68 (52.1), 46 (52.2).

Senate Executive Journal, Vols. I-XXV.

Senate Journal, (23.2), (46.3), (47.1), (48.1).

Senate Miscellaneous Documents
Nos. 80 (30.1), 9 (46.2), 42 (46.3), 12 (48.2).

Senate Reports
Nos. 355 (32.1), 368 (47.1), 952 (47.2), 1628 (49.2), 221 (50.1), 1944 (51.2), 2234 (51.2), 1142 (52.2), 1262 (52.2), 331 (53.2), 1 (57.1), 1663 (57.1).

Congressional Globe, Washington, 1834-1873.

Congressional Record, Washington, 1873—.

Consular Reports, Washington, 1880-1903.
Continued as *Monthly Consular Reports* (1903-1905) and *Monthly Consular and Trade Reports* (1905-1910).

Curtis, W. E., *Trade and Transportation between the United States and Spanish America,* Washington, 1889.

Halsey, Frederico M., *Investments in Latin America and the British West Indies,* Washington, 1918.

Hasse, A. R., *Index to the United States Documents Relating to Foreign Relations, 1828-1861,* 3 vols., Washington, 1914.

Malloy, William M. (ed.), *Treaties, Conventions, International Acts and Agreements between the United States of America and Other Powers, 1776-1909* [Published as *Senate Documents,* 357 (61.2), 2 vols., Washington, 1910.]

Moore, John Bassett, *History and Digest of International Arbitrations,* 6 vols., Washington, 1898.

———— *A Digest of International Law,* 8 vols., Washington, 1906.

Olney, Richard, *The Clayton-Bulwer Treaty: Memorandum,* Washington, 1900.

Opinion of the Attorney-General upon the Title Proposed to Be Given by the New Panama Canal Company to the United States, Washington, 1903.

Papers of the American Historical Association, Washington, 1894.

Papers Relating to the Foreign Relations of the United States with the Annual Message of the President, Washington, 1862—.

Report of Joseph L. Bristow, Special Panama Railroad Commissioner, to the Secretary of War, June 24, 1905, Washington, 1905.

Report of Hon. F. H. Morse, of Maine, from the Committee on Naval Affairs, H. R. in Relation to the Contract Made by the Secretary of the Navy for Coal and Other Privileges on the Isthmus of Chiriqui, Washington, 1860.

Richardson, J. D., *A Compilation of the Messages and Papers of the Presidents, 1789-1919,* 20 vols., Washington, 1897-1919.

Statement of Mr. A. G. Menocal before the Committee on Interoceanic Canals, United States Senate, Washington, 1902.

Statutes at Large of the United States of America, Concurrent Resolutions of the Two Houses of Congress, and Executive Proclamations, Washington, 1856—.

The Story of Panama: Hearings on the Rainey Resolution before the Committee on Foreign Affairs of the House of Representatives, Washington, 1913.

Sullivan, J. T., *Report of the Historical and Technical Information Relating to the Problem of Interoceanic Communication by Way of the American Isthmus,* Washington, 1883.

B. COLOMBIA

Arosemena, Justo, *The Panama Canal in the Light of American Interests,* Washington, 1880.

Biblioteca de historia nacional, 40 vols., Bogotá, 1902—.

Boletín de historia y antigüedades, Vols. I-XIV, Bogotá, 1902—.

Caballero, J. M., "Días de la independencia," *La patria boba* (Biblioteca de historia nacional, Vol. I), Bogotá, 1902.

Cadena, Pedro Ignacio, *Anales diplomáticos de Colombia,* Bogotá, 1878.

—— *Colección de tratados públicos de los Estados Unidos de Colombia,* 2 vols., Bogotá, 1883-1884.

Canal interoceánico: colección de artículos editoriales de "El Tiempo" de Bogotá, Bogotá, 1866.

Codificación nacional de todas las leyes de Colombia desde el año de 1821, hecha conforme a la ley 13 de 1912, por la sala de negocios generales del consejo de estado, 9 vols. Bogotá, 1925.

Colombia, departamento de contraloria—direción general de estadística, *Censo de población de la República de Colombia* [1918], Bogotá, 1924.

Colombia, ministerio de relaciones exteriores, *Documentos diplomáticos sobre el canal y la rebelión del isthmo de Panamá,* Bogotá, 1904.

Colombian Review (Bureau of Trade Information and Trade Propaganda), Vol. V, Washington, 1926—.

Colombian Trade Review (Bureau of Trade Information and Trade Propaganda), Vols. I-VI, London, 1921—.

Congreso de Cúcuta: libro de actas (Biblioteca de historia nacional), Vol. XXXV, Bogotá, 1923.

Documentos relatívos al canal interoceánico, Bogotá, 1870.

El precursor: documentos sobre la vida pública y privada del General Antonio Nariño (Biblioteca de historia nacional, Vol. II), Bogotá, 1902.

Escobar, Felipe, *El petróleo y la propiedad minera en Colombia,* Bogotá, 1919.

Finestrad, Joaquín de, *El vassallo intruído* (Biblioteca de historia nacional, Vol. IV), Bogotá, 1905.

Galán, A. M., *El comunero Galán* (Biblioteca de historia nacional, Vol. IV), Bogotá, 1905.

García de la Parra, Pablo, *Colombia en las conferencias Panamericanas,* Bogotá, 1926.

García Samudio, Nicolás, *Capítulos de historia diplomática,* Bogotá, 1925.

Guerra, José Joaquín, *La convención de Ocaña* (Biblioteca de historia nacional, Vol. VI), Bogotá, 1908.

Herrán, General Pedro A., *Protesta del General Pedro Alcantara Herrán, enviado extraordinario y ministro plenipotenciario de la confederación Granadina cerca del gobierno de los Estados Unidos de America, contra la dictadura del titulado "Presidente de los Estados Unidos de Colombia," Tomás C. de Mosquera* (n.p.), 1862.

Ibáñez, Pedro M., *Crónicas de Bogotá* (Biblioteca de historia nacional, Vol. XXXII), Bogotá, 1923.

Informe de la comisión de relaciones exteriores del senado, sobre el proyecto de ley "que aprueba las modificaciones introducidas por el senado norteamericano al tratado de 6 abril de 1914," entre Colombia y los Estados Unidos de América, Bogotá, 1921.

León Gómez, Adolfo, *El tribuno de 1810* (Biblioteca de historia nacional, Vol. VII), Bogotá, 1910.

Martín, Carlos, *Canal interoceánico. Informe para segundo debate de tratado celebrado en 1870,* Bogotá, 1870.

Martínez, Diego, *On the Treaty between the United States and Colombia,* Washington, 1916.

Mendinueta, D. Pedro, "Relación," *Relaciones de Mando* (Biblioteca de historia nacional, Vol. VIII), Bogotá, 1910.

Mendoza, Diego, *El Canal interoceánico y los tradados* (Anales de jurisprudencia), Bogotá, 1901.

Negociación: Santo Domingo Vila-Trescot, Bogotá, 1881.

Nueva Granada y los Estados Unidos de América: final controversia diplomática con relación a los sucesos Panamá del dia 15 de abril de 1856, Bogotá, 1857.

Núñez, Rafael, *Colección de artículos publicados en "La Luz" de Bogotá y "El Porvenir" de Cartagena de 1881 a 1884,* Bogotá, 1885.

Orjuelo, L., *Reseña Zipaquireña* (Biblioteca de historia nacional, Vol. IV), Bogotá, 1905.

Pérez Sarmiento, José Manuel, *Manual diplomático y consular Colombiano* [5th ed.], Bogotá, 1927.

Posada, Eduardo, *El 20 de julio* (Biblioteca de historia nacional, Vol. XIII), Bogotá, 1914.

────── y Pedro M. Ibáñez, *Vida de Herrán* (Biblioteca de historia nacional, Vol. III), Bogotá, 1903.

Protesta de Colombia contra el tratado entre Panamá y los Estados Unidos, Bogotá, 1904.

Protest of Colombia against the Treaty between Panama and the United States, London, 1904.

Restrepo, Antonio José, *Al pueblo Colombiano réplica a la legación Colombiana en Wáshington: labor por la paz, cuestión canal y cuestión constitucional; peligros imaginarios; la paz; intervención personal,* Madrid, 1902.

Rivas, Raimundo, *Relaciones internacionales entre Colombia y los Estados Unidos, 1810-1850,* Bogotá, 1915.

Samper, José M., *Note sur les sociétés ou enterprises fondées à Paris pour la colonisation ou la canalisation de l'isthme du Darién,* Paris, 1862.

Suárez, [President] Marco Fidel, *Tratado entre Colombia y los Estados Unidos,* Bogotá, 1914.

Uribe, Antonio José, *Anales diplomático y consulares de Colombia,* 6 vols., Bogotá, 1900-1920.

——— *Colombia y los Estados Unidos de América: el canal interoceánico: la separación de Panamá,* Bogotá, 1926.

——— *Cuestiones internacionales, económicas, politicas, y sociales,* Bogotá, 1925.

——— *La reforma administrativa,* Bogotá, 1903.

——— *Las modificaciones al tratado entre Colombia y los Estados Unidos,* Bogotá, 1921.

Urrutia, Francisco José, *Páginas de historia diplomática; los Estados Unidos de América y las repúblicas hispano-americanas de 1810 a 1830* (Biblioteca de historia nacional, Vol. XX), Bogotá, 1917.

Vargas Jurado, J. A., *La patria boba* (Biblioteca de historia nacional, Vol. I), Bogotá, 1902.

Zubieta, Pedro A., *Apuntaciones sobre las primeras misiones diplomáticas de Colombia, 1809-1830,* Bogotá, 1924.

——— *Congresos de Panamá y Tacubaya,* Bogotá, 1912.

C. MEXICO

Correspondencia de la legación Mexicana, Vol. III.

Guzmán, Jesús, y Raz Guzmán, *Las relaciones diplomáticas de México con Sud-América* (Archivo histórico diplomático Mexicano, Num. 17), México, 1925.

Orozco, Luis Chávez, *Un esfuerzo de México por la independencia de Cuba* (Archivo histórico diplomático Mexicano, Num. 32), México, 1930.

Peña y Reyes, Antonio de la, *El congreso de Panamá y algunos otros proyectos de unión hispano-americano* (Archivo histórico diplomático Mexicano, Num. 19), México, 1926.

D. PANAMA

Boyd, Federico, *The Secession of Panama,* Panama, [1911].

Boyd, Jorge E., *Refutation of Bunau-Varilla's Book*, Panama, [1913].

Velarde, F., y F. J. Escobar, *El congreso de Panamá en 1826*, Panamá, 1922.

E. VENEZUELA

Aspurúa, Ramón, *Biografías de hombres notables de Hispano-América*, 4 vols., Caracas, 1877.

O'Leary, Simón Bolívar (ed.), *Memorias del General O'Leary*, 32 vols., Caracas, 1883-1914.

Urdaneta, Amenodoro, *Bolívar i Wáshington*, Caracas, 1865.

F. GREAT BRITAIN

British and Foreign State Papers, London, 1812—.

III. UNOFFICIAL PUBLICATIONS

A. DOCUMENTS, CORRESPONDENCE, DIARIES,
MEMOIRS, AND TRAVELS

Adams, Charles F. (ed.), *Memoirs of John Quincy Adams, Comprising Portions of His Diary from 1797 to 1848*, 12 vols., Philadelphia, 1875-1876.

—— *The Works of John Adams*, 10 vols., Boston, 1850-1856.

Antepara, José María (ed.), *South American Emancipation: Documents, Historical and Explanatory, Shewing the Designs Which Have Been in Progress, and the Exertions Made by General Miranda, for the Attainment of That Object during the Last Twenty-five Years*, London, 1810.

Archivo Santander, 22 vols., Bogotá, 1913-1925.

Bache, Captain Richard, *Notes on Colombia Taken in the Years 1822-1823*, Philadelphia, 1827.

Baker, George E. (ed.), *The Works of William H. Seward*, 4 vols., New York, 1853-1861.

Biddle, Charles John, *Comunicaciones, entre el Señor Carlos Biddle, coronel de los E[stados] Unidos del Norte, i la sociedad amigos del país*, Panamá, 1836.

Bidwell, Charles T., *The Isthmus of Panama*, London, 1865.

Biggs, James, *The History of Don Francisco de Miranda's Attempt to Effect a Revolution in South America*, London, 1809.

Bingham, Hiram, *The Journal of an Expedition across Venezuela and Colombia, 1906-7; An Exploration of Bolívar's Celebrated March of 1819 and of the Battlefields of Boyacá and Carabobo,* New Haven, 1909.

Bishop, Joseph Bucklin, *Theodore Roosevelt and His Time, Shown in His Letters,* 2 vols., New York, 1919, 1920.

Blanco, José Felix (ed.), *Documentos para la historia de la vida del Libertador de Colombia, Perú y Bolivia,* 14 vols., Caracas, 1875-1877.

Blanco-Fombona, R. (ed.), *Cartas de Bolívar* (Biblioteca Ayacucho, Vols. LIX, LXII), Madrid, 1921.

Bolívar, Simón, *Un pensamiento sobre el congreso de Panamá,* Washington, 1916.

Bonny, Catharina Van Rensselaer, *A Legacy of Historical Gleanings,* 2 vols., Albany, 1875.

Brackenridge, H. M., *Voyage to South America Performed by Order of the American Government in the Years 1817 and 1818,* 2 vols., Baltimore, 1819.

Brown, Captain C., *Narrative of the Expedition to South America Which Sailed from England in 1817, for the Service of the Spanish Patriots,* London, 1819.

Bryce, Viscount James, *South America: Observations and Impressions,* New York, 1916.

Bunau-Varilla, Philippe, *Panama; The Creation, Destruction, and Resurrection,* New York, 1914.

—— *The Great Adventure of Panama,* New York, 1920.

Carrington, J., *The Passage of the Isthmus or Practical Hints to Persons about to Cross the Isthmus of Panama,* New York, 1849.

Chesterton, George L., *A Narrative of the Proceedings in Venezuela in South America in the Years 1819 and 1820,* London, 1820.

Childs, O. W., *Report of the Survey of a Route for the Proposed Nicaragua Ship-Canal,* New York, 1852.

Cochrane, Captain Charles S., *Journal of a Residence and Travels in Colombia during the Years 1823 and 1824,* 2 vols., London, 1825.

Colombian Legation at Washington, *In Honor of the Patriot Don Manuel Torres, 1764-1822* (Being the texts of speeches delivered at the unveiling of a tablet to his memory at St. Mary's Church, Philadelphia, July 20, 1926), Washington, 1926.

Colombian State Papers, Translated and Published from Official Copies, London, 1822.

Colton, Calvin, *Life and Times of Henry Clay,* 2 vols., New York, 1846.

Comegys, J. P., *Memoir of John M. Clayton,* Wilmington, 1882.

Cullen, Dr. [Edward], *The Isthmus of Darien Ship Canal,* London, 1852.

Cullom, Shelby M., *Fifty Years of Public Service,* Chicago, 1911.

Davis, Richard Harding, *Three Gringos in Venezuela and Central America,* New York, 1896.

Depons, F., *Travels in South America during the Years 1801, 1802, 1803, and 1804,* 2 vols., London, 1807.

Duane, Colonel William, *A Visit to Colombia in the Years 1822 and 1823,* Philadelphia, 1826.

Du Bois, James T., *Ex-Minister to Colombia, James T. Du Bois, on Colombian Claims and Rights,* Halstead, Pa., 1914.

Eckermann, Johann Peter, *Gespräche mit Goethe in den letzten Jahren seines Lebens,* Vol. III, Leipzig, 1899.

Edsall, John, *Incidents in the Life of John Edsall,* Catskill, N. Y., 1831.

Eustace, John Skey, *Official and Private Correspondence of Major-General J. S. Eustace,* Paris, 1796.

Fitspatrick, J. C. (ed.), "Autobiography of Martin Van Buren," American Historical Association, *Annual Report* (1918), Vol. II., Washington, 1920.

Ford, Paul L. (ed.), *The Writings of Thomas Jefferson,* 10 vols., New York, 1895-1899.

Ford, W. C. (ed.), *The Writings of John Quincy Adams,* 7 vols., New York, 1917.

Gage, Thomas, *A New Survey of the West Indies; or, the English American, His Travel by Sea and Land,* London, 1677.

Garella, M. Napoleón, *Projet d'un canal de jonction de l'ocean Pacifique et de l'ocean Atlantique à travers l'isthme de Panamá,* Paris, 1845.

Gisborne, Lionel, *The Isthmus of Darien in 1852*, London, 1852.

Gorgorza, Anthoine de, *Tracé d'un canal interocéanique sans écluses à travers le territoire du Darién, Etats-Unis de Colombie*, Paris, [1876?].

Gosselmann, Carl A., *Reise in Columbien, in den Jahren 1825 und 1826*, 2 vols., Stockholm, 1829-1831.

Hackett, James, *Narrative of the Expedition Which Sailed from England in 1817 to Join the South American Patriots*, London, 1818.

[Hall, Francis], *Letters Written from Colombia during a Journey from Caracas to Bogotá, and thence to Santa Marta, in 1823*, London, 1824.

Hamilton, John C. (ed.), *The Works of Alexander Hamilton*, 7 vols., New York, 1850-1851.

Hamilton, Colonel J. P., *Travels through the Interior Provinces of Colombia*, 2 vols., London, 1827.

Hamilton, S. M. (ed.), *The Writings of James Monroe*, 7 vols., New York, 1898-1903.

Harrison, General W. H., *Remarks of General Harrison, Late Envoy Extraordinary and Minister Plenipotentiary of the United States to the Republic of Colombia*, Washington, 1830.

Hendrick, Burton J., *The Life and Letters of Walter Hines Page*, 3 vols., Garden City, 1925.

Hippisley, G., *A Narrative of the Expedition to the Rivers Orinoco and Apure, in South America; Which Sailed from England in November, 1817, and Joined the Patriotic Forces in Venezuela and Caracas*, London, 1819.

Hughes, George W., *Letter in Answer to the Hon. John M. Clayton on Inter-Marine Communications*, Washington, 1850.

Hunt, Gaillard (ed.), *The Writings of James Madison*, 8 vols., New York, 1908.

Kelley, Frederick M., *On the Junction of the Atlantic and Pacific Oceans and the Practicability of a Ship-Canal without Locks by the Valley of the Atrato*, London, 1856.

———— *The Union of the Oceans by Ship-Canal without Locks, via the Atrato Valley*, New York, 1859.

King, Charles R. (ed.), *The Life and Correspondence of Rufus King*, 6 vols., New York, 1894-1900.

Letters from Theodore Roosevelt to Anna Roosevelt Cowles,
1870-1918, New York, 1924.

Liot, W. B., *Panama, Nicaragua and Tehuantepec,* London, 1849.

Lloyd, John A., *An Account of Levellings across the Isthmus of*
Panama, London, 1830.

Lodge, Henry Cabot (ed.), *Works of Alexander Hamilton,* 9
vols., New York, 1885, 1886.

Manning, William R. (ed.), *Diplomatic Correspondence of the*
United States Concerning the Independence of the Latin
American Republics, 3 vols., New York, 1925.

[Memorial edition], *The Writings of Thomas Jefferson,* 19 vols.,
Washington, 1904.

Mollien, G., *Travels in the Republic of Colombia in the Years*
1822 and 1823, London, 1824.

Moore, John Bassett (ed.), *The Works of James Buchanan,* 12
vols., Philadelphia, 1908-1911.

Morillo y Morillo, Pablo, *Mémoires du Général Morillo,* Paris,
1826.

Morse, J. T., Jr. (ed.), *Diary of Gideon Welles,* 3 vols., Boston,
1911.

Nelson, Wolford, *Five Years at Panama,* New York, 1889.

New Granada Canal and Steam Navigation Company, *Remarks*
on the Canal or "Dique" of Cartagena, New Granada,
and Its Navigation by Steam, New York, 1855.

Nicolay, John George, and John Hay, *Abraham Lincoln,* Vol.
VI, New York, 1917.

Nieto, Máximo A., *Recuerdos de la regeneración,* Bogotá, 1924.

Páez, José Antonio, *Autobiografía del General José Antonio*
Páez, 2 vols., New York, 1878.

———— *Memorias de General José Antonio Páez* (Biblioteca
Ayacucho, Vol. IV), Madrid, [1916?].

Panama Canal: A Collection of French and Dutch Newspapers
Published in 1879 Containing Articles on the Panama
Canal (Library of Congress).

The Panama Massacre: A Collection of Principal Evidence and
Other Documents Including the Report of Amos W. Cor-
wine, Esq., U. S. Commissioner, the Official Statement of
the Governor and Depositions Taken before the Author-
ities, Relative to the Massacre of American Citizens at the

Panama Railroad, Station on the 15th of April, 1856,
Panama, 1857.

Pombo, M. de (tr.), *Constitución de los Estados Unidos de América. Según se propuso por la convención tenida en Filadelfia el 17 le septiembre de 1787; y ratificada después por los diferentes estados: con las últimas adiciones. Precedida de las actas de independencia y federación traducidas del Inglés al Español por el cuidadano Miguel Pombo, e illustrados por el mismo con notas, y un discurso preliminar sobre el sistema federativo,* Bogotá, 1811.

Pombo, Manuel Antonio y José Joaquín Guerra (eds.), *Constituciones de Colombia,* 2 vols., Bogotá, [n.d.].

Poore, Benjamin P., *Reminiscences of Sixty Years in the National Metropolis,* Vol. II, Philadelphia, 1886.

Porter, Kirk A. (comp.), *National Party Platforms,* New York, 1924.

Quaife, Milo Milton (ed.), *The Diary of James K. Polk,* 4 vols., Chicago, 1910.

Rafter, M., *Memoirs of Gregor McGregor,* London, 1820.

Recollections of a Service of Three Years during the War-of-Extermination in the Republics of Venezuela and Colombia by an Officer of the Colombian Navy, 2 vols., London, 1828.

Report of the Honorable John Bigelow, Delegated by the Chamber of Commerce of New York to Assist at the Inspection of the Panama Canal in February, 1886, New York, 1886.

Restrepo, Antonio José, *Al pueblo Colombiano; réplica á la legación Colombiana en Wáshington. . . ,* Madrid, 1902.

Robertson, William Spence (ed.), *The Diary of Francisco de Miranda: Tour of the United States, 1783-1784,* New York, 1928.

Robinson, Tracy, *Panama: A Personal Narrative of Forty-Six Years, 1861-1907,* New York and Panama, 1907.

Roosevelt, Theodore, *An Autobiography,* New York, 1913.

────── *Fear God and Take Your Own Part,* New York, [1916].

Root, Elihu, *Addresses on International Subjects* (ed. Robert Bacon and James Scott Brown), Cambridge, 1916.

Rowland, Dunbar (ed.), *Jefferson Davis; Constitutionalist: His Letters, Papers, and Speeches,* Vol. III, Jackson, Miss., 1923.

Rush, Richard, *Memoranda of a Residence at the Court of London, Comprising Incidents Official and Personal from 1819 to 1825*, Philadelphia, 1845.

Sawvel, F. B. (ed.), *The Complete Anas of Thomas Jefferson*, New York, 1903.

Selections from the Correspondence of Theodore Roosevelt to Henry Cabot Lodge, 1884-1918, 2 vols., New York, 1925.

Sherman, John A., *A General Account of Miranda's Expedition, Including the Trial and Execution of Ten of His Officers*, New York, 1808.

Smith, Moses, *History of the Adventures and Sufferings of Moses Smith during Five Years of His Life: From the Beginning of the Year 1806, When He Was Betrayed into the Miranda Expedition, until June 1811, When He Was Nonsuited in an Action at Law*, Brooklyn, 1812.

La sociedad de los amigos del país (ed.), *Documentas importantes sobre la apertura de un canal fluvial entre océanos Atlántico y Pacífico por el istmo de Panamá*, Panamá, 1835.

Sparks, E. E. (ed.), "The Diary and Letters of Henry Ingersoll, Prisoner at Cartagena, 1806-9," *American Historical Review*, III, 674-702.

Squier, E. G., *Nicaragua . . . and the Proposed Inter-Oceanic Canal*, New York, 1852.

——— *Notes on Central America . . . and the Proposed Honduras Interoceanic Railway*, New York, 1855.

Stephens, J. L., *Incidents of Travel in Central America*, 2 vols., New York, 1852.

Steuart, J., *Bogotá in 1836-7, Being a Narrative of an Expedition to the Capital of New Granada and a Residence There of Eleven Months*, New York, 1838.

Stevenson, W. B., *A Historical and Descriptive Narrative of Twenty Years in South America*, 3 vols., London, 1825.

Strauss, Oscar S., *Under Four Administrations*, New York, 1922.

Strain, I. C., *A Paper on the History and Prospects of Interoceanic Communication by the American Isthmus*, New York, 1856.

Suárez, Federico González (ed.), *Escritos del Doctor Francisco Javier Eugenio Santa Cruz y Espejo* (cited in Gonzalo Bulnes, *Nacimiento de las repúblicas Americanas*, I, 78)

Sullivan, G. H. and W. N. Cromwell (ed.), *Compilation of Executive Documents and Diplomatic Correspondence relative to a Trans-Isthmian Canal in Central America*, 3 vols., New York, 1903.

Thayer, William Roscoe, *The Life and Letters of John Hay*, 2 vols., New York, 1915.

Thomson, James, *Letters on the Moral and Religious State of South America, Written during a Residence of Nearly Seven Years in Buenos Aires, Chile, Peru, and Colombia*, London, 1827.

Vane, Charles W. (ed.), *Correspondence, Despatches, and Other Papers of Viscount Castlereagh*, 12 vols., London, 1850-1853.

Washington, H. A. (ed.), *The Writings of Thomas Jefferson*, 9 vols., Washington, 1856.

Weatherford, W. D., *An Account of the Late Expedition against the Isthmus of Darién under the Command of Sir Gregor McGregor*, London, 1821.

Wharton, Francis, *A Digest of the International Law of the United States*, 2 vols., Washington, 1888.

Wheelright, William, *Observations on the Isthmus of Panama*, London, 1844.

Williams, Charles R. (ed.), *Diary and Letters of Rutherford Birchard Hayes*, 5 vols., Columbus, Ohio, 1922-1926.

B. OTHER BOOKS AND PAMPHLETS

Abbot, Brigadier-General Henry L., *Problems of the Panama Canal*, New York, 1907.

Abert, S. T., *Is a Ship Canal Practicable?* Cincinnati, 1870.

Acosta, Joaquín, *Compendio histórico del descumbrimiento y colonización de la Nueva Granada en el siglo décimo sexto*, Paris, 1848.

Adams, Ephriam D., *British Interest and Activities in Texas, 1838-1846*, Baltimore, 1910.

Aldana, Abelardo, *The Panama Canal Question: A Plea for Colombia*, Cardiff, 1903.

Álvarez, Alejandro, *The Monroe Doctrine: Its Importance in the International Life of the States of the New World*, New York, 1924.

Ammen, Daniel, *The American Interoceanic Ship Canal Question*, Philadelphia, 1880.

—— *The Errors and Fallacies of the Interoceanic Canal Question*, New York, 1886.

Angell, Hildegarde, *Simón Bolívar: South American Liberator*, New York, 1930.

Appeal to the Government and People of the United States, in Behalf of the Independent American Provinces (dedicated to Henry Clay), New York, 1818.

Appleton's Cyclopaedia of American Biography, 6 vols., New York, 1888.

Arboleda, G., *Historia contemporánea de Colombia*, 2 vols., Bogotá, 1918.

Arias, Harmodio, *The Panama Canal: A Study in International Law and Diplomacy*, London, 1911.

Arosemena, Justo, *Examen sobre la franca comunicación entre los dos océanos*, Bogotá, 1846.

Babson, Roger W., *The Future of South America*, Boston, 1915.

Bancroft, Hubert H., *The New Pacific*, New York, 1913.

Baralt, R. M., y R. Díaz, *Resumen de la historia de Venezuela*, 2 vols., Paris, 1841.

Bartholomew, Walter H., *Colombia, Its Resources and Potentialities*, New York, 1921.

—— *The Colombian Treaty*, New York, 1921.

Becerra, Ricardo, *Vida de Don Francisco de Miranda* (Biblioteca Ayacucho, Vols. XXII, XXIII), Madrid, [1916?].

Belly, M. Felix, *Canal intérocéanique de Nicaragua*, Paris, 1869.

Bemis, Samuel F., *Jay's Treaty: A Study in Commerce and Diplomacy*, New York, 1923.

—— (ed.), *American Secretaries of State and Their Diplomacy*, 10 vols., New York, 1927-1929.

Beveridge, Albert J., *The Life of John Marshall*, 4 vols., Boston, 1916-1919.

Biblioteca Ayacucho, 63 vols., Madrid, [n.d.].

Bidwell, Charles T., *The Isthmus of Panama*, London, 1865.

Bigelow, John, *Breaches of Anglo-American Treaties*, New York, 1917.

Bionne, M. Henry, *La question du percement de l'isthme de Panama devant un congrès international*, Paris, 1864.

Borda, José Joaquín, *Historia de la compañía de Jesús en la Nueva Granada*, 2 vols., Poissy, 1872.

Bourne, E. G., *Spain in America*, New York, 1906.

Bowers, Claude G., *Party Battles of the Jackson Period*, New York, 1922.

Briceño, Manuel, *Los comuneros; historia de la insurrección de 1781*, Bogotá, 1880.

Bruce, H. Addington, *The Romance of Expansion*, New York, 1909.

Bulnes, Gonzalo, *Nacimiento de las repúblicas Americanas*, 2 vols., Buenos Aires, 1927.

Burke, William, *South American Independence; or the Emancipation of South America, the Glory and Interest of England*, London, 1807.

—————— *Additional Reasons for Our Immediately Emancipating Spanish America*, London, 1808.

Burton, Theodore E., "Henry Clay," *American Secretaries of State and Their Diplomacy*, Vol. IV, New York, 1928.

Butte, George C., *Great Britain and the Panama Canal*, Heidelberg, 1913.

Callahan, James Morton, *Cuba and International Relations*, Baltimore, 1899.

Carr, I. N., "The United States Indemnifies Colombia" (Unpublished paper, Duke University).

Castellanos, Juan de, *Historia del nuevo reino de Granada*, 2 vols., Madrid, 1886-1887.

Centenario de la Universidad de Antioquia, 1822-1922, Medellín, 1922.

Chadwick, French Ensor, *The Relations of the United States and Spain*, New York, 1909.

Chapman, Charles E., *A History of Spain*, New York, 1927.

—————— *Colonial Hispanic America*, New York, 1933.

Chandler, Charles Lyon, *Inter-American Acquaintances*, Sewanee, Tenn., 1917.

Clarke, Francis E., *The Continent of Opportunity*, New York, 1907.

Condor, Josiah, *Colombia*, London, 1825.

Cooper, Clayton Sedgwick, *Understanding South America*, New York, 1918.

Cortissoz, Royal, *The Life of Whitelaw Reid*, 2 vols., New York, 1921.

Crichfield, George W., *American Supremacy*, 2 vols., New York, 1908.

Croly, Herbert, *Marcus Alonzo Hanna*, New York, 1912.

Crowther, Samuel, *The Romance and Rise of the American Tropics*, New York, 1929.

Curtis, W. J., *The History of the Purchase by the United States of the Panama Canal; The Manner of the Payment; and the Distribution of the Proceeds of Sale*, [Birmingham, Ala., 1909].

Dawson, Thomas C., *The South American Republics*, 2 vols., New York, 1904.

Denny, Ludwell, *We Fight for Oil*, New York, 1928.

Deschanel, Paul Eugène Louis, *La politique Française en océanie à propos du canal de Panama*, Paris, 1884.

Dewey, D. R., *Financial History of the United States*, New York, 1928.

Díaz, José Domingo, *Recuerdos sobre la rebelión de Caracas*, Madrid, 1829.

Duniway, C. A., "Daniel Webster," *American Secretaries of State and Their Diplomacy*, Vol. VI, New York, 1928.

Eckenrode, H. J., *Rutherford B. Hayes: Statesman of Reunion*, New York, 1930.

Eder, Phanor J., *Colombia*, London, 1913.

Enciclopedia universal ilustrada Europeo-Americana, Vol. LXII, Madrid, 1928.

Encyclopaedia Britannica, 14th ed., London, 1929.

Flinter, Major [George Dawson], *A History of the Revolution of Caracas*, London, 1819.

Freehoff, J. C., *America and the Canal Title*, New York, 1916.

Fuess, Claude M., *The Life of Caleb Cushing*, 2 vols., New York, 1923.

Fuller, Joseph B., "Hamilton Fish," *American Secretaries of State and Their Diplomacy*, Vol. VII, New York, 1928.

Galindo, Anibal, *El tratado de 14 de enero de 1869 para la escavación del canal de Darién*, Bogotá, 1869.

García Calderón, F., *Latin America: Its Rise and Progress*, London, 1919.

García de Sena, Manuel, *Historia concisa de los Estados Unidos desde, el descubrimiento de la América hasta el año de 1807,* Philadelphia, 1812.

———— (trans.), *La independencia de la costa firma justificada por Thomas Paine trienta años há: extracto de sus obras traducido del inglés al español,* Philadelphia, 1811.

Gil Fortoul, J., *Historia constitucional de Venezuela,* 2 vols., Berlin, 1907-1909.

Goebel, Dorothy B., *William Henry Harrison* (Indiana Historical Collection, Vol. XLV), Indianapolis, 1926.

Goebel, Julius, Jr., *The Recognition Policy of the United States* (Columbia University Studies in History, Economics, and Public Law, Vol. LXVI), New York, 1915.

Gonzáles Chaves, Nicolás, *Estudio cronológico de la guerra de la independencia en la antigua Colombia,* Paris, 1879.

González Valencia, José María, *Refutation of Misstatements and Erroneous Conceptions of Mr. Roosevelt in His Article entitled "The Panama Blackmail Treaty,"* Washington, 1916.

———— *Separation of Panama from Colombia,* Washington, 1916.

Goodwin, J. M., *The Panama Ship Canal and Interoceanic Ship Railway,* Cleveland, [1880].

Groot, José Manuel, *Historia eclesiástica y civil Nueva Granada,* 5 vols., Bogotá, 1889-1893.

Grotius, [Benjamin Johnson Darneille], *A Review of the Monroe Doctrine and the American Theory of the Panama Canal,* Washington, 1882.

Hall, Colonel Francis, *Colombia: Its Present State,* Philadelphia, 1825.

Haring, C. H., *Trade and Navigation between Spain and the Indies,* Cambridge, 1918.

Hart, Albert Bushnell, *The Monroe Doctrine; An Interpretation,* Boston, 1916.

Hasbrouck, Alfred, *Foreign Legionaries in the Liberation of Spanish America,* New York, 1928.

Henao, Jesús, y Gerardo Arrubla, *Historia de Colombia,* Bogotá, 1926.

Henderson, John B., *American Diplomatic Questions,* New York, 1901.

Hervey, John G., *The Legal Aspects of Recognition in International Law as Interpreted by the Courts of the United States,* Philadelphia, 1928.

Hildt, J. C., *Early Diplomatic Negotiations of the United States with Russia* (Johns Hopkins University Studies, Vol. XXIV), Baltimore, 1906.

Hill, Charles E., "James Madison," *American Secretaries of State and Their Diplomacy,* Vol. III, New York, 1927.

────── *Leading American Treaties,* New York, 1922.

Hill, Howard C., *Roosevelt and the Caribbean,* Chicago, 1927.

Huberich, Charles H., *The Trans-Isthmian Canal: A Study in American Diplomatic History, 1825-1904,* Austin, Texas, 1904.

Humbert, Jules, *L'occupation allemande du Vénézuéla au xvi siècle, période dite des Welser, 1528-1566,* Paris, 1905.

Humboldt, Alexandre de, *Essai politique sur le royaume de la Nouvelle-Espagne,* 2 vols., Paris, 1811.

Hutchinson, Lincoln, *The Panama Canal and International Trade Competition,* New York, 1915.

Ise, John, *The United States Oil Policy,* New Haven, 1926.

"I Took the Isthmus": Ex-President Roosevelt's Confession, Colombia's Protest and Editorial Comment on "How the United States Acquired the Right to Dig the Panama Canal," New York, 1911.

Jackson, B. Franklin (ed.), *A Brief Description of the Facilities and Advantages Which a Road across Central America from Chiriquí Lagoon or Admiral's Bay, on the Atlantic to Chiriquí Bay, on the Pacific Would Afford to the Commerce of the World,* Philadelphia, 1852.

James, Herman G., and Percy A. Martin, *The Republics of Latin America,* New York, 1923.

Johnson, Willis Fletcher, *Four Centuries of the Panama Canal,* New York, 1906.

Johnston, W. E., *The True History of the Panama Canal Scheme,* Paris, 1884.

Jones, Chester Lloyd, *Caribbean Backgrounds and Prospects,* New York, 1931.

Keasbey, Lindley M., *The Terms and Tenor of the Clayton-Bulwer Treaty,* Philadelphia, 1899.

Koebel, W. H., *British Exploits in South America*, New York, 1917.

Lallèment, G. N., *Histoire de la Colombie*, Paris, 1826.

Latané, John H., *The United States and Latin America*, Garden City, N. Y., 1921.

Lea, H. C., *The Inquisition in Spanish Dependencies, Sicily - Naples - Sardinia - Milan - the Canaries - Mexico - Peru - New Granada*, New York, 1922.

Lemly, Henry Rowan, *Bolívar: Liberator of Venezuela, Colombia, Ecuador, Peru, and Bolivia*, Boston, 1923.

Lindsay, Forbes, *Panama and, the Canal Today*, Boston, 1926.

Lockey, Joseph Byrne, *Pan-Americanism: Its Beginnings*, New York, 1920.

McCaleb, Walter F., *The Aaron Burr Conspiracy*, New York, 1903.

McCormac, Eugene I., *James K. Polk: A Political Biography*, Berkeley, Calif., 1922.

MacGeachy, Charles Edward A., *Who Started the Panama Canal and Its Railroad?* New York, 1915.

McFee, William, *Sunlight in New Granada*, New York, 1923.

McGregor, Rob Roy, "The Treaty of 1846: Seventeen Years of American-Colombian Relations, 1830-1846" (Doctoral dissertation, Clark University, 1928).

Malin, James C., *The United States after the World War*, New York, 1930.

Mancini, Jules, *Bolívar y la emancipación de las colonias españolas desde los orígenes hasta 1815*, Paris, 1923.

Manning, William R., *Early Diplomatic Relations between the United States and Mexico*, Baltimore, 1916.

Manson, N. J., *The Nicaragua Canal; Corporate Construction and Control against the Policy and Business Interests of the United States*, San Francisco, 1892.

Markham, Sir Clements, *The Conquest of New Granada*, London, 1912.

Martin, Charles E., *The Policy of the United States as regards Intervention* (Columbia University Studies in History, Economics, and Public Law, Vol. XCIII), New York, 1921.

Mateus, F. de P., *La victoria de los demócratos, lo que significa para Colombia*, Bogotá, 1913.

Medina, José Toribio, *La imprenta en Bogotá, 1739-1821,* Santiago de Chile, 1904.

——— *La imprenta en Caracas, 1808-1821,* Santiago de Chile, 1904.

——— *Historia del Tribunal del Santo Oficio de la Inquisición de Cartagena de las Indias,* Santiago de Chile, 1899.

Miller, Hugh Gordon, *The Isthmian Highway,* New York, 1929.

Mitre, Bartolomé, *Historia de San Martín y de la emancipación Sud-Americana,* 4 vols., Paris, 1890.

Mohr, Anton, *The Oil War,* New York, [1926].

Monteagudo, Bernardo, *Ensayo sobre la necesidad de una federación jeneral entre los Estados Hispano-Americanos, y plan de su organización,* Lima, 1825.

Morey, William C., *International Right of Way,* Rochester, N. Y., 1903.

Moses, Bernard, *Spain's Declining Power in South America,* Berkeley, Calif., 1919.

——— *Spanish America on the Eve of Emancipation,* New York, 1908.

——— *The Spanish Dependencies in South America,* 2 vols., New York, 1914.

Mosquera, Tomás C., *Memoir on the Physical and Political Geography of New Granada,* New York, 1853.

Mowat, R. B., *The Diplomatic Relations of Great Britain and the United States,* London, 1925.

Mulhall, M. G., *The English in South America,* Buenos Aires, 1878.

Nathaniel Niles' Plan for the Construction of a Ship Canal between the Atlantic and Pacific Oceans, New York, 1868.

Nietq Caballero, Luis E., *El dolor de Colombia,* Bogotá, 1922.

Niles, John M., *History of South America and Mexico,* 2 vols., Hartford, Conn., 1838.

Nimmo, Joseph, Jr., *The Proposed American Interoceanic Canal in Its Commercial Aspects,* Washington, 1880.

Nourse, J. E., *The Maritime Canal of Suez; and Comparison of Its Probable Results with Those of a Ship Canal across Darién,* Washington, 1869.

Offutt, Milton, *The Protection of Citizens abroad by the Armed Forces of the United States* (Johns Hopkins University

Studies in Historical and Political Science, Vol. XLVI, Baltimore, 1928.

O'Leary, Daniel F., *Bolívar y la emancipación de Sur-América*, Madrid, 1916.

Otero, Luis A., *Panamá*, Bogotá, 1926.

[Palacio Fajardo, Manuel], *Outline of the Revolution in Spanish America*, London, 1817.

Panama Railroad Company (a prospectus), New York, 1849.

Parra-Pérez, C., *Bolívar; contribución al estudio de sus ideas políticas*, Paris, 1928.

Paxson, Frederic L., *The Independence of the South American Republics: A Study in Recognition and Foreign Policy*, Philadelphia, 1916.

Peacock, George, *Notes on the Isthmus of Panama and Darién*, Exeter, 1879.

Peck, Annie S., *Industrial and Commercial South America*, New York, 1927.

Pereyra, Carlos, *Bolívar y Wáshington: un paralelo imposible*, Madrid, 1915.

——— *El mito de Monroe*, Madrid, [1914].

Perkins, Dexter, *The Monroe Doctrine* (Harvard Historical Studies, Vol. XXIX), Cambridge, 1927.

——— "John Quincy Adams," *American Secretaries of State and Their Diplomacy*, Vol. IV, New York, 1928.

Pezet, Federico Alfonso, *Contrast in the Development of Nationality in Anglo-America and Latin America*, Washington, 1916.

Pilling, William, *The Emancipation of South America* (condensed translation of Bartolomé Mitre, *Historia de San Martín*), London, 1893.

Pim, Bedford, *The Gate of the Pacific*, London, 1863.

Pinckney, the Rev. Charles C., *Life of General Thomas Pinckney*, Boston, 1895.

Pitman, Robert Birks, *A Succinct View and Analysis of Authentic Information Extant in Original Works, on the Practicability of Joining the Atlantic and Pacific Oceans, by a Ship Canal across the Isthmus of America*, London, 1825.

The Practicability and Importance of a Ship Canal to Connect the Atlantic and Pacific Oceans, with a History of the Enterprise from Its First Inception to the Completion of the Surveys, New York, 1855.

Pratt, Julius W., *The Expansionists of 1812*, New York, 1925.

Proceedings of a Meeting Held under the Auspices of the American Association of China to Consider the Question of an Isthmian Canal, Shanghai, 1899.

Radcliff, William, *Considerations on the Subject of a Communication between the Atlantic and Pacific Oceans, by Means of a Ship-Canal across the Isthmus, Which Connects North and South America; The Best Means of Effecting It, and Permanently Securing Its Benefits for the World at Large, by Means of a Coöperation between Individuals and Companies of Different Nations under the Patronage of Their Respective Governments*, Georgetown, D. C., 1836.

Rattenbury, J. Freeman, *Cession of Florida to the United States and the Necessity of Acquiring the Island of Cuba by Great Britain* (pamphlet), London, 1819.

Rebolledo, Alvaro, *Reseña histórico-político de la comunicación inter-oceánica, con especial referencia a la seperación de Panamá y a los arreglos entre los Estados Unidos y Colombia*, San Francisco, 1930.

The Recognition, the Loan and Colonization of Colombia (published by Baldwin, Craddock and Joy), London, 1822.

Reinach, Paul S., "Some Notes on the Study of South American History," *Turner Lectures in American History*, New York, 1910.

Restrepo, José Manuel, *Historia de la revolución de la república de Colombia en la América meridional*, 4 vols., Besanzon, 1858.

Restrepo, Juan Pablo, *La iglesia y el estado en Colombia*, London, 1885.

Reyes, Rafael, *The Two Americas*, New York, 1914.

Rhodes, James Ford, *The McKinley and Roosevelt Administrations*, New York, 1923.

Rippy, J. Fred, *The Capitalists and Colombia*, New York, 1931.

―――― *Latin America in World Politics*, New York, 1928.

—— *Rivalry of the United States and Great Britain over Latin America, 1808-1830,* Baltimore, 1929.

—— and Angie Debo, *The Historical Background of the American Policy of Isolation* (Smith College Studies in History, Vol. IX, Nos. 3, 4), Northampton, Mass., 1924.

Rivas, Angel César, *Ensayos de historia política y diplomática,* Madrid, 1916.

Rivera, Rodolfo Osvaldo, "Education in Colombia: Its Historical Development and Present Status" (Thesis, Duke University), Durham, 1930.

Robertson, William Spence, *Hispanic-American Relations with the United States,* New York, 1923.

—— *The Life of Miranda,* 2 vols., Chapel Hill, N. C., 1929.

—— *The Rise of the Spanish-American Republics as Told in the Lives of Their Liberators,* New York, 1918.

Robinson, W. D., *A Cursory View of Spanish America, particularly the Neighbouring Vice-Royalties of Mexico and New Granada, Chiefly Intended to Elucidate the Policy of an Early Connection between the United States and Those Countries,* Georgetown, D. C., 1815.

Rocafuerta, Vicente, *El sistema Colombiano, popular, electivo, y representativo, es el que más conviene á la América independiente,* New York, 1823.

Rodriques, José Carlos, *The Panama Canal: Its History, Its Political Aspects, and Financial Difficulties,* London, 1885.

Rojas, José María, *El General Miranda,* Paris, 1884.

Roldán, Salvador, *Relaciones comerciales entre los Estados Unidos de América i los Estados Unidos de Colombia,* Bogotá, 1870.

Roof, K. M., *Colonel William Smith and Lady,* Boston, 1929.

The Roosevelt Panama Libel Case against the New York World and Indianapolis News, New York, 1910.

Rutter, F. R., *South American Trade of Baltimore* (Johns Hopkins University Studies, Vol. XV, No. 9), Baltimore, 1897.

Salazar, José María, *Observations on the Political Reforms of Colombia,* Philadelphia, 1828.

Schurz, Carl, *Henry Clay,* 2 vols., Boston, 1896.

Scott, William R., *The Americans in Panama,* New York, 1912.

Scroggs, William O., *Filibusters and Financiers: The Story of William Walker and His Associates*, New York, 1916.

Scruggs, William L., *The Colombian and Venezuelan Republics*, Boston, 1900.

Sears, Louis Martin, *A History of American Foreign Relations*, New York, 1927.

Semple, Robert, *Sketch of the Present State of Caracas*, London, 1812.

Separation of Panama from Colombia: Reply to an Article Entitled "The Panama Blackmail Treaty," Published in the February Number of "The Metropolitan," 1915, Washington, 1916.

Shepherd, William R., *The Hispanic Nations of the New World: A Chronicle of Our Southern Neighbors*, New Haven, 1921.

Sherwell, G. A., *Antonio José de Sucre*, Washington, 1924.

Smith, John Lawrence, *Interoceanic Canal; Practicability of the Different Routes, and Questionable Nature of the Interest of the United States in a Canal*, Louisville, Ky., 1880.

Stephens, H. Morse and Herbert E. Bolton (ed.), *The Pacific Ocean in History* (Papers and addresses presented at the Panama-Pacific Historical Congress, San Francisco, Berkeley, and Palo Alto, Calif., July 19-23, 1915), New York, 1917.

Stephenson, Nathaniel W., *Nelson W. Aldrich: A Leader in American Politics*, New York, 1930.

Storey, Moorfield, *The Recognition of Panama*, Boston, 1904.

Stuart, Graham H., *Latin America and the United States*, New York, 1922.

Sullivan, Ward W., *A Study in the Relations between Colombia and the United States, 1900-1924* (Abstract of a doctoral thesis), Urbana, Ill., 1926.

Taussig, F. W., *The Tariff History of the United States*, New York, 1923.

Temperley, Harold W. V., *The Foreign Policy of Canning, 1822-1827*, London, 1925.

Thomas, David Y., *One Hundred Years of the Monroe Doctrine*, New York, 1923.

Thompson, Norman, *Colombia and the United States: A Judicial Study of Another "Scrap of Paper" and Its Supersession by the Colombian Indemnity Treaty for the Settlement of the Panama Question*, London, 1915.

Thompson, R. W., *The Interoceanic Canal at Panama: Its Political Aspects: The Monroe Doctrine*, Washington, 1881.

Travis, Ira D., *The History of the Clayton-Bulwer Treaty*, Ann Arbor, Mich., 1900.

Tyler, Alice F., *The Foreign Policy of James G. Blaine*, Minneapolis, 1927.

Uribe Echeverri, Carlos, *Colombia y los Estados Unidos*, Bogotá, 1921.

Urrutia, Francisco José, *El ideal internacional de Bolívar*, Quito, 1911.

Usher, Roland G., *Pan-Americanism*, New York, 1915.

Valdés, Ramón, *The Independence of the Isthmus of Panama, Its Antecedents, Its Causes, and Its Justification*, Panama, 1903.

Veatch, A. C., *Quito to Bogotá*, London, 1917.

Vejarano, Jorge Ricardo, *Orígenes de la independencia sudamericana*, Bogotá, 1905.

Vergara y Vergara, José María, *Historia de la literatura en Nueva Granada* (2nd ed.), Bogotá, 1905.

Verrill, A. Hyatt, *Panama, Past and Present*, New York, 1921.

[Vizcardo y Guzmán, Juan Pablo], *Lettres aux Espagnols-Americains*, Philadelphia, 1799.

Vicuña Mackenna, B., *El Wáshington del Sur; . . . Antonio José de Sucre*, Madrid, [1918?].

Villanueva, Carlos A., *El imperio de los Andes* (*La monarquía en América*, Vol. IV), Paris, [n.d.].

———— *Napoleón y la independencia de América*, París, [1912].

Walker, Alexander, *Colombia*, 2 vols., London, 1822.

Walton, William, *An Exposé of the Dissentions of Spanish America, Intended as a Means to Induce Mediatory Interference of Great Britain. . .* , London, 1814.

Warden, William W., and Charles A. Eldridge, *The Chiriquí and Golfito Naval Stations Matter*, Washington, 1882.

Webster, C. K., *The Foreign Policy of Castlereagh, 1815-1822*, London, 1925.

White, Elizabeth B., *American Opinion of France from La-fayette to Poincaré,* New York, 1927.

Williams, Alfred, *The Inter-Oceanic Canal and the Monroe Doctrine,* New York, [1880?].

Williams, Charles R., *The Life of Rutherford Birchard Hayes,* 2 vols., New York, 1914.

Williams, J. J., *The Isthmus of Tehuantepec,* New York, 1852.

Williams, Mary Wilhelmine, *Anglo-American Isthmian Diplomacy, 1815-1915,* Washington, 1916.

—— *The People and Politics of Latin America,* Boston, 1930.

Willson, Beckles, *America's Ambassadors to England, 1785-1929: A Narrative of Anglo-American Relations,* New York, 1929.

Wright, Benjamin C., *San Francisco's Ocean Trade, Past and Future,* San Francisco, 1911.

Yánes, Francisco J., *A Glance at Latin American Civilization* (pamphlet), Washington, 1924.

Ybarra, T. R., *Bolívar: The Passionate Warrior,* New York, 1929.

[Zea, Antonio], *Colombia, Being a Geographical, Statistical, Agricultural, Commercial, and Political Account of That Country, Adapted for the General Reader, the Merchant, and Colonist,* 2 vols., London, 1822.

IV. NEWSPAPERS AND PERIODICALS

Abbot, Henry L., "International Aspects of the Isthmian Canal," *Engineering Magazine,* XXII, 485-492.

Alexander, Thomas S., "Colombia, the Government, the Country and the People," *World's Work,* VII, 4336 ff.

*American Geographical Society, Transactions.**

American Historical Association, *Annual Report,* 1894—.

American Historical Review, New York, 1895-.

American Journal of International Law, Washington, 1907—.

American Political Science Review, Baltimore, 1907—.

American Society of Civil Engineers, *Transactions,* New York, 1872-1921.

Los amigos del país, Panamá, 1835.**

Ammen, Daniel, "American Isthmian Canal Routes," *Journal of Franklin Institute,* Dec., 1889.

―――"M. De Lesseps and His Canal," *North American Review*, CXXX, 130-141.

Andara, J. L., "The Bolívar Doctrine," *Inter-America*, IV, 40-46.

Annals of American Academy of Political and Social Science, Philadelphia, 1890―.

Arias, Harmodio, "The International Policy of Bolívar," *Inter-America*, II, 7-13.

Aurora, Philadelphia, 1822.*

Barrett, John, "The United States and Latin America," *North American Review*, CLXXXIII, 474 ff.

Becerra, Ricardo, "The Republic of Colombia," *Harper's Monthly*, LXXIX, 920ff.

Bishop, Joseph B., "Our Government's Course in Panama," *International Quarterly*, IX, 247 ff.

Borse, Max, "Colombia's Oil," *Chile Pan-Am.* (1931), XI, 7.

Brown, L. Ames, "À New Era of Good Feeling," *Atlantic Monthly* (1915), CXV, 99.

Bulletin of the Pan American Union, Washington, 1893―.

Burt, George A., "A Comparison of the Isthmian Canal Projects," *Engineering Magazine*, XIX, 19-26.

La caridad, Bogotá, 1869-1870, Vol. V.

Chamberlain, George Agnew, "The Cause of South American Revolutions," *Atlantic Monthly*, XCV, 822 ff.

Chamberlain, Leander T., "A Chapter of National Dishonor," *North American Review*, CXCV, 145 ff.

Chandler, Charles Lyon, "United States Commerce with Latin America at the Promulgation of the Monroe Doctrine," *Quarterly Journal of Economics*, XXXVIII, 466-486.

*Chile Pan-Am.**

La civilización, Bogotá, 1849.*

Cleven, Andrew N., "Some Plans for Colonizing Liberated Slaves in Hispanic America," *The Southwestern Political and Social Science Quarterly*, VI, 151-166.

Collins, Frederick, "The Isthmus of Darién and the Valley of the Atrato Considered with Reference to the Practicability of an Interoceanic Ship-Canal," *Transactions of the American Geographical Society*, V, 138-165.

Colné, Charles, "The Panama Interoceanic Canal," *Journal of Franklin Institute*, Nov., 1884.

"Colombia y los Estados Unidos," *Boletín de historia y antigüedades*, XIII, 513-645.

El colombiano, Caracas, 1824.*

Comercio-libre, Panamá, 1833.*

El continental, New York.*

Correo del Orinoco, Caracas, 1820.*

Cox, Isaac J., "Yankee Imperialism and Spanish American Solidarity: A Colombian Interpretation," *The Hispanic American Historical Review*, IV, 256-265.

Craven, W. F., Jr., "The Risk of the Monroe Doctrine," *The Hispanic American Historical Review*, VII, 320-333.

Crónica, New York.*

Crowninshield, A. S., "The Dream of Navigators," *North American Review*, Dec., 1897.

Current History, New York, 1915—.

Current Opinion, New York, 1888-1925.

De Bow's Review, New Orleans, 1846-1880.

Dennis, Lawrence, "Colombia and the State Department," *The New Republic* (1932), LXX, 75.

Deveros, Stephen, "Some Thoughts Relating to Our Conquests in America," *American Historical Review*, IV, 323-328.

Diario de Caracas, Caracas, 1896.*

Eads, James B., "The Isthmian Ship-Railway," *North American Review*, CXXXII, 223-238.

Edinburgh Review, Edinburgh, 1809.*

Editorial, "Amazing Concessions to Colombia," *Review of Reviews*, June, 1914, p. 651.

———"Another Chapter of Mr. Blaine's Diplomacy," *The Nation*, XXXIV, 93.

———"Belated Panama Scruples," *The Nation* (1904), LXXIX, 328.

———"Colombia and Oil," *The New York Times*, Jan. 18, 1932.

———"The Common Sense of the Isthmian Decision," *Engineering Magazine*, XXIII, 653-659.

———"Compounding a Felony," *The Outlook* (1914), CVI, 295-296.

———"Neighbor's Grievance," *Review of Reviews*, March, 1914, p. 264.

—————"Oil and Ideals in Latin Lands," *Literary Digest* (1913), XLVII, 1098 ff.

—————"Oil and the Monroe Doctrine," *Review of Reviews*, Jan., 1914, p. 23.

—————"Our Panama 'Regrets'," *Literary Digest* (1914), XLVIII, 1035 ff.

—————"The Settlement of Panama Questions," *The Independent* (1914), LXXVII, 289.

—————"The United States and the Panama Canal," *The Nation*, XXX, 90-91.

Engineering Magazine, New York.*

Engineering News, New York, 1874-1917 (title varies).

English Historical Review, London, 1885—.

Escobar, Francisco, "President Roosevelt's Message and the Isthmian Canal," *North American Review* (Jan., 1904), CLXXVIII, 122ff.

Evans, Walton W., "Interoceanic Canal Projects," American Society of Civil Engineers, *Transactions* (1880), IX, 1-20.

Ford, Worthington C., "John Quincy Adams and the Monroe Doctrine," *American Historical Review*, VII, 676-696; VIII, 28-52.

Foreign Affairs, New York, 1922.

Forum, The, New York, 1886—.

Fuertes, E. A., "The Interoceanic Canal," *Engineering News*, VI, 246.

Gaceta de Colombia, Bogotá.*

Gaceta de la cuidad de Bogotá, Bogotá.*

Gaceta del estado, Panamá.*

Gaceta de la Nueva Granada, Bogotá.*

Gaceta oficial, Bogotá.*

Gogorza, Anthony de, "Problem of Interoceanic Communication by Way of the American Isthmus: Proposed Unique Solution, 1866-1888," *Journal of the American Geographical Society*, XX, 502-513.

—————"Problem of Interoceanic Communication by Way of the American Isthmus," *Journal of the American Geographical Society*, XXI, 526-529.

Going, Charles B., "The Absence of Facts about the Nicaragua Canal," *Engineering Magazine*, XI, 416-417.

González, Eloy G., "The Dissolution of Greater Colombia," *Inter-America*, VI, 320-323.

Gordy, J. P., "The Ethics of the Panama Case," *The Forum* (1904), XXXVI, 115 ff.

Granger, Henry G., "The Stain on Our Flag," *The Independent* (1911), LXXI, 347 ff.

Grant, U. S., "The Nicaragua Canal," *North American Review*, CXXXII, 107-116.

Hackett, Charles W., "The Development of John Quincy Adams' Policy with respect to an American Confederation and the Panama Congress, 1822-1825," *The Hispanic American Historical Review*, VIII, 496-526.

Hale, Henry, "Bunau-Varilla, Engineer and Diplomat," *Review of Reviews*, XXVIII, 677 ff.

Harding, Earl, "Economic and Industrial Renaissance of Colombia," *Bulletin of the Pan American Union*, LV, 341.

—— "In Justice to Colombia," *World's Work*, XXVI 674 ff.

Harper's Monthly Magazine, New York, 1850—(title varies).

Haupt, Lewis M., "National Defense and the Isthmian Canal," *Engineering Magazine*, XV, 550-557.

Hazeltine, Mayo W., "The Clayton-Bulwer Treaty," *North American Review*, CLXV, 452-459.

Hispanic American Historical Review, The, Baltimore and Durham, 1918—.

Hoskins, Halford L., "The Hispanic American Policy of Henry Clay, 1816-1828," *The Hispanic American Historical Review*, VII, 460-478.

Hull, Amos G., "The San Blas Ship-Canal Project," *Engineering News*, XXIX, 580-582.

Hunter, W. Henry, "The American Isthmus and the Interoceanic Canal," *Engineering Magazine*, XVI, 711-728.

—— "A Review of the Nicaragua Canal Scheme," *Engineering Magazine*, XVI, 972-990.

Hunt's Merchants' Magazine, New York, 1844-1848.

Hurlbut, George C., "The Panama Canal from Within," *The Forum*, IV, 279-289.

Independent, The, New York, 1848-1928.

Inter-America, New York, 1917—.

Johnson, Emory R., "The Panama Canal," *The Independent*, LV, 764 ff.

———"The Panama Canal: The Title and Concession," *Political Science Quarterly*, XVIII, 199.

———"The Nicaragua Canal and the Economic Development of the United States," *Annals of American Academy of Political and Social Science* (Jan., 1896), pp. 38-48.

Johnson, Willis Fletcher, "Justice and Equity in Panama," *The Forum* (July, 1904), pp. 125 ff.

Journal of American Geographical Society, New York, 1859-1900.

Journal of Association of Engineering Societies, New York, 1888-1915.

Journal of Franklin Institute, Philadelphia, 1826-1917.

Latin American, "The Colombian Treaty: Its Legal and Moral Aspects," *North American Review* (Jan., 1916), CCIII, 55 ff.

Leigh, John George, "The Reports of the Isthmian Canal Commission," *Engineering Magazine*, XXIII, 1-14.

Lesseps, M. de., "The Interoceanic Canal," *North American Review*, CXXX, 1-15.

———"The Panama Canal," *North American Review*, CXXXI, 75-78.

"Letters of Bancroft and Buchanan on the Clayton-Bulwer Treaty," *American Historical Review*, V, 95 ff.

Lieber, Francis, "The Ship Canal from the Atlantic to the Pacific," *Hunt's Merchants' Magazine*, XIX, 676.

Lippincott's Monthly Magazine, New York, 1868-1916.

Literary Digest, The, New York, 1890—.

Living Age, The, Boston, 1844—.

Lloyd, E. M., "Canning and Spanish America," *Transactions of the Royal Historical Society*, New Series, XVIII, London, 1904.

Louisiana Historical Quarterly, The, Baton Rouge, 1917—.

Ludlow, William, "The Trans-Isthmian Canal Problem," *Harper's New Monthly Magazine*, XCVI, 837-846.

McCaleb, Walter F., "The Aaron Burr Conspiracy and New Orleans," *American Historical Association, Annual Report* (1904), I, 131-143.

McFee, William, "Hale Colombia," *World's Work* (1924), XLVIII, 622-629.

McLaughlin, A. C., "The Western Posts and the British Debts," American Historical Association, *Annual Report* (1894), pp. 413-444.

Mahan, A. T., "Was Panama 'A Chapter of National Dishonor'?" *North American Review* (1912), CXCVI, 549-568.

Manger, William, "Foreign Investments in the American Republics," *Bulletin of the Pan American Union* (1931), LXV, 1069.

Manning, William R., "The Nootka Sound Controversy," American Historical Association, *Annual Report* (1904), pp. 279-478.

Maxey, Edwin, "The Pending Treaty with Colombia," *Review of Reviews* (Feb., 1916), LIII, 191 ff.

Meagher, Thomas F., "The New Route through Chiriquí," *Harper's Monthly Magazine*, XXII, 198-209.

Menocal, A. G., "Intrigues at the Paris Canal Congress," *North American Review*, CXXIX, 288-293.

[Mill, James], "The Emancipation of Spanish America," *Edinburgh Review*, XIII, 277-311.

Mississippi Valley Historical Review, The, Jackson, Miss, 1914—.

Moore, Robert M., "Present Aspect of the Problem of American Interoceanic Ship Transfer," *Journal of Association of Engineering Societies*, VII, 37-52.

Morris, Charles, "The Isthmian Canal from the Beginning," *Lippincott's Magazine*, LXIX, 327 ff.

Moses, Bernard, "The *casa de contratación* of Seville," *Papers of the American Historical Association* (1894), pp. 93-125.

——— "Constitution of the Republic of Colombia," *Supplement to the Annals of the American Academy of Political and Social Science* (1903), pp. 3 ff.

——— "Social Revolution in South America," American Historical Association, *Annual Report* (1915), pp. 165 ff.

Munsey's Magazine, New York, 1892—.

Mussey, Henry R., "The Rights of Small Nations," *Annals of American Academy of Political and Social Science* (1917), LXXII, 172 ff.

Nation, The, New York, 1865.—

National Intelligencer, Washington, 1822.*

New Republic, The, New York, 1914—.

*New York Herald.**

*New York Times, The.**

*New York Tribune.**

*New York World.**

Niles' Weekly Register, Baltimore and Philadelphia, 1811-1849 (75 vols.).

Nimmo, Joseph, Jr., "The Nicaragua Canal in Its Commercial and Military Aspects," *Engineering Magazine,* XV, 720-726.

North American Review, Boston and New York, 1815—.

North Carolina Historical Review, Raleigh, 1924—.

Outlook, The, New York, 1893—.

Paine, Charles, "Concerning the Actual Condition of the Panama Canal," *Engineering Magazine,* XVIII, 681 ff.

*Panama Star and, Herald.**

Parks, E. Taylor, "The Colombian Treaty: A Triumph for Mr. Hull," *World Affairs* (March, 1934), XCVII, 48-50.

Parra-Pérez, C., "Bolívar and His Friends Abroad," *Inter-America,* III, 259-264.

Penfield, Frederic C., "Why Not Own the Panama Isthmus?" *North American Review* (1902), CLXXIV, 269 ff.

Pérez, Paul, "A Colombian View of the Panama Canal Question," *North American Review* (July, 1903), CLXXVII, 63 ff.

———"The Treacherous Treaty; A Colombian Plea," *North American Review* (Nov., 1903), CLXXVII, 934 ff.

Perkins, Dexter, "Europe, Spanish America, and the Monroe Doctrine," *American Historical Review,* XXVII, 207-218.

Phillips, Matilda, "Latin American Foreign Trade in 1930—A General Survey," *Bulletin of the Pan American Union,* LXVI, 113 ff.

Pierson, W. W., Jr., "The Political Influence of an Interoceanic Canal, 1826-1926," *The Hispanic American Historical Review,* VI, 212.

Political Herald and Review, London, 1785.**

The Popular Science Monthly, New York, 1872.

Public Opinion, New York-Washington, 1886-1906.

Quarterly Journal of Economics, Cambridge, 1887—.

Redfield, William W., "Sea Level Canal across the Isthmus of San Blas," *Journal of Association of Engineering Societies* (May, 1900).

Review of Reviews, New York, 1890—(title varies).

Reyes, Rafael, "Go Slow with Latin America," *The New York Times,* Sept. 21, 1913.

Rippy, J. Fred, "Colombia's New Régime," *Current History,* XXXII, 82 ff.

——"The United States and Colombian Oil," *Foreign Policy Association Information Service* (1929), V, No. 2.

Rives, M. L., "Spain and the United States in 1795," *American Historical Review,* IV, 62-79.

Robertson, William Spence, "First Legations of the United States in Latin America," *Mississippi Valley Historical Review,* II, 189ff.

——"Francisco de Miranda and the Revolutionizing of Spanish America," American Historical Association, *Annual Report* (1907), I.

——"The Juntas of 1808 and the Spanish Colonies," *English Historical Review,* XXXI, 573-583.

——"The Monroe Doctrine Abroad in 1823-4," *American Political Science Review,* VI, 546-563.

——"The Recognition of the Hispanic-American Nations by the United States," *The Hispanic American Historical Review,* I, 239-269.

——"The Recognition of the Spanish Colonies by the Motherland," *The Hispanic American Historical Review,* I, 70-91.

Romero, M., "The United States and the Liberation of Spanish America," *North American Review,* CLXV, 70 ff.

Roosevelt, Theodore, "How the United States Acquired the Right to Dig the Panama Canal," *The Outlook* (Oct. 7, 1911), XCIX, 314 ff.

Royal Geographical Society of London, *Proceedings,* London, 1856.

Royal Historical Society, *Transactions,* London, 1904.

Rublee, George, "The American Government and Colombia," *The New Republic* (1932), LXX, 21-22.

Ruggles, S. B., "The Nicaragua Canal," *Journal of American Geographical Society*, XI, 181 ff.

Saabye, Oscar A. F., "The Present Condition of the Panama Canal," *Engineering Magazine*, VII, 830-836.

*San Francisco Daily Herald.**

Scott, George W., "Was the Recognition of Panama a Breach of International Morality?" *The Outlook* (Dec. 19, 1903), LXXV, 947 ff.

Scott, James Brown, "The Treaty between Colombia and the United States," *American Journal of International Law* (1921), XV, 430-439.

Scribner's Magazine, New York, 1887—.

Scroggs, William O., "The American Investments in Latin America," *Foreign Affairs* (1932), X, 502-504.

———"William Walker's Designs on Cuba," *Mississippi Valley Historical Review*, I, 198-211.

Scruggs, William L., "Republicanism in Spanish America," *Magazine of American History*, XVII, 402 ff.

Shepherd, William R., "Bolívar and the United States," *The Hispanic American Historical Review*, I, 270-298.

Shirley, Elizabeth R., "Fernando Bolívar and the University of Virginia," *Bulletin of the Pan American Union* (Jan., 1929), pp. 1188 ff.

Silva Herrera, Gilberto, "The Dissolution of Greater Colombia," *Inter-America*, VI, 224 ff.

Southwestern Political and Social Science Quarterly, Austin, Texas.**

Stewart, Watt, "The Ratification of the Thomson-Urrutia Treaty," *Southwestern Political and Social Science Quarterly* (1930), X, 416-428.

Strong, Frank, "The Causes of Cromwell's West Indian Expedition," *American Historical Review*, IV, 228 ff.

Stuart, Graham H., "Simón Bolívar's Project for a League of Nations," *Southwestern Political and Social Science Quarterly*, VII, 238-252.

Taylor, Benjamin, "The Secession of Panama," *The Living Age*, CCXL, 389-397.

Temperley, Harold W. V., "The Latin American Policy of George Canning, *American Historical Review*, XI, 779 ff.

———— "The Relations of England with Spanish America," *American Historical Association, Annual Report* (1911), I, 231-237.

Thompson, S. A., "The Effect of Waterways on Railway Transportation," *Engineering Magazine,* XXIII, 583-590.

El tiempo, Bogotá.*

Troconis, Gabriel Porras, "The Dismemberment of Greater Colombia," *Inter-America,* V, 19-24.

Turpie, David, "Projects for an Isthmian Canal," *Harper's New Monthly Magazine,* XCVI, 351-358.

Van Norman, Louis E., "Latin American Views of Panama and the Canal," *Review of Reviews* (March, 1904), XXIX, 334 ff.

El vijía del istmo, Panamá.*

Washington Post, The, Washington (D. C.)*

Webster, Sidney, "The Diplomacy and Law of the Isthmian Canals," *Harper's New Monthly Magazine,* LXXXVII, 602-608.

Weld, Stuart F., "The Isthmus Canal and Our Government," *Atlantic Monthly,* LXIII, 341-353.

Whiteley, J. G., "The Diplomacy of the United States in Regard to Central American Canals," *North American Review,* CLXV, 364-378.

Wilcox, Marion, "Colombia's Last Vision of Eldorado," *North American Review* (Nov., 1903), CLXXVII, 919 ff.

Wilgus, A. Curtis, "Spanish American Patriot Activity along the Atlantic Seaboard, 1816-1822," *North Carolina Historical Review,* IV, 172 ff.

———— "Spanish American Patriot Activity on the Gulf Coast, 1811-1822," *Louisiana Historical Quarterly,* VIII, 193-215.

Williams, John N., "Panama and Colombia," *World's Work* (Jan., 1904), VII, 343.

Williams, Talcott, "Ethnic Factors in South America," *Annals of the American Academy of Political and Social Science,* XXII, 25 ff.

World Affairs, Washington, D. C.*

World's Work, The, New York, 1900—.

* Exact references in footnotes.

INDEX

Abadía Méndez, Miguel, 464 n, 468, 471

Abbott, John T., minister to Colombia, pessimistic regarding U. S. trade with Colombia, 266; reciprocity negotiations, 268, 270; presses Colón fire claims, 316, 316 n; on canal concessions, 380

Aberdeen, Lord, 196-198, 211

Acosta, Joaquín, 162-164, 197

Acosta, Santos, 344-347, 368

Adams, John, on Colombian independence, 36, 46, 48, 49; sends mission to France, 45

Adams, John Quincy, recognition of Colombian independence, 91-102, 142; and Torres's "American system," 99, 126; on U. S.-Colombian trade, 113; cool to idea of confederation, 127, 128, 131, 132, 138, 142; on incorporation of Cuba in U. S., 135; expresses regret over difficulties between U. S. and Colombia, 124-125; and Panama Congress, 141-143; mistrusts Bolívar, 153; opposes Harrison mission, 153-154; satisfied with claims negotiations, 165

Adams, John P., 324, 324 n

Adamson, Thomas, consul at Panama, 230, 244 n

Addington Ministry (British), 45

Aepli, Ebenbach and Salmon (Colón fire claimants), 308 n

Aguiar, Vicente de, 21

Aix-la-Chapelle, Congress of, 93

Aix-la-Chapelle, Treaty of, 33

Aizpuru, General (Panama), 229, 230

Alaskan-Canadian boundary dispute, influence on Anglo-American rivalry in Central America, 385-386

Alliance (U. S. vessel), 230

Almeida, José (U. S. citizen), privateer, 81-82

Almy, Admiral John J., 227

Alternativo del redactor (Bogotá), 25

Amador, Esteban de, 27

Amador Guerrero, Manuel (Panama secessionist and first president of republic), 397-399, 402, 419

Amar (Spanish viceroy), 64

Amaya, Ramón G. (Colombian officer), 401

American Atlantic and Pacific Ship-Canal Company of New York, 325

American International Corporation, 466 n

American Transport Line, 281

Ames, Oakes, 356 n

Amiens, Treaty of, 45

Ammen, Rear Admiral Daniel, 351 n, 356-359

Andean National Corporation, 468, 471

Anderson, Richard C., minister to Colombia, 104; regarding Colombian newspapers, 115; restores friendly relations, 124; negotiation of treaty, 132, 133; on Colombia and Cuba, 137; on confederation, 138; named delegate to Panama Congress, 141, 142; death, 142; claims negotiations, 165 n; obtains removal of early trade discrimination against U. S., 169

Andreas and Company of New York, 419

Andrés, Sebastián, 30

Anglo-Persian Oil Company, 468

Angostura, Santo Tomás de, 69, 71

Antioquia, 64, 65, 110, 111

Antonelli canal survey, 179

Appleton, Nathan, 358 n, 359-360

Aragua, Battle of, 66

Aranda (Spanish premier), 35

Arango, José A. (Panama secessionist), 397, 401-402, 419

Arango, minister from Panama, 434-435

Arbitration, 422-423

[531]

Argentina, 204, 267

Arias, Ricardo (Panama secessionist), 397 n

Arias, Tomás (Panama secessionist, 397, 401-402

Arias F., A. (Panama seccessionist), 419

Arosemena, Constantino (Panama secessionist), 397 n

Arosemena, Justo, 202, 287, 366

Arosemena, Pablo, 402 (*see also* Cortés-Arosemena Treaty, Root-Arosemena Treaty)

Arthur, Chester A., on reciprocity, 264-267; consular service, 265; advocates greater merchant marine, 265; on Pan American uniform currency, 265

Asch, Isaacs and, Colón fire claimants, 308

Asiento Contract (1713), 10

Aspinwall, William H., 272

Asuay, Department of, 123 (*see also* Ecuador)

Atlanta (U. S. vessel), 231, 400 n

Atlantic and Pacific Junction Company, 333

Atlas Steamship Company (British), 264, 281

Atrato canal routes, 179, 181, 330, 334, 351, 438, 440, 444, 452, 477 n

Ayacucho, Battle of, 72 n

Aznero, Vicente, 119

Bacchus (schooner), 51

Bache, Richard, 115, 181

Bacon, Senator A. O., on Panama secession, 427

Bailey, Commander, 223, 297

Bain, H. Foster, 471

Baker, Lieutenant Commander Asher, 385 n

Balboa, Vasco Núñez de, 4

Barbados (British), 33, 51

Bárbula, Battle of, 66

Barcelona (Colombia), 58, 61, 69

Barinas, 61, 66

Barranquilla, 5, 67

Barreiro (Spanish general), 70

Barrett, John, minister to Colombia, 431-434

Barrot, Chevalier (French), 349

Bastidas, Rodrigo de, 4, 178

Bay Islands, 326, 328, 331-332

Bayard, Thomas F., refuses extradition of Foyer, 248; on U. S. intervention, 259; claims, 309-315, 317

Beaupré, Arthur M., minister to Colombia, 403, 407, 409, 410, 428

Becerra, Ricardo, minister from Colombia, on U. S. intervention, 259; reciprocal agreements, 265, 266; Colón fire claims, 310, 312 n; Minister Jacob, 312 n; Protocol of 1881, 368; Minister Dichman, 369

Bee (schooner), 51

Beers, Captain J. R., 397, 398, 418

Belgium, 214, 462

Belize (British Honduras), 326, 328

Belly, Felix (French), 347

Benecia (U. S. vessel), 227

Berbeo, José Francisco (early revolutionist), 17, 20, 21

Bernardo, Archbishop, 433

Bernhardt, Sarah, and Panama Canal, 359

Bertrand (French), 34

Betancourt, Julio, minister from Colombia, 437; requests arbitration, 440; on Thomson-Urrutia Treaty, 441, 446-447

Betsy-Ann (U. S. vessel), 84

Biddle, Aznero and Company, 187, 194

Biddle, Charles A., mission of, 185-189; on Panama secession, 190

Biddle, Thomas, 301

Bidlack, Benjamin A., chargé to Colombia, arrives in Bogotá, 164; claims' negotiations, 168-169, 285; on Isthmian communication, 201, 202, 329; negotiation of Treaty of 1846, 202-206, 208-213, 327

Bidlake, John, 281

Bigelow, John, 377, 385 n

Billings, Fred, 356 n

Black, Doctor, 333

Black, Colonel William, 397, 419

Blackford, W. M., chargé to Colombia, appointed, 164; claims' negotiations, 167-168; trade treaty negotiations, 174-175

Blagge, Benjamin, 333

Blaine, James G., and reciprocity, 267-269; presses claims, 315-317; opposes European guarantee of canal, 370-371; attempts to modify Clayton-Bulwer Treaty, 372-373, 385

Bocas del Toro, 219, 231-232

Bogotá, Santa Fé de, 5, 11, 19, 25-26, 56, 58-60, 63-67, 70, 111, 118

Bogotá (gunboat), 401

Bogotá Street Railway Company of New York, 282-283

Bolívar, Fernando, 125

Bolívar, Juan Vicente, 86

Bolívar, Simón, deathbed statement, 15; his "Pan-Latin-Americanism," 25; fails in Venezuelan revolt, 62; flees to West Indies, 62; returns and joins patriot cause, 66; given title of *Libertador*, 66; is defeated and leaves Venezuela in hands of royalists, 66; forces Cundinamarca into confederation, 66; defeated again in Venezuela and flees to Jamaica, 67; returns to Venezuela, 69; famous march, 70-72; visits U. S., 73-74; and claims, 83-84; relations with U. S., 83-85; president of Republic of Colombia, 109; and education, 110; British on his staff, 113; absence from Bogotá and influence on government, 117, 118; returns to Bogotá, 118; opposition to, 119-123; death of, 123; receives certain Washington relics, 125; on Cuba and Puerto Rico, 136, 140; Monroe Doctrine, 139-140; U. S. in Panama Congress, 140, 143; and Panama Congress, 143-145; his idea of American confederation, 127, 143-144; temporarily checks separatist movement in Venezuela, 151; Watts's letter to, 151-153; letter from Clay to, 153; and Harrison mission, 154-157; Andrew Jackson, 158-159; his tariff decree, 170; opposes concession for canal, 181; commissions engineers to survey Isthmus, 182; influence on Panama, 190

Bolton, I., 117

Bonaparte, Joseph, 57, 58

Borah, Senator William E., 448, 451, 455, 456

Borda, Francisco de Paul, minister from Colombia, 437

Boston (U. S. vessel), 400

Boston Ice Company, 279, 283, 308 n, 310

Bowlin, James B., minister to Colombia, 223-224; opposes taxes on Isthmus, 237, 238; Herrán's protest against, 241; unsuccessful in claims negotiations, 286; and Panama Riot, 288-292, 295, 297; recommends seizure of Isthmus, 331; and canal, 336

Boyacá, Battle of, 70, 71

Boyd, A. B. (publisher of *Panama Star and Herald*), 279

Boyd, Federico, 397 n, 401-402

Brandegee, Senator Frank B., 448, 451

Brassy, Thomas, 333

Brazil, 263, 268

Briceño, Antonio Nicolás, 75

Briceño Méndez, Pedro, 110, 112, 145

Brión, Admiral, 83

Brissot (French), 40

Brown, Charles S., 281

Bruce, Sir F. W. A., 301

Bryan, William Jennings, on Colombian-U. S. reconciliation, 441; and Thomson-Urrutia Treaty, 442, 444

Bucaramanga, 5

Buchanan, James, and claims, 168, 297, 298; on Isthmian communications, 201, 329, 335-336; Treaty of 1846, 213; interest in Chiriquí Improvement Company, 274, 275; and U. S. intervention, 288; on Clayton-Bulwer Treaty, 328 n, 331, 332, 373

Buenaventura, sanitation of, 441

Buen Gusto, 25

Bunau-Varilla, Phillipe, 385 n, 398-399, 402, 416, 419

Bunch, Robert, 308, 349

Burke, William (British), 74, 75, 127

Burnside, Senator Ambrose E., 361

Burr, William H., 381 n, 385 n, 398

Burton, Allan A., minister to Colombia, on Panama independence, 225-228; taxes, 242-244; delay in presenting credentials to Mosquera government, 254; interpretation of Article XXXV, 255-256; on Negro colonization, 277 n; status of foreigners in time of civil war, 304; and claims, 305; canal, 337; on Mosquera and British, 340-341
Bustamente, General, 136
Butler, General Benjamin, 356 n

Caballero, General Lucas, 233, 403 n
Caballero y Góngora, Archbishop-Viceroy Antonio, 97
Caffery, Jefferson, minister to Colombia, 477
Caicedo, Domingo, 122, 160
Caledonia Bay route, 333, 351 n
Calhoun, John C., favors non-recognition pledge, 130-131; fears England in Cuba, 135; hostile to Panama Congress, 141-142; and claims, 168
Cali, Santiago de, 5
California, 219-221, 235, 250
Calvo, Bartolomé, 252
Cámara de Indias, 11
Campbell, George W., 93
Campbell, Patrick (British), 105
Canal commissions (U. S.), 351, 381, 386-387
Canal routes (*see* Isthmian communications)
Cannon, Joseph, 385 n
Capela, John, 305 n
Carabobo, Battle of, 71, 96
Caracas, Santiago de León, 5, 19, 29-30, 32, 35, 56, 58, 60-62, 66, 71, 75-76, 111, 118, 121
Caravan (U. S. vessel), 85
Cárdenas, Adán, 355
Cárdenas, Manuel, 333
Carib Syndicate, 467
Caro, Pedro José, 42-43
Carr, aide to General O'Leary, 156
Carrasco, Francisco, 26
Cartagena, 5, 9, 11, 33, 35, 44, 51-53, 63-67, 71, 110-111, 122-123, 280-281, 306-307

Cartagena-Magdalena Railway Company, 282
Cartagena Terminal and Improvement Company, 282
Casa de Contratación, 8
Casanare, 64, 68
Cass, Lewis, Panama taxes, 240, 241; and Chiriquí Improvement Company, 275; and Panama Riot claims, 297, 298
Cass-Herrán Treaty, 299-300 (*see also* Treaties of 1857 and 1864)
Cass-Yrisarri Treaty, 331
Cassano, Antonio María, 68
Castell (Calthel), Captain Clement, 77
Castellón, Francisco, 197-198
Castilla, Count Ruiz de, 59
Castilla de Oro, 4
Castillo y Rada, José María del, 110, 111
Castlereagh, Lord, 55-56
Castro, General, 401
Cauca Company of West Virginia, 282
Caudest, Charles, 336
Central America, and canal, 181-182, 184, 323-326, 382, 405; effect of dissolution on British loans, 326; Anglo-American rivalry in, 326-328; objection to Negro colonization on Chiriquí, 276
Central and South American Telegraph Company of New York, 280
Cerruti claim (Italian), 423
Chagres River, possible canal route, 178, 179; open to free trade, 185; Biddle, Aznero and Co., navigation concession, 187-188
Charles III (Spain), 10, 180
Charles V (Spain), 178
Chauncey, Henry, 272
Cherry, James, 282
Cheyne, Doctor, 155
Chile, 23
Chiriquí, Isthmus of, 257, 276, 277, 335-336, 362, 366
Chiriquí Improvement Company, 274-277, 335, 362
Chort (British), 28
Christie, Lieutenant, 77

Church, 10-13 (*see also* Dominicans, Franciscans, Jesuits)

Cincinnati (U. S. vessel); 232

Cisneros, Francisco J., 282

Civil War (U. S.), influence on U. S.-Latin American policy, 303-304; on canal policy, 332, 333, 337

Claims, 83 85, 165-169, 285-323

Clay, Henry, on distressed U. S. seamen, 78; advocates recognition, 95-96; friend of Torres, 97, 99; his portrait presented to Colombia, 125; and Panama Congress, 141, 142, 147; on American confederation, 126; and Cuba, 136, 137; and Watts, 152-153; and Harrison mission, 153-154, 157; interested in canal, 183

Clayton, John M., and canal, 185, 190, 214, 323, 329-330, 365 n; fears Great Britain on Isthmus, 215 (*see also* Clayton-Bulwer Treaty)

Clayton-Bulwer Treaty, 328, 329, 331-332, 339, 365, 372-374, 385-386

Clemente, General Lino de, 96, 97

Cleveland, Grover, on U. S. intervention, 230, 259; and Colón fire claims, 311, 315; and canal, 375-376, 378-379, 382

Clinton, George, 50

Club literario (Bogotá), 26

Cochrane, Admiral (British), 51, 72

Cochrane, Captain Charles S., 112-113, 181

Collins, Lieutenant Frederick, 351 n

Colombia, geography of, 3; discovery and settlement, 3-5; people of, 5-7; viceroyalty of New Granada established, 7-8; rule of Peninsular Spaniards, 7-8; early economic system, 8-10; church in, 10-13; parallels and contrasts between North American colonies and New Granada, 12-15; results of Spanish rule, 15-16; rumblings of discontent, 19; Quito uprising, 19-20; Europe and independence of, 21-23, 28, 31-32, 39-58, 60-61, 69, 74, 89, 91-94, 99, 103-105, 127-132; *Los Comuneros*, 20-23; *Los*

Precursores, 23-32; education in, 12, 25, 110-111, 162; early European interest and activities in, 33-35; early North American attitude and influence, 35-37; (*see* Miranda): U. S. and independence of, 37-54, 60-61, 73-75, 86-102; pawn on international chessboard, 40-49; Venezuelan Expedition of 1806, 49-54; Great Britain's chameleon policy regarding independence of, 55-56; Spanish revolt spreads to, 58-59; Quito launches revolution, 59-60; Caracas follows, 60-62; revolutionary contagion, 63-64; early attempts at self-government, 64-66; reconquest of, 67-68; triumph of patriot arms, 68-72; "United Provinces of New Granada," 65; "Republic of Colombia" established, 70-72; influence of U. S. upon, 73-75; trade with U. S., 75-76, 79-85, 115-117, 169-177, 262-271; North Americans in patriot service, 76-78; first North American mission to, 78-81; U. S.-Great Britain rivalry in, 78-81, 83-84, 112-115, 134, 145-147, 167-174, 176, 182, 183, 186, 263-264, 266-267, 290, 326-330, 345-346, 349, 443, 446, 453, 468, 477-478; privateers, seizures, and unsettled claims, 81-85; first official colonial diplomatic mission to U. S., 86; Constitution of La Gran Colombia, 96, 109-110; recognition by U. S., 102-103; Europe follows in granting recognition, 103-105; signs of progress and leadership in, 110-112; early governmental difficulties, 117-123; dissolution of La Gran Colombia, 122-123; early relations with U. S., 124-125; (*see* Monroe Doctrine); first treaty with U. S., 132-134; contemplated invasion of Cuba, 134-137; and P a n a m a Congress, 137-147; Watts's letter, 151-153; Harrison mission, 153-158; temporary rapprochement with U. S., 158-159, 162; formation of New Granada,

159-160; secession of Panama, 159, 183, 190-193, 224-234, 243, 339, 395-404; national renaissance under Santander, 161-163; friction with U. S., 163-164; friendly relations with U. S., under Herrán and Mosquera, 164; unsuccessful claims' negotiations, 165-169; initial Spanish interest in canal, 178-180; La Gran Colombia considers a canal, 181-182; (*see* Mosquito Coast); Biddle mission, 185-189; canal concessions granted, 185, 187, 194-196, 199-200, 333, 335-337, 351, 358-360; reincorporation of Panama, 195; (*see* European guarantee of canal routes); fear of British aggression on Isthmus and Mosquitia, 197, 199, 200, 204; (*see* Treaty of 1846); rumored Flores expeditions, 204, 250-251, 254; disturbances on Isthmus, 219-245, 353, 395; Panama Riot, 221-224, 288-302; (*see* Intervention); requests U. S. intervention, 229; Panama as federal department, 230-233; civil war, 231-233; passenger, tonnage, and mail taxes, 235-245; internal politics and Isthmian disorder, 235-245; United States of Colombia, 241; North American troops cross Isthmus, 245-247; North American prisoners cross Isthmus, 247-249; fear of foreign seizure of Isthmus, 250, 287, 310, 327, 329, 375, 378-380, 408; disturbances in Panama and at home, 251-254; U. S. recognition of Mosquera government, 253-254; President Arthur advocates reciprocity, 264-267; retaliatory reciprocity, 267-270; (*see* Panama Canal Co.); Chiriquí Improvement Company, 273-278; Joseph Gooding—road across Chocó, 278; A. de Gogorza and canal, 278-279, 356-358; (*see* Treaties of 1857 and 1864); influence of U. S. Civil War on relations with, 303-304; growing independence of, 304-308; Cartagena Riot, 306-307; *Montijo* Arbitration, 307-308; Colón fire claims, 308-317; interested in U. S. canal, 324; (*see* Panama Railroad Company); U. S. aggressive canal policy, 330-331; refuses to negotiate with U. S. regarding canal, 332; revival of canal interest, 339-340; Mosquera and British, 340-341; U. S. approached regarding guarantee, 341-342; unsuccessful canal negotiations with U. S., 342-354; Anglo-French influence in, 345, 346; Wyse (French) canal concession, 358-360; protests against U. S. vessels making soundings off Panama, 362 n; Protocol of 1881, 364-369; Secretary Clayton regarding Colombia and Panama, 365 n; U. S. fear of European guarantee, 369-372; U. S. and guarantee, 375-376; Colombia versus Nicaragua, 382-384; Spooner Act and, 387-388; (*see* Hay-Herrán Treaty); Panama secession, 395-404; independence of Panama recognized by U. S., 401-402; prevented from suppressing Panama revolt, 402-403; U. S. refuses to arbitrate with, regarding Panama, 403-404; legality and morality of U. S. course in Panama secession, 404-426; reconciliation with U. S., 429-441; -Panama boundary dispute, 434-435; (*see* Thomson-Urrutia Treaty); and oil, 443, 444, 449-457, 466-471, 474-477; economic renaissance in, 461-464; -U. S. rapprochement, 464-466; extensive borrowings, 471-480; depression, 473-480; U. S. interest in future of, 477-480; (*see also* Claims, Commerce, Intervention, Investments)

Colombian Petroleum Company, 467

Colón, 219, 221, 226, 229, 230, 232, 233

Colón fire claims, 308-317

Colorado Construction Company, 379

Columbus, Christopher, 3, 178

Colunje, Jil, 258

Commerce, 8-10, 14-15, 28, 33-34, 59, 75-76, 78-85, 115-117, 262-271; Anglo-American trade rivalry in Colombia, 112-115, 134, 169-174, 176, 263-264, 266-267; treaties of, 132-134, 161, 164, 171-175, 202-213, 235, 285; removal of early discrimination, 169; adverse legislation, 169-171; defective consular service, 176; volume of trade, 176-177, 262-263, 266, 270-271; passenger, tonnage, and mail taxes, 235-245; U. S. intervention to keep open transit, 249; President Arthur advocates reciprocity, 264-267; U. S. trade commission to South America, 264-265; (*see also* Claims and Reciprocity)

Compañía Fluvial de Cartagena, 282

Compañía Guipuzcoa na de Caracas, 19

Comuneros, Los, 20-23

Concha, José Vicente, 388-390, 406, 447-448, 457

Concord (U. S. vessel), 323, 400 n

Conlon, P., 36, 37

Consejo de Indias, 8, 29

Consular system (U. S.), early appointments, 116-117; in Colombia defective, 175-176; President Arthur advocates salary basis, 265

Contreras, Dionisio, 21

Cooper, Peter, 347, 344 n

Córdoba, General José María, 121, 156-157

Codazzi, General, 335

Coro, 29, 58, 61-62

Correo curioso (Bogotá), 25

Cortés, Enrique, 407-408, 430, 431, 433-436 (*see also* Root-Cortés Treaty)

Cortés, Manuel, 30

Cortés-Arosemena Treaty, 435

Corwine, Amos B., 223, 241, 287-289, 331

Costa Rica, 325, 390 n, 423

Cotesworth and Powell Claims Convention, 423

Cotterill, William Henry (British), 340-341

Cotton, John, 35

Cowdray, Lord, 444, 445

Craven, Lieutenant T. A., 336

Cromwell, Oliver, 33, 35

Cromwell, Captain B. J., 231

Cromwell, William Nelson, 398, 418, 435

Cuba, Napoleon willing for U. S. to take, 74; contemplated invasion of, 134-137; Bolívar and Panama Congress regarding, 140; British suspicious of U. S., 145-146

Cúcuta, Rosario de, 70, 71

Cúcuta, Congress of, 96

Culberson, Senator Charles A., on Panama secession, 427

Cullen, Dr. Edward (Irish), 333-335, 342

Cumaná (Colombia), 58, 61, 76

Cundinamarca, State of, 65, 66, 110

Curaçao (Dutch), 21, 31, 80

Curtis, Lieutenant Francis X., 77

Cushing, Caleb, 344-347

Dana, Charles A., 347, 344 n

Daniel, Senator John W., 427

Daniels (Danells), John Daniel, 76-77

Daniels (Danells), Simón Bolívar Daniel, 77 n

Danish West Indies, 338

Darién, Santa María la Antigua de, 11, 378

Darién canal route, 179, 190, 333, 336, 340, 342-344

Davie, William R., 49

Dávila, Pedrarias, 4-5, 11

Davis, Charles H., 340, 347

Davis, Jefferson, 252

Dawson, Thomas C., minister to Colombia, 435

Dayton, Senator Jonathan, 50

De Barco concession, 468, 470, 471, 476, 477

De Lesseps, Ferdinand, 337, 356-361, 363-364, 366, 369-370, 375, 377, 378, 380

Democratic Party, 287, 330, 382, 439

Dennis, Lawrence, 477

Derechos del hombre y del cuidadano, 29

Deveros, Stephen, 33-34

Días Herrera, Juan, 19

Dichman, Ernest, minister to Colombia, on Panama secession, 228;

passage of U. S. prisoners across Isthmus, 247-248; and canal, 360, 369; on anti-American feeling, 366, 369; trade with Colombia, 264

Dickinson-Ayón Treaty, 340

Dingley Tariff Act of 1897, 271

Dix, General, 347

Dixie (U. S. vessel), 400

Dodge, W. E., 356 n

Dominican Republic, 265, 268

Dominicans, 12 n

Douglas, Stephen A., 328 n

Doyle, Ensign John M., 77

Drexel, Morgan and Company, 364 n

Duane, William, 97, 181

DuBois, James T., minister to Colombia, on reconciliation, 437-439, 441; and Thomson-Urrutia Treaty, 442-443

Duesbury, Henry (British), 339

Duque, José Gabriel (citizen of U. S.), 397-398, 418

Dumouriez (French), 40

Dundas, British secretary of state for war, 44

Eads, Captain James B., 360, 380

Eaton, Senator William W., 361

Ecuador, incorporated in Colombia, 72; independence, 123; and U. S. claims against La Gran Colombia, 166, 167; and reported Flores invasion, 204, 250; and Panama Riot, 294 (*see also* Quito and Guayaquil)

Eder family, 283

Ehrman, Felix, 400, 402, 418

El Chocó (Colombia), 64

El redactor americano (Bogotá), 25

Ellsworth, Oliver, 49

El Rosario, College of, 25

Emerys (Boston), logging in El Chocó, 283

Enciso, Martín Fernández de, 4

Ernst, Lieutenant Colonel Oswald H., 381 n, 385 n

Escuela de la concordia (Quito), 26

España-Gual conspiracy, 30-31, 42

Espejo, Francisco Javier Eugenio Santa Cruz y, 24, 25, 127

Espinosa, Manuel, 397 n

Estrella de Panamá, 317-319

European guarantee of canal routes, 194-200, 210-212, 214-215, 296, 307, 329-330, 341-342, 365 n, 369-372, 413 n (*see also* Clayton-Bulwer Treaty)

Eutropélico, 25

Evans, Walton W., 360, 384 n

Evarts, William M., on trade with Colombia, 264; and canal, 344 n, 364-368, 371 n

Evening Telegram, The, see *Panama Star and Herald*

Everett, Edward, on foreign guarantee of Isthmus, 196-197

Extradition Treaty, 247-249

Fábrega, Francisco de, 222, 223

Falcmar (Swede), survey of Isthmus, 182

Fall, Albert B., 448, 449, 451, 452, 456

Family Compact (France and Spain), 34, 39

Fargo, William C., and Isthmian Canal Company of New York, 344 n

Farrand, Colonel, and canal legend, 357 n

Ferdinand and Isabella, 11

Ferdinand VII, 56-59, 64, 65, 67, 71

Fernández Madrid, Pedro, 199

Field, Cyrus, 347

Field, W. J., 308 n

Fish, Hamilton, on Panama protectorate, 227; intervention, 258; regarding foreign guarantee of Panama route, 307; and canal treaty, 351-355, 358

Flores, General Juan José, 122, 123, 204, 212, 250-251

Folger, F. J., 236

Fontainbleau, Treaty of (1807), 56

Foote, Thomas M., chargé to Colombia, instructions to, 215; on North Americans on Isthmus, 220; and canal, 333

Forsyth, John, on claims, 167; trade relations, 173-174; and Biddle mission, 185, 188

Forsyth, Dr. Samuel D., 84-85, 116, 165

Foster, John M., 117

Foster, John W. (secretary of state), on trade between U. S. and Colombia, 269, 270; and canal, 379-380

Foundation Company, 466 n

Fox, Charles, 333

Foyer, escaped Colombian prisoner residing in Arkansas, 248

France, pirates off coast of Colombia, 9; interest and activities in Caribbean area and Spanish Main, 34; and Colombian independence, 28, 39-41, 43-46, 48-49, 55-56, 58, 60, 74, 89, 92-94, 99, 103-105, 127-132; X. Y. Z. affair, 45-46; Napoleon underrates Spanish nationalism, 56-57; and monarchy in Colombia, 121; and contemplated invasion of Cuba, 134-135; and Isthmian canal, 180, 194-200, 324, 333-335, 337, 344, 348-349, 356, 363-366, 369, 374-375, 396, 398; (*see* European guarantee of canal routes); Colombia's fear of, on Isthmus, 201, 212; -U. S.-Great Britain protectorate over Panama suggested, 225, 227; on U. S. intervention, 253, 254; -U. S.-Great Britain, rivalry, 290, 345, 346, 349, 358-361, 374-375, 378-380, 382, 383; report of consul regarding Panama Riot, 294; on Panama Riot claims, 298; protests Isthmian taxes, 304; and Colón fire claims, 316; ordered out of Mexico by U. S., 338; De Gogorza delivers Panama to, 356-358; (*see* Ferdinand de Lesseps); U. S. opposition to, on Isthmus, 359-361, 378; and Panama railroad, 412; and Panama secession, 419; commercial interest in Colombia, 462; (*see also* Panama Canal Company and New Panama Canal Company)

Franciscans, 12 n

Franklin, Benjamin, 26 n, 27

Frelinghuysen, Frederick T., on reciprocity treaty, 265; on Clayton-Bulwer Treaty, 373-374, 385 (*see also* Frelinghuysen-Zavala Treaty)

Frelinghuysen-Zavala Treaty, 374, 376, 379, 382

Fudger, H. E., 176

Gaceta de Caracas, 60

Gage, Thomas, 33, 35 n

Galán, José Antonio, 21

Galena (U. S. vessel), 230

Gallagher, Mateo, 60

Gallatin, Albert, 160

Galvoa, Antonio, 179

Garay, José de, 197, 325

García, Mexican filibuster, 231

García de Sena, Manuel, 75, 89

Garella, Napoleón, 196-198

Garfield, James A., 368-369

Garrido, Manuel María, 222, 223

Garrido, acting-president of Colombia, 340

Germany, and Isthmian guarantee, 370; fear of Colombian aid to, unfounded, 448-449

Gerry, Elbridge, 45

Gibbes' Claim, 301-302

Gijón y León, Manuel, 180

Gisborne, Lionel, 333, 335

Goethe, Johann W. von, quoted, 183, 378

Gogorza, Anthony de, 278-279, 354, 356-358

Gomara, López de, 179

Gómez, Juan María, 198-199, 206

Gómez, General, commander of National forces on Isthmus, 232

Gónima, General, commander of government forces in Panama, 229

González, Florentino, 333

Gooding, Albert, 156, 278 n

Gooding, Joseph, 278, 333

Gore, Christopher, 49

Gorman, Senator Arthur P., 427

Grace, Eyre, Cragin Syndicate, 384, 386

Graham, John, 91

"Granadine Confederation," 241 (*see also* Colombia)

Granger, Henry, 282

Grant, U. S., on Chiriquí project, 277; relations with de Gogorza, 278; and canal, 347-351, 354-357, 360, 363-364

Granville, Lord, on European guarantee, 371-372; modification of Clayton-Bulwer Treaty, 372-374

Grenville, Lord, on Spanish American independence, 43, 44

Great Britain, piracy, 9-10; relations with the *Comuneros*, 21; and Colombian independence, 21-23, 28, 31-32, 41-58, 60-61, 69, 74, 91-94, 99, 103-105, 127-132; Nariño in, 28; Sir Thomas Picton and revolutionists, 32; interest and activities in Caribbean area and Spanish Main, 30-35; attack on Cartagena (1741), 35; Nootka Sound controversy, 38-40; volunteers in Venezuela (1818), 69; rivalry with U. S., 78-81, 83-84, 112-115, 134, 145-147, 159, 167-174, 176, 182, 183, 186, 215, 263 264, 266-267, 290, 326-330, 345-346, 349, 443, 446, 453, 468, 477-478; -U. S. coöperation 91, 92, 334-336, 385-386; officers in early Colombian navy, 112; aides in Colombian government, 113; and idea of monarchy for Colombia, 121; and contemplate invasion of Cuba, 134-137; and Bolívar's idea of a confederation, 143-144; consular service in Colombia, 176; and canal, 179, 182, 183, 196, 198, 199, 324, 333-336, 339, 344, 349; and Biddle mission, 186; possibility of Colombia turning Panama over to, for debts, 190; (*see* Mosquito Coast); Colombia fears aggression of, 197, 199, 201, 204; (*see* European guarantee of canal routes); and Treaty of 1846, 203-204, 206; aggression in Caribbean, 212, 213, 325, 326; intervention on Isthmus, 224, 332; France-U. S. protectorate over Panama suggested, 225, 227; on U. S. intervention, 253, 254, 332; blockade regarding "MacIntosh Loan," 290; rumor of attempt to secure naval base, 292; rivalry between U. S., France and, 290, 345, 346, 349, 382, 383; and Panama Riot, 294, 298-299, 314, 316;

Clayton-Bulwer Treaty, 328, 329, 331-332, 372-374; and U. S. rivalry in Caribbean, 325-330; treaties with Honduras and Nicaragua, 331-332; negotiations with Mosquera, 340-341; Hay-Pauncefote Treaty, 385-386; commercial interests in Colombia, 462, 468; loans to Colombia, 471

Greeley, Horace, 347

Green, James S., minister to Colombia, 236, 286, 330, 333

Gresham, Walter Q., 260, 271, 318

Griswold, J. H., 356 n

Guadalupe, Island of, 31

Gual, Manuel (early revolutionary leader), 30, 31, 42-44, 48

Gual, Pedro, 89, 97, 110, 111; attitude towards U. S., 124, 127; on American confederation, 132, 138, 146; on British in Colombia, 114, 146-147; and Treaty of 1824, 133-134; and Panama Congress, 141, 145; on claims, 165

Guatemala, 9 n, 268, 325

Guayana, 58

Guayaquil, Santiago de, 5, 33, 60, 67, 71-72, 111

Guizot, François, and canal, 196, 197; and Isthmian guarantee, 200, 211

Gulf Oil Company, 467, 468, 470, 476

Guzmán, Antonio Leocadio, 118

Habrahan (Habraan), Miguel, 221-222

Hains, Colonel Peter C., 381 n

Hale, Senator Eugene, 427

Hall, H. H., 360

Hamilton, Alexander, 36, 38, 39, 41, 45-48, 73

Hamilton, James (British), 113

Hamilton, Colonel J. P., 105, 114

Handy, Charles O., 84

Hanna, Mark, 387

Hannegan, Senator Edward A., 210

Hanseatic cities, and European guarantee of Isthmus, 214

Hargous, Peter A., 325

Harmony and López, 305 n

Harrison, Carter Bassett, 154

Harrison, General W. H., mission to Colombia, 153-158, 165, 170

Harrison, Benjamin, on reciprocal agreements, 266, 269-270

Harrison (Governor of Federal Reserve Bank of N. Y.), 474

Hart, Charles Burdett, minister to Colombia, on Colombian trade, 271; on claims, 318-319; and canal, 390

Hatfield, Captain Chester, 351 n

Haupt, Lewis M., 381 n

Hawley, Lieutenant, 77

Hay, John, and claims, 318-319; and Panama secession, 398, 399, 402, 403, 416, 428-431; and canal, 385 n, 406-410, 423, 426; on reconciliation with Colombia, 434 (*see also* Hay-Bunau-Varilla, Hay-Herran, Hay-Pauncefote Treaties)

Hay-Bunau-Varilla Treaty, 402, 422, 427

Hay-Herran Treaty, 388-391, 396-397, 403, 408, 412, 415, 423, 424, 426, 430, 433

Hay-Pauncefote Treaty, 385-386, 408, 424

Hayes, Rutherford B., on Chiriquí project, 277; and canal, 361-364, 366

Hebbard, R. W., and Company, 466 n

Hellert (or Ellet) (French), 197

Henderson, James, 333

Herrán, Pedro A., leader of opposition, 120; restores peace in Colombia, 163; alarmed at abrupt departure of U. S. charge Semple, 163-64; enlightened administration of, 164; on U. S. trade relations with Colombia, 174; policy on concessions, 195; fear of British, 197; representative to U. S., 209; on Treaty of 1846, 209-210, 213, 256; protests against actions of North Americans on Isthmus, 220; on taxes at Panama, 237-241; on passage of North American troops across Isthmus, 245-246; offers to mediate between Davis and Lincoln, 252; on Mosquera government, 252-253, 256; and Panama Railroad Company contract, 272; and Chiriquí Improvement Company, 274; on Panama Riot claims, 286-287, 290, 297-299, 300; and canal, 324; on Mosquitia, 327; on North American intervention, 332

Herrán, Tomás, chargé, on U. S. policy in Panama secession, 402; and canal, 390-391, 406-409

Herrera, Juan Días, 19

Herrera, Tomás, 191

Heuer, Captain W. H., 351 n

Higginson, John, 35

Hise, Elijah, 325

Hislop, Wellwood, 181

Hitchcock, Senator Gilbert M., resolution, 440

Hoar, Senator George F., 427

Holguín, Carlos, 368

Holguín, Jorge, 375, 403 n

Holland, 195

Honda, 5

Honduras, 268, 325, 331-332

Hooke, William, 35

Hoyt, E., 356 n

Howard's Sons, Benjamin (*see* Boston Ice Co.)

Howe, Lord, 38

Hubbard, Commander John, 233, 418

Huertas, Commander, 401

Hughes, Jr., Christopher, 83

Hughes, Charles Evans, 464

Hull, Cordell, 480

Humboldt, Baron von, 180-181, 334

Humphreys, General A. A., 351 n

Hurlbut, Stephen A., minister to Colombia, on extradition treaty, 247; trade with Colombia, 263; reciprocity, 268-269: U. S. violation of Treaty of 1846, 269-270; the *Montijo* arbitration, 307; and canal, 347-350

Hurtado, Manuel José, 117

Hurtado, J. M., minister from Colombia, and claims, 301, 311-315, 317-318

Hutin, director-general of New Panama Canal Company, 383

Hyde de Neuville, 135-136

Illinois (U. S. vessel), 221

Independence (U. S. vessel), 224

Index (Catholic Church), 11, 12

Indians, in Colombia, 5-7, 13; in uprisings, 19-23; education of, 111

Ingersoll, Henry, 52

Ingraham, J. H., 192

Inquisition, 11, 12

International Ocean Telegraph Company of New York, 280

"Inter-Oceanic Republic," 432

Intervention, U. S. on Isthmus, 219-234, 249, 253, 254, 257-261, 285, 288, 308, 310, 315, 317-319, 331-332, 353, 367, 372, 375-376, 389, 395-401, 416-418, 421-423

Investments (U. S. in Colombia), on Isthmus, 272-280; on Mainland, 116-117, 280-284, 466-479; loans, 284, 471-480; total (1913), 284, (to date), 478; protection of, 285-323, 389 (*see* Claims-U. S.)

Iowa (U. S. vessel), 232

Iroquois (U. S. vessel), 230

Irvine, Baptis, special agent to Angostura, 83-84, 165; offensive letters to Bolívar, 124-125

Isaacs and Asch (Colón fire claimants), 308

Isthmian Canal Company, 344 n

Isthmian Communications, early ideas of, 178-180; legendary accounts of, 179-181, 357; growth of idea: international, 180-181; Colombia considers, 181-182; North Americans manifest interest in, 182-193; canal surveys, 182 n, 196-199, 332-337, 351-358, 360, 429; Biddle mission, 185-189; increasing rivalry over, 197, 199; concessions granted, 185, 187, 194-196, 199-200, 333, 335-337, 351, 358-360; (*see* European guarantee of canal routes); revival of interest in, 323-326, 332-340; U. S. and canal (general), 180-198, 200-215, 278-279, 323-391; (*see* Clayton-Bulwer Treaty); Seward enthusiastic over, 342-347; Panama versus Nicaragua, 380-384; (*see* Hay-Pauncefote Treaty); (*see* *also* Atrato, Caledonia Bay, Chiriquí, Darién, Nicaragua, Panama, San Blas, San Juan, Tehuantepec canal routes)

Italy, 370

Jackson, Andrew, and Great Britain, 94; admiration of Bolívar, 158-159; and claims' negotiations, 166; on Biddle mission, 185, 188-189

Jacob, Charles D., minister to Colombia, 311, 312 n, 317

Jamaica, 56, 57, 67, 69

James and Company (Colón fire claimant), 308 n

Jastran, Colonel Felix, 76

Jefferson, Thomas, on Spanish American colonies and their independence struggle, 35-36, 39-41, 48, 50-53, 91, 126; contact with Miranda, 50, 73; and canal, 180

Jeffries, General Herbert O., 397

Jesuits, 11, 12 n, 19-20, 25, 37

John L. Stephens (steamer), 221

Johnson, Andrew, 341, 343-346

Johnson, Emory R., 381 n

Johnson, Senator Hiram, 455

Johnston, Colonel (British), 113

Johnston, W. E., 358 n

Jones, George W., minister to Colombia, 251-252, 299

Jouett, Acting Rear Admiral James E., 229, 230

Junín, Battle of, 72 n

Kaye, Captain, 34

Keith, Minor C., 283

Kelley, Frederick M., 278, 334-336, 340, 344 n, 360, 384 n

Kellogg, Frank B., 451, 455, 470

Kemmerer, E. W., 472, 474

Kennish, Captain William, 334

Kenyon, Senator William S., 455

Kersaint (French), 40

Ketchum, M., 356 n

King, Yelverton P., chargé to Colombia, 286

King, Rufus, minister to Great Britain, 42-43, 45-47, 49, 50, 52-53, 73

Klein, Mateo, 200

Morales, Juan Bautista, 21-22, 34
Morgan, Henry (buccaneer), 179
Morgan, Senator J. T., 381, 387, 427
Morillo, General Pablo, 67-69, 71
Morison, George S., 381 n, 385 n
Moro, Graetano, survey of Tehuantepec route, 197
Morse, Isaac E., 223-224, 290, 292, 294-295, 297
Mosquera, Joaquín, 122, 123, 127
Mosquera, Manuel M., 194-200, 214
Mosquera, Tomás C. de, restores peace to Colombia, 163; enlightened administration of, 164, 198; fails in negotiations for European guarantee, 198-199; turns to U. S., 200-202; on Treaty of 1846, 202, 203, 209; and Panama, 225, 251; defeat and revolution, 241, 300; on U. S. Civil War, 252; and Colombian civil war, 252-253, 256; U. S. recognition of, 254; and Chiriquí communications, 277; and Cartagena Riot, 306; on U. S. intervention on Isthmus, 332; and canal, 336, 342; and the British, 340-341; hatred of U. S., 341 n
Mosquito Coast (Mosquitia), Colombia and Great Britain claim, 182, 183, 194, 197-200, 210, 325-328, 331-332, 389
Murat, Joachim, 57
Murillo, Manuel, minister from Colombia, defeated for president, 241; in New York, 252, 254; and Chiriquí Negro colonization project, 276; and claims, 301, 304; suggested convention regarding rights of foreigners in civil war, 304; and canal, 337; mission of friendship to U. S., 342
Murray, Lord, 445
Mutis, José Celestino, 25

Napoleon I, 56-58, 74
Napoleon III, 198
Nariño, Antonio, 24, 26-30, 32, 36, 65-66
Narváez, José, 59
Nashville (U. S. vessel), 399, 400
National City Bank, 474, 476

Naval and coaling stations, 292, 335, 362, 366-367
Negro, in Colombia, 5-7; attempts to establish monarchy, 19; laborers on Panama railroad, 221; leader in Panama disturbance, 229; plan of sending, to Chiriquí to mine coal for navy, 275-277
Neiva, 5, 64-66, 70
Nelson, Consul, 280, 292
Nelson, Acting Master Thomas, 226
New, Senator Harry S., 454
New Granada (*see* Colombia)
New Granada Canal and Steam Navigation Company of New York, 281
Newlands, Senator Francis G., 427
New Panama Canal Company (French), 379-380, 382-384, 387, 396, 398, 408-412, 424, 434 (*see also* Panama Canal Company)
New York and South American Contract Company, 281-282
Nicaragua, U. S. reciprocal agreement with, 268; North Americans in, 296; friendly to U. S. and canal, 325; fears British aggression, turns to U. S., 327; Cass-Yrisarri Treaty, 331; treaty with Great Britain, 331-332; Dickinson-Ayón Treaty, 340; unsuccessful canal negotiations, 354-356; Frelinghuysen-Zavala Treaty, 374, 376, 378-379; (*see also* Nicaragua canal route)
Nicaragua canal route, 179, 181-184, 189, 194, 197-198, 202, 291, 323, 325-327, 340, 351-360, 362-364, 371 n, 372-374, 376, 378-379, 381-384, 386-388, 390, 408, 424-426, 477
Nicaragua Canal Construction Company, 379
Nicuesa, Diego de, 4
Noble, Alfred, 381 n
Noble, Henry (Colón fire claimant), 309
Nootka Sound Controversy, 38-40
Norris, Senator George W., 456
Nuestras costas incultas, anti-British pamphlet, 199

Núñez, Rafael, and possible secession of coastal states, 227; inauguration, 228, 258; on Panama, 230-231, 244, 310; loans to government of, by Panama Railroad Company, 284; sounds Scruggs regarding alliance, 375

Obaldía, Governor José de, 220

Obaldía, Governor José Domingo de, 401

Obando, José María, 121

Obarrio, Nicanor A. de, 397 n

O'Bryan, J. T., 282

Ocaña, 5, 67, 120

Ogden, Samuel G., 49, 52

Oil, and Thomson-Urrutia Treaty, 443, 444, 449-457; U. S. and Colombia regarding, 466-471, 473-477

Ojeda, Alonso de, 3, 4, 10

Olaya Herrera, Enrique, and Thomson-Urrutia Treaty, 457; as president, 473-480

Omaña, Nicholas Mauricio de, 88

Onís, Luis de (Spanish), 94

O'Leary, General, 121, 153

Oliver, Jack, 221

Olney Richard and claims 318; on Clayton-Bulwer Treaty 385

Oreo, Telésforo de, 86, 87

Orinoco River, 324

Ortiz, Tomás, 11

Ospina, Mariano, election of, 241; and Panama Riot claims, 298

Ospina, Pedro Nel, on Colombian mission to U. S. regarding Panama secession, 403 n; and U. S.-Colombian reconciliation, 437; in U. S., 464, 465; and finances, 472

Oyón, Gonzalo de, 19

Pacific Mail Steamship Company of New York, 236, 242, 280

Páez, José Antonio, 70, 117-119, 121, 122, 125

Page, Walter Hines, 445

Paine, Thomas, 38, 41, 75

Palacio Fajardo, Manuel, 88-89

Palmerston, Lord, 194, 335

Pamplona, 20, 23, 63-67, 70

Panama, 3-5, 7, 11, 33, 67, 71, 178; secession of, 159, 183, 190-193, 224-234, 243, 339, 395-404; ports opened to free trade, 185; Biddle mission to, 185-186; U. S. fear of British aggression against, 159, 183, 215; reincorporated in Colombia, 195; threatened Flores expeditions across, 204, 250-251, 254; revolution and disturbances, 219-245, 251-254, 353, 395; North American disruptive influence in, 219-221, 235; (see Intervention); Riot (1856) and claims, 221-224, 288-302; idea of foreign protectorate over, 225, 227-230; as a federal department, 230-233; passenger, tonnage and mail taxes, 235-245, 339; passage of U. S. troops across, 245-247; passage of U. S. prisoners across, 247-249; fear of foreign seizure of, 250, 287, 310, 327, 329, 375, 378-380, 408; influence of U. S. Civil War on Isthmian policy, 251-254; (see Treaty of 1846); U. S. steamship lines to, 262; importance of, in U. S. trade, 262; U. S. trade commission visits, 265; North American investments in, 272-280; strategic importance of, 285; *Montijo* arbitration, 307-308; Colón fire claims, 308-317; *Panama Star and Herald* and *Estrella de Panama*, 226 n, 279, 317-319, 398 n; French colonization of, 337, 374-375; Revolution of 1903, 395-404; U. S. recognizes, 401-402; Colombia prevented from suppressing revolt, 402-403; U. S. refuses to arbitrate with Colombia regarding, 403-404; legality and morality of U. S. course in Panama secession, 404-426; flag made in New York, 419; -Costa Rica boundary dispute, 423; Hay-Bunau-Varilla Treaty, 427; U. S. views on Roosevelt's Panama policy, 427-429; Colombia's attempt at reconciliation with U. S., 429-439; -Colombia boundary dispute, 434-435; (see also Panama Canal, Panama Canal Company, Panama Railroad Company, Thomson-Urrutia Treaty)

Panama Canal (*see also* Isthmian communications), Colombia considers a, 181-182; Biddle mission regarding, 185-189; (*see* European guarantee of canal routes); U. S. and, 200, 323-326, 329, 332-337, 356-391, 395-426; (*see also* Clayton-Bulwer Treaty); gaining in popularity, 332-340; French and, 196-200, 356-361, 377, 387-388; A. de Gogorza and, 356-358; U. S. opposition to a French, 359-361, 374-375, 379-380; U. S. approached on canal treaty, 341-342; Seward enthusiastic over, 342-347; Grant and, 347-350; Protocol of 1881, 364-369; versus Nicaragua, 380-384, 386-388; chosen by U. S., 386-388; U. S. negotiations with Colombia. over, 388-391; Colombia and U. S. reconciliation, 440-441; Anglo-American rivalry over oil concessions and, 468; (*see also* following treaties: of 1846; C l a y t o n-Bulwer; Hay-Herrán; Hay-Pauncefote; Hay-Bunau-Varilla; Thomson-Urrutia)

Panama Canal Company (French), 228, 273, 279, 309, 311, 377-380; (*see also* New Panama Canal Company)

Panama Congress, 137-147, 183

Panama Railroad Company, 226 n, 228, 238, 239, 242, 272-273, 280, 284, 291, 308 n, 309, 311, 324, 330-333, 336, 340-341, 348, 358, 380, 391, 411, 435 n, 438

Panama Riot, 221-224, 237, 246, 286, 288-302, 308, 312-313, 330-331

Panama Star and Herald, 226 n, 279, 317-319, 398 n

Pan American confederation, early ideas of, 127, 137-139; Monroe Doctrine, 125-132; Panama Congress, 139-147; Bolívar's ideas on, 143-144

Pan American Conferences, 267, 315, 432, 433

Pan American Society, 474

Pan American Union, 446, 447

Panaquire, 19

Pando y Sanllorente, Captain Juan José, 58

Panther (U. S. steamer), 232

Papel periódico de la cuidad de Santa Fé de Bogotá, 25

Paredes, Victoriano de, chargé from Colombia, 245, 250

Paris, Treaty of (1763), 34

Párraga, F., 276

Parrish and Company, 466 n

Pascal, M., 117

Pasco, Samuel, 381 n

Pasto, 5, 117

Patterson, Captain C. P., 351 n, 356 n

Patterson, William, 179

Pauncefote, Lord (*see* Hay-Pauncefote Treaty)

Paya, 70

Pearson, Admiral, 246, 255

Pearson, S., and Son, Limited (London), 444-446

Pensacola (U. S. vessel), 227

Penobscot (U. S. vessel), 226

Pérez, Santiago, 353, 358

Perry, Captain Oliver H., 84, 165

Perry, Captain Thomas, 232

Pershing, General John J., 464

Peru, 7, 9 n, 23, 71 n, 121, 204, 246, 250, 254, 339

Philip, Hoffman, minister to Colombia, 449-450

Phillip II, 179

Phillip III, 179

Pichincha, Battle of, 72

Pickering, Timothy, 46, 49

Pickett, J. C., 172

Picornell, Juan Bautista, 30, 31

Picton, Governor Thomas, 31-32, 43, 48

Pierce, Franklin, 287, 290, 292-293, 295

Piles, Samuel H., minister to Colombia, 469-470

Pinckney, Charles Coatesworth, 45

Pitá, Antonio, 21, 34

Pitt, William, 28, 38-40, 42, 44-45, 48-49

Poinsett, Joel R., 91, 143, 147

Poletica (Russian), 93

Polk, James K., on Colombian trade relations, 175; and Isthmian communications, 202, 324, 327; on Treaty of 1846, 207-209

Pombo, Lino de, and Isthmian communications, 184, 187; Colombo-American trade relations, 173-175; and Treaty of 1846, 206; on Panama taxes, 238-239; and Panama Riot, 289, 292-297

Pombo, Miguel de, 75

Pombo, Rafael, chargé from Colombia, 251, 297

Pomerene, Senator Atlee, 455

Pomeroy, Senator Samuel C., 275, 276

Popayán, 5, 11, 19, 25, 67, 70, 111, 121

Popham, Sir Home 36

Porter, Commander W. D., 224

Portland Cabinet (British), 55

Porto Bello, 9, 33, 185

Postal Convention of 1844, 243

Pownall, Governor, 34

Precursores, Los, 23-32

Prescott, H. G., 397, 418

Prestán, leader of Isthmian revolt, 229, 312

Primicias de la cultura de Quito, 24

Privateers, 81-85

Protection of U. S. citizens and property, 285-323

Protocol of 1881, 364-369

Providencia Island, 438

Prussia, 344, 348, 349

Puente Real, 20, 23

Puerta, Battle of, 66

Puerto Cabello, 58, 62, 71, 76

Puerto Rico, 56, 137

Quesada, Jiménez de, 10-11

Quevedo, Juan de, 11

Quijano Otero, J. M., 357 n

Quito, 5, 7, 19-20, 23-24, 26, 59-60, 63, 67, 71-72, 89 n, 109, 111, 123

R. R. Cuyler or *Rayo* (Colombian vessel), 306

Radcliff, William, 182-185, 189-193, 210 n

Ragonesi, Papal nuncio, 433

Railroads, North American investments in Colombia, 281-283; transcontinental, influence of their completion on canal, 355; suggested, from coast to Bogotá, 366; opposition of transcontinental, to canal, 364 n, 382

Rainey Resolution, 440

Randall, W. W., 283

Ranger (U. S. vessel), 232

Raspadura Canal legend, 179, 334

Rathbun, L. W. (Colón fire claimant), 308 n

Ravenga, José Rafael, 87, 152

Raymond, Henry J., 347

Raymond Concrete Pile Company, 466 n

Raynal, Abbé, 27

Raynor, J. A., 356 n

Reciprocity, U. S. offers, 171; early Colombian efforts for, 264; President Arthur advocates, 264-267; retaliatory, 267-270; Wilson Tariff Act of 1894, 270-271; Dingley Tariff Act of 1897, 271

Reed, Senator James A., 455

Reed, Thomas B. (speaker), 385 n

Reid, Whitelaw, 416 n

Rengifo, Julio, minister from Colombia, on claims, 318; and canal, 382-383

Republican Party, and New Panama Canal Company, 387 n

Restrepo, Carlos E., 437, 438

Restrepo, Felix, 112

Restrepo, José Manuel, 110, 152

Révérend, Doctor (French), 123

Reyes, Rafael, on U. S. and Panama, 403; and canal, 407, 409, 422; and Hay regarding Panama revolution, 428; reconciliation efforts with U. S., 429-437

Ricaurte, José Antonio, 27

Riohacha, 67

Rivas, Rafael, on Anglo-American rivalry, 214, 327, 329

Robinson, E. W., 117

Robinson, Tracy (Colón fire claimant), 308-310

Robinson, William, 76

Rodney, Caesar, 91

Rodríguez (Ramírez) de Arellano, Captain ———, 26

Rodríguez, minister from the Greater Republic of Central America, 382

Rogers, Lieutenant Charles C., 377

Roosevelt, Franklin Delano, 478, 480

Roosevelt, Theodore, and Panama secession and canal, 219, 233, 398-400, 402, 408, 412-417, 420-430; and Colombian reconciliation, 435, 437-439; and Thomson-Urrutia Treaty, 442, 443, 451, 452, 454-456

Root, Elihu, and canal, 424-425; and Roosevelt policy in Panama, 428, 431; and reconciliation with Colombia, 433-435

Root-Arosemena Treaty, 435

Root-Cortés Treaty, 435

Roscio, Juan Germán, 74-75

Rousseau, 26 n, 27

Rublee, George, 475, 477

Rundell, Bridge and Rundell (British), 113

Rush, Richard, 91

Russell, William W., minister to Colombia, 429

Russia, 92-94, 99, 125-132, 136-137, 330

Saavedra Cerón, Alvaro de, 178-179

Saint Aulaire, M. de, 196

St. Marys (U. S. vessel), 223, 224, 226

Salazar, José María, minister from Colombia, 104, 124-125; on Monroe Doctrine, 132; and Cuba, 136, 137; on U. S. and Panama Congress, 139, 141

Salazar, General Víctor M., 233

Salgar, Eustorgio, minister from Colombia, attempts to negotiate postal convention, 243; on interpretation of Article XXXV, 247; on claims, 301; and canal, 341-342, 368

Salomón, Augusto, and Company, 194-196, 199-200, 212

Salvador, 268, 325

Sámano, Juan, 68, 70

Samper, José M., 337

San Andrés Island, 438

San Bartolomé, college of, 25

San Blas canal route, 334, 351 n, 384

San Blas Conspiracy (Spain), 30

Sánchez, Cuban secret agent, 135

San Francisco, and Panama Riot, 286

San Juan (Nicaragua), British seize, 325-327

San Juan River, possible canal route, 179

San Martín, José de, 72

San Mateo, capitulation of, 62, 66

Santamaría, Miguel, 127

Santa Marta, 5, 11, 19, 21, 64, 66, 67, 462

Santander, Francisco de Paula, 69, 70, 111; vice-president of Republic of Colombia, 109; and education, 110; British on his staff, 113; decree of conscription, 117-118; appeals to Páez, 118; opposes Bolívar, 119-121; attitude on Monroe Doctrine, 131-132, 139; and Panama Congress, 139, 140; on Watts's letter, 152; chosen president, 160; return of, 160-161; attitude towards Moore and Jackson administration, 161, 172; administration, 161-163; U. S. and, 162-163; leader of anti-administration forces, 163; and canal, 182-185; and Biddle mission, 187

Santo Domingo, 51, 338

Santo Domingo Vila, General Ramón, 229, 317-318, 366-368

Santuario, Battle of, 123

Sarmiento, Joaquín, 357

Sayre, Stephen, 41

Scott, Alexander, 79-80

Scrafford, C. I., 247, 248

Scruggs, William L., minister to Colombia, and Panama secession, 227-228; on intervention, 258-259; and *Montijo* arbitration, 307-308; Colón fire claims, 311; canal, 353, 374-375

Selfridge, Commander T. O., 351, 358 n

Seligman, J. and W., 364 n

Semanario del Nuevo Reino de Granada (Bogotá), 25

Semple, James, chargé to Colombia, abrupt departure of, 163-164; and claims, 167; and Isthmian communication, 202; on trade negotiations, 173-174

Sergeant, John, 141-143, 147

Severs, Lieutenant Thomas, 77

Sevier, Senator Ambrose H., on Treaty of 1846, 209, 210

Seward, William H., not interested in Panama protectorate, 227; opposes Isthmian taxes, 241, 243; on right of U. S. to send troops across Isthmus, 246-247; avoids Isthmian discussion during Civil War, 251; on Anglo-French attitude towards U. S. intervention, 253, 254; on Article XXXV of Treaty of 1846, 255-256; on claims, 301, 305; his policy toward Colombia, 303; on rights of foreigners in country during civil war, 304; and Cartagena Riot, 306-307; and U. S. intervention, 332; and canal, 333-334, 341-347; as imperialist, 338-339

Seward, William H., Jr., and canal, 344 n

Shaler, Colonel J. S., 397, 418

Shelbourne, Lord, 38

Shenandoah (U. S. vessel), 229, 230

Sherman, John, 271

Shortridge, Senator Samuel M., 454

Shuber, H., and Brother, 279-280, 307

Shufeldt, Captain R. W., 351 n

Sickles, Major General D. E., 246-247, 277 n, 337

Sidney, Lord, 38

Sinclair Exploration Company, 475

Smith, Senator Marcus A., 449, 455

Smith, Colonel William, 38, 41, 49, 52, 54, 73

Smith, U. S. consul at Cartagena, 266

Smythe, Clifford, 429

Snyder, A. G., chargé to Colombia, 428-429

Snyder Banana Company of New Jersey, 283

La sociedad de los amigos de país, 186

La sociedad patriótica o escuela de la concordia, 24

La société civile internationale du canal interoceánique, 357

Socorro, 5, 20, 63, 64, 70

Soledad, 67

Soto, Francisco, 119

Spain, discovery and settlement of New Granada, 3-7; absolutism of Peninsular Spaniards in colony, 7-8; irrational colonial economic system, 8-10; powerful, exacting, and reactionary church in New Granada, 10-13; parallels and contrasts between colonial Colombia and English colonies, 12-15; results of rule in New Granada, 15-16; colonial revolts against, 19-32; interest and activities in Caribbean area and Spanish Main, 33-35; and Spanish American independence, 35-66, 68-72, 92-94, 102, 125-132; reconquest of Colombia, 67-68; triumph of patriots over, 68-72; and privateers, 82, 83; protests against U. S. recognition of Colombia, 102; and Cuba, 134-137; exploration of Americas, 178; and canal, 178-181; on foreign guarantee of Isthmus, 195, 370; reported assistance to Flores, 204, 250-251, 254; possible war with Peru, 246; U. S. war with, 271, 383

Spooner Act, 387, 389, 391, 406, 408 n, 409, 424

Sprague, Senator William, 347, 356 n

Squier, Ephraim G., 325

Standard Oil Company, 467, 475

Steele, J. W., 471

Stephens, John L., 189, 272

Sterling, Senator Thomas, 454

Stimson, Henry L., 474, 476

Stone, Senator William J., 409, 442, 448

Strain, Lieutenant Isaac C., 333, 335

Strauss, Oscar S., 414

Suárez, Marco Fidel, 450, 457

Sucre, Antonio J. de, advance on Guayaquil and Quito, 71; in Battle of Pichincha, 72; assassination of, 122

Sullivan, Peter I, minister to Colombia, and Cartagena Riot, 306; and canal, 342-347

Swain, Captain Joseph C., 77

Swatara (U. S. vessel), 230

Taboga (steamer), 221

Taft, William Howard, 437

Talleyrand, Charles Maurice de, 45, 49

Tallien, Jean Lambert, 28

Tanco, Mariano, 308

Tariff, discussion of discriminating, 169-175, 285; (*see also* Reciprocity)

Tayloe, Edward, 154-156

Taylor, R. W., 117

Taylor, Zachary, attitude towards Treaty of 1846, 235; and canal, 326 n, 327

Tehuantepec canal route, 179, 197, 323-325, 327, 360, 364, 376, 380

Teller, Daniel W., 339

El Telegrama (see *Estrella de Panama*)

Tennessee (U. S. vessel), 230

Texas Company, 475

The Hague Tribunal, 403, 422

Thierry, Baron de, 185, 186, 188

Thomas, Senator Charles S., 398 n, 451

Thompson, Ambrose W., 274-277, 335

Thompson, R. W., 364

Thompson, Doctor (of State Department), 50

Thompson (British), 113

Thomson, Thaddeus A., appointed minister to Colombia, 440; (*see also* Thomson-Urrutia Treaty)

Thomson-Urrutia Treaty, 408 n, 441-457, 466, 471

Tiger (U. S. merchant ship), 83

Tigre Island, 325-326, 339

Todd, Charles S., "confidential agent" to Bogotá, 84, 98-99, 103, 125; fears British influence in Colombia, 114, 183; on Gual's lack of cordiality, 124; and first Colombo-American treaty, 133-134; and American confederation, 138; and claims, 165; on commercial discrimination against U. S., 169

Torres, Don Manuel, residing in Philadelphia, 37; and recognition of Colombia, 97-103; suggests "American System," 126; discusses treaty with U. S., 132-134; on commercial discrimination against U. S., 169

Torres, Colonel, and Panama Revolution, 233, 401, 418

Totten, George H., 222, 223, 280

Tovar, Juan B., 401

Tovar, Commander, 401

Trautwine, T. C., 334

Treaty of 1824, 132-134

Treaty of 1846, 202-215, 285, 327, 342; Colombia's and U. S. attitudes towards, 235; protests under, 236-239; Article XXXV interpreted, 245, 254-261, 269-271, 389-390, 410, 417, 420, 431; influence on commerce, 262; and reciprocity, 269; inspires confidence and enlists North American capital, 272; Hurlbut and, 307, 349; claims under, 312, 314, 315; (*see* Treaties of 1857 and 1864); Garridos's fear of U. S. cancellation of, 340-341; renewal of neutrality guarantee proposed, 352; desire to supplant Article XXXV, 354-355; proposed cancellation, 360; Protocol of 1881, 364-369; and Clayton-Bulwer Treaty, 372; legality and morality of U. S. policy in 1903 under, 395-427; text of relevant clauses of, appendix, 485-491; (*see also* European guarantee, Interventions)

Treaties of 1857 and 1864 (claims), 241, 288-302, 313, 423

Trescot, W. H., 367

Trinidad (British), 31, 42, 43, 48

Tropical Oil Company of Pittsburgh, 467, 471, 475

Trujillo, 61, 66

Truxillo y Torres, Manuel (*see* Torres, Don Manuel)

Truxton, Commodore, 50

Tunja, 5, 64-66, 70, 110, 111

Tupac Amarú revolt, 21-23

Türr, General Étienne, 357
Tuscarora (U. S. vessel), 227
Tyler, John, 175

Uhlen and Company, 466 n
United Fruit Company, 283, 284
United Magdalena Steam Navigation Company, 281, 305 n
United Provinces of New Granada (*see* Colombia)
United States, parallels and contrasts between colonial Colombia and, 12-15; early attitude and influence, 35-37; X. Y. Z. affair, 45-46; Venezuelan Expedition of 1806, 49-54; and Colombian independence, 37-54, 60-61, 73-75, 86-102; citizens in Colombian patriot service, 76-78, 112; trade with Colombia, 75-76, 78-85, 115-117, 169-177, 262-271; protests against impressment of its sailors, 77-78; -British rivalry, 78-81, 83-84, 112-115, 134, 145-147, 159, 167-174, 176, 182, 183, 186, 215, 263-264, 266-267, 290, 326-330, 345-346, 349, 443, 446, 453, 468, 477-478; privateers, seizures, and unsettled claims, 81-85; recognition, policy of, 86-104; -British coöperation, 91-92, 334-336, 385-386; Colombian constitution compared with that of, 109; citizens in business in Colombia, 116-117; early relations with Colombia, 124-125 (*see* Monroe Doctrine); Treaty of 1824, 132-134; attitude regarding contemplated invasion of Cuba, 134-137; and Panama Congress, 137-147; Watts's letter, 151-153; Harrison mission, 153-158; temporary rapprochement with Colombia, 158-159, 162; attitude towards Santander, 162-163; Colombo-American friction, 163-164; rapprochement with Colombia under Herrán and Mosquera, 164; unsuccessful claims negotiations with Colombia, 165-169; and canal, 180-198, 200-215, 278-279, 323-391 (*see also* various canal routes); Biddle mission, 185-189; and Panama secession, 190-193, 395-404; attitude towards European guarantee of Isthmus, 194-200, 214-215, 296, 369-372 (*see* Treaty of 1846); citizens' disruptive influence on Isthmus, 219-221, 235; and Panama Riot, 221-224, 288-302; -Great Britain-France protectorate over Panama suggested, 225, 227; idea of Yankee protectorate, 227-230; Colombia asks intervention, 229; protests against passenger, tonnage, and mail taxes, 235-245; passage of U. S. troops across Isthmus, 245-247; passage of prisoners across Isthmus, 247-249; Colombia fears aggression of, 250; and rumored Flores expedition, 204, 250-251; influence of Civil War upon Isthmian policy, 251-254; recognition of Mosquera government, 253-254; President Arthur advocates reciprocity, 264-267; retaliatory reciprocity, 267-270; war with Spain, 271, 383; (*see* Treaties of 1857 and 1864); -France rivalry, 290, 345-346, 349, 358-361, 374-375, 378-380, 382, 383; (*see* Naval and coaling stations); Latin America fears aggression of, on Isthmus, 287; West Coast development and influence upon Isthmian policy, 285, 291-292; influence of Civil War on Colombian relations, 303-304; Colombia grows more independent towards, 304-308; Cartagena Riot, 306-307; *Montijo* arbitration, 307-308; Colón fire claims, 308-317; evolution of canal policy of, 323-395; British seizure of San Juan and Tigre Island and effect on canal policy, 325-326; (*see* Clayton-Bulwer Treaty); Cass-Yrisarri Treaty, 331; policy of "Manifest Destiny," 323, 338; Grant's futile canal negotiations, 347-350; Colombia offers canal treaty to, 351-354; unsuccessful Nicaraguan negotiations, 354-356; Gogorza delivers Panama to French, 356-358; turns definitely

to Nicaragua, 357; and De Lesseps canal project, 359-364; Protocol of 1881, 364-369; Cleveland turns provincial, 374-376; Nicaragua versus Panama, 380-384, 386-388; Hay-Pauncefote Treaty, 385-386, 408, 424; chooses Panama route, 386-388; Spooner Act and Colombia, 387-388; (*see* Hay-Herrán Treaty); and Panama secession, 395, 397-401; recognizes independence of Panama, 401-402; prevents Colombia from suppressing Panama revolt, 402-403; refuses to arbitrate regarding Panama, 403-404; legality and morality of U. S. course during Panama secession, 404-426; Hay-Bunau-Varilla Treaty, 427; Roosevelt's policy considered, 427-429; and Colombian reconciliation, 429-441; (*see* Thomson-U r r u t i a Treaty); and oil in Colombia, 443, 444, 449-457, 466-471, 474-477; commercial interest in Colombia, 461; -Colombian rapprochement, 464-466; interest in Colombia's future, 477-480; (*see also* Claims, Commerce, Intervention, Investments, Isthmian communications, Nicaragua, Panama, Tehuantepec)

United States Atlantic and Pacific Canal Company, 182 n

United States of Colombia (*see* Colombia)

Upham, N. G., 300

Upshur, Abel P., 175, 195

Urdaneta, General Rafael, 123, 158, 159, 170

Uribe, Antonio José, 457

Uribe, Carlos, 470

Urica, Battle of, 66

Urueta, Carlos A., minister from Colombia, 457

Valencia, 62, 111, 118

Van Buren, Martin, and Panama Congress, 141-142; on claims, 166, 167; and canal, 189

Vanderbilt, Cornelius, 242, 325

Vanderbilt, William H., 344 n

Vanegas, Ricardo, 333

Van Murray, William, 49

Van Rensselaer, Rensselaer, 154, 155

Vansittart, Nicholas, 42

Vargas Swamp, 70

Varon, Panama insurrectionist, 401

Vásquez Cobo, A., 434

Velasco survey, 179

Vendryes, Henry (British), 280-281

Venezuela, 5, 7, 19, 23, 77 n, 89 n, 117; independence movements in, 29, 30-31; Expedition of 1806, 49-54; United Provinces of, 61; patriots defeated in, 62; British volunteers and, 69; unites with Colombia, 70, 72, 109, Caracan revolution, 60-62; Bolívar and, 66, 69, 71, 118; Spanish control of, 66, 67; asks for U. S. revolutionary assistance, 79; U. S. sends aid to, after earthquake, 79-80; privateers, 82-84; requests U. S. recognition and alliance, 87-88; sends diplomatic representative to U. S., 96-97; first congress of, 111; withdraws from Colombia, 121-123; and U. S. claims against Colombia, 166, 167; U. S. trade with, 174, 177; fear of British aggression, 204; (*see also* Caracas, La Guayra)

Vera Cruz, 9

Vergara, Secretary, 156-158

Vespucci, Amerigo, 4

Vidalle, Luis, 21-23, 34

Villamil, José M., 76

Villavicensio, Antonio, 63

Vizcardo y Guzmán, Juan Pablo, 37

Voltaire, 27

Vroomans (of Philadelphia), 283

Walker, Rear Admiral John G., 381 n

Ward, Consul, on Isthmian taxes, 241; Panama Riot, 288-290, 297; Herrán complains of actions of, 220

Washington, George, and Colombian independence, 36, 38, 41; family sends relics to Bolívar, 125

Watson, Senator Thomas E., 456

Watts, Beaufort T., chargé to Colombia, on British in Colombia, 115; sounded on U. S. participation in Panama Congress, 141, 142; and Bolívar, 119, 151-153; on commercial discrimination against U. S., 169

Webster, Daniel, on James Semple, 164; claims, 167-168; recognition of Panama, 191-192; Isthmian communication, 200-201

Weckbecker, Alexander, 281

Wellesley, Sir Arthur, 55-57

Wheaton, Henry, 201-202

Wheelright, William, 182, 197

Williams, Ensign James, 77

Williams, Senator John Sharp, 455

Williams, Roger, 35

Williamson, J. G. A., consul at La Guayra, 117, 176

Wilson, Sir Arnold T., 468

Wilson, Patrick, 333

Wilson, Woodrow, on U. S. reconciliation with Colombia, 440;

Thomson-Urrutia Treaty, 441, 444, 446-449, 455

Wilson (U. S. vessel), 82

Wilson Tariff Act of 1894, 270

Winslow, Lanier & Co., 364 n

Wisconsin (U. S. vessel), 232

Wolcott, Senator Josiah O., 455

Woolsey, Dr. Theodore, 416 n, 428

World War, effect of, on Colombo-American relations, 446-449

Wright, C. L., 282

Wyoming (U. S. vessel), 400 n

Wyse, Lieutenant Lucien Napoleon Bonaparte, 357, 358, 360

X. Y. Z. Affair, 45

Yañes, Francisco Javier, 75

Yates, Colonel Henry, 468

Zapata, Felipe, 353, 357

Zea, Francisco Antonio, 24, 70, 84, 97, 104, 117, 181

Zipaquirá, 123

DATE